THE LITERATURE OF CHINA IN THE
TWENTIETH CENTURY

To Anders and Louise,
Torkel, Chris and Alex

二十世纪中国文学

杜博尼　雷金庆　著

BONNIE S. MCDOUGALL
KAM LOUIE

The Literature
of China in the
Twentieth Century

Columbia University Press, New York

Columbia University Press
New York

Copyright © 1997 Bonnie S. McDougall and Kam Louie
All rights reserved.
First published in the United Kingdom by C. Hurst & Co., Ltd., London
Printed in England

Library of Congress Cataloging-in-Publication Data

McDougall, Bonnie S., 1941–
    The literature of China in the twentieth century / Bonnie S. McDougall
and Kam Louie.
        p.   cm.
    Includes bibliographical references index.
    ISBN 0-231-11084-7   0-231-11085-5 (paper)
    1. Chinese literature—20th century—History and criticism.
2. Chinese literature—Western influences.   I. Louie. Kam   II. Title.
PL2303.M43   1997
895.1'09005—dc20   97-2533
                                                                         CIP

C 10 9 8 7 6 5 4 3 2 1
P 10 9 8 7 6 5 4 3 2 1

ACKNOWLEDGEMENTS

The authors would like to acknowledge with gratitude the assistance they have received from reference works, translations, institutions, colleagues, students and friends.

For factual information we have as much as possible relied on primary sources. We have also been enormously assisted by standard reference works, our main source being *Zhongguo wenxue da cidian* (Tianjin renmin chubanshe, Tianjin, 1991), supplemented by *Zhongguo da baike quanshu: Zhongguo wenxue* (Zhongguo da baike quanshu chubanshe, Beijing, 1986), *Zhongguo xiandai wenxue shouce* (Zhongguo Wenlian chuban gongsi, Beijing, 1987), *Zhongguo xiandai wenxue mingzhu cidian* (Sichuan renmin chubanshe, Chengdu, 1993), *Biographical Dictionary of Modern Chinese Writers* (Beijing: New World Press 1984) and *A Selective Guide to Chinese Literature, 1900-1949* (Brill, Leiden, 1988-90).

To make our book accessible to those who approach modern Chinese literature through English translation, we have paid particular attention to works which have been translated into English, and as a general rule adopt existing translations of titles and terms (despite some overall inconsistency). We should like to pay tribute to the many translators who have made this possible.

The institutions by which we were employed during the course of our work on this book are the University of Oslo, the University of Queensland and the University of Edinburgh: we wish to thank each for generous financial assistance for meetings in Oslo, Brisbane and Edinburgh, for travel to East Asian libraries and bookshops, for research leave and for manuscript preparation. We also wish to thank Professors Chiu Ling-yang and W.S. Leung of the University of Hong Kong for enabling access to the University Library, and Professor J. Watson and Nancy Hurst for access to the John K. Fairbank Center for East Asian Research and the Harvard-Yenching Library at Harvard.

Chen Maiping and Howard Goldblatt saw early versions of the drama and poetry chapters respectively, and Howard also offered pertinent criticisms and generous support throughout; Oliver Krämer compiled the greater part of the glossary and index and made many helpful comments on the text; Yang Lan permitted access to his unpublished doctoral thesis on Cultural Revolution fiction and gave substantial assistance on the glossary; Anders Hansson made the camera-ready copy of the glossary and many corrections to the text; Louise Edwards read the manuscript at several stages and made valuable suggestions throughout; Jenny Putin and Fang Yewjin checked the final draft manuscript; and Tommy McClellan, Chrys Carey, Raoul Findeisen and Michel Hockx offered information on Zhang Henshui, Feng Zhi, Huang Baiwei, Bian Zhilin and Hu Shi. We wish to thank all of the above for their painstaking and valuable contributions.

We are most grateful to our publishers, Christopher Hurst and Michael Dwyer, who took a great risk in taking on our project when the manuscript was far from complete, for their patience, understanding and ever-ready help with our questions and worries.

We are very conscious of the debt we owe our departmental colleagues at Olso, Brisbane and Edinburgh for their support and assistance in ways they may not yet be aware of.

We have no words to express the debt we owe to our families over the eight years since we made our first rough sketches for this book.

Universities of Oslo, Edinburgh and   B.McD.
Queensland, June 1997   K.L.

CONTENTS

1

INTRODUCTION

Classical Chinese poetry and the great traditional novels are widely admired by readers throughout the world. Chinese literature in this century has not yet received similar acclaim. Some works have been unjustly neglected, through lack of knowledge or good translation, but many may never gain a wide readership abroad purely on the basis of literary appeal. Nevertheless, modern Chinese literature provides insights into the lives of the largest population in the world. Our aim in this book is to provide a broad picture of the general history of Chinese literature from the beginning of this century up to its last decade, showing the ways in which Chinese people have expressed themselves through one of the most difficult, exciting and confusing periods in the long history of their culture and civilisation.

Literature in modern China

The relation between a literary work and the society in which it is produced and consumed is a matter on which Chinese critics, theorists and writers have held strong views, usually closely related to their political stance. It was less common for them to acknowledge that literary works are also related to each other: to the tradition from which they emerge, and to the other works which appear at roughly the same time. In practice, a literary work is usually viewed by its writer, reader and critic in the context of other literary works. Above all, writers and readers generally share unspoken assumptions of what 'literature' is.

The concept of 'literature' in modern China is heavily indebted to Western ideas dating from the early nineteenth century. Through the intensive debates of the 1910s and 1920s, it became understood as a body of written work comprising a certain set of genres –

1

chiefly fiction, poetry and drama – in which individual expression through consciously employed artistic techniques became the characteristic mode. Earlier Chinese and Western ideas of literature, or more avant-garde or radical concepts, were for the better part of this century generally ignored among the writers and critics who determined the boundaries of the literary world.

The idea of a canon of accepted literature, created and controlled by scholars, has existed from the earliest times in Chinese history: while the canon has changed in modern times, the authority of the educated elite to define it in their own interests and to preserve their own position as its creators and consumers has been jealously guarded. The democratisation of the literary canon, of its creators and of its audience, has been one of the major achievements of the reformist literary intellectuals in the twentieth century. Nevertheless, non-written literature – oral and performing literature of the villages and towns, including folksong and local opera – has continued to be excluded, along with popular entertainments of the cities such as commercial bestseller fiction and Peking opera, and the private or drawer literature of the elite (for instance, in the form of classical poetry). Despite the slogans of the reformers and revolutionaries, the majority of the Chinese population has been effectively barred from consumption of canonical works.

Despite this limitation, the modern canon is still the most discussed, studied and influential body of literature among educated readers in twentieth-century China, and works outside the canon make only brief appearances in this book. Film, which has functioned both as mass entertainment or instruction and as art cinema, and has often been closely related to written literature, belongs to the broader category of the arts generally and is not included as a central topic.

Literary genres

Modern Chinese literature, narrowly defined, consists mainly of published fiction, drama and poetry, with occasional special cases in manuscript or oral form. A few modern writers have crossed genres, writing both fiction and poetry or both poetry and drama, but on the whole the genres have remained distinct and followed differing lines of development. For this reason, the nine core chapters of this book are arranged by genre, reflecting in their different order in each of the three parts their relative importance in each period.

Traditional Chinese literature can be divided into two broad, overlapping groups according to the language in which it was written. At one end of the spectrum was the classical literature (chiefly poetry and essays), written in a highly developed literary language characterised by compressed syntax and an elaborate, allusive vocabulary; in the middle, short stories and novels written in a vernacular closely connected with the spoken language of their time; and at the other end, the oral literature of folksong and opera in stylised regional forms. Although the writers and readers of these two groups overlapped to a remarkable degree, literary scholars in imperial China recognised only the first as true, serious literature, while fiction and drama were classed as popular entertainment. In reality, the literary and vernacular languages were often employed even within one particular work, and the popular and elite traditions constantly interacted in the development of both serious and entertainment literature.

Fiction, especially in the form of short stories, has been by far the most popular mode of expression in the twentieth century and receives special emphasis in this book. Towards the end of the nineteenth century, noting the importance of fiction in current Western literature and the language reforms of an even earlier age, reform-minded scholars advocated a reworking of the canon to include fiction and to extend the use of the vernacular into poetry and literary prose. Initial opposition by conservatives was undermined by changes in society introduced by political reforms, and the new mainstream literature was firmly established by 1920. As part of the new respectability of fiction, the traditional vernacular language was transformed into a new written vernacular in which contemporary and colloquial forms were combined with elements of Western vocabulary and grammar; at the same time, it also claimed respectability as serious literature by virtue of its concern with reforming Chinese society. This kind of writing proved enormously popular, especially among young readers. At the same time as it was elevated into respectability, however, new fiction had little appeal to the less-educated sectors of the urban population, which continued to rely on entertainment fiction of a more traditional kind.

In most traditional societies, including China, poetry is the dominant form of literary expression, but while it has declined in popularity in Western countries, it has continued to be relatively important in China, especially at times of crisis. The use of the new vernacular in poetry, on the other hand, seems to have resulted in a slight drop in status: the formerly pre-eminent role of poetry was occupied by fiction, and the success of the new poetry continued to be questioned (though not successfully challenged). Classical poetry continued to be written and read, and at times enjoyed special recognition conferred by the elevated status of its authors – most notably, Mao Zedong. Folk poetry as oral composition and performance in the cities and countryside was largely ignored by professional writers in the early part of the century, but received new attention following the Japanese invasion and the dispersal of intellectuals to the countryside. Collections of folk poetry were popularised and imitated by established poets in the 1940s and 1950s, but propaganda aims led to such distortion that these published works cannot be considered genuine examples of folk poetry. From the point of view of most modern poets, both the classical and the folk tradition were linguistic and formal hindrances to the creation of a distinctive modern voice.

Drama in the form of plays with a written text for spoken performance on stage was a Western import which got off to a slow start early this century and only became an important genre for limited periods. Traditional Chinese drama comprised a wide diversity of theatrical forms in cities, towns and villages, in which the chief characteristics were the predominance of singing rather than recitative, musical accompaniment, elaborate costuming (including make-up and masks), stylised gestures, dance and acrobatics. In other words, it was more like Western opera, pantomime or vaudeville than post-Renaissance spoken drama. Traditional Chinese theatre was centred on performers rather than authors: little use was made of written scripts or scores, the plots were familiar to the audience in advance, and the didactic content reinforced rather than explored conventional moral and social attitudes. Twentieth-century reforms to drama brought it closer to the written play of the contemporary Western stage, notably in the use of a scripted, colloquial prose dialogue and socially reformist or morally subversive themes. Following Ibsen, Shaw and Brecht, Chinese reformers believed that stage performance could be a powerful means to present challenging views of social problems. The reformers, however, were largely unable to convince audiences that the new drama of ideas could be as theatrically exciting as the thematically and morally conventional but technically accomplished and sensuously appealing traditional forms. The most successful modern dramas were the five-act plays of the 1930s which combined the glamour of traditional staging with the sensationalism of Western plots, and where contemporary dialogue was interspersed with music and song in Western or Chinese styles. From the early 1940s, the stage was primarily for the presentation of accepted ideas, and writers and audiences shared a general sense of apathy about the theatre. At the end of the 1970s, however, a new impetus for social reform enabled language, staging and perspectives on social problems to be dusted off and given new life on the contemporary stage.

Other genres, including essays, journalism, reportage, diaries, letters, biography and autobiography achieved eminence only in the hands of a small number of writers, and are not included in this volume.

Writers

Since the majority of literary works in modern China are polemical, our chief concern in this book is not so much for trends or styles in writing but for literature as an expression of writers' engagement with their readers on a topic of overwhelming interest to them both: the nature, development and future of Chinese society. The core chapters of this book list the main writers of each period in chronological order with brief biographical sketches and accounts of their major works.

The contributors to the traditional literary canon were the scholars or literati, members of the highly educated gentry elite which occupied roughly one per cent of the population, along with a small number of women from the same social stratum or serving it as entertainers. Their successors in the twentieth century are the intellectuals, defined broadly as men and women educated to upper-secondary levels and associated with non-manual occupations (excluding business, the armed forces and government), who also occupy roughly the same one per cent of the population.

The creation of a new language for literature was part of an attempt by the new intellectuals to establish for themselves a leading role in a modernising society. The abolition of the traditional examination system in 1905 deprived Chinese scholars of automatic entry into the ruling administration by virtue of their abilities in writing classical poetry and prose based on the traditional canon. The descendants of the scholar–gentry class, who constituted the first wave of the new intellectuals, inherited the expectation of office without the guarantee of obtaining it. In order to justify their continuing claim to this heritage, modern intellectuals strove to create new forms, hierarchies and languages for literature in an attempt to reassert their identity as cultural and therefore social leaders.

Accepting the ideals of republican and representative government as opening up avenues for advancement, the new intellectuals advocated an extension of literacy and general education. A larger and more representative readership offered writers an informal mechanism for extended social influence. At the same time, and without necessarily being conscious of what they were doing, they set limits to the extension of education and democratisation of literature through the development of new linguistic and literary hierarchies, to establish their prerogatives as controllers of the new canon. To some extent, Western linguistic and literary formations replaced classical learning as an excluding device at the upper levels of education and culture.

Like the scholars, modern intellectuals largely control book and magazine publication among the elite, and, by virtue of their ability in literary expression, perceive themselves as the natural moral, social and political leaders of their country. The dominant literature of twentieth–century China has therefore been strongly author-centred and concerned with the problems of intellectuals in China's modernising society. In the first half of this century, writing by men and women could be distinguished by their preoccupation with social leadership, although women's writing showed less of a sense of anxiety and guilt engendered by lingering allegiance to premodern literati ideals. Excluded from that past, women writers were able to take a more detached view of the effects of social transformation on women and define the act of writing as an achievement in itself. By mid-century, literati ideals were submerged by class-based tensions from which women were not excluded, and the distinction between men's and women's writing became less clear.

The terminology and concepts with which writers variously defined their role in society in the early decades of this century were largely derived from Western models but nevertheless still consonant with this basic attitude. One early favourite was the role of the writer (or poet or artist) as a prophet, a Promethean or Byronic figure who by virtue of his literary sensibility envisioned the future and led his people towards it. During the 1920s, it became more common for writers to see themselves as observers or critics of life or society, standing outside society in order to reflect or criticise it more precisely. A third concept became accepted among left-wing writers from the 1930s on, though it was never entirely congenial to them: that is, the writer as a literary cog in the machine of society, whose master engineer was understood to be the Communist Party. The prophetic poet was almost invariably a male figure; the observers, critics and cogs were of both genders. As links with the traditional canon grew weaker, writers defined themselves and their works in Western terms, and references to the tradition became superficial and hack-neyed.

The warlord politics of the early republican central and regional regimes gave little scope to intellectuals as rulers or administrators, and the gap between literary intellectuals and governments was almost unbridgeable. Writers supported themselves with teaching or editorial salaries to supplement meagre royalties from hack journalism and translation in addition to creative work. With the establishment of the Chinese Communist Party and the revamped Nationalist Party in the early 1920s, the attractions of opposition politics under the umbrella of reformist or revolutionary political parties began to appeal to literary intellectuals. As party, government and national organisations achieved greater social respectability, particularly after the Japanese invasion of the 1930s, the writer as outsider, supported wholly from writing or teaching, became an infrequent and isolated figure.

The process of enmeshment was accelerated in the 1950s and 1960s, with the growth of two elites in China, government and intellectual, which met and crossed with ease at the upper levels as had the literati officials of an earlier time. As writers supported the state by producing politically acceptable work, staffing state and party cultural organisations, or simply even continuing to live on the mainland, the state supported writers with salaries, perquisites and status. When the Communist ruling elite fell from power in the Cultural Revolution, the intellectual and literary elite which had supported it fell with it; and both were revived together after the death of Mao Zedong in 1976. During the Cultural Revolution, however, younger intellectuals deprived of social expectations formed a new group of cultural and political dissenters, whose achievements laid the basis for the new literature and arts of the 1980s. This decade, with its loosening of social constrictions, led to redefinitions of the role of writers in society and eventually to a much wider social composition of both writers and their readers.

Periods in literary development

Twentieth-century Chinese literature can be divided into three major periods on the basis of changes within the structure of the literary canon. These periods form the three main parts of this book, each beginning with a chapter on general literary developments set against the historical background.

The first period, from 1900 to 1937, represents the beginning of a distinctively new literature in China, in which Western influence is a decisive factor in the growth of writing as a profession, in the creation of new concepts of literature, its styles and its languages, and in the development of a more broadly based readership.

The second period, from 1938 to 1965, can be seen as an interruption to the almost unchecked Westernisation of the earlier period. Under the impact of Japanese invasion, writers became more responsive to native Chinese traditions as they strove to reach a wider audience in the interests of national salvation. The consolidation of Communist Party power, spreading from its base in north-west China in the mid-1930s to become the ruling party on the mainland in 1949, also exerted increasing political restraints over the production and consumption of literary works. The tension between the native tradition, Western-style modernisation and the Soviet model of political control is the main characteristic of the literary world in this period.

The Cultural Revolution, dating from 1966 to 1976, by undermining the control of the Communist Party and the influence of the Soviet model, brought the second period to an end. The apparent victory of a heavily politicised voice in collectively written stage dramas based on traditional Chinese opera was offset by the growth of an underground literature in the 1970s which drew on the modern traditions of the 1930s and further Westernisation. As the Cultural Revolution came to an end, this underground literature set the tone for a new era in contemporary writing in the 1980s, and attempts by the authorities to reimpose the restrictions of the 1950s and 1960s were increasingly ignored. The experimentation of the 1980s and its openness towards books and readers from outside made this literature attractive to Western readers, and when the June Fourth massacre of 1989 forced many Chinese writers into involuntary exile, writing by Chinese abroad formed a new link between Chinese literature and the rest of the world.

China, Taiwan and Hong Kong

Throughout the years of warfare and economic turmoil in China from late imperial times up to 1950, migration was common in south and eastern China among the rural and urban poor. It was much less common among intellectuals, especially from the central, northern and western parts of the country. Even after 1949 when modern China became divided into two realms – the People's Republic of China on the mainland, the Republic of China on the offshore island of Taiwan, with a renewed influx of migrants into the British colony of Hong Kong – the vast majority of writers stayed on the mainland, while the development of literature in Taiwan, Hong Kong and Overseas Chinese communities took separate routes. The largely independent literatures of these communities have their own histories and will not be discussed in this book.

Part I. 1900–1937

2

TOWARDS A NEW CULTURE

On the morning of 5 August 1900, the Manchu Emperor, the Empress Dowager and a small entourage fled in disguise from the Imperial Palace, making their way westward to re-establish the court in Xi'an two months later. The group travelled either on foot or in donkey carts, and dressed as commoners to avoid detection. Their pitiable state was a telling symbol of the degree to which the once-majestic Qing Empire had declined. With only a few thousand men, European and Japanese forces marched into Beijing, meeting almost no effective opposition from either the imperial troops or their secret-society supporters, the Society of Harmonious Fists. The latter, known also as the Boxers, was an anti-foreign organisation which had laid siege to the foreign legations in the capital for nearly two months, enjoying the tacit support of the Manchu court. The subsequent plundering of Beijing by the occupying Allied troops and humiliating settlement agreed to by the Qing government demonstrated unmistakably to reform-minded Chinese that the Manchu rulers themselves were the chief obstacle to reform, and that a complete change in the system of government was the only hope for the country.

The Empress Dowager, obliged to acknowledge responsibility for the Boxer catastrophe, made a belated attempt to remedy the social, political and economic weaknesses that had led to their defeat. Her comprehensive reform programme, spanning the years 1901–5, covered the bureaucracy, education, military, and general social reforms. Specific changes included the abolition of the government examinations, the establishment of new ministries and the active recruitment of Chinese students abroad for government office. These reforms had a direct bearing on the changes in literature which followed.

The civil service examinations had a restricted subject–matter, the Confucian classics, and an even more restrictive prose style, known as the 'eight-legged essay'. Even during the nineteenth century, in the face of the Western incursion into China, the central and regional administrative bureaucracies continued to be staffed by traditional scholars trained within this classical mode. By the beginning of the twentieth century, it was obvious even to conservatives like the Empress Dowager that this kind of education was failing to equip China for the modern world. Curricular reforms in schools introduced foreign languages and studies of foreign governments alongside the Confucian classics. For speedier recruitment of modernised officials, the government also sponsored selected students for study abroad. By 1906, the number of Chinese students in Japan alone had reached 13,000. These young people imbibed not only Japanese culture but also a host of European ideas through Japanese translations of Western works. In turn, the students translated hundreds of Western and Japanese works into Chinese, resulting in the wide dissemination of foreign ideas and literary forms among educated Chinese.

The Empress Dowager's policies were not themselves innovative. In 1898, her nephew, the Guangxu Emperor, had instituted a reform programme, modelled after the Meiji reforms in Japan, on the advice of a group of scholars led by Kang Youwei and his student Liang Qichao. Kang Youwei and Liang Qichao were both educated in the classics but, coming from the southern province of Guangdong far from the conservative centre, also had ready access to the outside world. Advocates of change, they remained royalists, and their ultimate ideal was the establishment of a constitutional monarchy. The Empress Dowager, however, more sensitive to the threat of internal change than external aggression, suppressed the reform movement after one hundred days and placed the Emperor under house arrest. Most of the reformers fled to Japan, and some who remained, such as Tan Sitong, were executed.

The failure of both the Hundred Days Reform of 1898 and the Boxer Rebellion of 1900 brought drastic changes to the Chinese political agenda. While the most influential figure before 1900 was unquestionably Kang Youwei, whose revision of the Confucian classics as a vehicle for political change was matched by his loyalty to the Manchu Emperor, the early years of this century were dominated by a more radical advocate of change, Liang Qichao.

Now living in exile in Japan, Liang, through his contacts with Japanese modernisers and studies of European philosophical and political texts, developed the idea of a new 'nation-state' which would be home to 'citizens' rather than 'subjects'.

Like his mentor, Liang believed that this change, which he rightly called 'revolutionary', could be contained without altering either the dynastic structure or overthrowing the current ruling house. Other reformers demanded the overthrow of Manchu rule altogether and even the establishment of a republic. Led by Sun Yatsen, another radical political thinker from Guangdong, the latter group had perhaps a better claim to the term 'revolution' (*geming*). While its first known use, in *The Book of Changes*, implies a change in reign title only, its political import in the late nineteenth and early twentieth century came from the Japanese, who had borrowed the ancient term for the new Western concept. Tracts such as Zou Rong's 1903 *The Revolutionary Army* which called for the expulsion of the Manchus became a rallying point for political action.

While Liang Qichao did not endorse the demands of the revolutionaries, his acceptance of the term 'revolution' had momentous implications for the history of Chinese literature. On 25 December 1899, Liang advocated a 'revolution in poetry'; three days later he put forward the view that a 'revolution in literature' was required, and three years later, in 1902, he also coined the slogan 'revolution in fiction'. Liang's role as an innovator was enhanced by his own literary output (discussed below in Chapter 3). His combination of literary creation and literary theory not only heralded the rise of modern Chinese literature but established a pattern for twentieth-century literary intellectuals.

Liang Qichao's influence became widespread with the publication of his journals *Public Opinion* (1898–1902) and the *New People's Miscellany* (1902–7). As their titles suggest, these journals were targeted at a broad audience and Liang's writings were devoured by an eager public. Prior to 1900, the classical or literary language was the medium for serious writing of any kind. Scholars such as Yan Fu and Lin Shu, who translated Western thought and literature into Chinese in the late nineteenth and early twentieth century, prided themselves on the refined classical style of their translations. Lin Shu, although inevitably influenced by the European works he translated, derided Liang Qichao's journalistic semi-vernacular. The success of Lin's versions of novels by Dickens and H. Rider Haggard seemed to justify his attachment to the older tradition. Within a few years, however, it was the 'Liang Qichao style' which laid the foundations of a new language for literature.

The Liang Qichao style was based on the grammar and vocabulary of the old vernacular (the traditional language of most entertainment fiction) but drew also on both traditional literary Chinese and contemporary spoken Chinese. The magnitude of his achievement can be estimated by comparing his style with the dominant nineteenth-century writing styles, the Tongcheng School in prose writing and the Jiangxi School in poetry, both of which advocated antiquated models divorced from any conceivable spoken language.

Liang Qichao's ideas on the function of literature in society also laid the foundation for modern literary practice. Like many who went to Japan after the failure of the Hundred Days Reform, he was convinced that the success of the Meiji Restoration in Japan resulted from the willingness of the Japanese to imitate European ways. Japanese writers even claimed that Europe's modern governmental systems were due to the high regard in these countries for fiction, especially political fiction (for example, the novels of Disraeli and Bulwer Lytton). Liang was quick to seize on this notion, and his article 'On the Relationship between Fiction and Ruling the Masses', featured in the first issue of his new journal, *New Fiction*, in 1902, advocated the elevation of fiction to the status of a serious genre of vital importance to good government.

Liang Qichao also promoted Western literary criticism and theory, although he was not the first to practise Western methodologies. Wang Guowei (1877–1927), a conservative intellectual who had studied in Japan and was critical of Kang Youwei and Liang Qichao, drew on Schopenhauer's philosophy in his analysis of the traditional novel *Dream of the Red Chamber*. In poetry, Huang Zunxian (1848–1905), another scholar from Guangdong and a close friend of Kang Youwei and Liang Qichao, advocated the adoption of colloquial vocabulary and reference to objects in the modern world such as telegraphs and steamers. Ill-health prevented Huang's participation in the Hundred Days Reform in 1898, and he went on to enjoy a successful career as a diplomat in San Francisco, London and Singapore. An accomplished poet in the classical style, his familiarity with Western cultures encouraged him to explore Liang's 'poetry revolution' in practice.

A flood of translations and adaptations of foreign literary works and theories poured into China in the first decade of the twentieth century, leaving the late-Qing reformers stranded in a rapidly transforming society. The Qing court failed to understand the scope and nature of the new influences coming in from abroad, and even the more progressive among them, such as Li Hongzhang, refused to question the traditional reverence for Chinese culture as inherently superior and contempt for all others as barbaric. With the Guangxu Emperor's death in 1908, the last link between the imperial court and monarchist reformers such as Kang Youwei was broken. In its place, the revolutionary policies of Sun Yatsen and his followers gained further support.

The Qing rulers had become so inept that the revolutionaries succeeded in establishing the Republic of China with minimal bloodshed and within the space of a few years. The new era was proclaimed on 1 January 1912, with Sun Yatsen as provisional president. Lacking a substantial power base despite his Overseas Chinese and Triad links, however, Sun Yatsen was forced to relinquish his post to Yuan Shikai, the former Qing military commander who had been responsible for arresting the Hundred Days reformers in 1898. Owing no particular allegiance to republican ideals, Yuan tried to re-establish the monarchy with himself as emperor in 1915, but was promptly deserted by his generals who sought to proclaim their own independence in their provincial strongholds. When Yuan died in 1916, however, none was strong enough to capture and hold a centralising authority, and for the next ten years, China was divided and ruled by a succession of warlords in what was virtually a state of civil war.

While the warlord decade created political chaos in China, it also witnessed one of the most spectacular intellectual transformations in Chinese history. The warlords themselves were repressive and hostile to new ideas, but weakness at the centre meant that writers could operate in relative freedom in the provinces as well as in the foreign concessions in Shanghai and even in the capital itself. The unstable relationship between the warlords and foreign governments was also behind the ambiguous attitudes of

Chinese intellectuals towards Japan and the West. The young and impatient revolutionaries drafting their nationalist and anti-imperialist writings were aware that they were able to do so precisely because of their education in foreign countries and the protection they enjoyed thanks to foreign extraterritorial privilege.

One of the most prominent writers of this period was Chen Duxiu (1879–1942), the founder in 1915 of *New Youth*, a Shanghai-based journal dedicated to the creation of a vigorous new culture in China. Chen, who had studied for several years in both Japan and France, singled out Confucianism as the biggest stumbling block to the development of a new China. To replace it, Chen proposed allegiance to two Western concepts: science and democracy. To Chen and his followers, 'science' was not so much a body of scientific knowledge acquired by rigorous study but more a culture of experimentation and scepticism towards received ideas, while 'democracy' implied no more than limited suffrage for educated people.

Like Liang Qichao, Chen also tended to overestimate the role that literature could play in what became known as the New Culture movement, and encouraged Hu Shi, then a student of the American philosopher John Dewey at Columbia University, to publish his ideas for literary reform in *New Youth*. The modestly titled 'Some Tentative Suggestions for the Reform of Chinese Literature' appeared in January 1917. By today's standards, the eight principles put forward by Hu Shi seem commonplace, a series of admonitions against the use of clichés, stale literary phrases and writing without meaning or substance. In exhorting aspiring writers not to avoid using vernacular words and speech, however, Hu Shi initiated a movement which changed Chinese language and literature forever.

Although Hu Shi avoided the term 'revolution', his article nevertheless established the date for the beginning of China's 'new literature' and was followed by Chen Duxiu's call for 'literary revolution' in the February 1917 issue of *New Youth*. Without Liang Qichao's efforts, the literary revolution could not have been so universally and rapidly accepted, but where Liang Qichao stopped short of writing in the vernacular free of classical elements and of advocating the replacement of Chinese literary traditions with modern Western models, Chen had no such reservations.

Hu Shi's suggestions for the adoption of the vernacular in

literature may seem somewhat confusing, since traditional fiction had been written in the vernacular for several centuries; Hu Shi even drew readers' attention to the splendid achievements in premodern Chinese fiction and suggested that the older vernacular could be adapted for use in modern fiction. To contemporary readers, however, the new term used by Hu Shi, 'literature' (*wenxue*), understood to include fiction and drama, still meant primarily poetry and other high-minded prose writing, and the old respect for poetry still lingered. Hu Shi himself illustrated the use of the vernacular in literary writing by publishing several of his free verse poems in the same January issue of *New Youth*, to be followed over the next two months by short poems in the new style by Chen Duxiu and Liu Fu.

The work which is celebrated as the turning-point for modern literature, however, appeared in *New Youth* in May 1918: Lu Xun's 'Diary of a Madman'. This story, with its penetrating analysis of fundamental flaws in Chinese society, proved beyond doubt that vernacular fiction was a suitable vehicle for the expression of serious views in prose. Its distinctively new mode of expression and subject-matter not only launched a new literary tradition but also foreshadowed a period of sustained analysis of Chinese culture in general, which later became known as the May Fourth Movement.

The May Fourth Movement received its name from a demonstration of several thousand students assembled in Tiananmen Square on 4 May 1919. Carrying banners with slogans such as 'Boycott Japanese Goods' and 'No to the Signing of the Peace Treaty', the students marched to the Legation Quarter to protest against the world powers' agreements at the 1919 Versailles Peace Conference. The consequences of the First World War (1914–18), including the Russian Revolution of 1917, had a profound impact on the development of literature in China. The war effort in Europe temporarily distracted Western intervention in China, causing a rapid growth in local industry and commerce. In 1913, for example, there were only about half a million industrial workers in China, but by 1919, their number had grown to about 2 million. The new industries contributed to the development of urban centres into modern cities, whose populations benefited from the new educational policies of the 1900s and 1910s. By 1917, over 10 million people had received a modern education, forming a new class of readers distinct in their backgrounds and needs from the old scholar-official elite.

World War I also brought the realisation that European science and technology did not bring peace and happiness to their inventors. Furthermore, it became evident that Western values such as equality and democracy were for the exclusive enjoyment of countries which were strong and wealthy. China was neither. China had been on the side of the Allies against Germany, but despite this support, the Treaty of Versailles handed German-held concessions in China (most importantly, the Shandong peninsula) to another Allied supporter, Japan, on the basis of a secret treaty agreed between China and Japan dating back to 1915. The Allies' contempt for China's territorial integrity and the Chinese government's submission to Japan set off great indignation. The student demonstration in Beijing on 4 May 1919 quickly grew into a widespread patriotic movement throughout China incorporating a demand for a total re-evaluation of Chinese culture and civilisation.

The May Fourth Incident also marked the beginnings of an irreconcilable split between those who saw Chinese spirituality and Confucian values as the antidote to the moral disease of Western civilisation and those who sought national salvation through the Communist ideology of the Soviet Union. In the immediate aftermath of the May Fourth Incident, both camps still laid claim to the word 'revolution', but the aggressive activities of the Communist International instigated by the Soviet Union soon led to its appropriation by left-wing activists. Sun Yatsen's party, formerly known as the Chinese Revolutionary Party, was reorganised in October 1919 as the Chinese Nationalist Party, while the Chinese Communist Party was established by Chen Duxiu and Li Dazhao in 1921. The initial membership of the latter was fifty-seven; within six years it had grown to 57,963. The two founders of the Communist Party were both men of letters who had a very strong interest in literature, and Party members were an articulate and influential minority in the new literature movement of the 1920s.

The most significant achievement of the literary left in 1920 was to take control of the journal *Short Story Monthly*. Founded in 1910 and published by the Commercial Press in Shanghai, *Short Story Monthly* was a major outlet for popular fiction, including stories written in the literary language by such writers as Su Manshu.

The literary reformers regarded it as a commercial enterprise of little artistic or moral value, and a young left-wing employee, later to become famous as the novelist Mao Dun, persuaded the owners to appoint him as editor. Under Mao Dun's editorship the journal changed policy, attacking its former preference for apolitical entertainment and switching completely to the vernacular in 1921. *Short Story Monthly* became the best-known literary journal of the modern era: didactic and polemical in its early years, and yet receptive to a wide range of foreign literary theories and broad enough to include the majority of the most famous writers of the 1920s and early 1930s.

In 1921, the *Short Story Monthly* became an unofficial organ of the Literary Research Association, the first modern literary society to promote the new movement. Established in Beijing in January 1921, the Association boasted among its founders Mao Dun, Zheng Zhenduo and Zhou Zuoren, all to become prominent figures in the new literature. Literary journals sponsored by the Association included *Poetry* and *Drama*, the first of their kind in China. Out of touch with these developments, a group of students in Japan, including Guo Moruo, Yu Dafu and Tian Han, formed the Creation Society in July 1921. After moving its headquarters to Shanghai later the same year, the Creation Society prevailed on the Taidong Bookstore to publish its books and journals, such as *Creation Quarterly* and *The Deluge*. While there were more similarities than differences between the two groups, not to mention a great diversity of theories and styles within each group, the slogans by which they are best known indicate an allegiance to two broad alternatives: 'literature for life's sake' (or realism) for the Literary Research Association, and 'literature for art's sake' (or romanticism and expressionism) for the Creation Society.

New literary societies flourished in the 1920s: some of the more notable were the Popular Drama Society, the Unnamed Society, the Thread of Talk Society and the *Contemporary Review* group. Their main activity was to publish books and journals for their members, and by 1925, there were well over a hundred new literary magazines in all parts of the country, providing writers with ready outlets for their creative and theoretical or polemical work, and also space for translations of foreign works by Japanese, Russian, American and European authors ranging from the classics to the avant-garde.

The influx of new ideas encouraged an atmosphere of debate and controversy, to which personal and political rivalries sometimes added considerable bitterness. In the pages of the *Contemporary Review*, writers such as Hu Shi, Chen Yuan and Liang Shiqiu argued that good literature was free of class allegiances and should be independent of politics. They were denounced by left-wing critics including Lu Xun, who claimed that by denying the influence of class upon literature, these writers were acting as running dogs of capitalism. Even the most basic ideas of the new literature came under question from the *Critical Review*, established by the Harvard-trained scholars Wu Mi and Mei Guangdi in Nanjing in 1922, and *The Tiger Weekly*, published in Beijing by the Minister of Education, Zhang Shizhao. These journals tried to re-activate opposition to the vernacular movement, but since they wrote in the literary language, their journals had limited circulation and the new writers did not bother to mount a sustained counter-attack. Instead, in response to a series of national crises in the mid and late 1920s which polarised the political parties, the literary societies in turn became more intolerant of each other in their attempts to control the direction of the new literature.

Nationalists and Communists agreed that under warlord rule the national interest had become secondary to appeasement of foreign powers and industrialists. Foreigners filled important posts in the Maritime Customs and Postal Service, and the foreign concessions were a continual reminder of their privileges. Patriotic demonstrations by students and nascent trade unions became a common occurrence. On 15 May 1925 a Chinese worker was killed by Japanese police in Shanghai during one such demonstration. In protest, over 10,000 workers and students marched in the city's concessions on 30 May. The British officer in charge of a detachment of Chinese and Sikh police commanded his men to open fire, killing eleven demonstrators and wounding dozens more. Further protests took place across the country, and the literary journals joined in denunciations of the May Thirtieth Incident.

The brutality of the warlords in suppressing demonstrations made them equally a target of attack. On 18 March 1926, thousands of students and workers assembled in Tiananmen Square to protest against foreign (particularly Japanese) domination in national policy. The head of the Beijing ruling faction, Duan Qirui, ordered troops to open fire on the demonstrators: about fifty were killed and hundreds wounded. Among the many writers who expressed their rage and grief were Lu Xun and Wen Yiduo. These two incidents brought to a head several years of agitation by left-wing literary critics such as Mao Dun and Jiang Guangci for a more politicised literature. Guo Moruo's 'Revolution and Literature', published in *Creation Monthly* in May 1926, showed that the new 'revolutionary literature' was to be completely different to Liang Qichao's original concept. The function of literature, in the darkest days of warlord rule in the 1920s, could not be defined as a tool for the promotion of good government; writers were now encouraged to speak on behalf of the oppressed classes and help create a social revolution conceived in Marxist terms. The revolution in literature now having been achieved, left-wing writers were poised to use literature for revolutionary ends. Many were by this stage Communist Party members.

The split between the Nationalist Party and the Communist Party intensified the polarisation and politicisation of the literary camps. In alliance with the Communists, Sun had planned to establish a new national government with an assault on warlords from his base in Guangzhou. His death in 1925 brought Chiang Kaishek, a military officer, to the fore. After skirmishes with local Communist groups, Chiang set out in July 1926 as commander-in-chief of a National Revolutionary Army which included prominent Communists such as Mao Dun and Guo Moruo. With the help also of local Communist agents in mobilising support from peasants and workers, the Northern Expedition was a spectacular success. By March 1927, both Nanjing and Shanghai were taken, and a provisional government was set up in Wuhan.

Alarmed at the support for the left-wing even within his own party, Chiang Kaishek decided to abandon his Communist allies in order to win the support of the foreign powers and native capital. With the support of the notorious 'Green Gang', Communists and union leaders in Shanghai were rounded up and shot in April 1927. The Shanghai massacre drove the Communist movement out of the cities into the villages; at the same time, formerly non-aligned intellectuals were persuaded by Chiang's treachery to join the ranks of the left-wing. Chiang Kaishek's 'White Terror' was matched by warlords in other parts of China, equally ruthless in their attempts to exterminate left-wing influence:

in Beijing, for instance, Zhang Zuolin (a Manchurian general who protected Japanese interests in the north and north-east) arrested and hanged twenty Communists, including Li Dazhao.

The Communist response was first to find a scapegoat. Chen Duxiu, who had engineered the alliance with the Nationalists on orders from Stalin, was accused (in the current rhetoric) of being a Trotskyist and dismissed as secretary-general in August 1926. He was replaced by another intellectual and activist in the new literature movement, Qu Qiubai, who in turn remained in power for less than two years: at the Sixth Party Congress in June 1928, held in Moscow for reasons of safety, Qu was accused of opportunism and stripped of his post.

The foreign concessions in Shanghai still offered comparative security even at the height of the White Terror. The Communist writers Jiang Guangci and Meng Chao formed the Sun Society in 1928 to promote proletarian revolutionary literature. Much of their effort went into denouncing the failure of writers like Lu Xun and Mao Dun to produce literature that described the lives of, and was read by, the urban proletariat. Cheng Fangwu's essay 'From Literary Revolution to Revolutionary Literature' summed up the change in outlook in the Creation Society. Lu Xun also came under attack by Guo Moruo for counselling caution, and was ridiculed as an old man belonging to the leisured class. Lu Xun's riposte, that while all literature is propaganda, not all propaganda is literature, was evidence of his distance from the Communist-backed factions of this time. A debate between the Creation and Sun writers and Mao Dun (who by this time had let his membership of the Communist Party lapse), on the concept of proletarian literature, lasted until early 1929. The controversies among the left-wing writers and intellectuals during these years continued to reverberate half a century later.

Having successfully isolated the Communists in Shanghai's foreign concessions or in remote rural bases, Chiang Kaishek, in cooperation with the remaining local warlords, continued with the liquidation of the Communist Party and its sympathisers (about one million had been murdered by 1932). A further Nationalist push towards Beijing resulted in the assassination of Zhang Zuolin by the Japanese, who saw him as no longer able to defend their interests, and Beijing fell to the Nationalist forces in June 1928. Beijing (meaning 'northern capital') was renamed Beiping ('northern peace') and Chiang established a Nationalist government in Nanjing ('southern capital') on 10 October 1928 (10 October is still celebrated as China's National Day in Taiwan).

Stability of a kind was established with the taming of the warlords but economic and social conditions for workers and peasants deteriorated. A League of Nations study revealed that peasants paid about half of their harvest as land rental as well as other taxes. Mao Zedong's investigations in his home province of Hunan in 1927 (to where he was forced to retreat by the White Terror) showed much the same, and Mao concluded that the countryside – not the urban centres as decreed by conventional Marxism – could launch the Communist Chinese revolution.

Bickering among left-wing writers finally stopped in late 1929 when the Nationalist government began to terminate their organisations. The Creation Society was forced to disband in February 1929, soon followed by the Sun Society and other groups. Under pressure also from the Communist International to settle their differences, the two societies joined forces with Lu Xun in early 1930 to form the League of Left-wing Writers. The League was inaugurated on 2 March 1930 in Shanghai to an audience of over forty people, and Lu Xun gave the keynote speech. Branches were set up in Beijing and Tokyo, with sub-branches in Guangzhou and Nanjing. Mao Dun and Zhou Yang, who were not in Shanghai at the time, joined soon after, and Qu Qiubai became a leading member on his return from the Soviet Union in 1931. Altogether, nearly three hundred writers joined the League, amounting to a sizeable proportion of writers and critics in China at that time.

With so many experienced and popular writers and editors at its disposal, the League's publications became very influential. As well as being vehicles for their own members' work, journals such as *Pioneers* and *Sprouts Monthly* offered space to an even greater number of translations of Marxist and Soviet texts. The Nationalist government was so alarmed by these publications that a new code on censorship was announced in December 1930. As one League journal was closed, however, another was launched to take its place.

The popularisation of literature was central to the League, which took over the last few issues of *Mass Literature and the Arts*, a journal founded in 1928 by Yu Dafu and Xia Laidi. In 1931 and 1932 Lu Xun, Mao Dun and Zhou Yang conducted a detailed debate on the content, audience and language of proletarian literature, and Qu Qiubai's 1932 essays on mass literature summed up the League's position. Qu Qiubai believed that the May Fourth vernacular revolution had failed because the literature it produced was not welcomed by the masses. The style and even more the language of the new literature were Europeanised and therefore elitist, beyond the comprehension of the masses.

The gap between written and spoken Chinese is due partly to the largely non-phonetic nature of the Chinese script (that is, a script based on pictographs or ideographs as distinct from an alphabetic script). Another reason is the diversity of spoken Chinese in different parts of the country, where regional or even local dialects were unintelligible to outsiders. Qu Qiubai advocated the creation of a 'common language' (*putonghua*) which could be understood throughout China. As the country modernised and travel became more widespread, according to Qu, a common language had already begun to emerge at train stations and in the docks. This common language, which was very different to the vernacular language (*baihua*), only existed at that time as a rudimentary spoken form and needed to be popularised as a means of expression for all people in all parts of the country. Like the vernacular, it could also be written down using the old ideographic script, but Qu Qiubai and Lu Xun made the even more radical proposal that this script be replaced by a romanised (alphabetic) script in the interests of educating as many people as possible.

On 18 September 1931, Japanese troops stationed in north-east China attacked Shenyang (Mukden). Meeting virtually no resistance, they proceeded to occupy the whole north-east. This invasion of Chinese territory was followed by the punitive bombardment of Shanghai on 28 February 1932, and in May 1933 Japanese troops approached within ten miles of Beijing. Their own experience of Japanese aggression, combined with the testimony of refugees from the north-east, made national salvation a key issue among writers in the early 1930s and led to a new set of slogans such as 'revolutionary war literature', 'nationalist revolutionary literature' and 'national defence literature'.

Nationalist sentiments were also voiced by government supporters. A group under Huang Zhenxia, an army instructor, and Fan Zhengbo, the chief of police, declared war on the League under the slogan 'nationalist literature'. *The Vanguard Weekly* was launched in June 1930, followed by other publications such as *The Vanguard Monthly*, which carried in its first issue 'A Declaration by the Nationalist Literature Movement'. In direct opposition to the League, the declaration states that the relationship between individuals and class is superficial, and that the highest significance of literature is national. The term 'national' has racial overtones, and the notion of Chinese racial superiority is inherent in works written by members of the movement. Huang Zhenxia's 'Blood of the Yellow People' (1931), for example, describes the invasion of Russia by Genghis Khan's grandson.

At a time when Japan posed the main external threat, appeals by government supporters to racist emotions were calculated to sway public opinion. Left-wing writers, however, were alert to the implied subversion of the internationalism favoured by the League. Qu Qiubai, for instance, dismissed the Nationalist literary journals as nothing more than anti-Soviet propaganda, read by only the wives of their authors, while Lu Xun condemned the authors themselves as traitorous and despicable. The Nationalist Literature movement was clear evidence to League members that the government's chief aim was to wipe out Communism in China rather than to repel the invaders.

For its part, the dominance of the League crushed even moderate voices at this time. From 1931 to 1933, the literary critics Hu Qiuyuan and Su Wen, calling themselves 'free people' and 'the third kind of people', called for the non-interference of politics in literature and criticised the League for abandoning literary freedom for short-term political gains. Although their disquiet concerning the politicisation of literary debate was shared by many non-aligned writers, they were no match for the organised response from League members. Qu Qiubai and Zhou Yang in particular took the opportunity to promote the Leninist doctrine of literature as a tool of Party organisation. The combination of the Nationalists' repressive cultural policies and the threat of Japanese invasion effectively made arguments for a liberal and humanitarian approach to literature seem hollow.

While Shanghai continued to be the centre of left-wing literary activity, away from Shanghai the atmosphere was less militant. In Beijing, for example, Zhou Zuoren and Lin Yutang promoted non-aligned literature in their journals *Camel Grass* and *The Analects*, and although they received constant criticism, the attacks on them were less vindictive. Zhou advocated literature free from any kind of didactic purpose while Lin defended the role of humour and private feelings.

While the League may have dominated literary debates and publication outlets, it by no means had a monopoly on writing. Entertainment literature was still commercially successful in the hands of key writers such as Zhang Henshui. Mainstream May Fourth novelists and poets such as Ba Jin, Shen Congwen, Lao She, Wen Yiduo and Bian Zhilin kept their distance from the League, freely experimenting with both traditional Chinese and modern Western techniques. The cosmopolitanism of this time was even more noticeable in the theatre, where playwrights such as Cao Yu and Ding Xilin transplanted the European stage to China.

In the Jinggangshan area on the Jiangxi-Hunan border, meanwhile, literature was taking a very different path. After the failure of Mao Zedong's attempt to stage a peasant uprising in Hunan in 1927, he was joined later the same year in Jinggangshan by Zhu De, retreating from the unsuccessful Nanchang Uprising. Together they established a Communist base in Ruijin, which operated more or less independently of the Party's headquarters still located in Shanghai. While the urban-based Party continued to be dominated by the Communist International and to suffer from internal ideological division, Mao Zedong was both willing and able to ignore the Soviet Union and conventional Marxism. His base was the peasantry, most of whom were illiterate. To gain their support, Mao turned to traditional folksong and local opera as a vehicle for revolutionary ideas.

The new drama produced in Jiangxi shared with the Shanghai stage the message that revolution was needed to achieve improvements in living conditions, but because it was designed for performance rather than publication and for a local rather than a national audience, it remained almost unknown even to the left-wing in Shanghai. Nevertheless, over a hundred scripts are still extant, over forty of them in a complete form. Most of these plays or operas are quite simple, little more than straightforward propaganda on peasant struggles against landlords and battles waged by the Communist forces against the Nationalists or Japanese.

Their significance is mainly historical, as the forerunners of the new opera movement in Yan'an in the 1940s.

Even though conditions in Ruijin were far from perfect, the situation for Communists elsewhere in China was much worse. By 1931 Mao Zedong felt confident enough of his own relative success that he invited members of the Central Committee to attend the First National Congress of the Soviets in Ruijin. He also succeeded in being elected chairman of the Central Committee, and his policy of designating the peasantry as the primary element in China's revolutionary struggle was finally approved. This policy was further confirmed by Mao's ability to hold off repeated attacks by Chiang Kaishek's forces on the Red Army base between 1930 and 1934. Using German military advisers and superior firepower, Chiang's strategy was positional warfare, but Mao adopted guerrilla tactics which relied on massive local support.

Mao's unconventional tactics were frowned upon by Stalin, and Mao lost control of the Central Committee to Soviet-trained cadres known as the 'Twenty-eight Bolsheviks'. When Chiang Kaishek's Fifth Encirclement and Annihilation Campaign was put into operation in 1934, the new leaders switched from guerrilla warfare to conventional positional warfare. They were defeated so thoroughly that the Red Army was forced to evacuate the base which they had held for seven years. Qu Qiubai was among those ordered to stay behind to defend the base: he was captured and executed.

Some one hundred thousand soldiers and Party cadres broke through the siege in October 1934: the first stage of what was later to become known as the Long March had begun. In January 1935, Mao Zedong regained his position as chairman of the Party's Central Committee, a position he held for the rest of his life, and under his direction the Red Army moved further west and then north. The price for Mao's ascendancy was high: by the time they reached Baoan in the north-west province of Shaanxi a year later, there were only 8,000 survivors. The Long March, made under extremely difficult conditions and over scenic but inhospitable terrain, became a Communist legend, providing both inspiration and myth in countless literary works over the next fifty years. In December 1936, the Party moved its headquarters from Baoan to Yan'an, which became the base of the Red Army (and its successor, the Eighth Route Army) throughout the War against Japan. It was here that Mao implemented the literary theories developed by Qu Qiubai in Shanghai and later refined in Ruijin. His own formulation of Communist literary doctrine in 1942 was the culmination of trends that had been evolving in China since the beginning of the century.

3

POETRY: THE TRANSFORMATION
OF THE PAST

During the 1920s and 1930s, poetry was one of the most popular genres in the new literary movement, among both writers and readers. In one sense, it offered something particularly new: fiction had commonly been written in the vernacular, but poetry for the educated had previously been written in the literary language. The literary revolution in poetry was in this way more profound than in fiction, and perhaps for this reason took longer to achieve success. On the other hand, the link between poetry and social, philosophical or political concerns, which were the common preoccupations of twentieth-century writers, was much stronger than in the case of fiction: traditionally, poetry rather than fiction was the accepted mode of serious reflection.

The history of classical Chinese poetry shows many stages of change and development, in which the conventions of one period were seen to have become stale and in need of renewal. Typically, such renewal was achieved by introducing new prosodic rules, by incorporating elements of the spoken language, and by enlarging the thematic scope. Readers of classical Chinese poetry in translation may not be aware of these changes, since translations of Chinese poetry rarely take into account its basic formal structures and techniques. The changes which took place in Chinese poetry from before the fifth century BC to the late nineteenth century are therefore obscured in even the best translations, and the difference between traditional classical poetry and modern vernacular poetry are seen mainly in terms of theme and ideology. The differences in language and technique are nevertheless fundamental.

The concept of a revolution in literature in modern times begins with the 'revolution in poetry' of the late nineteenth century, an attempt to introduce the spoken language into classical verse.

The poets who composed this group, most notably the scholar-officials Huang Zunxian (1848–1905) and Xia Zengyu (1865–1924), inspired by the belief that English romantic poetry was written in a form closely approximating spoken English, advocated 'letting the hand follow the mouth' instead of writing in literary Chinese. The habits of literary Chinese as a written language, however, proved difficult to overcome, and their 'modern' poems were written in a simplified version of the literary language that had little to do with true spoken Chinese.

In literary Chinese, each word generally consists of a single syllable, and each syllable (with certain exceptions) has equal stress in the verse line; since the Tang dynasty, the rhythm of the line has been based not on stress (as in English poetry) or length (as in Latin poetry) but on a pattern of contrasts between tones (conventionally described as even or oblique, though the pitch qualities have now been lost and there is some doubt about their tonal nature). The equal weight of words in the line also allowed a set number of syllables per line rather than a set number of metrical feet per line as in English. The line length varied in different periods and different styles of Chinese poetry. In the earliest collection of Chinese poetry, *The Book of Songs* (which in its present form dates probably from the fifth century BC), the folksong-like poems of the 'Regional Airs' section were commonly four syllables per line, while lines of different lengths were more common in *The Songs of the South*, compiled in the second century AD but dating back to as early as the third century BC. The five-syllable line became standard between the second and third centuries AD, and was matched in the seventh century by a seven-syllable line. Around the late seventh century, tone patterns became regularised and mandatory in 'Regulated' poems. Whether in five or seven syllables, and whether regulated by tones or not, the literary language had become so condensed that the standard line in Tang poetry could only with great ingenuity be reduced to an equivalent length in English. A more flexible line length emerged again in the form known as 'Lyrics' in the tenth century, but the length of each line and the tonal contrast were predetermined in fixed patterns based on the literary language.

In vernacular Chinese, however, words are commonly made up of more than one syllable, and in the spoken language, some words or syllables are stressed and some are unstressed, as in

English. It is therefore virtually impossible to incorporate the vernacular into traditional verse forms, and the would-be revolutionary poets did not succeed in overcoming this barrier to verse that approximated speech.

Introducing neologisms for names and allusions from Western culture and the imagery of modern technology was a more manageable enterprise, and in this respect the poets were more successful. On the other hand, this practice restricted the audience for their work to a small group of reformist scholars with some Western education, such as Kang Youwei, Tan Sitong and Liang Qichao, who all tried their hand at the new style. The 'revolution in poetry' of the 1890s had little impact at the time and no direct successors. The next step towards a new poetry was made by a fundamentally different kind of character, Su Manshu.

Su Manshu (1884–1918)

Su Manshu's original name was Su Jian. He was born in Yokohama, Japan, to a Chinese father and his Japanese maid. He was sent to China in 1889, where he studied briefly at a village school and then spent two years in Shanghai before returning to Yokohama in 1898 to attend the Chinese school founded by Kang Youwei. In 1902 he went to Tokyo, where apart from his studies he joined three revolutionary Chinese student associations (Chen Duxiu was also a member of one). Returning to Shanghai in 1903 to carry out revolution in practice, he contributed patriotic poems, articles and translations (including a partial translation of Victor Hugo's *Les Misérables*) to the local press. He converted to Buddhism during a visit to Hong Kong, and travelled widely in East and South-east Asia between 1904 and 1912. After the 1911 Revolution, he returned again to Shanghai where he wrote his autobiographical novel, *The Lone Swan*, before taking off again for travels in China and Japan.

Su Manshu wrote poetry in classical Chinese, reputedly taught to him by Chen Duxiu. In 1908, he became a passionate admirer of Byron, whose poems he translated with an introduction for the Chinese reader. On the basis of his fiction, poetry, translations and unconventional life, he became a vastly popular, even semi-legendary precursor to the literary revolution of 1917. Although he identified himself with Western romanticism, his legacy included

Victorian ideas on art which became highly influential in the 1920s and 1930s. It was in Victorian times that the concept of pure poetry, occupying its own area as a realm distinct from practical experience or goals, became widespread. The conflict between self-sufficiency and instrumentalism in poetry, even more than in literature in general, is one of the main features of twentieth-century literary history. (*For Su Manshu's fiction see Chapter 4.*)

Hu Shi (1891–1962)

In the history of literature, a new movement or literary school is often best represented by its first writers: in the new literary movement of the May Fourth period, for instance, Lu Xun is at once its first and its best fiction writer and essayist. It was not so with poetry. Most of the early authors of May Fourth poetry were very young and wrote vernacular poems for a very short time; their efforts are remembered for their historical importance and because of their authors' achievements in other fields. Writing 'new poetry' for these authors constituted a claim for recognition as a 'new intellectual'. Hu Shi is a typical example of the short-term, part-time literary revolution poet.

Born in Anhui, he was the son of an elderly scholar–official, who died when Hu Shi was a child, and an illiterate countrywoman. He was first given a thorough classical education in the local village school (and illicitly discovered the delights of old vernacular fiction), then spent his secondary school years, from 1904 to 1908, in Shanghai obtaining a more modern schooling (and discovering the vernacular polemics of Liang Qichao). He left for the United States on a Boxer Indemnity Scholarship in 1910, entering first the Agricultural College at Cornell University before transferring to Arts and Sciences to study philosophy. After graduating in 1914, he continued his studies in philosophy at Columbia University.

As a student in the United States, Hu Shi was particularly attracted to Imagist poetry, one of the most innovative poetic schools of the time. Its use of concrete visual imagery, expressed in relatively simple language in free verse form, bore a superficial resemblance to the lyric poetry of the Song dynasty, and proved transferable both in theory and practice into modern Chinese.

Hu Shi was also impressed with the accessibility of serious literature in the United States, and adopted the concept of a single 'national literature' in China (as distinct from elite versus popular literature) as one of his chief aims. The new national literature was to be written in a language which the whole (educated) population could readily understand and to propagate new moral and philosophical views. The authors of this new literature, it went without saying, were to be the new intellectuals, with Westernised education and, in many cases, experience overseas.

Hu Shi advanced his 'tentative proposals' (later known as the 'eight proscriptions') for the reform of Chinese literature in an essay in *New Youth* in 1917:

1. Don't neglect substance in writing.
2. Don't imitate the ancients.
3. Don't neglect grammar.
4. Don't moan if you're not sick.
5. Don't use stilted language and outworn poetic diction.
6. Don't use allusions.
7. Don't use parallelisms.
8. Don't avoid colloquialisms.

The primary target of these negatives was clearly poetry – more particularly, the classical verse of the late-Qing period, which Hu Shi believed to be a degenerate epigone of Tang and Song poetry. In the following issue of *New Youth*, Chen Duxiu advocated the use of a modern vernacular along with a form of Western literary realism under the slogan of 'literary revolution', without much regard to genre. The staying power of the classical language was again shown by its use in both writers' proposals. Only in 1918 did *New Youth* switch from classical to vernacular throughout.

Hu Shi himself was more influential in theory and criticism than in his own poetry. He had been writing prose in vernacular Chinese since 1905 and began vernacular poetry in 1916. His poems in *New Youth* in January 1918, along with poems by Liu Fu and Shen Yinmo (1883-1971), were the first vernacular poems to appear in print, and his collection *Experiments* (1920) was one of the first collections of vernacular poetry. The first edition of *Experiments* consists of two sections of vernacular poetry, the first written before his return to China in September 1917 and the second covering the following two years. It also includes appendices of his classical verse, suggesting an inhibition about the literary revolution that is also conveyed in the tentativeness of the title. The poems themselves tend to bear out this supposition. In his preface to the second edition of 1921, Hu Shi noted that his early attempts at vernacular poetry were no more than 'vernacularised' old poetry, and that his true 'new poems' began with the poems written after his return to China. According to Hu Shi, conservative opinion at the time of publication regarded the first section as poetry and the second section as 'not poetry', and the same distinction was also made by his supporters using different terminology.

With the exception of elegies on lost friends, Hu Shi's poetry is characterised by detachment and impersonality. His adherence to American pragmatism led him to confine his themes deliberately to his limited personal experience, though some poems deal more generally with China's political and social problems. There is also a touch of pragmatism in his abandonment of the traditional rhyme categories (based on pronunciations from centuries earlier) for rhymes based on sounds in current spoken Chinese. As described above, the adoption of vernacular Chinese automatically implied rejection of the traditional five or seven-syllable (or word) line and the tonal patterns of classical regulated verse, and Hu Shi experimented with lines of different length to incorporate colloquial forms. He also included Chinese transcriptions of foreign names into his verse lines (e.g. Ibsen, Brieux and Edison), which caused some controversy. His use of modern colloquial Chinese, however, is limited, and much of his verse, in grammar, vocabulary and structure, remains close to the semi-colloquial forms of Song and Yuan lyric and dramatic verse.

'Dreams and Poetry' (1921) not only sums up Hu Shi's poetic credo but is perhaps also his most successful poem:

> *They are ordinary experiences,*
> *All ordinary experiences,*
> *Emerging by chance in a dream,*
> *They are transformed into strange new patterns!*
>
> *They are ordinary feelings,*
> *All ordinary words,*
> *Encountering by chance a poet,*
> *They are transformed into strange new verse!*

Once drunk we know wine's strength,
Once smitten we know love's weight;
You cannot write my poems,
Just as I cannot dream your dreams.

His insistence on pragmatism and individualism is here softened by such things as appeals to imagination and the senses, the use of significant form to give a mirror structure to the poem, and the use of repetition to lend musicality to the vernacular (compared with Guo Moruo's use of repetition to direct the reader's attention to the content of his verse).

Hu Shi's vernacular poetry has been called a bridge or a signpost to the new movement rather than successful examples of his principles. Nevertheless, his lifelong eminence as a critic and educator continues to draw attention to his work. From his youthful advocacy of literary revolution to the academic administration and scholarship of his last years in Taiwan, he was an example of the most successful of China's new professional intellectuals as successors to the former scholar-officials. (*For Hu Shi's influence on drama see Chapter 5.*)

Guo Moruo (1892–1978)

Guo Moruo, unlike most other May Fourth writers, knew little of the melancholy and depression typical of young men from declining gentry families. He came from a prosperous merchant Hakka family, recently settled in Sichuan, which aspired in the traditional way to higher status by educating its sons. As a child, he was schooled in the traditional classics, but Confucian learning no longer conferred office and he also attended modernised secondary schools in Jiading and Chengdu. From his early teens, he claimed, his pastimes included reading, revolution, fighting, drinking, masturbation and flirtations with male prostitutes, opera performers and fellow-schoolboys. In 1914 he went to Japan in preparation for a Western-style professional career as a new intellectual with scientific training: in his case, medicine.

Like other medical students in Japan, Guo Moruo's first foreign language was German, and as the study of medicine proved irksome and his readings in German literature led from romanticism to expressionism, he embraced with enthusiasm the concept that the function of literature was self-expression. Although he professed to believe that the cry of a child was 'pure poetry', Guo Moruo did not, however, isolate himself from the concern shown by other young writers with changes in Chinese society and the fate of modern intellectuals; according to his formulation, poets as creative writers were by nature revolutionaries seeking change. In this way, he managed to reconcile two apparently contradictory positions, giving reign to his desire for subjective freedom within a framework of aspirations for a role in social change.

By his own account, Guo Moruo started to write vernacular poetry in 1916. In 1918 he decided on a career as a poet (which for him at that time meant primarily cultivating his emotional sensibility rather than studying poetic technique or reforming society through the depiction of social evils), and his first poems were published in 1919 in the Shanghai literary supplement *Study Lamp*, edited by Zong Baihua. An important step in becoming a professional writer was to found the Creation Society with friends and fellow students in Tokyo in 1921, including Yu Dafu, Tian Han and Cheng Fangwu, rather than join forces with the Literary Research Association. The Taidong Press in Shanghai gave him a post as editor of the Creation books and journals, and the first Creation publication was his own *The Goddesses*, later the same year. Guo Moruo then returned to Japan to finish his studies, handing over local editorial responsibilities to Yu Dafu.

There is no evidence that Guo Moruo was inspired or influenced by Hu Shi, and he claims himself that his first sight of vernacular poetry was work by Kang Baiqing in *Study Lamp*; his poetry is seen best in relation to the classical tradition, as both reactive and assimilative. His first models were Tagore and Whitman, and his earliest vernacular poetry varies between extreme simplicity and self-conscious extravagance. References to Goethe (especially to the Faust legend), Byron and other Western writers are interspersed with Chinese mythological figures, poets and philosophers. The verbal exuberance and predilection for romantically vague mysticism in his first collection, *The Goddesses* (1921), recalls *The Songs of the South* and the Daoist classic *Zhuangzi*, but there are also echoes of *The Book of Songs* in his second and third collections, *The Starry Sky* (1923) and *The Vase* (1927). His fourth and fifth collections, *The Vanguard* (1928) and *Recovery* (1928) owe less to Chinese tradition and more to contemporary revolutionary rhetoric. The easy sentimentality of early enthusiasms for Rider Haggard and Walter Scott runs through his work.

Although in his essays Guo Moruo praised spontaneity, his poems are vehicles for specific beliefs, invoking the names of thinkers as varied as Zhuangzi, Spinoza and Kabir as part of his poetic vocabulary. His most prominent ideals are social justice, rebellion and iconoclasm, egotism and self-expression, pantheism, Marxism and internationalism. Romantic and sexual love was not an overriding interest in Guo Moruo's poetry. Soon after arriving in Japan he fell in love with a Japanese nurse who became his common-law wife and had five children. In the spring of 1925 he embarked on a brief affair with a young admirer, the result being the sequence of love poems which forms *The Vase*. Love poetry at that time was very much in vogue, but after 1925 it never again featured in Guo Moruo's work.

Professions of concern with social injustice were to become a cliché of twentieth-century Chinese verse, but at this time social criticism had a fresh, revolutionary quality in the context of current practice, continuing a Confucian sense of obligation as expressed in verse by the great Tang poets Du Fu and Bai Juyi and the Song poet Xin Qiji, but largely ignored by conventional Qing and early Republican poets. The use of mythology to express dissatisfaction with contemporary politics is clearly derivative from 'Encountering Sorrow' and the Qu Yuan legend (from *The Songs of the South*), to which Guo Moruo would turn again in prose drama; as in the traditional reading of 'Encountering Sorrow', the narrator-poet depicts himself as a noble hero frustrated by the evil politicians of his time. The ideas of rebellion, iconoclasm and self-conscious heroics have an obvious Western ancestry in Byron and Whitman but can also be related to Daoist eccentricity and a folk culture tradition of knight-errant swordsmen and secret society rebels. Guo Moruo's pantheism similarly draws openly on both Chinese and Western literature and philosophy, but his intense and exultant egoism is directly quoted from Nietzsche in lines like 'I am an idolator' (1920).

Marxism and internationalism are the most strikingly radical elements in his cluster of values, Guo Moruo being in this regard typical of younger Chinese intellectuals during the first decades of the century. The ideas are combined in the poem 'Victorious in Death', which gives a pretentious depiction of the poet as a warrior in solidarity with the international revolutionary cause. Guo Moruo's references to class struggle and self-identification as a 'proletarian poet' in *The Goddesses* and *The Starry Sky* are superficial and unconvincing; even after he earned his revolutionary credentials in the Northern Expedition, the focus of his poetry continued to be his own feelings in confronting specific examples of social injustice. His fervent internationalism, however, even if only in the form of name-dropping, is confirmed in almost every poem. Guo Moruo seems not to have been plagued by the sense of inferiority that caused writers like Lu Xun and Yu Dafu to revile themselves as belonging to a class and civilisation in decline; he saw himself as heir to world civilisation, his proud task as a twentieth-century Chinese poet being to pass on and add to this inheritance. His contribution, unacknowledged though it has been outside his own society, was the re-creation of a reworked Chinese mythology in modern verse.

Further, in spite of his praise of spontaneity, Guo Moruo was more innovative than Hu Shi in creating a new formal poetics. The first step was to replace the literary language with a new kind of written vernacular, borrowing from Western grammar, vocabulary and even proper names to create a distinctively new poetic diction. Occasionally whole words or lines in a foreign language were incorporated into the verse structure, as Yu Dafu was doing in fiction at the same time. This practice may have been copied from Eliot or Pound, but it is also possible that Guo Moruo and Yu Dafu invented the idea independently. The play of stressed and unstressed syllables in polysyllabic words and phrases in English verse corresponds roughly with stressed and unstressed syllables in spoken Chinese (in contrast with the predominantly monosyllabic line of classical verse), so that the vernacular line could with relative ease both copy and incorporate foreign words and rhythms.

The new diction, polysyllabic and with variable stress, inevitably meant rejecting the traditional verse line composed of a fixed number of words (or syllables). Guo Moruo experimented with a number of verse patterns, such as lines of roughly equal length and lines of greatly differing length, regular and irregular metres, stanzas of varying length, and rhymed and unrhymed stanzas, refusing to admit any rules of composition. Parallelism also had to be abandoned, as Hu Shi recognised, but while Hu Shi retained a classicist's dislike of repetition (which is found only in special cases in Lyrics and in some folk poetry), in Guo Moruo's poetics, repetition, with and without variation, is very frequent and sometimes the only structurally unifying device in a particular poem.

Again, unlike Hu Shi, Guo Moruo increased the range and frequency of allusion (by including Western culture as a source) instead of abandoning it in favour of images. He also introduced a new range of symbols, among which the most striking were the sun (rather than the moon, with its associations of eroticism, intoxication and mystery), the sea (rather than rivers, more familiar to inland Chinese) and blood (not previously associated with life), while the colour red, especially in his later poems, stood for revolution rather than fecundity. These symbols, which stand for inexhaustible strength, power and life, are not only relatively new to Chinese poetry but imbue it with uncharacteristic vigour. In Guo Moruo's poetics, exaggeration replaces understatement, explicitness replaces suggestion, and boldness replaces subtlety, in open repudiation of tradition.

As mentioned above, not all of Guo Moruo's poems exhibit the same stridency. 'Footprints in the Sand' is quiet, reflective and melancholy. It deals untypically with conflict between nature and man, but ends with man being absorbed into nature: his shadow and footprints are transitory; nature moves but is eternal. The thought is not original but the expression is modern, and Guo Moruo shows himself still a worshipper of nature even in his dismay at human impermanence.

The effect of Guo Moruo's innovations was vastly more dramatic than Hu Shi's restrained experiments, and he quickly became the centre of a group of like-minded literary revolutionaries, a model for budding writers, and a hero to a generation of Chinese students acquiring their first taste of Western culture. His essays on poetry, literature and art were just as Promethean as his verse, compensating for lack of consistency and logic with passion. His earliest slogans proclaimed simultaneously 'art for art's sake' and 'literature as self-expression', with social concerns as a kind of by-product of the poet's egotistic and individualistic expression. In fact, the Creation Society put forward a programme of literary study and translation not dissimilar to earlier recommendations by Chen Duxiu and Hu Shi. Guo Moruo's conversion to Marxism in 1924 was an extension of, rather than in contradiction to, his earlier views on literature: as Cheng Fangwu put it in 1926, it was a step from literary revolution to revolutionary literature. Most of Guo Moruo's radical enthusiasm was carried forward without pause, while his mythopoeic pantheism became subsumed in a similarly mystical concept of historical necessity.

In March 1926, after financial and other difficulties led to the suspension of the Creation periodicals, Guo Moruo went to Guangzhou, then a centre of left-wing activity, where he became dean of the College of Arts of the Sun Yatsen University. He regrouped the Creation Society there with Yu Dafu, Wang Duqing (who had just returned from France), Cheng Fangwu and Mu Mutian. In 1927, he joined the Northern Expedition as vice-director of the political training department, took part in the Nanchang Uprising in August and joined the Chinese Communist Party. Following the Nationalists' anti-Communist coup, he sought refuge first in Shanghai; in February 1928, he fled to Japan, where he remained for almost a decade. During this period he devoted himself to translation, autobiography and history but wrote no poetry. The second stage of his career as a poet began with the War against Japan: see Chapters 5 and 9 below.

Guo Moruo's poems, in *The Goddesses* especially, were immensely influential in the 1920s and 1930s. However, the qualities that were most ardently imitated, such as his experiments in free verse, his heavy-handed allusions to Western culture and current events, his hyperbole and extravagance, and his display of concern for social justice, soon lost their glamour in the further development of May Fourth literature. His later prominence in left-wing politics as an apologist for different factions in power kept his works in print longer than reader interest would have dictated. His pioneering role as poet, critic and literary activist, and his later studies in the origins of Chinese civilisation, also tend to obscure the immaturity of his creative work, which is consulted today only by literary scholars and historians.

Liu Dabai (1880–1932) and Liu Fu (1891–1934)

An early variation in vernacular poetry took *The Book of Songs* and contemporary folksong as a model. This trend was represented by Liu Dabai and Liu Fu, whose work appeared in early May Fourth publications such as *New Youth* and *Awakening* in the company of Hu Shi, Zhou Zuoren, Lu Xun and Guo Moruo. Liu Dabai, a graduate of the old examination system from Shaoxing and afterwards head of the department of Chinese at Fudan University in Shanghai, was an established poet in the classical tradition before becoming an enthusiastic convert to vernacular poetry after 1919. The most original poems in his collection *Old Dreams* (1924) are the imitations of folksongs, jingles and children's rhymes as vehicles for social protest in the voice of the poor. He also composed a large quantity of vernacular free verse and traditional lyric poetry on sentimental and moral themes, published in several volumes in the 1920s and 1930s. During this period, Liu Dabai enjoyed a successful career as a scholar–official, culminating with his appointment as Vice-Minister of Education in the Nationalist government.

Liu Fu (aka Liu Bannong), a student at Beijing University from 1917 to 1920 and in France from 1920 to 1925, was also much influenced by the current wave of interest in folksong. In 1919 and again in 1925, he published two groups of folksongs from his local region in coastal Jiangsu. His own poems in folksong style were written in 1920 and published in book form along with a selection of some of the originals under the title *The Clay Pot* (1926), in the same year as his own collection *Flourishing the Whip*. From the mid-20s on, he spent less time on poetry and more on his academic studies in linguistics.

Both Liu Dabai and Liu Fu used the four-syllable line from the 'Regional Airs' section of *The Book of Songs* as well as free verse forms. Like Hu Shi, they were not opposed to Chinese tradition in toto but with what they saw as the degeneration of elite literature in Ming and Qing. Paradoxically, their classical scholarship made them particularly able to exploit the folksong-like verse forms of the *Songs*.

Kang Baiqing (1896–1945), Zhu Ziqing (1898–1948) and Yu Pingbo (1900–90)

The Literary Research Association is best known for its fiction writers and publications like *Short Story Monthly*, but it also included members of a group around Hu Shi in Beijing writing and publishing vernacular poetry in 1918-20 for magazines such as *New Youth* and *New Tide*. These writers, who include Shen Yinmo, Liu Fu,

Yu Pingbo and Kang Baiqing, adopted other careers after graduation in the early 1920s, and, in some cases, abandoned vernacular poetry for classical. Many of them played an active role in the first years of the Literary Research Association, contributing to *Short Story Monthly* on its transformation into the Association's main organ and subsequently to its magazine *Poetry*, founded in January 1922. Edited by Liu Yanling and Ye Shengtao, with the assistance of Zhu Ziqing, Yu Pingbo and Zheng Zhenduo, *Poetry* is the first magazine devoted to vernacular poetry, and the Association's anthology *A Snowy Morning* (1922), featuring contributions by Zhou Zuoren, Guo Shaoyu and Xu Yunuo, as well as *Poetry's* five editors, was also the first of its kind. The most successful of the Association poets during this period were Xu Yunuo, Kang Baiqing, Zhu Ziqing and Yu Pingbo.

Kang Baiqing, originally from Sichuan, wrote large quantities of classical and vernacular poetry in 1919–20 for *New Tide* and *Young China* while a student at Beijing University. Published in book form in 1922 under the title *The Grass* by the Yadong Press in Shanghai (which also published Hu Shi's *Experiments* in 1920, Yu Pingbo's *Winter Night* in 1922 and Zhu Ziqing's *Traces* in 1924), and reprinted in two separate volumes in 1923 and 1924, the poems show the typical May Fourth characteristics of sentimentality, individualism, romanticism and patriotism. Kang Baiqing showed considerable inventiveness in devising a new written vernacular and relegated his classical verse to an appendix (in the style of Hu Shi). Apparently dissatisfied with his experiments, however, he gave up vernacular for classical poetry in the early 1920s.

Zhu Ziqing, a native of Shaoxing, was born in Donghai and brought up in Yangzhou. He studied at Beijing University between 1916 and 1920, where he came to identify himself with the literary revolution and the new intellectuals. After graduating he turned to school-teaching for a living, and his sense of futility and dismay at this inglorious end is echoed in his first collection of poetry and prose, *Traces* (1924). The most ambitious work in this collection is 'Destruction' (1923), a long philosophical poem which owes its structure to *The Songs of the South*. The poem shows considerable imaginative power, a wide range of poetic vocabulary and skilful use of the classical device of parallelism, but its disillusion is expressed with a somewhat bland pathos. His shorter lyrical poems are generally insipid and sentimental, but 'Postprandial' and 'The Modern Age in a Small Cabin' are convincing demonstrations of the author's middle-class sympathy with servants and fear of the potential for violence among the deprived. In 1925, Zhu Ziqing joined the staff at Qinghua University and afterwards wrote little poetry; he remained an influential scholar, critic, anthologist and essayist.

Yu Pingbo also introduced themes and motifs from *The Songs of the South* into his verse. His first poems, collected in *Winter Night* (1922), are typical of the early days of new poetry in their combination of classical and modern elements, experiments in line length, stanza length and rhyme, and themes of solitude, futility and nostalgia. After two more collections, *Returning from the West* (1924) and *Reminiscences* (1925), he devoted himself to academic research in traditional Chinese fiction.

Kang Baiqing, Zhu Ziqing and Yu Pingbo contributed only briefly to the new poetry movement, and their reputation as men of letters is based chiefly on their later scholarly books and occasional essays.

Xu Yunuo (1894– 1958) and Wang Tongzhao (1897– 1957)

Xu Yunuo was one of the most prolific and highly praised of the new poets but stood somewhat outside the group above. He made his literary début in Beijing in 1920 with a short story in the *Morning Post Supplement*, edited by Guo Shaoyu, and joined the Association under the sponsorship of Zheng Zhenduo. His poems appeared in each issue of *Poetry*, his was the largest contribution to *A Snowy Morning*, and his own collection, *Garden of the Future*, which has a preface by Zheng Zhenduo, was also published in 1922. His output dwindled after this impressive year and by 1926 he had fallen silent.

Xu Yunuo came from Lushan in Henan, an area where banditry was rife, and his schooling was irregular. At normal school in Kaifeng he came in contact with the New Culture movement through magazines like *New Youth*. After graduating in 1921, he taught in schools up and down the country, and though he enjoyed correspondence and personal acquaintance with members of the Association, he was not active in the literary circles of Beijing and Shanghai. His poem 'The Singer' laments the desperate conditions in his bandit-ridden home village, and melancholy and nostalgia are characteristic features of his work. Part of his appeal in the early 1920s was his identity as an independent and somewhat bizarre figure outside the urban literary intelligentsia. He took part in the resistance to Japan during the war years, then resumed his career as a teacher. He also took up writing again and became a member of the Writers' Association in 1956.

Wang Tongzhao was an outsider who quickly became an insider, a prolific writer and literary activist during the first half of the twentieth century. From a wealthy family in Shandong, he went to Beijing in 1918 where he took part in the May Fourth movement. While still a student he became a contributor and later an editor of the *Morning Post Supplement*. The only poet among the founding members of the Literary Research Association, he also edited *Short Story Monthly*, *Thread of Talk* and other literary magazines, and published six collections of vernacular poetry between 1925 and 1940, along with essays and fiction. His early romantic style gave way after 1927 to left-wing and then to patriotic verse. Between travels in Japan, the north-east, Egypt and Europe from 1927 to 1935, he returned to his home base in Qingdao. From 1935 through the war years he lived in Shanghai, writing and editing as circumstances permitted, and returned to Qingdao in 1945. (*For Wang Tongzhao's fiction see Chapter 4.*)

Zhou Zuoren (1885–1969), Lu Xun (1881–1936) and Yu Dafu (1896–1945)

Zhou Zuoren was more important as an activist in new poetry than as a writer: although he only published one volume of poetry (*Past Life*, 1930), he contributed prefaces to dozens of poetry collections in the 1920s and 1930s, and his essays and lectures on humanism and the new literature were very influential. His prose poems, published in *New Youth* and *Short Story Monthly*, helped introduce this form into China, but given the criticism that most of the early new poetry was too prosaic, it was not surprising that prose poetry failed to catch on in China. The one collection of prose poetry which has attracted considerable attention is Lu Xun's *Weeds* (1927). Partly this is because of Lu Xun's eminence in the new literary movement; partly it is due to the complex nature of the work itself.

Weeds consists of twenty-three short pieces published in *Thread of Talk* between 1924 and 1926, plus an introduction dated 1927. They include narratives, satires, reminiscences, dream sketches, a short play and even doggerel verse. It was a period when Lu Xun was on the one hand depressed about the current state of Chinese politics and also pessimistic about the ability of his former protégés and Chinese youth in general to come up with a better alternative, and on the other hand in the middle of a deeply satisfying love affair with a former pupil which held a promise of private happiness for the first time in his life. It was also a time of crisis in his creative work: his second collection of short stories proved to be his last, and for the remaining nine years of his life he produced mainly polemical essays and journalism. *Weeds* was a unique venture in a subjective, lyrical mode. Its common thread is Lu Xun's obsession with the 'powers of darkness'.

Yu Dafu is most famous for his fiction, but he also wrote poetry and essays. Vernacular poetry was mostly a young man's game: May Fourth writers typically turned to classical as they grew older. Yu Dafu is notable, like Lu Xun, for his lifelong habit of preferring classical to vernacular. His schoolboy interest in classical poetry was reawakened in 1922 while employed as a teacher at the Anjing College of Law and Administration (in addition to his editorial work on Creation publications). At the end of 1926, Yu Dafu (who had declined to take part in the Northern Expedition) was sent from Guangzhou to Shanghai to clear up Creation Society affairs. While so engaged he began an affair with the socialite beauty Wang Yingxia, and in August 1927 he broke completely with the Creation Society. The following year he became a co-editor with Lu Xun of *Torrents*, and in 1930 was a founding member of the League of Left-Wing Writers. In 1932 he withdrew from Shanghai life and politics, and in the relative seclusion of Hangzhou composed classical poetry; he also wrote essays with a traditional flavour, on every possible subject except politics. From 1934 on, he began to contribute mainly to Lin Yutang's magazines such as *The Analects* (of which he was editor from 1936 to 1937), and served briefly with the Fujian provincial (warlord) government in 1936. His classical poems on his marital crisis, written at this time, were published in Hong

Kong in 1939 to great scandal. He continued to write classical poetry during the war years, as he travelled first in China, then to Singapore and finally to Sumatra, where he was executed by Japanese security police. (*See also the sections on Lu Xun and Yu Dafu in Chapter 4.*)

Bing Xin (b. 1900)

Xie Wanying, best known under her pen-name Bing Xin, is the only woman poet of the new literary movement whose reputation outlasted the 1920s. This is in part because her exceptionally long life as a creative writer kept her name before the reading public, but the simplicity, sentimentality and conventionality of her poetry retained their appeal to youthful readers over several decades. One of the youngest poets to contribute to the new movement, she was also one of the earliest: her first two collections, *Stars* and *Spring Waters*, were published in the Literary Research Association's series in 1923. A third collection, incorporating the first two with additional poems, came out in 1933 under the title *Bing Xin's Collected Poems*, and has been available in different forms ever since.

The daughter of a naval officer, Bing Xin grew up in the coastal town of Yantai on the Shandong peninsula where she was tutored in the classics by her uncle. In 1914, after some years' schooling in her native Fujian, she went to Beijing where she studied at a Christian secondary school and later at Yanjing University. She took part in the May Fourth Movement as secretary to the female students' association at the university. Her essays, stories and poems were first published in the Beijing *Morning Post Supplement* and *New Tide*, and, from 1921 on, she also contributed to the Association's periodicals such as *Short Story Monthly*. Bing Xin's first and lasting model was Rabindranath Tagore (1861–1941), whose *Stray Birds* (English translation 1916) inspired a fashion for 'short poems' in the period 1919–22: many of her poems are only two or three lines, and few exceed the length of a sonnet. There seems little influence from the poet Li Qingzhao, whose lyrics she read as a child and who was the subject of her MA thesis at Wellesley College during her studies there in 1923–6. She published very little poetry after her return to China and appointment as a teacher at Yanjing but continued to be active as an essayist throughout her life.

Bing Xin's poems mostly describe the happiness of childhood and family life, the beauties of land- and seascapes, and the charm of animals and insects. Despite her youth, many poems begin with an apostrophe followed by exhortation: a poet is invoked and enjoined to follow nature; young people are advised to take thought for the future; fellow humans are asked to love one another; blades of grass are encouraged to feel proud of their ubiquity. The doubts or anguish that plagued Bing Xin's male contemporaries rarely appear in her poems, not so much because of any lack of sensitivity but because of different expectations. (*For Bing Xin's fiction see Chapter 4.*)

Zong Baihua (1897–1986) and Tian Han (1898–1968)

The short poem was also the preferred form of Zong Baihua and Tian Han, friends of Guo Moruo and early members of the Creation Society. Zong Baihua, originally from Jiangsu, studied German at Qingdao University and Tongji University in Shanghai. He took part in the May Fourth Movement and became an editor for *Young China* in Shanghai. He was the founding editor of *Study Lamp*, which during his six months tenure he made a platform for Guo Moruo, Tian Han and Yu Dafu. In 1920, he went to Germany for further studies, and after his return in 1925 withdrew from the literary world to build a successful academic career. His only collection was *Flowing Clouds* (1923), published by the Yadong Press. Like Bing Xin, Zong Baihua found the short poem a happy vehicle for describing nature, but his vision is more abstract and philosophical. Many of his poems are about love, usually represented by a red flower, but the passion is also universalised. Tagore and haiku were his twin inspirations.

Tian Han, better known as a dramatist, was one of the first new poets to explore the typographical possibilities of new poetry, using staggered line indentations and direct speech in quotation marks. His only collection of verse was *Spring in Edo* (1922), but he continued to write free verse throughout his life, although he broke off relations with the Creation Society, for personal reasons, in 1922. (*For Tian Han's plays see Chapters 5 and 9.*)

Wang Jingzhi (1902–96), Ying Xiuren (1900–33), Pan Mohua (1902–34) and Feng Xuefeng (1906–76)

Love poetry – rebellious, sensuous and erotic – became a dominant theme of the literary revolution in the early 1920s. Among the earliest to write new-style love poetry were four poets from Zhejiang and Anhui: Wang Jingzhi, a teacher; Ying Xiuren, a bank clerk; Pan Mohua, a normal-school student; and Feng Xuefeng. Wang Jingzhi's poems, published in *New Tide*, *New Youth*, *Short Story Monthly* and *Poetry* during 1921 and 1922, were the most notorious. After a chance meeting at Hangzhou, the four published a joint collection, *Lakeside* (1922), followed by Ying, Pan and Feng's *Spring Songs* (1923).

Written when he was barely twenty, Wang Jingzhi's free-verse poems advocate freedom of choice in love and marriage and denounce Confucian rules on family conduct. The publication of his first one-man collection, *Orchid Wind* (1922), was condemned as a bad influence on the young but defended by Zhu Ziqing (who wrote the preface), Ye Shengtao, Zhou Zuoren and Hu Shi for its defiance of social taboos. Wang Jingzhi's second and last collection, *The Lonely Country* (1927), shows the author moving in a new direction. Using rhyme and even line lengths for more forceful rhythms, the majority of the poems in *The Lonely Country* express frustration and despair, expressed theatrically in a language of doom with frequent reference to biblical imagery.

All four gave up poetry after the May Thirtieth Incident in 1925. Wang Jingzhi stopped writing after joining the Chinese Communist Party in 1925 and became a full-time academic after 1945. Ying Xiuren also joined the Party in 1925 and spent three years in the Soviet Union. He joined the League of Left-wing Writers in 1930 and later wrote stories for children about life in the Communist rural bases. He was arrested and died at the hands of Nationalist agents in Shanghai in 1933. Pan Mohua, after two years at Beijing University, went to Wuhan to carry out propaganda for the Northern Expedition, and joined the Communist Party in 1927; he was arrested in Tianjin in 1933 and died in prison the following year. Feng Xuefeng joined the Communist Party in 1927, became a prominent left-wing critic, and was Lu Xun's closest associate from 1928 to 1936. During two years in a Nationalist prison in 1941–2, he wrote his last collection of poetry,

Song of Reality (1943). He occupied a number of important editorial posts after 1949 but was expelled from the Party and excluded from literary life in 1958.

Xu Zhimo (1896–1931)

The May Thirtieth Incident of 1925 had a profound effect on many May Fourth poets: some abandoned poetry for scholarship, some escaped into pure poetry, and others became committed revolutionaries. Three notable collections of poetry were published that year, marking a new phase in the history of modern poetry: Xu Zhimo launched the Crescent school, Li Jinfa the symbolists and Jiang Guangci the proletarians. Xu Zhimo and Jiang Guangci both died in 1931, and Li Jinfa had already stopped writing by that time, but despite the brevity of their lives and careers, they are among the more influential Chinese writers of this century.

Xu Zhimo was born into a Zhejiang banking family which had been prominent in commerce and industry for several generations. He was given a traditional education at home followed by a semi-modern schooling. In 1910 he became Yu Dafu's classmate at Hangzhou Secondary School. After marriage in 1915, he attended Shanghai University, followed by Beiyang University in Tianjin and finally Beijing University in 1916. At this time, he became a personal disciple of Liang Qichao. In 1918, he left for the United States, where he first enrolled in Clark University in Massachusetts in banking and sociology then transferred to Columbia, where he obtained his MA in political science in 1920. Like most Chinese students abroad, he was active in student societies of a vaguely radical nature. In the autumn of 1920 he sailed for England, where he attended the London School of Economics before finding his spiritual home at Cambridge. He did not attend lectures but quickly formed friendships with such literary figures as E.M. Forster and I.A. Richards. Joined by his wife in 1921, he nevertheless started an affair with the daughter of a Chinese friend and sued for divorce the same year. It was at Cambridge that he finally decided on a literary career, admiring with equal fervour the philosophy and outlook of G.E. Moore, Walter Pater, Christian martyrs, Russian revolutionaries and Bloomsbury writers.

Returning to China in 1922, Xu Zhimo became a member

of the Literary Research Association and contributed poems to the leading literary supplements such as *Study Lamp*. In March 1923, with Hu Shi as a close friend and backer, he formed a private club at his house in Beijing, the Crescent Society (named after the title of a collection of Tagore's prose poems), and attracted national attention the next year as Tagore's chief interpreter and companion in China. In the autumn of 1924, Hu Shi managed to get him appointed professor at Beijing University, teaching English and American literature. Xu's flamboyant way of life also attracted attention. His former mistress was engaged to the son of Liang Qichao, and when Xu Zhimo attempted to resume relations with her in Beijing, he received a stern rebuke from his former teacher. A highly publicised affair with a married woman, Lu Xiaoman, made it expeditious for Xu Zhimo to leave the country, and in March 1925 he took the Trans-Siberian Express through the Soviet Union to Europe; back in England, he paid a visit to Thomas Hardy. Returning to China in August, he continued his affair with Lu Xiaoman, whom he married after her divorce the following year – and was again subjected to strong criticism from Liang Qichao.

In his first collection, *Zhimo's Poems* (1925), a privately circulated volume later reprinted by the newly-founded Crescent Press, Xu Zhimo was content to write the kind of free verse common in the early 1920s. What distinguishes the collection is the compressed power of his verse. His depiction of erotic love and the suffering in his homeland, sometimes combined in one poem such as 'This is a Coward's World', is unusually direct. The collection also exhibits a kind of optimism and enthusiasm unusual at the time, providing a suggestive link with Guo Moruo's work.

From October 1925 to October 1926, Xu Zhimo was the editor of the Beijing *Morning Post Supplement*, in which he set up two special sections, *Poetry* (April–June) and *Drama* (June–September). *Poetry* became a forum for the members of the revived Crescent Society (himself, Wen Yiduo, Zhu Xiang, Zhu Danan, Rao Mengkan and others) to explore new formal patterns for poetry. His second collection, *A Night in Florence* (1927), marks the first stage of his experiments with English metres.

At the end of 1926, as the Nationalist government began a campaign against the northern warlords centred in Beijing (where the alarmed administration suspended academic salaries), Xu

Zhimo, Hu Shi and other academic friends from the Anglo-American group moved to the relative safety of Shanghai. Here the Crescent Society was formally inaugurated (with Xu Zhimo, Liang Shiqiu, Hu Shi, Wen Yiduo, Ding Xilin and Rao Mengkan among the founders), the Crescent Press set up in spring 1927 and its journal, *Crescent Monthly*, launched in March 1928. Xu's manifesto in *Crescent Monthly* rejects all existing schools of poetry and speaks grandly of 'creative idealism' and 'the health and dignity of man's soul'. In his private life, however, he found the state of his soul suffering from the mundane cares of marriage and work, and over the next few years gloom and disillusion drifted into his poems. In the summer of 1928, he set out again for the United States, Europe and Britain, partly to collect funds to establish a rural settlement in China in imitation of Tagore's Santiniketan village, but the project collapsed not long after his return to China in 1929. *Crescent Monthly* turned to politics in 1929, and Xu Zhimo dropped out (along with Wen Yiduo), reappearing with the revived *Poetry* in 1931.

Xu Zhimo's third collection, *The Tiger* (1931), is written in more or less regular stanza form, occasionally rhymed. Although the title pays homage to William Blake, it also contains the first imitation of T. S. Eliot in Chinese verse, while the influence of Tagore can be seen in the verses in praise of smallness and humility, such as 'The Autumn Moon'. There are poems on the evils of civil war and social injustice in China, including 'By an Unknown Roadside', on poverty, and 'The Cricket', condemning commercialism. 'A Second Farewell to Cambridge' (1922), a descriptive poem highly praised for its polished technique, has become a standard anthology piece, especially in school textbooks. Romantic exoticism is here expressed as 'occidentalism' (the geographic reverse of 'orientalism'), but it is noticeable that the still-patriotic poet does not bring Cambridge 'clouds' back to China with him. Other often-anthologised pieces in the collection are love poems such as 'Pipa Tune in an Alley at Midnight'.

Early in 1931 Hu Shi returned to Beijing University as dean of the arts faculty and again arranged a teaching position there for Xu Zhimo. Not wishing to cut himself off from his other activities, Xu Zhimo, who loved to fly, travelled frequently by air between Beijing, Nanjing and Shanghai. He died in a plane crash in November, only a few months after his appointment.

Wandering in the Clouds (1932) is a posthumous compilation by Chen Mengjia from Xu Zhimo's last years and may include work that the author felt unready for book publication. It includes a long but unfinished narrative poem, 'Love's Inspiration', which marks a new stage in Xu Zhimo's development. The debt to Tagore is clear, as the poem describes a cycle of birth and death against a background of rural reconstruction as carried out by Tagore in Santiniketan, but there are also references to Christian religious practices and the storyline closely resembles *La Dame aux camélias*. The other poems are mostly lyrics: 'Don't Pinch Me, Pain', is the most erotic in Xu Zhimo's work. There is less colloquialism in this collection and more recourse to literary Chinese, and it is tempting to speculate that had he lived into maturity, Xu Zhimo may have contributed to a revival of classical poetry for the modern age.

Wen Yiduo (1899–1946)

Although Wen Yiduo and Xu Zhimo were close literary allies in the second half of the 1920s, they had very different personalities and came from very different backgrounds. Wen Yiduo was from a scholar-gentry family in Hubei and was educated in a traditional family school where he studied the Chinese classics. In 1912 he enrolled at Qinghua University in Beijing, where he began writing classical poetry. At Qinghua he came into contact with Western literature, and after taking part in the student movement, readily switched to the vernacular in 1920. His early interest in painting is evident in the striking colour imagery in poems written between 1920 and 1922, included in his first collection, *Red Candle* (1923), published by the Creation Society's Taidong Press. English romanticism, Anglo-American imagism and Tang classicism are easily apparent influences. Free verse in the May Fourth style dominates the collection, but some poems are rhymed and there are signs of regular metrical rhythms.

In 1922, Wen Yiduo went to the United States, where he studied painting and poetry at the Chicago Art Institute, Colorado College and the Art Students League in New York. His interest in Western poetry was stimulated in Chicago, where he met contemporary poets such as Harriet Monroe, Carl Sandburg and

Amy Lowell, and gradually he switched his main interest from painting to poetry.

Back in China in 1925, Wen Yiduo had a natural literary affinity with the Anglo-American group of returned students, but he was preoccupied with China's fate in a way unlike his friends. Hu Shi and Xu Zhimo moved easily in English and American schools, but Wen Yiduo had encountered racial prejudice in US Chinatowns. Like other students abroad from old gentry families, he resented being treated like a coolie by Americans who assumed that all Chinese worked in laundries or restaurants. The poem 'Laundry Song' (*c.* 1925) suggests that Americans with their soiled clothing are more unclean than the humble 'Chinaman' who washes them.

Wen Yiduo's attitude to the West was a divided one: he admired and imitated Western poetry but he detested Western imperialism and aspects of Western culture that he saw as destroying China. His attitude towards his own culture was just as complex: he admired traditional Chinese poetry but believed that China was obliged to modernise in order to resist conquest by the West. The tensions engendered by such conflicts resulted in Wen Yiduo's finest poems, written between 1925 and 1928 and published in *Dead Water* (1928) by the Crescent Press. During this period, Wen Yiduo began to develop his theories of art as an activity rather than a product: as an expression of social concern it could become an alternative to political action. Technical skill in writing was seen as both a source of creativity and a pleasurable activity in itself, compatible with both Western and Chinese classicism.

Wen Yiduo returned from the United States without a degree, and at first employment was difficult to find. Private tragedy and family troubles also burdened his life at this time, but on appointment to a teaching post at the Beijing Arts Academy, he organised a political group among young intellectuals like himself. In January 1926 he joined Xu Zhimo's revived Crescent Society and in March became the editor of *Poetry*, a section in Xu's *Morning Post Supplement*. The massacre of students in the March 18th Incident turned the first issue of *Poetry* into a denunciation of the authorities. In 1927, Wen Yiduo took part in propaganda work for the short-lived Wuhan government, but the devastation which followed the Nationalist coup made it advisable for him to retreat temporarily from active politics. That autumn he was appointed to teach English and American literature at Nanjing University, and spent his free time preparing a reaffirmation of his early ideals on art and literature. Practically, this meant compiling his second collection of poetry, *Dead Water*, and making plans with Xu Zhimo for the forthcoming publication of *Crescent Monthly* in Shanghai.

As the initial excitement of the literary revolution abated, many readers felt that the poems of the Literary Research Association circle were flat, boring and prosaic, while the Creation poets were shallow and (after 1923) narrowly political. Wen Yiduo's principles, developed in the mid-1920s, fall under three headings: pictorial beauty (images and symbols), musical beauty (rhyme and rhythm), and architectural beauty (regular stanzaic form). While showing no inhibitions about borrowing from the West, Wen Yiduo's proposals are based on the nature of modern spoken Chinese and the needs of modern Chinese readers.

In his own poems, Wen Yiduo moved from simple visual imagery to more complex symbols, rarely resorting to allusions from Western or Chinese culture except where the image itself added colour (for example, the red candle, borrowed from Li Shangyin). He was particularly critical of Guo Moruo for over-indulgence in references to Western culture, pointing out as early as 1923 the absurdity in replacing Confucius with Socrates. Admitting that his own early poetry suffers from the same fault, he believed that the new poetry should describe things specifically and recognisably Chinese, meaningful both to the poet and to the reader. At the same time he was anxious to avoid classical allusion, which he thought stale and out of place in new China; instead the poet should describe aspects of the modern age. Since the modern age itself was both bizarre and ugly, he introduced into Chinese verse the aesthetics of the grotesque as practised by French symbolists such as Baudelaire.

The operation of this principle can be seen in 'Laundry Song'. Instead of the vague generalisations and abstract symbols of Guo Moruo's political poetry, Wen Yiduo concentrates on details: dirt, sweat, stains, blemishes, soap and water: all are concrete but imply wider meanings. A more sophisticated essay occurs in his most famous poem, 'Dead Water', in which filth and stagnation are given a weird kind of beauty of their own.

Though he admired Guo Moruo's poetry for its strength and

spontaneity, Wen Yiduo believed that poetry had more impact when it observed formal rules of structure. Dissatisfied with the looseness of free verse, he experimented with the transplantation of English versification, including rhythm, rhyme, stanzas, repetition and refrain. His desire for musicality implied the use of rhyme, which he defended in modern verse because of the natural richness of homophones in spoken Chinese; his rhymes were based on contemporary pronunciation and not on the 'reading rhymes' used in traditional Chinese verse. He objected to the indiscriminate use of colloquialisms in poetry, arguing that poetic diction needed to be condensed and controlled for the sake of musicality.

Wen Yiduo's most influential innovation was in metre. The so-called natural rhythm of plain speech advocated by Hu Shi resulted in a poetic line no different from prose; on the other hand, the fixed patterns of stressed and unstressed syllables in English metrical feet, as first used by Xu Zhimo, were too rigid for vernacular Chinese. For a time he tried a fixed number of syllables per line, creating the so-called 'beancurd' effect (beancurd is sold in squares), the typographical neatness of which also appealed to poets like Xu Xu (see Chapter 7). His ultimate solution was a line based on a regular number of metrical feet (or 'sense groups') in which each foot consists of at least one stressed syllable plus a mixture of stressed and unstressed syllables. This happy balance of regularity and flexibility was adopted by many vernacular poets and has remained a standard device ever since. (The effect, of course, is lost in translation.)

Wen Yiduo's third principle concerned 'architectural beauty' in vernacular poetry. Traditional Chinese verse like English verse contains many variants of stanza length and rhyme patterns. (Some of these patterns, as Wen Yiduo knew, are also found in traditional Chinese folksong.) The earliest vernacular poets used a wide variety of stanza patterns, rhymed and unrhymed, native and imported, and Wen Yiduo's innovations in this regard are not so striking. He tended to favour the English quatrain, sometimes with a refrain or a repeated line, as in 'Laundry Song', but also used shorter rhymed stanzas and an undivided long stanza composed of rhymed couplets. The requirement for meaningful structure is impractical, since there is only a limited number of ways in which words can be arranged on a page, but Wen Yiduo managed to produce a few examples. In 'Laundry Song', the opening quatrains are repeated at the end in reverse order, closing one cycle and beginning another in the endless round of cleaning and soiling and cleaning. The last lines of the interior verses are not repeated but parallel. The lines are of precisely equal length, the second lines rhyming with the fourth, and after each quatrain comes a refrain. This structure is often used for ballads in English and is therefore very appropriate for this folksong-like protest, but perhaps only readers familiar with English literature appreciate its significance.

Wen Yiduo advocated purifying the subject-matter of poetry, returning it to traditional poetic themes such as love, nature and death, but the events of the outside world were not so easily excluded. Many of the poems in *Red Candle* and *Dead Water* are addressed to his wife (of an arranged marriage) and to the daughter who died while he was away (from home). Some of his most famous poems, such as 'Heartbeats' (aka 'Quiet Night') and 'Confession', present the impossibility of individual happiness in an unjust world. 'The Deserted Village', written immediately after the 1927 coup, when the Nationalists took back villages occupied by the Communists since the Northern Expedition, describes the contrast between the destruction of human life in the countryside and the continuing vitality of nature, a theme first made famous by Du Fu. 'Dead Water', also written after the coup, depicts China as a ditch of hopelessly stagnating water. More forcefully than the other poems, it prophesies change as possible only through destruction (i.e., revolution). His own role in this change remained ambivalent. In spite of the declaration in 'Heartbeats' that the poet cannot be content with individual happiness, he remains inside his room, unwilling to sacrifice his individual peace even knowing about the misery outside. In 'The Deserted Village', he calls on someone else to summon the villagers back home: he himself remains a sympathetic but passive onlooker. In 'Dead Water' as well he calls on intellectuals not to abandon China, so full of beauty and prosperity despite its present desolation; but again he cannot bring himslef to do more than to call other people's attention to its plight.

These three famous poems demonstrate a tightly interwoven social and aesthetic engagement: squalor depicted in its own perverse beauty. Wen Yiduo was the only one of his group able to master this combination of social protest and artistic technique, but the balance was unstable, as shown by the melodrama of 'Night Song'. Unable to reconcile his conflicting ideals, Wen Yiduo stopped writing completely after a final poem, 'Miracle', in 1930, which can be read as a repudiation of poems such as 'Dead Water'.

Wen Yiduo remained an editor of *Crescent Monthly* until it switched to politics in 1929, and he was also an editor of the 1931 *Poetry* with Xu Zhimo, Chen Mengjia and Zhu Xiang. After teaching classical literature in Wuhan and Qingdao, he returned in 1932 to Qinghua University, where as one of the most famous poets of his time he became a patron to many younger writers. He continued to be involved in new literature along with his colleagues Zhu Ziqing and Shen Congwen, but his main activity was the study of classical Chinese poetry (though he also lectured on foreign literature). He developed an interest in Qu Yuan and *The Songs of the South*, an interest which Guo Moruo in exile in Japan was still pursuing; Wen Yiduo was in a different kind of exile in Beijing. When finally he chose to engage in open political activity, he was shot dead. (*For details of Wen Yiduo's later life and tragic death see Chapter 8.*)

Li Jinfa (1900–76)

As shown above, the Literary Research Association and Zhou Zuoren came under criticism from Wen Yiduo and Guo Moruo for the prosaic poetry published under their aegis. The appearance of Li Jinfa's second collection, *Singing for Joy* (1926), in the Association's book series must have startled many readers but demonstrates Zhou Zuoren's dedication to cultivating young talent; Zhou Zuoren also sponsored Li's first and third collections, *Light Rain* (1925) and *The Retainer and Hard Times* (1927), both in the Beixin Press New Tide Society series. While Li Jinfa's poetry is too derivative to be called genuinely original, it is certainly unlike anything else published in China at this time. Just as unexpectedly as he first appeared, however, he also disappeared, another of the many young writers of the time who exhausted their talents within three or four years.

Li Jinfa was born in Guangdong and seems not to have had connections with the Beijing or Shanghai university-based cliques which dominated the literary scene of the 1920s. Most of his poems were written during his student years in Paris, Dijon and Berlin, and he stopped writing in 1927. Typically for his time and his age, they are love poems filled with frustration, hopelessness and gloom, so that the title *Singing for Joy* requires some explanation. Li Jinfa claims that his poems will encourage the ecstasy of sexual love in his prudish homeland. To this end, he employs a variety of shock tactics: suspension of logical and grammatical relationships, bizarre imagery, and irony. The model is French symbolism, chiefly Verlaine and Baudelaire; the mood is self-consciously decadent, featuring words denoting weariness, death and decay. For added exoticism, French and German words and allusions are freely (sometimes perhaps at random) scattered in the text. The poems aroused considerable controversy, but they also had their defenders and a small group of followers in the 1930s.

A sculptor as well as a poet, Li Jinfa had studied fine arts in Paris and on return to China became a professor of fine arts at several Shanghai universities. During the war he devoted himself to literary propaganda, and afterwards worked in the Chinese embassy in Iraq. From Iraq he went to the United States, where he wrote his memoirs and stayed for the remainder of his life.

Wang Duqing (1898–1940), Mu Mutian (1900–71) and Feng Naichao (1901–83)

Wang Duqing, Mu Mutian and Feng Naichao, three young poets who gravitated to the Creation Society in the mid-1920s, also sought a more technically sophisticated poetry along the lines of late-nineteenth-century French verse. They soon abandoned poetry for direct political activity in the Creation Society's later phase, and their initial experiments in poetry found few readers or imitators for another half-century.

Wang Duqing left his native town, Xi'an, after a newspaper he was editing became too barbed for official tastes. In Japan, he studied biology before deciding that his true passion was literature. Returning to Shanghai for the May Fourth Movement in 1919, he worked as an editor while taking part in the labour movement. In 1923, he went to Paris still with his biology books, but soon traded them in for Kant, Nietzsche and Spinoza. The title of his first collection, *Before the Madonna* (1926), prepares the reader for the Western flavour of its twenty-six poems, written between

1923 and 1925 during the author's three years in France. In correspondence with Guo Moruo and other members of the Creation Society, he endorses their principle of social reform through poetic creativity, but there is little evidence of this in his poems. Wang Duqing kept in touch with active student groups abroad, but much of his time was occupied by a love affair that ended with an unwanted child, and his despair at his own dissipation is his main theme. In 1925, receiving reports on the May Thirtieth Incident, he wrote 'About to Sail for Home', one of several farewells to decadence and the Latin Quarter; in 'I've Returned to My Country', he echoed the same theme between sketches of poverty and corruption in Shanghai. *Before I Die* (1927), a sequence of ten lovelorn poems probably written in Europe, is prefaced by a long poem, 'The Will' (1927), in which the poet again declares his intention to sacrifice his art for the sake of revolution. He took part in the Creation Society's campaign for revolutionary literature, helped edit the journals, and joined the others in Guangzhou as dean of the College of Arts and Sciences at Sun Yatsen University. His own work, however, in *Venice* (1928), *Fragments* (1932) and *Discipline* (1932), showed little sign of change. After the Nationalist coup in 1927, he retreated to Shanghai, only to be expelled from the Creation group as a Trotskyist.

Like Guo Moruo, Wang Duqing expresses modernity through allusions to Western high culture and Chinese mythology. The image of a Madonna in an Italian museum is compared, with the help of Sima Qian's *Historical Records*, to the virgin mother of Confucius, while Rome, with the help of lines from *The Songs of the South*, calls to mind ancient Chang'an (his native city). Like Guo Moruo, he implies elite education by including words and lines from exotic languages (French and Italian) in his verse, as in 'I Came out of a Café', 'Before Dante's Tomb' and 'About to Sail for Home'. He differs from Guo Moruo in his attempt to create musical effects with the least number of words, producing poems strongly influenced by Verlaine. In turning to regular rhyme, rhythm and stanza construction based on Western examples, Wang Duqing contributes as an independent to the trend initiated by Xu Zhimo and Wen Yiduo.

Mu Mutian's verse is also very much influenced by nineteenth-century French verse, but in his case he got no further abroad than Japan. A native of Jilin in Manchuria, he studied French at Tokyo University in 1923–6, and taught French on his return to China. Although he only produced one volume of poetry, *The Traveller's Heart* (1927), he remains one of the most technically inventive poets of the century. The themes themselves are the familiar ones of love and nostalgia; his experiments are auditory and visual.

Some of Mu Mutian's innovations are untranslatable literally: the juxtaposition of words of similar sound, the juxtaposition of characters written in similar ways, and the juxtaposition of internal and end rhymes. Others translate without difficulty: repetition of line beginnings and, most strikingly, blank spaces within verse lines as disconnectives between image sequences. His most famous anthology piece, 'Pale Chimes' (1926), in which most of these auditory and visual effects appear, also contains in its title an example of synaesthesia (blending of sense perceptions), another device borrowed from the French symbolists.

After joining the League of Left-wing Writers in 1930, Mu Mutian became more active politically, a change of direction also reflected in his poetry. He joined the Communist Party in 1932 but was expelled in 1934. In 1932 he also helped found the left-wing Chinese Poetry Society in Shanghai and spent the war years teaching, writing and publishing in the south-west. After the war he taught at Shanghai's Tongji University and transferred to Beijing's Normal University in 1952.

Feng Naichao was born in Yokohama to a Cantonese business family with close ties to Kang Youwei, Liang Qichao and Sun Yatsen. In 1923 he entered the philosophy department at Kyoto University, transferred to sociology at Tokyo University the following year, then changed his subject to aesthetics and art history. At Cheng Fangwu's prompting, Feng Naichao went to China in 1926 and afterwards played a prominent role in Creation activities. His early verse lacks the more obvious innovations practised by Li Jinfa, Wang Duqing and Mu Mutian, but the assimilation of symbolism perhaps goes deeper. His poems are collected in *The Red Gauze Lantern* (1928), a title which evokes a type of decadence familiar from traditional Chinese poetry. Of the Chinese writers of his generation he comes closest to Mallarmé's concept of 'pure poetry', where not a message but a mood is to be conveyed. His use of Christian imagery is presumably due more to technique than to faith, though it carried special appeal to the many readers who had received a missionary education and had not yet discarded its influence on patriotic grounds.

On joining the Communist Party in 1928, Feng Naichao gave up writing symbolist poetry. He taught at several left-wing universities in Shanghai, became a founding member of of the League of Left-wing Writers and edited several of its publications. He spent the war years engaged in propaganda work in the interior, and after the war moved from Shanghai to Hong Kong. After 1949 he enjoyed a succession of official appointments. Between 1951 and 1975 he was a professor at Sun Yatsen University, and in 1975 transferred to Beijing as an advisor to the National Library.

Jiang Guangci (1901–31) and Yin Fu (1909–31)

Jiang Guangci's poetry anticipated the later phase of the Creation Society. Born in Anhui, he was the son of a small shopkeeper, but as a student, poet and political activist, like Guo Moruo, he declared himself to be a member of the proletariat. He took part in the May Fourth Movement, joined the Communist Youth League and was sent to study in the Soviet Union in 1921. During his four years in Moscow, he wrote a number of poems celebrating the October Revolution, Communism, Lenin and Moscow. His main collections of verse are *A New Dream* (1925), dedicated to 'the revolutionary youth of the East', *A Lament for China* (1927), and *War Drums* (1929). He also published several novels in the late 1920s. The rhetorical flourishes and strident tone of Guo Moruo's revolutionary poetry are even more unrestrained in Jiang Guangci's work, although there is no evidence of direct borrowing. Jiang Guangci claimed as his heroes Byron and Heine and translated poetry by Nekrasov and Blok, but the interminable red banners in his work wave over adolescent fantasies: for all his actual revolutionary activities, his imagery remains curiously abstract and formulaic.

On his return to China in 1924, Jiang taught at the Communist Shanghai University, acted as translator to the warlord Feng Yuxiang's Soviet advisor in 1925, and then returned to Shanghai University. Towards the end of 1925, he joined the Creation Society; in 1926 he took part in the Northern Expedition and later joined the coalition government in Wuhan. After the

Nationalist coup, he took refuge in the foreign concessions of Shanghai, where after quarrelling with the Creation writers, he founded the Sun Society, dedicated to proletarian literature, in 1927. In 1929 he found it necessary to retreat temporarily to Japan, but returned to Shanghai after several months. In October 1930, after having offered to resign, he was expelled from the Communist Party as a petty-bourgeois writer who disobeyed party discipline. He died not long after helping to found the League of Left-wing Writers. (*For Jiang Guangci's fiction see Chapter 4.*)

Yin Fu left his Zhejiang village in 1927 for Shanghai, where he was soon arrested and imprisoned for three months. Back home, he was temporarily cut off from revolutionary activities: several poems from this period relate his complex feelings in regard to his past and future life. His identification of his mother as a 'Mary of the East' perhaps hints at his divided loyalties at this time. In 1928 he returned to Shanghai, studied German at Tongji University for a year and joined the Sun Society. The poems written in this year express a positive determination to celebrate the coming revolution and solidarity with the international proletariat. He left university in 1929 to work in the underground labour movement, was arrested again during a factory strike and released the same year. In 1930 he joined the League of Left-wing Writers, where he met Lu Xun, and compiled a selection of his poems from the 1920s under the title *The Children's Pagoda*. He was arrested by the Nationalists and executed the following year aged twenty-one. Thanks to Lu Xun, the manuscript survived, but only thirty-five of the original sixty-five poems were published in the 1954 Beijing edition of his works. According to the author's preface, the collection was to serve as a memorial to his early life before he had dedicated himself to the revolutionary cause, and includes love poetry written between 1924 and 1927.

Zhu Xiang (1904–33)

Zhu Xiang was among the most accomplished young poets who gathered around Wen Yiduo in the 1920s. As a child he was educated in the classics by a private tutor and later went to a village school in his native Anhui. He later studied engineering at a vocational college in Nanjing and learned English at night school, but in 1922 he vowed to read nothing but poetry. In

1924 he entered Qinghua University, where Wen Yiduo had been a student, and became a member of the Literary Research Association. After graduating in 1927, he went abroad to study at Lawrence University, the University of Chicago and Ohio University. On returning to China in 1929, he established links with Wen Yiduo and the Crescent group. He also taught English literature at Anhui University, but after a disagreement with the principal in 1932, he resigned and returned to Shanghai. From then until his suicide by drowning, he drifted from place to place without regular employment. Since he was the only May Fourth poet who committed suicide, the frequent mention of death in his poems should not be taken lightly.

During his short life, Zhu Xiang wrote prolifically. His poetry is collected in four volumes: *Summer* (1925), published in the Literary Research Association's series; *The Wilderness* (1927), in the New Writing series also sponsored by the Association; and two posthumously compiled volumes, *The Stone Gate* (1934), again in the Association's main series, and *Eternal Words* (1936). Despite his personal ties with Wen Yiduo and Xu Zhimo, he criticised both older poets for carelessness in technique and dismissed Hu Shi's poems as feeble.

Summer consists of twenty-six poems written between 1922 and 1924, about half the author's output. Most are descriptions of nature, frequently infused with a young man's melancholy, and the first three poems are about death and desolation. Several poems are dedicated or sent to friends. Although Wen Yiduo is the subject of one, the tone of another is borrowed from 'Encountering Sorrow' and Guo Moruo. A third group of very short poems expresses alienation and grief through images of a caged bird, a castaway, snow, the evening sky, and so on. In these early poems, the author shows both ingenuity and imitation: experiments with structure, perspective and mood in both English romantic and Tang classical styles.

The Wilderness consists of thirty-four poems written between 1924 and 1926. Although under this fashionable title the themes are again love, death and nature, the work as a whole is more impersonal than *Summer*. Descriptions of nature, for example, are invocations of sounds and scents rather than direct visual perceptions. Four long narrative poems accompany the usual short lyrics and ballads. The only poem referring to contemporary events is

'Lament for Sun Yatsen', written a few weeks after Sun's death; it is also one of the few occasions where the poet speaks directly in his own voice. Another example is 'A Life of Light', one of the last in the collection and serving as a preface, where he contemplates his own life and death.

The advance in technique in *The Wilderness* is striking. Drawing on Chinese and Western models, Zhu Xiang developed a wide range of verse patterns and a simplification of the written vernacular which mark him as one of the finest lyricists of his generation.

The Stone Gate is Zhu Xiang's longest collection; it is divided into five distinct sections, the arrangement and contents not necessarily reflecting the poet's own wishes. Part I consists of thirty-three short poems in the style of *Summer* and *The Wilderness*, but showing a wider range of language, voice and theme. There are more examples of reflection on the human condition and even current events – one poem describes refugees from the civil war in the countryside, and the impersonal voice has become bleak or even bitter instead of merely detached. (It is likely that by this time Zhu Xiang had become familiar with the poetry of T.S. Eliot and W.H. Auden.) Part III is a formidable display of craftsmanship, arranged according to verse patterns: one couplet, four quatrains, three triolets, one villanelle, three ballades, fourteen roundels, seventeen Elizabethan sonnets and fifty-four Petrarchan sonnets. The mood is again sombre, as the poet contemplates the joylessness and imperfection of human life. As appropriate to their form, many of the sonnets are addressed to or describe individuals: Hawthorne, Dante, Shaw, Homer, Don Juan, W.H. Davies, Rabelais and Xu Zhimo. The remainder of the collection can also be called experiments in form: a single narrative poem in Part II, three short prose poems in Part IV and a verse drama in Part V.

Perhaps the most notable advance in the collection as a whole is in language. Zhu Xiang's vernacular was compressed almost to the brevity of the literary language in *Summer*; in *The Wilderness* it became more directly colloquial, while in *The Stone Gate* there seems to be an attempt to create a new poetic diction based on Western vocabulary and grammar. No other Chinese poet has expended so much effort on exploring Western versification, and though later stages in the history of Chinese poetry brought few successors and few readers, nevertheless Zhu Xiang's achievement is remarkable.

Rao Mengkan (b. 1901), Shao Xunmei (1898–1975), Sun Dayu (b. 1905), Sun Yutang (b. 1910) and Chen Mengjia (1911–66)

In Beijing and Shanghai, from the mid-1920s to the beginning of the 1930s, Xu Zhimo and Wen Yiduo fostered the talents of a number of young writers. Among those who published with the *Morning Post* supplements and *Crescent Monthly* during this period were Rao Mengkan from Jiangxi, Sun Yutang from Jiangsu, and Shao Xunmei, Sun Dayu and Chen Mengjia from Zhejiang. Most of them gave up writing poetry in the 1930s for academic studies. Two other promising young Crescent contributors were Zhu Da'nan (d. 1931) and Fang Weide (d. 1935).

Rao Mengkan, a disciple of A.E. Housman, is best known for his poem '18 March' on the 1926 massacre of Beijing students.

Shao Xunmei ran the small press that published *Crescent Monthly*. From a banking family like Xu Zhimo, he also studied in England and was an admirer of Swinburne. His first collection of poetry, *Heaven and May* (1927), was reprinted the following year under the more fashionable title *Flowerlike Sin*; his short stories show the influence of Yu Dafu.

Sun Dayu was born in Shanghai, attended Qinghua University in Beijing and studied in the United States. On returning to China, he taught at universities in Wuhan and Beijing, becoming known for his translations from Shakespeare as well as for his own verse.

Sun Yutang, born in Wuxi, studied history at Qinghua University and at Tokyo University and later wrote historical drama. His best-known poem is 'The Precious Horse', an historical epic which won the *L'Impartial* literary prize for poetry in 1937.

Chen Mengjia, son of a Protestant clergyman, studied law in Nanjing before transferring to theology at Yanjing University. After the Japanese invasion of Manchuria, he moved to Shanghai to take part in anti-Japanese activities, then returned to Beijing where under Wen Yiduo's influence he turned to historical scholarship.

Feng Zhi (1905–93)

Feng Zhi's lifespan as a poet was exceptionally long for modern Chinese letters, from his student years until old age. Born in Hebei, he was a student at Beijing University from 1921 to 1927. He made his literary debut in 1924 in a Shanghai quarterly, *Hidden Grass*, published jointly by Feng Zhi and friends; it was followed by *The Sunken Bell* in Beijing, which appeared irregularly between 1925 and 1932. His first collection was published in 1927 by Beixin Press in Shanghai, in Zhou Zuoren's *New Tide* series, under the Blakean title *Songs of Yesterday*. With the exception of one long poem on the theme of necrophilia, these poems have been widely anthologised.

After graduating in 1927, Feng Zhi found employment as a teacher of Chinese in a Harbin secondary school but left after only one year. The poems from this period are collected in his second book, *The Northern Journey and Other Poems* (1929). Feng Zhi's start as a metaphysical poet is the poem entitled 'A Southern Night', a series of carefully graded images which culminate in the final couplet. The title poem, his longest, is a narrative of the poet's social education in Harbin in the 1920s, where his conscience was awakened by the sordid and brutal decadence of Chinese warlords, Russian exiles, Korean prostitutes and Japanese adventurers. The title recalls Du Fu's famous 'Northern Expedition' and the theme of a country ravaged by invasion and corruption is similar, but Feng Zhi's version of his frustrations is more sentimental and loosely constructed.

After his return to Beijing in 1928, Feng Zhi turned his attention to his academic work. He spent 1930–5 in Heidelberg and Berlin, studying German literature, art and philosophy. His doctoral thesis was on the poetry of Novalis. On returning to China in 1936, he was appointed professor at Tongji University, and he joined the South-west United University in Kunming in 1939. It was not until 1941 that he wrote for publication again. (*For Feng Zhi's later work see Chapter 8.*)

Dai Wangshu (1905–50)

From Hangxian, Zhejiang, Dai Wangshu attended secondary school in Hangzhou before getting his first taste of revolutionary education at Shanghai University in 1923. Dai Wangshu's earliest poetry is deeply influenced by his studies of Baudelaire, Verlaine and Jammes, whose works he read in French. His first collection, *My Memories* (1929), consists of twenty-six poems arranged in three sections. The images which occur throughout the collection are rain and mist, a wanderer, memories and dreams, dark graveyards and deserted gardens, broken hearts and pale faces. His most famous poem is 'The Rainy Alley' (1927), in which like Verlaine he achieves a delicate fusion of blurred images and sensations in brief, musical lines. The title poem is more severe in tone. The most unusual poem is 'A Severed Finger', about a relic in his possession: the finger of a friend who was arrested in a worker's home for revolutionary activity.

Between 1929 and 1932, Dai Wangshu moved away from these early imitations towards a more remote poetry which rejected the obvious appeal of musicality for unconventional expressions of mood. With Shi Zhecun, Du Heng and other friends, he established in 1932 the Modern Press, the *Modern Writing Series* and the magazine *Modern Times*; his own poems were collected under the self-dismissive title *Wangshu's Drafts* in 1933 in the series. Some of the earlier verse is reminiscent of Maeterlinck, whose poems Dai Wangshu was translating in 1929. The neo-symbolist Francis Jammes is also a strong influence, shaping dreams of non-existent people and things which form the poet's 'memories'. The poem 'Country Girl' was praised by Ai Qing for its venture outside the enclosed world of the poet's mind into the real world, but the 'girl' of the poem is just as imaginary as the naked woman of 'Come Here to Me'. Towards the end of the volume, the gentle melancholy of the early poems passes into a more restless, disturbed world of delirium and insomnia, but the technique remains basically the same: juxtaposed images, synaesthesia and a confused narrative progression.

Like Feng Zhi, Dai Wangshu established a reputation with his first two collections from the late 1920s and early 1930s, but is best known for his later work. (*For Dai Wangshu's poems from the 1940s see Chapter 8.*)

Feng Wenbing (1901–67), Cao Baohua (1906–78), Lin Geng (b. 1910) and Lu Yishi (b. 1913)

Feng Wenbing, who wrote under the name Fei Ming, is associated with Wen Yiduo, Zhou Zuoren and Lu Xun. After graduating from the English department of Beijing University in 1929, he stayed on as a teacher. During the war he went back to his native province of Hubei, resuming his position at Beijing University in 1945. His quiet, reflective poems from the 1930s show his strong attraction to Hardy, Buddhism and Daoism. He published one volume of poetry, *Riverside* (1944), a novel and a few collections of stories.

Cao Baohua dedicated his first collection to Zhu Xiang, a fellow-graduate of Qinghua University, and shared his interest in formal verse patterns such as the sonnet. He also resembles Dai Wangshu in his progress from symbolism to modernism and eventually to patriotic verse during the War against Japan. His first collection, *To the Muse* (1930), was published in Ba Jin's series *Literature Miscellany*, followed by *In Praise of the Setting Sun* (1931) and *Spiritual Fire* (1932) for the Crescent Press, and *Poems Without Titles* (1937), in the series edited by Ba Jin for the Culture and Life Press. After the war, he wrote little original verse but continued to translate.

Lin Geng is a native of Fujian but was born in Beijing where his father was a professor of Chinese and Indian philosophy at Qinghua and Beijing universities. After graduating from Qinghua in 1933, he stayed on as a teaching assistant in Chinese. During the 1930s, he produced three collections, *Night* (1933; with a preface by Yu Pingbo), *Spring Fields and the Window* (1935) and *Beiping Love Songs* (1936). Lin Geng wrote in free verse but achieved a classical restraint by dispensing with personal pronouns and punctuation and by careful composition in a style reminiscent of the ancient *The Songs of the South*. Although his poetic career was very short, it coincided with the rise and decline of the *Modern Times* school with which he was linked.

Lu Yishi's first collection, *Life Gone Through* (1935), contains poems written between 1933 and 1935 in Yangzhou and an epilogue by Shi Zhecun; most were first printed in *Modern Times*. The self-consciously 'modern' flavour of these poems is achieved by a relentless expression of nihilism and disgust with contemporary life. In Taiwan, where he has lived since 1948, he has also published verse condemning the government in Beijing.

Wang Yaping (b. 1905) and Pu Feng (1911– 43)

Events such as Guo Moruo's flight to Japan in 1928, Yin Fu's execution in 1931, the death of Jiang Guangci in 1931, Wang Jingzhi's immersion in politics after 1925, and the constant supervision of the Nationalist government left a notable gap in left-wing poetry at the turn of the decade. At a conference in Gutian in 1929, the Communist Party began the first of its attempts to re-introduce folksong and village drama into the new literary movement, but owing to the Nationalist blockade and also to the independence of the Shanghai left-wing, news of their success or failure took time to filter through to the urban proletarian poets. Under the direction of the League of Left-wing Writers, the young Communist poet, Pu Feng, along with the former Creationists like Mu Mutian, founded the Chinese Poetry Society in 1932 to advocate a 'song style' in order to popularise the new poetry.

Pu Feng, a native of Meixian in Guangdong, began a career in revolutionary poetry at an early age and with great haste, producing his four collections between 1935 and 1936. His poetry continues the sloganising typical of Sun Society poets such as Jiang Guangci within a more rhythmical form, based on Western and Chinese ballads.

Wang Yaping's poems on China's suffering masses have a more obviously traceable literary origin but are also based on the direct experience of a participant. From a Hebei peasant family whose fortunes were declining, Wang Yaping began his political career by being expelled from normal school; not long after, he fled to Beijing and Tianjin to avoid jail. After the Nationalist coup in 1927 he was obliged to go underground, and during the wanderings of those years he became aware at first hand of the Japanese encroachment of north and coastal China. In 1931 he was in Shanghai, where he met Pu Feng, Mu Mutian and other members of the Chinese Poetry Society. He returned to Beijing to set up the Hebei branch of the society, but his publications were banned and he was obliged to escape to Qingdao. In Qingdao, where he stayed for three years, he became acquainted with Wang

Tongzhao and Zang Kejia, who encouraged him to write. His literary education included the works of Lu Xun, Guo Moruo and Pushkin, whose influence is evident in his first collection, *Winter in the City* (1935), published by the left-wing International Press in Shanghai.

Winter in the City is divided into six sections: Miscellaneous Songs, Songs of the City, Songs of Night, Songs of Life, Songs of the Countryside and Storm Song. The main theme throughout is the suffering and despair caused by an unjust social system, conveyed through images of a cold, dark, wintry desolation. Wang Yaping's rhetorical devices include terse, clipped lines, repetition of words and phrases and frequent exclamations. Like much of Guo Moruo's verse, they are more convincing read aloud than on the printed page.

Pu Feng and Wang Yaping continued writing during the war years but produced little of lasting interest; the new left-wing poets who left their mark on the 1930s were Zang Kejia and Ai Qing.

Zang Kejia (b. 1905) and Ai Qing (1910–96)

Zang Kejia first took up politics when he joined the Northern Expedition straight from normal school in his native province of Shandong. After the Nationalist coup he entered Shandong University at Qingdao where, under the influence of Wen Yiduo and Shen Congwen, he became associated with the politically disengaged Crescent Society. His first collection of poetry, *The Brand* (1934), is noted for its intricate craftsmanship. While still at university, he gradually returned to his former left-wing outlook. In an essay written in 1934, he denounced Xu Zhimo, Wen Yiduo and Dai Wangshu for their aesthetic preoccupations. The poems in his second collection, *The Black Hands of Sin* (1934), written at Qingdao University in 1933 and 1934, declare his intention to confront the grimness of the real world with an unmodulated voice. After graduation in 1933, he taught at schools in the Shandong peninsula until the outbreak of war.

Zang Kejia's poetic persona in *The Brand* and the first part of *The Black Hands of Sin* is that of the outsider, the radical intellectual observing the lives of the urban poor and denouncing the system responsible for their misery. His descriptions of proletarian life are original, thoughtful and accurate, avoiding the empty clichés and posturing of the Creation and Sun revolutionaries. The second half of *Black Hands* concerns the peasantry, and was written after returning to his village for the New Year at the beginning of 1934, as the contrast between the noisy festivities of town and the silence of his home village provoked a series of reflections on the poverty of the Chinese countryside. In the first poems of this series, he is still an outsider, but soon the visitor reveals himself as a native son. He recalls a time when the villagers planted their crops with hope and when the old rituals were observed with faith and good will, in contrast to the present, where the ravages of civil war and natural disaster blight the land.

Zang Kejia rejected the more obvious foreignisms so beloved of most 1920s and 1930s poets: the foreign words, the allusions to Western culture, the devices of the symbolists, the experiments in Western verse form. He avoided the standard sentimental topics of love, death and nature, the delicate language of soft rain, fading roses, pale hands and deserted graves, even the passionate invocations and heroic exhortations of the rebels and revolutionaries. Nevertheless, although some of his lines echo the language and structure of traditional Chinese poetry and folksong, they are still clearly modern and vernacular, and the ideology informing his observations of urban and rural poverty is a product of Western thought.

Ai Qing produced only one collection before the outbreak of the War against Japan, but with it established an immediate name as a distinctive new voice. *Big Dike River*, a forty-one-page pamphlet containing nine poems and illustrations by Chagall and the author, was published at the author's expense by the Masses Magazine Company in Shanghai in 1936 (after having been turned down by the Culture and Life Press).

The first work in *Big Dike River* is 'Big Dike River – My Wetnurse', a portrait of Ai Qing's childhood nurse whose origins were so humble she was known only by the name of her birthplace, Big Dike River. It is followed by 'The Death of a Nazarene', a narrative of the Crucifixion. Two sketches of night scenes illuminated by points of light depict somewhat schematically the darkness inhabited by China's masses and their future hopes. 'Ballad of a Painter' and 'Reed Pipe' describe his debt to modern painting and poetry. The final two poems are portraits of Paris and Marseilles.

These poems were written during Ai Qing's imprisonment for 'seditious activity' in the French Concession in Shanghai in 1932–5, several years before the author joined the Communist Party. Although his left-wing sympathies are clear, he shows an uninhibited admiration for French painting, poetry and life as enjoyed in his student years in France (1929–32). Born in the last months of the Qing dynasty, he received an early education in the classics but is one of the few poets of his time to rely wholly on the modern idiom in his poetry. Throughout his life he remained consistently loyal to the free verse form of his youth, avoiding a tendency towards prose by devices such as dramatically varying line lengths, parallelism, repetition, enumeration and vivid colour contrasts.

Zang Kejia and Ai Qing continued to write during the war years and became state-subsidised poets after 1949. (*For their later work and careers see Chapters 8 and 13.*)

Bian Zhilin (b. 1910)

By the mid-1930s, the former division between Crescent poets and Moderns had blurred. The *New Poetry Monthly*, for instance, edited by Bian Zhilin, Sun Dayu, Liang Zongdai, Feng Zhi and Dai Wangshu in 1936, belonged to no specific school but published work of a generally Westernised aesthetic sensibility. Bian Zhilin was the most original of the contributors.

Bian Zhilin was born in Jiangsu in what he later described as a 'petty bourgeois' family. He received a traditional primary school education in his home town, followed by a modernised secondary schooling during which he became acquainted with the new poetry. His first greatly admired exemplars of vernacular poetry were Bing Xin's *Stars* and Guo Moruo's *The Goddesses;* Xu Zhimo's *Zhimo's Poems* and *Dead Water* were more lasting influences. After completing senior secondary school in Shanghai, he enrolled at Beijing University in 1929. In his second year, after extensive reading in English and French literature, he began to write 'new poetry' in earnest. Xu Zhimo, Wen Yiduo and Shen Congwen were his first patrons.

Bian Zhilin is the author of some of the most complex poems from twentieth-century China, and their publication history is similarly complex. His poems were written in a series of 'little waves' (his own words) but not published in book form in strict chronological order. The Crescent Press published *Leaves of Three Autumns* in 1933, but as Bian Zhilin moved towards modernism, his second collection, *Fish Eyes* (1935), was published by the Culture and Life Press in the series edited by Ba Jin, while his joint anthology with He Qifang and Li Guangtian, *The Han Garden* (1936), was published at Zheng Zhenduo's suggestion by the Commercial Press in the Literary Research Association's series. The later collections, however, include some of his earliest poems.

Bian Zhilin's first 'wave' was in 1930–2 (with a one-year interval following Xu Zhimo's death). Mainly introspective works like 'A Piece of Broken Ship' reflect his interest in late nineteenth- and early twentieth-century French poetry. In 1933–5, in imitation of the early T.S. Eliot, Bian experimented with the technique of dramatic irony in long narrative poems, such as his famous 'City in Spring', describing the city under threat of Japanese invasion. The last 'wave' of his pre-war poetry was in 1937, under the tutelage of Yeats, Rilke and Paul Valéry.

After graduating in 1933, Bian Zhilin taught in Baoding for one term before returning to Beijing. In 1935 he spent five months in Japan, and on returning to China taught at a senior secondary school in Ji'nan. The appearance of *Fish Eyes* and *The Han Garden* drew criticism from the left-wing for the poet's lack of political involvement, to which Bian Zhilin replied sharply. Like He Qifang, he pointed to the shallowness of what passed for left-wing poetry and denied that commitment to art implied indifference to society. In the summer of 1936 he was able to give up school-teaching and support himself as a freelance, writing, translating and travelling. Out of intensive study of nineteenth- and twentieth-century English and French literature (and his own much-praised translations), against a general background in classical Chinese poetry and Buddhist and Daoist philosophy, he had perfected a strongly individual style.

Part of this style involved strict attention to form, whether in short or long poems or in free or structured verse. He often used the metres invented by Wen Yiduo and Xu Zhimo for verse constructed in quatrains, but many of the shorter one-stanza poems are in carefully arranged irregular lines. By his own account, Bian Zhilin was meticulous about rhyme and other aspects of musicality, paying particular attention to the effect of pauses within the line (the caesura, a feature of classical verse) and at the end of the line (again, emphasised by the end-stops of classical prosody). What his poems are most noted for, however, is their opacity: with some exceptions, they seem not simply to tell a story, describe a scene, express an emotion, evoke a mood or deliver a message. Instead, they imply a perspective on the nature of human identity and the ego as imperfect guides to the illusory nature of the real world and the deeper reality behind it. For this reason, he is often labelled as a metaphysical poet.

Bian Zhilin continued to write poetry during and after the war, but his reputation rests on these poems of the 1930s. His readers were never many but he is one of the few writers whose poems remained in print throughout his lifetime. (*For Bian Zhilin's later verse see Chapter 8.*)

He Qifang (1912–77) and Li Guangtian (1906–68)

He Qifang was born into a wealthy landlord family in Wanxian, Sichuan. He studied the traditional classics in a family school but after contact with May Fourth literature at the local district school at the age of fourteen, he went to Shanghai to receive a modern education. There he devoted himself to French symbolist poetry, but on entering Beijing University in 1931, he elected to study Western philosophy. The Japanese invasion of northern China in 1931 and the bombing of Shanghai in 1932 registered only dimly as he absorbed the atmosphere of an ancient city and its modernist poets. Among his patrons in Beijing were Wen Yiduo and Shen Congwen, while a failed love affair and a visit back home in the summer of 1933 determined his poetic development.

He Qifang's first book publication was *The Swallow's Nest*, which is Part I of *The Han Garden* edited by Bian Zhilin and published in 1936. Drawn from poems written in 1931–2 and 1933–4, it appears again with other poems from the same period in He Qifang's 1945 collection *The Prophecy*. 'The Prophecy' (1931) is his most representative early poem, introducing the contrast between southern and northern landscapes and the undefined symbol of a 'young god' in flight from love, beauty and poetic inspiration. Other poems such as 'Do Not Wash Away the Red' suggest a similar sense of loss but in a more classical idiom. The second half of the selection contains several poems describing in melodramatic fashion the streets of Beijing. Their bleakness and desolation owe something to T.S. Eliot, his own private troubles and the overhanging threat of Japanese encroachment. Other poems such as 'Early Summer', expressing nostalgia for his native home, are more assured and subtle. The poems in this group are among his most carefully composed: following the example of Wen Yiduo and Bian Zhilin, he tried to re-create in colloquial Chinese the prosodic effect of the balanced classical line.

He Qifang's next group of poems date from the period 1934–5, when he was obliged to leave the relative seclusion of student life to teach at Nankai secondary school in Tianjin. Five of these poems are included in Part IV of the first and second editions of his collection of poetry, drama and essays, *Painstaking Work*, published in 1938 by the Culture and Life Press, and three are reprinted in *The Prophecy* (also published by Culture and Life). In 'Day of the Dust-storm', He Qifang follows Eliot in annotating his own work, which cites the Bible, Oscar Wilde as quoted by André Gide, Shakespeare, Dostoevsky and Pu Songling's *Strange Tales from Liaozhai*. 'The Fan', on the other hand, borrows its theme and imagery from the Tang poets Li Shangyin and Li He to suggest that even the re-created past brings only slight relief from present troubles. The two poems omitted from *The Prophecy* unfashionably quote from *Mencius* and *The Zuo Commentary* in even more elliptical expressions of the poet's dread of reality.

He Qifang's final group of pre-war poems consists of five poems written in 1936–7 in Laiyang, Shandong, where He Qifang taught for a year, published as Part III of *The Prophecy*. The general theme is the author's farewell to the world of poetry, expressed in bizarre or even brutal images and dramatic discordances. In 'Funerals' and 'Clouds', the author buries his former heroes Nerval, Esenin and Baudelaire in hope for his own rebirth as a worthy fighter in the War against Japan.

He Qifang's poetry gives an unusually vivid depiction of the author's progress through romanticism, symbolism, neo-romanticism, modernism and Russian futurism, from dreamer to patriot. Their popularity during the War against Japan led him to re-issue these poems in a single volume, but lacking comparison with the originals due to wartime conditions, the versions published in *The Prophecy* differ slightly in wording.

Li Guangtian's main contribution to the new poetry movement

is *Journeying Clouds*, Part II of *The Han Garden*. The first group of poems, written in 1933–4, describes his life as an exile far from home. The second group, dated 1931–3, continues the theme of nostalgia for home and childhood expressed in memories. Li Guangtian's reputation as a 'pastoralist poet' is largely based on 'Son of the Earth', where his longing for his native soil outweighs any desire for Heaven. The third group consists of three long poems all from 1934. In 'The Turk', the poet muses over the fate of a foreigner whose wanderings have brought him to a lonely grave in the Chinese countryside where the local people have given him a pauper's burial, and sympathises both with the lonely exile and the conservative but humanitarian villagers. 'Going To Heaven's Bridge' is a dramatic monologue on contemporary Beijing, complete with asides and dialogue in the manner of Bian Zhilin's and He Qifang's city poems, but his adoption of a small boy's persona is unconvincing.

He Qifang continued writing poetry throughout his life, although the quality of his work deteriorated considerably after 1942. Li Guangtian turned his hand to essays and fiction, but he wrote little original work of any kind after the 1940s. (*For He Qifang's later poetry see Chapter 8; for Li Guangtian's later fiction see Chapter 7.*)

Wang Xindi (b. 1912)

Wang Xindi and his brother Wang Xingu published a collection of poetry under the name *Pearls* in 1935. Wang Xindi's contribution consisted of poems written in 1933 and 1934 while he was a student at Qinghua University; together with poems from 1936 and 1937, it was reprinted as Part I of his 1948 collection *The Palm*. Wang Xindi, who was particularly well-read in Western literature, was already at this time familiar with Donne, Milton and Pope as well as nineteenth- and twentieth-century English and French poetry, the Russian novelists and the philosophers Spinoza and Schopenhauer. These early poems, mostly set in the streets of old Beijing, convey a message of the inevitability of human grief in vaguely metaphysical terms. At this period, he was in contact with Bian Zhilin's *New Poetry Monthly*.

After teaching in Beijing for one year after graduation, Wang Xindi left for study in Edinburgh in 1936. There and on vacation in Paris and London, he wrote a series of twenty-two poems (later published as Part II of *The Palm*) in which the vague melancholy of his Beijing days is replaced with the acute pain of homesickness. Although the author enjoys his visits to concerts and art galleries, his sense of alienation grows until he questions the reality of his own existence. The increasing abstraction of these poems is also due to the influence of Eliot, Auden, Spender and C. Day Lewis. Finally, the poet goes beyond nostalgia to the perception that life itself is a process of disillusionment.

The reality of war brought a temporary end to Wang Xindi's poetry, which he did not resume until after the victory over Japan in 1945. His poems from the late 1940s form the third and final section of *The Palm*. (*For Wang's later poetry see Chapter 8*.)

The typical poet of the 1920s and 1930s was a young man from a former scholar-gentry family in Zhejiang or Anhui, educated in the traditional classics at home or at a village school, introduced to modern Western thinking and May Fourth periodicals in Shanghai or Hangzhou, furthering his education at Beijing University or Qinghua University, and spending another two years abroad, in England, Europe, the United States or Japan, where his chief preoccupations were literature, romance and politics. He would have dabbled in writing classical verse in his early teens but switched to vernacular when he (like the century) was in his twenties. After joining one or two literary societies, teaching at a provincial secondary school if he were unlucky or, if he were very lucky, at Beijing or Qinghua universities, helping to edit one or two literary journals, producing translations of Western poetry and publishing a few volumes of his own work, he would give up vernacular poetry for academic studies; if he had started writing around the May Fourth Incident, this would happen around 1925; if he began writing around 1925, it would be around 1930. He would frequently quarrel with his fellow writers, especially with those in other societies, and would quite probably end up with a set of allegiances quite different to those with which he began. His preferred habitat was the secluded back lanes of Beijing or the foreign concessions in Shanghai.

The poems he wrote in his brief career would commonly have

a melancholy tone, and often show a fascination with death, decay and lost love. Love was an ideal which invited self–sacrifice, but reality brought disillusion; China, a country with a glorious past, was an oppressed nation in the modern world, but the poet was an heroic figure who could lead her to salvation; nature was a retreat where tired minds could find consolation and refreshment; the socially deprived, in the form of beggars, servants, coolies and occasionally peasants, were humble and passive in their suffering. If the poet came from a commercial background, there was liable to be a more optimistic or forceful note to his work; if he came from distant places like Guangzhou, he would have made his entry into literary circles from abroad. Whether or not he had studied abroad, he would sprinkle his poetry liberally with Western allusions (and sometimes Western words printed in alphabetic type) but confine his Chinese allusions to Qu Yuan, Zhuangzi and Tang poetry. He would experiment in a desultory way with Western verse patterns, and after he gave up vernacular poetry, he would continue to write classical verse and maybe translate sporadically throughout the rest of his life as a man of letters. The outstanding poets of the time, by definition not typical, shared some of these characteristics but also brought lifelong dedication to the craft of poetry.

Of the fifty writers whose lives have been briefly sketched above, twelve had died by the close of the May Fourth era: one (Zhu Xiang) had committed suicide, one (Xu Zhimo) died in a plane-crash, at least two (Lu Xun, Jiang Guangci) died of illness exacerbated by poverty and persecution, and three (Pan Mohua, Yin Fu, Ying Xiuren) died in prison or were executed. Only seven continued to write and publish in the 1940s, 1950s and 1960s; of the remaining thirty-one, most retreated into academic life, while some turned to politics.

Despite its narrow beginnings, however, the new poetry in this period showed a remarkable diversity of styles and kinds. Competition for the relatively small readership for new poetry encouraged individualism to flourish, and attempts at censorship or political control were largely frustrated by the chaos of the age. Poetry societies and clubs formed, coalesced, vanished and were not revived; poetry journals rarely lasted longer than two or three years. By the end of the period, free verse in vernacular Chinese dominated poetry in commercial publication, but both 'free verse' and 'vernacular Chinese' allowed a wide range of interpretations. And for all the crusading righteousness of its writers and critics, the new poetry co-existed, or even co-habited, with traditional classical poetry and folksong.

4

FICTION: THE NARRATIVE SUBJECT

In traditional Chinese society, the writing and reading of fiction were regarded by scholars as frivolous occupations, and not deemed part of literature proper. As its Chinese name, 'small talk' (*xiaoshuo*), implies, fiction had since very early times been thought of as idle chitchat. This derogatory use of the term persisted. Even major vernacular novels in late imperial China such as *The Romance of the Three Kingdoms*, *Water Margin* and *Golden Lotus*, written and read by the literati, were all first published under pseudonyms. Short fiction, known under rubrics such as 'records of the strange' (*zhiguai*), 'jottings' (*biji*) and 'tales of the wondrous' (*chuanqi*), traditionally dealt with matters considered trivial or unreal, and even stories written in classical Chinese were tainted by their association with tales of the supernatural, phenomena specifically excluded by Confucius from his teachings as not worthy of attention.

Attitudes towards fiction changed dramatically in the early twentieth century. Thanks mostly to Liang Qichao, who was influenced by the Japanese debate on the political novel at the end of the nineteenth century, fiction was the genre embraced by some of the best new writers as a means to propagate their political ideas. A striking feature of modern Chinese fiction is the predominance of the theme of social injustice. In part this can be attributed to the combined influence of traditional fiction, with its predilection for commenting on the evils of immoral officials and the degeneration of its own age, and of varieties of Western realism and naturalism; at the same time, modern Chinese writers have been witness to immense suffering and exploitation. Since the writers' personal experience was limited, the plight of rickshaw pullers as symbols of oppression was a common theme of early fiction. Fiction by and about women was even more common, and discussions of family and social reform were incorporated within stories about romantic and sexual love.

Social reform so dominated popular discourse that it even penetrated the world of commercial entertainment fiction. Writers called by their opponents the Mandarin Ducks and Butterflies school (because their novels always ended in marital harmony symbolised by paired ducks or butterflies) introduced modern themes and situations only to wrap them in comfortingly conventional morality. Mostly written in classical Chinese, novels of this kind were published in prominent journals such as *Short Story Monthly* until overtaken by the new fiction in 1920. In the hands of writers such as Zhang Henshui, popular fiction on modern themes continued to be published in urban centres throughout the 1930s and 1940s. Another popular genre, much despised by the literary reformers, was sited in a world of complete fantasy: the martial arts fiction of writers like Xiang Kairan. Unlike other forms of popular fiction, martial arts novels remained equally remote from themes of social injustice and the technical innovations copied from Western fiction.

European and European-influenced Japanese fiction was the main source of new models and techniques. First-person narrative was introduced into Chinese fiction by Wu Woyao in 1908. One of its purposes is to add a sense of authenticity to fiction, thereby elevating it above mere entertainment and demanding the reader's respect. Wu's use of this device is transitional, since in other respects it is an outgrowth of the traditional storyteller persona rather than a dramatised narrator in Western style.

Another innovation in new fiction was the diary format. Traditional fiction used prologues and epilogues to frame the central narrative, the frame implying closure and being suited for the narration of events leading to reward and punishment. The diary form, on the other hand, could be open-ended, often breaking off with the implied death (or moral transformation) of the fictional diarist. The diary format also provided a means of access into the inner world of the narrator's thoughts and emotions. The first modern work of fiction, Lu Xun's 'Diary of a Madman', uses both the diary format and a dramatised narrative persona; in addition, in a move that could be interpreted either as ironic or as ambivalent, the diary itself is framed with a post-facto prologue written in classical Chinese.

'Diary of a Madman' was Lu Xun's second short story; his first, written in classical Chinese in 1911 and published in *Short Story Monthly* in 1913, was not a success, nor were the early translations of Western short stories by Lu Xun and his brother Zhou Zuoren. The Western short-story form, however, quickly became popular. The term 'short story' (*duanpian xiaoshuo*) for serious short fiction was introduced in 1918 by Hu Shi. Even novels, which were traditionally multi-volumed and panoramic in their coverage of characters and events, gave way to shorter novels or novellas.

The rapid spread of shorter fiction was due to several factors. In the first two decades of the twentieth century, the new vernacular form, even for fiction, was unfamiliar territory, and most authors were still experimenting. The proliferation of literary journals during the 1920s further popularised the shorter form: stories had a better chance of acceptance if they could be printed or serialised over a few issues. The nature of the readership was also changing. The Western model itself was both an example and a symptom of a common trend: wider choices in modern societies meant that it was more difficult to hold the attention of readers over a multi-volumed work. The three-decker novel was abandoned in Britain in the 1890s in favour of single-volume novels, and short stories by Russian and French writers had a peculiarly fresh flavour to readers. In the 1930s, when novels began to replace short stories as the dominant mode in fiction in China, even works conceived of as trilogies were usually published as individual titles with a gap of several years between volumes.

The May Fourth spirit which typified the fiction of this period was on the whole robust and optimistic. Beyond the descriptions of poverty and alienation which characterise so many stories, there was a sense of common cause in appeals to rid the country of traditional constraints and foreign dominance. It was also a period of great diversity and growth, as traditional and foreign models were transformed into recognisably modern Chinese forms.

Liu E (1857–1909)

The son of a minor scholar-official, Liu E was born in Liuhe, Jiangsu. His interests were diverse. As well as writing fiction and poetry, he took an active interest in philology, mathematics and music. Liu E was also eclectic in his philosophical-religious beliefs. In 1880, he was converted to a sect known as the Taigu School, a mixture of Buddhism, Daoism and Confucianism. His career was also varied; among other occupations, he worked as a doctor and merchant as well as filling several administrative posts. In 1888 the Yellow River broke its dykes at Zhengzhou and he was placed in charge of repairing the damage. He was commended by the governor, Wu Dacheng, for the success of his work. Other important officials whom he either served or befriended included Zhang Yao and Fu Run. In 1896 he was attacked by conservatives for recommending to the governor of Zhili that a railway be built, and regarded as a 'traitor' the following year for representing foreign merchants wishing to carry out mining in Shanxi. Liu E's dealings with foreign merchants earned him many enemies during the Boxer Rebellion, including the arch-conservatives Yuxian and Gangyi. In 1908, he was banished to Xinjiang where he died the following year.

Liu E's friends and enemies in officialdom appear with very similar names in his most famous novel, *The Travels of Lao Can*, which was serialised under the pseudonym Hongdu Bailiansheng in 1903-7. The first thirteen chapters of the twenty-chapter novel were serialised in *Illustrated Fiction* in 1903-4. The next year, the *Tianjin Daily News* reprinted these chapters as well as completing the twenty-chapter series and adding a nine-chapter sequel. The twenty-chapter novel first appeared in book-form in 1907. This book then gained immense stature, mainly because it was vigorously promoted by champions of the vernacular movement such as Hu Shi in the 1920s. It was, for example, repeatedly chosen as a textbook in secondary schools.

The novel traces the travels of a respected eccentric, Tie Ying, who takes the sobriquet Lao Can (meaning 'Old Decrepit'). Lao Can wanders in the north of China, supporting himself by practising medicine. The first chapter serves as a preface in which a dream-tale is related. The dream is an allegory in which China is a sinking ship in stormy waters. The crew and passengers of the ship debate ways of saving the vessel, with some advocating the removal of the leaders responsible for the disaster. Lao Can in the dream is watching the ship with his friends Wisdom and Knowledge, and they offer less drastic solutions. Lao Can's moderate political stance reveals itself in this dream, as do his attitudes towards Westernisation and modernisation, because he proposes the use of technical instruments like the compass to put the ship on a right path. After he wakes up from this dream, Lao Can begins his travels, discussing the state of the world and how best to lead one's life with people he meets on the way. Chapters 2-7 and 13-20 relate his experiences in Shandong, and show the tragedies which result from the maladministration of corrupt officials such as Yuxian and Gangyi. Unlike many traditional tales where honest officials make just and correct decisions which bring happiness to the people, Lao Can witnesses the suffering caused by inflexible bureaucracy. Chapters eight to eleven are not about Lao Can's travels as such, but feature the visit to a recluse of great virtue by the nephew of one of his friends. This episode provides Liu E an opportunity to illustrate his vision of an ideal community. Lao Can also rescues ordinary people from oppression by officials and other injustices. In one episode, with the help of one of his friends, he redeems a talented and innocent courtesan from a brothel. Such incidents are meant to show the generosity and humanity of both Lao Can and his enlightened friends. The first six chapters of the sequel were later published separately in 1935. They are quite different in content to the first volume. Here, Lao Can and his newly-acquired concubine Huaicui tour Taishan (a famous mountain in central China) with another couple. It relates how Huaicui then becomes a nun at the sacred mountain. Chapters seven to nine are different in content yet again. The narrative switches to another dream sequence. Returning home alone, Lao Can dreams that he is visiting the underworld where he witnesses the dreadful tortures inflicted on the dead by King Yama. *The Travels of Lao Can* is not a literary masterpiece, but it is one of the first novels which is written in a language close to the vernacular and which also deals with problems of a modernising China around the turn of this century. These factors make it a popular novel for study even at the present time.

Li Boyuan (1861–1906)

Like Liu E, Li Boyuan (aka Li Baojia) was born in Jiangsu, and his concerns were also focused on reforming China in the modern world. His attempts to enter official life through the old examination system were unsuccessful, and in 1896 he went to Shanghai to become a journalist and editor. His fiction, which followed a few years later, was closely related to his professional standing as a 'new intellectual'. His most famous novels, *The Bureaucracy Exposed* (incomplete; serially published from 1903 and posthumously published in book form in 1906) and *Modern Times: A Brief History of Enlightenment* (1905) focus on the problems faced by his contemporaries in trying to introduce reforms in political and intellectual life in China. The former is a critical survey of the varieties and extent of corruption in the civil service under the influence of new commercial practices, and won its author immediate notoriety; *Modern Times* is a more relaxed satire on the efforts of young and old to profit from the trends in modern education, including Chinese students in Japan. The episodic style of Li's fiction makes for frustrating reading for late-twentieth-century readers, since character development as well as narrative structure disappear in the loosely-connected anecdotes or short stories which at the time were acceptable as full-length fiction; but passages such as those in which hypocritical scoundrels defend themselves are still highly amusing, while the portraits of contemporary figures and the depiction of manners in a rapidly-changing society are of lasting value to literary and social historians.

Wu Woyao (1867–1910)

Wu Woyao (a.k.a.   Wu Jianren) was born in Beijing, but his family originated in Foshan in Guangdong and he often used the pen-name Wofoshanren (Man from Foshan). His great-grandfather was a compiler in the Hanlin Academy and a famous scholar. The family moved back to Foshan when he was a child, and throughout his life he remained a Cantonese patriot. After his father died, Wu Woyao left home and arrived in Shanghai when he was in his late teens. He worked as a clerk but supplemented his income by writing some short pieces for the newspapers. He began his professional writing career in 1897 as an editor for the *Shanghai Literary Gazette*. The following year, he launched his own journal *The Trendsetter*. In 1902, he left Shanghai for Hankou and became an editor for the *Hankou Daily*. In the same year, Liang Qichao launched China's first specialised journal of fiction, *New Fiction* in Yokohama. Wu Woyao visited Japan in 1903, and his 108-chapter novel *Strange Events Witnessed during the Last Twenty*

Years began to appear as a serial in the new journal. Forty-five chapters had been published by 1905, when the journal ceased publication, and the final chapter was published in 1910. The impact of *Strange Events* was immediate and tremendous. It and Li Boyuan's *The Bureaucracy Exposed*, which was first serialised in Shanghai in 1903-5, became the forerunners of the fiction of social criticism in the late Qing. Wu Woyao later published many novels in rapid succession, including *The Sea of Regret, The Strange Case of Ninefold Murder* and *The Annals of Sorrow*. In the spring of 1905, he took up a post as editor of the Chinese section of the English paper *Central China Post*, which was run by Americans. He resigned from this post in the same year, in protest against the exclusion policy relating to Chinese coolies entering the United States. Returning to Shanghai, he continued to agitate for a boycott of American goods. In 1906, he became the chief editor of *Monthly Fiction* and published five novels in this magazine, including *The Secret of Becoming Rich* and *Ashes*. In 1907, the Cantonese Association of Shanghai established a Cantonese primary school and appointed Wu Woyao as headmaster. Wu held this position until the end of his life.

Strange Events remains Wu Woyao's best-known novel. The first vernacular Chinese novel written in the first person, it has a number of relatively modern psychological and structural innovations. Drawing on the Qing novel *The Scholars* as a satire on social hypocrisy, it develops the latter's episodic structure by introducing a unifying central character, Jiusi Yisheng (Nine Lives). The novel purports to be Jiusi Yisheng's memoirs, a record of his experiences and reflections over a twenty-year period from 1882 to 1902, a time of great social upheavals in China. A short prologue by a Sili Taosheng (Escapee from Death) claims that the memoirs were found in a marketplace and that the manuscript was then sent to *New Fiction* in Japan for publication: Wu Woyao in this way attempts to establish authenticity for the novel. In the memoirs, Jiusi Yisheng explains his unusual name by alleging that on reflection over the twenty years since he left home, he met only three kinds of people: vermin, predators and vampires. Despite this, he managed to survive; thus, he surmises, he must have nine lives. The number of people he meets in the novel is about a hundred and the 'strange events' about two hundred. They are found mostly in the bureaucracy and commercial world, but other social circles such as friends and family are also described as ruthless and immoral. At the beginning of the story, when Jiusi Yisheng is only a naive fifteen-year-old villager, his merchant father dies and leaves him a large amount of money. However, his uncle mercilessly tricks him and robs him of this inheritance. Jiusi Yisheng goes to Nanjing looking for his uncle. In the city, he finds work as a clerk in the magistracy. From this position, he is able to observe the many 'strange events' such as bribery, philandery and flattery which he gradually understands to be not 'strange' (i.e. not unusual) happenings in the China of his time but quite normal. Later on, he goes into business and travels the country. Through his observations and conversations with the people he meets, he concludes that 'all men are robbers and all women prostitutes'.

Not all of Wu Woyao's novels are panoramic pictures of society like *Strange Events*. He also wrote shorter didactic detective stories and sentimental love stories. One example of the former is *A Strange Case of Ninefold Murder* (published serially 1904–5), which is based on a case of murder and arson that occurred in the mid-eighteenth century. By depicting corruption in all levels of officialdom, Wu Woyao was able to cast doubt on the notion of a golden age in the Qing dynasty. Among his love stories, *The Sea of Regret* (1905) is a good example of the sentimental writing known as the Mandarin Ducks and Butterflies school (see above, page 83), which became very popular in the early twentieth century. It tells of the sorrows endured by two young couples when they are separated by the Boxer Rebellion. Of the young men, one becomes a hermit after discovering that his fiancée has become a whore; the other dies from opium poisoning while his fiancée becomes a nun. The tragic consequences of international and national turmoil on an individual's personal life described here foreshadow many stories in the late Qing and in the Republican era.

Zeng Pu (1872–1935)

Born into a wealthy Jiangsu family, Zeng Pu enjoyed a traditional education in classical studies, and had already completed a volume of poetry and a collection of essays in the classical style before he turned eighteen. In 1895 he published a scholarly work on the Later Han dynasty. This was also the year when China was defeated in the War against Japan, an event which had a tremendous effect on Zeng Pu. Moving away from classical learning, he enrolled in the College of Foreign Languages in Beijing to learn French and study Western culture. After the reformers were defeated in 1898, Zeng Pu went back to Jiangsu and established a modern school in his home town. He tried his hand at business in Shanghai in 1903, but failed and turned his attention to literature again. In 1904 he took over the writing of the novel *A Flower in an Ocean of Sin*, which was begun by Jin Songcen (1874–1947). From about 1908 to 1926, Zeng Pu was involved in provincial politics in Jiangsu. Even so, he managed to translate works by authors such as Victor Hugo into Chinese. Around 1930, he began his autobiographical novel *The Real Man*. It was to be a novel in six parts, but he only finished part one, *Love*, and sections of parts 2 and 6. Zeng Pu's career as a writer reflects the transitional nature of the times in which he was living: he began with classical poetry, continued with a semi-traditional novel of social criticism and ended with a modern confessional novel.

A Flower in an Ocean of Sin is by far the most influential of Zeng Pu's works. Through the adventures of the hero, Jin Wenqing, it presents a panoramic view of late-Qing life. As well as passing the Palace Examinations with the highest honours, Jin Wenqing travels to several European countries as China's ambassador, accompanied by his favourite concubine, Fu Caiyun. Jin Wenqing's successes, however, do not continue throughout his life. After returning to China, his fortunes decline and he dies in disgrace. Through the medium of Jin Wenqing's contacts with Western culture, Zeng Pu suggests to his readers that China may not be the cultural centre of the world and will have to adopt a more pluralistic system to survive in the modern age. How China was to achieve this became the key question in much of the literature of the twentieth century.

Su Manshu (1884 – 1918)

Su Manshu's father, Su Jiesheng, was a compradore from Xiangshan (present-day Zhongshan) in Guangdong who was resident in Japan; Su Manshu's natural mother, a Japanese maid, left the family's employ three months after giving birth, and the child was raised by Su Jiesheng's Japanese concubine. The child was taken to China for his early education by Jiesheng's wife, a Chinese woman also from Guangdong. At the age of fifteen he returned to Japan but did not see his 'mother', the Japanese woman who raised him, again until he was twenty-four. Although his fictional output consists of only five short stories and one short novel, these writings, combined with the myths surrounding his unconventional life, exerted a tremendous influence on the development of twentieth-century Chinese literature. His stories are written in the classical language, but he was the first Chinese novelist to indulge in his private feelings through the heroes in his stories.

Su Manshu's autobiographical impulse was already evident in his first completed short story, 'The Crimson Silk', published in 1915. Both the hero, Xue Mengzhu, and his friend Tanluan, the narrator, end up shedding all worldly desires and adopting Buddhism as a path to salvation. The interplay between religious enlightenment and sentimental attachments to mundane emotions is illustrated by the crimson silk scarf, which is used to wrap a piece of jade given to Mengzhu by his betrothed. He ostensibly rejects her affections by selling the jade at the market but keeps the silk scarf. Years later, he is found dead in a secluded temple, as a Buddhist monk, but clutching the scarf close to his heart. The ending suggests that although he may have reached religious enlightenment, he still longs for romantic love.

Su Manshu's only novel, The Lone Swan, is even more illustrative of psychological tension. In twenty-seven chapters, it was first serialised in 1911 and reprinted in Shanghai Pacific News in 1912. Many of the events and emotional experiences in the life of the dramatised narrator seem to have been taken from Su Manshu's own life. The hero is a young Japanese monk whose calling is no deterrent to the two women who fall in love with him, one of whom dies as a result of her devotion; the monk, who has grown up in China, otherwise spends much of his time looking for his Japanese mother. These three themes – romantic love, Buddhist denial and a lost mother – are central both to Su Manshu the man and his literary creations.

At the beginning of the novel, Saburō (Sanlang in Chinese) is living in a secluded monastery in Guangdong, but he falls into depression over the uncertainty of his parentage. Through a chance encounter with his former nurse, he learns that he is from a well-respected Japanese family. His father died when he was only a few months old and his widowed mother became a concubine to a Chinese merchant from Guangdong. When the merchant returned to China, mother and son accompanied him. He died shortly afterwards, and Saburō's mother was subjected to maltreatment from his Chinese widow. Finally she went back to Japan, leaving him in the care of the nurse, who was in turn driven away by the widow. Having learnt the truth about himself, Saburō decides to raise money by selling flowers to pay for the passage to Japan to search for his mother.

One day while sheltering from the rain, he is recognised by Xuemei, who was betrothed to him as a child by his Chinese stepfather. She pledges undying love and gives him enough money to travel to Japan. He is reunited with his mother, but his aunt's beautiful adopted daughter, Shizuko (Jingzi in Chinese), falls madly in love with him. Barely able to check his own passion, Saburō secretly returns to monastic life at Lingyun Monastery in Hangzhou. By chance, he learns that Xuemei has starved herself to death rather than marry someone else. He returns to Guangdong only to find that his former nurse has also died. The novel ends with the hero, after searching in vain for Xuemei's grave, declaring that his heart has turned to stone and that he will seek his original master to cut all ties with the human world. *The Lone Swan* was immensely popular during the 1910s and 1920s. It was rewritten as a play in 1925 by Huang Jiamo and was made into a film. It has also been translated into English, German, Japanese and Russian.

Su Manshu's other fictional pieces, such as 'The Broken Hairpin' (1916) and 'The Tale Which Is Not a Dream' (1917), are also mainly about the tragic consequences of desire. Loved by two women, the hero is unable to choose between them, and his indecision results either in death to all three, or death to the women while the hero becomes a monk. While the theme of love and its tragedies among talented men and beautiful women is common in traditional literature, and Su Manshu wrote in the classical language, he is nevertheless rightfully regarded as an important precursor of modern Chinese literature. His subjective technique was also employed for the purpose of self-expression by May Fourth writers such as Yu Dafu and Guo Moruo.

Although Su Manshu was born a few years after Lu Xun, his

literary output and resulting fame preceded Lu Xun's. Unlike Lu Xun, however, he is now read only by scholars for his place in literary history as one of the last of the classical-language novelists. (*See also the section on Su Manshu in Chapter 3.*)

Lu Xun (1881–1936)

Lu Xun is the pen-name of Zhou Shuren, a native of Shaoxing, Zhejiang. His grandfather, from a prominent local gentry family, was imprisoned for examination fraud when Lu Xun was only twelve, and the family fortunes declined sharply. When his father died after a long illness in 1886, his family became further impoverished. Nevertheless, he and his younger brother Zhou Zuoren retained a respect for learning, although not for the Confucian classics in which their early education had given them a firm grounding; as young adults, both went to Japan to study on government scholarships.

Lu Xun lived in Japan from 1902 to 1909. He began studying medicine but switched to literature after the Russo-Japanese War of 1904–5 because he felt that what China needed was a transformation of its national spirit, not simply a cure for physical ailments. Following Liang Qichao's example, he sought first to put forward his ideas in journalism, at the same time writing poetry to express his patriotic emotions. In a long essay written in 1907, he visualised the heroic spirit of romantic or demonic poets as the force to lead China out of darkness; to the same end, with the help of Su Manshu and others, he planned to establish a journal to propagate his ideas. The venture was aborted, however, and, together with Zhou Zuoren, he began work on translating and writing about Western fiction. Their joint collection of short fiction, mainly from smaller and oppressed countries in Europe, also failed to arouse public interest. After returning to China in the summer of 1909, Lu Xun taught in secondary schools in Hangzhou and Shaoxing. Cai Yuanpei invited him to work in the Ministry of Education in Nanjing in 1912, and he moved with the Ministry to Beijing later the same year. Here, he witnessed Yuan Shikai's attempt to dismantle the fledgling Republic and restore imperial rule. Depressed at this setback in reform, Lu Xun took to copying tombstone engravings and ancient classics 'to anaesthetise himself'. His first work of fiction, a story in the classical language, appeared in 1913 but went unnoticed, and Lu Xun's contribution to the literary revolution did not take place until three years later.

At the request of his friend Qian Xuantong, a member of the editorial board of *New Youth*, Lu Xun agreed to write for the magazine. His first short story in the vernacular, 'The Diary of a Madman', and a few poems appeared in *New Youth* in May 1918. After this, he published in quick succession a number of essays as well as short stories such as 'Kong Yiji' and 'Medicine'. By 1920 his reputation as a writer was firmly established and he took up part-time teaching posts at Beijing University and Beijing Women's Normal University. His most influential story, 'The True Story of Ah Q', appeared in 1921. These and a number of other short stories were collected in *Call to Arms* in 1923. His second collection, *Hesitation*, comprising eleven works such as 'New Year's Sacrifice' and 'Remorse', was published in 1926. Eight stories which use plots from classical texts such as *Zhuangzi* and *Mozi* form his final short story collection *Old Tales Retold*, published in 1936.

In all, Lu Xun wrote only about thirty short stories, most of which were thinly veiled attacks on various aspects of Chinese society such as the hypocrisy of Confucianism and the suffering caused by ignorance. Lu Xun was never able to reconcile himself with conditions in China, and he became extremely critical of both Chinese tradition and the current political situation. After the events of 1926–27, he turned to other forms of writing in his denunciation of 'things Chinese'. His iconoclasm found expression particularly in his satirical essays, and he used this form most effectively in polemics against his critics. Although the quantity of his fiction is not large, Lu Xun's short stories touched on issues which became central concerns for decades, such as the misery of women in modern society.

His first vernacular story, 'The Diary of a Madman', has a simple plot and is only about ten pages long, but its impact cannot be over-estimated. Although it is indebted to the Russian writer Gogol for its inspiration and title, it is a literary original in all senses of the word. For example, it is the first Chinese work to use the difference between the classical and the vernacular written languages as a political comment on the ethics of traditional culture. The diary, written in the vernacular, records the stages of the madman's paranoia as he becomes convinced that everyone, including his own brother and excepting only his five-year-old sister, wants to eat him. By reading Chinese history, he comes to the realisation that the whole of Chinese culture is based on cannibalism. An early entry in the diary reads, 'Twenty years ago, I trod on Mr Gu's old ledgers, and Mr Gu was most displeased': Mr Gu (Mr Ancient) stands for Chinese tradition. In another entry, the madman recalls one evening when, unable to sleep, he made a close scrutiny of a history book which had 'benevolence, righteousness, truth and virtue' scrawled all over; he read deep into the night until he discovered that hidden between every line of the book were the words 'eat people'.

The preface, written by a friend of the madman's family after his recovery, ostensibly serves to authenticate the madman's passage through mania back to sanity and an official appointment: also written in the first person, it employs the authority of the classical language. The juxtaposition of the two language styles in the diary and the preface suggests to the *New Youth* readership that it is the madman's view that is truly enlightened. The ending conveys the message that tradition can only be threatened very briefly and that the price of sanity is collaboration with the established order.

Lu Xun's detestation of Chinese tradition, reiterated in many later essays, is frequently linked with the theme of class injustice, for instance in his claim that 'our vaunted Chinese civilisation is only a feast of human flesh prepared for the rich and the mighty'. In the short story 'Medicine', 'eating people' is also practised among the poor and ignorant: the village teashop owner buys fresh human blood from a decapitated revolutionary in a futile attempt to cure his son's consumption. The idea of a 'man-eat-man' Chinese society was immediately seized upon by the iconoclasts of the May Fourth period, and scholars such as Wu Yu immediately tried to prove that Chinese people practised cannibalism in traditional times. The notion that 'eating people' was the central principle of Confucianism even found a late echo in the anti-Confucius movement of the early 1970s and again in the early 1990s.

Lu Xun became even more relentless in his denunciations of Chinese culture after 'The Diary of a Madman'. In this story, still influenced by the Social Darwinism he embraced while in Japan, Lu Xun managed to inject a degree of hope. For example, the famous last entry in the diary, 'Perhaps there are still some children who have not yet become cannibalistic? Save the children ....' also had immense appeal as it expresses a sentiment held by most Chinese intellectuals, who felt that only they had the right, the ability and the duty to lead the populace and to save China. In the May Fourth period, this evangelistic zeal was most evident among those who had some foreign education.

Typically, these new intellectuals saw traditional scholars as pathetic and ridiculous figures. The comic-tragic figure of Kong Yiji, in the story of the same name, illustrates their attitude to scholars whose learning is not relevant to the modern world. A failed member of the scholar-gentry class, Kong Yiji's bookishness only provides amusement to the local townspeople; crippled by a member of the gentry who has caught him stealing, he crawls away to die in a world indifferent to his plight. To some extent, Kong Yiji is not just a failed scholar but an archetype of the Confucian scholar: his surname is the same as the master's, Kong Fuzi (latinised to Confucius by early Jesuit travellers to China).

Lu Xun's major contribution to the dissection of the national character, also collected in *Call to Arms*, is 'The True Story of Ah Q'. Under the pen-name Ba Ren, it was serialised in the *Morning Post Supplement* between December 1921 and February 1922. It originally appeared in the entertainment column of the paper and its tone was initially facetious. As the story progressed, however, it became increasingly serious, and the final episode vacillates between tragedy and farce. In his preface to the Russian translation, Lu Xun said that he wanted to create a typical modern Chinese soul. Certainly, the subsequent popularity of the story suggests that readers recognised the protagonist Ah Q as an embodiment of the national spirit. Ah Q is an itinerant poor villager who hires himself out for casual labour. The story recounts his activities around the time of the 1911 Revolution. Constantly bullied by those stronger or more powerful than himself, he in turn picks on those who are weaker: cheered on by bystanders, for instance, he tries to molest a young nun. After this physical contact with a woman, his sexual longings are stirred and he makes a 'proposal' to his employer's widowed amah. For this he is beaten up and thrown out. He escapes for a short time to the county town, where he joins a gang of thieves. When he returns to the village he has money as well as (stolen) goods to sell. For a while the villagers treat him well. He even strikes fear in the hearts of the local gentry with the advent of the 1911 Revolution when he proclaims himself a revolutionary, vowing to take away the property and women of the wealthy. When the revolutionary forces finally enter the village, however, the local gentry become 'revolutionaries' themselves and forbid Ah Q to 'make revolution'. In the end, Ah Q becomes a scapegoat and is executed.

The story is the most outstanding of a series that Lu Xun wrote to show how little was achieved by the 1911 Revolution. The futility of the political and constitutional reforms is the theme of other stories from 1919 and 1920 such as 'Medicine' and 'Storm in a Teacup'. The latter is a light-hearted look at the disturbance caused in a hamlet when the last Manchu emperor, Puyi, was briefly restored to the throne in 1917. The anxiety endured by the boatman and his family is a result of rumours that pigtails, which all Chinese men were forced to wear under Qing rule and forced to cut off in the new Republic, would be compulsory again. The republican revolution is thus shown to mean little more than a change in hairstyles. Lu Xun does not place the blame for the failure of the revolution on the rich and powerful only. The poor and lowly are sympathetically but satirically portrayed as ignorant and pitiable, responsible to a large extent for their own unhappiness and the backward situation in China. For example, Ah Q only wants to join the revolution so that he can become an oppressor himself. His incomprehension about what the changes mean is illustrated by his mispronunciation of the 'Freedom Party' (*ziyou dang*) as the 'Persimmon Party' (*shiyou dang*).

More importantly, his ignorance is not confined to the political processes of Chinese society. He is also lacking in any sort of self-awareness, to the point of not even knowing his real name. He has no knowledge of his past, present or future. There are no descriptions of his appearance (apart from the scabs on his head), and he could truly be a Chinese Everyman. Spiritually and morally, he is also a vacuum: he lives by instinct alone, without thought, without love or hatred, and without desires above food, shelter and sex. Ah Q is a perfect example of an alienated individual in the Marxist sense: alienated from his society, his work, his family and himself. The 'Ah Q spirit' has become a popular term of derision in Chinese for people who, though weak, consider themselves superior. Self-delusion, the method used by Ah Q for consolation when he is humiliated by others, also describes what many radical reformers saw as the Chinese attitude towards the Western and Japanese powers at that time. While claiming spiritual superiority, China was being systematically degraded in its dealings with other nations.

The stories in *Call to Arms*, although critical of Chinese culture and society, still contain expressions of hope and compassion. The eleven stories in *Hesitation*, written after the initial enthusiasm of the May Fourth Movement had subsided, are dominated by despair. The first and most famous story in the collection, 'New Year's Sacrifice', is a good illustration of the bleakness of these stories. It relates the misfortunes of Aunt Xianglin, a twice-widowed peasant woman. After her first husband dies, Aunt Xianglin escapes to the narrator's home town, Luzhen, to work as a maid. She is eventually tracked down by her mother-in-law and sold into a second marriage. This marriage proves a happy one, and she has a baby. Then her husband dies and her baby is taken by a wolf. Back in Luzhen, Aunt Xianglin is considered unclean by the gentry and taunted by the villagers; at first sympathetic, they easily tire of her repeated attempts to relate her sad story. Towards the end of the story, she is reduced to beggary, wandering aimlessly among the New Year celebrations wondering what hell has in store for her. She asks the narrator about her fate in the afterlife: the narrator, a new intellectual, is confused and embarrassed by her questions and answers evasively. On New Year's Day, she is dead, a sacrifice to the gods so that people of Luzhen would have happiness. At the same time, the narrator salves his conscience by narrating the story for which its chief character was manifestly unable to find an audience, but in the retelling, the focus becomes the narrator's response to the woman's fate rather than the woman herself.

Aunt Xianglin is one of several woman characters in Lu Xun's fiction who act as the apparent protagonist but who die or otherwise disappear before the end of the story, leaving their stories to be told by inadequate male narrators. In 'Remorse', the apparent protagonist (the actual victim) is a liberated young woman who dares to defy convention and live with her lover. Her story is related by the young man, who despite his grief is unable to comprehend his own role in her death (he literally and figuratively deprived her of a voice) and remains preoccupied with his own narrative. The use of the inadequate narrator is one of the most powerful modern techniques introduced into Chinese literature by Lu Xun, although not all of his contemporary readers and imitators understood or supported its implications. When 'New Year's Sacrifice' was filmed in 1952, the narrator was retained but cleansed of any complicity in Aunt Xianglin's downfall: Aunt Xianglin remained a pathetic victim whose story had now become part of a state propaganda machine.

Lu Xun's last collection of short stories is very different to the other two in theme and style. These eight stories are based on legends and other historical writing, retold in a highly original way. Through these stories, Lu Xun re-evaluates major figures from the Chinese past: Laozi and Zhuangzi, for instance, the founders of Daoism, are presented as useless and hypocritical, and Mozi, traditionally the least respected philosopher, is a genuine fighter for justice and peace.

Lu Xun also contributed to the development of modern fiction by acting as editor of a number of literary journals and giving advice to younger writers. Despite his death at a relatively early age, his position as the most perceptive, innovative and challenging figure in modern Chinese literature remains undisputed. (*See also the section on Lu Xun in Chapter 3.*)

Xiang Kairan (1890–1957)

Xiang Kairan was a native of Xiangtan, Hunan. His first novel, *Studying in Japan* (1916), published a year after his return to China after seven years as a student in Japan, is also the first to depict the lives of Chinese students abroad. It has numerous characters and subplots, but is mainly centred around the adventures of Zhou Zhuan, an orphan raised by his uncle. Zhou is married at the age of sixteen but prefers to live by unscrupulous means rather than hard work. He manages to obtain false papers that enable him to go to Japan on a government scholarship. On his return a few years later, he abandons his first wife and marries the daughter of a shopkeeper. He then obtains another scholarship to Japan by unlawful means. Now thoroughly familiar with Japanese society, he joins a group of like-minded friends who lead immoral lives, seducing and marrying Chinese and Japanese women as well as spying on fellow students for Yuan Shikai's government. In the end, he is forced to return to China and is executed for his activities. Through Zhou Zhuan, therefore, Xiang Kairan was able to expose the corrupt and dissolute lifestyles of many Chinese students living abroad.

After Xiang Kairan returned to China, he spent most of his life as an officer in the military. He wrote prolifically, including more than twenty novels, mostly of the knight-errantry or martial arts genre. Although his novel on student life abroad had made him famous, he later became known as one of the best early-twentieth-century writers of martial arts fiction. The best example of his work is *Modern Tales of Chivalrous Heroes*. The novel again has a large cast of characters, most of whom are expert fighters specialising in different schools of Chinese martial arts. The protagonist, Huo Yuanjia, begins life as a weakling. His father is so ashamed of his delicate constitution that the family's special style of fighting, taught to all his brothers, is withheld from him. However, he learns it secretly by peeping into the room where his brothers are practising, and it is only when he is in his mid-twenties that his superior skills are revealed.

In the tradition of chivalrous heroes, Huo Yuanjia protects people in need, including Chinese Christians harassed by the Boxers. Many martial arts experts challenge him but he remains undefeated. Like all fighters who observe the martial arts code, Huo Yuanjia is also a patriot. He confronts and defeats fighters from Russia and Germany but dies after a bout with judo experts from Japan. The story implies that his death is the result of intentional neglect by a Japanese doctor who is treating his injuries rather than through fair combat. The novel contains all the elements of traditional martial arts fiction, including the defeat of foreigners, and in this case the barbarians are Europeans as well. It has given rise to a host of novels, stories and films about the adventures of Huo Yuanjia and his colleague, the swordsman Wang Wu.

Xu Dishan (1893–1941)

Xu Dishan, better-known under the pen-name of Luo Huasheng, was born in Tainan, Taiwan. His parents were devout Buddhists, and Xu Dishan himself was strongly influenced in his thinking and writing by the Buddhist faith. Before entering Yanjing University in Beijing in 1917, he taught in schools in Fujian and Burma. His first short story 'Bird of Destiny', was published in *Short Story Monthly* in 1921; 'The Vain Labours of a Spider' appeared in the same journal the following year. Between 1922 and 1926, he studied religion at Columbia University, Oxford and in India. After his return to Beijing in 1927, he taught religion successively at Yanjing, Beijing and Qinghua universities. He continued to write fiction and essays throughout this period, and his best-known story, 'Big Sister Liu', was published in *Literature* in 1934. Following personal conflict with the president of Yanjing University in 1935, he resigned and took up a post at Hong Kong University where he stayed until his death.

Xu Dishan's preoccupation with religion appears very early in his writings. The heroine of 'The Bird of Destiny' is willing to face death in her quest for Nirvana. Typically for Xu Dishan, the protagonist is a woman who chooses an independent path in life. The women in Xu Dishan's fiction are not weak victims of society, as commonly portrayed in modern Chinese fiction, but instead suffer because suffering is a necessary condition of life itself. As the heroine of 'The Vain Labours of a Spider' explains, people are like spiders: they labour to spin a web, not knowing when or how the web will be broken, but once the web is broken, they will wait for the first opportunity to spin another one. Although the heroine is a Christian, her attitude of resigned acceptance is also Buddhist. She lives up to her beliefs in relinquishing her share of the family property when her husband falsely accuses her of infidelity. When her husband later relents and requests a reunion, she goes back to him, only to find that through shame he has disappeared. Again, she accepts this as her fate, refusing to go and look for him. 'The Merchant's Wife' (1921) has a similar plot and theme.

In 'Big Sister Liu', Xu Dishan's Buddhist learning is used to great effect. The story is about the triumph of the human instinct over worldly morality. The heroine, Chuntao, whose husband Li Mao is forced into military service on their wedding night, survives by gathering wastepaper from garbage dumps. There she meets Xianggao and they begin a partnership, sorting out saleable items. They set up house together, but one day Li Mao appears, crippled and penniless. The men's indecision in this predicament causes much unhappiness, and in the end, it is Chuntao who shows how they can all live and prosper together under one roof. This story is unique in Chinese literature in affirming a woman's right to live by her own moral code, even if it means cohabiting with two men, and a direct challenge to Confucian concepts of chastity and patriarchal authority. Prototypes of Xu Dishan's women characters – strong, upright and independent – can be found in traditional Chinese fiction but are comparatively rare in the May Fourth period.

Ye Shengtao (1894–1988)

Ye Shengtao started his career as a writer with stories in classical Chinese but is now known only for his contributions to vernacular fiction dating from the May Fourth Movement. He changed his name from Shaojun to Shengtao after the 1911 Revolution. He became a primary school teacher in his home town, Suzhou, after completing secondary school in 1912, but was forced to leave two years later after conflicts with others in the school. Short of money, he submitted over ten stories in the classical language to journals like *Saturday*. He moved to Shanghai in 1915, where he taught for two years before he returned to Suzhou to teach at a primary school. After 1919, he supported the new literary movement, submitting vernacular short stories to journals such as *New Tide*, and became a founding member of the Literary Research Association in 1921. In the same year, he left Suzhou to teach first at Hangzhou First Normal University, then Beijing University and finally Fudan University in Shanghai.

Ye Shengtao's stories are mostly about urban dwellers and intellectuals, describing how social (more than political) change affects their lives. Twenty of these stories, all very brief but ranging in tone from lyrical to didactic, were included in his first collection, *Barriers*; published in 1922, it was the second modern short story collection after Yu Dafu's *Sinking*. They include one of his earliest stories in the vernacular, 'A Life', plus 'Lute Music on a Cold Dawn' and 'Bitter Crop'. In the same year, Ye Shengtao launched the first modern Chinese poetry journal, *Poetry*, with Zhu Ziqing and Yu Pingbo. He became an editor for the Commercial Press in 1923 and also published his second and third collections *Fire* and *The Scarecrow*. One of his best-known short stories, 'Mr Pan in Difficulty', appeared in *Short Story Monthly* in 1924. He took over the editorship of this journal in 1927. His most famous work (and only full-length fiction), *Ni Huanzhi*, was serialised in *Education Magazine* in 1928. He continued to write short stories, essays and poems throughout the 1930s and 1940s. After 1949, he was appointed to a series of official posts including Vice-Minister of Education, Deputy Director of the Publications Bureau and Director of the People's Education Publishing House.

Ye Shengtao's first story in the vernacular, 'A Life', is typical of fiction of that time in its criticism of traditional practices. It relates the life of a village girl whose parents cannot afford to keep her at home and arrange an early marriage for her. She bears a son, but when he dies she is maltreated by her husband's family and runs away. She finds employment in the city, but when her employers hear that her husband has died, they dismiss her in case his family should come to claim their widowed daughter-in-law. She returns to attend her husband's funeral, only to be married off again to defray the funeral expenses. She is still only about seventeen. Originally published under the title 'Is This Human?', the story questions the inequalities between male and female, city and country, rich and poor.

The most influential of Ye Shengtao's short stories is probably 'Mr Pan in Difficulty'. The story, told with great humour, is about the pretences involved in the making of heroes. The plot, as in most of Ye Shengtao's fiction, is simple. Mr Pan, a primary school principal, escapes from his village to Shanghai with his family because of fear of imminent civil war. In Shanghai, however, he worries that he may lose his job and so returns to the village. As it happens, the fighting does not come to his area, and after three weeks of anxiety, he is safe. He is then promoted by the local warlord as a hero and model. In another well-known story, 'A Posthumous Son' (1926), the initial humour sours: Mr Wenqing commits suicide after his failure to perpetuate the family line with a male heir, his concubine is deprived of her baby daughter and married off, and his wife's health and sanity deteriorate in the illusion of a false 'posthumous' pregnancy.

Many of Ye Shengtao's other works are about teachers or students, and he shows a genuine pedagogic concern with child development and the workings of children's minds. Ni Huanzhi, in the novel of the same name, is a teacher whose hopes for changing education and society are ultimately dashed. The novel was published in 1928, at the time of the White Terror. Against the background of the changing political situation in China between 1916 and 1927, Ni Huanzhi at the beginning of the novel is a young teacher with dreams of being part of the process of enlightenment in China. Sharing in the general optimism experienced by many intellectuals at that time, the principal of the school is also keen to effect a programme of reform, but they are both defeated by the opposition of the local landowners. Disillusionment also faces the hero at home, where his once idealistic wife is now interested only in their new baby and domestic duties. After meeting a radical student leader, Wang Leshan, Ni Huanzhi heads for Shanghai and participates in the upheavals of 1925–7, hoping to welcome the arrival of the Northern Expedition. When the White Terror instead claims Wang Leshan's life, Ni Huanzhi, despondent and broken, dies of typhoid fever. The only suggestion of hope for the future is that the hero's wife, who had earlier tried to deter him from engaging in political activities, vows at his funeral that she will carry on the struggle.

Zhang Henshui (1895–1967)

Born in Jiangxi but registered in Qianshan, Anhui, Zhang Xinyuan is best known under his pen-name, Zhang Henshui. A prolific writer, he produced a hundred and ten novels and stories, and most of his novels were bestsellers. Before becoming a fiction writer, he was a successful journalist. In 1918, only a year after beginning work, he was appointed as editor-in-chief of *Anhui Daily*. In the autumn of 1919, he moved to Beijing to work as editor for a number of papers. In 1924, he completed his first novel, *Life in the Capital*. Like all his early novels, it was mostly influenced by the Mandarin Ducks and Butterflies school of sentimental melodramas.

Life in the Capital tells the story of Yang Xingyuan, a young man who lives in Beijing. He falls in love with a courtesan, and when she dies, he buries her as if she were his betrothed. He then meets the beautiful and talented Dongqing at a friend's house. They have much in common and begin exchanging poems. They fall in love, but Dongqing has an incurable illness and tries to persuade him to marry a friend of hers instead. Yang Xingyuan vows that he will marry only Dongqing. When he falls ill, Dongqing rushes to his side so as to comfort him. They bid each other a tearful goodbye and he dies, still clutching his writing brush, after writing yet another poem for her. She wails bitterly and faints at his deathbed.

Fate in Tears and Laughter is the most famous of his early novels. Published in 1930, it became an instant success, and its popularity was further enhanced when it was made into a film. A variation on the ever-popular theme of the union between a talented man and a beautiful woman, it tells the story of Fan Jiashu, a young man who arrives in Beijing from Hangzhou in order to enter university. Fan Jiashu falls in love with a seventeen-year-old street singer who is exceptionally beautiful, but she is sold to a warlord and then driven insane by his maltreatment. Meanwhile, Fan Jiashu meets another woman who looks remarkably like her, the difference being that she is also very wealthy. She falls in love with him and the novel ends with them happily united. A lengthy work, with many twists and turns in the fates of the major characters, it also includes an element of knight-errantry involving a woman martial arts expert.

Zhang Henshui was largely unaffected by the political seriousness of the May Fourth writers, whose works were directed at students and young intellectuals. Zhang's fiction had a wider readership, partly because of its reliance on traditional modes of narrative, characterisation and plot. The vivid descriptions of Beijing life at all levels still lend interest to his work.

Yu Dafu (1896–1945)

Yu Dafu is the first fiction writer of the modern era to have started his career after the literary revolution of 1917. Born in Fuyang, Zhejiang, Yu Dafu lost his father when he was a young boy and was raised single-handedly by his mother as the family fortunes declined. Nevertheless he received a traditional early education and had read widely in traditional Chinese literature before he went to Japan with his elder brother to study when he was seventeen. Apart from a brief spell in 1920, when he returned to Fuyang to marry his first wife, Sun Quan, Yu Dafu stayed in Japan until he graduated in 1922. He first studied medicine, then switched to law and finally to economics at Tokyo Imperial University. He later claimed to have spent a considerable amount of time drinking and seeking the company of women, but he also estimated that he read over a thousand titles in European and Japanese fiction at this time. His first story to be published, 'Silver-Grey Death', appeared in July the same year, followed shortly after by 'Sinking' and 'Moving South'. These three formed Yu Dafu's first collection of fiction, *Sinking*; published in October 1921, it was also the first collection of modern vernacular fiction. These stories on the loneliness and sexual fantasies of Chinese students in Japan immediately caught the attention of a huge audience, especially the young.

Yu Dafu was a founding member of the Creation Society in Tokyo in 1921, and in 1923 he left Japan for Shanghai to organise the publication of the society's journals, *Creation Quarterly* and *Creation Weekly*. A new batch of short stories on life in Shanghai followed, including 'Nights of Spring Fever' and 'A Humble Sacrifice', in 1924. By the mid-1920s the Creation journals had been closed down, and Guo Moruo moved to Guangzhou to regroup. Yu Dafu joined him and other members of the society in 1926, but he was not happy with the Nationalist regime and returned to Shanghai the same year to clear up the society's affairs and set up the new journals, *The Deluge* and *Creation*. Internal dissension plagued the society and Yu Dafu quit in 1927. He became instead a close associate of Lu Xun, with whom he shared the editorship of *Torrents*. When *Torrents* was closed down in 1928, he became chief editor of *Mass Literature and the Arts* and was a founding member of the League of Left-wing Writers in 1930. His one novel, *She Is a Weak Woman*, was published in 1932. He resigned from the League and moved to Hangzhou in 1933. Living in semi-seclusion from 1933 to 1937, he wrote mainly poetry, essays and travel diaries. He left for Singapore in 1938 with his second wife, Wang Yingxia, whom he divorced two years later. When Singapore fell to the Japanese in 1942, he fled to Sumatra, where he remained and worked for the Japanese as a translator. He was executed shortly after the Japanese surrender in 1945.

The protagonist of Yu Dafu's first story, 'Silver-Grey Death', is a young man living in Japan. Depressed on hearing that back in China his wife has just died, he tries to pawn her ring so that he can go to a wineshop. He has become friendly with the wineshop owner's daughter, but on learning that she has just got married, he dies in the street, alone and forsaken. Typically in

Yu's early work, it focuses on loneliness, sexual frustration and guilt, emotions to which his young readers readily responded. The most popular of his stories is 'Sinking', whose protagonist appears to resemble the author in several significant details such as place of birth. A young Chinese student in Japan, he lives in an inn and has no close friends. His solitude is underlined from the opening scene in which he reads pastoral poems by Wordsworth. This solitude, however, is far from tranquil, as he is plagued by sexual desires and masturbates every night. In one episode, his sexual urge becomes so overwhelming that he goes downstairs to spy on the landlord's daughter in her bath. Racked by guilt, he moves into an isolated house in the hills. Wandering in a field one day, however, he accidentally overhears a couple making love, and returns to the city where he feels again that he is being treated with contempt by the Japanese. He visits a brothel but is overcome by guilt and longs for death. The story ends with his suicide and his final apostrophe to China, blaming his and others' deaths on the nation's poverty and calling on China to grow strong and wealthy for the sake of its children.

Adolescent sexual frustration is thus explicitly linked to national humiliation for the first time in Chinese literature. The validity of the link cannot be questioned, as the semi-dramatised narrator, who poses as a somewhat detached friend of the protagonist, intimates throughout that he is suffering from hypochondria and is not capable of objective assessments of either his own actions or those around him. Superficially, the hero is a decadent young man who has lost control of himself, but at a deeper level it is clear that he has a strong sense of morality. Beneath his sentimentality, likewise, he also has an idealised sensibility which he constantly tries to realise through the reading of Chinese and European poetry.

Yu Dafu's concern with idealised emotions is continued in two stories published in 1923: 'Nights of Spring Fever' and 'A Humble Sacrifice'. These are among the first in Chinese literature to deal with the interaction of intellectuals with the urban working class. The first-person narrator in 'Nights of Spring Fever' is a writer down on his luck who shares an attic in the Shanghai slums with a seventeen-year-old girl who works in a cigarette factory. He spends the day brooding and takes long walks at night. The girl suspects he may be a thief but remains friendly.

One day she invites him to share her meal and tells him of her difficult life at the factory, where the work is hard and she is constantly humiliated. One day the hero receives a fee for his translations, and after washing himself in a bath house and buying new clothes, he invites the girl for some snacks. At first, she advises him not to associate with thieves, but when he explains what he does for a living, she urges him to work hard so that he can prosper. The hero is intoxicated by her and wants to embrace her, but restrains himself for the sake of her purity and innocence. He then reflects gloomily that even though she is exploited and poverty-stricken, she can at least find work in a factory. He by contrast is unable to find any work at all.

'A Humble Sacrifice' is about the emotional response of a young, impoverished intellectual towards a rickshaw-puller. The first-person narrator befriends a rickshaw-puller struggling to maintain his family. The narrator tries to help out by giving him a watch, but the rickshaw-puller returns the present. Overworked and seeing no hope in the future, the rickshaw-puller drowns himself one stormy night. The narrator accuses the unfeeling crowd of being his friend's murderers, and he buys a paper rickshaw at the funeral as a humble sacrifice. Again, the narrator uses his friend's death to lament his own unhappiness. Even when Yu Dafu's semi-autobiographical protagonists commit noble acts, they quickly pass into self-indulgence and self-pity.

After joining the League of Left-wing Writers, Yu Dafu attempted to write in a less self-absorbed way, abandoning dramatised or intrusive narrative for conventional omniscient narrative and incorporating historical detail in place of overt autobiographical reference. *She Is a Weak Woman*, although not well-known, serves as a good example of his later work. The action takes place against the White Terror of the late 1920s and the Japanese attack on Shanghai in 1932. Yu Dafu's abiding interest in sexuality is here transferred to the relationship between three young women: Zheng Xiuyue, Li Wenqing and Feng Shifen. The main character, Zheng Xiuyue, falls in love with Li Wenqing, who has earlier tried to seduce Feng Shifen. Wenqing soon tires of Xiuyue, who then turns for solace to two of their women teachers. Xiuyue continues her affair with one of the teachers even after she marries, and is eventually found by her husband in a hotel with her lover; her husband blames himself for her behaviour. In 1932, when

Japan bombs Shanghai, Xiuyue is taken away by Japanese soldier. Unable to stop this from happening, all her husband can do is to shout that she should be forgiven, as she is a weak woman. A few days later her dead body is found in the street. Perhaps the subject-matter was too scandalous; the novel was never as popular as his early fiction. Yu Dafu's last story, 'Flight' (1935), draws on the background of civil war in a provincial town. A young revolutionary sinks into a degenerate way of life after being seduced by the daughter of a local landlord, but redeems himself by setting fire to the house owned by his wife's family where he has been living since their marriage. He flees to Shanghai, where he reads in the press that the fire has killed not only his wife and her parents but also her young brother and the maid. In the final sentence, the reader is implicitly invited to approve of 'the frank, unaffected smile' with which the hero greets this news.

Yu Dafu's early work is much studied by literary historians for its innovations in subject-matter and style. Modelled on Japanese confessional fiction, it is unabashedly self-referential and subjective. His experiments with narrative voice are not particularly successful, since most readers ignore the detachment or irony often present, and Yu Dafu was himself ambivalent about titillating his readers with revelations of his personal life. The full range of sexual preferences exhibited by his protagonists, however, cannot be attributed to their author, who is unlikely to have been so versatile, nor did he meet their fate (suicide or death by despair in the street); unlike them, he enjoyed an active social life and considerable success as a writer, editor and businessman. Now that the stories have lost their shock value, there is little evidence that they will continue to attract young readers. (*See also the section on Yu Dafu's poetry in Chapter 3.*)

Mao Dun (1896–1981)

Born in the same year as Yu Dafu, Mao Dun delayed writing fiction, first making his name as an editor and critic. It is no coincidence that when it finally appeared, his fiction was driven by ideology rather than subjectivity. A native of Tongxiang, Zhejiang, his father died when he was only nine, and he was brought up by his mother. She had a great respect for education and saw to it that he received a sound traditional education at home. By the time he entered a modern secondary school in Hangzhou in 1910, he had read most of the classic novels. He moved to Beijing in 1912 and enrolled in preparatory study at Beijing University, but financial difficulties forced him to give up after only two years, and he went south to work at the Commercial Press in Shanghai. At this time, he mostly used the name Shen Yanbing.

As well as editing and translating for the Commercial Press, he read widely in Western literature and literary history. After joining a Communist study group in 1920, Mao Dun became increasingly active in left-wing politics. Managing to get himself appointed as editor of the commercially successful *Short Story Monthly* at the end of 1920, he was chiefly responsible for its radical literary and political orientation until his resignation in 1923. His views on the relationship between politics and literature are summed in the influential essay 'On Proletarian Literature', published in May 1925. Over the next two years, he put theory into practice as an active participant on the Communist side in its complex relations with the Nationalist Party, working, for example, in the Shanghai Propaganda Bureau of the Communist Party in 1926. In 1927 he was chief editor of the *Nationalist Daily* in Hankou. When the left-wing Nationalist government fell later that year, he escaped to Shanghai, where between 1927 and 1928, he wrote the trilogy published as a single book under the title *Eclipse* in 1930, which had an immediate impact on the literary world. It was at this time he adopted the pen-name Mao Dun (using the Chinese term 'contradiction' to demonstrate his Marxist affiliation, but changing one character slightly to avoid censorship; roughly corresponding to 'Konrad Diction' in English).

Before heading for relative safety in Japan in July 1928, Mao Dun wrote several more short stories and essays. In Japan he completed his second novel, *The Rainbow*, as well as short stories such as 'Suicide' and 'A Woman' and major essays such as 'From Guling to Tokyo'. He returned to Shanghai in 1930 to help found the League of Left-wing Writers, and was appointed its executive secretary the following year. His most famous writings appeared in rapid succession between 1931 and 1937: 'The Lin Family Shop' and 'Spring Silkworms' were both published in 1932 and *Midnight* in 1933.

'Disillusion', the first part of *Eclipse*, is about the confusion experienced among university students after the events of summer and autumn 1927. The protagonist, Zhang Jing, is unhappy with the shallowness and hedonistic pursuits of her fellow students in Shanghai. Her close friend, Hui, a returned student from France, flirts with a young man, Baosi, who comes to Jing to say how hurt and bewildered he feels. Jing allows him to make love to her, only to find out the next day that he is a government agent sent to spy on the students. Doubly disillusioned, Jing falls ill, but her hopes are rekindled by news of the Northern Expedition. Eventually she journeys to the new government base in Wuhan, only to be disappointed again in both her personal and social life. The second part of the trilogy, 'Vacillation', is about the impact of the violent upheavals in a county town in Hubei in 1927 on young people. The main character, Fang Luolan, is a functionary in the left-wing faction of the Nationalist Party. He and his associates attempt to mobilise the masses in the town but are outmanoeuvred by a member of the old gentry, Hu Guoguang. The party members cannot take decisive action and are obliged to flee.

The third part, 'The Search', is even more despairing than the previous two. Centred on a group of friends who meet in Shanghai in 1928, it tells of dashed hopes and diminished ambitions. These friends have witnessed the counter-revolution, and while they still search for something for themselves, they have lost the will to build a better society. Through their individualism, they end up respectively as suicidal, alcoholic or self-absorbed and cowardly.

At the time *Eclipse* was completed, the White Terror had taken many lives; it was a period of extreme darkness for left-wing activists and their supporters. Mao Dun's trilogy offered very little in terms of brightness except to suggest that eclipses are always temporary and will be followed by sunshine. In literary terms, it set new standards as the first sustained effort in modern literature to give a coherent picture of a significant historical period in twentieth-century China.

By the time Mao Dun wrote the unfinished novel *Rainbow* in 1929, his mood was more positive. Although the situation in China was still tense, he wrote the novel far removed from the frontlines of the political and literary struggles. The novel traces the development of a young woman, Mei, during the momentous events from May Fourth to May Thirtieth. Like Jing in *Eclipse*, Mei is an educated woman dissatisfied with her life. She divorces her husband but becomes disappointed with her lover for being too weak-willed. She is not greatly inspired by the many new ideas with which she comes into contact either: individualism, socialism, anarchism and feminism. Finally meeting a Communist organiser, she is drawn to his sense of dedication and purpose. The novel ends with her transformation as she prepares to participate in the May Thirtieth demonstrations.

Mao Dun's understanding of Marxism led him to portray the international situation and its impact on peasants and small shop-keepers. One of his best short stories, 'Spring Silkworms', depicts the consequences of the conflict between China and Japan for the lives of Tongbao and his hard-working family. Lovingly tending their silkworms, providing them with choice mulberry leaves and warmth, to their great joy, they are rewarded with an abundant crop of good-quality cocoons. Their joy turns to despair, however, when they discover that all the silk factories have closed down and there is no demand for cocoons. 'The Lin Family Shop' shows the impact of the international economic situation on a small town on the outskirts of Shanghai, describing the futile efforts of a shopkeeper, Mr Lin, to avoid bankruptcy. Mr Lin is a shrewd businessman who tries his best to keep his drapery a going concern, but the combined pressure of Japanese dumping and the inability of his customers to pay prove too much for him. As well as creditors, he also has to watch out for the warlords, the Nationalist government and his own competitors. The plot is structured around a series of contradictions: the more he sells at his new low prices, the greater his overall loss; the more his creditors demand payment, the more they ensure his bankruptcy; pouring into the streets to maintain order, the police create a riot; his own wife and daughter treasure their Japanese clothes. Through contradiction, however, comes resolution: his wife and daughter reveal unexpected strength of character, and there is hope in the end for a new life for the family.

Although these stories would be enough to give Mao Dun an assured place in the development of literary realism in China, his best-known work is *Midnight*, a chronicle of the commercial and industrial scene in Shanghai in the summer of 1930 crammed with painstaking detail. Enthusiastically received by Communist critics such as Qu Qiubai as the first successful novel of Marxist realism, it is an ambitious work not easy to read or summarise. The main character is Wu Sunfu, a wealthy entrepreneur in the textile industry, who is convinced that national industries could become independent of foreign capital. Determined to fight for this goal, he seeks an alliance with Chinese industrialists who share his views. The ruin of a number of smaller operations does not dampen his spirits; on the contrary, he uses the opportunity to buy up more mills and factories. In the end, however, he is not able to prevent the forces of international capitalism and internal pressures from destroying his dreams. Wu Sunfu gets into debt because his factories are not profitable and tries to raise money by speculating heavily on the stock market. This action, the plot's main 'contradiction', only weakens his industrial base. He then tries to raise funds by lowering wages, but the workers go on strike and Wu Sunfu calls in the police, further weakening his control over his factories and holding up production. He finally meets defeat on the stock exchange through the machinations of his chief rival, Zhao Botao, a financier backed by international banking interests.

While *Midnight* can be read as the tragedy of an individual whose efforts are doomed to failure because of forces outside his control, it is also a statement of Mao Dun's understanding of the economic and political situation in China. Through the protagonist's ruin, Mao Dun implies that national salvation could not be achieved through national capital alone. China, in current Marxist analysis, was facing an economic crisis generated by feudalism and imperialism, and Wu Sunfu, like Mr Lin in 'The Lin Family Shop', struggles in vain against his historical destiny. The characters in Mao Dun's fiction face psychological stresses which in most cases defeat them. However, with some exceptions like Mei in *Rainbow*, his protagonists end the stories with little more understanding than they had at the beginning. In the stories of 1932–3, the characters were able to develop if they represented the emerging classes such as the petty bourgeoisie, but in these cases, they remained largely stereotypical characters rather than individual personalities. Through the experiences and interactions of these representatives, Mao Dun hammers home the message that Chinese society in the late 1920s and early 1930s was rent with contradictions which only a Communist revolution could resolve. (*For Mao Dun's later fiction see Chapter 7.*)

Wang Tongzhao (1897–1957)

Wang Tongzhao's first short story was published in 1918, the year in which he went to study in Beijing. His early writings are mostly concerned with the failure of his twin ideals, beauty and love, to exist in harmony together. In Beijing he became involved in the May Fourth Movement and was one of the founders of the Literary Research Association. *A Leaf* was published in 1922, and his most famous novel, *Mountain Rain*, appeared in 1933. After 1949, he became head of the Chinese Department at Shandong University and held a number of official posts in literary and cultural organisations.

A Leaf represents Wang Tongzhao's early attitudes towards life, which in an introductory poem he describes as a leaf fluttering in the wind. This naturalistic image is later evoked again as the hero, Li Tiangen, likens the vicissitudes of human life to a leaf floating in a stream, unable to determine its own course. This fatalistic vision of life was instilled in him when his childhood sweetheart, Wu Hui, was forced to marry another man while Li Tiangen was attending secondary school in the city; he returns home to find that his sweetheart has already died, her spirit broken. As Li Tiangen matures, his melancholy only deepens when events further destroy his dreams. For example, he is befriended at secondary school by a young teacher, Zhang Bairu, who advises him not to be so pessimistic about life, but in the end Zhang himself suffers from a series of misfortunes through no fault of his own, confirming Li's fatalism.

A Leaf is typical of the subjective, introspection fiction of the 1920s. By 1930, when Wang Tongzhao was writing *Mountain Rain*, the impact of social forces on people's lives dominated fiction. *Mountain Rain* shows the effect on the rural population of high taxes, abuse of power by the military, and foreign encroachment. The protagonist, Xi Dayou, seems to be sheltered from the difficulties burdening most of the peasants around him: he owns his own land and is happily married. However, his fortunes begin to decline when he becomes involved in an argument with an army officer. As a result of this dispute he is thrown in gaol and a large part of his land is sold to gain his release. To compound his predicament, he is subsequently wounded in a fight with local bandits, and the resulting hospital expenses bring his family to financial ruin. Ultimately, the once-proud Xi Dayou joins the ranks of impoverished villagers seeking work in the city and becomes a rickshaw-puller. (*For Wang's early life and poetry see Chapter 3.*)

Lao She (1899–1966)

The most famous novel on rickshaw men was by Lao She, a writer who simultaneously belonged to, and was distinct from, the new literary movement of the 1920s and 1930s. Manchu by birth, he was always conscious of his connection to the Qing regime whose overthrow was fuelled by racist hatred as well as political reforms. His father, a palace guard, was killed during the Boxer Rebellion in 1900, and he was raised by his mother in straitened circumstances. His original name was Shu Qingchun. On graduating from Beijing Normal School in 1918, his first job was as the principal of a local primary school. In 1922 he went to Tianjin to teach Chinese at Nankai Secondary School, where he wrote his first short story, 'Little Bell'. After only six months he returned to Beijing, working for the Beijing Education Society and teaching Chinese at secondary school. Becoming an active member of a Christian association, he also studied English, and in summer 1924, obtained a position teaching Chinese at the School of Oriental Studies at the University of London.

In London, Lao She read widely in English literature and wrote three novels under the inspiration of novelists such as Charles Dickens. The first, *The Philosophy of Lao Zhang*, was serialised in *Short Story Monthly* in 1926. The same journal serialised *Zhao Ziyue* and *The Two Mas* in 1927 and 1929 respectively. Lao She left for China in 1929. He stopped over in Singapore for six months, teaching Chinese and completing the fantasy *Xiao Po's Birthday*, on the life of a Cantonese child living in Singapore. He obtained a teaching post at Qilu University in Jinan, Shandong in 1930 and married Hu Xieqing the following year. His two satirical novels, *Cat Country* and *Divorce*, were published in 1932 and 1933, along with a number of short stories including 'Black Li and White Li' and 'The Crescent Moon'. By 1936 he was able to resign from teaching and concentrate on writing. In that year, his most famous novel, *Camel Xiangzi,* appeared.

Lao She's style took form during his years in London. The plot of *The Philosophy of Lao Zhang,* for example, one of Lao She's most significant novels, is modelled on *Nicholas Nickleby,* and its omniscient and intrusive narrator is also in imitation of Dickens. Set in Beijing in the years immediately after 1919, it makes no reference to the momentous political events of the time but focuses on individual characters whose lives are, for the most part, not tied to a specific period in history. The language, however, adopts the modern vernacular style promoted in the May Fourth Movement. The novel was extremely popular and has been constantly in print since publication. The central character, Lao Zhang, is a schoolteacher who also practises usury and owns a small shop, concerned mainly with money and status. Believing that a concubine would elevate his social standing, he tries to make the sister of one of his students his concubine in settlement of a debt. This sister is in love with another of Lao Zhang's students, and together they try to thwart Lao Zhang's machinations, but the young man is forced by his parents to marry someone else and the young woman dies, broken-hearted. At the end of the story, we are told that Lao Zhang becomes an official and acquires two concubines. Although the novel is meant to be a comedy, it ends in tragedy. To convey the novel's underlying sense of moral outrage, the despicable character of Lao Zhang is contrasted with a righteous rickshaw-puller, Zhao Si.

Lao She's second novel, *Zhao Ziyue,* is also set in Beijing during the aftermath of the May Fourth Incident. Unlike the previous novel, where students are shown as victims, the students in this work are depicted as lacking in substance. Their nationalist, Westernised mentality is condemned as superficial. Lao She wrote *Zhao Ziyue* while he was in London and this may have allowed him to distance himself from the political fervour of China during that time. The plot relates the activities of a group of college students, led by Zhao Ziyue, who advocate revolution and engage in strikes, but their actions are shown as destructive rather than constructive. The 500 students in the college are divided into 300 parties, and the only time they show any sign of unity is when they decide not to sit the examinations! Despite the slogans they mouth, their main concern is to obtain official positions on graduation. There is only one character, Li Jingchun, who embodies the values Lao She admired. Li is hard-working and upright, and avoids taking part in the students' political activities – with one telling exception: when the Temple of Heaven is in danger of being sold to foreigners, he does not hesitate to advise his friend, Zhao Ziyue, to take drastic action, including assassination.

The theme of *The Two Mas*, the last novel written by Lao She before he left London, is racial prejudice, especially the contempt shown by Westerners to the citizens of a poor and weak country like China. The plot relates the trials of Mr Ma and his son, Master Ma, who have come to London to take over a curio shop owned by Mr Ma's brother. The two Mas find it extremely difficult to find lodgings because the English believe that all Chinese people eat rats and smoke opium. Their friend, Mr Evans, a missionary who has lived in China, eventually manages to find them a place, where they are such good tenants that the landlady and her daughter learn to tolerate their 'strange ways'. Toleration turns to romance between the two couples, but ultimately the gulf between the two cultures proves too wide to be conquered by love. In the novel, only two kinds of foreigner, missionaries and traders, are depicted as having any knowledge of China. Yet, to the former, even after many years sojourn in China, the Chinese are no more than heathens whose souls need to be saved; and the latter look down on the Chinese because they are incompetent in managing their money.

On his return to China in 1930, Lao She found that his homeland was in even worse straits than he had imagined: Japan was poised to take over the country, China's leaders lacked integrity and her intellectuals were engaged in what appeared to him petty squabbles. *Cat Country* is a product of his despair. The dramatised narrator finds himself marooned on Mars and is captured by its inhabitants, the Cat people, who are lazy, cowardly and self-centred. They drag him off to Cat Country, which is dirty, crowded and ridden with inequality. The novel's chief target of attack is the education system, where students are automatically granted degrees. Intellectuals, political parties of both the right and the left, and members of the elite who take concubines and behave oppressively to women also face biting criticism. The satire in *Cat Country* is more bitter than funny, and Lao She was later harshly criticised for his comments on the political and social situation in China in the early 1930s. *Divorce*, written also in the early 1930s but set in Beijing, is a more personal study of domestic life in a changing society, but the 'divorce' of the title also stands for failed ideals and the breakdown of institutional structures. The hero, Mr Li, has little communication with his wife, an uneducated village woman, and blames his unhappiness on the system of arranged marriages. He falls in love with a beautiful neighbour who has been abandoned by her husband and dreams of a marriage based on mutual passion and understanding. The neighbour's husband, an arrogant and corrupt man who imagines himself a Marxist, has gone off with another woman, but in the end he returns and takes back his wife. Mr Li's illusions are shattered and his life is in ruins.

Many of Lao She's short stories have been reprinted in anthologies. A repeated theme is the hypocrisy of left-wing students. In 'Black Li and White Li', for example, Black Li is both a conservative and very kind-hearted, while his younger brother, White Li, is deeply involved in the revolutionary movement but has selfish tendencies. In the end, Black Li sacrifices his life to save his brother. Not surprisingly, stories such as this one were not reprinted after 1949. 'The Crescent Moon' is a straightforward tale of social injustice. Taking up a common theme in modern literature, the plot relates the defiant sufferings of a young girl whose mother is forced by poverty to become a prostitute; although she tries desperately to improve her life, the daughter's life also disintegrates and she ends up in prison.

In portraying the physical and moral decline of an individual in an unjust society, *Camel Xiangzi* stands out as Lao She's most penetrating social critique. In a departure from his usual practice, Lao She chooses a protagonist from the lowest stratum of urban society. At the beginning of the novel, Xiangzi is a proud and optimistic young man whose dream is to own his own rickshaw. He soon saves enough to buy one, but it is seized by marauding soldiers. He escapes, stealing a few of the soldiers' camels on the way, and his remarkable feat is celebrated in his nickname, 'Camel'. There is a suggestion, however, that this theft, no matter how excusable, departs from the hero's personal morality of decency and it sets the hero on his downward path. He starts saving again for a new rickshaw, but as soon as he gets enough the secret police rob him of his money. Xiangzi begins to lose some of his self-confidence. In this state, he is tricked into marriage by Huniu, the ugly and unscrupulous daughter of the owner of the rickshaw rental firm. They are thrown out by her disgusted father, but Xiangzi buys another rickshaw with Huniu's savings and recommences his rickshaw pulling. Tragedy strikes again when Huniu dies in childbirth and Xiangzi is forced once again to sell his rickshaw to pay for the funeral expenses.

By this stage Xiangzi is thoroughly discouraged. His only remaining hope is Fuzi, a young woman forced into prostitution to support her younger brothers. With the help of a former employer, the Dickensianly benevolent Mr Cao, Xiangzi seeks out the long-suffering Fuzi only to find that she has committed suicide. The novel ends with Xiangzi's final degradation, when he betrays the rickshaw union organiser to the secret police for a small sum of money. The organiser is publicly executed and Xiangzi continues along his hopeless path.

There are several versions of this novel, both in Chinese and in English translation. *Rickshaw Boy*, published in the United States in 1945 and named as Book of the Month, was given a happy ending; some post-1949 editions on the mainland simply cut the ending altogether. The different endings, however, testify to its popularity: in whatever version, the novel still provides an unrivalled picture of the life of the underprivileged in Beijing in the 1930s. Rickshaw-pullers, perhaps because of their visibility in the early twentieth century, are a favourite subject for many stories and poems. Unlike many other works of the modern period, which despite their concern with the suffering of the working classes are often extensions of the writers' own preoccupations or else glamorise the poor out of all recognition, *Camel Xiangzi* neither patronises or idealises the working man. Lao She shows in this novel the destruction of a strong and youthful spirit by an unrelenting and all-powerful system; rejecting the Communist solution, he offers no alternative to individual integrity. (*For Lao She's later fiction and drama see Chapters 7 and 9.*)

Bing Xin (b. 1900)

A precocious reader, Bing Xin read most of the classic novels as a child. Her first short story, 'Two Families', was published in the *Morning Post Supplement* in September 1919, followed by 'Personal Grief' in October. One of her most admired works is 'Superman', published in 1921. These stories are about the problems facing young intellectuals in a changing China, but in the 1930s she showed a wider range of characters in stories like 'Miss Winter'. A collection of essays, *Letters to Young Readers*, comprising thirty-nine letters relating her thoughts as a student in the United States, which was published in 1926 on her return to China, remained for many years a great success with children. Bing Xin published several more volumes of short stories and essays in the 1930s and 1940s, but her work after 1949 was mainly written for children.

Many of Bing Xin's stories are sentimental tales that idealise her childhood, and images of childhood innocence, mother-love, the moon and the sea are found throughout. Even when she writes about social problems, her characters tend to be young people. 'Personal Grief' is about two brothers who take part in a patriotic movement at their school. Their father, angered by their show of political activism, orders them to leave school and take office jobs, and the brothers reluctantly submit to his authority. In her treatment of inter-generational tension, Bing Xin sets forth common themes of youthful rebellion and paternal authoritarianism. In an age where social change generated difficult and dramatic conflicts, Bing Xin's writings represent a compassionate vision of life.

The hero of 'Superman', He Bin, is a young man who tries to reject emotions of love and sympathy. Under the influence of Nietzsche's then-fashionable philosophy, he isolates himself from people in an attempt to become a self-sufficient 'superman'. Despite his efforts, however, he cannot eradicate love from his life. One day, a young boy from a poor family living opposite breaks his leg. He Bin's sympathy for his suffering rekindles the love he had tried so desperately to deny. During the night's disturbed sleep, he dreams of his mother, flowers and stars. These symbols of love then inspire him to help fund the cost of the injured boy's medical expenses, and he comes to understand that 'all mothers in the world are good friends; and all sons in the world are also good friends'. Through the transformation in He Bin's attitudes, Bing Xin illustrates her belief in the power of love and goodness.

'Miss Winter' (1933) celebrates the independence of a young woman who triumphs over adverse circumstances. An affirmative portrayal of women at the lower levels of urban society, it consists of a widow's monologue about her daredevil daughter. There is no social criticism as such, and no reference to specific historical events. The daughter's emancipation is not due to intellectual influences, native or foreign, but is fostered by circumstance: deprivation can create courage as well as despair. Told in a colloquial, humorous style, it goes against the common May Fourth tendency to represent women as victims of social or family oppression.

Bing Xin is sometimes linked with Ling Shuhua, as two women writers born in the same year and both married to university professors. Since both tended to write about women and children in a domestic setting, their work is sometimes dismissed by male critics as narrow. Their lives and writing, however, were very different, and in their approach to social problems they belong on either side of the divide between the critical realists and the psychological ironists of the 1920s and 1930s. (*See also the section on Bing Xin in Chapter 3.*)

Ling Shuhua (1900–90)

Ling Shuhua was born in Beijing to a family from Panyu, Guangdong. She received a good education as a child at a private normal college for girls in Tianjin, and was admitted to the preparatory school attached to Yanjing University in 1921 to study foreign languages. She began writing when she was at university, but her fame as a writer came in 1924, when the short story 'After Drinking' was published in *Contemporary Review*. Graduating in 1926, she married one of its editors, Chen Yuan, the following year (professor of English at Beijing University, Chen Yuan was well-known for his conflicts with Lu Xun). She accompanied her husband to Wuhan University in 1929, continuing meanwhile to publish her stories in *Contemporary Review* and *Crescent Monthly*. Her first collection of stories, *The Temple of Flowers*, was published in 1928, followed in 1930 by *Women* and *Children*. In 1935 she published another volume of children's stories, *Little Brothers*, which incorporates all the stories in *Children*; although cleverly written, the thirteen stories collected here do not reach the standard of the stories in the first two anthologies. She wrote very little fiction after this promising beginning but developed a second career as a painter in the traditional style. In 1946, Chen Yuan became China's chief delegate to UNESCO and Ling Shuhua accompanied her husband to live in London, and the following year they moved to Paris. During the next forty-odd years, she travelled widely in Europe, Asia and America, and revisited the mainland in the 1980s.

The Temple of Flowers contains twelve stories which were first published in journals between 1924 and 1926. The title story is a provocative study of trust and desire in marriage. A young couple are deeply in love, but one day the husband arranges an assignation with another woman at a temple in the countryside; it turns out that the woman he is to meet has been sent by his wife to test his fidelity. Another story in the collection, 'The Eve of the Mid-Autumn Festival', is a finely detailed and unsentimental portrait of the collapse of a marriage, as a quarrel between husband and wife leads to the moral and physical degeneration of both; behind their estrangement is a semi-incestuous erotic relationship between the husband and his foster-sister. The disillusionment felt by young women in a rapidly changing society is most dramatically portrayed in 'Embroidered Pillows', which had a great impact on publication in 1925. A young woman in a declining gentry family, under instructions from her parents, spends six months meticulously embroidering a pair of pillow cases. This was to be her father's birthday gift to a high official in the hope that the official will be so impressed with her skill that he will betroth his second son to her. Two years later, her maid shows the still unmarried young mistress a pair of soiled but still exquisite pillow cases which she has obtained from a rich family. She has been told, and retells to her mistress, that at the birthday party where the pillow cases were presented, one pillow case was used to catch vomit and the other as a floormat. The story is a distanced observation of cruelty generated by changing times and anachronistic expectations.

'The Lucky One', written in 1924, is set in a wealthy family at an unspecified time in the recent past. It introduces several themes all of which became standard topics in modern literature:

the oppression of women in the Confucian family structure; conflict between women of different generations within the family; and the persistence of old conservative attitudes into modern times. Ling Shuhua chooses to adopt a traditional storyteller narrative persona – impersonal and omniscient but free to comment on the action of the story – but updates it by controlling the narrative perspective (only the Old Mistress is shown from the inside) and by the use of irony: in contrast to the narrator's clucking approval, the Old Mistress is shown by the action to be as vulnerable as any mere wife or concubine. In portraying her female protagonist as victim, Ling Shuhua echoes the conventional May Fourth line, but with the difference that as a matriarch she would be more commonly be placed among the oppressors. Ling Shuhua's independence in this respect, apart from her personal connections with the Hu Shi faction, caused her work to be neglected on the mainland for over thirty years.

The title story in *Women* describes the attempts of a wife and mother to prevent the husband/son from developing a romance with his student. It is typical of the stories in this collection in its portrayal of middle-class women in family situations. The trivia of daily life are used by Ling Shuhua to expose human foibles and psychological nuance. For example, 'The Send-off' consists only of conversations conducted mostly between two middle-aged women who are supposed to be seeing off a friend at the train station; between the lines of their polite chatter, however, these women reveal their insecurities about their husbands and themselves. The protagonist, Mrs Bai, takes every opportunity to scold the servants, a ritual by which she disguises her feelings of inadequacy despite her comfortable life. In the end, the women are too late to bid farewell to their friend. Ling Shuhua, who acknowledged the influence of Katherine Mansfield on her fiction, tempers sympathy with distance in her skilful and subtle sketches of the emptiness in women's lives.

Jiang Guangci (1901–31)

Jiang Guangci was the first writer to dedicate himself to revolutionary fiction, and both in his person and in his writing represented the kind of radical activist satirised by Lao She and Shen Congwen. Born in Anhui, Jiang Guangci went to Shanghai in 1919 to study

Russian. He joined the Socialist Youth League the following year, and in 1921 went to study at the Moscow Labour University. While in Moscow, he became friends with Qu Qiubai, joined the Communist Party, and read widely in Communist literary theory. He returned to Shanghai in the summer of 1924 and was assigned a teaching post at the Communist-run Shanghai University. He immediately published a series of essays and poems in left-wing journals such as *New Youth*.

His first novel, *The Young Wanderer*, and the short story 'On the Yalu River' were published in 1926. In August the same year he married. His only collection of short fiction was published the following year under the title *On the Yalu River*, and was dedicated to his wife who had just died. Jiang moved to the foreign settlement in Shanghai in 1927 to escape the White Terror. He was a founding member of the Communist-front Sun Society but his writing followed his own romantic tastes. *The Sorrows of Lisa*, published in 1929, was hotly attacked by left-wing critics such as Yang Hansheng for its sympathetic portrayal of the old Russian aristocracy and the implied questioning of the correctness of Soviet policies. Lisa is a White Russian aristocrat who has taken refuge in Shanghai; she works as a striptease dancer and a prostitute before meeting a pathetic and untimely end.

Jiang Guangci himself suffered from bad health and went to Japan for a few months to recuperate (and to avoid trouble over *The Sorrows of Lisa*). He continued writing prolifically, and published several novels during 1930, including *The Moon Breaks Out from Behind the Clouds*. In 1930, under continued pressure from the Communist Party to mend his 'petty-bourgeois' and 'romantic' ways, his health deteriorated and he wrote to resign from the Party. However, the Communist Party decided to expel him instead. His health finally gave way on him and he died the following year. Jiang Guangci's badly constructed plots, sentimental dialogue and clumsy use of language are typical of revolutionary literature in the late 1920s and early 1930s. In his novels, heroic young men struggle against wealthy and exploitative older men for the love of beautiful and tragic prostitutes: the pursuit of social justice is equated with romance.

The title story in *On the Yalu River*, for example, features a group of foreign students in Moscow talking about their romantic experiences; at the centre is a Korean student whose father and girlfriend both die as a consequence of their patriotic activities. Most of the other stories are equally tragic, with themes ranging from 'broken hearts', political instability caused by Japanese aggression, or inhumane social practices such as child betrothals. *The Sorrows of Lisa* is his most controversial work, but *The Young Wanderer* and *The Moon Breaking Out from Behind the Clouds* were more popular at their time, both running into several editions. *The Young Wanderer* is a melodramatic tale in which the orphaned protagonist wanders from place to place, failing to find employment but finally meeting a heroic death as a revolutionary.

Neither *The Young Wanderer* nor *The Moon Breaking Out*, one of his last works, is a mature literary work. The latter relates the experiences of Wang Manying, an unusual woman who joins a group of students in their revolutionary activities. When the group is forced to disband, she is left destitute and eventually becomes a prostitute. During this time, she has two clients. The first is the student who had initially persuaded her to join the group: he has become an official, betraying his ideals. The second is a wealthy debauched man who had tried to make her his concubine. She sleeps with both men, thinking that she had venereal disease which she would give them. She then meets another fellow student who has continued the struggle, and under his influence her fighting spirit is revived. She then discovers that she is not suffering from venereal disease after all but from a harmless discharge. She then has a romance with her revolutionary friend. It is easy to ridicule Jiang Guangci's novels but they did capture the imagination of the young at the time and their impact should not be underestimated. (*For Jiang's poetry see Chapter 3.*)

Shen Congwen (1902–88)

A member of the Miao ethnic minority, Shen Congwen was born in Fenghuang, Hunan. He went to primary school in the county town and stayed close to home until he was about fifteen. In 1918, he joined the militia and over the next few years drifted with his regiment from place to place in Hunan, Sichuan and Guizhou. During this time, he was able to see at first hand the natural beauty of south-west China, observe tribal customs in remote areas, and meet people from all walks of life, experiences which became invaluable raw material for his creative work. As a soldier, he witnessed extremes of brutality and heroism known only through books to urban writers.

Shen Congwen went to Beijing in 1923 and audited classes at Beijing University, where he came under the influence of the Anglo-American group of writers. At the same time he formed a triangular relationship with a young left-wing poet, Hu Yepin, and his lover Ding Ling, which gave rise to much gossip. From 1924 on, his fiction, plays, essays and poetry appeared regularly in the *Morning Post Supplement, Contemporary Review* and *Short Story Monthly*. By the time he left Beijing for Shanghai in 1928, he had already published two collections of his works. These early pieces, however, were uneven in quality. In Shanghai, Shen Congwen, Hu Yepin and Ding Ling jointly edited the journals *Red and Black* and *Red Black* and set up the Red Black Press. The projects were short-lived and the association soon foundered. Shen became a member of the Crescent Society and through Hu Shi obtained a teaching post in Shanghai. He later taught at various universities, including Wuhan, Qingdao and Beijing, and after the outbreak of the War against Japan joined the South-west United University in Kunming.

During these years Shen was extremely prolific, producing more than 200 short stories and ten novels. Many are based on his experiences as a soldier. In 'After Joining the Ranks', Shen Congwen pays tribute to the egalitarianism and freedom that can be found in army life. The plot is simple: a young prisoner becomes friendly with the squad in which the narrator is serving; they release him but he is recaptured and executed. In 'My Education', the narrator describes how his fellow soldiers execute alleged bandits or squeeze money from prisoners to supplement the pay which is frequently withheld by their superiors. Gruesome activities such as necrophilia and using severed heads for football are described in these stories, but the author maintains his distance and refrains from expressing moral outrage.

In stories of rural life such as 'Xiaoxiao', customs which would be considered feudal by radical left-wing writers are given a different perspective. For example, child marriage is practised in south-west China so that a poor family is relieved of the burden of having to feed a teenage daughter while the other family gains a babysitter. The orphaned Xiaoxiao accordingly is married at the age of twelve to a three-year-old boy. Xiaoxiao appears to be quite happy looking after her young husband, until she is seduced by a hired hand at the age of fourteen. When she becomes pregnant, her family is faced with a problem: traditional morality dictates that she should be drowned or sold as a prostitute, but her only remaining relative baulks at murder and in that remote area it is not easy to find a buyer. When the baby is born and turns out to be a healthy boy, Xiaoxiao is welcomed back into the family and her son is adopted as her husband's younger brother. Twelve years later, Xiaoxiao gives birth to another son, this time by her husband. Around the same time, the family gains another teenage daughter-in-law as Xiaoxiao's first son is married. The cheerful conclusion suggests that the country people's relationship to traditional ethics is much more ambiguous than many intellectuals would have us believe, and that faced with moral dilemmas, they can make choices which are both practical and humane. (Had the author chosen to make Xiaoxiao's first child a daughter, however, the outcome might have been very different.) The story was written in 1929 and revised for later publication in 1935; a film version was made in the 1980s.

The novella *The Border Town*, written in 1934, is one of Shen Congwen's most famous works. Set in the remote countryside of West Hunan and Sichuan, it continues the theme of pastoral innocence in the sexual awakening of a young woman. Cuicui has been brought up by her grandfather, an honest boatman. Her mother had committed suicide after falling pregnant to a young soldier whose love songs had won her heart. Cuicui's grandfather is determined that she should not ruin her life in the same way. On the opposite bank of the river is a border town, where two brothers live. Cuicui meets the younger brother at a festival, becoming offended when she misunderstands a harmless joke as an insult. The encounter stirs inexpressible feelings in her. At the same time, her grandfather ponders his own mortality, fearing for Cuicui's future.

The elder brother, who has also fallen in love with Cuicui, precipitates the action by sending a go-between to arrange marriage. Her grandfather, guessing that Cuicui prefers the younger brother, suggests a song contest so that she can choose the man she prefers. The younger brother sings first. Knowing that he cannot compete, the elder brother runs away and is drowned further downstream in an accident. His father then forbids the younger brother to marry Cuicui. Cuicui's grandfather also meets his death by drowning, and the story ends with the lovers still not united. Despite the pathos, there are no villains in the story, and the descriptions of the river and mountains suggest the idyllic beauty of traditional poetry and painting. Shen Congwen has also put to good use his knowledge of Miao customs in introducing the singing contest as a central element in the plot, evoking an atmosphere both nostalgic and exotic even to Chinese readers. The film version of 1984, which capitalises heavily on the natural beauty of the surroundings, won critical acclaim and a prize at Montreal but was less popular with Chinese audiences at home.

Shen Congwen liked to describe himself as a 'simple countryman' and the influence of traditional storytelling is apparent in the rambling plots, authorial intrusions and snatches of folksong that characterise his fiction. The cyclical construction of the stories and constant reference to the passage of the seasons reinforce a sense of inevitability. Most of the stories end with a harmonious resolution: the family circle is reconstructed and individual fate is merged with family survival. While the rural values of continuity and stability are upheld, human weakness is not condemned as sinful but tolerated and absorbed wherever possible. References to modern life are ironic and playful: the author is confident in the strength of the old ways. Shen Congwen rarely describes the physical appearance of his characters: his interest lies in their moral nature, which he describes with sympathy and even affection. (*For Shen Congwen's later fiction see Chapter 7.*)

Ba Jin (b. 1904)

Ba Jin is the pen-name of Li Feigan, who was born in Chengdu, Sichuan. It is generally accepted that the name Ba Jin is a composite of the transcriptions into Chinese of the first syllable of Bakunin and the last syllable of Kropotkin. Ba Jin was influenced by these two Russian anarchists during his youth and translated a number of Kropotkin's books while in his early twenties. During the 1950s, however, he denied this explanation of his pen-name.

In 1919, Ba Jin was a student at the Chengdu Foreign Languages School, where he was an eager reader of May Fourth journals such as *New Youth*. He entered college in Nanjing in 1923 and four years later went to study in France, where he stayed for over a year. His first novel, *Destruction*, was finished in 1928 and published in *Short Story Monthly* the following year. In the fifteen years between 1929 and 1946, he was a remarkably prolific writer, completing twenty novels and over seventy short stories. His early fiction is strongly influenced by anarchist ideals. In *Destruction*, the protagonist, Du Daxin, dies attempting to assassinate a martial law commander-in-chief; although the commander survives, Du's attempt on his life is depicted as heroic. The popularity of anarchism among students at this time was an indication of their despair at China's predicament and the difficulties in their own personal lives.

Ba Jin completed *The Family* (1933), the first novel in his *Torrent* trilogy and his most famous and influential novel, in 1931, when he was still only in his twenties. Like the traditional novel *Dream of the Red Chamber*, *The Family* describes the decline of a large, wealthy family and the dispersal of the younger generation. Just as the trials of the Jia clan in *Dream of the Red Chamber* have been read as reflecting social change in Qing China, so the trials of the Gao clan in *The Family* epitomise the decline of traditional gentry families in the modern age.

The youngest of the three Gao brothers, Juehui is the autobiographical hero of the novel: like Ba Jin, he is a rebellious young man who leaves home to create his own destiny. The Gao family is depicted as unbearably oppressive. Juehui's grandfather, despite his advanced age, still exercises all the formal powers of the head of a traditional family. The grandchildren, for example, are required to pay daily courtesy visits, despite their hatred of his authoritarian beliefs and practices. The author depicts the rituals associated with filial piety and other Confucian values as meaningless and hypocritical. In the end, the aged patriarch suffers a lonely and miserable death, deserted by his family who are already quarrelling among themselves for their share of the family inheritance.

While the grandfather represents the last vestiges of feudal authority, the greed and malice of Juehui's aunts and uncles exemplify a middle generation corrupted by social changes which have destroyed the old values without raising new ideals. The men indulge in vices such as prostitution, gambling and opium-smoking and the women engage in vicious gossip and attempts to eliminate their rivals. If there is any hope of improvement in the family and society in general, the novel puts that hope squarely on the young. This belief in the revolutionary potential of the young, especially students and young intellectuals, was common in the first few decades of the twentieth century. In *The Family*, however, the young are not without their weaknesses. For example, Juehui's eldest brother, Juexin, pays lip service to May Fourth ideals, yet he agrees to the marriage arranged by his elders. His cousin, whom he loves and had hoped to marry, dies as a result of his weakness. Juexin's wife is depicted as kind and loving, but she too dies when Juexin bows to family superstition which denies her adequate care during childbirth. Juehui himself, although intellectually enlightened, is shown to be superficial in his love for the maid Mingfeng. Immersed in his political activities, Juehui fails to notice his family's plans to marry her to an elderly lecher, leaving Mingfeng with no escape but to drown herself.

The Family is not a literary masterpiece but a melodrama in which the author blatantly manipulates the reader's emotions. Despite its shortcomings, its sympathy for young people under conflicting pressures at a time of rapid social change won from its readers an abiding affection both for the novel itself and for its author.

During the 1930s, Ba Jin wrote many other works including *Trilogy of Love* and collections of short stories such as *Gods, Spirits and Men*. Written between 1931 and 1935, *Trilogy of Love* consists of the novels 'Fog', 'Rain' and 'Lightning', which describe the revolutionary activities and romances of a group of young friends. The main characters are constantly faced with dramatic moral choices about how they should conduct their lives, balancing personal happiness and self-sacrifice. Many of Ba Jin's readers, both male and female, were inspired by these stories in making choices in their own lives. It is in this sense that Ba Jin was the most influential writer of his time. (*For Ba Jin's later fiction see Chapter 7.*)

Ding Ling (1904–86)

If Ba Jin was the first writer to show young men liberating themselves from family and social convention, Ding Ling in her early writing performed the same function for women. Ding Ling is the pen-name of Jiang Bingzhi, born in Linfeng, Hunan. Her father died when she was only four and she was raised by her mother, a self-educated and independent woman who supported the new ideas. At college in Changsha in 1919 (where one of her fellow students was Yang Kaihui, Mao Zedong's future wife), she actively supported the May Fourth Movement and eventually had herself transferred to a boys' school. In 1921 she broke formally with her family over their attempts to arrange a marriage for her and went to Shanghai, where she made friends with anarchists and left-wing activists including Qu Qiubai. In 1922 she enrolled in the People's Girls' School, founded by Chen Duxiu, and the following year entered the Chinese department at Shanghai University, a Communist Party organisation where Mao Dun was one of the lecturers, and began to learn Russian under the tutelage of Qu Qiubai.

Seeking a more formal education, Ding Ling left Shanghai for Beijing in 1924. For a while she audited Lu Xun's classes on Chinese fiction, but gave up her studies on meeting the young left-wing poet Hu Yepin, who became her *de facto* husband, and the older writer Shen Congwen who came to live with them. In 1926 she returned briefly to Shanghai to try out as a film star but did not meet with success. Her first short story, 'Mengke', based on this experience, was published in *Short Story Monthly* in 1927, and was followed the year after by 'Miss Sophie's Diary', Ding Ling's most famous work.

In the same year, Ding Ling went to Shanghai together with Hu Yepin and Shen Congwen to edit the literary supplement of *Central Daily, Red and Black*. The trio broke up in 1929 when Hu Yepin and Ding Ling went to Jinan for a year. They returned to Shanghai in 1930. Her novel *Wei Hu* was published the same year and her son was born in November. Hu Yepin joined the League of Left-wing Writers in 1930 and shortly after the Communist Party. In 1931 he was arrested as a Communist conspirator and executed. Ding Ling sent the infant to her mother in Hunan and went into hiding; later the same year she returned to the International Settlement and joined the League. Her stories at this time are on the theme of the role of writers in revolution, and her previous commitment to sexual liberation became increasingly diverted to the Communist cause. She became the chief editor of the League's journal *Big Dipper* and wrote *The Flood*, a proletarian novel which took on broad social issues rather than the concerns of the individual. Her novel *Mother*, celebrating her own mother's life, began to be serialised in 1932; the same year, she secretly joined the Communist Party. Ding Ling was arrested by Nationalist security agents in May 1933 and kept in detention in the house of the head of police in Nanjing for three years. During this time she was joined by her mother and child and had a second child by her new common-law husband. In autumn 1936, she escaped to Communist headquarters in Baoan where she was warmly greeted by Mao Zedong, who wrote two poems in her honour.

Ding Ling's early stories are on the theme of young women seeking an independent existence. 'Mengke' relates the experiences of a naive young woman from the countryside who comes to study art in Shanghai but ends up selling body and soul as a movie starlet, disillusioned with the glitter of the big city. The author's scathing condemnation of the Shanghai film world (which ignored her own talent) provides an excellent illustration of writing as revenge. Another early story, 'Summer Vacation', published in 1928, is about a group of young women teachers in a provincial school who can find no other outlet for their boredom in the oppressive summer heat than petty gossip and bickering; even their lesbian love affairs cannot relieve their frustration. The psychological barriers to female emancipation are explored in 'Miss Sophie's Diary', the work which established Ding Ling as the foremost writer on women's issues in modern literature. The diary in question covers a few months between December and March in the present. As her name implies, Sophie is an admirer of the emancipated heroines of Russian literature and revolution. Although she is suffering from tuberculosis, she has left her family and lives alone in a hotel room in Beijing, where unable to engage in regular work or studies, she indulges in introspection and fantasy. She keeps a diary in which she records the shifts and turns in her illness and in her moods. Among her friends is a young man by the name of Weidi, who is infatuated with her, but she feels that he does not understand her and takes pleasure in playing on his emotions; she is similarly harsh on a pair of friends who live together but abstain from sexual relations. Her own feelings are aroused by Ling Jishi, a business student from Singapore, who she nevertheless feels is not worthy of her. To be nearer to him she moves to a damp student hostel room which aggravates her illness. The diary entry of 18 January describes her journey to hospital; the next entry is for 4 March, in which we are told that her closest friend, Yun, has died; it is suggested that she and Yun once were lovers, and that Yun was forced into an unhappy marriage when the affair was discovered. The diary ends when Miss Sophie realises her greatest desire, to feel Ling's full red lips on hers. Although she feels victorious, the kiss also makes her feel degraded; full of self-pity, she decides to leave Beijing for the south.

The characters in 'Miss Sophie's Diary' are mostly confined to a small group of educated young men and women (servants appear fleetingly and are not dramatised). The Singaporean Ling, although wealthier than any of the others, is looked down on as belonging to an inferior social class (business people are rarely given a positive role in modern Chinese literature), and because he might return to Singapore, a liaison with him is also seen as vaguely unpatriotic. The suicide of Sophie's elder sister illustrates the penalty for failure in this difficult new world; Sophie's own illness is both realistic (TB claimed many young lives at this time) and a metaphor for suppressed anxiety at a betrayal of traditional morality. The use of the diary form gives the narrative full licence to concentrate on Sophie's contradictory, complex and even perverse states of mind. Before the kiss, writing is a therapy she practises to explore her conscious and unconscious desires; after the kiss, she no longer needs either the lover or the diary. Reaching a new stage in self-understanding, she quits Beijing (representing her old life, self-cultivation through formal education, political conservatism and the Anglo-American literary circle favoured by Shen Congwen), and goes south (i.e. to Shanghai, representing radical literary and social politics). The story offers no moral judgment on Miss Sophie's self-indulgent behaviour, nor is there overt social criticism. What the reader gains is both an unrivalled glimpse into the psychology of the new woman and a condemnation by implication of a society which lacks a social role for economically independent women and ignores their sexual needs. So persuasive is the story that readers who by this time should have become familiar with the conventions of first-person narration immediately assumed that the author was describing her own life, a confusion which was to dog Ding Ling for the rest of her life.

Ding Ling's first attempt at proletarian literature, *The Flood*, describes the disastrous floods in central China in 1931 which affected sixteen provinces. Although the physical suffering alone imposed unbearable hardship, the novel also relates the psychological trauma experienced by peasants affected by the collapse of the dyke and made desperate by the failure of the townspeople to offer them food and shelter. In the end, the peasants band together for mutual assistance and the novel concludes with an assault on the town granaries. Awakened through struggle, they recognise themselves as the exploited and assert that the grain is rightfully theirs for the taking. The novel *Mother*, based in part on the life of Ding Ling's own mother, is a story of political awakening at the beginning of the modern era. The heroine, Yu Manzhen, has become a widow after ten years of marriage. With a three-year-old daughter and a baby boy in her care, she decides to attend a new school for women after hearing about democracy and people's rights from her brother. She sells some land against advice from friends and relatives, sends her daughter to a kindergarten and enrols in the school, where she develops an interest in national affairs and undertakes physical training. In tune with the Republican Revolution of 1911, she unbinds her feet and swears a revolutionary oath of sisterhood with her friends. The novel remains one of the very few fictional works dealing with the transformation of a gentry woman into the 'new woman' of modern China. (*For Ding Ling's later fiction see Chapter 7.*)

Ai Wu (1904–1992)

Despite occasional stories set in the countryside, Ba Jin and Ding Ling are both urban writers. Like Shen Congwen, but from a left-wing point of view, Ai Wu introduced exotic borderland and foreign locales to readers in the 1930s. Ai Wu is the pen-name of Tang Daogeng, born in Xinfan, Sichuan. At the age of fifteen he was fired by the May Fourth Movement to seek an education. He first won a scholarship to a normal college in Chengdu, then moved to Yunnan to prepare for university entrance examinations but did not stay the course. Instead he crossed the border into Burma where he lived for several years until deported by the British colonial government for his political activities. On returning to China, he went to live in Shanghai. These experiences are retold in his first collections of short stories, *Travels in the South* and *A Night in the South*, written between 1931 and 1934 and published in 1935. The stories in the first collection are loosely autobiographical, set in Burma and narrated in the first person by a poor but educated wanderer much like Ai Wu himself. The second collection uses third-person narration and extends beyond Ai Wu's personal experience. 'The Night Xujia Village Roared', for example, relates Japanese atrocities in the north-east and the villagers' bloody revenge. Both collections contain detailed descriptions of local scenery in Yunnan and Burma, such as wild elephants wallowing in rivers like hippopotamuses.

As an active member of the League of Left-wing Writers in the early 1930s, Ai Wu depicts the minority people of south-west China with much sympathy as part of the oppressed masses. The inn in the Burmese story, 'I Curse That Smile of Yours', is frequented by people of diverse ethnic backgrounds. The narrator, who is employed at the inn, admires the beauty of the mountain women who come down to sell their handicrafts. One night he is asked to interpret for an Englishman who wants to buy the sexual favours of these women. The narrator tries his best to thwart his plans by showing him to rooms where only ugly old women are staying. The following morning, however, all the women are unhappy and a couple of teenage girls appear particularly depressed, and it is clear that the Englishman has achieved his goal.

Ai Wu occasionally uses urban settings to express his indignation at social injustice. The first story in *Travels in the South* relates the narrator's sojourn in Kunming after arriving on foot from Chengdu. With no money and no food, the narrator resolves in desperation to sell his straw sandals but has to resort to bargaining with rickshaw-pullers and hawkers. He tries to find a job, but finds that it is impossible even to be a rickshaw-puller without a guarantor. Staying in a cheap, disreputable inn, he has to share his bed with strangers, one of whom has scabies. When this unfortunate character is thrown out for failing to pay his rent, the narrator's new bedmate steals his old shoes. The story ends with the narrator forcing the hotel owner to replace his shoes but soon he is also thrown out of the hotel and the shoes turn out to be an inch too small. Ai Wu's foreign adventures are related in a critical realist mode and from a native Chinese perspective. The main representatives of true cosmopolitanism in the 1930s and 1940s were Shi Zhecun and Li Jianwu.

Shi Zhecun (b. 1905)

Shi Zhecun, pen-name of Shi Qingping and born in Hangzhou, was an active contributor to the Shanghai literary world in the 1920s and 1930s, chiefly famous as the author of psychological fiction about young men and women facing the temptations of modern urban life. Typically, neurotic men relate sexual fantasies in interior monologue, as in 'Evening Drizzle', 'Devil's Road' and 'At the Paris Cinema', or a third-person narrator explores the sexual repressions of young women, as in 'The Twilight Taxidancer', 'Fog' and 'Spring Sunshine'. A longer and more ambitious work is 'Kumarajiva', on the battle between desire and asceticism in the life of the Indian monk by this name (344–413), who travelled to China in the fourth century AD and became the earliest translator of Buddhist scriptures into Chinese.

By his own account, Shi Zhecun was influenced by Freud, Havelock Ellis and Arthur Schnitzler. For several years the editor of *Modern Times*, he was a member of the Anglo-American group whose influence waned in the late 1930s, and his career as a writer came to an end after 1949. From the 1940s until his retirement in 1986, he taught classical literature at a series of universities and colleges including Xiamen University, Jinan University and East China Normal University. Along with other neglected writers of the 1930s and 1940s, he saw a revival of interest in his work in the 1980s.

Zhang Tianyi (1906–85)

Zhang Tianyi (original name Tian Yuanding) came from a land-owning gentry family from Hunan whose fortunes were on the decline. The family frequently moved house as his father sought to support his many dependents. Zhang Tianyi himself was born in Nanjing and encountered people from different parts of China during his childhood. He became interested in foreign literature at secondary school, where he developed ambitions to become a writer. His first short story, 'New Poetry', was published in *Saturday* in 1922. He moved to Beijing in 1925 and entered the preparatory classes of Beijing University the following year. It was at this time he adopted the pen-name Tianyi and joined the Communist Party. He dropped out of university in 1927 and returned to Hangzhou, where he worked at various jobs such as clerk, reporter and school teacher.

Zhang's career as a writer was bolstered by approval from Lu Xun, who in 1929 accepted Zhang's short story, 'A Dream of Three and a Half Days', for publication in *Torrents*. Several novels, including *Ghostland Diary* (1931) and *The Strange Knight-errant of the Shanghai Concessions* (1933–4 in serial form), and over ten short story collections appeared in the 1930s. He wrote five novels for children and many of his adult stories are told from a child's perspective. For example, 'Tips' (1933) and 'Strange Encounter' (1934), are depictions of poverty as experienced by a child. His most famous stories are satires, the best example being 'Mr Hua Wei'. After 1949, Zhang was appointed to a series of official posts, including editor-in-chief of *People's Literature*. He continued to write, mostly didactic literature for children on good citizenship. The short story, 'The Story of Luo Wenying', published in *People's Literature* in 1952, won him first prize in the National Children's Literature competition in 1953.

Ghostland Diary is written in the form of a diary kept by Han Shiqian (a name homophonous to 'China Reality'), who has become stranded in Ghostland (a Chinese version of Lilliput). He gets involved in a debate between two political parties, whose major policy difference is that one party advocates lavatories where people can sit down and the other, lavatories where they squat. The parties become abusive, and when fighting breaks out, Han escapes back to earth. Ghostland is inhabited by Uppers, who live above ground, and Lowers, who live below. The Uppers include politicians, gentry and scholars and the Lowers include workers and peasants. Lowers cannot wander into areas reserved for the Uppers and many Uppers would rather commit suicide than become a Lower. Ghostland intellectuals who suffer from nervous disorders are considered modern: Sima Xidu, a decadent writer who decided at the age of five to become thoroughly modern, refuses to wash himself and is addicted to drugs and alcohol, while a symbolist poet talks in an incomprehensible and disconnected manner. In a preface to the diary, the narrator claims that there is no difference between Ghostland and China. Since most of Zhang Tianyi's readers were themselves politically active intellectuals of the type being satirised, the humour in the story presumably made his criticism more palatable. Compared with Lao She's *Cat Country*, *Ghostland Diary* is less subtle, but its humorous caricatures no doubt influenced the former, which appeared four years later.

Zhang Tianyi's skills at exposing hypocrisy are used to good effect in *The Strange Knight-errant of the Shanghai Concessions*. Set in the early 1930s, when the threat of Japanese invasion had become a reality and professions of patriotism became fashionable among educated people, it relates the adventures of a naive young man, Shi Zhaochang, who lives in a world of fantasy where the impossible feats of martial arts fiction are commonplace. As the Japanese prepare to bomb Shanghai, his family moves into the safety of the French Concession, but Shi Zhaochang, who has parted with some of his inheritance to learn Daoist magic, remains behind to face the enemy. He wonders why his Daoist friends do not join him, and is even more surprised when he is injured in the bombing despite his magic pills and magic knife. The hero, who ends up in hospital, is not the main object of the author's criticism: although misguided, he is at least prepared to act on his patriotism. The satire is directed instead at the middle–class characters who take advantage of the national salvation movement to benefit themselves. For example, members of a committee formed to raise money from Overseas Chinese patriots divert into their own pockets the generous donations intended to aid resistance to Japan.

This theme is continued in 'Mr Hua Wei' (1938). The story is related in the first person by Mr Hua's cousin, who appears to be praising Mr Hua's war effort but whose narrative reveals the discrepancies between his words and his actions. A committee member in many national salvation organisations, for instance, Mr Hua is only present at any of them long enough to utter a few clichés; he finds the time, however, to attend banquets and indulge his gluttony. At first the story reads as a satire on any officious bureaucrat, but towards the end it becomes evident, through Mr Hua's agitation about the imminent possibility of mass action, that he represents a particular type of official in the Nationalist government. It is said that 'Mr Hua Wei' was translated into Japanese to explain and justify the Japanese occupation of

China. The faux-naive narration admits a note of humour but also delivers a strong indictment of Nationalist preoccupation with defeating their left-wing rivals rather than with resisting the Japanese.

Zhang Tianyi's 1930s stories about children are social criticism in a sentimental mode. The chief character in 'Tips', Young Fuzi, is one of two apprentices exploited by their employer, the owner of a small restaurant, and his wife. When the couple abuse the boys they plan revenge, but in the end the only way out for Fuzi is to run away. Back at home, he finds that his family, now destitute, has been counting on him finishing his apprenticeship. 'Strange Encounter' is no less pathetic. A young child from a wealthy family one day visits her amah's home in the slums of Shanghai, where she is horrified to find that the amah's baby is dying. She is too young to understand why the baby's father cannot save the baby and calls him a monster. The reader is meant to understand that it is not the father but the social system, which prevents him finding employment, that is to blame. In contrast, the stories written after 1950 are entirely positive about the new society. In 'The Story of Luo Wenying', for instance, a naughty boy is transformed into a good Young Pioneer through the help of his classmates and a soldier: in this story, even the bad boys are clean and well-fed.

Zhang Tianyi is a versatile and resourceful writer whose stories range widely in theme and scope. He remains best remembered for his social satires of the 1930s, which despite their serious message and Marxist dogmatism still manage to entertain.

Li Jianwu (1906–82)

During his childhood, Li Jianwu's family was located in Beijing, and Li Jianwu was educated at the primary and secondary school attached to Beijing Normal University. His father, a well-known revolutionary activist from Shanxi, was assassinated in 1919, and Li Jianwu took part in political protests such as the May Thirtieth Movement in 1925. Li Jianwu was a precocious student, writing in his teens short fiction, plays and poetry for publication in the *Morning Post* literary supplement, *Literature Ten-daily*, then edited by Wang Tongzhao. He entered Qinghua University in 1925 and after one year in the Chinese department transferred at Zhu

Ziqing's suggestion to Western literature. After graduation in 1930, he was kept on as a teacher before leaving for Paris in 1931 to do research on Gustave Flaubert. On his return to China two years later, he continued his academic work, publishing translations and studies of Flaubert, and in 1935 was recruited as professor of French by Zheng Zhenduo, the newly appointed head of the literature department at Jinan University in Shanghai. He published several volumes of fiction in the 1920s and 1930s but afterwards concentrated his energies mainly on poetry, essays, literary criticism and translation. After 1949, he held a number of academic posts including that of research fellow at Beijing University's Literature Research Institute and the Institute of Foreign Literature in the Chinese Academy of Social Sciences.

Li Jianwu's first collection of short fiction, *Clouds over Xishan* (1928), comprises three short stories and a novella, the title story. The protagonist of 'Clouds over Xishan' is Xiao Fangbi, a university student who decides to quit city life for the Western Hills (Xishan) outside Beijing. At Xishan he falls in love with Zhuzhen, a washerwoman who was abandoned five years earlier on her wedding night by her husband. Although she has had no news of her husband during this time, Zhuzhen has been faithful to him, but with Fangbi she finds at last a chance of happiness. Then her husband returns, crippled by his service in the military. Trapped in an impossible situation, Zhuzhen commits suicide. 'Secret Love' is also about thwarted romance: a young street vendor is in conflict with a shopkeeper whose daughter he is secretly in love with. All these stories, except 'Secret Love', are set in the countryside, and in most of them, Li Jianwu reveals his ability to penetrate the minds of his characters.

Mental Illness (1933) further shows Li Jianwu's interest in psychology. Chen Weicheng has come to Beijing to study. He lives with his uncle and aunt, who treat him with disdain. He suffers from homesickness but cannot afford to visit his family, and his condition deteriorates when their financial support is suddenly cut off without explanation. He is so short of money that he often cannot afford to pay his tuition fees. Eventually he discovers that his uncle has been intercepting his family's remittances, and in his despair tries to commit suicide. This experience leaves him deeply disturbed, but his aunt's reaction is to speed up the marriage she has arranged for him before the girl's family (who believe themselves fortunate to have obtained a university student for a son-in-law) find out about his mental state. It is only on her wedding night that the bride discovers that her husband is insane, and she tries to hide from him in terror. In a sudden burst of clarity, Chen Weicheng realises that he is no longer his former self and disappears.

The consequences of arranged marriage is a common theme in 1920s and 1930s fiction; *Mental Illness* is only exceptional in the psychological depth of its portrayal. In his preface to the novel, Li Jianwu declares his intention to depict forgotten corners in society where people sicken and decay; because no-one bothers to explore these dark corners, they continue to poison the air and injure the health of everyone in reach, thereby falling behind in the march for progress. Like most intellectuals of his time, Li Jianwu believed that reform could be achieved through drawing attention to current social evils. After the outbreak of the War against Japan, he transferred his concern with individual redemption to national salvation within the same framework of enlightenment through education: the title story in his 1940 collection, *The Mission*, is about a group of teachers and students who march through the countryside with the mission of awakening the peasants to a sense of patriotism in the fight against foreign aggressors. (*For Li Jianwu's plays see Chapters 5 and 9.*)

Xiao Jun (1907–1988)

Xiao Jun is the pen-name of Liu Honglin, born in Yixian, Liaoning, a mountainous area where his father and uncles were farmers and craftsmen who later turned to soldiering and banditry. Xiao Jun grew up admiring masculine activities such as boxing and banditry and was expelled from various schools, including the North-east Military Academy. At the age of eighteen he joined the army, later becoming a cavalryman and then a junior officer. After the Japanese invasion of Manchuria on 18 September 1931, he enlisted in the Volunteer Army. Lacking a systematic education, Xiao Jun drew on his experiences in the army for material throughout his writing career.

Xiao Jun met the young aspiring writer Xiao Hong in Harbin in 1932: they immediately set up house together and began writing fiction. They produced a joint collection of short stories in 1933 and the following year went to Shanghai where they became Lu Xun's protégés. Lu Xun wrote a preface to Xiao Jun's first novel, *Village in August*, and helped arrange its publication in 1935. Its appearance marked Xiao Jun as the leader of the 'refugee writers' from the north-east after the Japanese invasion. Xiao Jun's confidence in himself had always been strong; believing that he had become far superior to Xiao Hong, he left her in 1938. Xiao Jun's literary status was further enhanced when his novel became the first work of contemporary Chinese fiction to be translated and published in English: it appeared in New York in 1942. His later work includes a well-known short story, 'Goats' (1935), and the polemical essay 'On "Love" and "Patience" among Comrades' (1942), which ultimately caused his political downfall. Three more novels appeared, including *Coal Mines in May* (1954), but they suffer from the author's attempt to redeem himself by attending to political demands.

Village in August is by no means an artistic masterpiece. Lu Xun, in his preface to the novel, notes that it is like a succession of short stories. There is no mistaking the intensity of Xiao Jun's emotional state or the forceful descriptions of different types of people. The novel is set in north-east China in the 1930s and chronicles the exploits of a guerrilla band led by their commander Xiao Ming. A self-styled 'people's army', they are not just patriotic fighters but have a revolutionary goal and are also known as the 'Anti-Japanese Revolutionary Army'. Despite their undoubted bravery and political consciousness, the soldiers are also shown to have endearing weaknesses. For example, an important motif is the place of love in the patriotic movement. Xiao Ming is in love with Anna, a former activist in the Korean liberation movement, but their romance is tested when the two of them need to part for the sake of the struggle. After a prolonged and deeply painful inner struggle, Xiao Ming in the end chooses continued participation in the revolution.

The conflict between love and revolution is even more starkly illustrated in the love affair between the former peasant, Pimples Tang, and his mistress, a widow who has already suffered at the hands of the Japanese. Tang inflicts heavy losses on his troops when he delays their retreat longer than is safe in order to look after his lover. The commander has no choice but to execute him; however, a stray Japanese bullet kills him first, and the terrible prospect of hero killing hero is averted. Nevertheless, the situation is clearly a reminder of the problems faced by those who choose to devote themselves to political struggle.

The overt theme of 'Goats' is the suffering inflicted on innocent people by an unjust society: the narrator, in gaol for an unspecified offence, relates the lives of the other inmates. Unlike *Village in August*, the story is plotless but carefully constructed into episodes that can be interpreted in several ways. The narrator begins with the story of two Russian children who are thrown into prison with him for a few days. The children long to return to their homeland when they are released because they believe it is much better than China. The narrator is touched by their patriotism; more importantly, the Soviet Union stands here as a symbol of a just society and the children represent hope. The second and third episodes are about two thieves. One is a simple and honest young man whose only crime is stealing a sheep; he dies as a result of the maltreatment he receives in prison. Representing less the Marxist caricature of rural idiocy than a Rousseauesque noble savage, he stands for the unawakened peasantry whose isolated acts against their oppressors are doomed to failure. The other is a professional pickpocket who specialises in stealing from foreigners. Unrepentant, he achieves an almost heroic status among the inmates because he justifies his theft by accusing foreigners of stealing from China. He represents the sharper wits of the semi-awakened urban rebel, whose random violence can achieve temporary successes. The lack of detail on the narrator's identity, along with his implied literacy as the author of the tale and the privileged treatment he receives (he is not required to do prison labour), would suggest to most readers at the time that he was incarcerated for a political offence, but embarrassed by the distance between them, he parries the other prisoners' attempts to characterise him as an intellectual.

This deflection of interest from the object (the other prisoners' fate) to the subject (the narrator), reminiscent of Lu Xun's experimental narratives, also suggests to experienced readers that this is yet another account of the dilemma of Chinese intellectuals, who, wishing to speak for the masses but unable to speak to them, end up as prisoners of their own literacy. Written after the imprisonment and execution of many political activists the author would have known or known of, the story unwittingly or otherwise is a poignant reminder of the survival of Chinese social castes even in gaol.

Wu Zuxiang (1908–94)

Originally from north China, Wu Zuxiang's family settled in Anhui in the twelfth century. The village where he was born was noted for having produced famous scholar-officials for many centuries. His own family were prosperous gentry landowners, and his father was for a time a teacher, so that Wu Zuxiang learned to love reading early in his childhood. He began writing short stories while still in secondary school, and his first published work appeared in the *Republic Daily* literary supplement *Awakening* in the early 1920s. In 1925 he moved to Shanghai, where he completed his secondary education and entered college. In 1927 he entered into a marriage arranged by his family; husband and wife already knew each other and the marriage seems to have been a happy one, but a long period of separation resulted after Wu resumed his studies in Shanghai and then entered Qinghua University in 1929. He first registered to study economics but his literary interests were already marked and he transferred to the Chinese department in his second year. During the 1930s, he continued to write and to make headway in his academic career.

Most of his stories are about peasants and gentry in Anhui, and a recurring theme is the impact of social injustice on the poor and powerless, especially women. One early story, 'Guanguan's Tonic' (1932), for example, depicts the gentry class as literally sucking dry the milk and blood of the peasantry. Guanguan is the spoilt son of a wealthy landlord. After a serious motor accident, he is brought back to health by blood transfusions from an ex-tenant and milk from the man's wife but shows not the slightest human feeling towards his benefactors. Guanguan mockingly describes the woman as smarter than a cow, and when her husband is later executed as a bandit, Guanguan's uncle remarks that his blood is now not worth a cent. The author narrates these stories of rural backwardness with an ironic distance. In 'The Verdant Bamboo Hermitage', a gothic tale published the following year, the narrator is autobiographically identified with the author. The narrator and his young wife become personally involved in the life of gentry women whose sexual frustrations take eccentric turns. Both these stories are in the collection *West Willow Village* (1934).

After-hours, which includes essays as well as the famous short story 'Fan Hamlet', appeared in 1935, and his patriotic novel *Duck Bill Fall* was serialised in *Resistance Literature* in 1941. After 1949, Wu Zuxiang's published work was mainly in literary criticism. From 1952, while professor of Chinese at Beijing University, he held a number of influential posts including the presidency of the *Dream of the Red Chamber* Research Society.

Two stories written in early 1934 and included in *West Willow Village* continue the theme of rural misery but can be seen as transitional in terms of Wu Zuxiang's perspective and style. The title of 'The World at Peace' refers to the characters engraved on three lances which crown the Fengtan Village temple. As in Lu Xun's 'New Year's Sacrifice', however, harmony is bought at a price, and the sacrificial victims in this story are Wang Xiaofu and his family. Wang Xiaofu is a diligent worker but when the shop where he is employed is bankrupted, he cannot find other work. Both he and his wife do everything they can to keep the family alive, but first his mother and then their children die of disease and hunger. In the end Wang Xiaofu himself dies while attempting to steal the vase on top of the temple which holds the three lances. Through no fault of his own except a certain gullibility, a hard-working man has been reduced to selling his wife's milk, then his home and finally his integrity. The story is told mainly in dialogue and from the perspective of Wang Xiaofu himself, but critics have pointed out the awkwardness that results from focusing on an inarticulate protagonist. 'Fan Hamlet', written two months later, reverts to a more traditional narrative style. This carefully structured story relates the misadventures of Xianzi, a young village woman who operates a roadside stall. Desperate for money to bail her husband from gaol, she robs and then kills her mother-in-law only to find out that her husband has escaped. Like Wang Xiaofu, Xianzi and her husband are driven by poverty to commit acts that defy the structures of family and religion, but they are too weak individually to undermine rural authority.

Wu Zuxiang's perspective on rural life changed dramatically after he left the sheltered environment of Qinghua University in summer 1934. This change is foreshadowed in 'Eighteen Hundred

Piculs', first published in January that year, which describes the assembly of the once wealthy Song clan at their ancestral temple. The meeting is to discuss the distribution of eighteen hundred piculs of rice and some ancestral land, managed by Song Botang. The clan members are now impoverished, and despite Song Botang's attempts to postpone a decision, an unpleasant quarrel breaks out. At this point, peasants who have been suffering from famine march into the compound and take the rice by force; by organised action in their own defence, they strike at the heart of rural authority. Compared to Ding Ling's *The Flood*, written around the same time, 'Eighteen Hundred Piculs' is also notable for its narrative skill: consisting almost entirely of dialogue, it contains sharply delineated portraits of a wide range of characters.

Shi Tuo (1910–88)

Shi Tuo is the pen-name of Wang Changjian, born in Qixian, Henan. He attended secondary school in the provincial capital, Kaifeng, where he developed an interest in literature. He moved to Beijing in 1931 and began submitting stories to journals such as *The Big Dipper* and *Literature Monthly*, based mostly on village life in his native province. His first book of short stories, *The Valley*, which won him the *L'Impartial* Literary Prize in 1936, was followed in 1937 by *Sketches Gathered at My Native Place* and *Light of the Setting Sun*. While his brutal and grotesque stories of rural life had already attracted the attention of the reading public, it was his 1947 novella *Marriage* which firmly established his reputation as a novelist.

The Valley contains seven stories. The title story, the longest in the collection, reflects the political concerns of most left-wing literature in the 1920s and 1930s. The hero, Huang Guojun, is a teacher in a mining settlement. When his colleague Hong Kuangcheng is arrested during a miners' strike, Bai Guansan, an acquaintance, offers to help buy his release. Huang does not know that Bai is an agent of the British-owned mining company and is having an affair with Hong's wife. When Hong is one of several protesters to be executed, his wife is left in despair. In the following riot, in which Huang takes part, Bai is beaten up by the workers, but when the police start shooting, the crowd disperses and Huang runs away in panic. While the unexpected action of the hero in running away holds some narrative interest, it is clearly not a very positive act.

Resolution through flight is also shown to be both wise and bold in another story in the same collection, 'The Underdog'. In this sober tale, a tenant farmer is unpopular in the village because he loyally guards the absent landowner's property. One day, he is devastated to discover that thieves have stolen some trees from the property during the night. He knows he will be punished for failing to keep guard but at the same time does not want to confront the villagers who are certainly shielding the thieves, so he decides to run away and start a new life. The first story in the collection, 'The Head', is about a likeable farm-hand who is suspected of theft by his employer. He is decapitated and his head is stuck on a tree in the village as a warning. The focus of the story is on the villagers' reactions, which range from expected feelings of hatred towards the employer to a mother's anger against the dead man when her young son falls ill at the sight of the head.

As the title suggests, the twelve sketches in Shi Tuo's second collection depict the inhabitants of his home town, written during and immediately after a visit in 1935. The protagonist of the first story, 'The Curse', is a jealous wife whose husband takes a concubine because she has failed to bear him sons. When the concubine becomes pregnant, the wife persecutes her until she commits suicide. The husband consoles himself by drinking until he is paralysed, and the wife is driven into insanity. As in most of the sketches, the narrator relates bizarre events with an ironic detachment, and although the plot sometimes descends into farce, there is no real humour. Unlike his patron, Shen Congwen, Shi Tuo shows no fondness for these exemplars of rural backwardness.

Xiao Qian (b. 1910)

Xiao Qian is the pen-name of Xiao Bingqian, born in Beijing of a Mongolian father and Han mother. His father died before he was born, leaving his mother dependent on the charity of her husband's family to bring him up. Through a Christian relative on his mother's side, Xiao Qian was given a place in a work-study school, working first in a rug factory and then in a dairy to pay for his tuition. In 1926 he was arrested for his involvement in a

Communist organisation at school, but thanks to his relative's intervention the school put up bail and he was released. He changed his name in 1928 when he took up a job as a teacher in Shantou, Guangdong, but stayed only a few months before returning to Beijing. After working as a publisher's assistant he decided on a career in journalism, which he studied at Yanjing University in 1931–5. His first short stories, written in 1933–6, were published with the title *Under the Fence* in 1936: they include 'Galloping Legs', 'The Philatelist', 'A Rainy Evening' and 'The Jiang Boy'. His second collection, published the same year under the title *Chestnuts*, includes 'When Your Eaves Are Low' and 'Cactus Flower'. His only novel, *Valley of Dreams*, was published in 1938.

Xiao Qian continued to write short stories during the 1930s but his time was increasingly taken up by his work for *L'Impartial* in Tianjin, Shanghai and Hong Kong. He obtained Lao She's former position at the School of Oriental Studies in London in 1939, and moved to Cambridge in 1942 for postgraduate studies in English literature. He covered the Western Front for *L'Impartial* in 1944 and 1945, and at the end of the war returned to China to take up a teaching post at Fudan University. In 1949 he was appointed deputy editor to *People's China*, and moved to Beijing where he has lived ever since.

In 1956–8 he was deputy editor of the *Literary Gazette* but lost this influential position in the Anti-Rightist campaign. Among his many translations are *The Good Soldier Schweik*, Lamb's *Tales from Shakespeare* and *Peer Gynt*. He now disowns the novel *How the Tillers Won Back Their Land*, written in English and published in 1955.

To avoid censorship, Xiao Qian often expressed anti-Japanese and anti-government sentiments by setting his stories among children. 'The Philatelist' relates the awakening of a young school-boy to the Japanese invasion of north-east China when he strikes up a friendship with a classmate in order to obtain new stamps for his collection. Shunned by the others because he seems completely self-absorbed, this boy receives letters from his family in Manchukuo, the Japanese puppet state. While the young philatelist does not at first concern himself with the reasons for his friend's moodiness, by the end of the story, when his friend returns to the north-east to face an uncertain future, he begins to sense that the stamps from Manchukuo have a sinister significance. The story is both a comment on Japan's threat to China and the indifference shown by many Chinese to its territorial integrity.

The day-to-day impact of Western imperialism in China is the theme of 'The Jiang Boy'. The young hero works for a dairy, where he becomes particularly fond of one of the goats. His delivery route includes foreigners, and one day an argument takes place between Jiang and a foreign cook. Jiang is accused of stealing milk and is dismissed, while his plea to keep his favourite goat is met with derision by his boss, the foreman and his fellow workers. The chief villains in this story are the Chinese who want to please their foreign customers. Again, it is the local Chinese who are the main target in 'Chestnuts'. The protagonist, who is the son of the Chief Constable of Beijing, has warned his fiancée that bloodshed may result from the anti-Japanese demonstrations she is organising. She joins the demonstrators regardless and is seriously wounded in a clash with the police. When he and his father visit her in hospital, she condemns them as traitors and refuses to have any more to do with them. 'Cactus Flower' is based on Xiao Qian's own experiences of humiliation as a child. A young boy's mother works in a missionary school so that he can receive an education there, but the other boys taunt him for being a 'spy' and a 'foreign child' because of his mother's subservience to Westerners. When anti-British demonstrations take place in Beijing following the May Thirtieth Incident in 1925, he is forbidden by the headmaster to take part in them, his mother pleads with him not to do so, and his schoolmates spurn him. Undaunted, he joins the demonstrators, and at the end of a long day when the others have exhausted their patriotic fervour, he is given the flag to carry. The next day, he is expelled from the school despite his mother's tearful entreaties but he himself rejoices in his liberation. The unflattering depiction of the young hero's classmates gives an edge to this tale of moral vindication, while the revulsion felt by the boy at the headmaster's physical appearance comes as an unwelcome shock to Western readers.

Injustice within the family is also a common theme in these stories. Both 'Under the Fence' and 'When Your Eaves Are Low' describe young boys with widowed mothers who are dispossessed by relatives, and society at large also shows no mercy. In 'A Rainy Evening', the young protagonist encounters a madwoman while sheltering from the rain. He subsequently learns that after having been abandoned by her husband she was raped by a stranger, but these misfortunes are regarded as crimes by the local people who deny her shelter: alone and homeless, she goes insane. A kinder note is struck in 'Shandong Deng', where an old street hawker, who gets his nickname from his lively street cries in a strong Shandong accent, is bullied by the school authorities but retains the support of his loyal customers through his honesty and courage. Its rich detail on Beijing street life in the 1920s gives this tale particular interest. One of the few stories set entirely in the adult world, 'Galloping Legs' is the tragedy of a rickshaw-puller who despite his hard work and pride loses his rickshaw and health. The story is lifted above the conventional by its attempt at narration from a street-level view of Beijing life.

As subsequently acknowledged by the author, *Valley of Dreams* is largely autobiographical, narrated in the first person as recollections of an unhappy romance. The hero, an impoverished young man, is expelled from school and goes south in the hope of finding a better living. Unable to speak Cantonese, he is at first very lonely. His life improves when he gets a job teaching Mandarin and falls in love, but his dreams come to nought when his beloved is claimed by the rich man who has supported her at school in preparation for her future life as his concubine. Despite his unhappiness, the narrator takes time out for lengthy descriptions of natural scenery and the unfamiliar bustle of life in a southern town. Xiao Qian's work shows considerable literary skill and subtlety in handling some of the major issues of his time, but by the 1940s his creative urge had been subsumed by his journalism.

Xiao Hong (1911–42)

Xiao Hong is the pen-name of Zhang Naiying, born in Hulan, Heilongjiang. Her stories are mainly set in the north-east, where she spent the first twenty years of her short life. She went to Beijing to study in 1930, in order to escape from an arranged marriage. Returning to Harbin the following year, she met Xiao Jun and they set up house together. Her first short story, 'The Death of Sister Wang', was written in 1933. Her first novel, *The Field of Life and Death*, was published in 1935 with the help of Lu Xun, who had taken a particular liking to both Xiao Jun and

Xiao Hong. The novel established Xiao Hong's reputation as a leading 'refugee' writer, and was followed by a series of influential short stories in 1936, such as 'On the Oxcart' and 'Hands'.

The Field of Life and Death relates in episodic fashion the struggle to survive in the tradition-bound countryside of north-east China. The first half of the novel deals with pre-war conditions in the villages, where the double-sidedness of the title is illustrated as birth scenes are transformed into death scenes. The fate of women in these backward areas is highlighted through characters such as Mother Wang, who is transformed from a despairing old woman to an active revolutionary. The second part of the novel takes place ten years in the future, and ends with the peasants organising themselves to resist the Japanese. The success of the novel is due to its focus on the realistic detail of individual lives as well as the author's overall vision of the significance of resistance.

Xiao Hong's concern with the effect of war on women is illustrated in short stories such as 'On the Oxcart'. The story of Sister Wuyun, whose husband has been executed for desertion, is told in her own words to the narrator through flashbacks as they ride together in an oxcart. She relates how she travelled to the military compound to see her husband only to find when she got there that he has already been executed. The contrast between the peaceful ride and the violence of the narrated events and between the narrator's and the protagonist's voices adds convincing colour to this story of social injustice. The protagonist of 'Hands' is a young woman whose family makes a living by dyeing clothes. In order to improve their lot, the family saves to send her to a private girls' school, but she is bullied by the other girls because the black dye on her hands cannot be scrubbed away. In the end, the principal does not allow her to sit for the examination and she is expelled. The story suggests that under the present social system it is impossible for the working classes to improve their lives. (*For Xiao Hong's later fiction see Chapter 7.*)

Although the period 1900–37 is only a brief moment in the history of Chinese literature, the fiction of this time showed an impressive creativity and diversity. The transitional interval (1900–17) is marked by novels written as social commentaries under the influence of Liang Qichao: Liu E, Li Boyuan, Wu Woyao and Zeng Pu had a common purpose in 'exposing' corruption and backwardness at the turn of the century. Their moral vision and concern for social processes show a direct line of inheritance from traditional Confucian scholar-officials, with whom they had much in common. They were all from gentry families, educated in traditional scholarship, and wrote in classical Chinese. On the whole, they were satisfied with traditional ethics, which they saw as misapplied by individual officials and scholars rather than intrinsically deficient, but their contacts with Western ideas and people gave them new perspectives for criticism. Su Manshu is perhaps the best illustration of the transitional writer at the turn of the century. Turning away from the group-oriented attitudes of most of his contemporaries, Su Manshu's romantic and individualistic pursuits took him into the modern age, but he continued to write in classical Chinese.

The formative decade (1917–27) was characterised by uninhibited experimentation with Western ideas and social practice. Although Chinese society was being fragmented by the upheavals of the previous decade, writers like Yu Dafu and Zhang Tianyi still pushed for faster change, and their impatience can be seen in the dominant form of fiction – short stories. After 1927, writers began to take a more sober approach to life. The decade 1927–37 was a period of maturation in fiction, during which the full-length novel emerged as the dominant literary genre. Novelists such as Ba Jin, Mao Dun, Lao She and Ding Ling developed objective and externalised modes of narrative, although the centre of their work, in many cases, remained subjective and frequently autobiographical. Most of them were still relatively young, but the machinations, betrayals and ruthlessness of the foreign powers and Chinese politicians in the previous decade had given them an early maturity. Their work mostly depicted individuals crushed by oppressive social forces beyond their control, and the protagonists were often women or the otherwise underprivileged; what made this fiction distinctively modern was their focus on the psychology of the protagonists.

5

DRAMA: WRITING PERFORMANCE

Traditional Chinese theatre included a wide range of forms, from acrobatics to reading scripts, and from operas by highly trained professionals at the imperial court to ribald or ritualistic performances by amateur troupes in the countryside. Such a broad and generous scope would seem to offer room for new types of performances, and yet Westernised drama took longer than the other imported genres to find audiences outside student groups. One reason for this lies in the specialisation of traditional theatrical forms, each with its specific audience that rarely strayed beyond its preferred type. The close bonds between these locally specific forms and their audiences constituted a barrier to the introduction of new elements, so that even within traditional forms, change and adaptation were very gradual. The Western theatre first experienced by Chinese audiences was, as it happened, particularly remote from Chinese theatrical tradition. Had would-be theatrical reformers encountered at first hand Shakespeare at the Old Vic, Racine at the Comédie-Française, or Verdi in Milan, cross-cultural transference might have been smoother, as signified by the later successes of Chinese and Japanese *Macbeths*. Late nineteenth-century Western spoken drama on social problems in the manner of Ibsen and Shaw was timely in its appeal to Chinese students abroad with their eyes fixed on social reform, but Chinese audiences took a long while to become used to the theatre as a medium for education in new ideas. Like the poetry revolution, the revolution in theatre got off to a false start, and the spoken play was still very much an alien form during its first few decades. Nevertheless, the potential effectiveness of drama for the propagation of new ideologies – in its reach and impact – was recognised long before an effective modern drama was created.

Although a literary theatre had existed in China since the Yuan dynasty, written drama was a relatively late development in China's long cultural history, and dramatic theory and criticism, with a few exceptions, lacked the great body of texts that supported the privileged status of poetry. Popular theatre, however, in its various forms, reached even wider audiences than fiction, including the illiterate and disabled, and the early reformers who saw fiction as a medium for transforming the ethics and customs of popular society soon recognised also the possibilities of drama. The first journal to devote itself to advocating a new theatre, *The Great Stage of the Twentieth Century*, was established in 1904 but expired after only two issues. Notwithstanding, the Enlightenment Dramatic Society was set up in 1906, and in the same year the dramatisation of an unfinished historical novel by Wu Woyao was published as a Peking opera libretto. There were several remarkable and innovative aspects of this modestly brief libretto: it was an adaptation of a novel, signifying its origins in written (rather than performance) literature; its intended audience was chiefly and possibly only readers (rather than spectators); it was a step in the direction of genre reform in that it contained long passages of dialogue in written vernacular (not the theatrical vernacular normally used in recitative in traditional opera); and by being published in a political rather than a literary journal, it took as its primary audience readers whose chief interest lay in social reform rather than literature as *belles-lettres*. Its publication can be seen as a response to calls by Chen Duxiu and Liu Yazi in 1904 for a drama 'to save the state and civilise the land', and its characteristics foretell the dominant trend in twentieth-century Chinese theatre.

If new poetry could be said to have had its beginnings in the United States, 'new drama' had its first performances in Japan and was from the outset heavily influenced by its immediate Japanese predecessor (*shingeki*). The Western spoken play had been introduced to Japan during the nineteenth century, and in 1906 the first performance of a Japanese new play was staged by a student drama troupe based at Waseda University. Inspired by this example, Chinese students in Tokyo formed the Spring Willow Society, an all-male amateur troupe, to perform in Chinese adaptations of plays which they had seen on the Japanese stage. Their productions consisted of one act from *La Dame aux camélias* by Dumas *fils*, staged as part of an exhibition in early 1907 to raise funds for famine relief in China, a stage version of Harriet Beecher Stowe's *Uncle Tom's Cabin* under the title *The Black Slave's Cry to Heaven* in June the same year, which received favourable notice from Japanese critics as well as applause from its mainly student audience, and finally a version of *La Tosca* by Victorien Sardou under the title *Hot Blood* in 1909. Enthusiastic improvisation might have compensated for inexperienced stagecraft: the main appeal was in the themes. China's Camille sacrificed herself for the sake of her lover's career in a quite traditional manner. On the other hand, the Christian message of *Uncle Tom's Cabin* was ignored in *The Black Slave's Cry to Heaven's* focus on rebellion against oppression – inevitably, in the anti-Manchu climate of the time, against racial oppression. *Hot Blood* similarly overlooked the romantic elements in *La Tosca* in concentrating on the hero's ambition to overthrow dictatorship and uphold the principles of liberty and equality. The Chinese Legation, agreeing that *Hot Blood* was disturbing to established order, threatened to cut off the students' stipends, and the society's activities came to a halt.

The overthrow of the Manchu dynasty in 1911 brought most of the students back to Shanghai. The Spring Sun Society, which had been briefly active in 1907 with performances of *The Black Slave's Cry to Heaven*, reassembled on the eve of the revolution as the Progress Troupe to stage both translated drama and new plays written by their own members. It broke up in 1912 but was replaced by the New Drama Fellowship until its disbandment in 1915. The titles of these and other amateur dramatic companies reflected the preoccupations of the 1911 reformers; the plays themselves were referred to as 'civilised drama' or 'enlightened drama'. Scripts for the new theatre were few and rudimentary, but the improvisation dictated by necessity also gave vitality and immediacy to the performances. Long speeches on current events interrupted the action, but to an audience used to the loose structure of traditional drama and filled with enthusiasm for radical change this was not a problem. The young, urban audience had a special fondness for family dramas concerned with generational conflict over themes such as free love (i.e. free choice in marriage). Stagecraft was of necessity still drawn from the Japanese, since very few Chinese had access to the Western theatre in Shanghai's concessions or abroad.

Yuan Shikai's regime soon turned its back on social reform

and banned plays which voiced social criticism, but by this time the commercial possibilities of the new theatre had been noticed, and domestic melodramas and adaptations of traditional fiction appeared both on stage and as scripts in the popular press. Popular culture was not developing as the reformers had wished, and intellectuals temporarily abandoned the stage as the medium of social transformation. Like its equivalent popular fiction, however, the new theatre continued to appeal to middle-class urban audiences, at the same time providing a livelihood for actors and other theatre personnel.

The appearance of *New Youth* in 1915 created a platform for debate on an alternative new theatre. The failure of the 1911 Revolution was underlined by the loyalty of urban audiences to traditional cultural modes, and foreign-educated reformers sought to detach themselves from popular tradition rather than try to work within it. In a special issue of *New Youth* on Ibsen in June 1918, Hu Shi and other contributors recommended close imitation of Western theatre, both in themes and performance styles; for the time being, they seemed content to address fellow students and new intellectuals like themselves. The critics and playwrights saw what they wanted in writers as diverse as Wilde, Galsworthy, Shaw, Ibsen, Bjornson, Maeterlinck, Brieux, Sudermann, Lady Gregory, Chekhov, Turgenev and Tolstoy; they cribbed liberally from Western commentaries but were not overly determined by them. Most strikingly, China's Ibsen turned out to be a social realist whose plays shaped both the literature and also the lives of his Chinese audiences: not only were the plays a literary model for China's new writers but Nora became a role model for Chinese women to emulate in discarding family ties (as much later, Peer Gynt became a generational symbol for morally compromised post-Cultural Revolution intellectuals).

Translations of Western drama (of which more than thirty appeared in 1918–21) smoothed the way for the new theatre of ideas, in which scripts became the basis of the production; stagecraft became secondary to faithful adherence to a preconceived and unalterable written form; authors dictated to actors; and exhortation replaced entertainment. In 1919–22 a new kind of playwright fashioned a new drama known as 'spoken plays', and the spoken word from a written script took centre stage. Chen Dabei, a veteran among the new performers, urged the establishment of amateur companies to bypass the call of the box-office, and new playwrights could be satisfied by a reading audience or amateur performance. The People's Dramatic Society was founded in Shanghai in 1921 by Ouyang Yuqian, Wang Zhongxian, Xiong Foxi and Chen Dabei, in tandem with the Literary Research Association's Shen Yanbing (Mao Dun) and Zheng Zhenduo, to promote new drama, and produced a monthly journal, *Drama*, dedicated to publishing original and translated scripts and criticism, which lasted for ten issues. Other groups followed in quick succession.

The academic bias of the new theatre was also shown in its attention to teaching. The first drama school, the Popular Arts Drama School, was set up in 1922 by Chen Dabei and others. In 1925 Yu Shangyuan and Xiong Foxi persuaded the Beijing Arts Academy to add a drama department, which under Xiong Foxi's direction until 1932 became a major centre for training new actors, directors and dramaturges. Another important centre in the 1930s was the department of Western languages at Qinghua University headed by Wang Wenxian, whose students included the writers Hong Shen, Cao Yu, Yang Jiang and Li Jianwu. More radical drama schools were to be found in Shanghai, such as Tian Han's Southern Arts Academy founded in 1928, which included among its staff and students Hong Shen, Xu Beihong, Tang Huaiqiu, Chen Baichen, Liao Mosha and Wu Zuoren. The authors, critics and amateur performers of spoken plays were almost all educated abroad and identified themselves as 'intellectuals'. Initially, only a small handful were professional actors, directors or theatre managers, like Ouyang Yuqian and Tian Han. Others, like Hu Shi and Ding Xilin, were writers or academics to whom drama was simply another vehicle for the expression of new ideas. Their common preoccupation was the relationship between the individual and society, whether this was seen as alienation from society as a whole (following the Russian model of the 'superfluous intellectual') or as personal liberation from outmoded social conventions (following Ibsenian models such as Nora and Dr Stockmann).

Ideological debate, at first directed against the traditional theatre, became livelier when stimulated by factions within the New Culture ranks. Wen Yiduo, although giving Guo Moruo his due as a pioneer in the new poetry, criticised his plays as verse or closet drama and for using figures from the past as mouthpieces for twentieth-century ideas. The Anglo-American group, consisting in this endeavour mainly of Yu Shangyuan, Sun Chuanfang, Xiong Foxi and Ding Xilin as well as Wen Yiduo and Hu Shi, advocated a 'little theatre' movement based on well-constructed plots, characterisation and stagecraft, expecting little in the way of audiences outside the universities. Yu Shangyuan provided a platform for this movement as editor of the drama supplement to the *Morning Post* in the mid-1920s, which after 1928 was succeeded by the *Crescent Monthly*. Apart from Guo Moruo and Tian Han, the Creation Society was preoccupied by the written word in its early days and tended to overlook drama. After its new left-wing orientation in the late 1920s, its only dramatist was Zheng Boqi (1915–79), whose plays, however, were seldom performed. His *The Track* is a typical proletarian play of its period, depicting revolutionary and anti-Japanese struggles by Chinese railway workers in 1928. Like the poetry of fellow Creationists like Jiang Guangci, it is little more than abstract rhetoric, with no apparent audience outside the author's own circle.

Poor attendance and censorship were major problems for the more ambitious left-wing groups. Even non-professionals found it hard to persevere against the continuing evidence that urban audiences outside the universities found the conversational dialogue, everyday costuming and didactic purpose of the new plays insupportably boring, whether Chinese or Western. The most famous case of audience rejection was the 1921 Shanghai performance of *Mrs Warren's Profession* (then banned in England), when a quarter of the audience walked out (some of them making obscene and abusive remarks as they did so) despite having professional actors like Ouyang Yuqian, Wang Zhongxian and Chen Dabei in the leading roles. The response was to inject more action, replacing intellectualised dialogue with passionate outbursts of emotion, tightening plot construction, and enlivening performance by borrowings from the traditional theatre. By the end of the 1920s, the growing audience for modern drama supported the rise of full-time professionals like Cao Yu, Hong Shen, Yu Ling, Xia Yan, Yuan Muzhi and Zhang Min, who variously combined the roles of actor, director, teacher and dramaturge. Although avantgarde New Culture activists such as Shen Yanbing found Western modernism profoundly exciting, and the influence of expressionism can be found in early work by Guo Moruo, Hong Shen and Cao

Yu, pre-war Chinese audiences were not prepared to accept these experiments; the writers complied by reverting to the conventions of the well-made play or employing native forms of non-realistic drama.

Women playwrights were few in the early period, reflecting their gradual exclusion from the theatre under the Qing. The first female actors appeared on stage in 1923, in a production by the Popular Arts Drama School of a play by Chen Dabei; by 1931, female impersonators were no longer required in modern drama. The New Woman as a character in male-authored and male-acted works was nevertheless one of the most familiar figures in the first modern plays, with a central role in representations of generational and gender conflict. The depiction of the New Woman in Western fiction and drama goes back to the 1880s and 1890s (the first London performance of *A Doll's House* was in 1889) and was variously interpreted. The Chinese New Woman was mostly portrayed as a wholly positive figure, scornful of conventions, rich in sympathy for the poor and oppressed in this world, well-educated and fully capable of leading an independent existence. She might appear as triumphant to Hu Shi, innocence betrayed to Tian Han, momentarily disconcerted by male wit to Ding Xilin, sexually aggressive to Ouyang Yuqian or sexually ambivalent to Guo Moruo, but between 1919 and 1925 she was generally there and as often as not the protagonist. After 1925, when literary revolution was displaced by revolutionary literature, the focus shifted from personal liberation – where a female protagonist could serve as a model to both genders – to class struggle – where male characters became dominant. After the mid-1920s, the woman in the piece was more often portrayed as a spoiled society beauty, a nagging wife or a passive victim of suffering. Chinese writers still regarded themselves as participants in world trends, and just as they had found models for the New Woman in plays by Ibsen and Shaw, they were now looking to the West and to Japan for male-centred models of proletarian and patriotic writing.

The adoption of left-wing goals was institutionalised by the founding of the League of Left-wing Writers in 1930 and the associated League of Left-wing Dramatists in 1931, as part of the Communist Party's new policy for bringing literature and the arts more closely under Party control (as in the Soviet Union).

Many of the early dramatists, such as Tian Han and Hong Shen, accepted the new direction; others, like Hu Shi and Ding Xilin, pursued other careers. Younger activists who carried out the footwork for the League included Yu Ling and Song Zhidi, joint editors of the League's *Drama News*. This trend had a particularly drastic impact on the new theatre, which was a major focus for Party attempts to influence public opinion. Unlike poets, who could still turn to commercial publishers or establish their own small presses for books and journals, dramatists discovered that performance venues were increasingly coming under the control of the League.

Professionalism in the sense of becoming financially self-supporting took a great step forward with the founding of the Travelling Dramatic Troupe of China in Shanghai in 1933. Under the direction of Tang Huaiqiu, the Troupe staged performances of *La Dame aux camélias*, Shaw's *Arms and the Man* and Wilde's *Lady Windermere's Fan* to receptive audiences in cities like Guangzhou, Nanjing, Suzhou and Beijing. Its greatest successes were with left-wing but not necessarily Communist plays such as Cao Yu's *Thunderstorm*. Professional skills were also boosted by the government-funded National Academy of Drama, founded in 1935 with the veteran Yu Shangyuan as its head; from 1936 to the outbreak of war, the Academy staged monthly performances of modern plays on a wide range of topics. Stanislavsky's acting methods were introduced in 1937, and almost four hundred translations of Western plays gave substance to a broad repertoire. So popular had the modern theatre become that the Carlton Theatre in Shanghai was converted from a cinema to help accommodate the demand. On the eve of war with Japan, new patriotic plays generated audience enthusiasm to such a peak that new drama came to seem the dominant genre of the day: 1937 was celebrated as 'The Year of Spoken Drama'.

Despite the attacks on traditional theatre by the New Culture activists, the new impetus for reform in the period had not left it untouched. Scripted versions of old and new opera stories, known as 'new opera', not only showed the close personal relations between certain scholars and actors but also signalled the gradual move of Peking opera into the modern age, while Mei Lanfang's reforms in the period 1913–18 not only introduced new themes and techniques from Western theatre and *kunqu* (an older form of drama, based in Shanghai), but also fostered a new sense of dedicated professionalism. Mei Lanfang's first overseas appearance was in Tokyo in 1919, where his performance was judged a great personal triumph and was followed by further tours in 1924 and 1926. The prestige of the traditional theatre was further enhanced by his successful tour of the United States in 1930, the first performances in the West by a Chinese theatrical troupe; on his tour of Europe in 1935, his acting made a lasting impression on Bertolt Brecht.

Although most regional and local opera continued to be regarded as vulgar and backward, a handful of classic forms such as Peking opera, Shaoxing opera and *kunqu* gradually became accepted by the new playwrights and directors as an intellectually respectable part of the national inheritance. From the 1930s on, some of the most successful new plays either borrowed plots from traditional fiction and drama or otherwise introduced elements of the traditional theatre into the stage presentation. Playwrights and actors like Ouyang Yuqian and Zhou Xinfang (a 'Southern', i.e. Shanghai, Peking opera performer) even crossed genres, a practice which became more common after 1949. The great bulk of writing on the theatre, however, ignored the continued vitality of the traditional theatre, and critical discourse was generally limited to the spoken play.

Ouyang Yuqian (1889–1962)

Ouyang Yuqian devoted his whole life and multifarious talents to the theatre, although his family background indicated a more traditional literary path. His grandfather was a famous scholar and reformer whose disciples included Tan Sitong and Tang Caichang, both executed at the failure of the 1898 reforms. Following family tradition, Ouyang went to Japan in 1907 intending to study commerce at Meiji University, but he soon moved to the more congenial atmosphere of Waseda. Persuaded of the educational value of a reformed theatre, Ouyang joined the Spring Willow Society in 1907 and took part in its productions of *The Black Slave's Cry to Heaven* and *Hot Blood*. Political and social reform were to remain constant themes in his life and work in the theatre.

On returning to China in 1911, he first attempted to found a new theatre movement at home. An active member of the

New Drama Fellowship in 1912 and its successor the Spring Willow Theatre in 1915, he realised that the shortage of written plays (including translations) impaired the company's professionalism and put a severe strain on the audience's patience. In 1916 he became a professional Peking opera actor, collaborating with Mei Lanfang on reforms to traditional theatre.

Ouyang turned his attention again to spoken drama after the May Fourth Incident. In 1921 he helped set up the People's Dramatic Society in Shanghai, followed in 1922 by the Shanghai Dramatic Association, which sponsored the first mixed-gender public performance. He also wrote several one-act plays for the Association, including 'The Shrew' and 'After Coming Home'. First performed in 1922 and published in 1925, 'The Shrew' focuses on the plight of the New Woman. In this case, the rebellious heroine is married to a businessman who turns his back on their former ideals and follows family tradition in taking a concubine. After denouncing him in front of the assembled family, the heroine somewhat improbably takes her baby and walks out, to live as a single independent woman. 'After Coming Home' (1924) presents a more complex depiction of a similar dilemma. This time the interloper is an assertive woman who met the husband while they were both foreign students in the United States, while the wronged wife is the daughter of a member of the rural gentry, a neighbour of the errant husband. Without much education but not without social status, she renounces her claim with dignity, declaring her wish to remain with her family in the countryside and let the Westernised couple return to the city and its ways.

There is a particular interest in Ouyang Yuqian's plays about the New Woman in that he specialised in female roles as a Peking opera performer. His expertise was more directly applied in works from the late 1920s and 1930s in which he introduced elements of traditional theatre into modern playscripts, in collaboration with fellow Southern Society members such as Hong Shen, Zhou Xinfang and Gao Baisui. The most outstanding of these was *Pan Jinlian*, performed in 1927 both as a Peking opera, starring Ouyang Yuqian in the lead role and Zhou Xinfang as Wu Song, and as a spoken play; the playscript was published in *Crescent Monthly* in 1928. Based on a famous episode from the classic novel *Water Margin*, it reverses conventional moral judgments by giving a voice to the adulterous uxoricide Pan Jinlian to denounce the system in which women are at the disposal of men. Following the conventions of Peking opera, the playscript consists of a succession of scenes without division into acts; it also omits several episodes in plot development since the audience can be expected to know the details. These traditional elements are nicely subverted by representational staging, sensational stage business (as Pan Jinlian bares one breast), colloquial language and psychological realism in characterisation. The play proved too challenging for most Chinese critics, however, and has been excluded from post-1949 editions of Ouyang Yuqian's works.

In 1929 Ouyang established the Guangdong Institute for Theatre Studies which he headed until its disbandment in 1932. One of a series of six short plays on the general theme of the wickedness of the wealthy that he wrote and produced at this time was 'Behind the Screen'. Borrowed from traditional plays such as *The Lute* and *The Wise Judge's Decision*, the plot creaks with age, and presumably no-one in the audience was the least surprised by the climax in which the seduced and abandoned heroine is confronted with the author of her plight, now the highly respectable chairman of the Society for the Preservation of Morality. The success of the play is at least in part due to the eminence of its progenitors.

Ouyang was a founder-member of the League of Left-wing Dramatists in Guangzhou in 1931. The following year he went on an extended European tour, and at a concert in Paris for Chinese students performed Chinese songs accompanied by Xian Xinghai on the violin. He returned to China in 1933, but increasing engagement in political activities obliged him to leave again for Hong Kong and then Japan. Back in Shanghai in 1934, he concentrated on film-making until the Japanese invasion forced him again to seek refuge in Hong Kong, where he wrote the script for the Shanghai film *Mulan Joins the Army*. From 1939 he spent the rest of the war years in Guilin.

Ouyang's last major work, *Peach Blossom Fan*, is an ambitious and complex project. Depicting historical events from the late Ming and early Qing, the plot is based on the play of the same name by the famous Qing dramatist Kong Shangren (1648-1718). Ouyang Yuqian's first treatment of the story was in his 1935 film *The New Peach Blossom Fan*, set in contemporary China. His next attempt returned to the original plot for adaptation as Peking opera in 1937, but it was banned after two performances because of its anti-Japanese tone. Ouyang Yuqian then redrafted the story as a Guangxi opera in 1939 in Guilin, but it was banned again. He finally rewrote it as a three-act spoken play for performance on tour in Taiwan in 1946, but the play was banned both in Taipei and the next year in Shanghai, this time for its anti-Nationalist sentiments. The main character in all versions is the heroine, a beautiful and talented courtesan who remains steadfastly loyal to the Ming dynasty after its overthrow. In his opera and play versions, Ouyang Yuqian's main contribution is to present her lover, a handsome and talented scholar-official who eventually comes to terms with Qing rule, as a coward and traitor. The courtesan's moral righteousness and patriotism (the Han imperial rule is identified in the script as 'the nation') doubtless required much courage and were much appreciated by contemporary audiences, but is also a step back from the bold unconventionality of Pan Jinlian. As will be seen also below, in wartime China, the sexually liberated heroine is replaced by a physically aggressive but morally virtuous female.

Apart from his scripts, acting and teaching, Ouyang Yuqian also exerted tremendous influence as a director responsible for some of the most highly regarded works of the time, including Ding Xilin's 'Oppression', Cao Yu's *Thunderstorm* and *Sunrise*, and Yu Ling's *Ballad of a Long Night*, as well as foreign plays such as Tretiakov's *Roar China!* His contributions to the development of pre-1949 cinema deserve a chapter of their own. After 1949 he was honoured with a string of titles, although in practice his work was mainly administrative, and he entered the Communist Party in 1955. His reminiscences relate the history of twentieth-century theatre which he had done more than anyone else to create.

Chen Dabei (1887–1944)

Chen Dabei joined the new theatre as an actor during his student days in Shanghai in 1910, and employment in Beijing at the Ministry of Finance in 1919 apparently allowed him leisure to pursue his interests. A founder-member of the People's Dramatic Society, Chen Dabei saw amateur theatre as the best way of introducing new plays and training new actors. He helped found the first drama school, enrolling both male and female students, and it was largely thanks to his lead that women increasingly took over female roles in new plays after 1923. Chen Dabei was also one of the most prolific playwrights of the 1920s, specialising in family themes in the tradition of 'civilised drama'. A typical portrait of the New Woman is given in his *Miss Youlan*, first published in 1921 and performed in 1922 with Li Jianwu as the lead. The play is typically disjointed, melodramatic and unconvincing as social criticism or individual tragedy, but its contemporary setting and fashionable stage design made it popular among young audiences. The comic possibilities of the Society for the Preservation of Morality, mentioned in the first act, were further exploited by Ouyang Yuqian (see above). During the War against Japan, he collaborated with the Wang Jingwei regime in Shanghai in producing pro-Japanese propaganda plays, and post-1949 cultural historians on the mainland tend to ignore his part in fostering the new drama movement.

Wang Zhongxian (1887–1937)

Wang Zhongxian was another pioneering actor in the early days of new drama who joined the People's Dramatic Society, and his one-act play *The Good Son* was published in its journal *Drama* in 1921. *The Good Son* was especially popular with Shanghai audiences because of the passages in Shanghai dialect spoken by its middle-class characters, who conform to the local stereotype by concerning themselves solely with money. A professional actor himself, he went to particular pains to create situations in which a great deal of lively stage business could be conducted. In a preface to the play, Wang Zhongxian noted that the play had a deeper political significance as an allegory for the exploitation of the nation by warlord rule. The large cast of characters and the farcical structure show the continuing influence of 'civilised drama', and after a successful performance in 1924, it was turned into a film in 1926.

Hu Shi (1891–1962)

Continuing in his role as the dedicated innovator of the New Culture movement, Hu Shi supported the new drama as vigorously as he supported the new poetry, and his one-act social comedy, *The Greatest Event in Life*, was China's first modern playscript. The story concerns a Chinese Nora who defies her parents and elopes with a thoroughly respectable young man whose only shortcoming is ineligibility according to the fortune-teller whom her mother consults and the ancient genealogies which her father consults. Hu Shi explained in a preface that the play was originally written in English for a performance by friends, but no respectable female could be found to play the lead role in either the original or the later Chinese version published in *New Youth* in 1919. It was eventually performed in 1919 and again in 1923 but, like his poetry, remains chiefly of historical significance. (*For details of Hu Shi's early life see Chapter 2.*)

Guo Moruo (1892–1978)

In drama as in poetry and criticism, Guo Moruo represents the opposite pole to Hu Shi within the New Culture movement. Although his dramatic oeuvre was much larger and has been more frequently performed, it would probably not have survived as more than a literary curiosity had it not been for his political prominence in the 1950s and 1960s. Although offering opportunities for colourful staging, their didactic speeches betray their origin as written texts rather than performance vehicles. Nonetheless, his nineteen plays (all but one on historical or mythological themes) made a significant contribution to the acceptance of spoken drama, and his translations of plays and novels by Goethe, Schiller, Upton Sinclair and Galsworthy opened new sources to young dramatists.

It took some time before Guo Moruo found his feet in the new drama. His only pre-war collection of plays, *Three Rebellious Women*, was published in 1926, although he had been working on the first of its three short pieces, 'Nie Ying', since 1920 and subsequently incorporated it into a longer work, *Twin Blossoms* (see below, Part II, Chapter 9). Guo Moruo started work on the first draft of 'Nie Ying' shortly after he had finished his translation of Part I of *Faust* but this two-act version was not completed until 1925. The main characters are two women of the fourth century BC who attire themselves as young men to seek Nie Zheng, brother of Nie Ying and beloved of the second young woman, an innkeeper's daughter. They discover that Nie Zheng has assassinated the ruler of the state of Qin, whose expansionist wars are alarming neighbouring states. In conventional Chinese historiography, Qin was regarded as a disturber of the old order, and it is not clear why at this point Guo Moruo the iconoclast should choose to depict the political murder of its ruler as a glorious act. The rebelliousness of the young women consists chiefly in cross-dressing followed by self-sacrifice as a gesture to publicise Nie Zheng's deed.

The second play, 'Wang Zhaojun', was written and first published in 1923. Wang Zhaojun's poignant story was well-known to Chinese readers and the subject of two other modern plays, Gu Yiqiao's *Zhaojun* and Cao Yu's *Wang Zhaojun*. Guo's version depicts Wang Zhaojun as a doomed woman who refuses to bribe the court painter to reveal her true beauty to the Han emperor Yuandi, strikes the painter across the face when he confesses his love for her, and abuses the emperor when he laments having promised her to the khan of the barbarian Xiongnu to secure the northern border. The painter's daughter takes Wang's side and accompanies her into exile, foreshadowing the travels of the two women in 'Nie Ying'. The heroine of the third play, *Zhuo Wenjun* (in three acts, also published in 1923), is equally famous in Chinese literary history as the young widow who gave up a comfortable but lonely life to follow an impecunious poet, Sima Xiangru: the audience knows, though the play does not state, that the couple worked in an inn before Zhuo's family finally relented. The couple's affair was abetted by a strong-willed maid (a conventional trope in Chinese literary romances), but in an unusual twist to the plot, the maid murders her own lover, who has betrayed Zhuo, and then kills herself, thereby shaming Zhuo into defying her father. Contemporary and later criticism tend to treat the plays as denunciations of feudal attitudes towards women, although there is little evidence in the texts to support this interpretation; Guo Moruo's preoccupation with cross-dressing, female bondage, sexual humiliation, betrayal and violence is ignored. Throughout his life, Guo remained fascinated by rebellious women, but his heroines are far removed from Hu Shi's positive

New Woman. (*For details of Guo Moruo's early life see Chapter 3; his later plays are described in Chapter 9.*)

Ding Xilin (1893–1974)

Ding Xilin's early plays are good-humoured satires on the changing mores of the new middle class. A physicist by profession, he had come into contact with contemporary British drama while studying in Britain. His favourite dramatist was Oscar Wilde, whose influence on his work is not hard to see. His secondary career as a dramatist was launched in 1923 with three one-act domestic comedies, 'A Wasp', 'Dear Husband' and 'After Drinking'. 'A Wasp' is a satire on modern courtship, contrasting the matchmaking efforts of the hero's mother with the independence of the New Woman who makes her own living as well as her own marriage choices. It was frequently performed in the 1920s and 1930s, and revived in 1979 in celebration of the sixtieth anniversary of the May Fourth Movement along with two later plays. *A Wasp* is typical of his early work in its small cast, reliance on dialogue rather than action and a neat climax like the sting in a wasp's tail. The son's predilection for teasing his mother leads to a nice intertextual passage where he takes dictation from her for a letter home, but without her noticing, substitutes the actual words she utters rather than transforming them into standard epistolary style; later, he complains to his mother that the New Woman is like 'poetry in the vernacular' – without interest. These mild jokes at the expense of the New Culture movement retain a certain documentary value.

'Dear Husband' and 'After Drinking' (the latter based on a short story by Ling Shuhua) are rather more daring in portraying unconventional sexual situations: the marriage of a young male poet to a male Peking opera star specialising in female roles, and the potential for a *ménage à trois* when a young woman toys with the idea of kissing her husband's friend as he lies asleep on their sofa after over-indulging in drink.

Ding Xilin's next work, 'Oppression', is a comic treatment of a serious issue. An excellent example of the well-made play, its first performance, directed by Ouyang Yuqian in Nanjing in 1927, was a great success, and it became one of the most popular items of the 1930s repertoire (on more than twenty occasions by the

Travelling Dramatic Troupe of China alone). An unmarried engineer in his forties and a young unmarried woman employee in the same company but unacquainted with him are competing for scarce lodgings in Beijing; in the end, under the banner of 'proletarian unity in the face of oppression', they conspire to a pretence of marriage so that both can share the rooms. It is based on a true incident in which a friend of the author's died in miserable circumstances after failing to obtain suitable lodgings. The sparkling dialogue, lively characterisation and ironies such as characterising the couple as 'proletarian' serve to make a brilliant comedy, while the single mention of the word 'oppression' hints at depth without portentousness. The Shavian element in this work foreshadows Ding Xilin's darker comedies of the war period.

'Oppression' was published in *Contemporary Review*, the journal of the Anglo-American group, in 1926. Ding Xilin was also one of the founder-members of the Crescent Society in 1928, but it does not seem to have stimulated his writing. His next work was 'Three Dollars, National Currency' (1941), a one-act comedy written and set in Kunming during the early period of the war; it is based on an incident witnessed by the author, in which a greedy and exploitative immigrant is given her come-uppance. It was restaged by the Beijing People's Art Theatre shortly before the Cultural Revolution. *Mount Miaofeng* (1941), also set in the south-west, has a wide range of social classes and an engaging bandit hero who leads the local resistance to Japan, but was not performed. Perhaps realising that he was writing for readers rather than audiences, Ding Xilin henceforth devoted himself to his academic work, but his early plays remained popular and have become a staple of school performances.

Tian Han (1898–1968)

Tian Han began writing plays as a student in Changsha Normal School (Mao Zedong's old school) in 1912. In 1917 he went to Japan to study first for the navy and then at Tokyo Higher Normal School. He quickly joined the radical student organisation Young China and published plays and literary articles in its journal. Introduced to Guo Moruo in 1920 by Zong Baihua, he was also a founder-member of the Creation Society. He returned to China in 1922 to work on Creation publications but left after a dispute with Cheng Fangwu.

Tian Han was one of the first Creationists to specialise in the new theatre, and his one-act sentimental dramas of thwarted young love among his contemporaries were performed by amateur companies in the 1920s and 1930s as fast as he could write them. Their popularity was partly due to their superficiality, compared with the hinted depths in Guo Moruo's plays, and also partly to Tian Han's active role in theatrical productions. An early member of the Shanghai Dramatic Association, he went on to found the Southern Society in 1928 with the support of other professionals such as Hong Shen, Ouyang Yuqian and Zhou Xinfang, touring Suzhou, Hangzhou, Guangzhou and Nanjing with plays by himself and other new writers. By managing his own troupe and journals, Tian Han was able to see these plays through to publication and performance to small but appreciative audiences, gradually building up his dramaturgical skills in the process. One of his most practical innovations was the 'small stage' movement which allowed students to earn a meagre living while at the same time gaining experience and knowledge of Western theatre.

'One Night in a Café' (1922) depicts a naive country girl deceived by a rich student, with a third, semi-autobiographical character providing narrative continuity, while 'The Night the Tiger Was Caught' (1922), set in the countryside, has a more robust depiction of a tiger-hunting oppressive father. Four one-act plays from the late 1920s incorporate brief passages hinting at the impact of contemporary political events on private lives: 'A Lakeside Tragedy' (1928), 'Return to the South' (1929), 'Death of a Star' (1929) and 'A Suzhou Night's Tale' (1929). In 'A Lakeside Tragedy' the protagonist, a young poet, mourns his beloved who 'dies' three times: as a companion to two girls killed in student demonstrations in Beijing; by a faked suicide when forbidden to marry the poet by her father; and finally by a real suicide as a sacrifice to love and art during the action of the play. The protagonist of 'A Suzhou Night's Tale', an older man, is a painter whose home was burned down and family dispersed during warlord fighting over Beijing in 1917. After taking part in the Northern Expedition in 1926, he goes to Europe (like the poet in the previous play), returning to China to earn a living as an art teacher. The play is marred by a contrived ending (father and daughter miraculously reunited), uneven tone (a sex farce opening followed by sentimental tragedy), and unconvincing characterisation (the lost daughter is a 'flower girl'). 'Returning to the South', a drama of the 'superfluous intellectual', features a mysterious Ibsenian stranger against a background oddly rich in Christian pastoral imagery; and 'Death of a Star' is the first of several works to achieve success by incorporating the glamour of Peking opera into a modern playscript. As if to prove the point in these plays that art could no longer stand aside from politics, the Nationalists closed down the Southern Society in 1930 after Tian Han's adapted version of Bizet's *Carmen*.

A short series of mood pieces in Chekhovian style were succeeded in the 1930s with left-wing plays such as 'The Rainy Season' (1931), 'The Alarm Bell' (1932) and 'The Moonlight Sonata' (1932). The main characters in these plays are workers, peasants and students suffering from feudal, imperialist and industrial oppression. One of the founders of the Left-wing League of Dramatists, Tian Han joined the Communist Party in 1932, was arrested for left-wing activity in 1935 and remained under house arrest in Nanjing until 1937. Political convictions do not of themselves guarantee authenticity, however, and Tian Han's proletarian plays are based on emotional sympathy and rhetoric rather than experience or understanding. It was also during the 1930s that Tian Han became very active in the film industry, sponsoring younger film artists and musicians like Xian Xinghai and Nie Er; Nie Er was later to write the music and Tian Han the words for China's post-1949 national anthem.

One of Tian Han's major legacies to Chinese drama began life as an outline for a one-act play adapted from an episode in Goethe's *Wilhelm Meisters Lehrjahre*. Staged by the Southern Society in 1928 under the title 'Miniang', it retained the European setting and kept to the original storyline: Wilhelm comes to the rescue of Mignon, a young girl hired to perform in a troupe of travelling acrobats.

Another version, performed the following year, gave the elderly leader of the troupe a new identity as Mignon's father, increasing the pathos of his role. The first written version of the play was in 1932 by Chen Liting with the help of Zhao Mingyi and Jiang Jingyu, who gave it a Chinese setting under the new title, 'Put Down Your Whip': this version depicted the sufferings of the Chinese at the mercy of rapacious local officials and natural calamities. A later version by the same authors with an anti-Japanese theme was staged by local members of the League of Left-wing Dramatists in Jiangsu in 1932. The following year, the dramatist Cui Wei staged a revised version near Qingdao under the title 'On the Hunger Line'; among the performers was the actress Li Yunhe, better known under her later pseudonym Jiang Qing. Tian Han returned with a three-act version under the name *The Song of Returning Spring* in 1935. Cui Wei rewrote the play again in 1936, reverting to the title 'Put Down Your Whip'; this became the standard version after publication in Aying's *Best Chinese One-Act Plays of 1936* (1937) and Shen Xiling's *Street Theatre* (n.d.). It became one of the most popular street plays of the war years, and its 'Ballad of September 18th', sung by the young performer, is one of the most famous songs of its time. Best described as a collaborative effort over almost a decade, it came to play a significant role in Chinese artistic and political history that its first Chinese begetter could not have foreseen. (*For Tian Han's later plays see Chapter 9.*)

Huang Baiwei (1894–1987)

Huang Baiwei's first three-act play was *Sophia* (1926), another variation on the New Woman theme with an amicable resolution. Her next three-act play, *Breaking Out of the House of Ghosts*, was published in 1928 in *Torrents*, a left-wing magazine edited by Lu Xun and Yu Dafu, but there is no record of performance. A convoluted drama of conflict and incest in a rural gentry family dominated by an evil tyrant, its central symbol is a decaying house from within whose crumbling walls the younger generation is unable to effect an escape; brother and sister are in the end murdered by their own father, while hope for the future is vested in the representatives of the exploited proletariat on the outside. Curiously foreshadowing the main action of Cao Yu's *Thunderstorm*, it lacks a strong female character to provide a credible antagonist to the overpowering father.

Hong Shen (1894–1955)

Dedicated to the theatre like Ouyang Yuqian but with an academic background more akin to Hu Shi's, Hong Shen began acting and writing plays as a student. His first performed work dates back to 1916, the year he graduated from Qinghua University in engineering. Later the same year he went to the United States, where he switched to drama, combining studies in dramatic theory with practical experience as an actor and director. On his return to China in 1922, he spent the next fifteen years teaching drama in turn at Fudan University, Jinan University (both in Shanghai), Sun Yatsen University in Guangzhou, Xiamen University and Beijing Normal University; he was also a member of the Shanghai Dramatic Association, the Southern Society and the League of Left-wing Dramatists. Among his special concerns were the replacement of female impersonators by female actors and greater artistic authority for directors. His production of Wilde's 'Lady Windermere's Fan' in 1925 was the first mixed-gender performance to the general public in China.

Hong Shen's plays have had a mixed reception. Academic critics and historians favour his *Yama Zhao* (published in *Eastern Miscellany* in 1923), one of the first adaptations of an O'Neill play in China. Hong Shen had seen the famous New York performance of *The Emperor Jones* with Charles Gilpin in the title role, which inspired him to create a counterpart in contemporary Chinese society. Zhao Da is a soldier in a warlord battalion who prides himself on the fierceness which inspired his nickname, King of Hell; at the same time, he tries to be an honest man in a world where goodness is rarely rewarded. When he robs his superior officer and decamps, his conscience will not allow him peace: he enters a dark forest where supernatural apparitions make him confront episodes from his past. The major part of the play consists of disjointed monologues in which the half-maddened former peasant admits his guilt while identifying the oppressive social forces that left him little alternative. As the scenes from his life recede in time, following the search for meaning in his disordered mind, episodes from the Boxer Rebellion and the imperial court of justice introduce on stage displays of weird rituals and costuming, enhanced by expressionist techniques in lighting and special effects. Hong Shen played the title role himself in the 1923 premiere, but finding audiences hostile to this venture into modernistic theatre, abandoned expressionism as a vehicle of social protest.

Marxist social theory formed the background to three short

plays written between in 1930–2 and published together in 1936 under the title *A Village Trilogy*. Written with the help of friends from the League of Left-wing Writers, they offer variations on the theme of resistance by peasants to their exploitation by the rural gentry. Hong Shen's best-known pre-war work is the one-act 'Smuggling', written in collaboration with Shen Qiyu and He Jiahuai in 1936 and frequently performed in the early war years. Following Nationalist government policy at that time, it was banned by the Shanghai authorities because of its exposure of the illegal trade fostered by Japanese-occupied Manchuria to the detriment of the local peasant economy.

After the outbreak of war, Hong Shen first worked under Guo Moruo in the drama section of the National Military Council Political Department in Wuhan, where he organised propaganda troupes in the interior; the rest of the war he spent in Guilin, Chongqing and Kunming. His main works of this period are *Leave It to Me*, a propaganda play about conscription first performed during a tour from Chongqing to Chengdu in 1939; and *Women, Women*, on the marriage problems of educated women, published in 1945. After 1949 he was a powerful figure in the cultural bureaucracy but wrote no more.

Yuan Changying (1894–1973)

Yuan Changying is remembered chiefly as the author of 'The Peacock Flies South-east' (1929), a dramatic adaptation of an old Han ballad of the same name. The original story depicts the tragic fate of a young woman who fails to gain the approval of her widowed mother-in-law and is cast out from the family to the grief of her devoted but powerless husband. The plight of women in the Confucian family system was a major theme of the New Culture movement, and several dramatisations of this well-loved ballad were written and performed in the 1920s and 1930s; they include 'The Peacock Flies South-east', performed by students of the Women's Normal High School in Beijing from a script by Chen Dabei published in *Drama* in 1922; *Rocks and Reeds* by Yang Yinshen, published in Shanghai in 1927; and *Lanzhi and Zhongqing* by Xiong Foxi, published in *Eastern Miscellany* in 1929; there were also two opera adaptations, including one by Ouyang Yuqian, and a film version in 1926. Yuan Changying's

1929 version is remarkable in shifting the emphasis from the victimised daughter-in-law to the mother-in-law, herself a victim of the system which prohibits remarriage for women and disregards the sexual and emotional needs of widows. It was published by the Commercial Press in Shanghai in 1930, with five other one-act plays.

Yuan Changying studied Western drama at Edinburgh University from 1916 to 1920. Returning to China in 1921, she began a distinguished teaching career at Beijing Normal Women's College. A further two years in France extended her knowledge of contemporary Western theatre, and on her return to China in 1929 she was appointed professor of Western literature at Wuhan University. After 1949 she became a member of the Chinese Democratic League and joined the Writers' Association in 1956. Apart from the six short plays published in 1930, she also wrote fiction, prose and academic studies of French literature.

Xiong Foxi (1900–65)

Xiong Foxi began acting in 'civilised plays' while a student at a missionary school in Hankou in the 1910s. In 1919 he went to Yanjing University to study education and literature, and was one of the first to join the newly established People's Dramatic Society in 1921. After graduating in 1923 he went to study drama at Columbia University in New York. On his return in 1926 he was appointed successively professor of drama at the Beijing Arts Academy, Yanjing University and Beijing University. Most of his work can be classified as comedy, and the author takes care to construct amusing dialogue uttered by believable, rounded characters. His chief purpose is nevertheless educational, as can be seen from his carefully constructed three-act plays of the mid-1920s. *The Foreign Graduate* (1926), set in the rural interior, exposes the pretensions of Chinese who have studied abroad and warns the local people not to be taken in. His depiction of bandits as upright figures in the class war suggests left-wing sympathies, but *The Foreign Graduate* avoids standard clichés. *A Patriotic Heart* (first performed and published in 1926) by contrast is set in a wealthy home in Beijing, where the conflict is not easily resolved according to clear-cut political criteria. Instead, the author seems to be warning that self-righteous nationalism of any kind can destroy families and individuals to no good end. The author's courageous depiction of the Japanese wife of a senior Chinese government official as a pathetic figure under attack within her own home, and as entitled to feelings of patriotism as her Chinese offspring, is unique for this period, and underlines his commitment to a humanistic outlook that was becoming increasingly rare. The play found an appreciative audience and was performed many times in the period leading up to the War against Japan.

Xiong Foxi's one-act plays, such as 'Drunk' (1928) and 'The Artist' (1928), were also successfully performed by the Travelling Drama Troupe of China in the late 1920s and early 1930s. The former, set in 1888, has as its protagonist an executioner who revolts against his trade but is unable to escape from the poverty that drove him to it. His wife and assistant get him drunk so that he can undertake one final execution to clear their debts, but instead he attacks an importunate rent collector and collapses. The milieu in the satiric comedy 'The Artist' appears to be more civilised, but again the protagonist is beset by greed and corruption inside and outside the home. Both short pieces portray a stereotyped nagging wife, while the artist shows dedication and integrity in the face of venality.

In 1932 Xiong Foxi left Beijing to head a theatre project in the Dingxian village movement in Hebei, an ambitious rural reconstruction initiative inaugurated as a modernising alternative to socialism and Communism. Dingxian had been a model village since 1914, and was also a centre for a form of northern drama which incorporated spoken dialogue, known as *yangge* (in some variants translatable as 'rice-sprout song'). Xiong Foxi wrote and directed several short plays in Dingxian. *The Young Man with a Hoe* (1932) depicts a free-thinking but hot-tempered young peasant who prefers to hunt and kill the local tiger to placating him with superstitious rites. Assisted by his female cousin, the resourceful and brave Qiulian, he despatches the tiger (and village superstition) with his hoe (the humble but effective weapon of the Chinese peasantry). *The Butcher* (written in 1932 and performed in 1933) shows how a clever bully can exploit credulous villagers but can in turn be brought to justice when he goes too far. *River Crossing* (written 1935 and performed 1936) preaches the message of change in the countryside through education and self-help to defeat the oppressive forces of the old society. These simple propaganda pieces are said to have been well received by the local audience, and following the Japanese invasion, Xiong led his troupe to Chengdu where they performed before large audiences. He returned to Shanghai after the war, and after 1949 was appointed to high-ranking posts in the Shanghai theatrical and cultural bureaucracy.

Cao Yu (1910–96)

Cao Yu's *Thunderstorm* is the most famous dramatic work of the pre-war period and possibly the most performed play in the modern Chinese theatre. It was first published in 1934 in *Literary Quarterly*, a prominent journal founded in January 1934 by Zheng Zhenduo and Jin Yi, and staged the same year by students in Jinan (Shandong). Later performances include Shanghai in 1935, directed by Ouyang Yuqian and Hong Shen; Tokyo in 1935; the Travelling Drama Troupe of China production by Tang Huaiqiu also in 1935; and the Nanjing production in 1936, which featured Cao Yu in the leading role. Two film adaptations appeared in 1938, in Hong Kong and in Shanghai. Tang Huaiqiu's production established his troupe as the first fully professional company for the spoken drama. With *Thunderstorm*, for all its flaws, the spoken play had come of age in China.

Cao Yu was born to a wealthy official family living in a large house in one of the foreign concessions in Tianjin. Tianjin is famous for its rich theatrical traditions, and as a child he was taken by his mother to see 'civilised drama' as well as traditional theatre. It was also his good fortune to have been a student from 1926 to 1930 at the Nankai Secondary School, which had one of China's most active student dramatic societies on campus. Cao Yu acted in works by Ding Xilin, Ibsen, Galsworthy and Molière, and one of his most praised performances was as Nora in *A Doll's House*; he was also co-translator of Galsworthy's *Strife*. From 1931 to 1934, he was a student at Qinghua, graduating from the Western literature and languages department, where he read Gorky, Chekhov, Shaw, O'Neill, Euripides and Aeschylus, and wrote *Thunderstorm* in his last undergraduate year. After graduation in 1933, he was kept on as a research student. He later taught at the Tianjin Normal College for Women and at Fudan University in Shanghai.

Thunderstorm is a skilful blend of psychological drama involving incest, repressed sexuality and generational revolt, the political drama of class struggle, and the old-fashioned melodrama of predestined fate, coincidence and bloody revenge – all it lacks is a scene from Peking opera. The protagonist is Zhou Puyuan, the wealthy owner of a coalmine in north China; ranged against him are his neurasthenic wife Fanyi, in love with her stepson Ping, and his former maid and mistress, Shiping, mother to Ping and to Lu Dahai (who unbeknownst to his father works in his mine), and also mother (by another man) to Sifeng who now works as a maid in the Zhou household. Ping rejects Fanyi but courts Sifeng, not knowing she is his half-sister; Lu Dahai heads a workers' revolt against his natural father. The play ends with a violent thunderstorm which precipitates the destruction of the family (and, by implication, of the doomed Confucian family and capitalist economic systems): Fanyi's son and Sifeng die by accident, Ping shoots himself, and Shiping and Fanyi end up in a mental asylum where a bowed Puyuan makes an occasional lonely visit. Attributions of foreign ancestry for *Thunderstorm* include Ibsen's *Ghosts*, Racine's *Phèdre*, Ostrovsky's *The Storm*, Galsworthy's *Strife*, O'Neill's *Desire Under the Elms* and assorted works by Euripides, Sophocles and Chekhov.

Later left-wing critics have emphasised the elements of class struggle in the play: the poor are either morally superior to the wealthy or else corrupted by them, while their exploiters are a doomed class in history's inevitable advance. Cao Yu, however, was not a Communist Party member, and as critics of the time such as Zhang Geng pointed out, the left-wing coloration is merely conventional. A feminist reading shows the persistence of patriarchy in the class war: the protagonist is punished by losing his women and children; the women lose first their lovers and children, then their lives or their sanity. As the instigator of the action, having summonsed Shiping to the household to remove her competition for her stepson's affections, Fanyi is a Iago-like antagonist and possibly the most complex figure on stage, but she shares her dramatic role with Shiping Zhou Puyuan remains the basic source of the dramatic conflict: it is his sexual and moral delinquency which sows the seeds of the family's destruction. Cao Yu's strongest plays are centred on the figure of the patriarch who destroys what he most wishes to extend, the family line, and it is perhaps this element in his work that Chinese audiences find the most profound and moving irony. In *Thunderstorm*, the means of destruction is incest, the gravest possible sin against the family; and Cao Yu punishes the profligate parent by depriving him of his children.

As was by now customary, *Thunderstorm* was accompanied by elaborate stage directions and requires elaborate staging, and this aspect has attracted massive commentary. Equally famous as a written script and in performance, it situates the spoken drama firmly in the theatre without sacrificing its claim to literary status. Its early popularity undoubtedly owes a great deal to its sensational themes, to which attention was drawn by frequent bans in pre-war years, and to the later prominence of the author, who became one of the modern theatre's most influential figures. Critics enjoy exploring its multiple meanings, and its place in the history of modern drama is assured.

Cao Yu's second play, *Sunrise*, was published in 1936 and won the *L'Impartial* award for the best drama that year. It was first performed in Shanghai in 1937 under the direction of Ouyang Yuqian, and appeared as a film the following year. Prefaced with one quotation from Laozi and eight quotations from the Bible, it resembles Xia Yan's *Under Shanghai Eaves* in its close-up of interlocking lives in contemporary Shanghai – a subject of never-failing interest to its local audience. Its protagonist is the standard 1930s figure of a failed New Woman: a society beauty whose social position has declined and who finally chooses death over degradation. A contrasting female role is given to a young prostitute, whose life is similarly doomed, while an idealistic intellectual who tries unsuccessfully to act as the saviour of both women survives to open a symbolic curtain at the end of the play and usher in the light of a new dawn. Controlling events in the background is a sinister financier with unlimited resources at his disposal, counterpoised by a gang of construction workers whose powerfully rhythmic pile-drivers seem to signify a new revolutionary force in society. The conventional Marxist reading of the plot is undermined by comments by Cao Yu that the intellectual is a self-righteous, bungling fool, and the construction workers are building an office block for the protagonist's patron, a banker on the verge of bankruptcy. The structure of the plot is looser than in *Thunderstorm*, and it portrays a wider collection of social types with more emphasis on relationships than action. Three young women, ranging in age from sixteen to twenty-two to thirty, illustrate the stages of degeneracy in the life of a prostitute; while the lives of three contrasting married women seem more stable, they are not very much to be preferred. In this urban society, the family hardly exists as a unit, but evil lurks everywhere, destroying lives whether worthy or unworthy. The sense of cosmic cruelty is stronger than in *Thunderstorm*, and the patriarchal figure is reduced to a background manipulator of events rather than a foregrounded active presence. Cao Yu noted that he was trying to avoid the 'well-made play' in this work, which has been compared to Chekhov's *The Cherry Orchard* and Ostrosvksy's *The Storm*, and to create interest through the fragmented depiction of parallel lives.

Cao Yu's third play, *The Wilderness*, has only recently attracted the same level of attention as its predecessors. Written in 1936 and performed in Shanghai in 1937, its expressionist techniques look back to Hong Shen's reworking of O'Neill's *The Emperor Jones*. Returning to Aristotle's recommendation of murder within the family as the strongest dramatic trope, the play shows a morally and physically deformed individual seeking private justice in a moribund society. Aided by a woman's love and confrontation in the Black Forest with apparitions from his past, he learns that the disadvantaged in an unjust society can never achieve justice by conventional means, and accepts that his revenge on the innocent is an historically necessary act. Entrusting his pregnant paramour (also called Jinzi, or Goldie, like Yama Zhao's wife) to the care of convict comrades residing in a fantasised Utopia, he frees himself of guilt and kills himself before his pursuers arrive. Although Cao Yu refers in the stage directions to the myth of Prometheus, the theme is closer to Hegelian metaphors of historical necessity; however, the supernatural and fantastic elements in the plot and staging did not meet the approval of left-wing critics at the time, and the hugely overwrought atmosphere had little commercial or artistic appeal. Less episodic and less reliant on monologue than Hong Shen's *Yama Zhao*, it is nevertheless Cao Yu's most sustained attempt at expressionism. Chinese audiences of the 1980s were more receptive to anti-realism, and Cao Yu revised the script for republication in 1982 and performances in 1984 by the Chinese Youth Art Theatre and the Central Academy of Drama. It was made into a film in 1981 and adapted as a Western-style opera by Wu Zuqiang in 1987. Its revival also owed a great deal to its author's personal standing. (*Cao Yu's later works are discussed below in Chapter 9.*)

Xia Yan (1900–95)

Xia Yan started his career as an activist in the May Fourth Movement while a young engineering student in Zhejiang. After graduation he went to Japan to continue his studies at Meiji University but was expelled from the country because of his association with left-wing organisations. Returning to China in 1927, he joined the Communist Party in Shanghai. Together with Feng Naichao and Zheng Boqi, he founded the Arts Troupe in 1929 and devoted himself to fostering left-wing drama and film. He was a founder member of the League of Left-wing Writers and primarily responsible for setting up the League of Left-wing Dramatists.

Xia Yan's first full-length play was *Sai Jinhua*, an historical romance loosely based on an episode in Zeng Pu's novel *A Flower in an Ocean of Sin*, on the life of a famous courtesan supposed to have played a prominent role in the Boxer Rebellion as the mistress of the German commander, Field-Marshal Count von Waldersee. Sai Jinhua had earlier lived in Europe as the wife of the Chinese ambassador to Germany, Russia, Holland and Austria. In the play, she is captured in the street by German soldiers during the siege of Beijing, demands to see the Count, intercedes with him to ease the situation in Beijing, and is later implored by Chinese officials to become his mistress in order to assist their negotiations for a peaceful settlement. The play ends with Sai Jinhua being punished for her association with foreigners by the very officials who had arranged it. In exposing the hypocrisy that lies beneath protestations of patriotism and honour, the play blends historical facts with subtle psychological profiling, astute political analysis and great dramatic irony; technically it is also innovative, for instance, in its use of cinematic projection. First staged in 1936, shortly before the death of Sai Jinhua herself, it attracted great attention and was the subject of a special symposium in Beijing in which it was praised as the first important work of the Theatre of National Defence. Like Xiong Foxi's version under the same name, it was banned in early 1937 by the Nationalists, and became a special target of attack during the Cultural Revolution.

Xia Yan next turned his gaze to the immediate present. In the three-act drama *Under Shanghai Eaves* (first performed in 1937 and published in 1941), he examines in naturalistic detail the interlocking fates of the poverty-stricken occupants of a Shanghai tenement from a Marxist perspective. Despite its technical accomplishments in stagecraft, dialogue and construction, the play is marred by sentimental characterisation: the frustrated intellectual, the good-hearted loose woman, the hen-pecked husband and nagging wife, and the by now obligatory Communist whose arrival sparks the action. Taking its inspiration from Gorky's *The Lower Depths* (adapted by Shi Tuo and Ke Ling as *The Night Inn*), *Under Shanghai Eaves* differs mainly in sticking to the middle-class characters that Xia Yan knew best rather than society's outcasts, and its main interest is in the triangular love story of a woman 'married' to two men. Partly thanks to Xia Yan's powerful position in Shanghai before and after the work, it became a standard work in the left-wing repertoire. Its resemblance to Cao Yu's *Sunrise* is probably due to shared parentage, and both set an example for Yu Ling's *Shanghai at Night* and Song Zhidi's *Chongqing in Fog*. (*Xia Yan's later plays are discussed below in Chapter 9.*)

Yu Ling (b. 1907)

Yu Ling joined the Communist Youth League in 1926 as a student at Suzhou Normal College. He entered the Law Faculty at Beijing University in 1931 and became a member of the League of Left-wing Writers and the League of Left-wing Dramatists in 1931. Over the next two years he was responsible for organising branches of the League in Tianjin, Jinan (Shandong), Taiyuan and Suiyuan. After joining the Communist Party in 1932, his work was directed towards the war effort, and between 1932 and 1945 he wrote over forty plays and filmscripts mostly on the theme of resistance to Japan. His main contribution to the Theatre of National Defence was the one-act 'The Traitor's Offspring'; Hong Shen, Zhang Min and Zhang Geng were co-authors of the script, which was first published in 1936 and revised in 1937. Staged in Shanghai in the second half of 1936 (and claimed by Hong Shen to have had the longest run of its kind), it depicts the protests by Chinese students against the older generation's complicity with Japanese interests. Yu Ling was also the chief organiser of the collective work *Defend the Marco Polo Bridge,* staged in July 1938 on the first anniversary of the Chinese resistance at Marco Polo Bridge which marked the beginning of the War against Japan. Nearly a hundred leading actors took part in the performance in Shanghai, which elicited an immediate response from the patriotic audience.

Yu Ling spent the early war years in Shanghai, where he continued to write anti-Japanese plays and filmscripts. *Shanghai at Night,* a sentimental melodrama on the life of refugees from the countryside, was performed in 1939 and made into a film in 1941. His next play, *Ballad of a Long Night,* returns to the genre established by Xia Yan: life in a Shanghai tenement from a left-wing perspective, with the hero and villain a school-teacher and currency speculator respectively, plus the obligatory underground Communist leader. It proved too much for the local censors, however, and was first performed in Chongqing in 1942 and then in Guilin in 1942, directed by Ouyang Yuqian. Yu Ling left for Hong Kong in 1941, and at the end of the war rejoined Xia Yan, Song Zhidi and Jin Shan in Chongqing before returning to Shanghai. After 1949, he wrote mainly filmscripts, of which the most notable was on the life of his old colleague Nie Er, and held a long series of high positions in the Shanghai drama and film world.

Li Jianwu (1906–82)

Not all audiences were prepared for unrelieved preaching, and Li Jianwu established a reputation as the most accomplished of the new dramatists with his well-crafted scripts of the 1930s. His plays combine strong left-wing loyalties with dramatic and literary skills developed from an early age. Li Jianwu's father was a well-known revolutionary activist who was assassinated in 1919. At the time, the family was living in Beijing where Li Jianwu was educated at the primary and secondary school attached to Beijing Normal University. He was a precocious student, writing in his teens short fiction, plays and poetry for publication in the *Morning Post* literary supplement *Literature Ten-daily,* then edited by Wang Tongzhao who became an early patron. He became attracted to the theatre as a student at secondary school, taking part in performances in female roles before women were permitted on stage.

As his reputation as a young actor grew, he became acquainted with other theatrical figures such as Xiong Foxi. He also took part in political protests such as the May Thirtieth demonstrations of 1925. He entered Qinghua University in 1925, where after one year he transferred to the Western literature department headed by Wang Wenxian, famous for its courses on Western theatre. In 1931, he went to France to study for two years. Back in China, he resumed acting, switching to male roles for Shaw's *How He Lied to Her Husband*. He also continued his academic work, and in 1935 was recruited as professor of French at Jinan University in Shanghai. His knowledge of Western drama was extensive: among others, he particularly admired Shaw, Lady Gregory, Synge and Wilde. His friends and associates in Shanghai included Huang Zuolin, Gu Zhongyi, Ba Jin and Zhang Tianyi.

Li Jianwu's early one-act plays featured working-class characters and were not performed. *Liang Yunda*, a bloody melodrama set in the countryside, was written in 1933 and published the following year in the leading independent journal *Literature*, edited by Ba Jin. His next play, *It's Only Spring*, a full-length work in three acts also written in 1933, was published in the *L'Impartial* literary supplement edited by Shen Congwen. The play is a comedy of manners whose protagonist is a beautiful but spoiled society hostess, married after an earlier disappointment in love to the chief of police, and the mysterious stranger whose arrival precipitates the action is, of course, her former lover turned revolutionary. Although the exposure of venality in the Beijing police force caused some early performances to be banned, the underlying message is not of class struggle but of moral turpitude among the rich and idle. The stranger, Feng Yunping, says at one point, 'At times I'm in danger of turning into a sentimental moralist' and the reference may be autobiographical (the play was written as a birthday present to Li Jianwu's fiancée). As might be expected under the circumstances, the wife defends herself passionately, showing true feeling despite her frivolous ways. Nevertheless the play is set at the time of the Northern Expedition, and the stranger from the south could in reality have lost his life.

This nice balance between political realities and romantic fancies appealed greatly to student audiences at the time. It was first staged by Chinese students in Tokyo in 1935, following Cao Yu's *Thunderstorm*, and rewritten in 1936 for school and other performances. A Shanghai production in 1939, directed by Chen Xihe (who directed the 1956 film of Ba Jin's *Family*), starred the author as the comic villain. Like Ding Xilin, Li Jianwu was able to create engaging theatre from serious issues. The one-act 'Thirteen Years', commemorates the execution of the Communist activist Li Dazhao in 1927; it was first staged in 1938 in Shanghai.

Li Jianwu's first attempt at pure comedy, *To Set an Example* (aka *A Pattern of Perfection*), was published in *Literature Quarterly*, the successor to *Literature* and also edited by Ba Jin, in the same issue as Cao Yu's *Thunderstorm*. It was prefaced by quotations from Confucius and Molière, an apt introduction for this French-style farce set in China. The protagonist is an elderly Confucian scholar whose old-fashioned rectitude threatens his family's survival. His discomfiture at the hands of the younger generation aided by scheming servants is well deserved, and yet at the end he is left as a pathetic figure whose rigid ways have harmed chiefly himself. As in all his plays, Li Jianwu does not shy away from stock characters and situations, but engages his audiences with lively dialogue, plenty of action and clever variations on familiar themes. It was produced in Chongqing by Zhang Junxiang in 1939 and in Shanghai by Huang Zuolin soon after. (*For Li Jianwu's early life and fiction, see Chapter 4; his last major work is discussed below in Chapter 9.*)

Part II. 1938–1965

6

RETURN TO TRADITION

From their garrison near Marco Polo Bridge, just outside Beijing, the Japanese army opened fire on Chinese troops during a military manoeuvre on 7 July 1937. The Chinese returned fire, setting in motion the War of Resistance against Japan. At first, Japanese victory was swift. Beijing and Tianjin fell within a month, and the evacuated capital, Nanjing, was the site of a terrible massacre of Chinese civilians in December 1937. Wuhan became the temporary Nationalist capital but was abandoned in turn on 25 December 1938. China's capital thereafter until the end of the war in 1945 was Chongqing in south-eastern Sichuan.

The Japanese invasion temporarily diverted Chiang Kaishek's attention from his anti-Communist campaigns. His allies from the Japanese-occupied north-east had for some time been putting pressure on him to form a broader political alliance against Japan. On a visit to Xi'an in December 1936, Chiang was imprisoned by troops from his own side and only set free through the mediation of Zhou Enlai, who acted as chief negotiator for the Communist Party. One of the conditions for his release was his agreement to a United Front in government and military affairs. Shortly after the Marco Polo Bridge Incident, the Red Army was – at least in name – incorporated in the national defence forces as the Eighth Route Army in the north-west and as the New Fourth Army south of the Yangtze River. The United Front was fragile, however, and both sides retained long-term plans for civil war. Although Chiang Kaishek repeatedly tried to weaken the Communist bases, his tacit recognition of their jurisdiction over the so-called 'liberated areas' meant a virtual Communist government in Yan'an and the border regions of Gansu, Ningxia and Shaanxi. China was therefore ruled by three distinct political regimes during the war: the Japanese in the major cities of the north, the coast, and the Yangtze River valley; the Communists mostly in the countryside in the north-west; and the Nationalists in the south and south-west.

Few writers chose to stay in occupied Beijing. A North China Writers' Association, headed by Zhou Zuoren, was established in 1942, but nothing of any note was produced under its auspices. In Shanghai, on the other hand, the foreign concessions offered limited protection for literary and artistic activity up until the end of 1941, when the International Settlement was taken over by the Japanese. Even under occupation, the city retained vestiges of its old cosmopolitan atmosphere. Performance arts in particular flourished, including the cabaret-style productions for which modern Shanghai is famous, as well as patriotic costume dramas and contemporary melodramas on the lives of chorus girls or refugees in Shanghai. In the absence of Hollywood films, over a hundred theatrical troupes competed for the attention of China's most sophisticated theatregoers.

Most left-wing writers fled Shanghai before the city fell in November 1937. One large group followed the central government first to Wuhan, where they formed the Chinese National Federation of Anti-Japanese Writers and Artists, and then to Chongqing in September 1938. The Federation was an impressive United Front organisation, its founding membership comprising ninety-seven representatives from non-capitulationist writers of all political colourings: the forty-five member executive included Guo Moruo, Mao Dun, Xu Dishan, Yu Dafu, Zhu Ziqing, Zhu Guangqian and Zhang Henshui. Lao She, one of the few well-known writers who owed allegiance to neither Communists nor Nationalists, was elected president. Lao She was also editor of the Federation's journal, *Resistance Literature and the Arts*, which ran from May 1938 and continued right through to June 1946. As the only literary journal which continued publication throughout the war, *Resistance Literature* exerted a strong influence. When Liang Shiqiu in 1938 asked for literary works that were not 'eight-legged resistance literature', he was so thoroughly denounced that he had to apologise and resign from the editorial staff.

Besides the publication of its journal, the Federation promoted the war effort through branches in other cities in the interior such as Chengdu, Changsha, Kunming and (until its fall in 1941) Hong Kong, holding workshops and seminars on topical issues such as the popularisation of literature. Under the slogan 'take literature to the villages; take literature to the army', over fifteen performance troupes and propaganda teams were sent to parts of the country still under Chinese control. These efforts grew out of the debates on mass literature held by the League of Left-wing Writers before it was dissolved in 1936, and many of those directing the campaign were Communists or had left-wing sympathies, so that much of their propaganda was directed at shortcomings in Nationalist-controlled areas. Song Zhidi's 1940 play, *Fog in Chongqing*, for instance, describes the disillusionment of students who made the journey to Chongqing only to find the city suffering under a corrupt regime. Works such as this were a manifestation of the still barely suppressed hostility between the Communists and Nationalists.

Despite dissatisfaction with the government and the privations of war, literary activity in Chongqing was in some ways more lively and diverse than in other parts of China. Non-Maoist Communist literature was supported by the July Society and its journal, *July*; Hu Feng was the leading theorist of the group, and Lu Ling and Duanmu Hongliang its best-known writers. *July* was banned in 1941 but was succeeded in 1945 by *Hope*. Nationalist intellectuals such as Chen Quan (1905–68) and Liang Zongdai (1903–83), on the other hand, reminded readers of China's ancient martial traditions as well as drawing on Nietzsche and Social Darwinism for inspiration in the Kunming-based *Annals of the Warring States* and its Chongqing successor, the 'Warring States' supplement to the *L'Impartial* (formerly in Tianjin).

An alternative for writers who found the atmosphere in Chongqing too repressive was Kunming, capital of Yunnan. Kunming was the site of the National South-west United University, a wartime amalgamation of universities from Beijing and Tianjin whose staff and students had travelled often by foot from the Japanese-occupied north. Material conditions were desperately poor, but the presence of respected teachers such as Shen Congwen, Wen Yiduo and Li Guangtian provided inspiration and support to students and budding writers.

On 7 January 1941, the Nationalists' Fortieth Division troops ambushed and all but annihilated the nine thousand men of the New Fourth Army in southern Anhui. This incident virtually destroyed the United Front, although both sides continued to pay lip service to it. Chiang Kaishek reinforced his economic blockade of the Communist 'liberated areas' and the Communists in turn redoubled their efforts in preparation for imminent confrontation. At this time, the Japanese were also resorting to more desperate tactics, having failed to build on their initial advance and capture of major cities in 1937 and 1938. A campaign of terror launched in 1940 to break the Chinese resistance by a 'three all' policy ('burn all, loot all, kill all') only stiffened the Chinese will to resist. In the face of a new wave of atrocities committed by the invaders, many people were dismayed at the latest evidence that Chiang Kaishek was more intent on fighting the Communists than the Japanese. To most intellectuals, this was an unforgivable crime.

Many writers had already gone to Yan'an at the beginning of the war, and many more joined them after the New Fourth Army incident. Most were attached either to the Lu Xun Academy of Art and Literature or to the Resistance University, both founded in 1938. Others worked for the Party newspaper, *Liberation Daily*, founded in 1941. Life in Yan'an, located in the barren loess plains of north Shaanxi, was difficult enough even without the war or economic blockades. The Communist base was under constant military threat not only from the Japanese, but also from the Nationalists and their local allies such as disgruntled landlords. Under conditions so precarious, Mao Zedong was able to turn his disparate recruits into a cohesive revolutionary force. To combat supply shortages, for instance, he put into practice a series of 'self-reliance' campaigns whereby the village economies were reformed by the establishment of mutual-aid cooperatives. These land reform strategies were accompanied in the ideological and cultural sphere by the intensification of the 'mass line' theories put forward by the League in the early 1930s and tested in the Jiangxi Soviet in Ruijin between 1931 and 1934. Now, intellectuals who claimed to be left-wing were required to demonstrate their solidarity with the masses by joining them in practice. Under the auspices of the Lu Xun Academy, performance and drama troupes were sent to the countryside to promote the war effort in conjunction with Communist policies, composing songs, poems and plays with a militant Communist flavour. Writers, who were now called cultural workers, were drafted to collect folksongs and other materials for their new compositions, to be published in new Yan'an journals such as *Mass Literature and the Arts* and *New Poems and Songs*.

The military isolation of Yan'an became even more severe in 1941 and 1942. After the Japanese bombing of Pearl Harbor on December 1941, the Second World War which had begun in Europe in 1939 opened a new front in the Pacific, with the United States entering the war as a major player especially in the East and South-east Asian theatres. The American commander in Asia, General Stilwell, became Chiang Kaishek's chief-of-staff, and aid totalling about US $1.5 billion poured into China. Most of the aid went directly to the Nationalist government, which pocketed much of it and diverted the rest to use against the Communists. The material deprivations at Communist headquarters exacerbated latent political tensions between the different groups in Yan'an. Intellectuals who had spent their lives exposing injustice in Shanghai and later in Chongqing began to say openly that Yan'an was also shrouded in fog. Mao Zedong responded by launching a Rectification campaign to enforce Party discipline in February 1942.

The literary intellectuals from the urban areas were particularly vocal in expressing dissatisfaction with social policies in Yan'an. In stories written in 1940 and 1941 such as 'When I Was in Xia Village', Ding Ling drew attention to the intolerable sacrifices women were forced to make for the war effort, without much sympathy or support from their own side. In March 1942, she followed this up with 'Thoughts on March Eighth', an essay commemorating International Women's Day, in which she argued that women in Yan'an still suffered from entrenched male prejudice, despite the Party's claims to support women's emancipation. Had the criticisms been restricted to women's issues, they may well have been let pass unnoticed, but the problem was broader. As editor of the literary supplement to *Liberation Daily*, Ding Ling also published essays by influential writers such as Xiao Jun, Ai Qing and Wang Shiwei, who criticised other kinds of inequalities in Yan'an and demanded more autonomy for artists and writers. Ai Qing's plea was to 'Understand Writers, Respect Writers'; Xiao Jun drew a line between politics and art in 'Politicians and Artists'; and most damning was Wang Shiwei's 'Wild Lilies', which described Yan'an as a class society where some people (i.e. political cadres) had much better living conditions than others (i.e. writers and artists) and where the leadership lacked concern for the ordinary people, especially the young.

These criticisms were a direct challenge to the Rectification campaign and Party control in the base areas. In May 1942, Mao Zedong summoned the Yan'an writers and artists to a conference to reaffirm Party authority over all spheres of life in the base areas. The conference was in session for twenty-three days: Mao gave the opening and closing addresses, and over two hundred participants attended a protracted series of workshops, public forums and lectures. Because Mao's were the only papers to be widely publicised, it is difficult to judge the degree of agreement or dissent which was reached at the conference. However, the difference in tone between Mao's 'Opening Remarks' and 'Concluding Remarks' indicates that considerable disquiet and even outright opposition were expressed. In the course of these three weeks, Mao Zedong clearly lost patience with what he saw as the writers' self-indulgent proclamations of their poetic inspiration, feminist grievances, sexual liberation, moral loftiness and political naivety.

In his 'Opening Remarks', Mao Zedong set out several issues for discussion: the writer's position, attitude, audience, work and study. The focus was clearly on the writer; the audience (here defined as workers, peasants and soldiers) had a subordinate, passive role, as the object for the work and study the writer has to undergo to be truly revolutionary. Most were agreed that the masses were to be led by enlightened intellectuals; the problem was how it could be done most effectively. Mao's underlying assumptions on this relationship were typical of the debates on social change, revolution and literature since the beginning of the twentieth century when Liang Qichao argued that fiction was an important tool for governing the masses. The most original and striking passages are in Mao's warning to intellectuals that they had to overcome their sense of superiority regarding manual labour and individual emotions. It seems likely, however, that these points were not heeded as much as he wanted during the discussions.

In his lengthy 'Concluding Remarks', Mao reverses the relationship between the writer and the audience: rather than enlightening the workers, peasants and soldiers, writers must learn to listen to the masses in order to deliver a better service. Instead of deliberating on what sort of attitude writers should adopt, Mao gives them no choice: literature and the arts are to serve the masses. Mao chastised the Yan'an writers for not making sufficient use of the conventions and rhetorical devices in popular art forms like folksongs and folktales. As most writers were from the cities and had relatively little experience behind the lines, they were far removed from the realities of the Chinese countryside; even the debates about proletarian and mass literature in the 1920s and 1930s were inspired by and based on European and Japanese sources. Mao Zedong, on the other hand, spoke with the confidence of his many years experience in rural China, his continuing fondness for traditional Chinese fiction about peasants and rebels, and his own practice in writing traditional poetry. Despite his polite phrases about the revolutionary potential of the May Fourth Movement, it can be estimated from Mao's remarks on the nature of literature that he thought little of the products of this movement.

Having admonished the writers and artists for their misplaced conceptions of the audience and themselves, Mao in the last sections of the 'Concluding Remarks' proceeded to lay down his prescriptive views on the relationship between politics and literature. If Mao's insight into the relationship between author and audience opened up new ways of looking at an old problem, his authoritarian approach to the functions of literature had the effect of closing the possibility of diversity in literary development. Mao unambiguously declared that all literature is class-based, and writers should not deceive themselves into thinking that any literature is independent of politics. From this, Mao further declared that all literature inevitably acts as a political tool. Writers who profess to be on the side of the masses should eulogise the masses in their writings, while exposure and condemnation are reserved for those elements opposed to the masses. By extension, proletarian literature should be a political tool of the Communist Party, which leads the masses. Communist writers should not only be responsible to the masses, but more importantly, they must serve the organisational needs of the Party. On the relationship between politics and art, Mao is again unambiguous: in all literary creations, politics comes before art for both readers and writers.

The authoritarian nature of the 'Talks' may not have seemed out of place in wartime. Whatever the intellectual persuasiveness of Mao's beliefs, the Yan'an writers had little choice but to accept or to leave, although the binding nature of these 'Talks' did not take effect immediately. A few days after the conference, the Central Political Institute held a series of meetings in which writers like Ding Ling, Xiao Jun and Ai Qing were required to make self-criticisms. As is common in these political campaigns, one person was scapegoated: Wang Shiwei spent the next five years in confinement, and when the Yan'an base was abandoned in 1947, he was executed. While this final punishment was not publicised, most writers would have been aware of it and from then on had to work under its shadow.

On publication a year later as 'Talks at the Yan'an Forum on Literature and the Arts', this document became the official policy of the Chinese Communist Party for the next forty-odd years. Targeted writers were enjoined to find their revolutionary identities by integrating with the masses, and many went to live with peasants or soldiers for periods of up to two years; some, such as Ding Ling, wrote very different works as a result of their experience. While the older writers were preoccupied with remoulding their ideology, new writers such as Zhao Shuli were encouraged to develop a new and very distinctive style, based on local forms of performance arts and delivering a very specific message to audiences in and around the base areas.

The new products of the 'Talks' repudiated the lachrymose tone common to most May Fourth literature, where writers mostly bemoaned the fate of the oppressed, typically portraying women and peasants as pathetic victims. Post-1942 works such as *The White-haired Girl* and *Wang Gui and Li Xiangxiang* still highlighted the sufferings of the oppressed, but peasant men and women are depicted as masters of their fate, overthrowing their oppressors under the guidance of the Party. Even when May Fourth modes were revived after 1949, positive endings continued to be mandatory: in works set in the past, the promise of resolution had to be made; in works set in the present, problems had to be resolved within the work.

Mao Zedong's ability to exert a high degree of literary control in the mid-1940s was a reflection of his dominating stature in the Communist Party, which now had a membership of over a million. At the seventh National Party Congress in April 1945 (the first since the 1928 congress in Moscow), Mao's leadership was unchallenged, and 'Mao Zedong Thought' was written into the new Party constitution. Although still nominally only referring to Party writers, the 'Talks' were circulated through the country as a guide to literary writing.

The Nationalist Party Congress in Chongqing the same month, on the other hand, was characterised by charges of corruption and inept leadership against Chiang Kaishek. As the international conflict was coming to an end and the two parties were positioning themselves to obliterate each other, it was clear that the Communists had the edge in terms of morale and popular support. In August, the Soviet Union launched an attack on the Japanese in north-east China and the United States dropped atomic bombs on Japan itself. Japan surrendered to the Allies on 2 September 1945, and China's long war of resistance was at an end.

The abrupt end to the war brought joy and hope. A few days before the formal declaration of surrender by the Japanese emperor, Mao Zedong flew to Chongqing to negotiate a post-war truce with Chiang Kaishek. He was extremely conciliatory, requesting only control over the liberated areas rather than a share in a national coalition government. Chiang Kaishek, after all, ruled two-thirds of China, was backed by a well-equipped army and had the support of the United States. Despite internal dissent from within his party, Chiang was in no mood to share power with his old enemies. In mid-1946, he ordered his 2 million-strong army against the Communists. Amid a series of initial victories, it pushed the Communist forces, now fighting under the name of the People's Liberation Army, into retreating from its head-quarters in Yan'an in 1947.

Both parties also stepped up the propaganda war and covert action against civilians. Nationalist agents resorted again to terror to wipe out opposition, including the self-styled 'third force' in post-war politics, the Chinese Democratic League. On 11 July 1946, Li Gongpu, a prominent Democratic League member, was assassinated by the secret police. At his funeral, Wen Yiduo, another League member and close friend, made an impassioned speech against this crime, daring the police to kill him too. He was shot and killed the same day.

Wen Yiduo was well-known as one of China's best modern poets and scholars, and his death aroused widespread indignation. It was also well-known that he was not a Communist, and his assassination became a symbol of the Nationalists' ruthless policies. Like their military strategies, where brute force gained territory but lost popular support, the assassinations silenced some opposi- tional voices in the short term at the cost of pushing previously uncommitted intellectuals into opposition. Disgusted by Chiang Kaishek's uncompromising tactics, the special US envoy, General George Marshall, who had been sent to mediate a truce between the two parties, returned home in January 1947.

By mid-1947, the course of the Civil War was turning in favour of the Communists. Where the victorious Nationalist army had over-extended itself, the Communists, forced to employ guer- rilla tactics once again, were able to gain support amongst the peasantry. The peasants took part in the strangulation of cities by cutting supply lines and other acts of sabotage. The most spectacular battle was fought in Manchuria in 1948, where the People's Liberation Army under Lin Biao defeated some 470,000 of Chiang Kaishek's best troops. Morale among the Nationalist soldiers quickly disintegrated. From there on, the People's Libera- tion Army overran one city after another in quick succession: Beijing in January 1949, Shanghai in May. The establishment of the People's Republic of China was declared on 1 October 1949, thereafter celebrated as National Day. The Nationalists fled south and then across the straits to Taiwan, which remains in Nationalist hands as the Republic of China to the present time.

The first step in mobilising writers and artists to support the new regime in Beijing was taken in July 1949 with a congress of 824 representatives of literature and the arts. Its importance was underlined by the participation of prominent politicians in- cluding Mao Zedong and Zhu De; the main address was given by the new premier-designate, Zhou Enlai, who urged the writers to adhere to the principles laid down in Mao's Yan'an 'Talks'. The main business of the congress was to approve the establishment of the Chinese National Federation of Writers and Artists and the appointment of Guo Moruo as president, flanked by Mao Dun and Zhou Yang as vice-presidents. Guo Moruo and Mao Dun were there by virtue of their contributions to poetry, drama and fiction as well as their prominence in the literary societies of the 1920s and 1930s. The real power in the Federation was held by Zhou Yang, whose literary contributions were limited to translations and some early poems but who had been the chief organisational force in the League of Left-wing Writers (after Qu Qiubai), in the Lu Xun Academy in Yan'an, and in the Party's Department of Propaganda. The Federation's organ, the *Literary Gazette*, was edited by Ding Ling, and well-known writers like Ba Jin, Xia Yan and Feng Zhi were given official positions as the Federation established branches in other cities in China. Nominally an autonomous body promoting the interests of writers and artists of all kinds, it was one of the chief means of control over literature and the arts, and its senior officials reported directly to the Department of Propaganda.

Affiliated to the Federation were the professional associations: the Chinese Writers' Association, the Chinese Dramatists' Association, the Chinese Film Artists' Association and so on, each with its corps of full-time administrative officers, editorial staffs and salaried professionals. The Writers' Association, for example, published *People's Literature* and *Poetry* at the national level. Both the Federation and the member associations had branches in all the provinces and major cities, each with its own staff and publications, providing an immense network of career opportunities for intellectuals willing to support the new regime. Writers also found employment in newspapers and journals published directly by the Party's Publications Bureau, such as the national *People's Daily*. Some worked for similar organisations such as the Central Film Bureau or the Women's Federation, while others taught or held administrative posts in schools and universities throughout the country.

Many of the May Fourth writers had fought for some three decades for a left-wing government and were eager to try out their ideas on a national platform. Holding joint appointments in senior government and bureaucratic posts meant they were placed in policy-making positions. On 1 October, Mao Dun was appointed Minister of Culture and Guo Moruo, Director of the Cultural and Educational Commission; non-Party writers like Ba Jin were appointed to the People's Political Consultative Committee. Guo Moruo continued to write, but most of the older writers confined themselves to administrative and ceremonial duties. The reasons were complex: some baulked at the difficulty of writing about the new prescribed topics or in the new prescribed styles, while others were presumably satisfied that they had achieved their career goals. As a consequence, the literature of the early

1950s was left to younger writers whose careers were launched in Yan'an and whose works, almost without exception, were optimistic and didactic: common themes included land reform and the 1950 Marriage Law.

For those who harboured uncertainties about the new era, the early 1950s brought a succession of thought reform and political study sessions. Literature and the arts were a rich source for political education. For example, in 1951, the *Literary Gazette* criticised the film *The Life of Wu Xun* for its glorification of its hero, Wu Xun, a Qing dynasty educationalist. Wu Xun came from a poor background but was famous for begging for donations from the ruling classes to educate the poor. According to the film's critics, Wu Xun lacked resolve in class struggle, and the rich and powerful should not have been depicted as willing to help the poor. Mao Zedong's intervention in a letter to the *People's Daily* in support of the criticisms led to a campaign against the film.

Political campaigns involving criticism and self-criticism sessions on the Yan'an model appeared to be an effective mechanism for remoulding the ideological outlook of wavering intellectuals and other subversive elements in society. Similar methods used on prisoners-of-war taken by the Chinese during the Korean War of 1950-3 left a lasting impression on American public opinion throughout the Cold War of the 1950s and 1960s, 'brain washing' being regarded as a peculiarly vicious aspect of Communist rule. In retrospect, it appears that intimidation rather than remoulding was achieved, but the thought reform endured by intellectuals was nowhere as brutal as the 'struggle meetings' held against people considered 'counter-revolutionaries' and former capitalists during the 'Three Evils' and 'Five Evils' campaigns in 1950-2. It is difficult to estimate the human cost involved in the building of New China, but anecdotal evidence suggests that during land reform (the redistribution of land in the villages in the late 1940s and early 1950s), a million landlords alone were killed, and millions more were humiliated, terrified or imprisoned. However, because they had no access to publishing either inside or outside China, their stories were never told in literature until the 1980s. They were, after all, only a fraction of the population. Nonetheless, the scale of state intimidation was clearly visible even to those not directly involved.

Emboldened by the relative ease with which the early reforms were implemented, the Party leadership launched the First Five Year Plan (on the Soviet Union model) in January 1953. Although it started rather haphazardly, by the end of the period, official figures showed that targets were overfulfilled. Economic success led to continued efforts on the ideological front, and a four-volume *Selected Works of Mao Zedong* was published in 1953 to provide the correct orientation. The chief document for writers was the 'Talks at the Yan'an Forum on Literature and the Arts', reprinted with minor revisions, as guidelines for all writers and all readers in the new society. From the early 1950s until the early 1980s, this text was used to intimidate or condemn writers and had more weight than government policy or law, so that the history of literature in this period became defined in terms of departures from the 'Talks'. At the Second Congress of the Federation, in September 1953, the theory and practice of 'socialist realism' became official policy in literature and the arts, signalling both dependence on the Soviet Union (where the term originated in the 1930s) and the determination of the authorities to have the controlling voice in the production of a new socialist literature for the new age.

The first full-scale campaign against a writer was the attack led by Lin Mohan and He Qifang on Hu Feng in 1953 for supposedly advocating individualism and bourgeois ideas in literature. Hu Feng condemned the exclusive reliance on Marxism as the criterion for judging literary work and predicted that such a policy would lead to a literature divorced from reality. Over the next two years, the campaign widened to include over 80,000 writers and other intellectuals, accused of supporting Hu Feng in anti-Party activities. Western humanistic scholarship also received a battering when two young researchers, Li Xifan and Lan Ling, attacked Yu Pingbo, by now known as an authority on *Dream of the Red Chamber*, for neglecting class analysis in his studies on the novel. Hu Shi also came under attack at the same time. Such assaults by politically ambitious and self-righteous young men on older theorists became a common phenomenon in the 1960s.

Intellectuals who longed for more autonomy and better living conditions were heartened by political relaxation in the Soviet Union in spring 1956, following Khrushchev's denunciation of Stalin. The Chinese leadership deliberated briefly on their response to the Soviet thaw, and Mao seized the opportunity to undermine the trend towards professionalisation in the bureaucracy and the arts which had been of growing concern to him. In a speech on 2 May (but not published at the time), he proposed a policy of supporting diversity in literature, theatre, scholarship and thinking generally, under the attractively traditional slogan, 'Let a hundred flowers blossom, let a hundred schools of thought contend'. Despite misgivings from those who saw China's future in efficient modernisation, the new strategy was announced two weeks later by Lu Dingyi, the head of the Propaganda Department, in the form of a political campaign in which intellectuals were encouraged to speak their minds and explore new ideas. The Eighth Party Congress of the Communist Party was convened in September to give its approval, and in what may have been a compromise move, Mao Zedong Thought was dropped as the guiding principle for the Party in the new draft of the Party constitution. The Hundred Flowers campaign gathered momentum in the remainder of 1956 and early 1957. With respect to literature, it implied that while the Yan'an guidelines were still in force, politics were not the sole criterion for the assessment of literary works. Hitherto uncommitted writers, such as Feng Zhi and Bian Zhilin, and intellectuals of all ranks were persuaded that the Party was best positioned to protect their interests and became members. In November 1956, a ten-day conference was held in Beijing by editors of journals to decide on what they should do in response to the new environment. *Poetry*, one of several new journals inaugurated in January 1957, carried in its first issue eighteen classical poems by Mao Zedong to illustrate that even traditional styles were permitted.

The Hundred Flowers debates were conducted chiefly through the Party's own journals, which offered the greatest diversity of opinion since the Party was founded. Critics such as Zhou Bo, Ba Ren and Chen Yong argued that literature should shake off dogmatism and include topics of human interest. Qin Zhaoyang, brought in as editor of *People's Literature* to liven up the journal, set the tone with his September 1956 article, 'Realism – The Broad Road'. Qin claimed that literary critics had become political watchdogs, with power and influence going to those who could best use slogans and labels to oppress others. He suggested that 'socialist realism', the Soviet formula for politically conventional writing which had been adopted in China, should be replaced by 'critical realism' to reflect changing realities (that is, to question aspects of Party and government policy and its implementation). As examples of critical realism he published stories by the young writers Wang Meng and Liu Binyan which immediately became controversial.

The purpose of the Hundred Flowers campaign was not simply to enliven literary production: its chief aim was to throw light on problems within the Party by people on the outside. It is debateable how aware the Party leadership was of the risks they were taking in inviting comment: certainly they were taken aback at the vigour of the response. Intellectuals, students and workers throughout China began to air their grievances against basic Party policies as well as individual erring cadres. A Democracy Wall was created in Beijing University for posters criticising the Party, and similar protests occurred in other campuses. Party officials had never before been subjected to so much scrutiny. Mao Zedong may have been willing to sacrifice any number of lower-level cadres in order to cleanse the Party of corrupt and incompetent officials, but others (including Deng Xiaoping) had been opposed all along to any weakening of Party authority. By mid-1957 the Party conservatives forced a halt to the Hundred Flowers campaign, and those who had been active or outspoken were branded as 'rightists', anti-Communists or counter-revolutionaries.

The Anti-Rightist campaign of 1957-8 generated bitter divisions and resentment for many years. By the end of 1957, over 300,000 intellectuals, from famous writers to obscure primary school teachers, were labelled as rightists and sent 'to experience life' in remote towns and villages. The young and not so famous suffered most: in many cases, the campaign brought an end not just to their careers but to their lives. Wang Meng, Liu Binyan, Liu Shaotang and Gong Liu were among the younger writers banished for indefinite periods; older writers such as Ding Ling, Ai Qing, Feng Xuefeng, Xiao Qian and Wu Zuguang were punished even more severely with gaol sentences. Even though nearly all of these writers returned to privileged positions in later years (or perhaps because of this), the Anti-Rightist campaign had a far greater impact than the much more violent and bloody campaigns around 1950. It is an indication of Party omnipotence that henceforth, literary debates were confined to factional competition over interpretations of doctrine.

Shrugging off the failure of the Hundred Flowers campaign, Mao turned next to an earlier model to rid the Party of its impurities: the Yan'an mass line. The international situation also strengthened the tendency to look inwards and backwards. Tensions with the Soviet Union were becoming noticeable, and the United States continued to undermine China's international position with its support for Taiwan. The main thrust of the new campaign, known as the Great Leap Forward, was to force huge increases in industrial and agricultural production by far-reaching structural changes. In the countryside, peasants were mobilized to transform the socialist collectives of the early 1950s into much larger and semi-autonomous 'people's communes' at an intoxicating pace. Writers were required to make their own leaps forward not only by increasing their output, but more significantly by renewed spells in the countryside among the peasants to collect materials and to compile folksong collections. A new theoretical Party journal, *Red Flag*, was set up in June 1958, featuring Zhou Yang's article 'New Folksongs Have Blazed a Trail for Poetry', and millions of people in farms and factories all over China were encouraged to take time off from their work to compose poetry. A revival of local opera also took place at this time, but just as folksong was seen as complementing Mao's classical poetry, Peking opera also flourished briefly alongside it. By implication, May Fourth literature was being denigrated, although neither Zhou Yang nor Guo Moruo appeared to mind. On 9 June 1958, the *People's Daily* announced that 'a cultural revolution has started'.

The *People's Daily* was uncannily accurate in reporting that the seeds of a cultural revolution had sprouted. For reasons including natural disasters and the break with the Soviet Union as well as the leadership's erratic and irrational policies, the Great Leap Forward brought not prosperity but the Three Hard Years (1959–61), when over 30 million died of starvation and millions suffered. Nobody dared to address the facts of the disaster openly, let alone its causes. At a Party conference at Lushan in July 1959, the Minister of Defence, Peng Dehuai, alone expressed unease: he was dismissed, and the economy continued to deteriorate.

In a typical move, Mao had recourse to a new literary slogan. At the Third Congress of the Federation, held in 1960, 'socialist realism' was replaced by a call for 'the combination of revolutionary realism plus revolutionary romanticism', a slogan which not only implied criticism of the former Soviet-based line but also gave leeway for even more idealised depictions of life in China since 1949. The new line was embraced with enthusiasm by Guo Moruo but for most professional writers it represented an even more pronounced retreat from the liberalisation of the Hundred Flowers period.

In 1961–5, different factions in the ruling hierarchy jostled to position themselves in new alignments of power. Two main factions emerged: the populists, who backed Mao's voluntaristic leftist line; and the conservatives, who advocated cautious economic development under disciplined Party leadership, represented by Liu Shaoqi and Deng Xiaoping. Each faction had its followers competing for dominance in the literary world, the conservatives holding power in Beijing, and the populists finding their support in Shanghai.

Belated support for Peng Dehuai, and by implication criticism of Mao Zedong's role in the Great Leap Forward and Peng's dismissal, appeared in disguised form in a number of literary works in the early 1960s. The most controversial of these was the Peking opera *Hai Rui Dismissed from Office* by Wu Han, published in *Beijing Literature* in January 1961 with the support of Wu Han's patron, Peng Zhen, mayor of Beijing. *Hai Rui Dismissed from Office* illustrates the paradox that several of the most influential literary works of twentieth-century China – influential in the sense of affecting peoples' lives and the course of political history – were not written by professional writers but by academics or others with primary interests elsewhere. Hu Shi was an example from the New Culture movement; Wu Han is an example from fifty years on.

Wu Han was a prominent historian active in politics with the honorary position of deputy mayor of Peking. Peng Dehuai had voiced the concern of many senior Party personnel with Mao's populist and voluntarist policies which attempted to bypass bureaucratic procedures and the intellectuals who administered them. Wu Han, who had joined the Party in 1957, was joined by two such senior figures, Deng Tuo and Liao Mosha, in writing a series of essays critical of Mao's policies under the collective pseudonym Wu Nanxing, *Random Notes from the Three Family Village*, between 1961 and 1964 (published in book form in 1979). Even more outspoken, and more widely read, were another series of short essays by Deng Tuo under the unassuming title *Evening Chats at Yanshan*, first published in *Beijing Evening News* in 1961 and in book form in 1963 (a fuller edition appeared in 1979). Veiled attacks on Mao's policies were also contained in fiction, poetry and literary criticism. For example, Shao Quanlin, a vice-president of the Writers' Association and an influential literary critic in Liu Shaoqi's faction, promoted 'middle characters' in fiction, moving away from the Yan'an model in direct defiance of Mao's new directive, 'never forget class struggle'.

Faced with the opposition of his party colleagues, Mao's next move was to recruit his wife, Jiang Qing, defying a ban placed in Yan'an on her active involvement in politics. From 1961 on, Jiang Qing became increasingly powerful as Mao's agent, with her most immediate impact being on drama. A former actress in Shanghai, she denounced the survival of traditional theatre and set about creating a new theatre based on contemporary revolutionary plots featuring workers, peasants and soldiers. The first of these to appear was *The Red Lantern* in November 1963; described as a 'revolutionary Peking opera', it was followed in 1964 by two more operas, *Shajiabang* and *Taking Tiger Mountain by Strategy*, and the revolutionary ballet *The Red Detachment of Women*. Party leaders opposed to these developments tried to block them either by not attending the performances or by using their bureaucratic powers to delay their appearance.

While Mao's opponents were reluctant to air their disagreements in public, preferring passive resistance and innuendo, Mao's supporters were now on the offensive. In 1965, on Jiang Qing's instructions, one of her Shanghai radicals, the critic Yao Wenyuan, wrote 'A Critique of the New Historical Play *Hai Rui Dismissed from Office*'. History as allegory is a game in which more than one can play, and Yao Wenyuan was able very effectively to attack Hai Rui as a defender of a corrupt, 'feudal' regime – a reading to which there was little answer. Yao Wenyuan also claimed that in praising Hai Rui as a moral hero, Wu Han ignored the Marxist principle that it was the masses who made history, not individuals. Using rhetoric rather than logic, Yao Wenyuan then accused Wu Han of wanting to bring back the rule of the landlords and bourgeoisie. When Peng Zhen, who openly expressed his preference for traditional opera, managed to block publication of Yao Wenyuan's article in Beijing, Mao's next move was to use his Shanghai base, where the article was published in Shanghai's main newspaper, *Wenhui Daily*, in November 1965. A debate was conducted in the national press between December 1965 and February 1966, in which the Peng Zhen group succeeded in turning the focus away from the play towards a more general criticism of the level of historical studies.

Mao Zedong was not satisfied by the February report on Wu Han, and the campaign was re-launched in April and May 1966 with attacks by Yao Wenyuan and others on the *Three Family Village* and Deng Tuo's *Evening Chats at Yanshan* as well. Big-character posters were organised through the schools to criticise the three targets, even though the students had little idea at the time of the factional struggle behind the campaign. The Central Committee's Circular of 16 May, marking the beginning of the Cultural Revolution proper (although not published until 1967), renewed the attack on the three and extended it to include Peng Zhen by name. In this way, a skirmish conducted in terms of a literary debate signalled the commencement of one of the most spectacular dramas in Chinese history: the Great Proletarian Cultural Revolution.

Looking back over the previous seventeen years on the eve of the Cultural Revolution in November 1965, Zhou Yang defined the five great battles in literature and the arts as the *Life of Wu Xun* campaign, the criticism of *Dream of the Red Chamber* studies, the campaign against Hu Feng, the Anti-Rightist campaign targeting Ding Ling and Chen Qixia, and the campaign against the domination in the theatre of old operas in 1961–2. Even then, few people predicted the upheaval that was soon to come.

7

FICTION: SEARCHING FOR TYPICALITY

The War against Japan made a significant impact on Chinese fiction, as the patriotic mood generated by the war effort prompted many authors towards a more politicised mode of writing. Even those not in Yan'an, such as Ai Wu and Sha Ting in the south-west, and Xiao Jun, Duanmu Hongliang and Xiao Hong, who were based in the north-east, became sympathetic to the Communist cause. Ding Ling is a good example of those who followed the Yan'an line: after her autobiographical and subjective fiction of the late 1920s and experiments in politicised writing of the 1930s and early 1940s, she adopted the Yan'an model in the late 1940s. After 1949, however, even Ding Ling stopped writing fiction, along with most other May Fourth writers, although she continued to be active in literary politics. The field belonged to a younger generation of writers such as Zhao Shuli and Zhou Libo, who began their careers in the 1940s. With the exception of a few short stories such as Ru Zhijuan's 'Lilies', most fiction from the 1950s and 1960s has little literary merit. Most of the highly publicised writers of the 1950s and 1960s, such as Liu Baiyu (b. 1916), Du Pengcheng (b. 1921) and Wang Wenshi (b. 1921), gained prominence through their ability to write according to current policy. Other writers, including Ru Zhijuan, Hao Ran, Liu Binyan and Wang Meng, were not necessarily more skilful or creative but attracted more attention beyond China because of their challenges to political orthodoxy. What the two groups shared was a common preoccupation with politics, as increasingly after 1949 Liang Qichao's belief that fiction can make a difference to a nation's political fortunes was accepted as fact by both writers and politicians. The fact that the merging of the two activities led to a decline in writing skills and diversity was tacitly ignored by both.

Non-Communist writers either adopted other careers after 1949 or left China: Shen Congwen and Qian Zhongshu are examples of the former, Zhang Ailing of the latter. Other writers living outside the mainland in 1949 stayed there even though they were not necessarily anti-Communist: Xu Xu and Jin Yong, for example, became very popular in Hong Kong and among overseas Chinese, but since Jin Yong became prominent only after he left the mainland, his work is not discussed here.

Mao Dun (1896–1981)

Mao Dun's first collection of fiction after war broke out was *Fog*. He left Shanghai in 1938 and for the next few years travelled widely, stopping in Changsha, Wuhan, Guangzhou, Xinjiang, Yan'an, Chongqing, Hong Kong and Guilin. The novel *Decay* was published in 1941, during his stay in Hong Kong. In 1949 Mao Dun went to Beijing to join in preparations for the establishment of the People's Republic. He became the first Minister of Culture for the new government in 1949 and for the rest of his life (with an interruption during the Cultural Revolution) enjoyed numerous official posts in literature and arts. He continued to write essays and literary criticism, but his creative output came to an end in the 1940s.

The seven stories in *Fog* describe urban life in the north-east after the Japanese invasion in September 1931, revealing the sufferings endured by ordinary people such as clerks and rickshaw-pullers. *Decay*, by contrast, is about the life of secret agents in Chongqing between September 1940 and February 1941. Written in diary form, it is a study of the psychology of betrayal within the context of the political struggle between Nationalists and Communists during the resistance years. In the preface to the novel, the author claims to have found the diary in an air-raid shelter in Chongqing. The diarist is Zhao Huiming, a young woman who works undercover for the Nationalist government, and her entries record both her moral decay as she carries out her assignments (shown here as the persecution of innocent victims) and her inner confusion and conflicts. Her final awakening comes when she is made to spy on her true love from better times, who has been arrested for Communist activities. With her unwilling complicity, he is arrested, tortured and executed. Zhao Huiming's attitude then begins to change, and she decides to alert a university student who is about to be recruited by the secret police. The abrupt end to the diary at this point suggests that she too has been executed. Despite its setting, the novel is not a thriller but a fairly routine exercise in anti-Nationalist propaganda.

Mao Dun's later career as a literary politician and bureaucrat ensured that his fiction became a central part of the literary canon, and it continues to attract the attention of literary scholars. While his place in literary history is assured, however, he has little appeal to contemporary readers. (*For Mao Dun's early fiction see Chapter 4; for his plays of this period see Chapter 9.*)

Lao She (1899–1966)

At the outbreak of war in 1937, Lao She left Jinan for Wuhan and then Chongqing. Free from close identification with either the right or the left, he was a unanimous choice for president of the newly formed Chinese National Federation of Anti-Japanese Writers and Artists. During the war years, Lao She wrote mostly poetry, plays and essays. After the war came to an end, he set about writing what he hoped would be his greatest work: *Four Generations under One Roof*, published in three volumes between 1946 and 1950.

In 1946 Lao She and Cao Yu were invited to make a lecture tour in the United States. Cao Yu returned at the end of the tour but Lao She stayed on. Invited personally by Zhou Enlai in 1949 to serve in the new government, he returned to Beijing in December and was awarded important posts in cultural affairs. Unusually for writers in his age group, he also kept up an impressive literary output over the next few years. The most interesting of his fictional works is his last, *Beneath the Red Banner*, an unfinished novel written in 1961–2 but not published until 1979. Shortly after the onset of the Cultural Revolution, Lao She was beaten up by Red Guards in circumstances which suggest backing from higher authorities, and he became so despondent that he committed suicide.

Despite its length, *Four Generations under One Roof*, a description of life in a Beijing lane during the Japanese occupation, is not a great work. Lao She's anti-Japanese propaganda work had clearly left a strong impression on him: patriots suffer tremendously only to triumph in the end, while traitors and collaborators meet the fate they deserve. The Qi family enjoys the traditional good fortune of sheltering four generations in a large compound. Most of its members are reasonably honest and hard-working, and it has its fair share of good and bad characters. The Qi family could thus be said to represent Chinese families in general. Among their neighbours is the Guan family, in which only the master's concubine and his eldest daughter are innocent of treachery. Mr and Mrs Guan obtain power and wealth by betraying people such as their neighbour Qian Moyin, a middle-aged poet who is tortured by the Japanese but who escapes to lead an underground resistance movement. Also in the novel is a host of ordinary Beijing people such as teachers, waiters, removalists, policemen and rickshaw-pullers. The patriotic message dominates the characterisation, however, and the novel lacks the vitality of *Camel Xiangzi*.

An autobiographical fragment consisting of only eleven chapters, *Beneath the Red Banner* describes life in a Manchu banner (clan) at towards the end of the Qing dynasty. Banner men were hereditary imperial guards: while they were originally fierce soldiers who had conquered China, by Lao She's time they led dissolute lives in the cities. Because their actual duties and salaries may be minimal, banner men from wealthy families become useless and effete while poorer families find it difficult to survive. While the narrator himself does not leave the city, he reports the experiences of a younger Boxer from Shandong, so that the conflict between the Boxers and their foes – missionaries and Chinese Christians – is worked into the narrative. Rituals and customs of Manchu and other Beijing families are described in vivid detail. The novel breaks off when the narrator is still a child, but the reader is left with a fascinating account of life in a bygone age and the factors which caused it to disappear. (*For Lao She's early fiction see Chapter 4; for his plays in this period see Chapter 9.*)

Shen Congwen (1902–88)

Like Mao Dun, Shen Congwen stopped writing after 1949; unlike Mao Dun, he also withdrew from all political activities. He spent most of the war years in Yunnan as a teacher at the South-west United University. On the way to Yunnan he travelled extensively in Hunan, and *The Long River*, published in 1943, is a product of this time. In the same year, he published two short story collections and a collection of essays. After the war, he took up a teaching post at Beijing University, and thereafter devoted his time and energy to the study of Chinese artefacts, publishing several detailed works on subjects such as ancient Chinese costumes and art.

According to Shen Congwen, *The Long River* records what he heard and saw during four months in a small town along the river Yuanshui, as an idyllic society in the relatively untouched south-west copes with the momentous social changes that follow modernisation and resistance to Japan. The first chapter provides an overall view of the people who live here, from students to boatmen. The novel then focuses on Teng Changshun, who owns an orange grove, and his daughter Yaoyao. Their serene existence is threatened by the captain of the security forces, a city man who despises the local populace but lusts after Yaoyao. Shen Congwen captures the moment of change between modernity and tradition, showing the vulnerability of simple rural virtue to exploitation from the outside.

Shen Congwen's nostalgic pastoralism, shunned during the 1950s and 1960s, was revived as a target for attack during the Cultural Revolution. In the changed atmosphere of the 1980s, his work experienced a great revival, and his influence on writers such as Wang Zengqi and Ah Cheng is marked. (*For Shen Congwen's early fiction see Chapter 4.*)

Ding Ling (1904–86)

By the beginning of the war period, Shen Congwen and Ding Ling had long since parted company. On arrival at the liberated base area in 1936, Ding Ling was personally welcomed by Communist leaders such as Mao Zedong and Zhou Enlai. Among the positions she assumed, the most important were as head of the Chinese Literature and Arts Association and editor of the literature and arts supplement of *Liberation Daily*. She also continued to write short stories, reportage and polemical essays. As her power and influence increased, she was often the spokesperson for women and youth in cultural matters. At that time, she was accompanied by Chen Ming, who became her first legal husband. This also caused some scandal in Yan'an, since he was ten years younger than her.

Although her writings in the late 1930s and early 1940s moved away from the feminist and individualist concerns of her early works, they retain her concern for the plight of women and the ambiguous role of intellectuals in the revolutionary struggle. Her 1942 essay, 'Thoughts on March Eighth', expresses dismay at the inequality of women in the liberated areas; for her dissident views in this and other essays, Ding Ling became one of the major targets at the Yan'an Forum, held a few weeks later. Ding Ling accepted the criticism and although she disappeared from public view for several months, was able to continue writing. Over the next few years, she wrote mostly reportage on labour heroes and peasants, such as 'The Eighteen', on the heroic deeds of eighteen soldiers trapped behind enemy lines, published in July 1942. Eight stories based on her visits to the front were published under the title *Scenes from Northern Shaanxi* in 1948, the same year as her last novel, *The Sun Shines over the Sanggan River*. With this novel, Ding Ling's fame and prestige were restored: it won a Stalin Prize for Literature in 1951 and was translated into many languages. She went on an official visit to Moscow and Prague in 1949, and over the next few years held numerous official posts. As editor-in-chief of both the *Literary Gazette* and *People's Literature* she exerted considerable power on the formation of the new literary canon. As such she posed a threat to Zhou Yang's faction, and was criticised in 1955 as leader (with Chen Qixia) of an anti-Party clique. After the collapse of the Hundred Flowers campaign in 1958, she was banished to the Great Northern Wasteland (a desolate area in northern China), accompanied by Chen Ming. From this time, Ding Ling remained either in labour camps or in gaol until the end of the Cultural Revolution.

Ding Ling returned to Beijing in 1979 and resumed political life as a vice-chair of the Writers' Association. She visited the United States, Canada, France and Australia in an official capacity in the early 1980s, writing about her travels and giving many interviews. To the surprise of many who identified her as a liberal voice in the 1940s and 1950s, she was one of the very few literary figures who gave active support to the 1983 campaign against spiritual pollution, turning on younger writers who questioned the orthodoxies of that time. This made her extremely unpopular among writers in general, and at the Writers' Association congress in January 1985, she failed to be re-elected to the executive board. Realising how times had changed, she founded a new literary magazine *China* in 1985, inviting contributions from former underground writers such as Bei Dao, and courting controversy to the extent that the magazine was closed down in 1986, shortly before her death.

Ding Ling's engagement with Party politics throughout her life was characterised as much by orthodoxy as by dissent. A series of short stories extolling the virtues of Communist soldiers, including a sketch of General Peng Dehuai, appeared in 1936, followed the next year by one of several stories about young people during the war, 'The Unfired Bullet'. Based on a real event, this is the story of a young soldier who has lost touch with his unit in the Red Army and is given shelter in a village. His identity is revealed when Nationalist troops occupy the village, and the commanding officer gives the order to shoot him. The boy asks to be executed with a knife so that the bullet could be saved for fighting the Japanese invaders; moved by his patriotism, the officer spares his life.

Several of Ding Ling's Yan'an stories concern women. 'When I Was in Xia Village', published in 1941, is told in the first person by a narrator easily identified with Ding Ling herself. At Xia Village, where she is sent to recover her health, the narrator befriends Zhenzhen, a young woman who has just returned from the occupied areas where she has been operating as a spy for over a year. Zhenzhen tells the narrator her story. About to become ordained as a Catholic nun, she was raped by Japanese soldiers. She managed to escape, and after making contact with Red Army guerillas, she agreed to go back to the occupied areas and gather intelligence. Zhenzhen has returned to the village to receive treatment for the venereal disease she has contracted. The reaction of the villagers to her plight range from admiration from the younger people to downright hostility from the majority. An uplifting story of heroic self-sacrifice, at the same time it is also a reminder of traditional attitudes entrenched in the Chinese countryside. The protagonist is a triple victim of exploitation and discrimination: used by the Japanese and the guerillas, and shunned by the villagers. Like Ding Ling's earlier woman characters, the protagonist is not passive, however, and speaks up boldly in her own voice. An underlying theme of the story belongs to the narrator, whose loyalties are to her gender as a woman and to her profession as reporter, as well as to the Party. An entirely different type is the male reporter in her 1940 story 'Entering the Ranks': this reporter is depicted as a contemptible coward in sharp contrast to the ordinary rank and file soldier.

The woman reporter in 'Xia Village' suggests that the war effort and the Party are best served by honest and independent witness, but Ding Ling became more critical of intellectuals in her post-1942 fiction. *The Sun Shines over the Sanggan River*, the most famous novel of land reform in north China during the post-war period, contains a stinging portrait of an educated rural cadre, Wen Cai. Based on Ding Ling's personal experiences as a member of several land reform teams, the novel gives a panoramic view of the personalities and issues in the implementation of the reforms in a single village. A three-member land reform team arrives in Nuanshui in the summer of 1945. Problems begin immediately when the team leader, Wen Cai, refuses to take advice from the other team members, and the chair of the peasants' association is corrupted by his affair with the niece of the most powerful landlord in the village, Qian Wengui. Instead of rallying together against Qian Wengui, the peasants and cadres confiscate property from less powerful landlords, including the village head. The situation is only resolved when a county-level cadre arrives on the scene and Qian is overthrown. The novel closes with the villagers celebrating their victory over the landlords.

Ding Ling has never been renowned as a stylist, though in her early years she showed interest in narrative and characterisation, and the quality of her fiction is uneven. Her active political engagement and the scandals attached to her life and works have both contributed to her standing as China's most famous woman novelist. In her best writings, however, she drew public attention to aspects of women's lives that few other writers dared to tackle. (*For Ding Ling's early fiction see Chapter 4.*)

Ba Jin (b. 1904)

Ba Jin travelled a great deal during the war years, staying in turn in Guangzhou, Guilin, Kunming, Shanghai and Chongqing, but kept his distance from Yan'an. Unfettered by political restrictions, he also kept up a very respectable output during the war. The second volume in the *Torrents* trilogy, *Spring*, was published in 1938, followed by the final volume *Autumn* in 1940. Collections of essays and short stories also followed, and the novella *Pleasure Garden* appeared in 1944. Two years after this, two of Ba Jin's finest works, *Ward Four* and *Cold Nights*, were published: the latter was first serialised in *Literary Renaissance* and then published in book form the following year. *Ward Four* is based on his experiences in a hospital in Guiyang two years previously. It depicts the callousness and inhumanity in a ward for poor patients, where suffering and death pass unnoticed. The ward is clearly meant to be a microcosm of Chinese society at that time.

After 1949 Ba Jin was given important positions in United Front bodies like the People's Political Consultative Committee. To support the new regime he wrote a series of sketches praising Chinese soldiers in the Korean War in 1952 and 1953 but after this he more or less withdrew from creative writing. Persecuted with ferocity during the Cultural Revolution, he became one of the most highly regarded of the old guard in the 1980s, and was elected to the chair of the Writers' Association in January 1985. His *Reminiscences*, published serially during the 1980s, were warmly received.

Spring and *Autumn* continue the story of the Gao clan featured in *The Family*. In the former, two young women, Shuying and Hui, are brought up in large traditional families to be obedient young ladies. Although they come from similar backgrounds, Hui bows to authority while Shuying, under the influence of Juemin and Juehui, rebels. *Autumn* traces the final decline of the Gao family, a tale of bullied maids, suicide, failed marriages and broken families. Although the same themes are raised, the treatment is hackneyed and neither work reached the same level of popularity as *The Family*.

Like much of Ba Jin's fiction, *Pleasure Garden* is semi-autobiographical. According to Ba Jin, the garden itself is his childhood home and one of the central characters is modelled on one of his uncles. Even the name of the narrator, Mr Li, is a homonym of Ba Jin's real name (Li Feigan). Mr Li is depicted as a kind man who wants to do good in the world. Returning to his home town for the first time in sixteen years, he takes up residence in the Pleasure Garden, a mansion belonging to an old school friend, Yao Guodong. Yao's son, who neglects his schooling and leads an undisciplined life, is drowned in a storm. The narrator also encounters a grandson of the previous owner. The boy's father, Yang Mengchi, has squandered all his money and now lives in an old temple. When the narrator wants to help, however, Yang Mengchi runs away and dies in prison. The novel depicts the decline of the two families, prone to tragedy because they have lost the ability to manage their own lives.

By the time Ba Jin wrote *Cold Nights*, his anger at the Chinese middle classes seems to have softened. Whereas their decline has been depicted as a consequence of immorality in the *Torrents* trilogy or ineptness in *Pleasure Garden*, *Cold Nights* depicts the hardships imposed by war as an unavoidable factor in the destruction of individuals' hopes and dreams. *Cold Nights* also features a young woman, Zeng Shusheng, who runs away from her family. However, in this case, her husband Wang Wenxuan is not a tyrant but a weak man dying from tuberculosis. Both husband and wife have received a tertiary education, and initially live together unmarried as an act of conscious defiance of traditional morality. When they do get married and have a child, their family life is marred by poverty, job insecurity and constant quarelling between Zeng Shusheng and her mother-in-law. As Wang Wenxuan's health deteriorates, he loses his job as well, and life at home becomes unbearable. Zeng Shusheng decides to leave for Lanzhou with her boss. His wife's departure to follow her career is the final blow, and when she returns in disillusionment only a few months later, Wang Wenxuan is already dead. His son and mother have left Chongqing and cannot be found. While the atmosphere throughout the novel is thoroughly depressing, it represents a more mature approach by Ba Jin to human relationships, where superficial emancipation is not so much a solution to problems but their cause. (*For Ba Jin's early fiction see Chapter 4.*)

Sha Ting (1904–92)

Sha Ting (also known as Sha Ding) is the pen-name of Yang Zhaoxi, a native of Sichuan. Born into a landlord family, he was exposed to revolutionary ideas as a young man and joined the Communist Party in 1927. In 1929, he went to Shanghai, where he met Ai Wu, a former classmate. The two young writers sought the patronage of Lu Xun and Sha Ting joined the League of Left-wing Writers in 1932. After the War against Japan broke out, he worked for a short spell in Chengdu, then went to Yan'an in 1938 with He Qifang and Bian Zhilin. While in Yan'an, he worked briefly in the Lu Xun Academy before returning to Chongqing in 1939, which was his home until his death. From 1949 he was president of the Sichuan branch of the Writers' Association but produced little original work.

Sha Ting's most significant works were written in the early 1940s. Published in December 1940, the short story 'In Qixiangju Teahouse' is one of the best satirical portrayals of local politics in this period. Fang Zhiguo, the Ward Chief (i.e. the village head appointed by the local government), gets into an argument with Loudmouth Xing, a member of the local gentry. Hearing that the newly appointed county magistrate intends to reorganise the military, Fang sends him an anonymous letter informing him that Xing's son has earlier managed to avoid being drafted. As a consequence, the son is called up. Fang and Xing square off in the village teahouse and eventually come to blows. At this point they are told that Xing's son has been released, and it is clear that the magistrate has accepted a bribe from the powerful Xing family. Through the brawl between Fang, representing local officials, and Xing, representing the local gentry, Sha Ting reveals the contradictions within the middle classes in Nationalist China. The setting is in a typical Sichuan institution, the teahouse, and the action is confined within this space, but the message has national relevance.

Gold Rush was written the year after 'In Qixiangju Teahouse' but not published in book form until 1943. Set in a Sichuan gold mine during the War against Japan, it relates the conflict between competing interests to control the mine. The three main characters, He Guamu, Lin Yaochangzi and Longge, represent the landlords, the secret societies and the local gentry respectively. These people and their supporters use all sorts of methods to gain financial advantage. Even the secret societies, which are supposed to be righteous and just in their dealings with ordinary people, are shown to be facades for the ambitions of the leaders of popular movements. The novel is a fierce indictment of the middle-ranking ruling clique in Nationalist China.

Li Guangtian (1906–68)

Li Guangtian came from a poor family in Zouping, Shandong, and only managed to achieve an education after much struggle and privation. In 1921, he was accepted as a trainee teacher and was hired to teach in the local primary school. Abandoning his village, however, he entered the provincial normal college in Jinan, where he encountered the new literary movement. After graduation he joined the Communist Youth League and was arrested for spreading revolutionary propaganda; he was only saved from execution by the downfall of the warlord Zhang Zongchang in 1928. In 1930 he entered the Foreign Languages department at Beijing University, where he became friends with Bian Zhilin and He Qifang and published his first poems and prose. After graduation in 1933, he taught at a secondary school in Jinan, and spent most of the war years at the South-west United University in Kunming. His only novel, *Gravitation*, was published in Kunming after the war. Li Guangtian joined the Communist Party in 1948. In 1949-52 he taught at Qinghua University, then took up the post of chancellor at Yunnan University. Labelled a Rightist in 1959, his career never recovered, and his early death in 1968 was due to persecution during the Cultural Revolution.

Li Guangtian's poems and essays are known for their perceptive observation and deceptively simple style. His fictional output is not large, consisting of only two collections of short stories in addition to his novel. Many of the thirteen stories in *Pot of Gold*, published in 1946, read more like reminiscences or anecdotes than fiction. Li Guangtian's main subject is the lives of the poor and unfortunate in villages or small towns, whose individuality has been so thoroughly suppressed that they are defined only as members of a social matrix. In the story 'Nameless People', for instance, a village couple are known as 'Little Gu's pa' and 'Little Gu's ma'. Gradually they drop the 'pa' and 'ma', and continue to call each other by their son's name even after Gu dies. When the old man himself dies, nobody can remember his real name. Other stories introduce a note of fantasy. 'The Man Who Ate Stones', which contains references to Lu Xun's theme of cannibalism and to the Russian Revolution, relates the encounter between a Daoist monk who professes to eat stones and a group of schoolboys. 'A Sunless Morning', written in 1945, is the only story directly on the theme of class struggle in the countryside.

Gravitation describes the gradual conviction of the heroine, Huang Menghua, that she should leave her mother and her job as a school teacher in Japanese-occupied Jinan to join her husband, Lei Mengjian, in the interior. After much hardship, she arrives in Chengdu only to find that her husband has already left for a 'better place', leaving for her a note condemning the Nationalist government. Realising that she has only quit one dark society for another, she decides to follow Lei. Li Guangtian's attempt at full-length fiction was not a great success. Even though the novel is set in a time of tremendous social upheaval, events are only described as they impinge on the mind of the protagonist in a curiously detached third-person narrative. Huang Menghua is said to be based on Li's own wife who travelled from Jinan to join him in Kunming during the war, and the transformation of her compassion for individuals into political awareness is shown in depth. No other characters are developed, however, and the novel as a whole lacks pace.

Although he has been called a peasant writer, Li Guangtian is very much within the May Fourth stream of modern writers, educated to tertiary level and finding a career in academic life. To represent writers with a close involvement with the working life of the rural poor, we need to look writers from very different backgrounds who were fostered in the Communist base areas during the War against Japan. One of the first was Zhao Shuli. (*For Li Guangtian's poetry see Chapter 3.*)

Zhao Shuli (1906–70)

Born in Qinshui, Shanxi, Zhao Shuli is one of the most accomplished writers from the Chinese rural interior. Usually also described as coming from a peasant family, his father did not work in the fields but made a living as an itinerant fortune-teller, selling herbal medicines and entertaining villages audiences with the local form of storytelling known as 'quicksticks' (rhyming couplets, often satirical, chanted to regular beats of a pair of clappers). After graduating from the local primary school in 1923, Zhao Shuli first taught in a village school before entering teacher's college in 1925. It was at this time that he first came in contact with the May Fourth Movement and began to take part in political activities. In 1926 he was expelled for his part in a student protest movement and in 1929 was imprisoned for over a year on suspicion of being a member of the Communist Party (to which he was admitted in 1937). He began publishing short stories after his release from prison in 1930, at the same time polishing his skills as a storyteller in local performance troupes. His early fictional pieces were about peasant life and the anti-Japanese war effort. Moving to Communist headquarters in Yan'an, he was first employed as a journalist, one of many local people recruited and trained to work as low-level cadres. At a conference in January 1942, shortly before the Yan'an Forum, Zhao Shuli strongly supported the popularisation of art and literature among the peasantry, and his own writing career received a great boost as a result of the policies adopted after the Forum. Two of his most famous works, 'The Marriage of Young Blacky' and 'Rhymes of Li Youcai', were published in 1943, followed by a playscript, two short story collections, *Land* (1946) and *Lucky* (1947), and the novel *Changes in Li Village* (1947). His literary output was praised by the Communist leadership for its success in describing the peasants' struggles in a sympathetic and lively manner, using traditional story-telling techniques and incorporating the Communist Party's political line, and well into the 1950s Zhao was regarded as a model writer.

After 1949, Zhao Shuli was appointed to a number of important positions in literature and the arts, such as president of the Folk Art Workers' Association and editor-in-chief of the monthly journals *Story-telling* and *Performance Arts*. It was in the former that some of his most significant short stories of the 1950s first appeared, such as 'Registration'. He also wrote story-telling scripts, essays and influential novels such as *Sanliwan* (1955). Zhao Shuli came in for criticism in the early 1960s, partly for his association with Shao Quanlin's promotion of 'middle characters' (his 1958 short story 'Improve Yourself through Training' was said to contain an abundance of 'middle characters') and partly also for continuing to feature traditional characters, such as Lord Guan (the god of war) talented scholars and beautiful courtesans in *Performance Arts*. He was subjected to even stronger criticism during the Cultural Revolution, despite his Yan'an credentials, and he died in Taiyuan in 1970, apparently as a result of harsh treatment while under house arrest.

Zhao Shuli's fiction celebrates the triumph of socialist policies over traditional thinking and practices in rural areas. Although his stories promote the new society, their popularity among audiences and critics was largely due to his adaptations of traditional themes and techniques. The frustrations experienced by young people whose wedding plans are blocked by superstitious parents is a theme which can be found in traditional literature but is particularly associated with May Fourth, where it often appears as tragedy. Zhao Shuli gives an old story a new twist. The two lovers in 'The Marriage of Young Blacky', Young Blacky and Xiao Qin, are well matched in their progressive views as well as by their youth and wit. By contrast, Blacky's father, nicknamed Kong Ming the Second after the cleverest strategist in Chinese history, believes in astrology, while Xiao Qin's mother, a shaman whose nickname is Immortal Fairy the Third, wears heavy make-up and flirts with the young men who flock around her daughter. Blacky's father opposes his marital plans because the young couple's astrological signs are inauspiciously matched; Xiao Qin's mother wants to marry her off to an army officer. The parents find support in a pair of local reactionaries who collaborate with the Japanese. In keeping with Yan'an directives, the story ends happily when Communist Party officials come to the rescue and in the process of aiding the marriage also arrest the collaborators.

The timely intervention of Communist cadres is also featured in 'The Rhymes of Li Youcai', on the transformation of remote and poor villages under Communist rule. Li Youcai is a poor herdsman who is also the most accomplished storyteller in the village. Employing the local style 'quicksticks', he comments on the action and characters throughout the story. The most powerful landowner in the village, Yan Hengyuan, has retained his power by bullying the poor peasants and fooling the young cadre left in charge. Li Youcai's witty rhymes help the villagers keep up their fighting spirits, but the situation is only solved with the arrival of the experienced revolutionary Comrade Yang, who finds out what is happening by mixing with the poor peasants. The characterisation is strictly aligned with class status (poor peasants are good, rich peasants are bad, and those in the middle are in the middle) but the characters themselves are credible and sympathetic. A major policy directive of the Rectification campaign, on the importance of mass action under Communist leadership, is adroitly incorporated in what thereafter becomes a formula for post-1942 fiction and drama. In form, the story also follows Yan'an directives. The tone of the third-person narrative is in harmony with the story-telling style practised by Li Youcai himself, creating the illusion that narrator, characters and audience are all members of the same big village: there is minimal description of the characters and setting, for example, implying both that we are all familiar with them and at the same time that it is a story which could take place in any village in China. The use of language is particularly skilful, blending oral/colloquial and written/literary expressions, employing localisms only to the extent that they are self-explanatory, and mixing traditional references with contemporary political terminology. It avoids on the one hand the vulgarity and obscenity characteristic of traditional folk narrative and at the same time the Westernised vocabulary and grammar of standard May Fourth writing. The narrator rarely strays outside the world portrayed in the story even in regard to narrative tone: the narrative sticks to the convention in traditional fiction in making no attempt to portray the characters' inner states of mind (for example, by interior monologue), and the metaphors employed in the narrative, dialogue and rhymes are mostly of a work or domestic nature. This internal consistency helps to convince readers of the author's familiarity with village life and adds greatly to the local colour that gives the story its main appeal.

The same formula is adopted in *Changes in Li Village* but the narrative is more conventionalised as the author addresses himself to a national audience perceived as readers rather than listeners. The novel relates the long-standing conflict between Zhang Tiesuo, a poor peasant, and Li Ruzhen, the local landowner, against the background of class struggle in the village, warlord and Nationalist rule, the War against Japan, and the impending Civil War. The long-suffering peasants unite under the guidance of a Communist organiser as the village is attacked in turn by Japanese and Nationalist troops. In the end, the peasants win and Li Ruzhen is executed.

Zhao Shuli returns to the theme of love and marriage in 'Registration', written shortly after the new Marriage Law was promulgated. Xiao Fei'e discovers on New Year's Eve that her daughter Ai'ai has exchanged tokens of love with a young man according to local custom. She recalls how she had done the same as a young girl but was later married to another man who took offence at her indiscretion and beat her brutally. Xiao Fei'e and her husband want to arrange a marriage for their daughter but Ai'ai refuses. Her friend Yanyan, who is facing a similar problem, persuades the parents to let Ai'ai choose her own husband, but the village administration withholds the marriage certificate because the official in charge is the uncle of the man whom Ai'ai has refused. The introduction of the new Marriage Law at this point in the story allows Ai'ai and her sweetheart to marry without having to get permission from the authorities, and Yanyan also persuades her mother to let her do the same.

The new modes of courtship and marriage are also central to *Sanliwan*, where the action takes place against the collectivisation movement in the villages in the early 1950s. The novel shows how three young couples gain political awareness in the course of their romantic entanglements. As they sort themselves out, their families also learn to be less selfish and to support the collectivisation programme.

'Improve Yourself through Training' is Zhao Shuli's response to a 1957 Rectification campaign aimed at village cadres whose selfish or compromising attitudes slow down rural reform. The story begins with Yang Xiaosi, deputy leader in the village brigade, launching the campaign with a big-character poster criticising 'Sore Leg Muscles' and 'Always Hungry', the nicknames of two women who hang back from participating in productive labour. The poster causes a storm, and the brigade leader, Wang Juhai, whose main concern is to maintain the peace, is prepared to compromise. In the end Yang Xiaosi is appointed leader and a meeting is held to criticise the two women. As a result, the political consciousness of the commune members is raised and production goes up.

Zhao Shuli's support for the literary politics of the 1950s and early 1960s ensured the mass publication of his works at that time. In the 1980s his work was generally dismissed by critics as little more than propaganda, but it seems likely that his Yan'an fiction will be remembered for its contribution to the creation of a new written language to represent peasant speech in modern Chinese fiction. Writers of the 1950s and 1960s like Zhou Libo built on Zhao Shuli's achievements while lacking the knowledge and experience that made Zhao's early work lively and persuasive.

Zhou Libo (1908–79)

Zhou Libo is the pen-name of Zhou Shaoyi, born in Yiyang, Hunan. After finishing secondary school, he taught arithmetic in a primary school in Yiyang before going to Shanghai in 1928 with his friend Zhou Yang, also from Yiyang. He entered Shanghai Labour University the following year but was expelled shortly after for his political activities. In 1933 he was arrested for taking part in a strike, and joined the Communist Party after his release in August 1934.

Zhou Libo also joined the League of Left-wing Writers in 1934, translating Russian fiction into Chinese and editing League journals. Between 1937 and 1939 he travelled widely in China, collecting materials on behalf of the Communist Party in places including Xi'an, Guilin and Wuhan. He arrived in Yan'an in 1939, and stayed there for the remainder of the war years. His first story, 'Water Buffalo', was published in 1941, and he was appointed editor of the literary supplement of *Liberation Daily* in 1944. In 1946 Zhou Libo was transferred to north-east China to take part in land reform, and wrote up his experiences in *The Hurricane*, a two-part novel published in 1948 and 1949. Zhou Libo's literary reputation was confirmed when his novel was awarded a Stalin Prize in 1951.

Zhou Libo's second novel, *The River of Iron* (1955), based on a few months' stay at Shijingshan Steel Plant in 1951, had little impact and Zhou moved back to Yiyang, where he produced idealised stories of peasant life such as 'The Family on the Other Side of the Mountain' in 1958. His major work is *Great Changes in a Mountain Village*, published in two parts in 1958 and 1960. During the Cultural Revolution he spent some time in prison, but on his release in the late 1970s returned to Beijing to became a powerful figure in the literary world. His award-winning story on the 1945 victories of the Eighth Route Army, 'A Night at Xiang River' (1978), was his last work, and he died the following year.

Zhou Libo's novels are all based on national policies current at the time of writing. In Part I of *The Hurricane*, the peasants under the leadership of the Communist Xiao Xiang successfully carry out the first stage of land reform at the expense of the local landlord, Han Laoliu. Part II illustrates the difficulties in adjusting to the new life, as the leader of the Peasants' Association uses his position for personal gain. The characterisation follows closely the Yan'an directive that poor peasants must be presented in a positive light, and the novel comes to a triumphal conclusion. Zhou Libo's naturalistic descriptions of village life and his use of the north-east dialect show the influence of both Zhao Shuli and the May Fourth realists of the 1930s.

The River of Iron depicts the reconstruction of the industrial sector in the early years after 1949. The protagonist, Li Dagui, a former scout for the PLA, approaches his duties at the factory with the same dedication, working tirelessly for the Communist cause. He encourages his fellow workers to repair a generator in record time so that production can continue and at the same time defeats enemy agents with his wit and courage. The novel also features a demobilised PLA political commissar, Liu Yaoxian, who though having no knowledge about the industry soon becomes an expert. The same is not true of the author.

Great Changes in a Mountain Village is a long polemic on the collectivisation movement in a remote village. Deng Xiumei is given a nine-day briefing session on collectivisation before going to Qingxi Village as Deputy Party Secretary. On her way she meets peasants cutting down bamboo plants to sell before they are taken over by the collective, while rumours that even wives are to be shared are causing poor peasants to oppose the move. Under her guidance, the collective eventually takes shape with Liu Yusheng as leader and Xie Qingyuan as his deputy. Xie Qingyuan's enthusiasm is undermined by the villain, Gong Ziyuan, whose background is not known by the villagers. When Xie Qingyuan changes his mind again, his wife leaves him, and his misfortunes are compounded when his water buffalo is attacked. Despondent, Xie tries to kill himself but is saved by Liu Yusheng, who further proves his valour by risking his life when the village is flooded. In the end, Gong Ziyuan is unmasked as a Nationalist agent and former merchant-landlord, and the village makes further progress towards collectivisation.

'The Family on the Other Side of the Mountain' is a good example of Zhou Libo's skilful use of local idiom and customs. While delivering the message that the new society promotes simple weddings, the story also conveys the joyous mood of the young men and women on their way to the wedding party, and the descriptions of traditional customs are given with sympathy and understanding. Zhou Libo is almost unread today, but like Zhao Shuli his writing may be popular again when the political themes in his fiction no longer raise painful memories.

Ouyang Shan (b. 1908)

Ouyang Shan is the pen–name of Yang Fengqi, a native of Jingzhou, Hubei. He moved to Guangzhou in 1922 where he attended middle school, and in 1924 wrote his first short story 'That Night'. He went to Beijing in 1925 but returned to Guangzhou to participate in the Guangdong–Hong Kong general strike. He founded *Guangzhou Literature* in 1926, and attended Lu Xun's lectures at Sun Yatsen University in 1927. He wrote several novels and short story collections in the late 1920s and early 1930s, including the novel *Bamboo Ruler and Iron Hammer* (1931). These early works were heavily influenced by European thinking and syntax. Following the Communist Party's call to write in a language closer to the masses, Ouyang also tried to write in the Cantonese dialect, his 1933 novel *One-eyed Tiger* being the best known example.

Ouyang went to Shanghai in 1933 and became a member the League of Left-wing Writers. He joined the Communist Party in 1938 and in 1940 went to Yan'an. After the Yan'an Forum he took part in land reform in a Shaanxi village, which became the setting for *Uncle Gao* (1947). Ouyang Shan returned to Guangzhou after 1949 where he was appointed president of the South China Literary Association and editor-in-chief of *Literary Works*. *Romance of a Generation* is his most ambitious project of the post-1949 period: Part I was published in 1959 and a further three parts had appeared by 1964. Some two hundred chapters still in manuscript form were lost during the Cultural Revolution, when Ouyang Shan was at a cadres' school, but he completed three more volumes, which appeared in 1981, 1983 and 1985.

Although Ouyang Shan's writings span several decades and he has produced over thirty books, he is best known for his Yan'an fiction. *Uncle Gao* was the first major work by Ouyang Shan to follow Yan'an Forum directives: it incorporates Shaanxi dialect and is set wholly within the contemporary struggles in the transformation of the countryside. Big Uncle Gao, the deputy head of the Renjia Valley cooperative in 1941, sets up a medical unit which is so successful that he expands its activities into other areas. He meets opposition from several quarters: the co-op head who suffers from bureaucratic inertia, a village sorcerer who practises traditional medicine and feels threatened by the new methods, local gangsters and sundry rascals. In the end, Gao persuades the villagers that the cooperative can be made economically viable. Like most fiction of this period, the peasant and Party characters are portrayed as realistic types, with human weaknesses as well as strengths.

Romance of a Generation provides a panoramic view of China between 1919 and 1949 through the experiences of a working–class intellectual, Zhou Bing. The first part, published under the title *Three Family Lane*, is set in a lane in Guangzhou inhabited by three families: the landlord gentry He family, who occupy a grand mansion; the compradore-capitalist Chen family, who live in a three-storey house; and the working-class Zhou family, who live in a shack. In Part II, *Bitter Struggle*, Zhou Bing goes to Shanghai in an unsuccessful attempt to establish contact with the Communist Party but finally joins up on returning to Guangzhou on the eve of the War against Japan. In Part III, *Bright Flowers among the Willow Shades*, Zhou Bing organises the Guangzhou textile workers but is arrested during a demonstration calling for a boycott of Japanese goods. He escapes and joins the anti-Japanese resistance, where he meets up with Hu Xing, the heroine, who has led a group of young people to Yan'an. Zhou Bing and Hu Xing fall in love in Part IV, *The Sacred Land*, which covers the period from the War against Japan to the Civil War. Zhou Bing and Hu Xing take part in land reform in the north-west in Part V *Evergreen*, which ends with their marriage and the reunion of three generations in *Three Family Lane*.

Xu Xu (1908–80)

Xu Xu was born in Cixi, Zhejiang. After graduating in philosophy from Beijing University in 1931, he stayed on a further two years to study psychology. He then moved to Shanghai to begin his literary career as an editor, collaborating with Lin Yutang on the journals *The Analects* and *This Human World*. Later he co-edited their successor, *Airs of the Universe*, with Lin Yutang's brother in Shanghai and Hong Kong. He left for France in 1936 for further studies in philosophy, and obtained a Ph.D. from the University of Paris. He returned to China after the outbreak of the War against Japan, moving from Shanghai to Chongqing, and from 1944 to 1946 worked in the United States as a foreign correspondent. He left the mainland in 1950, and spent his last years as dean of the School of Arts at Hong Kong Baptist College.

His writing career was long, spanning several decades and producing numerous works of fiction, poetry and prose. His most famous works are *Ghostly Love* (1937), *The Rustling Wind*, which became a bestseller on publication in 1944, and *Characters in Society* (1960). Xu Xu also wrote poetry, switching back and forth between classical and vernacular styles. Five short volumes of poems written between 1942 and 1944 were published in 1948 under the collective title *Poetry at Forty*: his achievement here is to write poetry in the vernacular within rules of formal structure as strictly applied as in classical verse.

Xu Xu's popularity as a writer comes partly from placing traditional themes in modern settings. The narrator of *Ghostly Love*, for example, relates in a thoroughly modern manner one of the oldest plots in Chinese fiction. One night he encounters a mysterious woman who tells him she is a ghost. Fascinated by her beauty but also frustrated because of her distance, he seeks solace in pleasures of the flesh and solitary drinking. By chance he meets her one day dressed as a nun. She explains that she was formerly a revolutionary, but that after her lover was executed she has become dead to the world. She then disappears and he collapses: although she sends flowers during his illness, they never meet again.

Another reason that Xu Xu's novels became bestsellers is their ability to entertain. Despite his interest in psychology, Xu Xu does not indulge in the soul-searching or social analysis characteristic of May Fourth fiction. *The Rustling Wind*, set in Shanghai under Japanese occupation, exploits the tense atmosphere mainly as the background to intrigue and romance. The narrator, whose surname is Xu, counts among his wide acquaintance foreigners, socialites and entertainers. He suspects Baiping, a beautiful nightclub hostess, of being a Japanese spy because she entertains Japanese army officers, and tries to obtain secret documents from her. When he finds out that Baiping is an undercover agent for the Chinese government, she is killed by a Japanese spy (another beautiful woman). The narrator escapes to the interior while another friend, also a beautiful Chinese agent, remains in Shanghai to continue her espionage work. As this summary shows, the plot is contrived but the pace and glamour were very appealing to younger readers.

Like his associate Lin Yutang, Xu Xu has never been regarded as a major actor in literary circles, since detachment, wit and lightness of spirit have always been his preferred tone. Nevertheless, both his poetry and fiction remain consistently in print.

Qin Shou'ou (b. 1908)

Qin Shou'ou is the pen-name of Qin Hao, born in Shanghai. After studying in several business colleges in Shanghai he had a succession of jobs including teaching and editorial work. He was also a prolific writer in the Mandarin Ducks and Butterflies style. His best-known works include the novel *Endangered City*, the screenplay *Couples in Adversity* and the novel *Begonia*, later adapted as a play and as a film. First serialised in *Shen bao* in 1941, *Begonia* was published in book form in 1942, and several revised editions appeared within the next few years. Qin moved to Guilin in 1944 and to Hong Kong after 1949.

The plot of *Begonia* begins in the early 1920s as a young Peking opera performer known by his stage name Qiuhaitang (Begonia) finishes his training as a specialist in female roles. Despite the dubious reputation of female impersonators, Qiuhaitang is a morally upright man who does not encourage advances from suitors of either sex. He appears to compromise himself, however, by falling in love with the concubine of a local warlord. After their affair is discovered and she gives birth to his child, the warlord takes vengeance on Qiuhaitang by disfiguring him. His acting career in ruins, he retreats into the countryside with his daughter Meibao, living on his savings and working as a peasant. Meibao grows up into a beautiful young woman. They return to Shanghai where Qiuhaitang falls ill with tuberculosis and Meibao secretly finds work as a singer in a Shanghai teahouse to support them. There she is found by her mother, who has been looking for her since the warlord died some years before. Mother and daughter rush back to Qiuhaitang, but in true melodramatic fashion, they find him lying dead after having leapt from a rooftop. The plot details vary in several respects in different versions of the tale, especially in the ending, but the essential nobility of the three central characters is upheld. Qin also wanted the social message of the novel to be taken seriously, and although warlords and their retinues are easy targets, the contrast between the social degradation of the hero and heroines and their inner purity is both dramatically striking and psychologically convincing. (*For* Begonia *on stage see Chapter 9.*)

Jin Yi (1909–59) and Yao Xueyin (b. 1910)

Jin Yi and Yao Xueyin can be grouped together with Qian Zhongshu as academics who wrote serious fiction without excessive tendentiousness. Jin Yi is the pen-name of Zhang Fangxu, who was born and brought up in Tianjin. After graduating from secondary school he moved to Shanghai where he studied foreign trade at Fudan University. Together with Ba Jin and Zheng Zhenduo, he edited a succession of literary journals in the 1930s such as the *Literature Quarterly* and also published several short story collections. Jin's early work focuses on interpersonal relationships and shows a tendency towards sentimentality. *Snowstorm in the Faraway Sky* (1937), for example, is a collection of stories dedicated to the memory of the author's mother. Although they can be read independently, the stories explore the emotional bonds between mother and son. Jin Yi became increasingly left-wing in the late 1930s, and his 1942 novel *Before Dawn* shows the effect of the War against Japan on members of a large urban family. After 1949, Jin Yi was appointed secretary of the Writers' Association and held several important editorial posts, but he wrote little creative work.

Before Dawn is about the changes which beset the wealthy Huang family as a result of the Japanese invasion: the family's decline parallels national events and the characters stand for a range of contemporary social types. Huang Jianzhi is a former high official from the old society who grieves over his lost status. He has one son and five daughters, who are educated in modern schools and universities. Under the influence of Schopenhauer's philosophy of pessimism and denial, the son neglects his wife, and it is only when she dies in childbirth that he realises he loves her. He ends up joining the guerrilla forces to fight the Japanese. Two of the daughters revel in the pleasures of high society, and one marries a collaborator. Two other daughters respectively try to save the family and to establish her own life. The youngest daughter is the heroine of the novel: she is an idealistic revolutionary who takes part in the resistance movement. With the outbreak of full-scale war against Japan, however, the family is doomed. The message of the novel is that personal liberation can only come as a result of national salvation.

Yao Xueyin was born in Dengxian, Henan. His first contact with politics took place when he attended preparatory classes at Henan University, when he was briefly imprisoned for taking part in the student movement. One of his first literary works to gain attention was the short story 'Half a Cartload of Straw Short' (1938), which shows the increasing participation by peasants in the anti-Japanese war effort. Anticipating the Yan'an Forum directives, Yao successfully incorporated elements of the northern dialect in representing peasant speech. He was appointed associate professor of North-eastern University in 1945 and became a full-time writer in 1951. Labelled a Rightist in 1957, he began planning a five-volume historical novel, *Li Zicheng*, on the famous peasant insurrection at the end of the Ming dynasty. Volume 1 was published in 1963; Volume 2, which won a 1982 Mao Dun Literary Prize, in 1977; and Volume 3 in 1981; the remaining two volumes are still being written. The novel generated heated debate among historians in the 1960s and 1970s on the proper interpretation of peasant leaders in the past.

Qian Zhongshu (b. 1910)

Born in Wuxi, Jiangsu, Qian Zhongshu graduated from the foreign languages department at Qinghua University in 1933 and spent several years in Europe, studying literature at Oxford and the Sorbonne. He returned to China in 1938 and taught foreign languages at various universities. The short story collection *Men, Beasts and Ghosts* was published in 1946, followed by the novel *Fortress Besieged* which was serialised in 1946–7. After these two works, he published mainly essays and literary criticism. Like Shen Congwen, he gave up creative writing after 1949 and concentrated on classical studies. Beginning with a volume on Song poetry in 1950, he wrote a number of books on traditional and comparative literature. He has also held many influential academic positions since 1949, including a professorship in Qinghua University and a research fellowship at Beijing University, and since 1982 he has been a deputy president of the Academy of Social Sciences.

Qian Zhongshu displays his knowledge of Western and Chinese literary traditions very clearly in his two volumes of fiction. The first story in *Men, Beasts and Ghosts*, 'God's Dream', is a satirical version of creation myths. God has a dream in which he first creates a man and a woman from clay, and then creates animals in order to subdue the humans. Athough he is omnipotent, however, he finds himself unable to control either the people or the animals. The theme of dream and illusion in contrast to reality is also evident in 'Inspiration', where reincarnation is used as a device to portray the vanity and mediocrity of writers in the 1920s and 1930s. 'Souvenir' is an example of Qian's cynicism about love and marriage. A conceited young woman has an affair with her husband's cousin and becomes pregnant; when the cousin dies, her husband, unaware of his wife's infidelity, wants to honour him by naming the baby after him. The longest and most influential story in the collection, 'The Cat', shows the futility and emptiness of Westernised intellectuals. Aimo is a graduate of a modern women's college run by Americans, and her husband, Li Jianhou, had studied in the United States. Bored with his life of leisure, Li Jianhou engages a young writer, Qi Yigu, to help him record his reminiscences of his travels abroad, but Qi Yigu is attracted by Aimo, who flirts with him. Li Jianhou is disgusted by this behaviour and takes another woman to Shanghai. In the end, both husband and wife feel deceived and unsatisfied.

Qian Zhongshu's unflattering portrayal of pretentious intellectuals is sustained in *Fortress Besieged*. The protagonist, Fang Hongjian, has spent four years in three universities in Europe. He returns to China on the eve of the War against Japan with a fake Ph.D. certificate. On the boat home, he is attracted to Su Wenwan, but when this does not lead anywhere, he has an affair with a Hong Kong woman. When he arrives in Shanghai, he meets Su Wenwan again and tries to strike up a relationship with her cousin. After this fails, he obtains a position in a university in Hunan, where he has a series of romantic entanglements with other staff members, finally marrying the devoted Sun Roujia. At the same time, he makes powerful enemies at the university and is dismissed. The couple, already estranged, return to Shanghai, but more family problems arise and eventually Sun Roujia leaves him. Fang Hongjian and his associates are shown to be pathetic individuals lacking in any moral strength. Even when they want to lead honest and decent lives, they lack the ability to do so successfully.

In principle, Qian's critique of contemporary intellectuals could have been interpreted as a Marxist attack on the petty bourgeoisie, but left-wing intellectuals found his unremittingly sarcastic tone uncomfortably close to the mark. It is not surprising, therefore, that although *Fortress Besieged* has been highly praised by critics for its elaborate structure and brilliant metaphorical flourishes, it was not available in China until a revised version was published in 1980.

Xiao Hong (1911–42)

The north-east was represented by two writers during this period, Xiao Hong and Duanmu Hongliang. Xiao Hong went to Japan for a few months in 1936 to recover from an illness. She returned to Shanghai in the beginning of 1937 and later the same year moved to Wuhan, where she edited the monthly *July* jointly with Duanmu Hongliang and Hu Feng. In 1938 she divorced Xiao Jun and married Duanmu Hongliang. As Wuhan fell to the Japanese, Xiao Hong and Duanmu Hongliang fled to Chongqing, and then finally in 1940 to Hong Kong, where she died two years later. Xiao Hong was extremely productive during the early war years. Her last short story collection, *A Cry in the Wilderness*, was published in 1940, followed by the two-part novel *Ma Bole* and her most famous work, *Tales of Hulan River*, in 1941.

The title story in *A Cry in the Wilderness* is typical of Xiao Hong's short stories in its presentation of the personal ordeals of ordinary people during the War against Japan. An old couple are greatly troubled one stormy evening, fearing that their only son has gone to join the anti-Japanese forces. He returns carrying two pheasants and claims to have been out hunting, and the old couple relax, not knowing that he has been making preparations to sabotage a Japanese train carrying ammunition. The story ends with the news that some railway workers have been arrested for causing the derailment of a train. The old couple are again deeply troubled, looking and praying for their son.

Ma Bole also takes as its background the War against Japan but is set in a well-to-do family, which becomes the target for the author's satire on middle-class hypocrisy. Ma Bole's father is a member of a former gentry family from Qingdao who has converted to Christianity in order to appear Western, and his son grows up amid protestations of Christian love as a cover for the family's selfish ways. Educated in a Westernised school, Ma Bole likes to think of himself as a modern left-wing intellectual and aspires to fame as an anti-Japanese writer. As the enemy advances, however, he is exposed as a coward, running from one city after another.

In the semi-autobiographical *Tales of Hulan River*, written in Hong Kong, Xiao Hong returns to a mood of nostalgia for the north-east where she grew up. While some of the sketches portray the backwardness still to be found in provincial towns, the reminiscences of her grandfather show the author's attachment to country people and her respect for their ability to survive the harsh conditions in Heilongjiang. These people are trapped in their superstitious beliefs and lead alienated lives, but there are heroic individuals among them who are prepared to defy tradition. Despite Xiao Hong's original rejection of this society, distance has softened her attitude to such an extent that the sketches are as poetic and haunting as their probable model, Turgenev's *A Hunter's Notes*. Her death through illness was a sad loss. (*For details of Xiao Hong's earlier life and work see Chapter 4.*)

Duanmu Hongliang (1912–96)

Duanmu Hongliang is the pen-name of Cao Jiajing, born in Changtu, Liaoning. He attended secondary school in Tianjin but was expelled in 1931 for his anti-Japanese activities. In 1932 he went to Beijing to study at Qinghua University. He began writing in the early 1930s and became a member of the League of Left-wing Writers in 1932. His first collection of short stories was published under the title *Hatred* in 1937, followed by the novel *The Sea of Earth* in 1938. In the same year he was appointed to teach at Fudan University, which had moved to its wartime location in Chongqing. His best-known novel, *The Korchin Banner Steppe*, which had occupied him for several years, was published in Shanghai in 1939 along with his second short story collection, *Fengling*

Ferry. He moved to Hong Kong in 1940 with Xiao Hong, and after her death in 1942 travelled widely, visiting Guilin, Wuhan, Changsha and Shanghai. He returned to Beijing in 1949 and was appointed deputy director of the Publications Bureau and editor of *Beijing Literature*. Since 1949 he has written little apart from traditional opera scripts and historical novels.

Most of Duanmu Hongliang's stories are set in north-east China under Japanese occupation in the late 1930s and early 1940s, and feature cruelty and violence. Many are written from the perspective of children, highlighting the message that those who are most affected by the violent times are the innocent. The title story is about a boy who is so incensed by the sadistic behaviour of two of the local landlord's agents that he sets a shack on fire when the men are inside. Other stories in *Hatred* depict the Japanese invaders as the source of the hatred and sorrow that permeate the book. Hatred against the Japanese is also the theme of the title story of *Fengling Ferry*, which ends with a fisherman laughing wildly as he and two drunken Japanese soldiers drown in the surging waters of the flood-swollen Yellow River. The other main theme in *Fengling Ferry* is the difficulty of personal relationships in the corruption of the modern city.

The Sea of Earth is set in a small village in the north-east on the eve of Japanese occupation, and begins with an extended description of the land and its inhabitants. While their way of life is depicted as primitive, it is nevertheless idyllic, but the natural order is shattered by the invaders. The central characters are an old man and his two sons. Both sons love the same woman, Xingzi, and the tension between them is aggravated when one son collaborates with the Japanese while the other hates them. The moral depravity of collaborators is implied when one of the most powerful pro-Japanese characters murders Xingzi. The villagers rise up against the Japanese but the rebellion is suppressed. The patriotic father and son take to the hills and eventually join the anti-Japanese Volunteer Army.

Not published until 1939, *The Korchin Banner Steppe* was completed in 1933 when Duanmu Hongliang was only twenty-one. It also ends with one of the heroes joining the anti-Japanese forces, but its main theme is the rise and decline of the wealthy Ding family in Liaoning, a region which under the Qing had been assigned to the Mongols of the Korchin banner (clan). The protagonist, Ding Ning, is a young man who has returned from studying in the south, where he has come into contact with the new ideas of freedom and liberation. Ding Ning is repelled by his family's abuse of power and disgusted with its moral depravity, especially as revealed by the sad lot of its women. When his father dies, Ding Ning nevertheless assumes his role as head of the family. Disgust turns to depression when each of the two young women he befriends meets a tragic death, and his maid, whom he has made pregnant, is forced by his mother to drink poison. In the final chapter, when the Japanese forces arrive in 1931, they are met with resistance by Chinese soldiers. Among them is Huang Dashan, Ding Ning's cousin and friend who has distanced himself from the exploitation and corruption of the Ding family, but Ding Ning is nowhere to be found. Huang Dashan's appearance as a revolutionary patriot gives the ending a note of optimism although the long conflict has only just begun. As early as 1933, Duanmu Hongliang prophesied the Japanese invasion as spelling the end to the traditional power structure and the emergence of a new kind of hero.

Among the many short stories and novels dealing with the Japanese occupation, Duanmu Hongliang's work stands out by its striking characterisation of a wide range of personalities, its historical scope and its close association with the land and way of life in the north-east. Although his early work is weakened by clumsy plot construction, his novels at their best bear comparison with nineteenth-century Russian fiction. Critics have also drawn attention to the influence of traditional Chinese fiction in his portraits of heroes.

Lu Ling (b. 1923)

Lu Ling is the pen-name of Xu Sixing, born in Jiangsu and educated in Nanjing. After the outbreak of the War against Japan, he travelled first to Wuhan and then to Sichuan. In 1938 he became a student again but was soon expelled because of his leftist political views; he then worked in a series of clerical and teaching posts in Chongqing. In 1939 he met Hu Feng and later became a contributor to Hu Feng's short-lived journals *July* and *Hope*. Hu Feng was a prominent left-wing critic who opposed what he saw as formulaic writing by most left-wing writers, especially after 1937.

Under his influence, Lu Ling turned his attention to nuanced psychological studies of soldiers, factory workers, vagabonds and women without means of support. Similarly, members of the exploitative classes are generally depicted as victims in their own way of a society that is incapable of righting social injustice. His first major work in this vein is the novella *The Starving Guo Su'e*, published by Hope Press in 1942 and reprinted the next year. His short stories of 1944–6, most of which appeared first in the journal *Hope*, were collected in two volumes, *In Search of Love* (1946) and *In Iron Chains* (1949). His major work is the long novel *Children of the Rich*, published by Hope Press in two parts in 1945 and 1948.

Despite his refusal to follow the Yan'an directives of 1942, Lu Ling continued to write fiction after 1949. His best-known story is 'The Battle of the Lowlands' (1954), based on his experiences as a visitor to the Korean front in 1952. As editorial adviser at the Chinese Youth Art Theatre in Beijing, he also wrote several plays, but none of his post-1949 work reached the standards of his earlier efforts. In 1955 he came to the defence of Hu Feng with a four-part essay 'Why This Kind of Criticism?' in the *Literary Gazette*. For this he was sentenced to gaol, and shortly after his release in 1966 he was returned to prison for another eight years, 1967–75. The verdict on Hu Feng was reversed in 1980 and Lu Ling was allowed to return to his former post as a dramatist, but his health had been seriously damaged and he was unable to work.

The eponymous heroine of *The Starving Guo Su'e* is an orphan married to an opium-addict more than twenty years her senior. His addiction impoverishes them both, and Guo Su'e survives by selling cigarettes outside a factory. She has an affair with Zhang Zhenshan, a worker who becomes the leader of an emerging labour movement in the factory. She is also pursued by a relative on her husband's side, Wei Haiqing, who hopes to marry her when her husband dies. When Wei finds out that Guo and Zhang are intimate, he exposes the relationship to her husband. Driven to desperation by her husband's plans to punish her by forcing her into prostitution or selling her off to a rich pervert, Guo tries to make a stand, but the village authorities are on her husband's side and she is tortured to death. Zhang Zhenshan, who had previously refused to elope with Guo Su'e, is dismissed from the factory on the pretext of scandal and comes to take her away, but he is too late. Wei Haiqing is also filled with remorse after her death, and dies after a fight with the local lout who assisted in Guo's torture. The Sichuan countryside is depicted as a place where exploitation, mistrust and lust dominate human relationships.

Children of the Rich, a semi-autobiographical account of the disintegration of a former gentry family under the pressure of Japanese invasion and political corruption, describes a very different world. In Part I Jiang Jiesan, a former Qing official, loses control over his property and his family in parallel with China's loss of territorial integrity with the Japanese invasion of the north-east in 1931 and the bombing of Shanghai in 1932. His eldest son commits suicide while the other children are left destitute, and his own death at the end of Part I goes unnoticed. The action moves between Shanghai, Suzhou and Nanjing, the centre of China's commercial and business life but facing collapse through the policies of the Nationalist government. In Part II the family moves inland ahead of the Japanese advance, encountering on the way not only the suffering of refugees but also the hypocrisy of the left-wing anti-Japanese war effort. The novel is a powerful document on the struggle for survival in the 1930s, its grimness lightened by the idealism of the main character, Jiang's third son.

Lu Ling's story of the Korean War, 'The Battle of the Lowlands', is typical of the war propaganda produced at the time by professional writers even including Ba Jin, the former anarchist. The story is told from the standpoint of a soldier, Wang Yinghong, who un-thinkingly obeys his superior officers. When a young Korean woman falls in love with him, his commanding officer cautions him to be careful about his feelings. When Wang finds a pair of socks in his pocket, given to him by the Korean woman, he reports the incident and returns the socks. Just before going into battle, he again discovers the socks in his pocket, this time with an extra embroidered pattern on them. He is killed in the fighting and the blood-soaked socks are returned to the Korean woman with his photograph.

The political orthodoxy of 'The Battle of the Lowlands' is beyond reproach. However, even though it seems that Lu Ling was willing to accept direction in the early 1950s, he did not escape criticism and there was plentiful of ammunition for the campaign against him in 1955 to be gathered from his earlier work. In this way he can be regarded as representative of writers who were launched on promising careers in the 1950s only to have them abruptly terminated under the new regime.

Yuan Jing (b. 1914) and Kong Jue (1916– 66)

Born in Beijing, Yuan Jing began her political life at an early age, joining the Communist Youth League at sixteen and the Communist Party at twenty-one. Her writing career began as a propagandist in youth organisations during the War against Japan. She went to Yan'an in 1940 where she began to write in several genres, including the opera *Reducing Rent* (1944) and the playscript *The Lawsuit Brought by Liu Qiaor* (1945), which was later made into a film. In the late 1940s she entered a writing partnership with Kong Jue which resulted in their best-known works, *The Case of the Blood-stained Corpse* (1947), *Daughters and Sons* (1947) and *Fate* (1951). Yuan Jing then turned to children's literature, such as *The Story of Little Black Horse* (1958) and *Red Communications Route* (1959). Her career revived in the 1980s with award-winning stories such as 'Fangfang and Tom' (1982) and 'Heroes and Little Troublemakers' (1983).

Kong Jue is the pen-name of Zheng Zhi, from Wuxian, Jiangsu. He trained and worked as a surveyor before embarking on a literary career. He went to Yan'an in 1938 and studied at the Lu Xun Academy of Art and Literature. His best-known individual works are 'Chairman of the Peasants' Association' (1939), 'Miserable People' (1942) and 'Father and Son' (1942). After 1949, Kong Jue was appointed to high-ranking official positions as adviser to the Sino-Soviet Friendship Society and editor at the Central Film Bureau. He was expelled from the Communist Party in 1952 for immoral conduct, and drowned himself at the Summer Palace at the beginning of the Cultural Revolution.

Daughters and Sons follows faithfully the Yan'an directives in regard to form and content. Set against the background of the War against Japan, it traces the victory of the peasants over the landlords and their lackeys in the area of Baiyang Lake in Hebei. Yang Xiaomei is married to Zhang Jinlong, an underling of the local landlord. It is a poor match, since the couple also have opposite views on life, and Zhang Jinlong mistreats his wife. Yang is attracted to Niu Dashui, who shares her determination to fight the Japanese and who joins the local guerrilla forces. The focus is on their personal relationship as much as political events, and the couple marry after much hardship. The title is taken from a famous nineteenth-century popular novel, *A Tale of Heroic Sons and Daughters*, and it incorporates features of the traditional novel such as verses introducing each chapter. First published in 1949, it was much praised in the early 1950s and made into a successful film.

Zhou Erfu (b. 1914)

Zhou Erfu was one of the most successful novelists of the 1950s. Born in Nanjing, his career as a writer began at the YMCA secondary school in Nanjing. He went to Shanghai in 1933 to study English at Guanghua University, and after graduating in 1938 went to Yan'an where he wrote short stories and worked for several literary organisations. In 1942 he made a name for himself with an essay on Norman Bethune, a Canadian doctor who worked in the Communist base areas and died of an infected wound after an operation. After moving to Hong Kong in 1946, he extended this essay into a full-length novel, *Dr Bethune*. He returned to China in 1949, settling first in Shanghai before being recalled to Beijing in 1959. Altogether he produced many volumes of fiction, poetry, plays and essays. His major work is the four-volume *Morning in Shanghai*, published between 1958 and 1980. Immediately after the Cultural Revolution he became a powerful figure in the literary world, and during the early 1980s he made many visits abroad as deputy president of the Chinese People's Association for Friendship with Foreign Countries. His indiscretions on a visit to Paris caused him to be expelled from the Communist Party in 1983, and he never regained high status.

Morning in Shanghai can be seen as a successor to Mao Dun's *Midnight*, providing a detailed portrayal of industrial and commercial life in Shanghai between 1949 and 1956. The novel has a wide cast of characters, drawn mostly from the Hujiang Cotton Mill and including cadres, shopkeepers and factory workers. As in *Midnight*, however, the central figure is a former capitalist, Xu Yide, the owner of the mill. Volume 1 relates the response of capitalists like Xu Yide to the economic and political policies of the new Communist government. Xu Yide and his deputy, Mei

Zuoxian, discuss ways of transferring their money and equipment to Hong Kong. They bribe the deputy of the previous workers' union, Tao Amao, to join the leadership in the new union in order to further their cause. Xu Yide also makes use of compulsory political study meetings to make contacts with other industrialists. Such activities precipitate the government's 1952 campaign to eradicate their influence within local government and industry. By the end of Part I, as a result of the campaign, one former capitalist, Ye Naichuan, has committed suicide, setting off unease and even panic among the others.

In Part II the Chinese Volunteer Army in Korea orders a large amount of medical supplies from the Fuyou Pharmacy, owned by Zhu Tingnian. Zhu, whose financial guarantor is Xu Yide, sabotages the war effort by delaying supplies and sending fake medicine. As work teams visit shops and factories to explain to the workers how they have been exploited, Xu Yide pretends that he is now enlightened and writes a confession, but the work team exposes his wrong-doings and he is isolated.

Part III depicts the reforms that follow the campaign. Xu Yide tries to get rid of the link between himself and Zhu Tingnian, who by now has been arrested, but continues to attend the meetings of industrialists and businessmen. He also tries to distance himself from the day-to-day running of the mill, and is baffled when large number of workers at the mill suddenly fall sick and are diagnosed as suffering from food poisoning. The workers become more politically aware, thanks to re-education by the work team, and many apply to join the Communist Party. Xu Yide's son, Xu Shouren, becomes involved with hooligans and is arrested for theft.

In Part IV the process of industrial reform is reaching its conclusion and the subplots in the previous volumes are resolved. Xu Yide tries to secure the release of his son through his connections, but Xu Shouren sees the error of his ways and obtains an early discharge through good behaviour and reform through labour: he is even admitted into Fudan University, while the workers are accepted into the Communist Party. Zhu Tingnian is found guilty of criminal activities and executed. Tao Amao, who turns out to be a Nationalist agent responsible for many acts of sabotage including poisoning the canteen food, is caught in the act of arson. Most importantly, the government succeeds in transforming the private ownership of enterprises into joint state-private ownership, and most of the former capitalists agree to stay on as owner-managers within the new system.

Yang Mo (1914 – 95)

If Zhou Erfu is Mao Dun's successor as the chronicler of Shanghai capitalism, Yang Mo can be seen as Ba Jin's successor in portraying the turbulent love lives of young revolutionaries. Yang Mo was born in Beijing. Her father, Yang Zhenhua, founded a private university but it ceased operation when Yang Mo was twelve, and the Yang fortunes declined. Her parents arranged a marriage for her when she was still in school, but she refused to oblige and found employment as a primary school teacher in a village on the outskirts of Beijing. She audited classes at Beijing University and began writing essays for publication in 1934, followed two years later with short stories. She joined the Communist Party in 1936 and was sent the following year to the Communist base areas in the north-west to work in women's associations. She also worked for Communist newspapers such as *The Dawn Daily* in the 1940s. Her novella *Life on Reed Lake* (1950) is a typical post-Yan'an effort. Based on the encirclement campaign waged by the Japanese against the Eighth Route Army in the Reed Lake region, it shows how the local guerillas under the guidance of the local Party Secretary act as decoys so that the regular army can launch a counter-attack.

Yang Mo returned to Beijing in 1949 and was appointed to a high-ranking position in the Women's Federation. Because of ill-health, however, she was transferred to work as an editor in the Central Film Bureau in 1952. Yang Mo is best-known for *The Song of Youth*, which became an immediate bestseller when it appeared in 1958 (surpassed only by Qu Bo's *Tracks in the Snowy Forest*). Her fame became even greater when *The Song of Youth* was made into a film and released as part of the tenth anniversary celebrations of the founding of the People's Republic. Yang Mo became a full member of the Writers' Association but produced only a few short stories in the next few years. During the Cultural Revolution, between 1972 and 1976, she wrote *Dawn in the East*, on the internal struggles of the Communist Party and the changing position of intellectuals during the War against Japan; a revised version was published in 1979. A sequel to *The Song of Youth* appeared in the mid-1980s but failed to attract readers.

The Song of Youth is largely based on the author's early experiences but has an interesting variation on the formulaic characterisation by class background which is purely her own invention. Her protagonist, Lin Daojing, is shown throughout the novel as torn between good and evil, a conflict directly attributed to her mixed-class descent: her father is a wealthy landlord who raped her working-class mother. This device also introduces romantic complications as Lin dithers between two men, Yu Yongze (who represents the unreliable bourgeois intellectual elite) and Lu Jiachuan (a revolutionary working-class intellectual). The story begins when Lin's adopted mother arranges for her to marry the son of the head of the Nationalist secret service. Lin effects an escape to Beidaihe, where she tries to commit suicide by plunging into the sea. She is rescued by Yu Yongze, at that time a student at Beijing University, they fall in love, and Lin finds work as a teacher. Lin also meets Lu Jiachuan, who is involved in underground work for the student movement, and they become close friends. When the Japanese invade north-east China in 1931, the Beijing students organise a protest delegation to the Nationalist government in Nanjing. Lu is appointed deputy leader of the delegation and is obliged to leave Lin on her own, while Lin returns to Beijing to cohabit with Yu Yongze. Yu and Lu are on opposite sides of a heated political debate at Beijing University, with Yu's faction taking Hu Shi's line that the students can best serve their country by devoting themselves to their studies, and Lu taking the Communist line advocating student participation in active resistance to the Japanese. Lin, who is becoming disenchanted by Yu, agrees with Lu, and when he is imprisoned she takes over his distribution of Communist pamphlets. When Yu tries to stop her, she breaks off relations with him altogether. She herself is detained but on release becomes even more active in her political work. She is arrested again and locked up with other women political prisoners, including a young girl and a seasoned Communist revolutionary. Inspired by their courage and revolted by the cruelty of the prison guards, she joins the Party after her release. The novel finishes with her working underground for the anti-Japanese student demonstration of 9 December 1935.

The novel's popularity among young readers provoked some criticism from orthodox Party authorities who denounced its emphasis on 'petty bourgeois' feelings; critics were also on safe ground in pointing out that the novel ignored the customary attention paid to working-class and peasant participation in the revolutionary movement. Other writers, including Mao Dun and He Qifang, praised the novel's accurate and often moving depiction of student life in Beijing in the 1930s, while at the same time acknowledging the novel's shortcomings in characterisation. Like most Chinese authors at this time, Yang Mo relies heavily on descriptions of physical attributes as a clue to intelligence and morality: good characters such as Lu have broad faces, thick eyebrows and large eyes, while as Yu's standing in the heroine's eyes declines, his own eyes change from being 'bright' to 'small and beady'. As a consequence of the debate, the novel became even more widely read, and even experienced a minor revival in the 1980s.

Yan Wenjing (b. 1915) and Qin Zhaoyang (b. 1916)

Yan Wenjing and Qin Zhaoyang both found their way to Yan'an in 1938 and membership of the Communist Party at an early age, and both became prominent players in the literary world after 1949, enjoying a reputation as liberals within the orthodox power structure. Yan Wenjing was born in Wuchang, Hubei. He quickly established a reputation in Yan'an as a children's writer with his 1941 collection, *Nannan and Uncle Whiskers*. His 1944 novel, *One Man's Troubles*, is one of his few works for adults. He returned to children's stories in such works as *Dingding's Strange Journey* (1949), the short story collection *A Story of Earthworm and Bee* (1950) and the novella 'Tang Xiaoxi in Next Time Port' (1958). 'Next Time Port' is the attractive name of an ultimately sinister place where all action is postponed, and Tang Xiaoxi is a young boy who is always putting things off. The author shows young readers the perils of procrastination by introducing Tang Xiaoxi into a fantastic world in which everything is still, even the sea and clouds.

Yan Wenjing's adult fiction is also didactic. The hero of *A Man's Troubles* is a young intellectual, Liu Ming, whose idealism and enthusiasm ends in disillusionment and aimlessness. Set during the early phase of the War against Japan, the novel depicts Liu

Ming as a typical intellectual who fails to live up to the challenge of his time. Unable to cope with hardship and frustration, he withdraws from active life, his good intentions undone through lack of courage and stamina.

Qin Zhaoyang was born in Hubei and went to secondary school in Hankou. From an educated family background, he taught in a primary school before attending teachers' college in Wuchang in 1934. After graduating, he went to Yan'an, where he studied at the Lu Xun Academy. After a spell in the border areas between Hebei and Shanxi, Qin Zhaoyang was sent to central Hebei in 1943, turning his experiences in the countryside into typical Yan'an-style fiction, essays and plays. His short stories of this period, collected under the titles *On the Plains* (1949) and *Happiness* (1950), were enough to establish him as a literary figure after 1949 but otherwise made little impact on readers. His fairytale, 'The Adventures of Little Swallow' won a national prize for children's literature in 1952; it was followed by similarly orthodox works such as *Village Sketches* (1954), a collection of fifteen stories, and *Marching Forward in the Fields* (1956), his first novel. The stories in *Village Sketches* are modest in scale, illustrating the impact of social change on individuals like the peasants in 'Sacrifice to the Kitchen God' with fresh touches based on personal observation.

Qin Zhaoyang came to fame during the Hundred Flowers campaign in 1956. Appointed as editor of *People's Literature* in January that year to usher in a more relaxed style of writing, he published Liu Binyan's critical reportage 'At the Bridge Site' in April and 'Confidential Report on Our Paper' in June, followed by Wang Meng's 'A Newcomer to the Organisation Department' in September and his own 'Silence' in January 1957. Most controversial of all was his own essay, 'Realism – The Broad Road', published under a pseudonym in September 1956, which advocates less control over literature by the Party. As an example of what he considered the true function of literature under socialism, 'Silence' is an attack on Party doctrinarism in the countryside, depicting the damage caused by village cadres acting against the advice of knowledgeable peasants. On another level, the story can also be interpreted as an attack on Party officials in the literary world who denied freedom of expression to writers. Under heavy pressure, Qin recanted in March 1957, criticising Liu Binyan and Wang Meng as well as himself, and in September that year he was declared a Rightist. In 1959 he was sent to Guilin, where he was eventually allowed to write and work in local cultural organisations under a different name.

Yan Wenjing's fate was very different. For many years the editor-in-chief at the People's Literature Press in Beijing, he survived the political movements of the 1950s and 1960s to emerge in the late 1970s and 1980s as a patron of the new unofficial writers such as Zhao Zhenkai. Referring for the first time in public to his Christian upbringing, he defended humanistic values while retaining his high posts until retirement in the late 1980s.

Qin Zhaoyang returned to Beijing in 1975 with his health much impaired, but he continued to write and to accept important if nominal positions such as editor-in-chief of the influential literary quarterly *Contemporary*. His novel *The Big Land* won a literary prize in 1984.

Fang Ji (b. 1919)

Fang Ji was born in Shulu, Hebei. He began auditing classes at Beijing University in 1935, at the same time founding the Wind and Sand Literary Society as a vehicle for his own essays and poems. He joined the Communist Party in 1936 and was assigned work in Changsha, Guilin and other places in the south. He went back north to Yan'an in 1939 where he worked as an editor and translator, and after 1949 was appointed editor of the literary column in *Tianjin Daily*. He continued to write fiction, essays and poems on safe topics such as the Yangtze River and Chairman Mao, and his novel *Tales under the Old Mulberry Tree* (1950) describes land reform and resistance to Japan in the Hebei countryside. His reputation as a controversial author rests on the 1958 short story 'The Visitor', for which he was declared a Rightist. He suffered further persecution during the Cultural Revolution and as a result is still paralysed on the right side of his body. His work enjoyed a revival in the 1980s, some of it revised by the author for re-publication.

'The Visitor' is related by two first-person narrators, the frame narrator and the protagonist. The frame narrator is a member of the Party Committee at an unspecified journal: he is not named and readers are invited to identify him as the voice of the author. One day he is asked to see an unemployed man aged twenty-eight by the name of Kang Minfu; he is startled by his visitor's peculiar appearance and demeanour but allows Kang to tell his story. Kang then takes over the narrative, which proceeds abruptly and in fragments. The previous year, Kang was a student and teaching assistant at a Beijing university. On a visit home to see his sick mother in Tianjin, he fell in love with a beautiful drum singer performing in the traditional popular Tianjin theatre. Persuaded that his only aim is to save her from the degradation of an immoral life, he shuttles frantically between Beijing and Tianjin to see her. To her foster-mother he is an unwelcome caller, but the young woman is won over by his devotion and moves in with him. After they have lived together for a while, his contempt for her profession and lack of sympathy for the sacrifice she has made for his sake become unbearable and she leaves him. In agony at her departure, he tracks her down, and her refusal to return to him drives him to attempted suicide. Reaching the end of his story, Kang becomes very agitated and rushes from the office. The narrator then institutes enquiries and is assured that the woman is a respectable performer and Kang an irresponsible playboy. It is the time of the Anti-Rightist campaign, and the narrator is relieved to find that Kang has by now given himself up for rehabilitation through labour. His last information about the affair is that Kang has visited the woman in hospital after she has given birth to a daughter, and when she still refuses to marry him, threatens to take the child; she slaps him, he flees, and everyone feels that the episode has been satisfactorily resolved: Kang has been brought to a sorry end through giving way to selfish desires. The frame narrator lets his position remain ambiguous, however, and different readings can be taken of the implied message. As a depiction of sexual obsession it is a powerful psychological study at a time when psychology and sexology were forbidden zones for both writers and scientists, but even more controversially, it is related against a background of exploitation and bohemian behaviour which could not be tolerated in a socialist society. From any point of view, it is one of the most bizarre stories to appear in the 1950s. Unlike the critical fiction written by the more famous Rightists of the time, Qin Zhaoyang, Wang Meng and Liu Binyan, 'The Visitor' is a truly radical work.

Zhang Ailing (1921–95)

Zhang Ailing, also known as Eileen Chang, was born in Shanghai but spent part of her childhood in Beijing and Tianjin as well. Her family was wealthy but troubled; her father was addicted to opium, and her mother divorced him and left for France when their daughter was still very young; she did not return to China until 1937. Zhang Ailing went back to Shanghai in 1929, and attended St Maria's Women's College in 1937-9. In 1939 she went to study at the University of Hong Kong. She returned to Shanghai in 1942 after the fall of Hong Kong and established herself as a writer with stories in journals such as *The Cosmos* and *Heaven and Earth*.

Zhang Ailing's reputation grew with the novella 'The Golden Cangue' (1944) and other stories. She continued to write fiction after 1949, despite her guarded support for the new regime: *Eighteen Springs* was serialised in the newspaper *Yi bao* and published in book form in 1951, and she attended the First Congress of Literary Workers in Beijing. In 1952 she left China for Hong Kong and then moved to the United States in 1955, settling there permanently with the help of friends such as Hu Shi. Her experiences on the mainland are the basis of two novels, *Love in Redland* and *The Rice-sprout Song*, both published in Hong Kong in 1954. While she is highly regarded in Hong Kong and Taiwan, where her works have remained in print, her condemnation of life under Communism meant that in China itself her writings have until very recently been ignored.

'The Golden Cangue' is a psychological study of a destructive personality over a thirty-year period from the beginning of Republican China. The protagonist, Cao Qiqiao, is married to an invalid son of a wealthy family, by whom she has a son and daughter. Cao was forced into the marriage by her elder brother and feels no love for her husband. She falls in love with her husband's younger brother, but he does not return her affection, reasoning that it would not serve him well, and the embittered woman turns to the pursuit of wealth and power. Ten years later, when Cao's husband dies, she is only able to inherit a portion of his wealth and becomes further embittered. Her brother-in-law, who has squandered his own property, tries to re-ignite her passion, and she takes her revenge in humiliating him. Over the years of denial Cao has become cold and callous, finding satisfaction only in controlling others despite the cost to herself. She engineers the deaths of her son's wife and concubine, and deliberately destroys her daughter's chances of marriage. At the end of the story she is alone and insane in the 'golden cage' she has constructed around herself. Skilfully using symbols such as the golden ring worn by Cao since her marriage, Zhang Ailing shows the corrupting influence of money in China's transition to a modern commercial society and its damage to an individual's body and soul.

Eighteen Springs is another tale of thwarted love, set this time among the poor. Gu Manzhen, a factory worker in Shanghai, is in love with her fellow worker, Shen Shijun. Shen's sister, who works as a hostess in a bar, helps her lover, Zhu Hongcai, to abduct and rape Gu Manzhen. Gu has a child by Zhu Hongcai, and Shen Shijun is told that she has married someone else. In despair, Shen goes to Nanjing where he marries. After 1949 Gu Manzhen meets Shen Shijun and his wife, and the three decide to involve themselves in revolutionary work in the north-east. A revised edition appeared in Taiwan in 1969 under the title *Half a Life*, in which the final two chapters, where the main characters decide to go to the north-east, are deleted and the words 'after Liberation' are replaced by 'after the War'. In either version, the story is not as subtle as 'Golden Cangue' and has not received the same critical acclaim.

Zhang Ailing's experiences in China were not happy, and when she left, she no longer gave her tales a happy ending; in her next two novels, human tragedies under Communism are not relieved by love or friendship. *Love in Redland* shows how the Communist Party betrays both its own supporters and the people in general, peasants as well as intellectuals suffering because of government policies. In addition, the personal ambitions of Communist Party members were already corrupting the system from within even in the 1950s, and the author depicts the sacrifice of the innocent. The novel was later translated into English by its author under the title *Naked Earth*.

The Rice-sprout Song is set in a village near Shanghai. Yuexiang, a model worker, returns home after three years in the city to find that there is widespread starvation. When the village cadre, Wang Lin, visits their home unexpectedly, their porridge happens to be a little thicker than usual, and this 'luxury' causes her husband, Jin'gen, to feel extremely uneasy. As the spring festival approaches, Wang Lin urges the peasants to contribute meat or cash for the families of soldiers. Jin'gen refuses, but Yuexiang surrenders her savings to try and pacify the bullying Wang Lin. When Jin'gen joins rioting peasants in an attempt to obtain grain, their child is trampled to death and Jin'gen is seriously injured. The novel ends with both husband and wife dying, while the unhappy villagers, forced to perform the Yan'an-style 'rice-sprout song', awkwardly celebrate Chinese New Year with the soldiers' families. The criticism levelled against Communist society in this story is stark, and the reception of the novel has mostly been determined by reaction to its political message. In style it is a continuation of the anti-Nationalist fiction common in the late 1930s.

Zhang Ailing remained a prolific writer to the end of her life. Although her prophetic critiques of Communism won renewed interest in the 1980s, she is best remembered for her earlier studies of women in destructive relationships, for which she draws on the traditions of the great Chinese novels of the past as well as modern psychological realism.

Qu Bo (b. 1923)

Born into a peasant family in Shandong, Qu Bo joined the Eighth Route Army in 1938 and became a member of the Communist Party the following year. At first a cultural worker, he rose quickly to the rank of political instructor. In 1943 he entered the Anti-Japanese University in Jiaodong, where he wrote plays for student performance. On his return to active service in 1945, he led a small detachment against local bandits in the mountains and forests of the north-east. He was transferred to accompany the PLA in its drive south but was wounded in battle. After 1949 he worked as Party Secretary in a locomotive factory and then was transferred to the Ministry of Railways as an official. He wrote fiction in his spare time and achieved great success with the novel *Tracks in the Snowy Forest* in 1957. Episodes from the novel were the basis for a series of other works, including a film of the same name, a Peking opera and eventually the revolutionary model opera *Taking Tiger Mountain by Strategy*.

Tracks in the Snowy Forest is divided into three main sections, each ending with victory over a different group of bandits during the Civil War in 1946–7. The Nationalist troops had been routed in the north-east but remnants joined with local bandits to make isolated attacks on the PLA and to raid villages under its control. The novel begins with a massacre of Communist workers and sympathetic peasants by a local band. The PLA decides to change its tactics and instead of launching a counter-attack, sends a detachment of thirty-six men under the command of Shao Jianbo to deal with the bandits. The detachment ascertains that the culprit is Horse Cudgel Xu, a bandit chief on Breast Mountain. The scout platoon leader, Yang Zirong, captures Xu's adjutant, Luan Ping, and learns from him that Breast Mountain is extremely treacherous, with only one entry into the bandit stronghold. With the help of a local mushroom gatherer, the PLA soldiers use ropes and other climbing gear to descend into the bandit stronghold, catching them by surprise and wiping out most of the gang.

The next section describes the conquest of Tiger Mountain. Obtaining a map of the gang's underground contacts, and pretending to be Luan Ping, Yang Zirong is sent into the bandit camp on Tiger Mountain with the excuse of presenting the map. He wins the trust of Vulture, the bandit chief, and is even appointed a gang leader. Luan Ping escapes from captivity and makes his way up to Tiger Mountain on the day that Vulture is celebrating his sixtieth birthday. Yang Zirong maintains that he is the true Luan Ping and, after a battle of wits, convinces Vulture, who orders Luan Ping's immediate execution. The party continues and Yang Zirong encourages them to get drunk. With help from Yang Zirong, Shao Jianbo leads his men into the bandit stronghold, captures Vulture alive, and destroys the Tiger Mountain gang. The last section relates the detachment's valiant engagements with bandit troops led by the Nationalist agents, Hou Diankun and Ma Xishan. Shao Jianbo is wounded, but in the end all the remnant Nationalists and bandits are wiped out.

The enthusiastic welcome by readers and audiences to this tale is partly due to the well-paced action but even more to the techniques adapted by Qu Bo from traditional novels like *Three Kingdoms* and *Water Margin*. Some passages are reworkings of famous episodes, most notably in the second section. Yang Zirong's encounter with a tiger on his way to the bandit stronghold, for instance, would be familiar to most readers as a modern version of Wu Song's encounter with a tiger in *Water Margin*, and the differences are as instructive as the similarities. The strength and courage of the original hero, Wu Song, are enhanced by his drunkenness, but the modern hero, Yang Zirong, cannot afford this weakness. Nevertheless Qu Bo's portrait convinces us by allowing Yang moments of fear and irresolution. The novel also charms readers with its humour and lively language: again, Yang Zirong swears like a trooper to convince the bandits of his identity, and the battle of wits in the bandit cave adds amusement and tension – both rather rare experiences in Communist fiction.

Ru Zhijuan (b. 1925)

Born in Shanghai, Ru Zhijuan lost her mother while she was only three and was raised by her grandmother. Although she only had four years of formal schooling, she loved literature and published her first story, 'Life', in *Shen bao* in 1943: the protagonist is a university graduate who cannot find work and in a rage tears up his graduation certificate. When the story appeared in November, she had already joined the New Fourth Army with her elder brother. At first a member of the theatrical troupe, she was subsequently appointed deputy group leader of a creative writing group and wrote ballads, 'rice-sprout song' scripts and poems. In 1947 she joined the Communist Party and also won a literary award.

Ru Zhijuan continued to write short stories after 1949, gaining national attention with 'Lilies' in 1958. Her first collection, *Tall Aspens*, containing ten short stories and five poems, was published in 1959, followed in 1962 by *The Quiet Maternity Hospital*, a collection of ten short stories. Many of these stories were translated into foreign languages during the 1950s and early 1960s, as Ru Zhijuan became the best-known of the new women writers.

Set in the time of the PLA offensive against the Nationalists in autumn 1946, 'Lilies' is told in the first person by a member of a theatrical troupe who has been sent to the front as a first-aid assistant. A young PLA soldier is assigned to show her the way to the clinic, and she notes with sympathy his shyness and dedication. He fails to obtain bedding for the clinic from a newly married woman in the village although the narrator has no trouble getting a new quilt from her. While the soldier mumbles that the village woman is feudal in her attitudes, it is clear that the two young people are awkward in each other's company. Shortly after, the young soldier dies when he throws himself on top of a grenade in order to save his comrades. The bride wraps her new quilt, embroidered with lilies, around the dead soldier as his funeral shroud. Ostensibly on conventional themes such as the interdependence of the PLA and the ordinary people, the emotions shown by the soldier and the young bride hint at stronger, if hidden desires, and Ru Zhijuan herself in 1980 claimed that it was a love story in which love is absent. Contemporary readers feel free to appreciate the author's depiction of the tenderness and sorrow felt by women faced with the death of loved ones, even a blushing stranger who dies after just one meeting. (*For Ru Zhijuan's later fiction see Chapter 12.*)

Liu Binyan (b. 1925)

Liu Binyan was born in Changchun, Jilin, and grew up in Harbin. He became politically active soon after finishing secondary school, joining the Communist Party in 1944. The Russian presence was very strong in the north-east immediately after the war, and Liu Binyan taught himself Russian and began translating Russian literary works. In 1951, he was transferred to work at *Chinese Youth News* in Beijing, where he became an investigative journalist. Two of his reports, 'At the Bridge Site' and 'Inside News', both published in 1956 during the Hundred Flowers campaign, immediately attracted attention and Liu Binyan was admitted to the Writers' Association the same year. During the backlash the following year, he was labelled a Rightist and expelled from the Communist Party. From then until the late 1970s, when the verdict on him was reversed, publication of his work was forbidden.

In 1977 Liu Binyan returned to work as a special correspondent for the *People's Daily*. As a journalist, he specialised in investigating the more sensational cases, as seen in his reportage 'People or Monsters?' (1979), which won him a national award. In 1987 he was once again expelled from the Party as a major target of the campaign against bourgeois liberalisation. He went to Harvard University as a Nieman Fellow in 1988. Since then, he has remained in America, touring worldwide to lecture on Chinese problems and distributing anti-government material from his base in Princeton.

'At the Bridge Site' appeared in the April issue of *People's Literature*. It is based on an investigation of a building site at the Yellow River Bridge in 1955 in which Liu Binyan took part. His report exposes the complexities in the bureaucracy which controlled the site. Zeng Gang, engineer and team leader, designs a series of measures which if adopted would make construction more efficient. However, not only are these plans not adopted, they are criticised for being immature and reckless by the brigade leader, Luo Lizheng. After a bitter struggle between the two, in which the conservative Party cadre accuses the young engineer of not observing discipline and even being anti-Party, Zeng Gang is transferred to another workplace.

Liu Binyan's most daring move was not simply in exposing a particular case of mismanagement but his penetrating analysis of Luo Lizheng. A committed Communist and bridge-builder since well before 1949, Luo Lizheng feels he has made his contributions to socialist construction, and his main concern now, after some six years as a high-level cadre, is to stay in power. This means not taking any risks or adopting new strategies. The idealism which fuelled his youth is long gone, and he spends most of his time at his hobbies, hunting and repairing watches. His motto now is 'not making mistakes is achieving victory'. Responding to the Hundred Flowers call for intellectuals to criticise Party cadres, Liu Binyan went further than most in depicting the self-serving complacency which had already overtaken the new Communist bureaucracy. In the conclusion, Luo Lizheng's tactics pay off: by doing nothing, he remains in power; it is Zeng Gang, who is prepared to risk his life for the sake of the construction project, who is transferred. Liu Binyan's narrative sympathies are clearly on the side of ambitious young professionals who are impatient with uneducated cadres whose main qualification for senior rank is length of service to the Party.

'Inside News' followed two months later in the same journal and proved even more controversial. An enthusiastic young reporter, Huang Guiying, finds herself pitted in her first job against her boss at the news agency, a conservative bureaucrat by the name of Chen Lidong. Chen is a tireless worker and punctilious in the extreme in implementing all directives from the political leadership. He considers his greatest merit is his devotion to the Party, and insists on the same dogged orthodoxy in the staff in his office. The newspaper becomes so boring that sales are nearly halved. Huang's protests are ignored by Chen, and in the end she too admits defeat.

Although he writes reportage rather than straight fiction, Liu Binyan is generally classed with the fiction writers of the 1950s, given the semi-documentary nature of 1950s fiction. Compared with the average short story of the time, Liu's reports tend to be more prolix, including more background material both in regard to technical detail and also political theory. The dialogue is stiff, as are the main characters, but the very clumsiness of the writing appeared to readers as a kind of guarantee of the report's authenticity. Compared to Wang Meng, who impresses readers with his cleverness, Liu Binyan achieved a wide following who cared more about investigative truth than for the most imaginative and technically skilled fiction. Liu Binyan and Wang Meng are the most outstanding examples of the Rightists who were only able to re-establish their careers after the Cultural Revolution.

Wang Meng (b. 1934)

Wang Meng was born and educated in Beijing. The son of a professor of philosophy, he came into contact with Communist ideas while he was still at school, and joined the Communist Party in 1948. After 1949, he had a series of posts as Party Secretary in branches of the Communist Youth League. He began writing the novel *Long Live Youth* in about 1953 and completed the final draft in 1956, but because of his downfall in the Anti-Rightist campaign, the novel was not published until 1979. *Long Live Youth* is set in the early 1950s and describes how a group of senior school students band together to help the daughter of a former capitalist and the adopted daughter of a foreign missionary to overcome the disadvantage of their backgrounds and to devote themselves to the new Chinese state. A short story published in 1955, 'Little Bean', is equally inoffensive.

The story that made Wang Meng famous, 'The Young Newcomer in the Organisation Department', was published in *People's Literature* in September 1956. Like Liu Binyan, Wang Meng seemed set to become an important writer, only to fall victim to the Anti-Rightist campaign of 1957. He wrote only one other short story, 'Winter Rain', before being labelled a Rightist. In 1957 he was sent to the countryside near Beijing for five years of manual labour. The Rightist label was removed in 1961 and Wang Meng returned to the city to teach at Beijing Normal College. In 1963, however, he was sent to Xinjiang, returning to Beijing only in 1979.

'The Young Newcomer in the Organisation Department' is similar to Liu Binyan's reports in its criticism of inertia and incompetence in the Communist bureaucracy. Through the conflict between the newcomer, Liu Zhen, and the Deputy Bureau Chief, Liu Shiwu, the story highlights the tensions between younger and older cadres and the differences in the way they carry out their work. A few days after he takes up his new assignment, Lin Zhen realises that the factory manager is irresponsible and dutifully reports this to his superiors. Much to his dismay, he finds that leaders like Liu Shiwu are reluctant to take action, saying that the manager's problem is his lack of education and it is not a matter for disciplinary action. When Lin Zhen reports to Liu Shiwu the behaviour of other inactive bureaucrats, Liu defends them on the grounds that cadres' past merits must be emphasised, not their shortcomings. Liu's praise for Lin Zhen's initiative and enthusiasm turns out to be hollow. Even when investigations prove that the factory manager is indeed at fault and is penalised, Lin Zhen is shocked by the lack of interest in the affair shown at executive committee meetings.

Although rather long for a short story, 'Newcomer' shows promise in the author's characterisation of the clash between ambitious youth and conservative old Party officials, one of the main themes of the Hundred Flowers campaign. Without reference to its very specific context, however, the story's high-flown abstract dialogue and caricaturistic portraits appear banal and affected. In this sense, it can also be read as a typical literary product of the 1950s, written for a specific campaign purpose and having little independent existence outside that purpose. (*For Wang Meng's later fiction see Chapter 12.*)

Hao Ran (b. 1932)

In the wake of the Anti-Rightist campaign and the Great Leap Forward that followed, the literary authorities were at pains to encourage new writers to replace those disgraced and silenced.

Amateur writers were given training in writers' workshops, and their works redrafted by professional editors for publication. Of the new writers who rather suddenly found themselves famous in the late 1950s, Hao Ran (pen-name of Liang Jinguang) is among the most talented and eventually the most controversial.

Born in Zhaogezhuang, Tangshan, Hao Ran was brought up from the age of seven by his widowed mother in her brother's family in Hebei. He became a correspondent for the *Hebei Youth* in 1949. After a stint at the *Hebei Daily*, Hao Ran was transferred to Beijing in 1956 to work for the Russian-language *Friendship Daily*. In the same year, he published his maiden short story 'Magpies Perch on Branches'. He joined the Writers' Association in 1959 with two short story collections already to his credit and continued to publish large numbers of stories and essays over the next few years. His first major work, the three-volume novel *Bright Sunny Skies*, was begun in 1960, and completed and published in 1965. Adopted by the radical left as a model of new fiction, it was one of the very few works from the 1960s available in bookshops during the Cultural Revolution, and was made into a film in 1973.

One reason for Hao Ran's success is his ability to convey the familiar details of peasant life in a clear and sympathetic manner, noting the conflicts as well as the achievements of radical structural change in the countryside in the 1950s and 1960s. This corresponded neatly with Mao's insistence in 1961-2 that class struggle was still 'the key link' in China's socialist transformation. Again, Hao Ran's choice of female protagonists with a high level of political consciousness was very welcome to Jiang Qing for her own agenda in cultural politics. For example, 'Magpies Perch on Branches', set at the time of the new Marriage Law, is about an independent young woman who devotes herself to productive labour. Anxious about her future, her parents are uncertain whether or not they should arrange a marriage for her. When told that his daughter has met someone she likes in a neighbouring village, her father decides to go and find out about this young man. On the way he happens to meet a young man whom he likes very much; the reader is not much surprised when it turns out that the young man is his future son-in-law. 'The New Daughter-in-Law' is also about changing marital customs. At her wedding, the fiercely independent bride refuses to follow the traditional rituals, and her father-in-law is displeased. In the end he discovers that she is extremely hard-working and is universally liked by other villagers, and is persuaded to forget his prejudice.

Hao Ran's early short stories follow the Yan'an line in emphasising positive heroes in village life and reflect the general emphasis on the increasing prosperity of the countryside. The element of class struggle, which requires villains as well as heroes, makes an appearance in the early 1960s and becomes the main theme of the novels for which Hao Ran is most famous. Stereotypical heroes and villains are unambiguously divided along class lines, and conflicts between people are invariably explicable in class terms. *Bright Sunny Skies* is set in a village near Beijing during the summer harvest of 1957. This was at the height of the collectivisation effort in the countryside, when private enterprises were to be abolished in favour of a collective economy. The novel is a panoramic study of the way people from different backgrounds react to these changes. The three central characters are Xiao Changchun, Party Secretary of the collective, Ma Zhiyue, the former Party Secretary who has been demoted because he has committed a mistake, and Ma Xiaobian, a former landlord.

The novel traces the struggles between these three men and their respective supporters. Just before the harvest, Xiao Changchun carries out the policy of division of produce according to collectivised principles whereas Ma Zhiyue wants to continue the principle of dividend on land shares in which peasants benefit according to their original shares. After careful propaganda work, and with the support of the poor peasants, Xiao Changchun wins the battle. Just then, a rumour is started where the peasants are led to believe that higher authorities will come to take their produce. Many secretly sell their goods. In the end, however, the rumour is revealed as a malicious attempt to foil the new policies. In Volume 2, the former landlord Ma Xiaobian, supported by Ma Zhiyue, tries to instil further dissatisfaction among the peasants, persuading them to argue for more grain during distribution time. In Volume 3, the struggle intensifies: Ma Xiaobian murders Xiao Changchun's young son but is caught and his wrongdoings come to light. The County Party Secretary also comes to investigate and reaffirms that Xiao Changchun's policies are correct.

The language of this novel is particularly noteworthy. Based on the colloquial language of north China (which is close to standard modern Chinese), it avoids difficult localisms and in principle at least is intelligible to the literate peasantry throughout China (although there is little evidence to suggest it was read by anyone other than urban educated youth). By the time of writing *Bright Sunny Skies*, Hao Ran had learned how to enrich this language with references to traditional culture (of an approved kind) and to differentiate characters by their speech habits as well as their personalities. As if to assert the author's own status as one of the educated class, the third-person narration remains in the standard written language. (*For Hao Ran's later fiction see Chapter 12.*)

From the outbreak of the War against Japan to its end in 1945, different centres fostered a range of styles and themes in fiction. Writers in the south and south-west continued to explore individual psychological and moral states, while writers in the north-west increasingly gave voice to group emotions such as patriotism and class consciousness, their post-1937 works echoing the militant optimism of the revolutionary left. Diversity became even more pronounced during the Civil War but was one of the casualties of Communist victory in 1949. Throughout the 1950s and 1960s, fiction writers followed closely the political dictates of the day, and the use of fiction as a campaign weapon was rarely questioned. The writers who began their careers in the late 1940s and 1950s had received their training in wartime conditions, and their views of the world in many respects coincided with the government line which stressed the hostility of the outside world towards China. At the same time, they shared in the early pride and enthusiasm for building a new society, but when the regime exerted its control by means of punishment as well as rewards, formulaic writing quickly became the dominant mode. Whether under the rubric of socialist realism or the combination of revolutionary realism and revolutionary romanticism, from the mid-1950s on, the ubiquitous and usually omniscient third-person narrator spoke with all the authority of the state as writers conscientiously strove to eliminate irony, ambiguity and ambivalence from their work.

8

POETRY: THE CHALLENGE OF
POPULARISATION

By the outbreak of the War against Japan in July 1937, the battle for the new poetry had been won in the universities and in commercial publishing. Poetry continued to be written in classical metres by scholars and practised as folksong in the countryside, but readers with pretensions towards progress took it for granted that the poetry of the modern age was to be written in the vernacular. The tendency for the pioneers of the literary revolution to revert to more traditional styles was hardly noticed as more and more volumes of vernacular poetry filled the shelves. The new poetry must have seemed irresistible, a movement that no individual could stop. Although at the outset of the War against Japan, the division between the political poets and the independents seemed at first only to continue the trends set in the early 1930s, the fate of two of the older poets, Wen Yiduo and Guo Moruo, showed the impossibility of fixing rigid boundaries between the strands of twentieth-century poetry.

The War against Japan brought Wen Yiduo back into public life. He joined the exodus of university staff and students from Beijing, travelling with Qinghua University first to Changsha in Hunan, where he lost most of his books, and then further south, traversing on foot the mountains of central China towards the relative safety of Kunming. At the newly-formed South-west United University in Kunming, Wen Yiduo continued to teach Chinese literature and carry out research on its origins. It was a time of great hardship and suffering: life in the ivory tower was just not possible. In 1943, Wen Yiduo publicly repudiated his own highly refined style in favour of what he called the drums of the new age. He wrote an essay to support a new kind of partisan poetry, exemplified in Tian Jian's declamatory verse, which

261

openly took sides in the struggle. For this he has been much praised, although a more detached observer might now reflect that patriotism, like other kinds of ideology, can fool even the most perceptive critics. In 1946 he joined the Chinese Democratic League, a 'third force' of intellectuals neither Nationalist nor Communist. Although not a Communist, he criticised Nationalist corruption and was subsequently assassinated by the secret police —an act which further alienated writers and intellectuals from the Nationalist cause.

The fate of Guo Moruo, from Wen's assassination until the end of the 1970s indisputably China's senior poet, was very different. From his radical phase in the 1920s, he moved gradually into a form of scholarship which lent itself to support first for the revolutionary cause and eventually for successive government policies after 1949. His career in poetry similarly took dramatic turns over these years.

During the first five years of the war, it is estimated that over a hundred collections of poetry were published in pamphlet form and a total of half a million lines was written. Much of it took the form of declamatory verse, usually performed on street corners and in other open venues, and would long ago have perished but for the need of Chinese governments and writers after 1949 to force attention to the patriotic credits then accumulated. There seems no clear evidence that this poetry ever had much effect as propaganda except possibly to keep up the morale of the poets themselves at a time of much hardship and danger. Some of the new poets who made their reputations at this time, such as Tian Jian, continued to write after the war; others, like Gao Lan, one of the most famous of the declamatory poets, returned to academic life.

Meanwhile, the efforts of the Chinese Communist Party to foster a propaganda corps based on local art forms were showing some success. When the clash between writers and Party leaders came to a head in Yan'an in 1942, Mao Zedong could point to a new direction: reworkings of the folksong traditions of the countryside. Mao remained reluctant, however, to publicise his own preferred writing style, the classical poetic forms that dated back a thousand years or more.

The policies set forth in Yan'an became mandatory for left-wing writers there and beyond after 1942, although with decreasing force outside the Communist-controlled area. The main alternative centre for poetry was in Kunming, where under the tutelage of Wen Yiduo, Feng Zhi, Shen Congwen, Bian Zhilin and Li Guangtian, a cluster of younger poets who were to dominate the late 1940s were encouraged to work at improving their poetic skills without descending into trivial or frivolous conceits. Elsewhere in China, war poets such as Su Jinsan and Fang Jing continued to follow May Fourth patterns, simplifying the language, strengthening the didactic element, widening the vocabulary and focusing resolutely on the travails of village life in wartime. Although the end of the war was soon followed by Civil War, the period between 1946 and 1948 at least offered new possibilities for literary study, writing and publication. The most promising work was by a group of poets known collectively as the Nine Leaves: Hang Yuehe, Chen Jingrong, Mu Dan, Zheng Min, Wang Xindi, Du Yunxie (b. 1918), Tang Qi (b. 1920), Tang Shi (b. 1920) and Yuan Kejia (b. 1921); other poets who published in their journals, *Poetry Creation* and *China's New Poetry*, included Zang Kejia and Li Ying. The Nine Leaves were attacked by Hu Feng's July group for their unwillingness to adhere to the Party line or to give prominence only to Party writers. During Hu Feng's initial spell in power in the early 1950s, he managed to have them banned from writing poetry, and though he himself fell from power in 1955, the Nine Leaves group were not given recognition again as poets until the end of the 1970s.

The establishment of the People's Republic in 1949 brought with it a state apparatus that required the support of cultural activities and a cultural bureaucracy to administer the performance of those duties. In urban centres, this bureaucracy was staffed mainly by writers (including poets) who had already established their claim by the publication of one or more volumes of literary works. With such excellent career prospects, writing as a profession attracted many new writers during the 1950s and 1960s. This chapter ends with those whose first works coincided with the launching of the new regime.

The establishment of literary journals and literary columns in general interest journals and newspapers gave generous space to the publication of single poems, and the publishing houses established in each province also offered fully subsidised book publication for established poets. The centre of official poetry was the monthly journal *Poetry*, which initially ran from 1957 to 1964. Its editor throughout these years was Zang Kejia, and members of the editorial board were mostly practising poets, including Tian Jian, Ai Qing, Bian Zhilin, He Jingzhi, Li Ji and Guo Xiaochuan. The first issue featured the first authorised publication of eighteen poems by Mao Zedong, as well as a letter from Mao to the effect that he did not wish the classical forms of his poems to be imitated by the new generation. In subsequent issues, the majority of the poems were written in free verse, with a limited number in regulated Western style, folksong and classical Chinese forms. Most journals ceased publication around May 1965, at the onset of the Cultural Revolution, but *Poetry* was by then already defunct.

Throughout the 1950s and 1960s, poetry continued to be a political battleground. The first skirmish was fought over the issue of form in poetry: among the main contenders were He Qifang and He Jingzhi. Mao then fired his secret weapon: his own poetry was released in batches starting in 1957. The populist policies of the Great Leap Forward were translated into literary terms with the poetry campaign of 1958–9, where the whole population of the country, from peasants to factory workers to professors were obliged to take time off to write poetry in the form of folksongs (for most purposes, this meant a four-line stanza in simplifed classical Chinese, with five or seven syllables per line and end rhymes). Zhou Yang and Guo Moruo lent their names as editors to the official anthology, *Songs of the Red Flag*, which contained 305 of these 'new folksongs' in conscious emulation of *The Book of Songs*. The market reforms introduced by Liu Shaoqi and Deng Xiaoping after the Three Hard Years (1959-61) allowed the cultural bureaucrats, primary among them Zhou Yang and Guo Moruo, to restore the professional autonomy they had earlier enjoyed. In 1966 the Cultural Revolution removed these bureaucrats from office, often violently, and the literature they favoured disappeared from view for several years: its replacements were classical verse by Mao Zedong and other aging generals and a new wave of pseudo-folksongs modelled on the 1958 poetry campaign. The May Fourth tide that had seemed irresistible only thirty years earlier now seemed at its last ebb.

Guo Moruo (1892–78)

Returning to China in 1937, Guo Moruo spent the war years in the Nationalist areas, occupied mainly in anti-Japanese propaganda. His best-known work from this period is historical drama, but he also rushed into publication with *The Sound of War* (1938), a collection of twenty-one poems (some in classical styles), followed by *Cicada* (1948), war poems from 1939 to 1947. Between 1950 and 1966, he published eight collections of poems in praise of government policies; among these, poems in 1961 and 1963 drew responses from Mao Zedong. He also contributed both vernacular and classical poems in support of Vietnam in 1964. A poem dedicated to Jiang Qing at the beginning of the Cultural Revolution ('Dear Comrade Jiang Qing, you are the fine example for us to follow ...') later caused some embarrassment, and after the fall of the 'gang of four' in 1976 he wrote several poems denouncing them. Most of his poetry is in *Moruo's Complete Works* (17 vols, 1957-63), supplemented by *Guo Moruo's Selected Works* (3 vols, 1979). *(For Guo Moruo's early work see Chapters 3 and 5; for his plays see Chapter 9.)*

Mao Zedong (1893–1976)

It was during the War against Japan that Mao Zedong's predilection for writing poetry in classical forms became known. In terms of their influence over four decades in shaping Chinese ideals of the self, society and revolution, they can hardly be overestimated. The influence of the form in which he chose to write is a more difficult matter. Although he was not the only senior intellectual and Party leader to write classical verse, he strongly discouraged the practice, so that with some exceptions, classical verse was not openly published until the last years of the Cultural Revolution and its aftermath. The earliest of his poems published during his lifetime is dated 1925, and his last 1965. They were formally published in four batches: eighteen in 1957, six in 1962, ten in 1964 and two in 1976, although most were circulated privately soon after writing. The timing of each release was a tactical assertion of Mao's right to exert cultural and moral leadership as well as political power. Since his death, more of his poems have been published in what is a tribute both to his new powerlessness and continuing influence.

As dictated by the genre, Mao's poems are written in the literary language, in an extremely compressed grammar designed for reading comprehension. They are frequently reproduced in Mao's own handwriting, a free, bold style which adds an extra flourish to the words. The rhythmic forms he adopted are in themselves highly musical, so the poems are also striking read aloud, and were set to music during the Cultural Revolution. Unfortunately, several of the most characteristic features of the poems are lost in the currently available translations. For example, the use of parallelism in the original is frequently ignored, so that the sense of balance and comprehensiveness is lost. Again, since in the literary language, the subject, number, tense and gender are also frequently not specified, the translations usually remove some tantalising ambiguities in the originals. Finally, the unconventional blending of literary and colloquial diction is also largely obscured in translation.

Of the thirty-six poems published during his lifetime, eleven are written in the Regulated style of the Tang dynasty and the rest in the Lyric style of the Song (for these terms, see Chapter 3). These two genres are the most restrictive in Chinese poetry, with fixed rules on the length of lines, the tone patterns of words in the line, the number of lines in the poem, the rhyme patterns and so on. The challenge is like chess: to use the rules to create originality, not to stifle it.

'Loushan Pass', written in 1935, is a typical Lyric poem in eight lines, with a refrain after the opening couplet in both stanzas. The first stanza sets the time and place: the 'west wind' in the first line indicates the season (autumn), which is confirmed in the second line with 'geese' and 'frost'. The first two lines blend tactile, aural and visual images, while the last two consist of a contrasted pair of aural images. The action is presented in the second stanza: the political message, one of defiance of Nationalist military power and natural obstacles, is stated in the first couplet, and the colour parallelism in the final couplet emphasises the will to victory.

'Snow', a Lyric dated February 1936, is probably Mao's most famous poem. Again, the first stanza sets the scene – the brilliant spectacle of north China in winter; and the second delivers the message – the grandeur of China's destiny. In addition, the first describes space – the vast expanse of China; and the second emphasises temporality – the length of China's history. The first stanza contains sets of contrasting images: surface textures (silver snakes and wax-hued elephants); colour contrasts (red against white); mobility and restraint (locked-in ice and whirling snow; a swift current stilled; mountains dancing and highlands charging). The general impression is of immense energy held in check: the power of the masses in revolution, or of Mao's own ambition. The second stanza lists five historical characters: Qin Shi Huang, founder of the Qin dynasty; Wudi, powerful early emperor of the Han; Taizong, founder of the Tang; Taizu, founder of the Song; and Genghis Khan, founder of the Yuan (Mongol) dynasty. Implying that both military and civil (or civilised) genius is necessary to maintain a dynasty, Mao claims that the 'truly great men' belong to the present age. In Marxist terms, this should refer to the proletariat, the only class in history to initiate class struggle conscious of its historical role; in the circumstances of its composition and release, it could be read as meaning either Chiang Kaishek and Mao Zedong, or Mao Zedong alone.

'Beidaihe', a Lyric written in 1954, describes in its first stanza the seaside resort established by foreigners in the 1920s and since the 1950s used as a summer retreat by China's new rulers. Its position near the sea-end of the Great Wall and proximity to the harbour named after Qin Shi Huang also provide reminders of China's ancient power. The second stanza refers more directly to the historical past, and proclaims again that the time has come for China to break free of its ancient pattern of cyclical dynasties to create a new era. 'Swimming', a Lyric poem written in 1956, celebrates the achievements of the new era, and at the same time establishes his own vitality, in a similar two-stanza form.

A more personal poem is 'Reply to Li Shuyi', a Lyric written in response to an old war comrade in 1957. Li's husband, whose surname was Liu (meaning willow), was killed by the Nationalists in 1933; Mao's second wife, whose surname was Yang (meaning poplar), was executed in 1930. 'I lost my proud Poplar and you your Willow', the poem begins: one husband and one wife stand for all the martyred couples of the long years of civil strife. It finishes on a triumphal note as the couple in heaven witness the defeat of the enemy. 'The Immortals' Cave', a Regulated poem written in 1961, was inscribed on the back of a photograph taken by his fourth wife, Jiang Qing.

The more recent poems address the present rather than the past, and show an aging man's impatience as well as fading vigour in their relatively colloquial language and commonplace imagery. A poem in reply to Guo Moruo in 1963 contains the well-known lines 'Seize the day, seize the hour' and 'Away with all pests!'; a Lyric from 1965 is still defiant with 'Nothing is hard in this world If you dare to scale the heights,' while the last poem, a Lyric from the autumn of 1965, taunts Krushchev's Communism with the boast that 'the world is being turned upside down.'

Like the quotations in the 'little red book', Mao's poems became one of the texts of the Cultural Revolution: 92 million copies were distributed by 1968. Schoolchildren learnt them off by heart, and by the end of the Cultural Revolution, other old generals like Zhu De, Chen Yi (posthumously) and Ye Jianying, or senior intellectuals like Guo Moruo and Zhao Puchu, were also emboldened to publish their classical poems.

Ke Zhongping (1902–64)

Originally from Yunnan, Ke Zhongping joined the Creation Society as a student in Beijing. He then moved to Shanghai where he took part in underground Party trade-union work. He started writing poetry for the Creation journals as early as 1924, drawing little attention outside his own circle, although his verse drama *Wind and Fire Mountains* (1930) had the distinction of being banned by the Nationalist authorities in Shanghai. In 1930 he joined the Communist Party and later the same year was arrested and sentenced to execution, but his sentence was commuted and he was released in 1933. Between 1934 and 1937 he lived in Japan, returning to China at the outbreak of war. He immediately made for Yan'an where he was readmitted to the Party in 1938. His absence from the left-wing literary circles of Shanghai in the 1930s may have influenced his readiness to abandon the professional autonomy fostered by the literary associations and magazines which flourished in the relatively free atmosphere of the International Settlement.

Ke Zhongping took part in the declamatory and street poetry movements of the late 1930s but is best-known for two long narrative poems written in 1938 and published in Chongqing in 1940. In Yan'an he had quickly taken the side of the populists who advocated the adaptation of 'national forms' against the professionals (who included He Qifang) who tried to preserve the internationalist spirit of May Fourth. At Mao Zedong's prompting, he organised the Masses' Opera Troupe in 1938 to perform old opera with new revolutionary content. His own long poem, 'The Border Region Self-Defence Corps' was set to a folksong tune: Mao Zedong praised it warmly, but it was criticised by He Qifang. In 1940-2, Ke Zhongping was chiefly engaged in fostering a village-based drama movement though his own Masses' Opera Troupe, which again was singled out for praise by Mao Zedong at the 1942 Forum and generously rewarded for its achievements. After the war, Ke Zhongping lived mainly in Xi'an, where he continued to write while occupying a series of senior academic and administrative posts.

Zang Kejia (b. 1905)

Zang Kejia was one of the most prolific of the war poets, consolidating his position as a leading left-wing writer with several collections of short poems and a few long ones, most of which appear in the collection *Poems of a Decade* (1944). Spending the war years away from Yan'an, he managed to maintain his prewar style largely intact. In the period of Civil War after 1945, he became a member of the Nine Leaves group and wrote several satirical poems of which the best-known are included in the collection *The Zero Degree of Life* (1947). At this point, Zang had already sunk to the banality of lines like 'My heart will never rest in peace, As long as someone is unhappy.' He continued to write voluminously in the 1950s and 1960s and, as editor of *Poetry*, established in 1957 with poems by Mao as its inaugural attraction, exercised great power in the literary world. His career as a poet and cultural bureaucrat was revived along with *Poetry* in 1975. (*For Zang Kejia's early work see Chapter 3.*)

Feng Zhi (1905–93)

Not all poets found it necessary to express their patriotism in propaganda. Feng Zhi, who like Wen Yiduo had several years earlier abandoned poetry for academic life, concentrated initially on his duties as a teacher, joining the exodus to the south-west and spending the rest of the war years in Kunming. In 1941, he suddenly produced a series of twenty-seven sonnets, published simply as *Sonnets* in 1942. Some are addressed to individuals, like Lu Xun and Goethe; more are triggered by a humble patch of wild flowers, or a string of pack-horses. Many are reflections on the evanescent nature of temporal and spatial restrictions on life and the mind, with obvious reference to the displacements suffered by his contemporaries under war conditions. These poems, which in their restraint suggest his debt to Rilke, are generally considered his finest achievement in verse. During the 1950s and 1960s, he maintained a discreet silence as he continued his academic studies on German literature. The sonnets were excluded from *Feng Zhi's Selected Poems* of 1955, to be restored in 1980 along with his reputation as one of the new literature's best poets. (*For Feng Zhi's early work see Chapter 3.*)

Dai Wangshu (1905–50)

Among the more direct victims of war was Dai Wangshu, who in 1938 fled to Hong Kong. Together with Ai Qing, he founded a poetry magazine with the futuristic title *Acme*, whose first and last issue appeared in Guilin in 1938, and the few poems he wrote at this time continue the modernist strain of his earlier work and are not vehicles for propaganda. His main activity was in editing and journalism, and following the Japanese occupation of Hong Kong, he was imprisoned briefly in 1942.

After the war, he returned to Shanghai, where his final collection of poetry, *Years of Disaster*, was published in 1948. Some of these late poems lament the disasters that occurred in his private life; although he later remarried, his first marriage broke up in 1939 when his wife left him, taking their daughter with her. Better-known are the two patriotic poems, 'Written on a Prison Wall' and 'With My Injured Hand', which infuse the bitterness of the defeated with the courage to hope for final victory. The simplicity and restraint of the poems in this collection, despite their sombre tone, have made them the poet's most popular work. After another brief visit to Hong Kong in 1948, Dai Wangshu returned to Beijing in 1949 to take part in the first writers' and artists' congress, but died of illness the following year. (*For Dai Wangshu's early work see Chapter 3.*)

Su Jinsan (b. 1906) and Fang Jing (b. 1914)

Su Jinsan was one of several older poets who tried to adapt to the new requirements of the Yan'an Forum without much success. Although he started writing new poetry during the May Fourth Movement, he did not gain a wider audience until the publication of his war poetry. His best-known work is *Outside the Window* (1949), mostly long descriptive poems incorporating dramatic monologue dating from 1943–6. A physical education teacher at Henan University in Kaifeng at the outbreak of war, he moved with the university to south and west Henan. His poems describe the suffering in the countryside caused by the war with less rhetoric and more attention to local detail than the more prominent war poets. In 1948 he went to the Communist-controlled area in Hebei, where he worked at the Literary Research Institute in Shijiazhuang and came into contact with Ai Qing. He returned to Henan in 1949 and embarked on a new career as cultural bureaucrat. In 1957 he was declared a Rightist and his poetry disappeared from view until after the Cultural Revolution.

Fang Jing could be seen as Su Jinsan's west China counterpart, although he joined the Communist Party as early as 1938. A close friend of He Qifang, Cao Baohua (both fellow-Sichuanese), Bian Zhilin and Li Guangtian, his first two collections of poetry, *Rainscapes* (1942) and *Sounds* (1948), drew little attention beyond his own circle, but he became better-known for his 1948 and 1949 collections of war and post-war poetry, *Songs of a Stroller* and *Victims' Verses*. At this time he also had strong links with the Nine Leaves poets in Shanghai, Hang Yuehe and Chen Jingrong. He published little thereafter, although he continued to correspond in poetry with his old friends, and enjoyed a respected academic career in the south-west.

Gao Lan (1909–87), Tian Jian (1916–85) and Zou Difan (1917–95)

The vogue for declamatory poetry took hold of the popular imagination in the temporary wartime capital Wuhan in 1937: on the first anniversary of Lu Xun's death, Gao Lan, a poet from the Japanese-occupied north-west, used abbreviated, repetitive lines to arouse resistance to the enemy. His radio broadcasts spread the new style, and a collection of nineteen of his poems was printed under the title *Gao Lan's Verses for Declamation* in 1937.

Tian Jian's first collections of poems, *Before Dawn* (1935), *Chinese Shepherd Songs* (1935) and *Chinese Village Tales* (1936), were worthy but unremarkable representations of village life. The outbreak of war found him in Japan, but he hurriedly returned to China to support the war effort. Having come across Mayakovsky's poems in Japan, Tian Jian became an enthusiastic convert. He organised the 'street poetry' festival in Yan'an in 1938 and joined the Communist Party the same year. His most innovative works are the long poems 'For the Battlers', written in 1937, and 'She Too Will Kill' (1938), which won extravagant praise from senior writers including Wen Yiduo. To suggest the rhythm of war drums, Tian Jian shortened each line to a few words or syllables, extending the length to encompass dramatic narrative: the transformation of a simple peasant woman into a resistance fighter. Although the poem at times seems absurdly naive, it is a careful adaption into Chinese of the futurist poetry of Mayakovsky and other Soviet poets. 'The Biography of a Cart Driver' (1946), another epic poem, was more intricate and elaborate, also experimental but less innovative.

Zou Difan began his career as a poet in 1936 with left-wing verse in the style of Zang Kejia. His first collection, *Dust* (1938), was unremarkable, but the collection of narratives in *The Carpenter's Shop* (1940) established his reputation as a war poet. After the war he continued to write and occupied important posts in the new cultural bureaucracy. In the brief period of relaxation of the early 1960s, he showed a talent for lyric verse.

Tian Jian also continued to produce throughout the next three decades (with a brief interruption in the first phase of the Cultural Revolution), but never rose again above the conventional output required from a powerful cultural bureaucrat. Gao Lan published only sporadically during the 1940s and 1950s, and exerted little influence outside his academic post.

Ai Qing (1910–96)

The War against Japan brought Ai Qing to prominence as a leading propagandist for the resistance outside the Communist base in the north-west. His best-known collection from this period is *The North* (1939), written in Guilin in praise of the suffering peasants in the Japanese-occupied north. A more optimistic note characterises the long poem *Towards the Sun* (1940), celebrating the spirit of resistance in Wuchang in 1938. *Announcement of Dawn* (1943) is a miscellaneous collection of poems written in 1939 and 1940, in which political themes chase descriptions of life in China's cities and villages. Persuaded to go to Yan'an by Zhou Enlai, he arrived there in 1941, at a time when morale in the Communist headquarters was at an all-time low. For Ai Qing, it seemed that the solution lay in turning over to professional writers and artists like himself the responsibility for the spiritual life of the people, a suggestion that aroused deep opposition from Mao Zedong.

The severe criticism dealt out to Ai Qing in 1942 seemed to achieve its desired effect; he joined the Communist Party in 1945 and his poetry over the next decade and a half was thoroughly conventional. In the first years after 1949 he enjoyed the life of a celebrity, appointed as deputy editor of *People's Literature* and travelling to the Soviet Union and Chile. In 1957, however, he was branded a Rightist and banished from Beijing for the next two decades (of which sixteen years were spent in Xinjiang). On his return to Beijing and his career as a poet and cultural bureaucrat, he soon succumbed to the temptation to inflict a similar measure of severity to the new poets of the 1970s and 1980s. (*For Ai Qing's early work see Chapter 3.*)

Bian Zhilin (b. 1910)

Even for those who tried to respond to the challenge, the transition to wartime conditions and then to life under Communism was not easily reflected in their writing. In 1938 Bian Zhilin went to Yan'an from where he travelled to the front with a writers' 'comfort' group, composing poems which addressed the needs of the times and gathering material for a novel. In 1940 he left Yan'an for the more congenial atmosphere of Kunming, where he spent the rest of the war teaching literature. The 'comfort poems' formed the last part of his final collection, *Poems of a Decade* (1942). During the 1950s and 1960s he published only a small handful of poems, which, despite his efforts to conform, were not well received. The more relaxed period of the 1980s saw the recognition of his achievements as poet, translator and scholar. (*For Bian Zhilin's early work see Chapter 3.*)

He Qifang (1912–77)

For He Qifang, the war years confirmed the decisive change in his life which had taken place in 1936–7. Returning to Sichuan from the Japanese stronghold in Shandong in 1937, he spent an uncomfortable few months in Chengdu teaching and writing before leaving in 1938 with Bian Zhilin on a visit to Yan'an and then to the front. Unlike Bian, He Qifang decided to join the Communist Party and remain in Yan'an, where he soon became a leading member of the literary establishment as an academic, critic and administrator. The rigours of wartime life under the discipline of the Communist Party both exhilarated and depressed him. His inner conflicts are best expressed in a series of poems called 'Night Songs', written in 1940 and forming the centrepiece of the collection *Night Songs* (1945 and 1950; the first edition is incomplete). In these poems, as well as in longer narrative pieces written between 1938 and 1942, he attempted to simplify his language and make his poetry more accessible to less educated readers. Although he manages to achieve a more colloquial tone, the effect is not convincing, and it seems impossible for him not to refer again and again to his beloved Western poets even as he declares his intention to undergo 'an agonising rebirth'. After the Yan'an Forum of 1942, he was obliged to suppress his nostalgia for an earlier way of life, and the 'Night Songs' were re-edited and rearranged for publication in 1952 under the title *Night Songs and Songs of Day*.

During the 1950s and 1960s, He Qifang wrote steadily but not abundantly, dividing his time mostly between academic research and, increasingly, the multifarious duties of the cultural bureaucrat. Some poems were occasional pieces, written on demand, such as his contributions to the Great Leap Forward poetry of 1958 and his Vietnam poems of 1964; others are private exchanges with friends, published after his death. From a poet who consistently defended the May Fourth poetics of Wen Yiduo and Xu Zhimo, it is remarkable that these private poems, and even a few public ones, are written in classical forms. (*For He Qifang's early work see Chapter 3.*)

Wang Xindi (b. 1912)

The end of the war inspired Wang Xindi to write again. The ten poems written in 1946 and 1947 form the third and final section in *The Palm*, marking a premature end to his creative life. The contrast between his privileged social status as an intellectual (and son of a wealthy banking family) and the desperate plight of most Chinese became his main theme, echoing the poems written a few years earlier by He Qifang in Yan'an. 'The Palm' introduces a longer, looser line into his verse, to announce his intention to harden himself in the cause of post-war reconstruction. His professed humility is less convincing when, as in 'The Cuckoo', he lapses into current political jargon, and his earlier pessimism returns more darkly in an intuition of a final 'Day of Judgement' when 'human feelings, and faith in the light' are lost from civilisation ('Has Civilisation Shaken Out the Candlelight?').

Xindi (as he generally signed his work) also became active in promoting post-war literature, presiding over the Nine Leaves group as its oldest member. Employed as a banker in the service of the state in the 1950s and 1960s, he re-entered the literary world in the 1980s to handle foreign liaison work for the Shanghai branch of the Writers' Association and later became council member of the national Association. (*For Wang Xindi's early work see Chapter 3.*)

Hang Yuehe (1917–95)

Among the poets who shaped the direction of poetry after the end of the War against Japan, Hang Yuehe was one of the most active and influential. A native of Yixing, he was first educated at the provincial Pottery School, then at Jiangsu Normal College after which he taught in a local primary school. After the outbreak of war, he went to the north-west, where he studied briefly in Yan'an and travelled to the border areas. In 1940 he went to

Chongqing and became involved in left-wing publishing (including two volumes of Pushkin's poetry and essays on Zang Kejia). His first collection, *Picking Star Grass*, was published in 1945.

After the war, Hang Yuehe first went to Shanghai, where together with Zang Kejia and Fang Jing he founded one of the most influential post-war literary journals, *Poetry Creation*. He was also a founder, with Wang Xindi and Chen Jingrong, of *China's New Poetry*. Both journals aimed at reviving the Westernised free-verse styles of the May Fourth period, with particular attention to the craftsmanship of the *Crescent* and *Modern Times* poets. Although they tried to free poetry from the insistent political demands of the left, the strong element of social criticism in their work was considered subversive by the Nationalist government, and both journals were closed down in November 1948. Hang Yuehe then fled to Hong Kong (also the refuge of Zou Difan).

One of Hang Yuehe's main accomplishments was his attempt to create a new poetic idiom for the 1940s, blending old sayings, folk ballads, documentary extracts, contemporary speech idioms and Western syntax. He experimented with writing sonnets and then returned to exploring the rhythmic possibilities of free verse, including both short lyrics and longer narrative works. His themes were strictly contemporary, especially in his post-war poetry, showing a debt to Auden as well as to his Chinese colleagues. His main collections are *Records of a Nightmare* (1947), *The Burning City* (1948) and *The Revived Earth* (1949).

Hang Yuehe returned to the mainland but was effectively prevented from publishing poetry again until the 1980s. He retained his literary connections through his work as a book designer in the 1950s, 1960s and 1970s, under his real name, Cao Xinzhi, and was an early supporter of the new poetry of the 1980s. His close associate, Yuan Kejia, was one of the main official backers of the modernist tendency in the 1980s.

Chen Jingrong (1917–89)

Chen Jingrong started writing poetry in the 1930s, but her main activity as a poet dates from the post-war period as a co-editor on *China's New Poetry* with Hang Yuehe. Her early translations of poetry by Rilke and Baudelaire developed her inclination towards philosophical poetry, encouraged by her fellow Sichuanese, Fang

Jing. Her first collection, *Poems of Grace* (1948), includes work from 1935-45. Some of the early poems, set in Beijing, recall He Qifang's city poems of 1933 and 1934. On the outbreak of war, she returned to Sichuan, where she wrote characteristically introspective poems – mostly in a sombre mood, but with a more hopeful note emerging towards the end of the war.

Her second collection, *A Symphony* (1948), of poems from 1946 and 1947, shows a change of direction. The first section dates from a short stay in Chongqing and continues the romantic tendency of the previous volume. The second and third sections were both written in Shanghai, where disillusion with post-war civil strife penetrates her private world. Sometimes despair leads to melodrama, as in 'Process' with its maggots, garbage, flies and scabs; more often the poems express inner disquiet and hesitation before the final expectation of hope.

As a member of the Nine Leaves group, Chen Jingrong was prevented from publishing her own work in the 1950s, although she was admitted into the Writers' Association in 1956. She continued writing, however, and finally achieved book publication in the 1980s.

Mu Dan (1918–77)

With Beijing and Shanghai under Japanese occupation, and Chongqing and Yan'an competing capitals of the Nationalists and Communists, life in the remote south-west offered artistic autonomy to alleviate the hardships of war, homelessness and poverty. One of the most outstanding of the new writers in Kunming was Mu Dan, whose first collection of poetry, *The Exploration Team*, was published in 1945. The self-published *Mu Dan's Collected Poems*, consisting of sixty poems from between 1939 and 1945, appeared in 1947, and twenty-five of these poems, from the period 1941-5, were then republished as *The Flag* in 1948.

Mu Dan is the pen-name of Zha Liangzheng. Born in Tianjin and educated at Nankai Secondary School, he went to Qinghua University in 1935 originally to study geology, but soon found his true vocation in poetry and transferred to foreign languages and literature. He joined the university's wartime trek to Kunming and graduated from the South-west United University in 1940. In 1948 he went to the University of Chicago for a master's degree in English. He returned to China in 1952, and in 1953–8 taught English literature at Nankai University and published highly regarded translations of poetry by Pushkin, Byron, Shelley and Keats. On being labelled a Rightist, he spent the remainder of his life as a library assistant at Nankai. The end of the Cultural Revolution gave him the chance to write again, but he was not formally rehabilitated till after his death.

Mu Dan's war and post-war poems show the continuing role of Rilke, Eliot and Auden in aiding Chinese poets to convey their disillusion and despair at the world's chaos. To Mu Dan, the end of the war in 1945 did not bring promise of a better world, and his later verse is imbued with bitter irony: '... the best of us, Show vacant eyes; the happiest, Die, but die without a bridge' (from 'The Besieged', 1945). To communicate his complex thoughts and emotions, Mu Dan preferred a longer line than is common in modern Chinese verse, and employed Westernised syntax to give structure to his expression. The longer line is also flexible enough to contain reported speech, allowing the poet to stand outside the poem as an observer. Like the left-wing patriotic poets, Mu Dan finds it hard to avoid banality in his attempts to sound positive and optimistic, as in 'The Flag'; his individual voice is more distinct in his comments on the waste and destruction of war. His most remarkable lines, however, are in the considered reflections of his 1976 poems like 'Self' and 'Autumn'.

It was Mu Dan more than anyone who established the identity of the Nine Leaves group. Despite his youth and small output, he was then and is again now regarded as a highly distinctive presence in new poetry.

Guo Xiaochuan (1919–76) and Ke Lan (b. 1920)

Guo Xiaochuan joined the Eighth Route Army in 1937 and became a member of the Chinese Communist Party the following year. His literary abilities were soon noticed, and he was sent to study literary theory in Yan'an in 1941–5, taking part in the 1942 Forum on Literature and the Arts. His first collection of poetry, dating from his Yan'an years, was published in 1950. A string of administrative and journalistic posts followed, and in 1953 he moved from Tianjin to Beijing to work in the Party's

Propaganda Department. In 1955 he was admitted into the Writers' Association, and published another nine verse collections between 1956 and 1965. During the latter part of the Cultural Revolution, he continued to write poems glorifying Mao Zedong, and one of his last works was a long poem in 1976 commemorating Zhou Enlai's death. Most of his work is a more or less perfunctory performance dictated by Party policy, although his response to the encouragement of artistic professionalism in the mid-1950s shows a willingness to explore a world beyond mundane duties. His preferred poetic form was free verse incorporating an elaborate vocabulary partly derived from classical sources.

Like Guo Xiaochuan, Ke Lan also joined the Eighth Route Army in 1937 and the Communist Party in 1938, studied literature in Yan'an and spent the latter part of the war as a journalist and editor. His post-war base was in Shanghai, where the film industry became one of his many administrative interests. After the Yan'an Forum, Ke Lan had experimented with writing fiction in traditional styles but reverted to the conventional modern format after 1949. He is unusual among modern poets in writing prose poetry. His essay 'Echo in the Valley' was the basis for the 1984 film *The Yellow Earth*.

Zheng Min (b. 1920)

Another of the new talents fostered in Kunming was Zheng Min, whose sixty-two poems, written in 1942–7, were published in 1949 as *Zheng Min's Poems*. Her studies in German philosophy, augmented by Feng Zhi's lectures on Goethe and his own Rilkean sonnets, lend her verses a sense of tranquillity and detachment that seems far removed from war. She does not escape sentimentality, however, in poems like 'Evening Appointment', and it is disconcerting to find at this late stage yet another meditation on a rickshaw-puller. The longer poems suggest a more delicate sensibility, pondering the symbolism of journeys in the lives of individuals and nations. Zheng Min is one of the very few Chinese poets, like Guo Moruo before her and Yang Lian after, to attempt a panoramic vision of Chinese culture, although her versions are more subdued.

Born in Fujian, Zheng Min graduated in philosophy at Southwest United in 1943 and went to Brown University in the United

States. In 1950 she began postgraduate studies at the State University of Illinois, obtaining a master's degree in English literature in 1951. On returning to China in 1956, she was appointed a teacher at Beijing Normal University. Like Yuan Kejia, she seemed to have enjoyed some protection in her academic post. Following a thirty-year silence, she began to write and publish poetry again in 1979.

Li Ji (1922–80)

When Mao delivered his opening and closing speeches at the Forum on Literature and the Arts in 1942, he was drawing on the confidence and experience of his own poetic practice as much as on the current line in Soviet literary policy as reported by Zhou Yang and his other advisors. Compared to May Fourth writing, from the hindsight of the 1940s, China's classical and folk traditions seemed much nearer to each other than either to the Westernised new fiction, drama and poetry. The success of the Party's propaganda teams in adapting local opera provided a model for a future direction in creating a genuinely proletarian literature and art, and at the same time undercut the pretensions of the urban writers who sought to establish their own power-base in Yan'an. The poets who took part in the Forum dutifully collected folksongs (like He Qifang) and tried to incorporate folk elements into their poetry (like Tian Jian), but were either unable or unwilling to abandon their early allegiances, while Mao's more enthusiastic supporters such as Ke Zhongping were more successful as organisers than in their own writing. The new mass poetry was to come from another generation, of whom the foremost representative was Li Ji.

Li Ji's credentials were exemplary. Originally from a peasant family in Henan, he had only one year's schooling before he joined up with local guerrillas. He came to Yan'an in 1938 to study at the Military Academy and joined the Communist Party the following year. After some years travelling with the Eighth Route Army, he lived in 1942–7 in a north Shaanxi town near the Great Wall as a school-teacher, editor and local administrator. His literary career started after the Forum, but struck fame only with the publication of his long narrative poem *Wang Gui and Li Xiangxiang* in 1946. Based on the *xintianyou* ballad form, it was given an ecstatic welcome at the time as the first product of the Forum and the beginning of a new era in poetry.

One of the most popular folksong genres of the north-west, the *xintianyou* (roughly meaning 'free flowing') ballad consists of rhymed couplets, of which the first line creates an image and the second line relates a story or delivers a message. Traditionally an extempore performing art, in the hands of a skilled practitioner it could produce remarkably inventive and powerful effects. Self-evidently suitable for narrating stories of village life, it was also easily adapted to the post-Forum demand that literary works should promote class struggle among the masses. The plot is simple, a classic tale of lovers suffering oppression, set during the Civil War in the 1930s. Wang Gui is a village lad in service to an evil landlord who has killed his father, and Li Xiangxiang is his sweetheart. The landlord, Cui Erye, proceeds to torture the son for joining a Communist guerrilla unit as well as being Li Xiangxiang's lover. Wang Gui's comrades rescue him and the couple are married, but the landlord escapes. He returns to the village with government troops to support him, kidnaps Li Xiangxiang and forces her to marry him. In the nick of time Wang Gui then reappears with the guerrillas to rescue Li Xiangxiang, and the landlord is taken away.

Li Ji does not manage to sustain the convention throughout the 378 couplets, and not all first lines provide good matches for the second: for example, 'A flock of goats [or sheep] follows the goat at the head, Throughout north Shaanxi the Communists spread'. Other conjunctions are happier: for example, 'Fresh round grains on maize you'll find, Li [Xiangxiang's father] was old but his heart was kind.' Popular sayings were also incorporated into the text, along with local expressions which were nevertheless comprehensible to a wider audience. Saturated with local colour, impeccably correct in sentiment and yet lively and appealing, the poem was given considerable publicity as a model throughout the 1940s and 1950s. It failed, however, to produce successors, and suffered a final indignity when the English translation, first published by the Foreign Languages Press in Beijing in 1954 as a high point of literary achievement under Communist Party leadership, was marketed in the 1980s as a children's story. Li Ji continued to write during the 1950s and 1960s, and occupied important editorial positions in the 1970s.

He Jingzhi (b. 1924) and Li Ying (b. 1926)

Born in Shandong, He Jingzhi fled to Hubei at the outbreak of war to study, and then followed his school to Sichuan where he began taking part in resistance activities, including war poetry. He went to Yan'an in 1940 and joined the Communist Party the following year. His first notable literary achievement was co-authorship of the opera *The White-haired Girl* in 1945, following Mao Zedong's directive at the 1942 Forum to adapt local art forms to propagandistic aims. He occupied increasingly important Party and government posts in the 1950s and 1960s, accompanied by a steady stream of poems celebrating the achievements of the new regime. His best-known works are his long poems 'Return to Yan'an' (1956), 'Song of Lei Feng' (1962), 'China in October' (1976) and 'Song of August 1st' (1977). 'Return to Yan'an' is based on a simplified folk ballad form; the later poems are mostly in free verse, with short exclamatory lines and highly-coloured rhetorical flourishes. The culmination of his career was his appointment in September 1989 as Minister of Culture following Wang Meng's resignation after the June Fourth massacre.

Li Ying started writing as a student at Beijing University in 1945. On graduating in 1949, he became a reporter attached to the People's Liberation Army on its southern advance and joined the Communist Party. Back in Beijing, he joined the People's Liberation Army headquarters and covered the Korean front in 1950. A series of poetry collections in the 1950s led to his admission into the Writers' Association in 1956, after which he became even more prolific. Like He Jingzhi, he continued to write and publish during the Cultural Revolution, and like him also celebrated its end with poems such as 'The Unforgettable 1976'. Again like He Jingzhi, he wrote little thereafter. His preferred poetic style is a conventional balladic form, mainly sentimental rhapsodies in praise of soldiers and their commanders.

Of the fifty poets mentioned in Part I who were active in the twenty-five years 1912–37, only seven were still sufficiently active to be included in Part II. Twelve had died, and of the remaining thirty-one, most had retreated into academic life while some turned to politics. Only twenty-five poets are represented for the thirty years from 1938–68: perhaps as many were writing, but the pressures of war and Communism diminished the amount of poetry that might be expected to outlive its age. Of the twenty-five one was assassinated and one died shortly after being released from prison camp; the remainder survived the war period although not necessarily as active writers. Apart from Mao himself, whose death defined the end of the Cultural Revolution, the other twenty-two also lived long enough at least to celebrate – genuinely or dutifully – its conclusion.

Discounting the factor of the natural death rate, it is notable how few of these writers suffered a violent or premature death through illness caused by poverty or persecution in the years 1938–68 compared to the preceding two decades. Considering the drop-out rate of the earlier period, however, it is not surprising that only a handful of those active at the beginning of the War against Japan continued to publish more than occasional verse after the founding of the People's Republic of China (the occasional versifiers including the indefatigable old warriors Guo Moruo and Mao Zedong).

Several reasons can account for the relative silence of the older established poets during the 1950s and 1960s. As in the earlier period, it is noticeable that Chinese poets of this century who built their reputation on new literature turned to classical forms of writing in their old age – much, perhaps, as Chinese scholars in imperial times are said to have turned in their old age from Confucianism to Daoism. Since this kind of writing was not considered suitable for general circulation, what they wrote was rarely published. (Younger writers whose writing was formed in the folk-styles of Yan'an also found themselves unfashionable in the 1950s and 1960s but seemed to find little difficulty in switching to the bastardised May Fourth free verse that dominated this period.)

Ideological control over such elements as themes, character portrayal and language, whether in the form of pre-publication censorship or command directives, was a substantial factor in the silence of writers from all age groups, either reluctant or unable to change their literary allegiances. A third factor was factional politics, including guilt by association: the most prominent loser in this game was Ai Qing; the unluckiest were the Nine Leaves poets. Many older writers excused themselves on the grounds of pressure from adminstrative or academic duties; some of these may have felt that having qualified for such positions in a kind of literary apprenticeship, there was no need to continue to prove themselves.

What was most distinctive about the 1940s, 1950s and 1960s was the beginning of a conscious divide between public and private selves, which was to become even more striking in the 1970s. In these decades, we see poets coming easily or painfully to terms with the need for public witness and private concealment. In the 1940s, poets still had room for choice: to move to another part of the country, to retire into academic life, to write for private publication. In the following two decades, little room for manoeuvre was permitted. Given the strict controls over what was deemed suitable for publication, it is remarkable how many of the older generation, accustomed to their pre-war autonomy, still chose to write at all. Some may have given way to pressure; some were undoubtedly confident of being duly awarded for their efforts; others may simply have been propelled by the age-old motive of professional writers: dislike for other kinds of work. It is hard not to wonder if they ever considered the personal risk to themselves, or felt embarrassed at the rubbish that poured out, not only for the domestic audience but also for consumption abroad. By their own account, many writers believed that they were serving the cause of the masses, or helping to establish a powerful intelligentsia, or contributing towards world recognition of China as a great power, all of which the cultural achievements of the first half of the twentieth century had failed to secure.

9

DRAMA: PERFORMING FOR POLITICS

Under pressure of Japanese aggression, playwrights turned to street theatre to reach new audiences, a movement which started as early as 1932 in Shanghai and was renewed and extended in 1937 and 1938. By definition a limited form, street theatre may have lost its intended audience – the urban proletariat and semi-urban peasantry who did not normally patronise the new theatre – before its writers. Following geographical shifts in the population in the face of expanding Japanese power, the new theatre broke off into independent areas: Japanese-occupied Shanghai, the north-west Communist Party headquarters in Yan'an, and the Nationalist south-west from Chongqing to Guilin. Of the thirteen troupes organised in August 1937 in Shanghai, two stayed in Shanghai while the rest took to the provincial towns and villages. A year later, Guo Moruo, as head of literary propaganda for the United Front's Military Affairs Commission, reorganised these troupes into ten Anti-Japanese Drama Companies, providing employment for three hundred drama workers as well as moral support for amateur groups of all kinds to take part in theatre-based propaganda.

In Chongqing and Guilin, writers and performers of the new theatre quickly regrouped to stage satires on the greed and corruption of the Nationalist government. A theme of particular interest was the plight of the middle-class, obliged because of the war to resettle in the south-west but frustrated by the inaction of the government on the war front and the difficulty of making a decent living as a teacher, doctor or owner-manager of a small business or factory. Examples are Cao Yu's *Metamorphosis*, Chen Baichen's *Men and Women in Wild Times* and Tian Han's *Autumn Song*. The reinstitution of strict political censorship in the early 1940s was probably a factor in nudging playwrights to explore the psychological dimensions of this theme, as the old order was

285

overturned and new elites profited from the war, shown in Cao Yu's *Peking Man*, Xia Yan's *Fragrant Flowers on the Horizon*, Hong Shen's *Women, Women* and Song Zhidi's *Chongqing in Fog*.

Another response to Nationalist censorship was the revival of plays on historical subjects. Costume drama had been popular since the 1930s among politically aware audiences and playwrights including Li Jianwu, Xia Yan, Yang Hansheng, Chen Baichen and Song Zhidi, and during the war years it flourished again in the hands of Guo Moruo (who wrote no other kind) and Yang Hansheng. Apart from the relative safety for authors in criticism cloaked in historical melodrama, the past was also plundered for its audience appeal, both in terms of national pride in heroic episodes from Chinese history and in the colour added by classical literary texts, costuming and pageantry. Even plays with modern settings, such as Tian Han's *Autumn Song*, incorporated material from the past.

A by-product of costume drama which became increasingly evident was the blurring of the formerly distinct line between new and traditional theatre. Lao She's attempts at modern story-telling scripts and Ouyang Yuqian's experiments in semi-operatic drama helped to merge and expand theatre audiences. According to Tian Han, by 1940 there were 2,500 drama troupes in Chong-qing and Guilin with over 75,000 members (including actors, playwrights, producers and musicians). Increasing professionalism in the theatre, and its reputation as an effective educational medium, encouraged established novelists based in Chongqing such as Mao Dun and Ba Jin to try their hand at drama, although without notable success. Mao Dun's five-act play *Around the Time of Qing-ming*, an attack on the Nationalist government for its failure to protect China's industry and commerce, was first performed in Chongqing in 1945 under the direction of the actor Zhao Dan who also took the lead role. Because of its author's fame it attracted much attention, but the biggest hits in Chongqing in 1938–45 were by professionals: *Metamorphosis* by Cao Yu, *The Nation above All* by Lao She and Song Zhidi, *The Fascist Baccillus* by Xia Yan, *The Song to the Spirit of Honour* by Wu Zuguang, and *Qu Yuan* by Guo Moruo.

Despite the prevalence of anti-Nationalist propaganda, censor-ship was relatively rare in the early war years in Chongqing and almost non-existent in Guilin. The theatre in Shanghai presented special dangers and opportunities. Strict censorship was imposed on all forms of theatre starting from the summer of 1937. Traditional theatre was allowed to resume performances in the autumn, but troupes were kept under close surveillance and stars like Mei Lanfang and Cheng Yanqiu either retired or moved away. Most of the writers and performers in the modern theatre fled to the interior, and the remaining underground resistance was brutally suppressed. The French Concession enjoyed limited autonomy as an Axis member after 1940, offering some protection to its Chinese residents, but the International Settlement lost its autonomy after the outbreak of the Pacific War at the end of 1941 when it was directly governed by the Japanese until handed over to the Wang Jingwei government in Nanjing in 1943. In the summer of 1942, however, the theatre was booming, as writers and performers discovered that censors could be bribed or fooled.

By far the most popular genre was costume drama with a message for contemporary audiences: this was signalled as early as 1939, when Yu Ling's new resistance play *Night in Shanghai*, a critical but not a box-office success, was outperformed commercially by an historical allegory with the same patriotic message, *Sorrow for the Fall of the Ming* by the critic Aying (Qian Xingcun, 1900–77). Aying went on to write several wartime plays with women warriors, like Ouyang Yuqian in *Peach Blossom Fan*, identifying the Japanese invasion with the Manchu attack on the Ming empire. Confirmation of this trend was secured by Wu Zuguang's *The Song to the Spirit of Honour* in 1940, Yao Ke's *Malice of Empire* in 1941, and *Wen Tianxiang* (i.e. *The Song to the Spirit of Honour* under a new title) in 1943. Hua Mulan, the most famous of China's women warriors, also appeared in a filmscript by Ouyang Yuqian in 1939, *Mulan Joins the Army*, later performed in Shanghai and Chongqing as a play.

A variation on historical drama proper consisted of plays with a contemporary setting but featuring Peking opera stars, such as the 1942 stage adaptation of Qin Shou'ou's *Begonia* and Wu Zuguang's *Return on a Snowy Night* in 1943. Costume drama not only blurred the lines between traditional and modern theatre but also broke down the barriers between commercial and art audiences in a way that was probably only possible in a large cosmopolitan city like Shanghai (the absence of a powerful left-wing organisation was also a factor). Even a purely commercial piece like *Begonia* had a message of moral corruption in high places and the virtues of the oppressed, as did the sensationalist, well-constructed plays of Zhou Yibai (1900–77) like *The Canary*, the story of a high-class prostitute, and his costume drama *Hua Mulan*.

Foreign rule in Shanghai had always given the city minimal censorship in regard to sex, and Shanghai audiences were not averse to being titillated. Women were often the protagonists of Shanghai drama and film, and their sexual exploitation or exploits were a common theme. Running a close second to prostitutes as main characters were cross-dressers such as the woman warriors Hua Mulan and Ge Nenniang, the aspiring scholar Zhu Yingtai, and Peking opera actors specialising in female roles. The plays with the longest runs during these years were Wu Tian's adaptation of Ba Jin's *The Family* (cross-class romantic love and family conflict), *Sorrow for the Fall of the Ming* (historical cross-dressing and patriotism), *Malice of Empire* (patriotism, generational conflict and doomed love, all in an historical setting), *Begonia* (cross-dressing and social oppression) and *Wen Tianxiang* (patriotism in an historical setting, the only example where the love theme is secondary).

Socially conscious and psychological realism was best represented by adaptations of Western plays. The prevalence of (or need for) these adaptations has no counterpart in modern Chinese fiction or poetry, although more or less conscious plagiarism was common enough. In many cases they were made by directors, most notably Huang Zuolin and Fei Mu, who were acutely aware of the need to keep the customers pouring in. Other factors included the requirements of the foreign concessions, the dearth of local playwrights, and the lack of competition from new books and imported films. The novelist Shi Tuo's *The Big Circus*, adapted from Leonid Andreyev's *He Who Gets Slapped*, was a big success in 1942–3, and his *The Night Inn*, co-authored by Ke Ling and based on Maxim Gorky's *The Lower Depths*, was published in 1944 and staged after the Japanese surrender; both plays were directed by Huang Zuolin. Even as noted a dramatist as Li Jianwu spent most of the war years on adaptions from Sardou and other French playwrights, although Fei Mu's production of his new work, *Juvenescence*, was well-received despite its lack of reference to the war. On the whole, the psychological dramas of the Chongqing stage did not transplant easily: the Shanghai Theatre Arts

Association put on plays like Li Jianwu's *This Is Only Spring*, but Yang Jiang's anti-romantic *Windswept Blossoms* was not performed.

The blurring of distinctions between audiences in Yan'an took a rather different form. The Communist Party had a long history of fostering local drama or folk opera for propaganda and educational purposes, going back to the Northern Expedition of 1926 and the implementation of mass-line policies on the use of traditional cultural forms in Ruijin in 1931–4. Educated youth from the cities introduced spoken drama to the Jiangxi Soviet as early as 1930, but theorists like Qu Qiubai stressed the need to reform spoken drama to make it more familiar and acceptable to workers, peasants and soldiers, the main objects of Red Army recruitment and propaganda. Soon after the establishment of Red Army bases in the north-west, the Communist Party set about active recruitment of students and intellectuals, who began arriving in Yan'an in large numbers in 1937 and 1938.

Two parallel tendencies in drama coexisted in 1936–42. On the one hand, a large number of locally based drama troupes trained by Red Amy veterans from Jiangxi operated in the countryside, with higher-level troupes in Yan'an such as the Masses' Opera Troupe headed by Ke Zhongping. On the other hand were small touring corps presenting 'street theatre' to rural areas, staffed by urban intellectuals trained in the spoken drama; one of the best known of these was the North-west Battleground Service Corps, headed by Ding Ling. Both sorts were avowedly propagandist and took the rural masses as their audience.

The rapid expansion of numbers in Yan'an was meanwhile creating a more sophisticated audience. Although Party leaders like Mao Zedong and Zhu De enjoyed Western musical and dramatic performances, they were also fond of traditional Chinese opera, and in response to Mao's impromptu suggestion in 1938, Ke Zhongping founded a professional troupe for the reform of traditional opera with revolutionary content. Known as the Border Region Masses' Opera Troupe, it appears to have performed chiefly in Yan'an for the edification of cadres, soldiers and the local peasants, and its mixture of musical styles from different levels of regional and village operas formed the prototype of a new Chinese 'opera' (*geju*, literally 'song-drama', a term previously reserved for Western opera). At the same time the newly founded Lu Xun Academy, whose drama section was headed by Zhang

Geng, set up the Experimental Drama Troupe to perform both spoken drama and Peking opera. The Lu Xun Academy followed the Shanghai pattern of enlivening modern drama with techniques borrowed from classical Chinese music and opera, appealing to the new elites in both the cultural and political sphere. 'The Yellow River' cantata, based on a poem by Guang Weiran with music by Xian Xinghai, was another Academy success in 1939.

Up to the Rectification campaign of 1941–2, the intellectuals were gaining the upper hand in Yan'an cultural life. Students at the Lu Xun Academy were trained on Stanislavsky's methods and masterpieces of the Western and May Fourth tradition by Molière, Gogol, Chekhov and Cao Yu, while leaders relaxed to performances of Western classical music performed by musicians in white tie and tails. Nevertheless, experiments in local opera and folk dance were continuing in the areas outside Yan'an, and some success had been achieved in the *yangge*, a folk dance which incorporated short sketches containing some spoken dialogue, known in many varieties and under different names throughout north China (Dingxian was another centre). In accordance with Engel's theory on the origins of art in labour, the word *yangge* was taken to mean '[rice-]sprout song'. It was traditionally performed around the New Year (i.e. early spring) as part of fertility rituals, and the sketches were heavily erotic in content and presentation. Reformed *yangge* kept the dance steps, lengthened the sketches, cleaned up the content, and substituted everyday village types for the traditional roles. After Mao's 1942 speeches, the reformed *yangge* was introduced to Yan'an drama workers, whose attention was directed towards developing *yangge* into plays for performance in towns as well as the countryside. The Lu Xun Academy, leaning heavily on the efforts of Ke Zhongping's troupe, launched several new *yangge* plays in 1943 for local consumption. This in turn led to *The White-haired Girl*, an opera by He Jingzhi and Ding Yi incorporating *yangge* elements which became one of the best-known works of the modern Chinese theatre. Other Yan'an works include the spoken drama, *Comrade, You've Taken the Wrong Path!* (1944), and the Yan'an Peking Opera Company's *Driven to Join the Liangshan Rebels* (1944), which earned Mao's personal congratulations.

Although the term 'socialist realism' was borrowed from the Soviet Union for use in Yan'an and after, Mao's 'Talks' reveals an older conception of literature. Socialist realism implies an optimistic representation of current social forces successfully carrying out Party policy, written and overseen by professionals, while the 'Talks' requires the adaptation of existing popular cultural forms to embody Party thinking expressed through characters who typify Communist ideals. Mao Zedong's understanding of 'typical characters' was entirely compatible with role stereotyping in traditional Chinese theatre, from amateur peasant performances in villages, such as *yangge*, to the highly professional *kunqu* (a highly literary operatic form from the Shanghai area) and Peking opera styles. The blurring of lines between traditional and modern theatre, between elite, commercial and folk audiences, and between art and propaganda, was the chief bequest of the war years to the development of new drama.

The theatre was taken very seriously by the new regime, which for organisational as much as ideological reasons brought all forms together within the new Ministry of Culture. In 1950 the Ministry sponsored a national conference of theatre personnel, bringing together modern playwrights, traditional performers and state and Party cultural personnel. Professional associations, schools and troupes were established or re-organised under state and Party supervision to regularise education, training, employment and welfare, all of which were heavily subsidised. Financial support and political control were complementary, according to long-held policies which saw the arts generally as the responsibility of the state; the theatre, like the cinema, was a branch of the arts which was always dependent on considerable investment. As the theatre became primarily a medium of programmed political education, professional performers and theatre artists of all kinds were regarded alike as 'intellectuals', a welcome rise in status at the time but one that was to have drastic personal consequences in the 1960s. Spoken drama, traditional theatre (especially Peking opera), modern Western-style opera, dance-drama and various folk arts were brought closer together than ever before, and interchangeability of genre was fostered by common political aims.

The spoken drama, whose personnel and audiences were most closely aligned with the new cultural bureaucracy, was initially a favoured genre, and critics were found to aver that spoken drama had its roots not in the West but in plays, now lost, dating from the Tang dynasty. State subsidies were given to up to a hundred professional spoken drama companies, and prominent May Fourth figures such as Tian Han, Lao She and Cao Yu were encouraged to stage new plays on contemporary themes. The former National Academy of Drama was moved from Nanjing to Beijing and reorganised as the Central Academy of Drama in 1950 with Ouyang Yuqian at its head and a generous complement of Soviet advisers. The Beijing People's Art Theatre, established in 1952 to perform spoken drama, was headed by Cao Yu as president and Jiao Juying as director, and the Capital Theatre was purpose-built for it in 1956. The continued unpopularity of spoken drama with broader audiences, especially in the countryside, was met with suggestions for reform by the Shanghai director Huang Zuolin, but the kind of modernism he urged, a strange blend of Brecht, Stanislavsky and traditional Chinese opera, had a limited attraction apart from drama students and professionals.

The traditional theatre came under more critical attention, although swings in direction reflected the ambivalence felt by many senior Party members. Mao Zedong was a well-known patron of the traditional theatre, and is thought to have coined the Hundred Flowers slogan at this time to allow the traditional theatre to survive by discarding only its most blatantly backward aspects. Almost three thousand opera companies were given state support, and the Beijing School (later, Academy) of Traditional Drama was set up in 1952 to train performers and writers. On the other hand, the new Ministry of Culture established a Committee for Theatre Reform headed by Zhou Yang in 1950 to weed out 'harmful' plays from the repertoire, starting with an immediate temporary ban on fifty-five plays. In 1952, the Committee published a list of twenty-six banned works; another sixty-three said to have been revised; fifteen drastically revised; and more than 200 permitted to continue unchanged. Limited encouragement was given to regional opera: at the First National Festival of Traditional Drama in Beijing in 1952, more than a thousand people presented nearly a hundred works in over twenty operatic forms (out of approximately 350 regionally or locally based forms or styles). Prize-winners included *Liang Shanbo and Zhu Yingtai* (Shaoxing opera), *Love under the Willows* (Sichuan opera) and Tian Han's *The White Snake* (Peking opera).

Reform of the traditional theatre was slow, despite pressure exerted by the authorities which disbanded troupes or dismissed performers. The proscribed plays represented only a tiny proportion of the opera repertoire, and even the bans were not treated very seriously. Audiences and performers continued to prefer the old favourites, and in October 1953, Guo Moruo praised the traditional theatre as a treasured part of the national inheritance. Filming of traditional opera commenced in 1953, forming an important archive for training and extending the opera audience, as well as systematic transcription and recording for research. A conference on Peking opera in November 1954, attended by Ouyang Yuqian, Tian Han, Mei Lanfang and Cheng Yanqiu, advocated the retention of techniques such as painted faces but the elimination of 'unhealthy' elements such as the kowtow and continued use of Western-style backdrops and scenery. The chief focus was still on content, and texts and plots were altered to suit the new policies. Theatres remained largely in private hands, but theatre companies were gradually brought under state control, along with other urban enterprises, between 1952 and 1956. In his report on the achievements in drama by 1955, Tian Han, president of the Dramatists' Association, presented a statistically staggering record of performances and attendances.

At the beginning of 1956, Liu Shaoqi announced the beginnings of a new, relaxed policy on both traditional and modern drama, but quantity rather than quality was the first result. Forty-nine new plays were performed at the First National Festival of Spoken Drama held in Beijing in March–April 1956, mostly humdrum propaganda pieces of no particular merit: the most notable were the prize-winning *Bright Skies* by Cao Yu and Lao She's *Looking West to Chang'an* (based on Gogol's *The Inspector-General*). More encouraging was the national conference on drama in June 1956 in Beijing, attended by writers, performers and officials. Traditional opera was given firm support, the entertainment value of the theatre was defended, and the interference of Party authorities condemned. Many previously banned plays were re-instated (*The Butterfly Dream*, *Si Lang Visits His Mother*), and works thought to have a positive message were highlighted, such as Lao She's revised version of the *kunqu* opera *Fifteen Strings of Cash*. Although the latter is rich enough in entertainment value not to need further justification, its plot involves the same kind of upright late-Ming official invoked by Wu Han as a cover for attacks on Mao Zedong in the early 1960s. (Its revival as a film in the late 1970s was greeted as a very direct attack on the Cultural Revolution.) A more innocuous work, *The Wild Boar Forest* by Li Xiaochun, a Peking opera adapted from an episode in *Water Margin*, was performed as politically orthodox entertainment rather than for the purpose of factional politics, although it was criticised during the Cultural Revolution for its 'feudal' theme. A second conference in February 1957 lifted all restrictions on traditional theatre and paid tribute to the masses' ability to distinguish between 'flowers' and 'weeds'. Tian Han's statement that bad plays were no more than a tiny fraction of the entire repertoire was a common enough sentiment at the time, although it was to be held against him personally in 1966. Figures published in April 1957 announced that more than 51,000 traditional plays had been discovered in different parts of the country, of which over 14,000 had been transcribed and 4,200 re-edited for performance.

The revival of old plays was very popular and the crowds flocked to the theatres again. Fearful of a backlash, famous performers including Mei Lanfang, Cheng Yanqiu and Zhou Xinfang warned theatre management not to ignore modern opera but they were not taken seriously. At a drama conference in June and July 1958, as part of the Great Leap Forward, Zhou Yang confirmed that opera was still a primary weapon of propaganda: the work of re-editing old opera was to be resumed, but more importantly, new opera was to comprise half of the entire repertoire. Among the new Peking operas prepared at this time was an adaptation of *The White-haired Girl* with Du Jinfang as Xi'er and Yuan Shihai as the landlord, and *Taking Tiger Mountain by Strategy*, excerpted from the novel by Qu Bo, *Tracks in the Snowy Forest*. During the years 1959–62, however, only a handful of new operas was ever staged, while the old operas gained the status of popular classics. At the National Day celebrations in 1959, Peking opera stars Mei Lanfang, Ma Lianliang and Yuan Shihai were joined by Hongxiannü and Ma Shizeng representing Cantonese opera, Yu Zhenfei representing *kunqu*, and Xu Yulan representing Shaoxing opera; all showcased classic pieces. By 1960, an archive of reminiscences by famous performers included contributions from Mei Lanfang (who died in 1961), Cheng Yanqiu (died 1958), Ouyang Yuqian and Zhou Xinfang.

Following the Hundred Flowers campaign, modern spoken drama continued its close entanglement with politics, but with the difference that the state was now actively involved as a sponsor rather than merely a censor. At the same time professional dramatists and other intellectuals continued to use drama to defend their own status and interests. The latter trend culminated in the historical plays and operas of the late 1950s and early 1960s: Lao She's *Teahouse* (1957), Tian Han's *Guan Hanqing* (1958), *Princess Wencheng* (1960) and *Xie Yaohuan* (1961), Meng Chao's *Li Huiniang* (1961) and Wu Han's *Hai Rui Dismissed from Office* (1961).

Mao Zedong's sensitivity to criticism through literature, theatre or cinema had a long history. One of the first instances was the case of the film *The Secret History of the Qing Palace*, produced in Hong Kong in 1948–9 from a script adapted by Yao Ke from his very successful wartime costume drama *The Malice of Empire*. The film was very popular not only in Hong Kong but also on the mainland, where it was released for general distribution on the authority of a committee which included Lu Dingyi, Zhou Yang and Hu Qiaomu, and whose superior was Liu Shaoqi. A scene at the end of the film showed the Qing emperor, in flight from the Boxers and the foreign siege of Beijing, being advised by loyal but long-suffering peasants along the route to pay more attention to the nation's problems. It is likely that the film-makers who added this scene to the original filmscript intended it as a criticism of Chiang Kaishek, but Mao Zedong took it to be a reflection on himself, whether intentionally or otherwise, and in 1950 overrode the decision to release the film; an internal memo from Mao in 1954 also denounced the film, implying criticism of the four originally responsible. A similar incident, in which Jiang Qing was directly involved, occurred in 1951 over the release of the film *The Life of Wu Xun* (1950), a project personally supervised by Xia Yan. There is no evidence to show that Mao's sense of personal insult had any foundation in these two cases, but from 1956 onwards criticism of Mao's policies was frequently expressed through historical allegory on stage.

In *Guan Hanqing* (1958; revised edition in book form, 1961) Tian Han delivered a warning on the displeasure felt by intellectuals at the power structure around Mao Zedong. There was a very personal element in this: Jiang Qing had long been a potential threat to Tian Han, their enmity going back to the 1930s, and the prospect of her rising influence in the theatre could have caused him only dismay. The appeal in the play to the populace and historical inevitability are conventionally Marxist. What is distinctive is the portrait of the disaffected scholar who uses the arts – in this case, the theatre – to justify to himself and to the regime his right to social status and power. The message in 1958 was veiled; the re-publication of the script in 1961 was a clearer statement. In the play, Guan Hanqing refuses to cut offending lines and is punished by banishment. Tian Han was to face a more terrible fate.

Wu Han's *Hai Rui Dismissed from Office*, an historical allegory for the dismissal of Peng Dehuai in 1959 because of his opposition to Mao's Great Leap Forward policies, had an even more tortuous history, and its author also lost his life on its account. The opera implies not only that Hai Rui was an upright figure, but also that the morality which he upheld was still valid for contemporary China. This moral conservatism on the part of modern scholar officials was deeply offensive to Mao, and Wu Han became the first target in a campaign against the group around Peng Zhen, Wu Han's patron. Mao's irritation at the covert attacks on him personally was conveyed in a message to Xia Yan by Jiang Qing in July 1962, but the message was ignored. Jiang Qing then turned her attention to more active methods for promoting Mao's views, eventually finding allies among theatrical reformers and an operational base in Shanghai.

The persistence of traditional ideologies had become a matter of sharp disagreement within the Party, with Mao attempting a comeback to the frontline of Party policy-making. A national conference on drama and opera in Guangzhou in March 1962, addressed by Chen Yi, had re-affirmed the new relaxed line, and Mao decided to make reform of the performing arts a priority. Jiang Qing, who had begun investigating the repertoires of Peking opera companies in Beijing and Shanghai in 1961, highlighted the absence of operas on contemporary themes; she also advocated a ban on *Hai Rui Dismissed from Office* in July 1962. Early in 1963 Mao Zedong criticised the Ministry of Culture for its support of 'emperors, generals, scholars and beauties' and its failure to back Jiang Qing's new revolutionary works. Under pressure, the Ministry announced a ban on plays about 'ghosts' in March. Ke Qingshi, mayor of Shanghai, at Jiang Qing's request, sponsored the East China Festival of Spoken Drama in Shanghai from December 1963 to January 1964 with twenty new plays on modern themes by nineteen troupes. By tacit agreement, this festival was a disaster, and Jiang Qing lost interest in spoken drama. More promise was shown at the Festival of Peking Operas on Contemporary Themes in June and July 1964, at which thirty-five new Peking operas from twenty-seven national and provincial troupes were presented, four under Jiang Qing's personal sponsorship. Performers included Ma Lianliang, Zhao Yanxia and Yuan Shihai. Peng Zhen, as mayor of Beijing, presided over the festival, which was also attended by Mao Zedong and Zhou Enlai, and both Lu Dingyi and Jiang Qing made speeches. Jiang Qing's first complaint was that of the 3,000 theatre companies currently registered with the state, 2,800 performed traditional opera and only ninety performed spoken plays; and that between them both the old and the new stage were dominated by characters from the past or foreigners. She also demanded a decisive role in the creation of scripts for political leaders and the masses as well as theatre professionals. The final demand was for greater attention to be paid to positive protagonists, who typically tended to be overshadowed by the more interesting villains or 'middle characters'. Jiang Qing's speech was not reported at the time, however, and Peng Zhen continued to resist her demands for a complete ban on all old operas.

During the next year, many new Peking operas were written and performed. There were several reasons for making Peking opera the focus of the populists' campaign. It was the most widely performed and most popular of all the performing arts and yet the preponderance of old plots featuring the old imperial rulers made it the most incompatible with Mao's mass line. Its formal presentation and techniques were far removed from Soviet-style socialist realism, but its role stereotyping made it an excellent vehicle for moral propaganda. Finally, despite the patronage of Party leaders like Wu Han, Tian Han and Peng Zhen, the performers themselves were not as firmly tied to the Party apparatus as in the spoken theatre.

Jiang Qing's involvement was not confined to opera. The National Day celebrations in October 1964 featured three dance-dramas, *The East Is Red*, *The Red Detachment of Women* and *The White-haired Girl*. Dance-drama was a hybrid form which only became prominent in the early 1960s. Its origins lie both in traditional Chinese dance, which had almost disappeared from the modern stage, and in Western modern dance and ballet. Introduced by the White Russian refugees of the 1920s in Shanghai as an art form for the foreign community, ballet had gained a place in Chinese society during the war years thanks to the efforts of Dai Ailian, born in Trinidad in 1916 and trained in Britian. The new régime installed ballet as one of the state-supported arts when Soviet influence was at its height in the early post-1949 years. In December 1959, the National Dance School (later, Academy), founded in Beijing five years earlier with Dai Ailian as its head and a large number of Soviet advisers, set up its own experimental ballet troupe. Its repertoire in the early 1960s consisted chiefly of items like *Swan Lake*, *Le Corsaire* and *Giselle*. After the Sino-Soviet split, British, French and Swedish ballet companies toured China in place of the Bolshoi and Kirov; at the same time, 'dance-drama' was devised as a kind of sinified ballet, combining ballet routines with traditional Chinese dance forms accompanied by an orchestral backing. *The East Is Red*, which combines informal and traditional dance routines with singing as a major element, was the first full-length dance-drama to achieve national prominence on its premiere at the Great Hall of the People. *The White-haired Girl* and *The Red Detachment of Women* are more properly described as ballets. Jiang Qing took a close interest in both but was not involved in *The East Is Red*. Finally, Jiang Qing tackled the Central Philharmonic Society in Beijing, and in the face of understandably stiff resistance, commanded them in 1964 to turn the score of *Shajiabang* into a symphonic suite. Declared a success in September 1965, it was raised to the status of a model in 1966. The transformation of the theatre in all its forms was complete. The definitive operas and ballets of the Cultural Revolution, as well as the radically different plays that replaced them, are discussed below in Part III.

Guo Moruo (1892–1978)

Like Hu Shi, Guo Moruo directed his energies towards academic studies up to the outbreak of war, and thereafter to the war effort. On his return to China in 1938, he was appointed head of the Third Section (literary propaganda) in the Political Department of the Military Affairs Commission, an organisation created to oversee Nationalist-Communist cooperation in which Zhou

Enlai played a leading role. From this position, Guo was able to foster patriotic and left-wing theatre. In 1940 worsening political relations caused the Nationalists to abolish the Political Training Bureau, but Guo Moruo continued as chairman of the Cultural Work Committee, although with diminished influence. In 1941, after the New Fourth Army Incident, as the Nationalists instituted stricter censorship over the theatre, Guo Moruo's response was to produce historical drama on contemporary themes. Between December 1941 and February 1942, he wrote three new plays and rewrote another, all of which have since been frequently performed and much studied. Given his aptitude for seizing upon themes of national significance and his boundless energy in factional politics, the sheer awfulness of most of his writing – and nowhere is it more awful than in his historical plays – seems irrelevant. This is true of *Qu Yuan*, one of his most famous works, in which he re-created the myth of Qu Yuan as a loyal statesman of Chu and author of China's most celebrated collection of early poetry after *The Book of Songs*. Far from being the author of these poems, which were most likely shamanistic in origin, there is no contemporary evidence that Qu Yuan ever existed, but for generations Chinese readers have accepted the heroic portrait given in Sima Qian's *Historical Records* (dating several centuries after the events). With a few exceptions, traditional scholars and modern intellectuals alike have identified themselves with Qu Yuan's protestations of unrequited loyalty and righteousness, and Guo Moruo's version of the myth found a ready audience.

Qu Yuan was written and first performed under the direction of Chen Liting with a cast that included China's most famous actors. It is set in 313 BC in the Chu capital, where Qu Yuan enjoys the confidence of the king and the reputation of a great poet. As the queen and her adviser plot to rid the court of his patriotic counsel, however, Qu Yuan is deserted by all except his faithful maid. When she dies in gaol drinking poison prepared for him, Qu Yuan sets fire to the palace and flees north into exile. Guo Moruo had been attracted to the figure of Qu Yuan since his first attempts at new poetry, incorporating a short sketch depicting Qu Yuan in exile in *The Goddesses*; in defensive exile himself in Japan between 1927 and 1938, he regarded himself as a modern Qu Yuan. In the play, the story works as an allegory of contemporary China, with intrigue at the southern Chu court representing the Nationalist government in south-west Chongqing (Chiang Kaishek depicted as a manipulated puppet and his wife, Soong Meiling, as a vicious schemer), the north standing for Communist headquarters in Yan'an, and the threatening state of Qin as Japan. He also uses the story to identify the figure of the poet as prototype of the intellectual as statesman and voice of the people, the poet's survival being central to the survival of the nation. As a script and in performance, *Qu Yuan* took full advantage of its origins: modernised versions of the poems are cleverly integrated into the action and add to the atmosphere of grand tragedy. At the same time, the storm scene and Qu Yuan's temporary madness have been compared to *King Lear*, and the five-act construction is along classical European lines. Not the least of its accomplishments is the link it provides between the modern and the traditional theatre. After Wen Yiduo's assassination by agents of the Nationalists, Guo Moruo compared him to Qu Yuan, the highest tribute he could pay to this contemporary martyr.

The Tiger Tally, another five-act historical drama based on a biography in the *Historical Records*, was also the subject of a traditional novel. An account of resistance to aggression set in the kingdom of Wei in 267 BC, in Guo Moruo's version it refers transparently to the struggle against Japan. The chief character, Lord Xinling, believes that conciliation to a militarily superior force can only result in disaster, but while an army can be brutalised into victory, in the end loyal troops fighting in a just cause will prevail. The play also introduces two notable women: the Dowager Consort, a dignified and upright figure, was created at Zhou Enlai's suggestion to portray the traditional eastern concept of an ideal mother; Ruji, the royal concubine who aids her brother-in-law Xinling, on the other hand, is a typically passionate and courageous New Woman. Between them, Xinling and Ruji variously commit or abet theft, deception, conspiracy, treason, suicide and murder, all in the name of patriotism. In the *Historical Records*, Xinling is said to feel shame for his acts but the play shows no such qualms. Despite some entertaining dialogue from the play's lower-class characters and some musical interludes, the play is marred by programmatic characterisation and long, self-righteous speeches.

Peacock Gall is Guo Moruo's last major play of the war years.

Set in Yunnan in 1362, towards the end of the Yuan dynasty, it depicts the uneasy relations between the Mongolian rulers and their Chinese subjects. Intrigue and violence enliven the action but the play as a whole is undistinguished. 'Nie Ying' was revised in 1937 and again in 1941 to establish a clear political direction, in which the wicked king represents Chiang Kaishek and the aggressive Qin the Japanese. This version was performed in Chongqing in 1942 under the title *Twin Blossoms* and directed by Ling He.

The establishment of the People's Republic of China brought new roles for Guo Moruo as a senior official in the cultural apparatus, but he retained his interest in historical drama. *Cai Wenji* was written in 1959. Set at the end of the Later Han dynasty, it relates Cai Wenji's return to the Han court after twelve years of marriage to a tribal chief in the north and her subsequent remarriage to a Han official. Its most attractive feature is the interweaving of the famous Han ballad 'Eighteen Airs for the Fife', and its most innovative aspect is the re-evaluation of the general and later prince Cao Cao as a hero. An even more radical re-evaluation came in *Wu Zetian*, written in 1960 and revised in 1962, which depicts the famous Tang empress, usually vilified as a tyrannical and depraved usurper, as a capable and energetic ruler whose reputation suffered at the hands of conservative scholars whose lands and privileges were threatened by her economic and social reforms: it is the pro-Mao counterpart to the anti-Mao plays of the early 1960s. *Tiger Tally*, *Cai Wenji* and *Wu Zetian* were all performed at the Capital Theatre under the direction of Jiao Juyin between 1956 and 1966 in deference to the author's high position. (*For details of Guo Moruo's early life see Chapters 3 and 5; for his later life see also Chapter 8 above.*)

Lao She (1899–1966)

After the outbreak of war, Lao She turned to the theatre as a vehicle for anti-Japanese propaganda. Of the four plays he wrote at this time, all on contemporary themes, none survived its original purpose. *Lingering Fog*, based on an earlier short story and first performed in 1940, compares unfavourably with Song Zhidi's *Chongqing in Fog* of the same year. His next play, *The Nation above All*, also first staged in 1940, was commissioned by the

Patriotic Association of Muslims to strengthen national unity and written in collaboration with Song Zhidi. In 1942 he collaborated with a young woman, Zhao Qingge, on *Peaches and Plums in the Spring*, whose first performance, directed by Wu Yonggang, won a government award for its patriotic and impeccably Confucian sentiments. Lao She was not particularly skilful as a dramatist at first, and none of his nine full-length plays from the war years can be called outstanding. He also wrote librettos on patriotic themes for traditional-style storytellers and Peking opera scripts.

Lao She's best-known plays belong to the 1950s; like Ba Jin, he did not refuse the new government its entitlement to official patronage. *Dragon Beard Ditch*, written in 1950 and performed by the Beijing People's Art Theatre, uses the central image of slum clearance to represent the change in people's lives brought by the new regime – an apparent answer to Wen Yiduo's famous poem of China in the 1920s, 'Dead Water'. In the first act, set in 1948, Dragon Beard Ditch is a malodorous slum in the southern suburbs of Beijing; by the second act, in the months immediately before and after October 1949, the area has been cleaned up; and in the third and final act, not only sanitation but problems of livelihood are finding solution. Lao She also elaborates on the role of a character whose lapse into madness allows him to voice penetrating truths and whose status as a folk artist not only provides the opportunity for popular songs to enliven the script but also the stature and nobility to give depth to the madman's utterances.

During the 1950s Lao She turned out a number of uninspired plays on contemporary themes. The only one to have aroused controversy is *Looking West to Chang'an*, written in 1955. Based on a true incident revealed in a speech by Luo Ruiqing, Minister of Public Security, it relates the story of a young imposter who penetrates the upper circles of the Party. It was performed at the the First National Spoken Drama Festival in 1956, where it was rumoured to be written at the express invitation of Luo Ruiqing.

Official sanction of traditional opera encouraged Lao She to revise the old *kunqu* play *Fifteen Strings of Cash* for performance in 1956 by the Kunqu Opera Company of Zhejiang. The original libretto by Chen Suchen was based on a Ming story which in turn was based on a Song storyteller's tale. The hero is the upright

Prefect of Suzhou, Kuang Zhong, referred to in the script as 'a second Judge Bao'. Suspecting that the prisoners entrusted to him for execution might be innocent, the Prefect asks leave of the Governor to conduct an investigation. The Governor resents the implied aspersion on his administration but eventually gives in, and the identity of the guilty party is established. The magistrate responsible for the false conviction is shown as foolish rather than corrupt, as is the Lieutenant who tried to deny the Prefect audience with the Governor, while the Governor himself is shown as not only indifferent in the pursuit of justice but, by implication, morally derelict in failing to come forward to approve the verdict's reversal. This portrayal of social irresponsibility by middle-level officialdom is very much in line with the criticisms voiced in fiction and poetry in the Hundred Flowers campaign.

Lao She's most powerful drama is *Teahouse*, written in 1956 and first performed by the Beijing People's Art Theatre in 1957 under Jiao Juyin's direction. Apparently an exposure of the evils of the old society, it can also be seen as skilfully disguised criticism of the new regime. As the play begins, the late-Qing setting provides a rich backdrop: signs and bustle and wealth abound, despite the play's message of social oppression. As the action moves into the early Republic (1917) and then to the post-war years (1945), the stage becomes progressively barer, but what remains throughout is an official notice saying 'Discussion of state affairs is prohibited'. The official debate on the play (which included Jiao Juyin, Chen Baichen, Lin Mohan, Wang Yao, Zhang Henshui, Li Jianwu and Zhang Guangnian) in 1958 stressed its failure to provide a positive ending, but most of the criticism was deflected into secondary areas such as the lack of a narrative plot and the supposed problem created by the large cast of seventy. A more devastating attack in 1966 preceded the author's suicide by only a few weeks. When the play was restaged in 1979 by the Beijing People's Art Theatre, the unwritten comment on everyone's lips was that the play actually consisted of four acts: the last act (i.e. the 1950s) was a blank. The play worked well enough without this coded message, however, and had a successful tour in Europe and the United States. In the mid-1980s Lao She's reputation rose even higher with a film version of *Camel Xiangzi* and a wildly popular television serialisation of *Four Generations under One Roof.* *(For Lao She's early life and work see Chapters 4 and 7.)*

Chen Baichen (b. 1908)

Compared with other dramatists of the period, Chen Baichen had little formal education. He studied stagecraft under the auspices of Tian Han's Southern Society but was arrested soon after joining the Communist Youth League and remained in prison in 1932–5. From prison he wrote short stories and plays for publication in *Literature, Literature Quarterly* and *The Modern Age.* His first major success was with an historical play on the last years of the Taiping Rebellion, *Shi Dakai's Road to Ruin,* staged in Shanghai in 1936 as an attack on Nationalist inaction in the face of Japanese aggression. (Yang Hansheng continued the Taiping theme to the same purpose in his *Death of Li Xiucheng* in 1937.) On the outbreak of war, he organised a travelling company to stage propaganda plays in the interior, such as his own *Autumn Harvest. Men and Women in Troubled Times,* a satire on early wartime chaos in the interior first performed in 1940, made effective use of exaggeration and the grotesque to convey the sense of outrage and frustration felt by refugees from the Japanese in their encounters with local and Nationalist officials. *Wintertide,* a drama of wartime life in the interior, was staged by Chen Liting in Chongqing in 1946 and subsequently in Shanghai in 1947–8, confirming his reputation as a leading dramatist. He returned to satire with *How to Get Promoted,* based on Gogol's *The Inspector-General* and imaginatively staged by Huang Zuolin in Shanghai in 1946.

When Chen Baichen returned to Shanghai in 1946 he turned his attention to film. His most famous project was as head of the writing team for *Crows and Sparrows,* which was begun in 1947, suspended by the Nationalist authorities, and completed a few days after the People's Liberation Army entered Shanghai. Chen joined the Communist Party in 1950, and occupied high administrative and academic posts as well as continuing to write short plays during the 1950s. His last work was the historical play *Song of the Great Wind* in 1977.

Cao Yu (1910–96)

Cao Yu was one of the earliest arrivals in Chongqing and one of the first to write a full-length propaganda play. *Metamorphosis* (1940), first performed in 1939, is set in a wartime hospital which suffers as much from inefficiency and corruption as Japanese air raids. *Peking Man*, written in 1940 and first published and performed in 1941, is a more thoughtful and original work, and has attracted much critical attention as well as misunderstanding; not the least of the controversy about it was its lack of reference to the war. Set in the Beijing mansion of an old wealthy family in decline, it shows the demise of the old order in China under the pressure of new economic forces, while hope for the future is borne by the younger generation, who move forward to revolution with inspiration from China's most ancient past – Peking Man. Cao Yu's use of imagery is powerful rather than subtle – coffins, rats and a broken kite symbolising decay – but his characterisation is carefully individualised in a way rare on the Chinese stage. The women in the family, for instance, who include a woefully de- pendent married daughter, a strong-minded but frustrated and spiteful daughter-in-law, a self-sacrificing idealistic unmarried niece, a rebellious granddaughter and a tomboyish neighbour, ranging in age from thirty-eight down to sixteen, have variously left the New Women stereotypes of the 1920s and 1930s far behind. The Peking Man image is markedly ambiguous: he is both the admired object of study by Yuan Rengan, an anthropologist who represents enlightened scientific knowledge, and a modern-day primitive, a truck driver who helps Yuan get rid of the money collectors who pester the failing patriarch. Cao Yu's 1947 revision removed the modern-day 'Peking man' but retained the speech praising his primitive freedom from the restraints of conventional moral codes. Yuan and his Peking Man are effectively contrasted with the middle-aged son, a 'superfluous man' with a distinct family resemblance to nineteenth-century Russian intellectuals. The patriarch is a weaker figure than in *Thunderstorm*, both in stage presence and plot structure. His sin against the family amounts to little more than conservatism, and he is punished less dramatically: a son commits suicide again, and a great-grandchild is aborted, but a grandson survives and another son is on the way. The old generation is doomed, but the new generation will cleanse itself:

through personal sacrifice and cutting strings with the past, there is hope for the future. Not only the Japanese but even class struggle are ignored; goodness is seen to reside even in this landlord family. Again, a comparison with *The Cherry Orchard* shows the same theme of inevitable social change.

In his third and last portrait of a patriarch, Cao Yu adapted Ba Jin's *The Family* for stage performance in 1941; its themes of generational conflict and free choice in marriage, with three dead women and striving sons, still had Chongqing audiences in tears. Next came *The Bridge*, first performed in 1947, a conventional drama of love and frustration in factory management. In this play, first published in *Literary Renaissance* in 1945, the dedication of engineers, scientists and professionally trained managers is contrasted with the venality of the capitalist class. During the war years, Cao Yu also translated *Romeo and Juliet* and taught in the National Academy of Drama in Chongqing.

In April 1946, along with Lao She, he went to the United States for a year at the invitation of the State Department. On his return to China he was appointed to script and direct the film *Sunny Skies* at the Wenhua Studio in Shanghai. Among his most influential positions in the 1950s, he was director of the Beijing People's Art Theatre. In 1954 he began to write the three-act *Bright Skies*, which was published in 1956 by the People's Literature Press and won first prize at the National Modern Drama Festival in 1956 in a performance by the Beijing People's Art Theatre. Set in Beijing Union Medical College in the years 1948–52, it shows a Chinese doctor awakening to the evils perpetrated by the Americans in germ warfare in Korea and by the American Dr Jackson who formerly ran the hospital. Having in this way paid for his US trip, Cao Yu shortly afterwards joined the Communist Party.

Cao Yu's prestige was at its height during the early 1960s: *Thunderstorm*, *Peking Man* and *Sunrise* were frequently performed at the Capital Theatre and elsewhere to full houses. In 1961 he tried his hand at historical drama with the five-act *The Gall and the Sword*, directed by Jiao Juyin for the Beijing People's Art Theatre and published in *People's Literature*. Cao Yu was only one of several prominent intellectuals who ventured into historical drama at this time to express criticism of Mao Zedong's voluntarist policies of the Great Leap Forward and his attempt to regain power after the Lushan conference. *The Gall and the Sword* is set in the period 492 to 473 BC, during the long conflict between the states of Wu and Yue. It shows the King of Yue not unfavourably as a monarch whose patriotism is beyond question but who needs the wise counsel and encouragement of loyal officials and the masses to achieve the goal of defeating the arrogant Wu. According to Mao Dun, more than a hundred plays on this topic of this episode appeared between 1958 and 1962, and of the fifty that he had read himself, Cao Yu's was the only spoken play and also the best play. It is likely that Mao Dun was referring to the implied theme. Most plays concentrated on the episode where the King of Yue sends the famous beauty Xishi to distract the King of Wu, but in Cao Yu's play this is only one of several stratagems practised by Yue. More significant references are to the drought in Yue, an unmistakeable reference to the severe famine in China in the years 1959–61, and to the skilful manoeuvres of the minister Fanli, who could stand for either Zhou Enlai or Liu Shaoqi. Wu might be either the United States or, more likely at this time, the Soviet Union; in one episode the King of Yue's daughter is given as hostage to Wu, which recalls the death of Mao's son in Korea, a conflict forced on China by the Soviet Union.

Cao Yu's final work was *Wang Zhaojun* in 1979, an undistin-guished end to a remarkable career. His multiple influences from Western drama have been exhaustively studied, although his debt to other contemporary Chinese dramatists has been overlooked, and he is everywhere acknowledged as China's leading playwright of the twentieth century. After his rehabilitation after the Cultural Revolution, he became one of the chief celebrities of the new regime, defending it on frequent overseas tours as well as at home. He was one of the very few intellectuals who did not take part in the democratic movement in spring 1989 and who praised the use of force to crush the movement in June. (*For details of Cao Yu's early life and work see Chapter 5.*)

Tian Han (1898–1968)

Tian Han joined the war effort in Wuhan as head of the drama and film unit in Guo Moruo's Literary Propaganda Section of the National Military Council, but his forays into the countryside were not particularly fruitful and he spent most of the war in Guilin. His best-known original work of this period is the five-act *Autumn Song*, depicting the lives of refugee intellectuals in the south-west; performed in Guilin in 1941, it includes the text of Ouyang Xiu's prose poem of the same name from the Song dynasty as well as the brand-new cinematic technique of flashbacks on stage. Apart from incorporating music in spoken plays, Tian Han also experimented with musical theatre during the war years and was responsible for tours of Peking opera in the interior. At the end of the war he returned first to Shanghai and then to Hong Kong, rejoining Communist forces in the north-east in 1948.

Tian Han moved into important positions of power in the theatre after 1949. His first post-1949 work was a new Peking Opera called *The White Snake*. The legend of the White Snake, thought to go back to the Tang dynasty, has been presented in many different literary and operatic forms. In one of the earliest written versions, set in the twelfth century around the famous West Lake in Hangzhou, the White Snake is portrayed as a female demon who preys on men. Her character is more complex in the most famous literary version, a short story included in Feng Menglong's anthology *Stories to Startle the World* (c. 1620). In Feng's story, her victim is a young man, Xiu Xian, who lends the White Snake and her sister, the Blue Snake, an umbrella in a rainstorm. She falls in love with him and proposes marriage, and although her thefts cause him to be twice imprisoned, she rescues him both times and persuades him of her good faith. When he realises that she is a spirit, he eventually decides to appeal to a Daoist monk, Fa Hai, for help, and between them they imprison both spirits under the Lei Feng Pagoda, near Hangzhou. The monk explains that the snake spirit has defied heaven by wanting to experience human love, and must be imprisoned in order to avoid harm coming to men through deviance from heaven's law. Over the next three hundred years, dramatic versions add details such as the White Snake's pregnancy, further humanising her as a woman fighting to save her marriage. In all versions, the fundamental theme is that humans and spirits inhabit two different worlds and can never be wholly united, possibly an allegory for human male–female relationships. Tian Han's version, on which he is said to have worked for some thirteen years, overturns this tradition by showing the White Snake as a powerful but good woman striving for freedom in love, Xiu Xian as well-meaning but easily swayed, and the monk Fa Hai as an evil force representing moral and religious conservatism. The official explanation was that the White Snake represented the masses, although she can equally well be seen as an updated version of the New Woman, and naturally there is a happy ending as the Blue Snake rallies the masses to overthrow the pagoda's guardian. First performed in 1952, *The White Snake* was the most widely distributed of the new operas. The script, a mixture of dialogue, recitative and arias in sixteen scenes, was published by the Writers' Press in 1955.

Tian's next work was a costume drama, *Guan Hanqing*, a full-length work in twelve scenes about a famous Yuan dynasty dramatist, China's first named writer of full-length playscripts. In 1958 Guan Hanqing was chosen as a major subject for commemoration; his most famous work, *The Sorrows of Dou E*, was performed in its original version, and Tian Han's biographical play was written and performed at the Capital Theatre the same year. Historical detail on Guan Hanqing is sparse, and Tian Han felt free to elaborate, for instance, on his attachment to a famous courtesan and actress, Chen Zhulian. The play takes full advantage of the opportunity afforded by costume drama for music and spectacle, including excerpts from *The Sorrows of Dou E*, other plays by Guan Hanqing and a verse from Wen Tianxiang's 'Song to the Spirit of Honour', but is far from being popular entertainment. The violence (a young actress has her eyes gouged out; she later asks for them to be hung on the city wall so that they can witness the fall of her assailant, who has been cut down by an assassin) is all off-stage, and there is not much action between the long speeches. An unusual feature is the detailed reference to the techniques of Yuan drama as well as more familiar literary and historical allusions. When another famous Yuan dramatist, Wang Shifu, is drawn into the plot for no obvious reason, it is clear that Tian Han is addressing a highly literate audience. More significantly, the play draws attention to Guan Hanqing's use of historical allegory in *The Sorrows of Dou E* to criticise Kublai Khan's government, and the theme of *Guan Hanqing* is the duty of intellectuals to criticise the ruling powers, preferably indirectly through literary or other artistic forms. The original version allowed the hero some consolation for his heroic defiance, as Chen Zhulian follows Guan Hanqing into exile; in the revised 1961 version, the lovers are separated at the last moment. In a preface to the English edition, Tian Han notes that the Russian translation has the happy ending, while the English has the sad one.

Other post-1949 works by Tian Han are the adaptions of old plays like *The Western Chamber* (1958) and his own play, *Princess Wencheng* (1960). His last work, the Peking opera *Xie Yaohuan* (1963), was also seen as a veiled attack on Mao Zedong. Tian Han was one of the 'four villains' to be singled out for attack in 1966, and *Guan Hanqing* formed a major part of the evidence against him. He died in jail and was posthumously rehabilitated in 1979; several of his works, including *Xie Yaohuan*, were restaged over the next few years. (*For details of Tian Han's early life, see Chapters 3 and 5.*)

Xia Yan (b. 1900)

At the outbreak of war Xia Yan left Shanghai for Guangzhou, Guilin and then Hong Kong; after the fall of Hong Kong in 1941, he moved on first to Guilin and then to Chongqing, where he spent the remainder of the war years. *The Fascist Bacillus*, first performed in Chongqing in 1942, is his best-known war play, but despite some interest provided by the diverse settings, from Tokyo in 1931 to Shanghai in 1937 to Hong Kong in 1941 to Guilin in 1942, and the new topic of the subordination of science to politics, it remains a typical propaganda piece. *Fragrant Flowers on the Horizon*, on love and marriage among refugee intellectuals in wartime Guilin, is unexpectedly Confucian in its attitudes towards stability and harmony within the family, possibly because of its semi-autobigraphical nature. It was performed in Chongqing in 1945 under the direction of Jin Shan.

At the end of the war, Xia Yan returned to Shanghai where he became an influential member of the post-1949 cultural bureaucracy, culminating in his appointment as Vice-Minister of Culture in 1955. He continued writing plays such as *The Test* (1953; performed by the Beijing People's Art Theatre), about factory life in a northern industrial town in 1953, but spent an increasing amount of time in film work. Among his best-known filmscripts are adaptations of Lu Xun's 'New Year's Sacrifice' and

Mao Dun's 'The Lin Family Shop'. During the 1930s, Xia Yan had been involved in disputes with Lu Xun, and this became a pretext for a prolonged attack on him in 1966. The severity of his treatment (he was imprisoned and tortured) was more likely due to his poor relations with Jiang Qing during the 1950s. Restored to power in 1978, he gave a moving speech at the Fourth Congress of Writers and Artists in which he acknowledged the abuses of power practised by him and his colleagues before the Cultural Revolution. This did not stop him from attacking young theatre and cinema artists during and after the campaign against spiritual pollution (see Chapter 10), but he began to express disquiet about increased repression after 1987 and was a supporter of the democratic movement in 1989. (*For details of Xia Yan's early life see Chapter 5.*)

Song Zhidi (1914–56)

Song Zhidi has been described as coming from a poor peasant family in Hebei, but he managed to proceed from a local education to enter the Law Faculty at Beijing University in 1931. Under the influence of Yu Ling, seven years his senior, he became a member of the League of Left-wing Dramatists the following year. His political activities attracted the attention of the Nationalist government, and in 1933 he fled to Shanghai, only to be arrested later the same year for taking part in a demonstration. He was released a year later but then detained for another year. The first of his plays to make an impact was the historical drama *Wu Zetian* in 1937.

After the outbreak of war, he organised anti-Japanese resistance troupes in the interior, ending up in Chongqing. His *Chongqing in Fog*, a psychological drama of life among the capital's refugee intellectuals like himself, was a success on its first performance in 1940. During the Chongqing years he collaborated with Cao Yu on *Twenty-eight Black Letters*, with Chen Baichen on *Long Live the Chinese People*, and with Lao She on *The Country above All*. An unusual event of 1943 was a play on the history of the spoken drama of 1921–37, *Annals of the Theatre*, jointly written by Song Zhidi, Xia Yan and Yu Ling: of more interest to historians than to readers, it is a rare inside look at the drama within the new drama.

In the late 1940s Song Zhidi incorporated Yan'an elements into his work, not only the themes of peasants taking an active part in revolution but also motifs such as the 'rice-sprouts song'. He joined the Communist Party in 1948 and was given a series of influential posts in the People's Liberation Army. He continued to write for the theatre and play an active role in literary politics up to his early death.

Wu Zuguang (b. 1917)

Wu Zuguang comes from a gifted family: his brother, Wu Zuqiang, is a noted composer. He was also precocious: he was a teacher at the National Academy of Drama in 1937–41, and was still only twenty-three when his first play, *The Song to the Spirit of Honour*, was staged in Chongqing and Shanghai. Based on the last years of the Song patriot Wen Tianxiang, it takes its title from a poem of the same name composed by Wen shortly before his execution at the order of Kublai Khan (a prose version is supplied in the play). It was restaged in Shanghai with a change of title in 1943, and made into a film in Hong Kong in 1948. His next play was *Return on a Snowy Night*, performed in Chongqing in 1942, in Shanghai the following year, in Kunming in 1946, and several times in different versions after 1949; a film version was made in 1947. A melodrama about moral corruption in the modern age, it is set in the backstage world of Peking opera, and the costumes and singing which adorn many scenes are un-doubtedly part of its audience appeal. Ambiguous sexuality is an underlying theme: both hero and heroine – an actor of female roles and a concubine who describes herself as a prostitute – are objects of rich men's lust.

Wu Zuguang had always been interested in the traditional theatre, and during the war he had written scripts for *pingju* (a north China regional opera). The famous *pingju* actress Xin Fengxia had performed in one of his plays, and their wedding in 1951 was attended by Ouyang Yuqian, Lao She, Guo Moruo and Mei Lanfang. In 1957, he was labelled a Rightist and sent to the north-east, but Xin Fengxia (whose reminiscences of her early life as a performer became a bestseller in the late 1970s) courageously supported him throughout. On his return to Beijing in 1960, he was assigned by Xia Yan and Qi Yanming to write Peking operas.

He managed to complete six of these between 1963 and 1966, of which the best-known is the collectively written *Wu Zetian* (published in 1978). His wartime plays were restaged by the Chinese Youth Art Theatre in the early 1980s, and his essays on modern life won a devoted readership. He openly denounced the repression of the late 1980s, and became a vocal supporter of the democratic movement in spring 1989.

Qin Shou'ou (b. 1908)

After the performance of *Return on a Snowy Night* in Chongqing but before its Shanghai appearance, a play with a similar theme, *Begonia*, became the major hit of the war years at Shanghai's famous Carlton Theatre. First published as a novel, it was adapted as Shanghai opera and played to full houses for six months. In 1942 Gu Zhongyi, Huang Zuolin and Fei Mu rewrote it again as a modern drama, which played again to full houses for almost four months with Shi Hui in the starring role, and the first film version appeared soon after. Qin Shou'ou published a revised version of the script under his own name in 1946, and a second film was made after the war. A romance between a Peking opera star and a warlord's concubine, its combination of sentimentality and operatic interludes guaranteed popular success. The novelist Eileen Chang (Zhang Ailing) noted at the time 'the humilating fact' that the new theatre had only managed to outperform traditional theatre by taking over the colour and atmosphere of its rival. (*For Qin Shou'ou's early life and his fiction see Chapter 7.*)

Yao Ke (1905–91)

Another major commercial success of the Shanghai wartime theatre was Yao Ke's *The Malice of Empire*, in four acts and a prologue, directed by Fei Mu in 1941. The story relates the conflict between Cixi, the Dowager Empress, her son the Emperor, and his favourite concubine Zhen. Set within the Qing court against a background of events including the Sino-Japanese War, the reforms of 1898 and the Boxer Rebellion, the story seemed highly relevant to current struggles – with the Empress Dowager variously standing for the Japanese, Chiang Kaishek and even Mao Zedong. On its opening night in Tianjin in 1942, it was banned by the Japanese authorities, but it was revived in Shanghai in 1944 and again after the end of the war. A film adaptation was made in Hong Kong in 1948–9 under the name *The Secret History of the Qing Palace*, with changes added by the producer, Li Zuyong, and director, Zhu Shilin, over the author's protests. The play's subsequent history suggests that it can be read as a study of tyranny in other forms; alternatively, it can also be read as a well-crafted melodrama on the standard New Culture themes of generational revolt, free choice in marriage, the New Woman, and the nobility of idealistic reformers, all enhanced by the glamour of high position and national tragedy. The characterisation is conventional, the dialogue feeble and the history superficial, but there is plenty of action and even high drama as the Empress Dowager spits out her despotic commands.

Despite the differences between them, the film and play each boosted the other's popularity and both were targeted by mainland critics; the blurring was accentuated by the adaptation of the play into traditional opera. Between 1949 and 1953 the publishers were instructed to withdraw all copies of the play from circulation and performances were officially proscribed, but in 1954 it was performed as Shaoxing opera in Shanghai, and over the next few years in local styles in Shanghai, Nanjing, Hangzhou and even Beijing in 1957. The prohibition was renewed in 1958, but even then the play in various formats and under different titles continued to be performed up until 1963. The main controversy, however, was over the film, and it was renewed with even greater ferocity in 1966, culminating in the re-release of the film in June 1967 as instruction by negative example. The play was revived in China in 1977 and looks set to continue as a popular classic.

Born in Xiamen to a family of scholar officials from Anhui, Yao Ke (also known as Yao Xinnong) was given a Confucian education followed by Western learning in secondary school. He entered Suzhou University as a student of international law, but his passion for the theatre led him to switch to the department of Chinese literature, where he graduated in 1931. While on a tour of the Soviet Union and Europe he represented China at an International PEN conference in London in 1937, and the following year went on to study drama at Yale. After his return to China in 1940, he devoted himself to incorporating elements from the traditional Chinese stage into modern drama and film. In 1948 he moved to Hong Kong and, between 1964 and 1967, was head of the department of Chinese language and literature at the Chinese University of Hong Kong. He spent most of the Cultural Revolution years teaching in the United States, returning to Hong Kong in 1976 but going back to San Francisco on his retirement.

Li Jianwu (1906–82)

After the Marco Polo Bridge Incident, Li Jianwu moved to Shanghai's French Concession for safety. Along with other Shanghai stayers at this time such as Aying, Xia Yan and Yu Ling, he founded the Shanghai Theatre Arts Association to sustain serious drama under the occupation. His main contribution to the war effort was the full-length play *Juvenescence*, produced by Fei Mu 1944, which has no reference at all to war. Set in the north China countryside during the closing years of the Qing dynasty, *Juvenescence* is a village *Romeo and Juliet*, with comic touches to a serious theme; the human misery resulting from rigid adherence to convention and prejudice. Authentic local dialect enhances the dialogue. Although written in a modern form, it has a timeless quality that allowed a successful adaptation as a traditional farce in the north China genre known as *pingju*. The script was published in *Literary Renaissance* in 1946. Towards the end of the war, Li Jianwu was arrested by the Japanese authorities in Shanghai, suffered torture and was released on bail after twenty days. After his release, he concentrated mainly on translations from Shakespeare and Molière. Li Jianwu is also known for his many adaptions of works by Scribe and Sardou for performance in the French Concession in the early 1940s, further strengthening the well-made play repertoire. The most notable of these is *Qin Xiaoyu*, based on *La Tosca* and featuring a Peking opera star in the main role. Li Jianwu remained active in the theatre as a translator, critic and educator, but *Juvenescence* was his last major original work. (*For an account of Li Jianwu's earlier works see Chapters 4 and 5.*)

Yang Jiang (b. 1911)

Yang Jiang was born in Beijing but educated in Shanghai and Suzhou. In 1932 she became a research fellow at Qinghua University, where she met and married the academic and novelist Qian Zhongshu. The couple went abroad in 1935 and on returning to China in 1938 settled in Shanghai, where Yang Jiang began her literary career as a writer of short fiction and essays. During the war years she wrote three plays for the Shanghai theatre. The first two are comedies which have enjoyed a modest success on stage. Her third play was the unperformed *Windswept Blossoms* (1946), which brought psychological drama to a new level of anti-romantic irony. Set in the countryside, it treats the disillusionment of young intellectuals who had hoped that out of agrarian and educational reform a New China would arise. Not only are their goals frustrated by the advent of war and local resistance to change, but they become aware of their own flawed personalities as a triangular relationship develops between the heroine, her husband and their closest colleague. The play gives a new perspective on the New Woman several years on, one who has acted in accordance with her ideals and yet nevertheless is caught in an emotional trap in which idealism becomes irrelevant. There seems little reason to write it as a play rather than a novel, however, despite the violence at its climax and the heroine's passionate exchanges with her husband and lover. Yang Jiang herself commented that it was simply a potboiler, but the sense of inevitable tragedy has led to comparisons with Ibsen's *Hedda Gabler* and *The Wild Duck*.

After 1950 Yang Jiang devoted herself to academic studies and translations, but the appearance in the late 1970s of her *Six Chapters from a Cadre School*, on the experiences of herself and her colleagues from the Academy of Sciences (including Li Jianwu) during the Cultural Revolution, re-affirmed her reputation as an author of great sensibility and talent. She was an open supporter of the democratic movement in spring 1989.

Yao Zhongming (b. 1914)

Written with the assistance of Chen Boer and Sai Ke, Yao Zhongming's *Comrade, You've Taken the Wrong Path!* was one of the first spoken plays to emerge after the Yan'an Forum. Set in north China behind the Japanese lines, it treats the problem of United Front tactics with the local Nationalist forces in the cause of resistance to Japan, its main characters representing views advanced by Mao Zedong, Wang Ming and even Chen Duxiu in the abstract language of political rhetoric. Except for colour provided by the villains (the Nationalist officers), the play is even more stilted and long-winded than the 'proletarian literature' of pre-war Shanghai. Nevertheless, it was backed by Zhou Yang, and its first performance in 1944 was considered a successful launch of new spoken drama. It was restaged by the Beijing People's Art Theatre in the 1950s.

He Jingzhi (b. 1924) and Ding Yi (1913–54)

The most successful drama from the Yan'an period is undoubtedly *The White-haired Girl*. Designed to take the *yangge* play to a further stage of development as a full-scale modern opera, it was the Lu Xun Academy's contribution to the 1945 Party Congress, and was personally supervised by Zhou Yang and Zhang Geng. The three-act script is now attributed to He Jingzhi and Ding Yi, but contemporary accounts stress the contributions not only by all members of the troupe but by the Yan'an population at large. He Jingzhi already had some reputation as a revolutionary poet. Ding Yi had joined the Party in 1936 and had a long history as a propagandist attached to the armed resistance. Both had taken part in the Academy's 1943 *yangge* effort. Wang Bin was also listed as an author in a 1946 edition of the play, and the composers were Ma Ke, Zhang Lu and Qu Wei.

The plot was said to be based on a true story circulating in the Communist-controlled areas since 1940. In a small village in Hebei, which had been 'liberated' some years earlier, a district cadre was dismayed when the villagers failed to show up for elections. On investigation, they were found in a nearby temple, supposedly inhabited by a white-clad goddess who had commanded them to make sacrifices twice a month. Concealing himself in the temple at night, the cadre saw a young woman snatching food from the altar; he chased her back to her dwelling, a cave, where she told her story. Raped and threatened with murder by the local landlord, she had escaped and given birth in the mountains.

She had managed to survive by stealing food, but her hair had turned white from privation.

In the 1945 opera version, the story begins one New Year's Eve, when a tenant farmer is forced by the local landlord, Huang Shiren, to hand over his daughter, Xi'er, in payment for his debt. New elements in the story include the father's suicide, resistance by her sweetheart, a young peasant who then joins the Eighth Route Army and is present when Xi'er is discovered, the threat of prostitution rather than murder, a confrontation at the temple between Xi'er, now a white-haired 'ghost', and her tormenters, and a final scene with Huang Shiren being publically castigated at a mass meeting of the villagers.

At the première, attended by Mao Zedong and other leaders, *The White-haired Girl* was proclaimed the first 'new opera' and a great success in both form and content. However, the Academy was directed to change the ending 'in response to the demands of the masses', and in all subsequent versions the villain was shot. Over the next few years, *The White-haired Girl* was performed throughout the Communist-controlled areas in north and central China and new works were constructed on its model. Although the term opera has now stuck, it would be technically more appropriate to call *The White-haired Girl* (and its imitations) a musical, since it contained a large element of spoken dialogue, given in the local vernacular rather than the stylised recitative of traditional Chinese opera. The score consisted of a mixture of folksong, *yangge* and local opera set in a framework of Western orchestration (both as an accompaniment to the arias and as incidental music), and the singing was based on Western open-throat technique in place of traditional Chinese folk and opera voice production. There was a minimum of stage props, and the instrumentation and dialogue could be adapted to local needs and customs.

The White-haired Girl also satisfied the Party's requirements on theme and direction. Set in the present, it highlights the peasants' active struggle against oppression which becomes effective under Party leadership. Class background determines character, and class background dictates the plot. Some of the peasant characters are shown succumbing to fear and supersition but more importantly, all are fundamentally good while the landlord and his accomplices are portrayed as hypocritical villains. The opera is clearly directed at a peasant audience, accustomed to the black-and-white morality and the positive resolution of traditional opera; there was enough realism in the plot to persuade them that the cause was indeed their own. There is not an intellectual or other member of the petty bourgoisie in sight, although the two writers were originally from a left-wing May Fourth background. Over the next four years, details were added or changed in order to reinforce the realistic and didactic elements and to eliminate any remaining ambiguity, and the definitive version of the script was published in 1949. It was filmed in 1950, awarded a Stalin Prize in 1951, and performed as a spoken play, as regional opera and as Peking opera during the 1950s. Its further transformation during the Cultural Revolution is discussed in Part III. (*For an account of He Jingzhi's poetry see Chapter 8.*)

Wu Han (1909–69)

Wu Han began his career as one of Hu Shi's protégés. He studied history at Qinghua University and soon made a name for himself as an authority on the Ming dynasty. He spent the war years in Kunming where he became a member of the Chinese Democratic League. Returning to Beijing at the end of the war, his cooperation with the Communist Party in aiding the student movement eventually forced him to seek refuge in the Communist-held areas. During the 1950s, he was appointed head of the history department at Qinghua while continuing to be active in politics.

Wu Han's involvement with Peng Zhen's anti-Maoist faction goes back to 1957 (the year he became a Party member), when he criticised the Hundred Flowers campaign and supported closing Party ranks. Two years later, his special expertise became unexpectedly relevant. In March 1959, Mao happened to mention two Confucian officials as models for present-day bureaucrats, Wei Cheng (580–643) and Hai Rui (1515–87), and instructions were sent out to compile anthologies of both. With Zhou Yang's encouragement, Zhou Xinfang began to write a play about Hai Rui, and took part in the performance in October 1959. At the same time, a 'leading comrade' (possibly Zhou Enlai, or even Mao Zedong himself), asked Wu Han to publish under a pseudonym a vernacular translation of a famous rebuke by Hai Rui to the Jiaqing emperor, urging him to be more responsible in the execution of his duties. It is possible that the example of these Confucian officials might have goaded Peng Dehuai into opposing Mao Zedong's Great Leap Forward policies at the Lushan conference in July that year, a position which led to his replacement as Minister of Defence by Lin Biao a few weeks later. One of Peng Dehuai's supporters was Peng Zhen, Wu Han's superior as mayor of Beijing. On Peng Zhen's behalf, Hu Qiaomu approached Wu Han with the suggestion that the historian might employ his specialist knowledge to write further on Hai Rui. The ensuing article 'On Hai Rui' carefully distanced the author from Peng Dehuai but retained the message that upright officials should dare to speak their mind. In 1960 Wu Han composed a new version of Hai Rui's story in the form of Peking opera, a genre with a ready-to-hand trial format for one of the key scenes. Instead of the emperor, who does not appear, Hai Rui's antagonist is a former prime minister, retired but still powerful – in other words, a figure closely resembling Mao in the early 1960s. Hai Rui is shown as a man of principle who insists on upholding justice even when it conflicts with personal loyalties, and it is because of his incorruptibility that he is falsely condemned. Even after he has been dismissed, however, he still proceeds to execute the guilty son of his former superior and restores ownership of land to the peasants whom the son had cheated out of it. In this final version, Hai Rui has become a mythic figure comparable to Qu Yuan: an upright paragon of virtue, an outstanding representative of the official scholar class.

Wu Han's choice of Peking opera over spoken historical drama can be explained as a conciliatory gesture towards Mao himself. The message was meant for Mao to understand and accept: it was not veiled in an attempt to evade censorship while reaching a wide but knowledgeable audience, as in the costume drama of the 1930s and 1940s, but in order to keep it within the closed circle of the cognoscenti. Another reason for chosing opera might have been the need to cast Hai Rui as irreproachable, a role type not easily credible in spoken drama. The close association of the opera with contemporary history makes appraisal difficult, but for that very reason it may find a place in the standard Peking opera repertoire. The opera was staged in February 1961, but the text was not published until the campaign against the work had reached its height in 1966. Wu Han died in a Beijing prison three years later.

Three famous playwrights of the 1950s and 1960s died in gaol. This alarming statistic is partly contingent (Lao She was previously best-known as a novelist; Wu Han was primarily an historian), but due attention should also be given to the unusually prominent role of the theatre in modern Chinese politics. The private predilections of political leaders for the traditional theatre; the identification of the spoken historical drama with the reformist and modernising efforts of Party intellectuals; the unmistakeable impact of audience reaction, so immediate and so demanding in terms of the entertainment values of spectacle and skill; the need for a support network of training schools and performance venues: all these factors combined to give theatre an unusual claim on the attention of politicans, bureaucrats and ambitious intellectuals. For these reasons, the theatre became the main stage for displaying the cultural products of the Cultural Revolution, its achievements as well as its failures.

Part III. 1966–1989

10

THE REASSERTION OF MODERNITY

The Great Proletarian Cultural Revolution was a political event which had drastic effects on literature and the arts: the works, their authors and their audiences. In the period 1965–7, literary works, especially in the theatre, were not so much weapons of propaganda for official policies as screens behind which factions attacked their political opponents. The outcome of the battle remained unclear for several months. Yao Wenyuan's critique of *Hai Rui Dismissed from Office* in November 1965 achieved its immediate goal: Wu Han capitulated on 30 December in an article in *People's Daily*, agreeing that he had neglected Mao Zedong's theory of class struggle. The real targets, Peng Zhen and Liu Shaoqi, then took steps to deflect the attack. Peng Zhen set up a committee to investigate the Hai Rui affair in February 1966, and the committee's report, approved by Liu Shaoqi, criticised Wu Han but treated the whole issue as an academic debate. Liu Shaoqi's attempt to diffuse tensions in the Communist Party was met with a counter-attack by a meeting in March in Shanghai organised for the express purpose of denouncing Mao's opponents in literature and the arts.

The document which came out of the Shanghai meeting, 'Summary of the Meeting on People's Liberation Army Work in Literature and the Arts Held by Jiang Qing with the Endorsement of Lin Biao', put forward Mao's new programme for cultural reform. Lin Biao was the Minister of Defence who had replaced Peng Dehuai: by this stage he had extended his base in the People's Liberation Army into the security apparatus as well. By enlisting his support, Mao Zedong now added powerful sections of the military to the group of eager young writers cultivated by Jiang Qing since the early 1960s. The 'Summary' denounced as 'black' the literature of the seventeen years since 1949 in three aspects:

325

theories, works and writers. Although the 'Summary' was not published until 18 April 1966 (in *Liberation Army Daily*), the meeting itself had an immediate effect: on 26 March 1966, Peng Zhen disappeared from public view.

Yet Liu Shaoqi still seemed to underestimate the danger to his faction and himself. On the same day that Peng Zhen disappeared, Liu went to Pakistan and Afghanistan on a state visit for two weeks, leaving Beijing in the hands of the Maoists. Lin Biao quickly gained control of the capital, and the Maoists promptly extracted confessions of guilt about ignoring class struggle from the city's Municipal Party Committee. By the time Mao Zedong returned to Beijing from Shanghai in July, his faction had won domination over both Party and central government. In August 1966, Mao called Lin Biao his 'closest comrade-in-arms' while Lin reciprocated by describing Mao as 'our great teacher, great leader, great supreme commander and great helmsman'. Parts of this formula would find their way into almost every song and poem written over the next few years.

During 1966 and 1967, stage and film works from the early 1960s or before continued to be used for factional politics, preparing the ground for the final exposure of their ultimate targets while the denunciation and imprisonment of theatre artists and bureaucrats were foregrounded. Tian Han, Xia Yan and Yang Hansheng, later known collectively as the 'four villains' along with Zhou Yang, came under open attack in February and March 1966; of the three, Tian Han was treated the most harshly. In April, Liu Shaoqi's supporters Wu Han, Deng Tuo and Liao Mosha were denounced in *Beijing Daily* (now in the hands of the Maoists) as the authors of the 'Three Family Village' and *Evening Chats at Yanshan* essays, and the attack was repeated in May by Yao Wenyuan in *Liberation Daily*, of which he was now editor. Although not yet by name, Liu Shaoqi was accused of protecting 'obscene' operas and foreign works such as *Swan Lake*, and Zhou Yang of promoting *La Traviata* (the opera based on *La Dame aux camélias*) as well as secretly backing the historical plays criticising Mao; open attacks on Zhou Yang as a sponsor of *Hai Rui Dismissed from Office* came in July. Other named targets in the theatre in 1966 and 1967 were Zhou Xinfang, Yu Ling, Xie Jin, Zhang Geng and Qi Yanming. Again on Jiang Qing's instructions, Yao Wenyuan made public Mao's earlier criticism of the film *The*

Secret History of the Qing Palace in *People's Daily* in January 1967; again, Yao Wenyuan found it easy to attack the peasants' advice to the fleeing Manchu emperor as misplaced feudalism, while the portrayal of the Boxers as a destructive force was also out of line with Maoist historiography on peasant rebellion. The named target in this article was Zhou Yang, but a follow-up by Qi Benyu in March in *Red Flag* made it clear that the main target was Liu Shaoqi. Up to this point, the focus had been on the film without reference to the original play and its author, but after the director died in January 1967 (the producer had died seven years earlier), it was widened to include Yao Ke, who at the time was living in Hong Kong, giving the campaign international notoriety. On a Voice of America broadcast in April, Yao Ke stated (perhaps with the benefit of hindsight) that in 1941 he had regarded the Japanese, Chiang Kaishek and Mao Zedong as representing different kinds of authoritarianism but that the play was intended to draw attention to despotism of all kinds.

Despotism needs its backers, and in May 1966 Mao turned to a third source of support: university and secondary-school students. Organised into units which waged war on each other as well as Mao's opponents, they were known collectively as Red Guards after the youthful adjuncts to the Red Army. Starting in August 1966, Mao Zedong and Lin Biao staged spectacular parades at Tiananmen Square in which the young Red Guards were told to struggle against the 'four olds' (thought, culture, customs and habits) as well as revisionists within the Party. Schools and universites were closed down in June 1966, and public transport was placed at the disposal of the Red Guards so that they could rally at centres around the country. Throughout 1967, Red Guard units reached every corner of China, attacking anyone considered to be hindering the realisation of Mao Zedong Thought. Adult intellectuals from famous writers to primary school teachers were the main victims, since anyone with a traditional or Western education was automatically suspected of counter-revolutionary thoughts, and were ritually humiliated and physically abused. From 1966 to 1968, the enthusiasm and euphoria of the Red Guards were matched with confusion and fear among writers, teachers and other intellectuals.

To signal the new direction in literature and the arts, Mao Zedong's Yan'an 'Talks' were reprinted in *Red Flag* in July 1966;

immediately afterwards, literary organisations were closed down and all literary journals except the *Liberation Army Literature and the Arts* ceased publication. Literary criticism, both positive and negative, was conducted in non-literary outlets such as the *People's Daily*, *Red Flag* and *Liberation Army Daily*, where Jiang Qing's political theorists, headed by Zhang Chunqiao and Yao Wenyuan, put forward new guidelines such as the principle of the 'three prominences'. Based perhaps on the concentric hierarchies of 'democratic centralism', it was not such a bad prescription for creating new operas, but it was much less appropriate for fiction and wholly inapplicable to poetry. Between 1966 and 1968, Jiang Qing's attention remained fixed on the theatre, and little new fiction or poetry was published.

Liu Shaoqi was formally dismissed from all Party and government posts in November 1968, along with Deng Xiaoping and Zhu De. Zhou Enlai was the only political figure who seemed to have managed the impossible in avoiding attack, but even he was kidnapped in Wuhan by 'ultra-leftists' in summer 1967 and only released on army intervention. Factions were formed and reformed in quick succession, so that thousands upon thousands of bureaucrats and intellectuals were in turn the accusers and then the accused. As a result, profound bitterness and resentment was widespread, and few came out of the experience unscathed.

The chaos caused by Red Guards and other factional battles reached its height in 1967–8, and in the worse-affected areas the People's Liberation Army was called in to impose control. Among other measures adopted in the summer of 1968 to restore order, millions of urban educated youth, many of them currently or previously active Red Guards, were sent to the countryside, supposedly to be re-educated by the peasants; many were still there a decade later. Schools re-opened in the autumn, and the following year universities with newly designed recruitment policies and curricula accepted a new batch of students. The end of the Cultural Revolution was announced in 1969 as some degree of normality returned to public life. A handful of magazines resumed publication in 1970, and some intellectuals were permitted to return to the cities after re-education in 'cadre schools' in the countryside.

The military's new role had brought increased power to Lin Biao, and he was designated Mao's successor at the Ninth Party Congress in 1969. The position next to the top is often a precarious one, and at a conference of Party leaders at Lushan in 1970, Mao attacked Chen Boda, a powerful supporter of Lin Biao, as an 'ultra-leftist' and 'political swindler'. Sensing that the political tide was turning, Lin Biao plotted a direct seizure of power. When the conspiracy was uncovered by Mao's personal guard, Lin Biao took flight, but his plane crashed in Mongolia, apparently en route to the Soviet Union, in September 1971. The news was not released to the Chinese public for another year and the details are still unclear, but the absence of Lin Biao in the National Day celebrations in October told its own story.

Lin Biao's fate was also related to changing international alliances. During the 1960s, the Western and Soviet blocs had managed between them to isolate China from the international community. In the 1950s, Chinese intellectuals had been able to obtain information about developments in the rest of the world from Soviet sources, but even this conduit was blocked during the Cultural Revolution. The nationalistic and belligerent nature of Chinese foreign policy during this period was reflected in literature, with its motifs of spies and class enemies. Domestic and international politics converged in July 1971 at a secret meeting between Henry Kissinger and Zhou Enlai. Kissinger's visit was the result of a daring move by Mao Zedong to improve relations with the United States, a gesture not welcomed by Lin Biao's faction which preferred rapprochement with Moscow. Richard Nixon's equally dramatic state visit to China in February 1972 was followed by a stream of other foreign visitors, and governments with whom China had previously had no diplomatic relations, such as Japan, West Germany, New Zealand and Australia, recognised China in rapid succession.

The trend towards cultural relaxation was accelerated in 1972 with the revival of national magazines, such as *Cultural Relics* and *Archaeology*, and provincial and city literary magazines. A small number of literary works were re-issued or published for the first time at the Spring Festival, including new work by the poets He Jingzhi, Li Ying and Li Xueao. Reinstatement of former Party and government officials continued as Zhou Enlai re-established the central administration, and Deng Xiaoping was among those returned to office in 1973.

As premier, Zhou Enlai had his base in the state bureaucracy, but the Maoists still controlled the Party and through it the national media. At the Tenth Party Congress in 1973, Zhang Chunqiao and Wang Hongwen were appointed to the five-member Standing Committee of the Political Bureau, which itself included Jiang Qing and Yao Wenyuan among its members. These four, later labelled 'the gang of four', launched a new campaign under the slogan 'criticise Lin Biao, criticise Confucius'. The link between Lin Biao and Confucius was a scroll containing a saying by Confucius advocating 'restoration of the past', said to have been found among Lin Biao's possessions; Confucius was accused of having wanted to restore slavery in ancient China. The real target was Zhou Enlai, whose successful foreign and domestic policies had won him much support. The campaign brought forth a flurry of activity as scholars produced new studies of ancient philosophical texts to prove the case of their political bosses, but while it may have contributed to a revival of classical studies it failed to dislodge Zhou Enlai.

In January 1975, Zhou Enlai announced a reformist policy of 'four modernisations' in agriculture, industry, the armed forces and science and technology; the same month, the Ministry of Culture was restored with Yu Huiyong (chief artistic creator of the model operas) as its head. In the summer, perhaps as a result of criticism by Deng and others, an attempt was made to stimulate greater literary productivity by reviving the national literary magazines. Older writers such as Zang Kejia, Feng Zhi, He Qifang and Mao Dun (under his former pen-name Shen Yanbing) made ceremonial appearances and were published; younger writers included Ru Zhijuan, Shen Rong and Liu Xinwu as well as the Cultural Revolution's prize novelist, Hao Ran. The return to power of former high-level cadres with extensive experience in administration and politics clearly threatened the radicals, and Mao Zedong turned to literature to provide the means to topple Deng Xiaoping again. Among his favourite books was the Ming novel *Water Margin*, with its large cast of bandits and rebels. One of the rebel leaders, Song Jiang, was known for his short stature and conciliatory gestures to the throne, and when the radicals initiated a campaign to criticise him as a 'capitulationist', Chinese readers quickly realised that Song Jiang was meant to represent Deng Xiaoping, and, by implication, Zhou Enlai. Literary scholars were instructed to examine other works in similar fashion, so that splits in the Jia household in *Dream of the Red Chamber*, for instance, were analysed in allusion to the factional fights in the central leadership. In the end, it was the death through illness and old age of the two main players that brought a conclusion to the political struggle by literary proxy.

Zhou Enlai died in January 1976. Mao Zedong was absent from the state funeral, at which Deng Xiaoping gave the eulogy. He even failed to issue a personal message on his old colleague's achievements. In a covert protest at his insulting coldness towards one of China's most skilful twentieth-century politicians, and also to demonstrate their hostility towards Mao and his followers, some 100,000 people gathered in Tiananmen Square on 5 April 1976 to pay tribute to Zhou Enlai's memory at the national festival of mourning, Qingming. Hundreds of poems were pasted on the walls around the Martyrs' Monument in the centre of the Square and wreaths were piled up at its foot; some of the slogans around the wreaths bore disparaging remarks about women rulers such as Indira Gandhi and the late-Qing Empress Dowager, in an obvious reference to Jiang Qing. Similar demonstrations occurred in cities throughout the country. The spontaneity and extent of support for Zhou Enlai provoked an immediate response. Mourners were arrested and gaoled, and Deng Xiaoping was again stripped of all his Party posts two days later. The new premier was Hua Guofeng, a relatively unknown figure whom both factions tried to manipulate.

Momentum for change was not so easily stopped. Republication of the literary magazines went ahead more or less on schedule, with *People's Literature* appearing in January and followed in March by *People's Theatre*, *People's Cinema*, *People's Music*, *Dance* and *Fine Art*. Writers and artists reappeared in the cities, and publication of new fiction and poetry began to approach pre-Cultural Revolution levels. But signs of the coming political battle were everywhere: support for Deng Xiaoping's policies, for example, was shown by tying small bottles to trees around Beijing (Xiaoping is homophonous with the expression 'little bottles' while the word for 'tree' (*shu*) also means 'establish'). To the superstitious, the devastating earthquake in August in Tangshan, not far from Tianjin and Beijing, was even more ominous.

Mao Zedong died on 9 September 1976. On 6 October his wife Jiang Qing and her colleagues Wang Hongwen, Zhang Chunqiao and Yao Wenyuan were arrested and charged with crimes against the state. Jiang Qing was vilified in particularly vicious terms, and her involvement in literature and the arts bitterly condemned by those who had survived it. Opponents of the 'gang of four' at first based their criticisms on the frameworks established in the immediate past years. For example, still using the terminology of the *Water Margin* campaign, critics accused the 'gang of four' of being followers of Song Jiang's capitulationist line. It was also claimed that the model operas were inspired and guided by Mao Zedong, not Jiang Qing. In 1977 the Cultural Revolution was declared to have ended, while its cultural theories and products were attributed to the 'gang of four' and therefore open to repudiation.

The period 1977–9 was remarkable not simply for the reintroduction of past practices but also for a determination on the part of many political and literary actors to investigate and correct the errors of the past that had led to the Cultural Revolution. The rehabilitation of former politicians and bureaucrats came first. Deng Xiaoping was once again restored to his former posts in July 1977, and the Third Plenum of the Eleventh Central Committee held in December 1978 resolved the Party's intention to 'right the wrongs' of all the politicians, bureaucrats and intellectuals who had been condemned since 1957, restoring them to their former status. By such means, Deng enlarged his own power base as well as gathering support behind a renewed drive for the 'four modernisations'. He also consolidated his support among intellectuals by encouraging them to denounce Cultural Revolution policies.

Literary intellectuals were prominent among those restored to power, although many familiar faces were missing. Writers and critics who had been killed or died in gaol during the Cultural Revolution included Lao She, Tian Han, Wu Han and Shao Quanji; Guo Xiaochuan died in 1976, He Qifang in 1977 and Guo Moruo in 1978, just in time to keep his status intact. Many more, such as Zhou Yang and Ba Jin, were restored to their former positions of power or prestige, and soon found themselves sharing platforms with former Rightists such as Ai Qing, Ding Ling, Wang Meng and Liu Binyan. Once-condemned works, such as *Heroes of Lüliang Mountains*, were reissued and performances of Tian Han's anti-Maoist plays were widely publicised. *People's Daily* sponsored a forum to criticise 'gang of four' literature, and

Hao Ran was attacked in *Guangdong Literature*. Yu Huiyong committed suicide.

The keynote for the new literature was struck with the publication of 'Class Teacher', a short story by Liu Xinwu in *People's Literature* in November 1977, its condemnation of the educational and cultural policies of the previous decade complemented by its praise for intellectuals. It was followed in 1978 by 'The Scar', by Lu Xinhua, a Shanghai university student, on the emotional stress and domestic tragedies caused by the Cultural Revolution. Dubbed 'scar literature', these stories dwelled on the mental or physical scars left by the Cultural Revolution, although their analysis of the causes was superficial. Perhaps for this reason, Liu Xinwu and Lu Xinhua became overnight celebrities, and while many critics wrote in defence of their exposés of problems in socialist China, nothing was published attacking them.

Another result of the Third Plenum in 1978 was the promulgation of two new principles to guide political behaviour: 'practice is the sole criterion of truth' and 'seek truth from facts'. These principles encouraged writers to become even more daring in their works, and throughout 1978 and 1979 it became fashionable to break into 'forbidden areas'. Thus, topics such as love and sex as well as the re-evaluation of the campaigns of the 1950s became popular in fiction and drama. The expected backlash against 'scar' or exposé literature was belated and isolated; only Tian Jian among prominent figures was prepared to take a stand. In 1979 an article entitled ' "Praising Virtue" and "Lacking Virtue" ', criticising current literature for having departed from Yan'an precepts by describing the darker aspects of life under socialism, was published in *Hebei Literature and Art*. The author, a young unknown writer by the name of Li Jian, was subjected to immediate denunciation by influential critics such as Wang Ruowang, and even the editor of *Hebei Literature and Art* was attacked; not one critic raised a voice in Li's defence. Li Jian had clearly misread the political mood of that time: the following year, he wrote a series of short stories which outdid those he had criticised in depicting the 'dark side' of contemporary Chinese life.

Limits were still drawn, however, and overstepping these limits led to outright repression. Some of the activists of April 1976 began to circulate 'unofficial publications' containing underground literature from the early 1970s along with new work expressing dissatisfaction with the failure of the new regime under Deng Xiaoping to redress all the mistakes of the 1950s and 1960s. In November 1978, posters appeared on a wall at a busy intersection in Beijing calling for the introduction of democracy as the 'fifth modernisation'. Dubbed the 'Democracy Wall', it also attracted a new kind of literature which similarly repudiated the literary products of post-1949 China. The most prominent of the new literary magazines was *Today*, co-edited by Bei Dao and Mang Ke, two former underground poets. The poems in *Today* quickly became known as 'obscure poetry'; the short stories set the style of 'ruins fiction'. This literature, much of which was first written and circulated during the Cultural Revolution, differed from 'scar literature' by the greater depth of its analysis of China's political troubles as well as by its search for new modes of literary expression. In the spring of 1979, Deng Xiaoping closed down Democracy Wall in Beijing and its counterparts in other cities and arrested its chief activists. Wei Jingsheng, an educated youth from a prominent political family (but at the time employed as an electrician), was sentenced to gaol for fifteen years on trumped-up charges of revealing classified information. *Today* produced a few more issues before closing down in 1980; by then, however, changes in the official literary world enabled many of its writers to find publication in official outlets.

To celebrate the new Dengist era, the Fourth Congress of Writers and Artists was held in Beijing in October–November 1979. Attended by over 3,000 writers and artists, the congress sought to provide guidelines for the 1980s. Deng Xiaoping himself made a speech in which he promised an end to interference in artistic creation, a sentiment welcomed by all speakers including the cultural politicians and bureaucrats present such as Mao Dun, Zhou Yang, Xia Yan, Ding Ling, Wang Meng and Liu Binyan. Calls for emancipation in thinking and the exploration of new modes of expression were also warmly applauded. Deng Xiaoping also urged those present to learn from Western writers in the drive towards modernisation, confirming a trend which was just re-emerging and which was to have a huge impact: the translation and dissemination of foreign literature.

Throughout the 1980s, Chinese readers were introduced to literary developments since the 1950s and 1960s in the rest of the world from Europe, the Americas, Japan and the Soviet Union.

Fiction writers imitated Garcia Marquez; poets copied René Char. The influence of the West was to become even more decisive when, as part of the modernisation programme, China decided to send students abroad. In 1978, 480 students were sent to twenty-eight countries. This number grew rapidly so that numbers reached tens of thousands within a few years, especially when privately funded students were allowed to further their education overseas. As well as students, hundreds of bureaucrats and business people also began to go on study trips or official visits abroad, thus further opening the horizons of many Chinese readers. Deng Xiaoping himself went to the United States in January 1979.

The open-door policy was essential both for the modernisation drive and for a reassessment of the Cultural Revolution and Mao Zedong. Deng Xiaoping needed to repudiate Maoist policies in order to legitimise his own leadership but it was a sensitive matter which he handled carefully. The first part of his strategy was to isolate the 'gang of four' and their supporters as chiefly culpable for the excesses of the Cultural Revolution. Between November 1980 and January 1981, the 'gang of four' and those close to Lin Biao such as Chen Boda were brought to trial; key episodes were shown on television and watched by millions. The accused played their parts to perfection: most looked unkempt and weary. As expected, Jiang Qing put into words what everyone knew but thought prudent not to say, that she had only followed Mao Zedong's orders. It was almost as if she did not know that the Cultural Revolution had over the past four years been thoroughly discredited. By proclaiming that Mao was responsible, she helped bring all of Mao's policies into disrepute.

Deng Xiaoping's victory was secure. At the Sixth Plenum of the Eleventh Central Committee in June 1981, Deng Xiaoping and his protégés, Hu Yaobang and Zhao Ziyang, between them took control of the top posts in the Party, state and military. The plenum also issued a long document which defined the Cultural Revolution as a movement which lasted from 1966 to 1976 and which brought great damage to the Party and country. It also described Mao as having made errors, in the cautious ratio of 70 per cent right, 30 per cent wrong. With the Cultural Revolution behind them and Mao's supporters behind bars, the new leadership pressed ahead with plans for modernisation. Dissatisfied intellectuals were no longer needed to expose the wrongdoings of the Communist Party or the People's Liberation Army, and a new set of guidelines, known as the 'four cardinal principles' (the socialist line, proletarian dictatorship of the Communist Party, Marxism-Leninism and Mao Zedong Thought), began to take precedence over 'seeking truth from facts'.

As far as official writers were concerned, cultural policy remained fairly relaxed throughout 1980 and 1981. Influential figures such as Zhao Dan published articles under titles such as 'Watched Too Closely, Literature and the Arts Have No Hope', and writers and critics such as Dai Houying and Zhou Yang promoted humanism as a basic philosophy for literature. The new controls became more obvious in April 1981, with an attack on a filmscript by Bai Hua and Peng Ning, 'Unrequited Love' in *Liberation Army Daily,* invoking the four cardinal principles. This tale of an overseas Chinese painter who had returned to China after 1949 only to be humiliated, and ultimately to die as a criminal during the Cultural Revolution, asked the question: what had China done to its artists? This took the place of the more usual formulation: what could artists do for their country? Bai Hua, an army writer, was the main target in the first personal attack on a writer since the Cultural Revolution, but the attack remained verbal only. Many people, including influential figures like Liu Binyan, openly supported Bai Hua and in the end the campaign petered out, leaving writers with the sense that their resistance had been unexpectedly effective.

After the plenum the Communist Party began to assert itself more openly. In December 1981, a prominent party theorist, Hu Qiaomu, revived the attack denouncing works such as 'Unrequited Love' as examples of 'bourgeois liberalisation', and Bai Hua was obliged to make a further self-criticism in November 1981. Nevertheless, he was allowed to continue writing, and in December, Hu Yaobang, who had earlier indicated his wish to restrict the campaign, now declared the matter to be settled. Works which challenged the status quo continued to appear in 1982 and early 1983. Critics and scholars came out in support of the new literature in articles such as Wang Ruoshui's 'A Defence of Humanism' and Xu Jingya's 'Rising Poets: On the Modernist Tendencies in Chinese Poetry'.

In response to such challenges, and also to new social trends such as hooliganism in the streets and Western fashions in dress, a campaign to eliminate 'spiritual pollution' was launched in the autumn of 1983 by Hu Qiaomu with Deng Xiaoping's backing. Among the chief targets in literature were humanism, alienation and modernism, in works by Bei Dao, Dai Houying and Jia Pingwa. Younger writers and critics found themselves particularly vulnerable. Under heavy pressure from public security agents, Xu Jingya was forced to a self-criticism in March 1984 in which he confessed to having been influenced by bourgeois liberalism in his support for 'obscure poetry'. The campaign evoked deep concern among writers as a possible forerunner to a new Cultural Revolution, and Liu Binyan and Xiao Qian were among those who refused to take part in the persecution of named targets; Wang Meng's participation was low-key; Ai Qing, Tian Jian, Zang Kejia, Xia Yan and Ding Ling lined up behind Hu Qiaomu. In the end, however, Deng Xiaoping chose to place economic growth above ideology.

China's economy had been growing at a phenomenal rate since 1978. In the agricultural sector, after the communes were dismantled and a contractual system introduced for land use, rice and wheat yields had risen by 50 per cent in less than ten years. Reforms in heavy industry were limited by the constraints of state ownership, but light industry and some manufacturing were dramatically transformed by Deng's open-door policy. To attract foreign capital, 'special economic zones' where foreign firms were given preferential treatment were established in south China, while Japanese, American and, more importantly, Taiwanese and Hong Kong joint ventures found inexperienced but eager partners in most urban areas. By 1983, much of China's economic development was tied directly to contacts with Western business along with their supporting framework of legal, commercial and cultural practices. These contacts undermined belief in Communism as an economic system and gave rise to doubts about its political and cultural supremacy. As tens of thousands of influential middle-level officials as well as top leaders had personal contacts with Western countries, it became increasingly difficult to persuade either these officials or the populace to take seriously the anti-foreign propaganda in the campaign against spiritual pollution. When foreign business interests began to complain that the campaign was damaging foreign investment, even the ideologues were forced to withdraw in the early summer of 1984.

Although the campaign was over by the end of the summer, it took longer for writers generally to recover confidence in the Party leadership, especially as it became widely known that Deng Xiaoping had personally been responsible. But the failure of the campaign was also interpreted as showing the Party that the public would no longer countenance this kind of bullying. At the Fourth National Congress of the Writers' Association in December 1984 and January 1985, the mood was one of pride in the autonomy that writers had defended or at least not easily surrendered, and a sense of shared identity among writers of all kinds as a patriotic literary intelligentsia was established. Xie Mian, a Beijing University academic who had championed obscure poetry, Shu Ting, one of the young poets, and Jia Pingwa were elected to the national council, while Ding Ling suffered public humiliation. Wounds were healed when Ding Ling switched sides by founding a new literary journal, *China*, in December 1985 with support from both reformist and avant-garde writers.

Modernisation in the economy also brought conspicuous wealth among some sections of the population, and cases of corruption and mismanagement quickly became public issues. In mid-1985, for example, officials in Hainan Island were exposed as having been involved in fraudulent activities totalling millions of dollars. They were, however, simply demoted and much of the money could not be traced. This scandal revealed the degree to which corrupt practices were part of the liberalisation process, particularly in the 'special economic zones'. Contacts with foreign countries also brought foreign images and ideas from the Western media to Chinese screens and magazines. At the height of foreign influence in 1985–6, writers, artists and film-makers were ready to make a direct appeal to the foreign market. They included young men who had spent years in the countryside as educated youth in the 1960s and 1970s who now sought out the primitive or basic elements of Chinese culture.

Literary criticism in the mid-1980s was dominated by attempts to replace Maoism with Western theories of subjectivity and post-modernism. Liu Zaifu, the editor of *Literary Review*, set the trend with his two-part article 'On the Subjectivity of Literature' in November 1985 and January 1986. Still relying on a Marxist terminology, he argued that the relationship between writers and their fictional characters is dialectical, and that both writers' creative impulses and audience reception are determined by subjectivities: the subjectivity of the writer, the characters and the reader. This theory was attacked by conservative critics such as Lin Mohan and Chen Yong, but their response only served to enhance Liu Zaifu's status among his followers.

As a consequence of Liu Zaifu's success in promoting subjectivity in literature, many critics, including Liu himself and Wang Ruoshui, also supported humanism as the basic philosophy for new literature, although the new avant-garde writers had already discarded humanistic sentiments. Wang Meng's belated narrative innovations of the early 1980s were now looking decidedly old-fashioned, and it caused no great surprise when he was appointed Minister of Culture in June 1986. Of more concern to conservatives were essays and reportage by Liu Binyan and Wang Ruowang which openly questioned whether Communism really was better than capitalism in bringing wealth and prosperity to China. Apprehension turned to alarm in December 1986 when student demonstrations in fifteen major cities in China protested against Party manipulation in the 'elections' of government representatives. Drawing on popular urban support, the students went on to demand freedom and democracy (it would seem they understood these terms to mean less interference in their private lives and greater participation in politics by intellectuals). The students' demands were taken up by writers and scholars, the most outspoken being the astrophysicist Fang Lizhi, who highlighted the moral dimension by denouncing Party leaders for their unethical behaviour.

Many in the Communist hierarchy were in favour of stopping the spread of 'bourgeois liberalisation' through the usual means; Hu Yaobang, however, saw greater participation by intellectuals in government as a way of replacing the septuagenarians and octogenarians in top Party positions so that reforms could be pushed through more quickly. Deng Xiaoping, who was himself in his eighties, settled for economic development without political or cultural change. As part of a new campaign against 'bourgeois liberalisation' within Party ranks in January 1987, Hu Yaobang was relieved of his post as General Secretary and outspoken critics such as Wang Ruowang, Fang Lizhi and Liu Binyan were expelled. In a related move, Liu Xinwu was dismissed as editor of *People's*

Literature, and once again fears of a new Cultural Revolution began to pervade the literary world.

The advance warning signals leading up to the 1987 campaign against bourgeois liberalisation had again gone unheeded, thanks to the confidence that the literary intelligentsia now generally enjoyed. But although limited in scope, the effects of this campaign within the literary world, where it was conducted largely by reformists against fellow-reformists, went even deeper. Writers became convinced that lack of political reform would result in a constant succession of campaigns as in the early decades of Party rule. Even the upholders of cultural orthodoxy (with the notable exception of Zang Kejia) lapsed into a kind of negative passivism. Bureaucrats as well as creative writers lost confidence in the political elite, and the political leadership lost confidence in the literary intelligentsia. To the Party, writers had misused their freedom, not just in criticising the Party but ignoring or misunderstanding the fundamental problems of agricultural productivity, population control, urban growth and national identity. To the literary intelligentsia, the Party had lost its credibility as an authority able to provide a stable environment of predictable rewards and punishments, in which they could pursue their public and private concerns. More than ever, temporary or even permanent life abroad for themselves or their children became the preferred way out for literary intellectuals of all kinds.

Deng Xiaoping continued to identify himself in public as a moderate by reiterating on a number of occasions in 1987 the importance of the open-door policy and the need to curb the excesses of previous campaigns. This was confirmed when no reprisals were taken against the thousand-plus Chinese students in the United States who signed an open letter to the Communist Party and the State Council to express indignation at the suppression of intellectuals. The premier, Zhao Ziyang, also attempted to reduce the impact of the campaign in a speech to cadres in charge of propaganda work in May 1987. By the time the Thirteenth Congress met in October, the Party seemed to have worked out a compromise between reformers and conservatives (the old terms 'left' and 'right' having long since ceased to have any meaning). Zhao Ziyang became the new General Secretary of the Communist Party, and more than ninety Party elders, including the conservatives Peng Zhen and Deng Liqun, were forced to retire. On the other hand, Li Peng, Zhou Enlai's foster-son who had close connections with the conservative faction, was appointed acting premier. Soviet-trained, Li Peng was not opposed to orderly economic progress and endorsed the modernisation programme.

The Thirteenth Congress was remarkable in Communist history as the first time that a group of political leaders voluntarily relinquished official positions to a younger generation. In policy terms, Zhao Ziyang advanced the notion that China was at a 'primary stage of socialism'. He explained this concept by building on Deng Xiaoping's idea of 'socialism with Chinese characteristics'. Because China had not passed through the capitalist stage experienced by European countries, a rapid expansion of the commodity economy had to take priority, and making money was therefore a primary duty. The new emphasis on market forces also affected literature. Popular culture from Hong Kong and Taiwan, including Jin Yong's martial arts fiction and Qiong Yao's romantic novels, was already widespread in south China, and even literary writers were beginning to produce popular fiction for the mass market.

The primacy of economic development was underlined when Zhao Ziyang made two inspection trips to the coastal areas of Shanghai, Jiangsu, Zhejiang and Fujian immediately after the Congress. These areas were instructed to work towards economic prosperity and to strengthen foreign investment through joint ventures. Entrepreneurial initiatives were encouraged throughout the country, and people who became rich were featured as models in the media. Some people did become very wealthy. On the other hand, inflation was beginning to affect millions of people, especially salaried urban workers, as deregulation allowed prices of basic commodities to climb. Unofficial estimates put the inflation rate in the second half of the 1980s at 20-30 per cent a year, and although wages also increased with fast economic growth, they could not keep up. Unchecked commercialism and corruption in government as well as in private business, sometimes indistinguishable from each other, fed resentment and frustration, and the pervasive atmosphere of cynicism and opportunism was exploited in fiction by explicit descriptions of sex and violence.

Conflict and confusion within the Party were manifested in its loss of credibility on moral and political issues. The Party journal *Red Flag*, which had for many years been studied by millions for political and moral instruction, ceased publication in June 1988. Even Party theoreticians like Su Shaozhi, the former head of the Marxism-Leninism-Mao Zedong Thought Institute, openly denounced the 1983 and 1987 campaigns against spiritual pollution and bourgeois liberalisation. Non-Party intellectuals took these signs of the times as encouragement for further action. In January 1989, Fang Lizhi wrote an open letter to Deng Xiaoping urging a general amnesty for political prisoners such as Wei Jingsheng on the seventieth anniversary of the May Fourth Incident, and a large number of similar open letters by academics and prominent people in China, Hong Kong, Taiwan and the United States followed. The Party leadership's response was simply to ignore them or dismiss them as meaningless.

The top leadership had other concerns to attend to in preparation for the visits of the US President, George Bush, in late February and the General Secretary of the Soviet Communist Party, Mikhail Gorbachev, in May. Both visits, intended as celebrations of a decade of economic progress, instead focused attention on the Party's political weaknesses. At the state dinner hosted by Bush, Fang Lizhi was among the invited guests but was prevented at the last minute from attending. This high-handed action by the Chinese leadership increased the determination of pro-democracy activists to press for political reforms.

The death of Hu Yaobang on 15 April 1989 proved the pretext for an open expression of discontent, in a manner disturbingly reminiscent of the demonstrations of April 1976. Within two days, thousands of students from universities in Beijing gathered in Tiananmen Square, laying wreaths and putting up posters eulogising Hu Yaobang and making indirect attacks on government and Party leaders such as Li Peng. At the memorial service in the Great Hall of the People on 22 April, some 200,000 demonstrators gathered outside, pleading in vain for Li Peng to speak to them. In an editorial in *People's Daily* on 26 April, the students were threatened with reprisals if they continued their protests, which had included strike action and the seizure of campus broadcast stations. Undeterred, the students continued their demonstrations and rallies, which became more numerous and bigger each day, and they were joined by workers in campsites across the Square.

Gorbachev's impending visit also bolstered the students' resolve, since unlike Deng Xiaoping and Li Peng, he had placed political reform ahead of economic liberalisation. To the bitter humiliation of his hosts, he arrived on 15 May to find the streets full of demonstrators and Tiananmen Square a sea of students, among whom 3,000 were on hunger strike. Gorbachev's visit also brought hundreds of reporters from all over the world, most of whom continued to report on events in Tiananmen Square after Gorbachev left. By 17 May the number of protesters had increased to over a million. Writers and intellectuals signed petitions and marched in the streets alongside the students, and Ba Jin, president of the Writers' Association since 1984, also declared his support. It became obvious that the Party was split between reformers represented by Zhao Ziyang, and hard-liners represented by Li Peng, so the demonstrators shouted slogans such as 'Li Peng resign!' and 'Long live Zhao Ziyang!' Similar mass rallies and demonstrations were held in most major cities throughout the country.

On 19 May Deng Xiaoping called an enlarged meeting of the Military Commission at which he was assured of support from the military. On 20 May, Li Peng and Yang Shangkun declared martial law and ordered the People's Liberation Army to restore order. Over the next two weeks, army units in and around Beijing were mobilised, but the streets leading to Tiananmen Square were blocked by people urging them not to enforce martial law. Their temporary success in forestalling military action gave the students renewed courage, but Deng Xiaoping and Yang Shangkun also used the time to prepare a massive operation. In the early hours of 4 June 1989, tanks rolled into the square and troops shot at civilians all over the city: hundreds were killed and thousands injured. Within hours, 'order' was restored. Those who could, went abroad; others were sentenced to long terms of imprisonment; and some were labelled 'hooligans' and executed. Wang Meng resigned as Minister of Culture, and literary publication by well-known authors was delayed for several years. Smashing 'small bottles' on the anniversaries of June Fourth had to take the place of verbal political comment.

The repercussions of the June Fourth massacre in Beijing and other cities continued to be felt into the 1990s. Although universally condemned for the use of terror against unarmed students, the Party leaders showed no sign of remorse. Policy remains as before, with even more emphasis on economic prosperity and military might, and an uneasy balance between moderates and hard-liners.

Although Yang Shangkun was demoted, the military has grown in strength and influence. Li Peng stays in office, and Zhao Ziyang has been replaced by Jiang Zemin, closer in temperament to the moderates than the hard-liners. Despite his lack of formal status, Deng Xiaoping exercised ultimate power right up to his death in early 1997. He continued to promote modernisation without losing the 'Chinese characteristics' which have been so central to all conservative attempts at reform since the end of the nineteenth century. In the age of the information super-highway, this dream may seem an impossibility, but the power of cultural pride and nationalistic sentiments should not be underestimated.

Current orthodoxy in China draws an absolute line between the literature of the Cultural Revolution and that which succeeded it, dubbed 'new era literature'. As the following chapters show, there was more continuity than might be expected in regard to writers, themes, styles and audiences. Although the intensity of political controls varied, even in periods of relaxation attitudes tended to persist, and it was only towards the second half of the 1980s that a genuine diversity became evident again. The closing years of the twentieth century bring many of the same dilemmas of a hundred years before. Thousands of Chinese students, along with hundreds of writers and artists, are again resident in Western countries, which again provide the major avenue for new ideas and new approaches. Most of them will return to China, providing a further avenue for change, and there is no shortage of talent in China itself. The dominant trends of the 1990s suggest that popular culture in its various forms will also provide indigenous sources for the literature of the twenty-first century, and new readers are there in ever-greater numbers.

11

DRAMA: REVOLUTION AND REFORM

As the Cultural Revolution got underway and cultural institutions of all kinds were dismantled, theatre and film, because of their capital-intensive and public nature, were the most drastically affected of all the arts. Between 1968 and 1971, with a few hand-picked exceptions, training schools and research institutes were closed, troupes were disbanded, actors were humiliated and forbidden to perform, and writers were kept occupied in writing confessions. Like other intellectuals, theatre personnel were sent to the countryside for re-education. At the same time, the new power-holders around Jiang Qing organised new performance groups, whose members were still periodically obliged to seek re-education but who also enjoyed the privileges and perils of state employment over the next decade, as the theatre became the main stage for the emergent new culture. The spoken play, seen in the early years of the century as a revolutionary displacement of traditional theatre and largely subordinated to the purposes of left-wing and patriotic propaganda over the previous three decades, was now subordinated to traditional opera. It was not until after the Cultural Revolution that spoken drama recovered its earlier role in spearheading social criticism and protest, and traditional opera its time-honoured function as entertainment.

In February 1966, Jiang Qing with Lin Biao's support convened a forum in Shanghai on literature and art in the armed forces, at which she put forward preliminary versions of the concept of model works and the theory of the 'three prominences'. In its final form, developed in association with Yu Huiyong over the following decade, this theory required scriptwriters and directors to give prominence to the positive characters, to give even greater prominence to heroic characters; and to give greater prominence still to the principal hero/heroine.

New plays, operas and dance-dramas and other forms of theatre swept across the stage in 1966–7, mostly disappearing without trace. By the end of 1966, five Peking operas had emerged as standard-bearers of the new cultural revolution: *The Red Lantern*, *Taking Tiger Mountain by Strategy*, *Shajiabang*, *On the Docks* and *Raid on the White Tiger Regiment*; joining them were two ballets, *The White-haired Girl* and *The Red Detachment of Women*, and the symphonic suite based on *Shajiabang*. These eight works were collectively designated as models in December 1966, and were performed as a group in May 1967 for the twenty-fifth anniversary of the Yan'an Forum in Beijing; some were also part of a broader programme in Shanghai. The final texts of the five operas and two ballets appeared between late 1969 and 1971. After a short interval, another twelve items (some of them variants of the original group) appeared in 1972: they include three new Peking operas, *Azalea Mountain*, *Song of the Dragon River*, and *Fighting on the Plains*; another ballet, *Ode to Yimeng*; a symphonic suite based on *Taking Tiger Mountain by Strategy*; the piano concerto *The Yellow River* (based on Xian Xinghai's 1939 cantata); and a piano accompaniment to Peking opera arias from *The Red Lantern*, written in 1967 and performed by Yin Chengzhong. A final model opera, *Boulder Bay*, was addded in 1976.

The long time taken to produce these models and their small number were not simply a matter of correct content: although the line changed in some respects over these seven years, none of the models needed to be withdrawn on this account. The problem lay in the adaption of traditional techniques to portray contemporary life – the same problem that had faced Mei Lanfang half a century earlier. In order to become an effective medium of propaganda, the model works had to be effective as opera. The most obvious gulf between traditional practice and modern needs was in movement. Peking opera movements were intimately linked with traditional costuming, including elaborate headware, wide sleeves and shoes with high platforms; through skilful manipulation of these props, emperors and palace ladies showed not only status but also emotion, and their skills were watched closely by an expert and critical audience. Brand-new sets of movements had to be designed for workers, peasants or soldiers, however, since previously (if they appeared at all) they had been confined to minor, comic roles. New tunes and singing styles also had to be devised, especially for female roles, and Western music was introduced to provide more stirring accompaniment for contemporary heroes than was thought possible through traditional music. Other Westernised elements included backdrops and representational stage scenery, and the adoption of gestures from the international proletarian movement such as the clenched-fist salute.

The ballets and the symphonic suites naturally owed even more to Western influence. Despite innovative sinification, the ballets were never as widely accepted as the new Peking operas. The combination of classical ballet routines with Chinese dance steps was a more difficult feat than Western choreography applied to traditional Chinese dance and opera movements. It is unlikely that Chinese audiences ever really saw any reason for dancing on points. On the other hand, the addition of singing offended only a very small handful of purists, and was neatly justified under the slogan 'When politics is in command, even the ballet has a voice.'

Other technical aspects were transferred from traditional opera to the model works without too much trouble. Role stereotyping, embodying extremes of good and evil in characterisation, was the most obvious example: to audiences used to painted face performance, the application of red make-up for heroes and green for villains was not a problem. The use of dramatic pauses in the action allowing the hero or heroine to strike a pose was also fully within the tradition. Some inventions were very effective, such as the skiing movements in *Taking Tiger Mountain by Strategy*. In a reasonable compromise with reality and the new political line, the peasants wore neatly patched clothes rather than rags, and more colourful effects were introduced wherever possible – for instance, the capes worn by the soldiers on skis.

The chief creative talent behind the model works was the musician Yu Huiyong, who served as Minister of Culture during the latter part of the Cultural Revolution. (Jiang Qing's role is still disputed; her involvement in 1964 and 1965 is documented, but from November 1956 to late 1967 she was mostly engaged in direct political struggles.) Although the creation and production of the model works were in the hands of an educated elite, there was an echo of traditional practice in the collective authorship and constant revision of the scripts and staging. Certainly there was a deliberate shift away from the author-centred plays of May Fourth drama, where publication of playscripts might precede performance and property rights were exerted through royalties and box-office returns. Also traditional was the predictability of the plots, especially when distribution reached saturation levels, so that theatre audiences inevitably concentrated their attention on performance skills.

Having gone to such great lengths to create these works, the authorities demanded, as much as was feasible in local conditions, their exact duplication in performance. In a radical departure from traditionally unscripted opera, handbooks recorded the scripts, musical score, detailed descriptions of costumes and stage properties, and stage directions. The film versions were especially valuable for national standardisation, even using the same props as the stage performances. Further publicity was given to the model works by television and radio broadcasts, gramophone records, posters, paintings and sculptures. Book publication and performances were prefaced with quotations from Mao Zedong's works and, especially after repeated performances of the same work, the ancient ritualistic role of the theatre was re-invoked.

Peking opera was basically an urban form which had spread to the main provincial cities, but the aim of the Cultural Revolution authorities was to reach into the villages, creating a genuinely national audience. To do this, it was necessary to use regional and local opera forms. Around 1971, troupes specialising in regional styles were revived, first adapting model operas and then introducing new or revised pieces along the same lines. *The Red Lantern, On the Docks* and *Shajiabang* were performed as Cantonese opera in 1972, with some success in the singing parts, less in spoken passages.

The transplanted variants and new models of 1972–4 were only part of the revival in literature and the arts after the fall of Lin Biao, which included new spoken plays along with regional opera. A notable signal was the re-introduction in November 1972 of programmes featuring excerpts rather than complete works. Theatre also continued to be a battleground for factional struggles. One of the highlights of the North China Theatrical Festival in Beijing in January–February 1974 was a new Shanxi opera *Thrice Ascending Peach Peak*; said to show support for Liu Shaoqi, it was then vigorously attacked in the campaign against Lin Biao and Confucius. Exclusive performances of old Peking opera for top leaders and visiting dignitaries were staged from 1973 on but still banned to the public at large.

In the end, the fatal problem of the model works was their over-exposure not just in the cities but also in the countryside, where attendance was made compulsory by village cadres. As early as 1971, rural cinema audiences had to rely for light relief on faults in the power supply or the vagaries of pedal-operated generators and projectors. By the mid-1970s, the dearth of new works provided opponents of the authorities with an effective weapon. Almost equally damning was the failure of the models to work in other genres. Some spoken plays appeared during 1967 and again in the mid-1970s but none were elevated to the state of models; fiction and poetry were even more resistant.

Tours by Western companies provided limited but welcome relief at least for urban audiences. The Vienna Philharmonic visited China in April 1973, and featured at one of its Beijing concerts Yin Chengzhong playing *The Yellow River* concerto and a short piece by Schubert. Deng Xiaoping, then deputy prime minister, attended the concert and afterwards praised Beethoven, Mozart and Schubert; a press attack on Schubert followed immediately after. Eugene Ormandy took the Philadelphia Orchestra to Beijing and Shanghai in 1973. The première on 16 September was attended by Jiang Qing, wearing Western dress, and at the request of the hosts, it also featured Yin playing *The Yellow River* concerto.

Further relaxation in 1974–5 was demonstrated by a series of drama festivals, in which altogether forty-eight local operas adapted from the models, over fifty new local operas and thirty-five new spoken plays gave over a thousand performances to audiences totalling nearly two million people: none of these works survived Mao's death in 1976 and the end of the Cultural Revolution.

The model works caused some embarrassment to the new ruling group after the arrest of Jiang Qing and the 'gang of four', since they had been publicly praised by Mao Zedong and Zhou Enlai. The first tactic was to downplay Jiang Qing's role and give the credit to others. In August 1977 Hua Guofeng criticised them only for dominating the stage, but the formulaic characterisation and other aspects had come under fire even earlier, and before long the model works disappeared from public performance for almost a decade (and Chinese ballets disappeared altogether). Another tactic, dating from late 1977, was designed to stress the legitimacy of the new ruling group as a continuation of the former regime: the earlier, displaced opera and film versions of *The White-haired Girl* and *The Red Detachment of Women* were revived, and the Yan'an opera *Driven to Join the Liangshan Rebels* was chosen to commmemorate the thirty-fifth anniversary of the Yan'an Forum. Plays which had been criticised by the 'gang of four' took longer: *Hai Rui Dismissed from Office* was revived in 1979, although since criticism of the Cultural Revolution was still limited, the pretence was maintained that Yao Wenyuan's attack had been a distortion, followed by Tian Han's *Xie Yaohuan*.

Western theatre returned in March 1979 with a performance of Brecht's *Das Leben des Galilei* in Beijing, and *Much Ado about Nothing* in Shanghai. Regional opera also grew rapidly, and by 1979 the number of locally based troupes approached the level set two decades earlier. New plays on historical themes were hurried along by the authorities. The first of these was *Yang Kaihui* in 1977, on Mao's second wife, who was assassinated by the Nationalists in 1930. Very obviously in an attempt to distance Mao from Jiang Qing, this play was also the first to represent on stage any of the major political leaders of the past decades. Several other plays with actors in the roles of Mao and Zhou Enlai were performed in the late 1970s and 1980s, and regulations were issued to ensure their proper respectful treatment: for instance, the actors must substitute Standard Modern Chinese for the politicians' actual local (dialect) pronunciations. The very small amount of new work by elderly authors was also encouraged. Cao Yu's *Wang Zhaojun*, published in November 1978 and per-formed in July 1979, was given extensive publicity and official praise, although by some accounts audiences were lukewarm.

More to the taste of audiences in Beijing and Shanghai were new plays on contemporary life. Drama can be quicker than fiction to react to current events, but since the stage must to some extent be public, there was no underground theatre during the Cultural Revolution, nor even playscripts. Its post-1976 recovery, however, was both remarkably rapid and, in taking contemporary urban tragedies as its main theme, remarkably bold.

Shanghai was the first site of the resurgence of new plays strongly influenced by the pre-war theatre. The first nationally acclaimed work was the solemn *In a Land of Silence*, written by a former educated youth, now factory worker, Zong Fuxian; it was followed by a series of lively satires. At a meeting to discuss the exposure of corruption in the theatre in January 1980, Hu Yaobang ordered performances of the popular Shanghai play *If I Were Real* to be halted for revision. Hu Yaobang's speech was the first active intervention of the authorities in the arts since the end of the Democracy Wall, and the expression 'social effect' was regarded by some as a portent of a new Cultural Revolution. The controversy continued throughout the year, Sha Yexin vigorously defending himself with the backing of Ba Jin, and was revived again in the debate over the filmscript 'Unrequited Love' in 1981.

The centre of new drama in the early 1980s shifted to Beijing, where the leading theatre was for several years the Chinese Youth Art Theatre, the site of innovative productions of foreign plays from *Das Leben des Galilei* in 1979 to *The Red Nose* by the Taipei playwright Yao Yiwei in 1982, of revivals of pre-war successes such as Wu Zuguang's *Return on a Snowy Night* and of controversial plays on the theme of love by the former actress and resident writer Bai Fengxi in 1981 and 1983.

The long-delayed introduction of modernism reached the Chinese theatre in the early 1980s. The ground had been laid by Huang Zuolin, who as a student in 1936 had first encountered Brecht's impressions of Chinese theatre from Mei Lanfang's European tour. Soviet Russian influence in the 1940s and 1950s had led to the dominance of Stanislavsky's theatrical methods in Yan'an and, after 1949, in Beijing and Shanghai, but Huang Zuolin remained fascinated by Brecht's anti-realism. In 1962 Huang Zuolin proposed a cautious amalgam of Chinese and Western dramatic traditions to build a non-realistic theatre, but non-realism was to develop along other lines: the campaign against Stanislavsky in 1969 offered only Jiang Qing's formulations in its place. It was not until the end of the 1970s that Huang was able to advocate undiluted Brechtian method as an appropriate way forward.

The other main source of experimental drama in the early 1980s came from the French theatre of the absurd as interpreted by Gao Xingjian, whose plays became smash hits among younger intellectuals. The 1983–4 campaign against spiritual pollution seemed at first to spell an end to modernist experimentation, and Gao Xingjian's comeback in 1985 introduced primitivism to the

Chinese stage. Modernism was further served by Wang Peigong's *W.E.* and Tao Jun's *The Magic Cube* in 1985–6.

Productions of Western plays by guest directors became an established practice in the early 1980s as a short-cut in training a new generation of performers to discard both the semi-operatic styles of the Cultural Revolution and the Stanislavskian method that preceded it. Arthur Miller's 1983 production of *Death of a Salesman*, with Ying Ruochen in the starring role, played to full houses at the Capital Theatre and was a *succès d'estime*, but for audiences it was outclassed by the Central Academy of Drama's production of *Peer Gynt*, directed by Xu Xiaozhong from Xiao Qian's translation and starring Zhang Xinxin as the Woman in Green. (The Academy's *Anna Christie*, on the other hand, directed by the O'Neill specialist George White in 1984, was a flop.) Chinese cities also played host to large numbers of touring Western orchestras, ballets, opera and drama troupes. In this atmosphere, revivals of plays from the 1950s and early 1960s fared poorly: audience boredom was manifest at a highly touted performance of Guo Moruo's *Cai Wenji* in 1982. Unreformed Peking opera, *kunqu* and other regional forms made a triumphant comeback, only to face a different kind of modernisation in order to win younger audiences.

Throughout the first half of the 1980s, the theatre was able to compete successfully with the cinema, also newly revived, as one of the liveliest media for new ideas and new forms of expression. The steady extension of the contract system for theatre groups from early 1983 allowed greater freedom of choice in repertoire and styles. After 1985, both theatre and cinema came increasingingly under pressure from commercialisation in the face of audience preference for television and video. Sporadic censorship between 1981 and 1988 if anything helped redirect attention to the stage, but the end of the decade saw the end of unprecedented change and experimentation in all forms of drama.

Taking Tiger Mountain by Strategy: A Modern Revolutionary Peking Opera (1970)

The model version of *Taking Tiger Mountain by Strategy* was developed by the Peking Opera Troupe of Shanghai; consisting of ten scenes, the final script is dated July 1970 and was published by the People's Press in September. The music was composed by Yu Huiyong. In the best tradition of popular drama, the earliest version of a key passage in this opera goes back to the scene in the novel *Water Margin* where the drunken hero Wu Song encounters a tiger on a mountainside and kills it single-handedly. A variation of this episode was incorporated into the novel *Tracks from the Snowy Forest* by Qu Bo, an account of the fighting in the north-east after the end of the War against Japan, where the tiger-killer is Yang Zirong, a PLA scout on a mission to penetrate the bandits' lair on top of the mountain. The episode was then in turn performed as a play by the Beijing People's Art Theatre in the 1950s, and became one of the first Peking operas on a contemporary theme during the Great Leap Forward in 1958. A revised version of the opera made under Jiang Qing's supervision was presented at the 1964 Festival. It was named as one of the original five model operas in 1966, and further revisions took place in 1967 and 1969. Released in October 1970 as the first model opera film, it starred the original performer, Dong Xiangling, as Yang Zirong.

A gang of bandits in the north-east, led by Vulture (called Eagle in some early English translations), have established a reign of terror over the local inhabitants from their stronghold on Tiger Mountain. Chang, a hunter whose wife and mother were killed by the bandits, and his daughter, Bao, who masquerades as a mute boy for protection, are forced to hide in the forest. When the People's Liberation Army arrives to organise resistance to remnant Nationalist troops, Chang Bao and her father join up. Yang Zirong, the leader of a scout platoon, disguises himself as a bandit to gain entry to the enemy's camp. The rest of the platoon follows and the gang, which has links with the Nationalists, is routed.

On the way up the mountain, Yang Zirong encounters a tiger and kills it, then uses the incident to gain credibility for his cover story. In the *Water Margin* version, Wu Song is surprised by the tiger because he is very drunk, and it is only because he is drunk that he dares wrestle with it. In the *Snowy Forest* version, Yang Zirong is very much on the alert, and is even singing obscene ditties to keep in character, in case he is being watched. In the 1964 version, the obscene ditties are deleted, and instead he sings heroic arias to demonstrate his strength of purpose. Also cut are two scenes about superstition and murder, and his flirtation with the bandit chief's licentious daughter, which were written to play up the negative roles; they are replaced with 'speaking bitterness' scenes for the masses (the hunter and daughter) and Yang Zirong. Further editing took place in 1965, emphasising Yang's integration with and reliance on the people. Another change was Yang's demeanour in the bandit's lair: instead of telling ribald stories and otherwise trying to blend in with his company, in the model version he holds himself apart through contrasts in make-up and posture, and is followed by the spotlight even when he stands to one side of the stage. In general, the changes tend to disregard realism for the sake of stronger character contrasts and moral clarity.

Some plot details have a specific political function: the tiger killed by Yang Zirong represents the 'paper tiger' of imperialism, and the struggle in the north-east is supposed to have been a strategy proposed by Mao but opposed by his 1960s adversary, Peng Zhen. Male-bonding is an important sub-theme, suggesting Jiang Qing's dependence on the army at this stage. In this respect it can be compared with the 1956 Peking opera from *Water Margin, The Wild Boar Forest,* whose heroes live apart from the world of ordinary peasants, who seek revenge for injustice only as a matter of private or brotherly honour, and who indulge freely in gluttonous eating and drinking. In *Tiger Mountain* the soldier heroes work closely with the local people, seek to overthrow a social class rather than wicked individuals, and are as chaste in their ingestion as in their sexual relationships. The two bands of heroes have in common a fierce devotion to loyalty and justice. The two operas have in common vigorous action and singing, enhanced in the case of *Taking Tiger Mountain by Strategy* by boldly imaginative choreography and costuming. It has always been one of the most popular of all the model operas, and was one of the first to be revived in the 1990s.

The Red Lantern: A Modern Revolutionary Peking Opera (1970)

The model version of *The Red Lantern* was developed by the Peking Opera Troupe of China; consisting of eleven scenes, it is dated May 1970 and was published in September by the People's

Press. Originally a Shanghai opera, it was first arranged as Peking opera in 1963 under Jiang Qing's direction and shown at the 1964 Festival. The script was by Wang Ouhong and Ajia, a veteran of the Lu Xun Academy in Yan'an, and the cast included the well-known performers Qian Haoliang as Li Yuhe, Liu Changyu as Tiemei and Yuan Shihai as Hatoyama. It was restaged in 1965 and was soon the best-known of the new operas. Piano music to accompany the most famous arias became a model work in its own right in 1968, and the film version was released in 1970, starring the original cast. Posters of Tiemei holding aloft the red lantern were popular pin-ups for several years.

The opera is set in north China during the early years of the War against Japan. Li Yuhe is a railway worker living with his foster-mother and his adopted daughter; none of them have any living family. An underground Party member, he is asked to deliver a secret code to the Communist guerrilla forces but is betrayed and handed over to the Japanese army of occupation. The chief of the Japanese military police, Hatoyama, used to work as a doctor in China and once treated Li Yuhe, but now he has no compunction in using torture on his former patient. When Li refuses to yield, Hatoyama fetches the old woman and the seventeen-year-old girl Tiemei to make him talk. The three still refuse to capitulate, and Li Yuhe and the old woman are executed. Tiemei, the only one left alive, outwits the Japanese spies and delivers the code, finding her way by the light of the red lantern belonging to her natural parents, killed in the 1923 massacre of the Beijing–Hankou railway strikers. Communist guerillas then kill Hatoyama and the Chinese traitor. In earlier versions, Hatoyama was treated more sympathetically and dominated the action, while Li Yuhe was apt to seek refuge in drink.

Shajiabang: A Modern Revolutionary Peking Opera (1970)

The model version of *Shajiabang* was developed by the Peking Opera Company of Beijing; consisting of ten scenes, it is dated May 1970 and was published in September by the People's Press. Wang Zengqi was chiefly responsible for the libretto and Li Muliang for the music. Under the title *Sparks amid the Reeds*, it first saw life during the Great Leap Forward in 1958 as a Shanghai opera.

In 1963 Jiang Qing approached the First Peking Opera Troupe of Beijing with the script and asked them to make it into Peking opera. An early attempt, under the title *The Underground Liaison Agent*, is said to have had a female impersonator playing the title role. The script was revised for performance at the 1964 Festival, with Zhao Yanxia as Aqing. After undergoing further extensive revison in 1965, including a change of name suggested by Mao Zedong, it was adopted as a model in 1966. The film was released in 1971, with the 1964 cast playing their original roles. A Cantonese opera version was developed in 1972 and made into a film in 1974, starring Hongxiannü.

The story is set in Shajiabang, an area of lakes and marshes in Jiangsu, during the War against Japan. Eighteen wounded New Fourth Army soldiers come to the village, which is behind enemy lines, to recuperate until they are well enough to rejoin their unit. Their main local contact is Aqing, a refugee from Shanghai who now runs a local teashop to provide cover for her underground Party work. Warned of an approaching Japanese raid, the political instructor, Guo Jianguang, leads his men to hide in the reeds. The villagers put up a fight, and the Japanese commander, Colonel Kuroda, orders puppet troops, commanded by Hu Chuankui, to search for the wounded soldiers. Hu Chuankui announces himself as willing to work for three sides: Chiang Kaishek, the Japanese and secret societies. In a battle of wits with Aqing, however, he and his chief-of-staff are outmatched, and the wounded soldiers are led to safety. The puppet troops torture and kill the villagers to find out who helped the soldiers, but a commando platoon led by Guo Jianguang returns to Shajiabang to capture the villains.

Shajiabang was one of the most popular of the model operas, and its main arias were frequently performed at concerts and sung as popular tunes. The martial exploits of the New Fourth soldiers also provided the opportunity for splendid displays of acrobatics, but the battle of wits between the heroine and the villain is almost as entertaining. The patriotic theme was one which most people could identify with, and the characterisation was robust enough to allow the villains some good lines. The prominence given to Aqing in some of the earlier versions was lessened to highlight the army's role: it was not until after the fall of Lin Biao that true female protagonists emerged in the model operas.

The Red Detachment of Women: A Modern Revolutionary Dance-drama (1970)

The model version of *The Red Detachment of Women* was developed by the Dance Troupe of China; consisting of six scenes with a prologue and interlude, it is dated May 1970 and was published in August. The first full-length ballet on a contemporary theme, *The Red Detachment of Women* was said to be based on a true incident. It appeared first as a local Hainan opera and was made into a film, *Qionghua*, by Xie Jin in 1960. A Peking opera version was staged at the 1964 Festival, and a *kunqu* version appeared in 1965 under the same name. Jiang Qing supervised the ballet version, which was first presented at the National Day celebrations in 1964. The film was released in 1971 and shown at the Venice Film Festival the same year (this was the first time that a model film had been shown outside Third World countries). A new Peking opera version by the Peking Opera Troupe of China was also made a model and released as a film in 1972. President and Mrs Nixon, along with Henry Kissinger and entourage, saw a performance in February 1972, hosted by Zhou Enlai with Jiang Qing, Guo Moruo and other high officials in attendance. The American party afterwards expressed their reaction as a mixture of boredom and astonishment.

The heroine is a bondmaid, Wu Qinghua, who is imprisoned and beaten by her employer, a wealthy Hainan landlord, for trying to run away. She escapes again, is apprehended, beaten fiercely and left for dead. At dawn the next day, she is discovered by Hong Changqing, a Red Army cadre for the women's detachment of the local partisans. On Wu's first assault on the enemy, she loses control of her fierce emotions and the mission is aborted. Under the Party's guidance, she learns discipline in the women's company and becomes a model soldier. During a battle at a mountain pass, the Red Army and the partisans are able to repel the enemy, but Hong is captured and put to death by fire by the landlord. The Red Army and partisans swoop down on the enemy's mansion, and Wu kills the landlord and dedicates her life in place of Hong's.

The incongrous combination of classical ballet routines and Chinese dance steps in this work was accentuated by the extraordinary costume of the women soldiers in their skin-tight shorts and flesh-coloured tights. The script was even more melodramatic than the other model works, and the stage effects were exaggerated to the point of being grotesque, as for instance when Hong is being burnt at the stake. Fighting and beatings made plenty of action on stage, but this was offset by the improbability of episodes such as his show of defiance when helpless and surrounded on all sides.

The White-haired Girl: A Modern Revolutionary Dance-drama (1971)

The model version of *The White-haired Girl* was developed by the Shanghai Dance School; consisting of eight scenes, a prologue and an epilogue, it was published in 1971. *The White-haired Girl* appeared in several different forms after 1949, most notably as a Peking opera during the Great Leap Forward in 1958, starring Zhao Yanxia. The Shanghai Dance School was much younger, founded only in 1960. The success of *The Red Detachment of Women* encouraged it to develop a dance-drama of its own under the direct supervision of Jiang Qing. The ballet *White-haired Girl* started off as a half-hour production in June 1964, performed in an extended version for National Day the same year. The first performance of the full-length production was at the Shanghai Spring Festival in May 1965, and it was raised to the status of a model in summer 1966. The film of the model ballet was released in 1972.

Major changes to the plot included the death of Xi'er's father while resisting the landlord's lackeys (rather than by suicide), less attention to the romance between Xi'er and Dachun, her successful resistance to rape, the on-stage execution of the landlord, and Xi'er's induction into the Eighth Route Army. Much of the original score, including the principal songs, is retained, but more Chinese instruments and tune-types from Peking opera were added, along with new songs. (*The early history of this work is given above in Chapter 9.*)

On the Docks: A Model Revolutionary Peking Opera (1972)

The model version of *On the Docks* was developed by the Peking Opera Troupe of Shanghai; consisting of seven scenes, it is dated

January 1972 and was published in May. It first appeared in 1963 as a *huaiju* opera (a form of traditional opera popular in the Shanghai area), and at Jiang Qing's suggestion was arranged as a Peking opera in 1964. Liu Shaoqi is said to have suggested revisions to the *huaiju* version for performance in 1965, and Jiang Qing was stung into a second attempt. The music was composed by Yu Huiyong. The model opera film was released in 1972.

The only one of the original five model operas to tackle a post-1949 setting, it depicts the attempted sabotage of a shipload of seed rice for Africa in a Shanghai dockyard in 1963. The villain is a dispatcher (i.e. an educated worker), and manages to put a sack of export wheat mixed with fibreglass into the rice shipment by tricking a young docker who has had a secondary-school education and dreams of becoming a seaman. The heroine, the Party Secretary Fang Haizhen, with the help of the other dockworkers, recovers the tampered sack, re-educates the careless youth, and gets rid of the saboteur.

From the beginning, *On the Docks* was always the most unsatisfactory of the model works. The main flaw is that, following custom, the saboteur is made up to look like a villain to the audience, while to the characters on stage his true nature is supposed to be hidden throughout most of the two-hour performance. Equally unconvincing is his identity as a spy concurrently in the employ of the Americans, the Japanese and the Nationalists. Compared with the gory plots of the other model works, the sabotage seems trivial: despite the Party Secretary's attempts to convince the dock workers of the importance of their task, the audience might remain sceptical. It is hard to see even the urban population getting very worked up about whether the seed grain gets to Africa in time for the sowing season, and some might reasonably harbour a wish that the dastardly accountant had succeeded in getting the fibreglass aboard the Scandinavian ship for the sake of the profit. The action is limited, and the only violent episode, the fight between the villain and the brigade leader, occurs off-stage.

The adaption of Peking opera to twentieth-century industrial work should not in principle be any more insoluble than in other areas of modern life, but costuming, make-up, movement and postures in this example are all unimpressive. These shortcomings were noted at the time but there was not much that could be done to save it. Politically, it reflects two main preoccupations:

the foregrounding of the main female role, and the association of education with moral deficiency. The internationalist theme is of interest but remains an abstract issue rather than part of the action.

Raid on the White Tiger Regiment: A Modern Revolutionary Peking Opera (1972)

The model version of *Raid on the White Tiger Regiment* was developed by the Peking Opera Troupe of Shandong. First produced as Peking opera during the Great Leap Forward in 1958, it was revised for the 1964 Festival. A story of Korean War 'volunteers', it has plenty of action but little human interest. Political needs of a rather special kind dictated its changing emphasis. Originally a straightforward depiction of the evils of US imperialism in Korea, the final script needed accommodation to the current negotiations between China and the United States over an end to the conflict in Vietnam. The film was released in 1972. Unlike *Taking Tiger Mountain by Strategy*, *Raid on the White Tiger Regiment* never caught hold of the popular imagination and tended to be staged less frequently even at the height of the Cultural Revolution.

Song of the Dragon River: A Modern Revolutionary Peking Opera (1972)

The model version of *Song of the Dragon River* was developed by the Peking Opera Troupe of Shanghai; consisting of eight scenes and an epilogue, it is dated January 1972 and was published in May. Set in 1963 in a commune in the south-east coastal region, in many ways it resembles *On the Docks*: the chief character, the Party Secretary, is a woman, and the villain is 'a class enemy concealed within the brigade'. It also suffers from the same problems, only slightly modified by its rural setting (more suitable for traditional theatrical styles) and given dramatic interest by some tricky stage business in the form of a human barricade against the river current. The army is present only in its boy-scout role. The film version was released in 1972.

Azalea Mountain: A Modern Revolutionary Peking Opera (1973)

The model version of *Azalea Mountain* was developed by the Peking Opera Troupe of Beijing; consisting of nine scenes, it is dated September 1973 and was published later the same year. The script was written by Wang Shuyuan and others. It was reworked over two years from an earlier version shown at the 1964 Festival. The film version was released in 1974.

The story is set in the spring of 1928 in the border region between Hunan and Jiangxi. The hero, Lei Kang, is a member of an independent 'self-defence corps' (i.e., virtually indistinguishable, at this stage, from a bandit group) who has managed to escape from the clutches of the local landlord, known as Viper. Hearing that a Communist representative from Jinggangshan has been captured, Lei Kang, wearing a deerskin waistcoat and holding a trident from which hang a fox and some rabbits, leads a small posse to the rescue. All are taken aback to discover that the Communist is a woman, Ke Xiang, whose poise is such that the armed guards cower when she glares at them. Brought back to the corps, Ke Xiang, a miner's daughter whose family was slaughtered by capitalists, causes some anguish among the members of the group as she counsels long-range tactics in the class war rather than the traditional banditry of disaffected peasantry. This leads to a somewhat fatuous passage: when the enemy appears to be setting fire to a much-revered old village woman, Ke Xiang decides to call a meeting 'to analyse the enemy situation'. In the end, the traitor within the ranks is exposed and killed, while the landlord and his men are defeated in battle.

Azalea Mountain is certainly one of the better works in the model repertoire. There is a great deal of action on stage, and some fine dramatic clashes between the members of the corps, stimulated not only by the hidden traitor but also by the sexual tension created by the attractive and extremely competent heroine. The discrepancy between the characters' and the audience's perception of the traitor within the ranks is not as great as in *On the Docks*, and his ability to manipulate the group is more credible. The costuming and the make-up are neither particularly colourful nor uncomfortably out of place. Politically the work is of interest in embodying the new historiography in which a sharp distinction is made between traditional peasant rebellions and communist revolution, and as the first portrayal of a pre-1949 woman communist leader (referring perhaps to Jiang Qing's pre-1949 credentials). It has also been seen as a rebuke to the military adventurism said to have been practised by Lin Biao.

Ode to Yimeng: A Modern Revolutionary Dance-drama (1973)

The model version of *Ode to Yimeng*, consisting of a prologue, four acts and an epilogue, was published in 1973. A depiction of the close relations between the army and the peasants during the civil war of 1946–9, its most startling action is when the village heroine Ying goes behind a rock, expresses milk from her breast, bottles it, and then reemerges to feed it to the wounded soldier, all performed to a throbbing violin solo. The last of the model dance-dramas based on ballet, it signals the decline of the genre.

Zong Fuxian (b. 1947)

Zong Fuxian came from an educated family, but his own education was interrupted by the Cultural Revolution, and at the time of writing *In a Land of Silence* in 1978, he was employed as a factory worker. Transferred to Beijing in November after its Shanghai première, it became the first play to attract national attention since the 1960s. Appropriately enough it bears a strong resemblance to Cao Yu's *Thunderstorm*, set in a rich and powerful household, and featuring the return of the exile, the overthrow of the patriarch and a conflict of loyalties within and outwith the family. Of daring topicality, dealing with the roles of Mao Zedong and Hua Guofeng in the Tiananmen Square demonstrations of 1976, within three years it had been left behind by Party historiography. The script was published in *People's Theatre* in 1978.

Sha Yexin (b. 1939)

In the spring of 1979, news of a scandal touching on corruption in high places broke in Shanghai. A local educated youth still living in the countryside had tried without success to buy a ticket to see *Much Ado about Nothing*, but mistaken for the son of the Deputy Chief of Staff of the People's Liberation Army, he found himself being admitted to the theatre. Encouraged to continue the deception, he enjoyed life at the highest levels of society for several months before being arrested. In July, a short farce based on this incident, *The Artillery Commander's Son*, written by three students at Fudan University, Zhou Weibo, Dong Yangsheng and Ye Xiaonan, was staged to a student audience and shortly after won first prize at a Shanghai drama competition. A longer play on the same theme appeared in August, playing at first to a restricted audience. Written by Sha Yexin together with two other members of the Shanghai People's Art Theatre, Li Shouceng and Yao Mingde, *If I Were Real* was an immediate hit. It was performed in Beijing later the same year during the Fourth National Congress of Writers and Artists and was the main target in a hastily convened seminar on satiric plays in 1980. Over the next few months, it was alternately banned and re-released but remained unrevised, and the text was only published in Hong Kong in 1980.

Even several years later, the boldness of the authors' attack on official corruption is impresssive: as contemporary commentators noted, the 'good' cadre and happy ending are unconvincing, perhaps deliberately so. One of the most innovative aspects of the play was to feature an anti-hero as protagonist, Li Xiaozhang, the first since 1949 and a dramatic repudiation of Cultural Revolution orthodoxy. Although the audience is asked to feel sympathy for Li as the victim of social forces, he is nevertheless shown as a willing fraudster. The play also breaks away from Party puritanism: his girlfriend's pregnancy is shown as not a problem of morality but an offence against convention. The play escapes some of the self-indulgence in typical 'scar' writing: it is not the cadres' better material conditions that the young lovers hanker after, just a chance to marry and set up a home.

Intertextual references to theatres and audiences give the play additional interest: Gogol's *The Inspector-General* is foregrounded as Li Xiaozhang's inspiration (it is not clear if the authors were also aware of Lao She's *Looking West to Chang'an*). Also very effective is a Brechtian breakdown between stage and audience. The prelude, for instance, discovers Li Xiaozhang seated among the audience, from where he is removed by public security officers:

an event which may have caused an authentic shiver among many of the audience. The dialogue is brisk and clever, and still reads well today.

Instead of revising *If I Were Real* in the light of the January criticism, Sha Yexin started work on his next play, *Mayor Chen Yi*, a straightforward eulogy of a proment victim of the Cultural Revolution containing little of special interest. Published and staged in 1980, *Mayor Chen Yi* won official approval, but Sha's third play, *The Secret Life of Marx*, stirred up controversy once again in 1983. An attempt to humanise Marx by showing his private life at the time of writing *Das Kapital*, it pleased neither orthodox critics nor less conventional audiences, and despite minor technical innovations and even denunciation in the campaign against spiritual pollution, it was eclipsed by Gao Xingjian's new plays.

Gao Xingjian (b. 1941)

Gao Xingjian studied French at Beijing University and was employed as a French translator at the Foreign Languages Press before being transferred to the Writers' Association in the late 1970s, and his early work is heavily influenced by French modernism and the theatre of the absurd. The author of several short stories and plays, in 1981 he was appointed as a scriptwriter to the Beijing People's Art Theatre. The first of his plays to be staged was *Warning Signal*, co-authored by Liu Huiyuan; it was peformed as theatre in the round in the small upstairs auditorium of the Capital Theatre in October 1982 under the direction of Lin Zhaohua. The hero is a petty thief, brought to see the error of his ways by his more conventionally minded girlfriend and a wise old worker. Set in the guard's van of an old-fashioned steam train, a major part of its audience appeal lay in its excellent light and sound effects; the acting, in a mixture of styles, was less successful and the plot only mildly innovatory.

Gao's second play was *The Bus-stop*, also directed by Lin Zhaohua and staged in the same auditorium in June 1983, after preliminary publication of the playscript in May. The performance is preceded by Lu Xun's playlet *The Passer-by*, one of Lu Xun's last expressions of the evolutionism he preached in the 1910s, and its protagonist, transformed into the Silent Man, takes his place in the bus queue which forms the opening scene in *The Bus-stop*. *The Bus-stop* can be seen as a Chinese *Waiting for Godot* plus Social Darwinism: while a cross-section of Beijing society waits foolishly for buses that never come or never stop, the Silent Man sets off alone on his arduous journey. Skilfully employing the liveliest Beijing slang to be heard on stage since Lao She's *Teahouse*, Gao Xingjian satirises the passivity, vacillation and superficiality of key types in 1980s society, including a young hoodlum from the suburbs, a housewife preoccupied by the rising cost of food, a young woman fearful of growing too old to attract a husband, and a jovially corrupt factory boss. As the play reaches its climax, surreal effects are created by disco lights and frantic music. After endless argument (introducing the first polyphonic episode on the Chinese stage), the characters in the queue agree to walk into town, but when the stage lights darken, they are still irresolutely in place.

Preparing for his next play on the eve of the campaign against spiritual pollution, Gao Xingjian instead became one of its main targets, and the first performance of *The Wild Man* was delayed until spring 1985. During the Cultural Revolution, Gao had spent some time in the south-west, and it was from this area that much of *The Wild Man* was derived. Another source was in traditional dramaturgy, not so much from the classical forms of Peking opera and *kunqu* but from descriptions in written records of earlier prototypes. Under Artaud's influence, Gao sought to recreate on stage some of China's most ancient myths and legends as a backdrop to his portrayal of a middle-aged intellectual, concerned with the break-up of his marriage, the political chaos of the post-revolutionary period, and the growing damage to the environment ignored by an apathetic urban government. Audience opinion on *The Wild Man* was mixed. Some praised it as a major contribution to the new movement towards primitivism in the arts; noting the long speeches and unmistakeable autobiographical references, others saw it as self-indulgent, sentimental and modishly didactic. Only the extraordinary sets, designed by the Yunnan sculptor Yin Guangzhong and dominating the stage of the Capital Theatre's main auditorium, won universal praise.

The increasingly repressive atmosphere after 1986 led to prohibitions on Gao's new work. After travelling to Europe in 1987, he settled in Paris where he continues to write fiction and drama.

Wang Peigong (b. 1940)

In the early 1980s Wang Peigong was an airforce writer of conventional works such as *Ardent Hearts* (1983; in collaboration with Li Dongcai and Liu Dianchen). He became famous to a different audience in the summer of 1985 with an experimental modernist drama under the title *W.E.* A depiction in loosely connected scenes of the frustrations of China's educated youth in 1978–84, it set a new level of frankness, both in language and in topic, and was an immediate hit with Beijing's younger intellectuals. The strange title (which involves three levels of punning) was very disturbing to one Party official, who regarded the use of alphabetic initials as aping the West. A hurried ban was placed on its performance, and the director demoted from his airforce post. Wang Peigong had his supporters, including Wu Zuguang, who spoke up in his defence, and the script was published in *Playscripts* in September. Sha Yexin, the newly appointed director of the Shanghai People's Art Theatre, promptly arranged its Shanghai première in October. Performances resumed in Beijing later the same month, but a new ban was imposed again in November.

Wang Peigong was an open supporter of the democratic movement, resigning his Party membership in May 1989, and was briefly under arrest after 4 June.

Tao Jun (b. 1959)

The momentum for experimental drama was carried forward by *The Magic Cube*, by a young amateur playwright in Shanghai, Tao Jun. Named after Rubik's Cube, the title refers to the variability of the play's nine segments, which are not connected in theme or style. The only unifying factor is the spirit of enquiry (in the current jargon, 'exploration'): leaning heavily on existential theory, the characters ask themselves the meaning of life in an absurd society. Moving to Beijing, it was produced by the Chinese Youth Art Theatre in December 1985 under the direction of Wang Xiaoying. The play's main popularity was based on its implied criticism of Deng Xiaoping's increasingly erratic and repressive rule.

The crackdown in literature and the arts which followed the June Fourth massacre had a particularly devastating effect on the avant-garde theatre, and there seems to be little sign of a renewal in the 1990s; theatre managers play safe with commercial and nostalgic revivals. The promoters of the model operas had attempted, with (it must be said) some limited success, to create a single national theatre in China for a single national audience. What replaced it in the 1980s was possibly the most fragmented audiences ever in Chinese history, reflecting not only massive urban populations and increasing levels of education but also the rich diversity of regional styles and preferences. The revolutionaries had also aimed to replace the author-centred elitist modern drama of the 1950s and early 1960s with an audience-centred populist theatre, with the important reservation that the 'audience' was measured in terms of political expediency rather than actual audience response. Their efforts were curiously matched in the 1980s by the revival of traditional regional theatre, the commercial box-office plays of the mid-1980s and even the avant-garde chamber plays where the line between authors, players and audiences was deliberately blurred. The Cultural Revolution indeed performed a service in ridding the Chinese stage of the lamentably poor literature of the 'seventeen years'; in the case of drama (but not in fiction or poetry), it even produced something to take its place. Now that the political context of the model theatre has become history and its products are obliged to compete in the marketplace, *Taking Tiger Mountain by Strategy* and *The Red Lantern* may even outlive their more literary successors from the 1980s.

12

FICTION: EXPLORING ALTERNATIVES

Fiction during the Cultural Revolution was not a favoured genre. Nevertheless, at least 126 novels were published during the decade: taken on an annual average, this figure is not significantly lower than the average over the previous seventeen years. In addition, a great quantity of shorter fiction was produced and published in magazines, collections and anthologies. Most of this fiction was on agricultural themes; military and industrial fiction was also common, but the life of students or intellectuals in the cities, a frequent subject in previous decades, was conspicuously absent, as was foreign travel or other residence abroad. The time setting was invariably the present or the immediate past: historical fiction set in premodern China had fallen into disfavour after the Hai Rui case, and anything before the 1930s was suspect.

In line with current innovations in theatre, the major emphasis in fiction was on the creation of heroic characters as models: whether they were true to life was a secondary consideration, and 'middle characters' disappeared in the extreme polarisation of heroes and villains. Heroes were mostly unmarried younger men and women; they were invariably from a humble peasant or working-class background and had limited formal education. They were portrayed as perfect specimens, physically and morally: tall and strong, with marked facial features, abundant and glossy hair, bright eyes and red lips, they also shared qualities such as generosity, honesty, modesty, reasonableness, level-headedness and courtesy. With unerring instinct, to the Party they were loyal and submissive; to obstructionists within the Party they showed rebelliousness; and to the enemy they were implacable.

As with other characteristics of Cultural Revolution fiction, these portraits of heroes differed little from the main characters seen in fiction since the 1940s, but idealisation was pushed to superhuman levels and ambiguous characters more thoroughly excluded. The moral qualities shown by the heroes go back even earlier, and their prototypes can be found in premodern as well as contemporary martial arts fiction. The main innovation is the aesthetic interests attributed to peasant, worker or soldier characters: Cultural Revolution heroes were frequently inspired by scenes of natural beauty to write poetry, compose music or paint pictures.

Another feature of Cultural Revolution fiction was the type of language used in both narrative and dialogue. This included metaphors derived from military affairs, politics and economics. Contrary to expectation, however, there is less use of dialectic expressions, folk proverbs and vulgar or abusive terms, and greater recourse to bookish expressions such as literary proverbs and quotations from classical verse. In this respect, the language of fiction differed from the language style of other Cultural Revolution products such as 'big character posters' and slogans. This tendency can best be related to the pressure towards standardisation and control in political life, so that language as well as character was to be evaluated in terms of didactic effect. What seemed to matter least to the authorities was actual audience response, and there is little evidence to suggest that the fiction whose production they supervised so carefully during this decade was read by anyone other than themselves, other writers, and educated youth.

Fiction was also featured in the underground and unofficial movements of the 1970s, some of it resurfacing in official magazines after 1979. In reaction to the standardisation and idealisation of the official product, this fiction tended to value authenticity, individuality and originality. It also had a very direct relationship to its audience, who were simultaneously its publishers and distributors. Some of this fiction was exploratory and experimental, such as *Waves* by Bei Dao and other 'ruins' fiction like 'Open Ground' by Chen Maiping (b. 1952); other works, like the sentimental *The Second Handshake* and the spy thriller *Plum Blossom Party*, were frankly populist. When this fiction came above ground in the late 1970s and early 1980s, magazines specialising in fiction were quickly established or revived to meet popular demand. By the end of 1980 there were 180 literary magazines at the national and provincial level, mostly or exclusively featuring new fiction. In addition, literary magazines were also published by municipal and local cultural bureaux, the armed forces, and student societies.

Some of the national level magazines had a circulation of up to a million; among the most prominent were *October* in Shanghai and *Flower City* in Guangzhou. Some magazines, like *Yangtze Literary Compendium* in Wuhan, had fewer issues per year but more pages per issue to accommodate longer work. Within a few years, fiction had reclaimed its place at the centre of literary production and consumption.

The first new kind of fiction to emerge, 'scar literature' (also translated as 'wound literature'), which lasted from the end of 1977 till 1979, was new only in terms of its themes, and few of its writers or works survived the immediate need for fictional denunciations of the recent past. An exception was Liu Xinwu, who played a significant role in introducing the controversial theme of humanism in a socialist society. The most celebrated and criticised example of fiction on a socialist form of humanism was Dai Houying's (1938-1996) *Ah, Humanity*, which was published in 1980. In the same year, love stories dominated the literary scene, and as literary censorship retreated in the mid-1980s, sexuality in most of its forms received increasingly explicit attention. Feminist issues in subjects ranging from family relationships to discrimination against women in the workplace, the social ramifications of economic reform, and the sexual and emotional needs of women in an officially puritanical society, were explored by women such as Zhang Jie, Zhang Kangkang and Wang Anyi, while men like Zhang Xianliang, Zheng Wanlong and Liu Heng respectively dealt with images of masculinity and impotence. Depictions of sexual customs in the countryside and among ethnic minorities also became a major element in the mid-1980s' 'root-seeking' fiction by Ah Cheng, Han Shaogong and Jia Pingwa, while the theme of national identity invited descriptions of outlandish customs in general against a background of non-Confucian aspects of Chinese tradition. Urban fiction also flourished, with depictions of street crime and new technology as its major preoccupations. Both urban and rural writers were captivated by the opportuntities for fantasy and irrationality offered by 'magic realism', one of the most significant influences on fiction in the late 1980s, and post-modernism made an appearance in works by Can Xue and Yu Hua (b. 1960).

The increasing tendency towards images of death and decay in the second half of the 1980s turned many readers away from the serious fiction in the literary magazines in favour of commercial fiction, where writers like Wang Shuo cleverly exploited similar themes of alienation and concern with the rising crime rate with humour and sensationalist plots. Novels on Overseas Chinese life, knight-errantry, secret societies and science fiction also became popular in the new open market in publishing. The middle ground, meanwhile, was occupied by Mo Yan and Su Tong, who gained international recognition through the film versions of their works. By the end of the 1980s, both serious and commercial fiction showed a preference for non-standard or substandard language in narrative as well as dialogue, with a superabundance of dialect, slang and abusive expressions as well as interlardings from traditional narrative terms, while stylistic innovations such as fragmented narrative and stream of consciousness were no longer the exclusive preserve of elite readers and writers. In the end, the creation of a mass audience for fiction, which had remained no more than an empty slogan thoughout the 1960s and 1970s, was achieved in the late 1980s.

Wang Zengqi (1920–97)

One of the very few writers to span the period before, during and after the Cultural Revolution was Wang Zengqi, whose lyrical style and pastoral settings are often compared to those of Shen Congwen. Born in Jiangsu, Wang Zengqi was educated at the South-west United University. After graduation he worked as a secondary school teacher, in a museum and then as a literary editor. In 1962 he was seconded to the Peking Opera Troupe of Beijing as a writer, where his main accomplishment was the libretto of *Shajiabang*. After the Cultural Revolution, he went back to writing short fiction. His most famous short stories are 'The Love Story of a Young Monk' (1980) and 'A Tale of Big Nur' (1981), which both won literary awards.

According to Wang Zengqi, he wrote 'The Love Story of a Young Monk' to illustrate his ideals of beauty and health, paradoxically choosing monkhood to show how human desires are natural and should be treasured. The story is simply told and invokes the innocence of rural childhood and religion. When Minghai is seven years old, his uncle, a monk, decides that he should become a monk too. Both the boy and his family think this is a good idea, since monks are guaranteed food and education, and he is inducted at the Biqi Temple at the age of thirteen. The scenery around the temple is picturesque and life is peaceful. With little else to occupy them, the monks ignore prohibitions against eating meat, gambling and sex.

Minghai teams up with Yingzi, a young girl who lives next to the temple. Her family do not object to their friendship, and the pair spend most of their time together. When Minghai goes to the Shanyin Temple for his initiation ceremony, Yingzi rows him there and collects him again two days later when the ceremony is over. Full of curiosity about his experience, she asks whether or not the burns on his head hurt, whether or not the abbot's young concubine is pretty, and so on. Minghai answers matter-of-factly, and as the conversation drifts, Yingzi asks if Minghai will marry her. In astonishment, Minghai stares at her for a moment and then shouts 'yes!' At a time when most literature was preoccupied with the horrors of the Cultural Revolution and the backwardness of Chinese culture in general, this idyllic portrayal of innocence and religion by a former Cultural Revolution writer was a welcome change of tone.

'A Tale of Big Nur' is set in a village at the side of a lake ('*nur*' is Mongolian for 'lake'), whose inhabitants are described at the beginning of the story as enjoying a relaxed and harmonious life untroubled by orthodox Confucianism. A community of tinsmiths, they provide mutual help and protection at a time of great social change and unrest. Women choose their own husbands and extra-marital affairs are tolerated. The main character is Huang Qiaoyun, whose mother had eloped with a passing actor when she was only three years old. Qiaoyun, now a beautiful young woman, is in love with a handsome young tinsmith, Shiyizi, but she is raped by the leader of the local militia, Trumpeter Liu, and Shiyizi is beaten up. The tinsmiths then stage a demonstration, forcing the prefectural government to get rid of Trumpeter Liu. With its echo of Shen Congwen's 'Xiaoxiao', this story is an example of Wang Zengqi's narrative skills in the art of understatement and naturalistic ethics.

Ru Zhijuan (b. 1925)

During the Cultural Revolution, Ru Zhijuan produced little apart from a few essays in 1975 and 1976, but her career revived immediately afterwards. A short story, 'Coming Out of the Mountain', appeared in 1977, and two short stories published in 1979, 'A Story Out of Sequence' and 'The Path through the Grassland', both won national awards. While her early fiction was drawn mostly from her experiences in the Civil War, her new works covered a wider scope. Nevertheless, her concern for the emotional life of young people is still evident in stories such as 'The Love of Sons and Daughters' (1980). She is now a vice-president of the Writers' Association and editor of *Shanghai Literature*.

While 'scar literature' focused on the horrors of the Cultural Revolution, 'A Story Out of Sequence' points to the Great Leap Forward as the starting point of the disasters to come. The hero, an old peasant by the name of Shou, contrasts the relationship between Party and peasants before and after 1949 through a series of flashbacks. He recalls how peasants voluntarily made great sacrifices in the 1940s for the Communist forces: Shou himself donated four bags of grain, his family's whole supply. The Communist commander, Gan, however, quietly left two bags behind so that the family would not starve. This relationship of mutual help and love has disappeared since the Party has come to power. While Shou remains a peasant, Gan builds a career as a government official by making false reports about harvests at the expense of the peasants. He also orders the commune's pear trees to be cut down in obedience to the misguided land-use policies of the late 1950s. Shou knows the folly of this move but is labelled a stumbling block when he tries to object. The story was considered very controversial when it first appeared and was also praised for its originality in non-sequential narrative.

Ru Zhijuan further questioned the motives of Communist officials in 'The Love of Sons and Daughters'. The main character is a high official near to death who worries about her son's future, since he and his girlfriend dress smartly and seem to be determined to lead a bourgeois life. The story suggests that the younger generation see old revolutionaries as a dying breed, raising poignant questions about China's future direction. There is little doubt that her own sympathies lie with the young. (*For Ru Zhijuan's earlier fiction, see Chapter 7.*)

Gao Xiaosheng (b. 1928)

Gao Xiaosheng represents the new type of peasant writer who came into favour after the Cultural Revolution: like Ru Zhijuan, he traces the beginnings of mistaken policies on land-use to the 1950s. Born in Jiangsu, he received an old-fashioned education and enjoyed reading traditional fiction such as Pu Songling's *Strange Tales from Liaozhai*. He went on to study economics and journalism in Shanghai and Wuxi, and after 1949 worked as a clerk before being appointed as editor to the literary supplement of *Xinhua Daily*. A collection of poems as well as a co-authored libretto for Wuxi opera appeared in 1953, and his 1954 short story, 'The Broken Betrothal', was also well received. Written for a campaign to publicise the new Marriage Law, it describes how a young peasant extricates herself from an arranged marriage.

Gao Xiaosheng was labelled a Rightist in 1957 and spent most of the next twenty-two years in his home village, first as a peasant labourer and then as a teacher. He re-entered the literary arena in 1979 with the short story 'Li Shunda Builds a House', which quickly established his reputation as a writer on the problems faced by ordinary peasants. Adopting a traditional story-telling narrative persona, he tempers his indignation with humour. A series of short stories around the character Chen Huansheng followed, of which the most famous is the first, 'Chen Huansheng's Adventure in Town', published in 1980.

In 'Li Shunda Builds a House', the story of one man's attempts to improve his life is narrated in the context of political changes in China since 1949. Li Shunda's class background could not be more correct: he is from a poor family which has never owned its own house. When the new government tells him that the poor can now look forward to a better life, Li Shunda mobilises his entire family to sacrifice everything in order to save for a house. Their hard work and self-denial pays off: by 1957 they have saved enough to buy the building materials. To his dismay, these materials are suddenly confiscated in the drive for collectivisation. Li Shunda does not give up, however, and starts saving again, this time more cautious about how he is to use his money.

Then the Cultural Revolution comes, and he is again cheated of his savings and falls into trouble for having so much money. In a spirit worthy of the most patient battler, Li Shunda saves again. At the end of the Cultural Revolution, the house is not yet built, but he has learnt to bribe and use connections, and it is understood that the house will eventually be built. Despite the humour, the story is a bitter attack on policies which denied peasants their most basic needs. Li Shunda's reactions are portrayed with apparent naivety. For example, when his bricks are taken to build the collective furnace and pigsty, the narrator comments that he has agreed to give the collective what it wanted because his thinking is 'totally liberated'.

Gao Xiaosheng also tackled the problems arising from the 1978 reforms, when peasants were allowed to sell their own produce to make money. In 'Chen Huansheng's Adventure in Town', the hero goes to the county market to sell home-made fried dough and plans to buy a new hat with his profit. Business is good but he catches a chill and is too ill to go home. The local Party Secretary drives him to a hotel, and after a night's sleep he is better again. Thinking that he is the Party Secretary's friend, the receptionist is at first polite, but when she finds out that he is an ordinary peasant, insists on his paying the full five dollars for the room. Chen Huansheng is angry at having to spend a whole day's work on one night's sleep, but the story ends on a happy note. Back home everyone is impressed by his adventures, especially his ride in the Party Secretary's car, and his standing in the village rises. Among several themes in the story, the contrast between the differences in living standards between village and town is particularly well handled.

Deng Youmei (b. 1931) and Liu Shaotang (b. 1936)

Deng Youmei and Liu Shaotang were both victims of the Anti-Rightist campaign who resumed their literary careers in the late 1970s and went on to produce nostalgic accounts of earlier days in the 1980s. Born in Tianjin, Deng Youmei came from a relatively poor family and had only four years of primary education before attempting to join the Eighth Route Army in 1942. He was sent back to Tianjin the following year because of his youth and was then taken to Japan as a labourer. He returned just before the

Japanese surrender in 1945 and this time managed to join up as a reporter. After 1949, he was appointed to work in the Federation of Writers and Artists in Beijing and his first short stories date from the following year. 'At the Precipice', the story of a young dancer who almost embarks an affair with his partner, brought him to national attention in 1956, but he was labelled a 'poisonous weed' in 1957, and with the exception of one short story published in 1962, his writing career was interrupted for over twenty years. On returning to literature, he kept at first to politically safe topics, and 'Our Army Commander', in praise of General Chen Yi, who had recently regained his political standing, won an award in 1978. Of greater interest are his later stories on old ways and eccentric characters in Beijing, the most famous of which is the novella *Snuff-bottles* (1984).

Liu Shaotang comes from Tongxian on the outskirts of Beijing. His first collection of short stories, *Green Branches*, was published in 1953 and he joined the Communist Party in the same year. He entered Beijing University in 1954 but left after one year to work at the Chinese Youth Publishing House. Since his rehabilitation in 1979, he has written many short stories and novellas, the best-known of which, *Catkin Willow Flats*, won an award in 1980.

Catkin Willow Flats is set in a small village on the banks of the North Canal in the summer and autumn of 1936, and devotes nine of its twelve chapters to careful portraits of local characters. The unifying feature of the novella is a six-year-old boy, He Manzi. His grandmother, who is physically stronger than several young men put together and who can swear and fight with the best of them, saves the life of Wang Rilian, whose house has been bombed by the Japanese and whose sweetheart, Zhou Qin, has been abducted by warlord soldiers. But all ends happily with the lovers' marriage. The interest of the story is not so much in the predictable plot but in the loving evocations of the small pleasures of rural life.

Hao Ran (b. 1932)

Unlike the great majority of established writers, either prohibited from writing or voluntarily silent during the late 1960s, Hao Ran produced two more novels and several collections of short stories. Hao Ran's special position was due in part to his class credentials: he was precisely the kind of writer that the Cultural Revolution authorities wanted to encourage, and his familiarity with peasant life made his work suitable for promoting as mass literature. As a relative newcomer to the literary scene, he was not an important member of any literary faction, and while others in the cultural bureaucracy were stripped of their power and prestige, Hao Ran prospered. The Cultural Revolution was already underway by the time the third volume of *Bright Sunny Sky* was published, and his second novel, *The Golden Road*, was published in 1972–4. Like *Bright Sunny Sky*, it was made into a film and became very influential as a model for younger writers. His third novel, *Sons and Daughters of Xisha*, appeared in 1974 but it is considered an inferior work even among his supporters. Hao Ran's prominence declined after the Cultural Revolution but he continued to write, adapting his stories to the new circumstances. As if to underline his marginalisation, his children's stories won several national awards in the 1980s.

The Golden Road is the most famous novel of the Cultural Revolution, and in keeping with the spirit of the times, Hao Ran claimed that it was written with the inspiration and help of peasants and workers. Set during the land reform and collectivisation movements of the early 1950s in a north China village, Fangcaodi, it is peopled by idealised characters representing types which could be identified in contemporary political debates on the class structure in the countryside. The hero, Gao Daquan, is from a poor peasant background: young and courageous, he always takes the correct political line. His antagonists are former landlords, new bourgeois elements and rich peasants.

Volume 1 begins with a rich peasant, Feng Shaohuai, buying a mule to increase the productivity of his landholding. He has the approval of the village head, Zhang Jinfa, who wants to encourage families to become prosperous. Gao Daquan, who sees in Feng's move a renewed attempt by the enemy to oppress the poor, criticises Zhang Jinfa for not putting the country and socialism first. Zhang dismisses Gao's objections and goes ahead with his plan to make money by hiring out his tools during the spring sowing season. Gao Daquan, meanwhile, organises the peasants to cooperate among themselves, convinced that collective effort is the only way to raise the living standards of the poor peasants. His belief is reinforced when he visits other villages which have successfully carried out collectivisation, and on his return forms the first mutual-aid team in Fangcaodi.

Volume 2 continues the theme of class struggle. The Party and government have provided Fangcaodi with money to assist its efforts towards collectivisation. Spurred by Zhang Jinfa, however, one of the middle peasants wants the money to be divided among individual peasants. Gao Daquan sees through the plot and instead of antagonising the middle peasants, persuades them to form a new co-operative. The frustrated class enemies resort to increasingly extreme measures, but Gao Daquan and the masses expose them in the end and the cooperatives are formed as planned.

The character of Gao Daquan is designed as a model rather than as a realistic hero and the plot is based on an idealised historiography of the land reform movements. Unlike Hao Ran's 1950s stories where class conflict is muted, his Cultural Revolution tales emphasise class struggle and in this regard allow the author to detail conflicts that must have been commonplace during the land reform and collectivisation movements. Compared with *Bright Sunny Skies*, not only the characterisation but also the language is flatter: references to traditional culture are fewer and narrower in range, and vulgarisms are no longer to be found in the positive characters' dialogue. Compared with other Cultural Revolution fiction, or even some fiction of the early 1960s such as Liu Qing's well-known *The Builders*, however, the density of ideological expressions is relatively low.

Sons and Daughters of Xisha, situated in the Xisha Islands in the South China Sea, is less convincing. In Volume 1 Cheng Liang is a poor fisherman whose wife is beaten to death by the local tyrant. Cheng Liang joins the Communists, captures the tyrant (who is also a collaborator) and fights the Japanese invaders. In Volume 2 Cheng Liang is in the navy and his daughter, Ah Bao, leads a group of young people to form a local militia; the hapless enemy this time are the invading Vietnamese. The novel ends with Ah Bao's marriage. As a wedding gift, her father presents her with a famous photograph taken by Jiang Qing of Lushan, and the young couple look at the photograph several times a day as a source of strength and inspiration. This episode may account for the particularly vicious criticism of the novel after Jiang Qing's arrest. Such personal considerations aside, the novel represents a further deterioration in Hao Ran's fiction. Although he visited Xisha, it is clear that he had only a cursory knowledge of local customs and language, and in general the novel shows little of his former skills. (*For Hao Rau's earlier works see Chapter* 7.)

Wang Meng (b. 1934)

During his years in Xinjiang, Wang Meng learned to read and speak Uygur and spent several years translating Uygur works into Chinese; judging from the maturity of his later writing, he learnt more than just a new language. In 1978, the year before his return to Beijing, he took advantage of the new relaxation in the arts by releasing his long-suppressed creative energies in new fiction, including a novel, *The Scenery Here*, serialised in *Xinjiang Literature and Art*. The story which won an award in 1978 and made him once more a nationally famous writer, 'The Most Precious', deals with a theme that was to be dominant in his writing thereafter: lost innocence. A high Party official is told that his son was responsible for the downfall of a colleague during the Cultural Revolution, and is forced to realise that his son, having lost his youthful idealism, is now only interested in pursuing a career. Described as the most precious quality for young people, the destructive power of idealism is avoided in the author's conventional lament for the effect of the Cultural Revolution on educated youth.

The novel, *Long Live Youth,* written in the mid–1950s but only released in 1979, reads as a laboured enthusiasm for the new society. Its message was out of date by the time of its eventual publication. A warmer welcome was given to 'Bolshevik Salute', which was considered stylistically innovative in 1979. Wang Meng developed this style more fully in three stories published in 1980, 'Butterfly', 'Voices of Spring' and 'Kite Streamers'. The new stories provoked a heated discussion on writing techniques in 1980-81, in which Wang Meng was credited with being the first official writer of the new era to use non–linear time sequences and interior monologue (usually described as 'the stream of consciousness technique'). Although mildly experimental in style, the content of the stories remained cautiously reformist, and Wang Meng was rewarded with appointment as editor of *People's Literature* in

1983. In 1985 he became a member of the Central Committee, and in 1986 left *People's Literature* in the hands of his protégé, Liu Xinwu, to become Minister of Culture. Even in his new post, works such as the controversial novel, *The Man with Movable Parts* (1987), continued to appear. He resigned as Minister of Culture after the June Fourth massacre, and his distaste for the new regime was evident in 'Stubborn Porridge', published the same year. Wang Meng frequently travelled abroad throughout the 1980s, and these experiences are also incorporated in his fiction.

'Bolshevik Salute' is a psychological exploration of one person's experiences in the context of the political changes of 1950–80. Like the author himself, the hero of 'Bolshevik Salute', Zhong Yicheng, becomes a Communist organiser in 1949 at the age of seventeen. He falls in love with Xue Ling, also a staunch Communist, but his faith in the Party is tested in 1957 when he is branded a Rightist. He is expelled from the Party and is sent to a remote mountainous area for reform through labour. Strengthened by his marriage to the steadfast Xue Ling, Zhong Yicheng works hard in the hope that his loyalty to the Party will be rewarded, but misfortune continues to dog him, and during the Cultural Revolution, he suffers mental and physical abuse. Re-admitted to the Communist Party in 1979, Zhong Yicheng salutes the new political leaders, despite feeling that twenty years of his life have been wasted. By juxtaposing episodes from different times in the past, Wang Meng contrasts the idealism of his youth with the despair of Cultural Revolution days and his joy in his new life.

'Butterfly' follows the reveries of a middle-aged Party official, Zhang Siyuan, as he returns to Beijing after a visit to the village where he had been sent during the Cultural Revolution. He remembers how in 1949, when he was twenty-nine and already a high-ranking official, he rejoiced in his boundless energy and power. Married to a young student leader, he divorced her when she was declared a Rightist in 1957 and married a woman who was fully supportive of his devotion to his career. During the Cultural Revolution he was imprisoned and lost his high positions: he was like a butterfly without a place to settle. It was only when he lived among the peasants that he learned to accept himself as a person. Even after being re-instated, he remains aware of what he has learnt about the meaning of life, pondering the Daoist paradox in Zhuangzi's famous anecdote: is it the philosopher dreaming he is a butterfly, or is it the butterfly which dreams it is a philosopher? This dreamlike quality matched Wang Meng's interest in subjectivity in the early 1980s.

One of Wang Meng's most attractive stories is 'Kite Streamers', which defends the right of young lovers to find a place where they can be together in private in the city's overcrowded apartment blocks. 'Voices of Spring' is notable not only for its references to Germany (the title refers to a Strauss waltz popular in China) and its richly detailed descriptions of contemporary life, but also its skilful use of metaphor in portraying the China of the 1980s as a train where travellers are jammed into a boxcar hitched to a brand-new diesel engine.

Elements of fantasy and black humour mark Wang Meng's late-1980s' fiction. In *The Man with Movable Parts* the hero Ni Zao visits a friend of his father's in Europe, where certain household items trigger memories of his childhood in the 1940s. His parents were ill-matched and, unable to obtain a divorce, his father slipped away in secret and joined the Communist forces. After his victorious return to Beijing, he divorced his wife and married again, but remained discontented with his lot. Ni Zao remembers a foreign toy which his father gave him: it is a figure with movable parts, and each different position gives rise to a different human form. As a metaphor, the toy implies that people are twisted by circumstance into weird and unhappy creatures. Because the novel spans the period both before and after 1949, it suggests that Wang Meng sees misfortune as a constant state of being in any society. (*For Wang Meng's earlier work see Chapter 7.*)

Shen Rong* (b. 1936)

Like Wang Meng, Shen Rong spent most of her life close to positions of power: her father was a judge in the Nationalist Supreme Court, and in the 1980s her husband was editor-in-chief of *People's Daily*. Shen was born in Hankou but spent most of her childhood in east Sichuan. After a brief period working in

---

* The standard pronunciation of Shen Rong's surname is Chen, but the author herself prefers her native Sichuan pronunciation, 'Shen'.

a bookshop in Chongqing, she was sent to study at the Institute of Russian Language in Beijing, where she graduated in 1957; she was then assigned work as an editor and translator at the Central Broadcasting Station. In 1962 she stopped work because of ill health, and in 1963 was living in a village in Shanxi. She returned to Beijing in the following year, but went again to a village near Beijing in 1969. Shen Rong began to write fiction in 1972, and her first novel, *Everlasting Youth*, a typical Cultural Revolution tale of peasants opposing privatisation, appeared in 1975. In 1973 she returned to Beijing and taught Russian at Number 5 Secondary School. *Brightness and Darkness* appeared in 1978 and the novella *Spring Forever* in 1979. Her reputation was made by the novella *At Middle Age* in 1980, which won first prize in the first National Novella Competition for 1977–80. Praised for highlighting the difficult circumstances of intellectuals in the aftermath of the Cultural Revolution, it has been included in numerous anthologies and made into a successful film. Other stories won national literary awards throughout the 1980s for their thoughtful analyses of problems faced by professional women under pressure from commercialisation and other social changes. 'Ten Years Deducted' (1986) is one of her more experimental efforts, describing the bizarre outcomes when the authorities declare that because the Cultural Revolution had wasted ten years of people's lives, everyone is to be officially ten years younger.

The protagonist of *At Middle Age* is Lu Wenting, a forty-two-year-old ophthalmologist. Because medical training was suspended during the Cultural Revolution, doctors in her age group have no juniors to relieve them, while the seniors are too old for intricate operations; all the work and responsibilities fall on the shoulders of the middle-aged. Lu Wenting's burden is made even heavier by domestic duties, since her husband, a scientist, although helpful and understanding, is busy as well. When one of her children develops a temperature, Lu Wenting is too busy to take time off and go home. Among her patients is a vice-minister whose wife, dubbed 'Mrs Marxist-Leninist', constantly interferes. After the operation on the vice-minister, Lu collapses from exhaustion and goes into a coma. The story ends on a happy note as Lu recovers and returns home with her husband, but the issues raised in the story are not resolved. Despite her dedication and expertise, Lu barely makes enough to live on: their flat is cramped and her husband's singlets are full of holes. Her uncomplaining self-sacrifice is contrasted with the vice-minister's wife, who uses her position to win privileges at the expense of ordinary people. Lu's best friend at the hospital has decided to migrate to Canada, declaring she would be better off doing manual labour in a Western country, and while Lu regrets her decision she cannot condemn her for it.

At Middle Age made a profound impact among professional workers of all kinds, for whom the end of the Cultural Revolution and the restoration of their status in society had not yet brought tangible benefits, and the particular plight of the middle-aged became a matter for national attention. Unlike Zhang Jie, Shen Rong does not identify herself as a feminist: her women characters experience the same problems as intellectuals in general, but as women are even more virtuous in their capacity to endure suffering.

Zhang Xianliang (b. 1936)

Zhang Xianliang, another 1950s' Rightist, became one of the most notorious writers of the 1980s with his explicit coupling of sex and politics. Born in Nanjing, he started writing as a secondary school pupil but instead of going to university when he finished in 1955, he was sent to a Party training college in Gansu. 'Song of the Wind', a poem published in 1957, landed him in a state farm for reform through labour for two decades. In 1976 he was allowed to work as a teacher on a state farm and began to write stories based on his experiences. In 1980 he was appointed to work on the staff of *Ningxia Literature*. His award-winning 'Flesh and Soul', published in 1980, made him nationally famous when it was made into the film, *The Herdsman's Story*. *Mimosa* (1984) and its sequel, *Half of Man Is Woman* (1985), are his most famous works, followed by *Getting Used to Dying* (1989).

Published at a time when the 'blood-line' theory that class loyalty is passed from one generation to the next was under attack, 'Flesh and Soul' was part of that process. The protagonist, Xu Lingjun, was abandoned by his father when he was only eleven, and his mother died not long after. He is raised in a state orphanage and becomes a teacher after finishing secondary school, but because his father lives abroad, he is labelled a Rightist in 1957 and sent to a remote state farm where his only companions are the farm animals. After being cleared of wrongdoing, he chooses to remain on the farm as a herdsman, marries and has a son. After thirty years' separation, his father comes back to China and begs his son to go abroad to inherit the fortune he has built up. The herdsman refuses out of patriotism and a kind of pantheistic identification with nature. At a time when all Chinese who could were trying by any means to leave the country, audiences enjoyed the sentimentality but found the hero's behaviour risible.

Mimosa and its companion piece *Half of Man Is Woman* discard the idealised descriptions of life in a state farm. *Mimosa* is the tale of an intellectual, Zhang Yonglin, who is released from a labour camp in 1961 to work on a state farm. Despite his emaciation and although conditions are even worse than in the prison camp, he goes to sleep happy at the thought that he is now a free man. He is befriended by Mimosa, a young woman who also works on the farm and who feeds him from her secret store of grain and other food provided by the men who admire her beauty. Zhang Yonglin cannot catch animals or make goods for her, but she loves to listen to his stories and theorising. The brigade's carter, Hai Xixi, who is tall and strong, also pays her daily visits. As Mimosa shows her preference for brains over muscles, the two men get into a fight which neither win. Zhang Yonglin emerges as the victor by default, and Hai Xixi runs away.

Mimosa advises Zhang Yonglin to study hard and promises that they will marry when the difficult times are over, but Zhang Yonglin is accused of having been instrumental in Hai Xixi's running away and is imprisoned. When he is released six years later, he discovers that Mimosa has returned to her home in Qinghai with her daughter. The novel ends in Beijing in 1983, when Zhang Yonglin remembers how the simple labouring people such as Mimosa helped him become a more complete person. The novel created a stir when it first appeared. Readers were impressed with the depiction of an intellectual as a thoroughly masculine hero who defeats his peasant rival, with the analyses of the hero's state of mind, and with the titillating descriptions of the devoted Mimosa.

Zhang Yonglin's story continues in *Half of Man Is Woman*, in a labour camp in 1967. Every night the prisoners talk about sex, swapping stories of dreams where they copulate with ghosts, as their sole diversion from the bleak surroundings. Zhang Yonglin comes across a woman prisoner bathing in a creek, getting a clear view of her naked body. She also sees him but lets him continue to gaze at her. Eight years later, Zhang Yonglin is released and works in a state farm herding goats. The Party Secretary, Cao Xueyi, arranges for this same woman, Huang Xiangjiu, to come and help him. They marry, but on their wedding night he finds that years of denial have made him impotent. He wants a divorce, but she refuses. Discovering later that she is having an affair with Cao Xueyi, he buries himself in Western and Chinese philosophy in frustration and bitterness. A flood at the farm enables Zhang Yonglin to become a hero, and Huang Xiangjiu is especially attentive to him that night: finally he achieves an erection, and from being 'half a man' becomes 'whole'. Having regained his potency, he treats Huang Xiangjiu with open contempt but she responds with renewed tenderness and affection.

The novel contains the most explicit descriptions of sex ever in overground fiction, and the debate on whether or not it was pornographic caused an immediate sensation and gave the novel instant prominence. The link between sexual impotence and political repression was also a contentious topic, with some critics claiming that the labour camps were meant to represent the whole of Communist society during the 1950s and 1960s. Zhang Yonglin's ethics were also much discussed, and to a lesser extent his literary characterisation. Zhang Xianliang's later work continued to explore repressed and aberrant sexual behaviour supposedly caused by Maoist sexual puritanism, but his portraits of sexually aggressive men and their admiring women became increasingly stereotyped. His novels are among the few to have won critical attention and commercial success abroad.

Zhang Jie (b. 1937)

Zhang Jie shared Shen Rong's concerns with the poor living conditions of Chinese intellectuals but focused her attention on the emotional damage suffered by women in the new society; her protagonists are flawed but articulate and active on their own behalf. Born in Beijing, Zhang Jie spent some of her childhood and youth in Guilin and Shaanxi before returning to Beijing to study economics at People's University. After graduation in 1960, she worked at one of the industrial ministries in Beijing before being sent to a training school in the countryside in 1969. She returned to Beijing in 1972 where she has lived ever since. Her first publication was the award-winning 'The Child from the Forest' (also translated as 'Music of the Forest') in 1978, and her next story 'Love Must Not Be Forgotten' raised her to celebrity status. Despite its clumsy structure and awkward language, the story created a sensation by its proclamation that love should be the primary consideration in marriage. 'There Is a Youth' (1980) tackles love and morality among the young, and *Leaden Wings* (1981) describes the reform movement of the early 1980s. Zhang Jie returned to women's issues in *The Ark* (1981), and like Shen Rong tried her hand at more experimental writing in the mid-1980s with 'What's Wrong with Him?' (1986). Now a full-time writer, she receives royalties from the many translations of her work abroad as well as a salary from the Writers' Association.

'The Child from the Forest' is formulaic 'scar literature' in its denunciation of the Cultural Revolution for the suffering endured by artists and intellectuals. A professional musician, Liang Qiming, has been assigned to work in a lumberjack team where he can only play his flute in his spare time. A young boy with perfect pitch is captivated by his music, and Liang Qiming, who is dying from cancer, decides to teach the boy all he knows. The boy finally is accepted into the Central Conservatory of Music, where his style of playing persuades Liang's old friend and former colleague that Liang's spirit lives on in his disciple. The sentimentality of the story attracted much admiration among younger readers but did not itself break any new ground.

By contrast 'Love Must Not Be Forgotten' is one of the first stories in the new era to expose the inadequacies of married life in modern China. The narrator of the story describes the tragedy of her mother and the man she loves, who both contract marriages out of duty and even fail to consummate their love when they are free to marry at the end of their lives. When the narrator reads the words 'Love must not be forgotten' in her mother's diary, she delays her own impending marriage until she can be sure it is based on love. The debate surrounding the story revealed a variety of opinion, from those who were dismayed by unbending rectitude in loveless marriages to those who condemned the mother for her platonic but extra-marital romance.

In *The Ark*, Zhang Jie describes the lives of three women who refuse to rely on men to support them. In the 1920s Lu Xun claimed that China's Noras would either fall into prostitution, go back to their husband or starve, but Zhang Jie's modern women are educated and have employable skills. As single women living together, however, they are the targets of gossip and harassment. Cao Jinghua is a Party member and theoretician. During the Cultural Revolution, she is sent to a forestry area where she marries an uneducated timberworker. She returns to Beijing, ill and alone, only to be attacked again because she has written an essay criticising aspects of the new era. However, she refuses to lose heart, and turns her skills to practical use by making all the furniture in the flat. Liu Quan is an interpreter who has also been divorced by her husband. Her beauty now makes her the target of unwelcome advances from her superiors at work, and she suffers from prolonged depression. The third member of the household, Liang Qian, is not divorced but has left her husband because of his hypocrisy. An assistant film director for over ten years, she is given her first opportunity to direct a film after the Cultural Revolution, but the film is banned because the main actress has breasts that are unacceptably large. The three women decide to continue to support each other in their struggles to live as normal people.

Jiang Zilong (b. 1941)

Born in Hebei, Jiang Zilong went to secondary school in Tianjin where he harboured ambitions to be a writer. Instead, he was taken on as an apprentice at the Tianjin Heavy Machinery Plant. He enlisted in the navy in 1960, learnt to be a draftsman and began writing for publication. Demobilised in 1965, he returned to the factory in Tianjin to work as a foreman. In 1972–5 he established himself as an amateur writer, but 'A Day in the Life of the Head of the Electrical Equipment Bureau', written in 1975, was criticised for not following the current political line. His next story adhered to Cultural Revolution guidelines but his timing was poor and the story became an easy target for post-Mao critics.

Jiang Zilong finally redeemed himself in 1979 with 'Manager Qiao Assumes Office' on the stagnation of industry under the 'gang of four' and the difficulties of economic reform. This award-winning story captured the attention of readers throughout China for months: hundreds of people wrote about it and seminars on its significance were held in many work units. 'Pages from a Factory Secretary's Diary' (1980), which depicts another kind of manager, also created a sensation. 'All the Colours of the Rainbow' (1981), which focused on workers rather than managers, was made into a successful film. Jiang Zilong was rewarded with many official posts, and was appointed president of the Tianjin Writers' Association. He also tried his hand at writing about topics outside industry, but although he won prizes for works such as 'Elegy of Yan Zhao', his later writings never achieved the influence of his early work.

The emphasis on ideology above efficiency throughout the 1960s and 1970s meant that management practices in industry were poor and productivity low. In 'Manager Qiao Assumes Office', a simple and effective solution is proposed and put into action. At the end of the Cultural Revolution, Qiao Guangpu is returned to active life and chooses to take charge of a large electrical machinery plant. The factory's Party Secretary, Shi Gan, a former colleague, explains that no-one in the management team is willing to take responsibility and the workers are lazy and incompetent. Against everyone's advice, Qiao Guangpu implements a series of controversial measures including individual assessments for every employer. On the basis of the results, those who fail are demoted and those who pass are promoted. This brings him enemies and supporters. He also marries his old sweetheart, a Russian-trained engineer, who becomes the chief technical assistant. His bold and decisive management style is depicted as generating positive outcomes. The sequel 'More about Manager Qiao' continued the theme of the tough but progressive manager. Throughout the early 1980s, Qiao's style became a model for managing economic reform for thousands of readers.

The protagonist of 'Pages from a Factory Secretary's Diary', Jin Fengchi, adopts a completely different approach, spending most of his time making contacts and trying to satisfy everyone in the factory. Jiang Zilong shows some sympathy for this slippery character, whose family life is in ruins and who ends up drowning his problems in alcohol, but clearly indicates his shortcomings as a manager. 'All the Colours of the Rainbow' compares the fate of two young workers, Xie Jing and Liu Sijia. Xie had won promotion as an activist during the Cultural Revolution, but now that the political climate has changed, she decides to leave her office job and become a team leader of a transportation unit. The drivers under her control, who include Liu Sijia, are considered hooligans and they make life particularly hard for her because of her past. Liu Sijia is a cool character who runs a food stall in front of the factory before work, and yet he does not keep any of the profits. He makes Xie Jing drunk by putting spirits into her beer, but he does not take advantage of her, taking her home instead. Inevitably they fall in love, conveying to readers the message that both young radicals and hooligans can still be responsible and patriotic under the right conditions.

Feng Jicai (b. 1942)

Like Jiang Zilong, Feng Jicai's transition from Cultural Revolution writer to 'new era' writer was relatively easy. Born in Tianjin, he showed his many talents from an early age. When he was forced to drop out of the municipal basketball team after an injury, he joined the Tianjin Fine Arts Association as a painter and also wrote art criticism. In 1974 he began to work at the Tianjin Fine Arts Factory and taught concurrently at the Tianjin Arts and Crafts College. After his historical novel *The Boxers*, jointly written with Li Dingxing, appeared in 1977, he was transferred to the Tianjin Writers' Association as a full-time writer. He was very prolific as a full-time author. His short story 'The Carved Pipe' and the novella 'Ah!' both won national awards in 1979. The emphasis on his later fiction is on the bizarre, such as the novella *The Miraculous Pigtail* in 1984 and *Three-inch Golden Lotus* in 1986.

The hero of 'The Carved Pipe' is an artist, Mr Tang, who, denied the opportunity to paint during the Cultural Revolution, whiled away his time carving pipes. One day, he goes to a greenhouse to see a flower show and is recognised by an old gardener. The old gardener notices Mr Tang's carved pipe and expresses his admiration. Mr Tang offers it to him, but he adamantly refuses such a handsome gift. When Mr Tang is restored to favour, he has no time for the old gardener, who continues to deliver flowers to him. One day, the old gardener hesitantly asks for one of his pipes. Mr Tang gives him one of the most amateurish ones in his collection, thinking that the old man would not know the difference. Not long after, Mr Tang is in trouble again, and his guests stop coming. Then the old gardener dies, with his last request being that he be buried with the pipe in his mouth, and Mr Tang is filled with remorse and guilt.

Feng Jicai continued to build his stories around a central symbol. In *The Miraculous Pigtail*, set at the turn of the century, a young man known as Shaer (Second Simpleton) has learnt from his father a martial arts technique that involves swinging his pigtail with great force and skill. With this technique he vanquishes in turn a local bully, an old champion, and a Japanese samurai. When the Boxers come to Tianjin, Shaer joins them but is defeated by the Westerners' bullets. Like everyone else, he is forced to cut off his pigtail when the Qing dynasty collapses. Although the pigtail has been cut off, it remains part of his 'spirit', and Shaer becomes a crack marksman. Appropriately for its subject and setting, the novel incorporates elements from traditional story-telling. Its popularity was enhanced by the widely distributed film version.

In *Three-inch Golden Lotus*, Ge Xianglian's frailty and bound feet capture the attention of a shopkeeper who takes her into his home as his daughter-in-law. She learns from him how to make her feet even smaller. Eventually, she becomes the most powerful person in the family. Her own attitudes toward foot-binding are mixed. When the movement to abolish foot-binding begins she argues against it, but in secret, she allows her daughter to have 'liberated feet'. Like Shaer's 'spiritual pigtail', Ge Xianglian's foot-binding is ambiguous. On the one hand, the practice of sexualising deformed female feet can be interpreted as symbolic of a warped mentality. On the other hand, the implicit acceptance of tradition can also be seen as endorsement. In an essay describing his purpose in writing the story, Feng Jicai claims that he uses the absurd to ridicule the absurd practices of Chinese culture.

Liu Xinwu (b. 1942)

Liu Xinwu was the first of the writers from the 1960s to make his name in the post-Mao era. Born into a well-off family in Chengdu, Sichuan, Liu Xinwu moved to Beijing in 1950 when his father took up a post there. After graduating from Beijing Teachers' College in 1961, he taught at secondary school for fifteen years and began to write literature in his spare time. By 1966 he had contributed over seventy essays, short stories and other literary pieces to *Beijing Evening News*, *People's Daily* and *Chinese Youth Daily*. At the beginning of the Cultural Revolution, he was sent to the countryside but returned to Beijing in 1972. His 1975 novella *Open Your Eyes* relates the adventures of young people fighting against class enemies, and follows closely the political requirements of the time.

Liu Xinwu returned to the classroom in 1976 and was then transferred to Beijing Press. His most famous work, 'The Class Teacher' (also translated as 'Class Counsellor'), published in November 1977, heralded the literary thaw of the 1980s. Other controversial stories followed, including 'The Place of Love' and 'Awake, My Brother'. The novella *The Flyover* (1981) was a pioneering attempt to shift attention from the 'scars' of the Cultural Revolution to the hardships faced by ordinary citizens in post-Mao Beijing. Praised by critics as realistic and mature, it marks Liu's transition to a less sensational but more informative style. In 1984 the award-winning novel *The Drum Tower* was serialised in *Contemporary*.

From the late 1970s to the mid-1980s Liu Xinwu was editor of *October* and served on the editorial boards of *Beijing Literature* and *Ugly Duckling*. As editor of *People's Literature* in 1987, he lost his job over the publication of a story by Ma Jian, said to have offended Tibetans because of its indecent descriptions of Tibetan sexual customs. It was generally believed that his support for 'bourgeois liberalisation' was the real reason for his dismissal, and his reputation as an intellectual prepared to stand up to political repression for the sake of artistic freedom was enhanced. Liu Xinwu has travelled abroad frequently in response to invitations as well as on official business, but his work is not well known to non-specialist Western readers.

'The Class Teacher' was the first story officially published in China to expose the damage inflicted on young people by the Cultural Revolution. The teacher, Zhang Junshi, agrees to admit Song Baoqi, a young hooligan, into his class but is opposed by his student, Xie Huimin, the Party Secretary of the Youth League branch. Zhang Junshi discovers that Song Baoqi's delinquency is caused by parental neglect. His parents are ordinary workers, and his crime is the stealing of banned books. Among the books in Song's possession is *The Gadfly* (1897) by Ethel Lillian Voynich (one of Zhang's favourite novels). Xie Huimin believes that any book not found in bookshops must be politically unorthodox or even pornographic, and condemns *The Gadfly* as a 'poisonous weed'. Zhang Junshi fails to persuade her to be more flexible, and the story ends with an echo of Lu Xun's appeal 'to save the children'. Readers gave an enthusiastic reception to this defence of literacy, and a spate of stories followed where intellectuals were favourably compared with radical youth and uneducated workers.

'Awake, My Brother' depicts a young man who loses faith in Communism because although he tries everything to prove his devotion – including piercing his chest with a Mao badge – his family background prevents him from being accepted by his peers. 'The Place of Love' is the pathetic story of a young woman so insecure about herself that she seeks advice from an old widow whether it was proper for her to have feelings for a young man who has been friendly with her.

The Flyover takes place in a small apartment in Beijing in the course of one Saturday night. The apartment is occupied by an old worker, Hou Qinfeng, his wife and their psychologically unstable daughter. During a visit from his two sons a family squabble about housing takes place, and his daughter is rushed off to hospital. The elder son and his family teach in a country school; they would like to return to Beijing but cannot obtain permission; further complicating matters they cannot settle in the country either because their official residence is still in Beijing. The younger son has transferred his residence status to the country where he lives with his wife, the daughter of a high-ranking official, but he resorts to bullying his own family in his attempt to return to Beijing. The story shows the erosion of morals and values resulting from poor living conditions.

The Drum Tower details the activities of the Xue family who live near the Drum Tower in Beijing. The most dramatic event in the story is the wedding of the youngest son, Xue Jiyao, when one of the drunken guests reveals that the elder Xue used to work in a brothel. During the festivities, some money and a watch are stolen. Otherwise the story describes the pleasures, fears and vexations felt by various members of the family as the day progresses. By incorporating references to local sites and local language, Liu Xinwu shows how people rationalise traditional modes of behaviour with their desires for a better future.

Gu Hua (b. 1942)

Gu Hua (pen-name of Luo Hongyu) addressed the problems of the 1970s and 1980s in a more melodramatic fashion. The mountainous area around his birthplace in Jiahe, Hunan, is famous for its folk songs, and Gu Hua was steeped in folk traditions from an early age. His father died when he was only ten and he spent his childhood doing odd jobs like tending water buffalo. He taught in the local primary school for a year after graduating from secondary school, and was transferred in 1961 to an agricultural research institute where he worked for fourteen years. His first published story was 'Sister Apricot' in 1962, followed by more short stories and songs as well as a novel. In 1975, he was transferred to the Zhengzhou Song and Dance Troupe as a script writer. After the Cultural Revolution, his writing specialised in descriptions of Hunan folk customs set against criticisms of Cultural Revolution policies. His most famous works are 'The Log Cabin Overgrown with Creepers' and *A Small Town Called Hibiscus*, both published in 1981. The latter was made into a very popular film, and Gu Hua became president of the Hunan Writers' Association in 1980. He migrated to Canada in the late 1980s where he still lives.

'The Log Cabin Overgrown with Creepers' is set amid the densely wooded Wujie Hills in Hunan. Wang Mutong is the warden of a state forest called Green Hollow, where he lives with his wife Azure and two young children. They are secluded from the rest of the world, so that even when the Cultural Revolution is in full swing, they continue undisturbed until they are joined by a one-armed educated youth, Li Xingfu. When Azure and the educated youth become attracted to each other, Wang Mutong beats her and tries to intimidate him. After many tribulations they elope, and Wang Mutong accuses them of having started a forest fire. He is made a hero and joins the Communist Party; Li Xingfu and Azure are declared class enemies but are never seen again.

A Small Town Called Hibiscus is also set in the mountainous areas of Hunan during the Cultural Revolution. The story begins in 1963, when a small measure of private enterprise is permitted under policies drawn up by Liu Shaoqi and Deng Xiaoping. A vivacious and energetic young woman, Hu Yuyin, opens a bean curd stall with her husband, Li Guigui. Her good looks and pleasant manners ensure that the stall is well patronised, and husband and wife begin to prosper. In the state-run canteen, by contrast, customers are few, and the manager, Li Guoxiang, becomes jealous of Hu Yuyin's success.

By 1964, Hu Yuyin and her husband have saved enough money to build a house, but Li Guoxiang and a local idler, Wang Qiushe, label the young couple as capitalist roaders and confiscate the new house. Li Guigui in anger commits suicide. As the Cultural Revolution approaches, Li Guoxiang and Wang Qiushe gain power while Hu Yuyin's patrons are disgraced. During this difficult period, she falls in love with a Rightist, Qin Shutian. The situation only returns to normal in 1979, when the former village officials are returned to power. While the Cultural Revolution is a convenient setting for this melodrama of passion and betrayal, it could just as well be set in any time of great social change. The details of local customs and scenery add an extra dimension to the appeal of the novel.

Zheng Wanlong (b. 1944)

Zheng Wanlong spent his childhood among Oroqen huntsmen and Han goldminers in the remote forest areas of Heilongjiang. Although he moved to Beijing at the age of eight after his mother's death, his childhood experiences provided a wealth of material for his later fiction. After leaving school, he worked in a factory and wrote poetry in his spare time. In 1974 he was transferred to work at Beijing Press, where like Liu Xinwu he began his writing career in earnest. Zheng Wanlong's stories of the late 1970s and early 1980s are mostly about young people and their attitudes towards life and love; representative works include *Trilogy of Contemporary Youth*, which consists of three separate but inter-related stories and was written over 1980–3. *Red Leaves over the Mountains* was published in 1982 and *Contemporaries* followed in 1983. When 'root-seeking' became popular in the mid-1980s, Zheng Wanlong wrote a series of short stories and novellas under the title 'Strange Tales from Strange Lands', whose descriptions of the Oroqen tribes and their rites captured the imagination of critics and readers. The first ten stories from this series were published in 1986 in a collection titled *The Totems of Life*.

Most of these 'strange tales' are sketches of masculine frontiersmen in the wilds of Heilongjiang. In 'Old Stick's Wineshop', a hunter known as Three Kick Chen boasts of forty-three scars on his body, presumably from as many fights. The last wound, however, has not healed, and it looks to be serious. Instead of recuperating in the inn as Old Stick suggests, he wanders out into the heavy snow and certain death, preferring to be remembered as a hero who does not die of illness. 'Yellow Smoke' describes how an Oroqen tribe believe that a volcanic crater is a sacred site and offer human sacrifices there. Zhebie, a brave young man whose father was one of the victims, discovers that the yellow smoke comes from fissures in between the rocks. The elders in the tribe are furious and he is knifed to death. In some stories, barbaric Oroqen customs are contrasted with Han civilisation. 'Clock' is about a forbidden romance between a young man, Molitu, and the beautiful daughter of an ostracised widow. A bad hunting season is blamed on their affair, and Molitu is expelled. He ends up in a Han settlement, where the sound of a clock drives him crazy. Returning home, he finds that both his sweetheart and her mother have been killed by the tribespeople.

By attributing brutal practices to the Oroqens, Zheng Wanlong satisfied the thirst of readers for the exotic and erotic. The tales have also been seen as Chinese 'Westerns', and the tough-man image owes a lot to the 1980s craze for Westerns and martial arts films. Zheng Wanlong was promoted to influential positions such as deputy editor of *October* and has also written successful television series.

Zhang Chengzhi (b. 1948)

Another primitivist writer is Zhang Chengzhi, a member of the Hui (Muslim) ethnic minority. Born in Beijing, he was sent to Inner Mongolia in 1967 and spent several years on the steppes. He later attended the Chinese Academy of Social Sciences where he studied the history of minorities in north China as well as some of the major languages. His first story, 'Why Herdsmen Sing about Mother', won an award in the national short story competition for 1978. The narrator of this story is an educated youth who goes to Mongolia and stays with a local family. Eji (which is the Mongolian word for 'mother'), the head woman of the house, takes him as her adopted son. She is described as kind and selfless, to the point of using her own sheepskin coat to keep the narrator from freezing during a snowstorm, and thus becoming paralysed herself from the cold. The self-sacrificing spirit of Mongolian women is seen as a national characteristic and celebrated in Mongolian folksong.

In 1982 Zhang Chengzhi won another national award for his novella *Black Steed*. The relatively straightforward story is again set in Mongolia. The hero of the story loses his mother when he is only eight, and his father sends him to live with another family. He and the daughter of this family (they are the same age) grow up together, fall in love and get engaged. When he is seventeen, he is chosen to study husbandry at the commune. While he is away studying, his fiancée is raped and he leaves the village for the city to work in a veterinary college. After nine years, he returns on an official trip and runs into his old sweetheart again. She is now a mature mother who leads a poor and simple existence. However, like the other Mongolian 'mothers' in Zhang Chengzhi's stories, she remains a hard-working, good-natured and honest woman.

Zhang Chengzhi's use of mother figures to symbolise the un-complaining, toiling masses is not very original. 'Rivers of the North', published in 1984, is much more innovative and became his most famous story. It is ostensibly a hymn to the great rivers of north China. The protagonist is a geologist who reports on his thinking and feelings as he investigates the Yellow River. He meets a young photographer who shares his awe at the natural beauty and might of China's rivers, and recalls his experiences during the Cultural Revolution. In his preface, Zhang declares that no matter how naive or mistaken his generation were, their future is still bright. As a rebuttal of the negativism in 'scar literature', the story created a sensation when it first appeared. Zhang Chengzhi became then identified with a group of 'educated youth writers' such as Liang Xiaosheng and Shi Tiesheng who observed that their experiences during the Cultural Revolution were not all bad.

Zhao Zhenkai (b. 1949)

Three writers all born in 1949 went very different ways: Zhao Zhenkai, better-known under his pen-name Bei Dao, began his career as an undergound writer in the early 1970s; Liang Xiaosheng was one of the first 'scar' writers of the post-Mao period; and Ah Cheng's first published story ushered in the root-seeking style of the mid-1980s. Zhao Zhenkai's first effort in fiction was a long short story written in 1972 but was destroyed by its author as immature. His next attempt was *Waves*, a short novel first drafted in 1974, revised and printed in *Today* in 1979, and reprinted in *Yangtze Literary Miscellany* in 1981. The longest, most complex and most philosophical of Zhao's fiction, it was also a pioneer in reintroducing subjectivity, multiple narrative and interior monologue into contemporary Chinese fiction. His next two stories, 'In the Ruins' and 'The Homecoming Stranger', were expressly written for the first and second issues of *Today* in 1978 and 1979. 'Melody' and 'Moon on the Manuscript' followed in 1980, and his last two stories, 'Intersection' and 'No. 13 Happiness Street', were first published in overground literary journals in 1982 and 1985 respectively.

The main themes of *Waves* are search beyond the actual, hope beyond despair and integrity beyond fate. The text is composed of a number of episodes as perceived by each of the five main characters in turn. The most compelling of these five is Xiao Ling, a young woman with a secret, and although her embittered views on life are occasionally challenged by others, including her lover Yang Xun, their criticisms of her fade in the face of her compassion, her disgust with brutality, and her love of poetry and music. Xiao Ling is from a family of intellectuals, and the memories of her old home keep her from falling into nihilism. After repeated experiences of betrayal, half-reluctantly she falls in love with Yang Xun, son of high-ranking Party officials. Yang Xun has also suffered during the Cultural Revolution, but his parents have managed to protect him from a jail sentence. This selfish, vacillating young man, a direct descendant of Lu Xun's narrator in 'Regret for the Past', precipitates Xiao Ling's tragic death because of his inability to accept the existence of her illegitimate child. Her fate is sealed when Lin Dongping, a leading Party official in the provincial city where the story is set, takes it on himself to protect Yang Xun from her degradation: it is eventually revealed that he had earlier conducted an adulterous affair with Yang Xun's mother, and is possibly his father. Offering a contrast to Yang Xun is a young hooligan, Bai Hua. Despite his drug-running and other criminal activities, he offers protection to the weak and abandoned, including Xiao Ling. The fifth narrator is Lin Dongping's daughter: spoiled and capricious, she flirts with both Yang Xun and Bai Hua. A document of its time, *Waves* is the most vivid depiction of official corruption and social breakdown written in the 1970s, and its fragmented composition conveys its characters' desperate attempts at fleeing reality.

'In the Ruins' does not differ greatly at first reading from scar fiction. Its protagonist is a middle-aged, Western-educated professor of history, who would rather hang himself than face public denunciation by Red Guards. After walking to the Old Summer Palace, where he meets a village girl whose father has been killed for stealing a melon, he decides to face his tormentors, whose future repentance he can visualise. His reflections on the nature of time, history, death and forgiveness give the story depth, as does also a concealed message that the true protagonist of the story is the Red Guard. 'Intersection' is little more than a brief character sketch showing the alienation between factory workers and management under socialism. As in *Waves*, and still uniquely for its time, Zhao Zhenkai captures in dialogue the cynicism of the disadvantaged expressed in credible street slang. 'No. 13 Happiness Street' is the first depiction in China of the thin line between dissidence and madness in an authoritarian society, with strong echoes of Kafka and Solzhenitsyn. (*See also the section on Bei Dao in Chapter 13.*)

Liang Xiaosheng (b. 1949)

Born in Harbin, Liang Xiaosheng went to Heilongjiang at the beginning of the Cultural Revolution as an educated youth, working in various jobs such as teacher and journalist. He joined a literary study group in 1971, began publishing stories and essays in the magazine *Fighters' News*, and entered Fudan University to study Chinese in 1974. After graduating in 1977, he was appointed editor and scriptwriter at the Beijing Film Studio, and was transferred to the National Children's Film Studio in the early 1980s.

One of his first published stories is 'The Jet Ruler', a cloying romance in a proletarian setting. His short story 'A Land of Wonder and Mystery' won a national short story competition award in 1982 and was made into a successful film. The novella *There Is a Snowstorm Tonight* also won an award the following year, and his novel *Snow City* (1986) was highly praised by critics.

'A Land of Wonder and Mystery' is about a group of educated youth who try to conquer the 'devil's swamp' in the Great Northern Wastelands. This land has never been cultivated, and the team face fierce blizzards and bottomless swamps. Innocent teenagers on the verge of love and desire, many fall victim to natural disasters. The story uses heroic language to evoke the terrible beauty of the north. *There Is a Snowstorm Tonight* also relates the tremendous sacrifices made by educated youth in the wilds, and shows how the survivors had matured into heroes by 1979 when orders came for their return to urban areas. The post-1979 fate of educated youth is also the subject of *Snow City*, as some 400,000 educated youth in Heilongjiang return to the provincial capital. The Political Instructor Yao Yuhui, whose father is mayor, is already thirty, but for eleven years in the wilderness she has denied her femininity. She quickly learns that although she has vowed to retain her independence on her return to urban life, she has to rely on her father's position to survive. Other educated youth also reject their former idealism in the struggle to find employment and raise families. These stories have a definite historical significance, but their appeal will wane as the generation whose experiences they chronicle passes.

Of more lasting interest may be Liang's later stories, showing the squalor and violence in Chinese life since the 1960s. Although clumsy and melodramatic like all his work, reliant on improbable coincidences and overheard conversations, they are among the most convincing depictions of China's poverty-stricken interior, from which the only escape is through education. Going against the tide of 'scar literature', first-person, autobiographical stories such as 'Father' and 'The Black Button' show the educated escapees as cold hypocrites, while the families and friends left behind, despite ignorance and superstition, are heroic in their endurance. More powerful still is 'Ice-dam', whose villagers would be recognisable by writers of the 1920s and 1930s such as Lu Xun and

Zhang Tianyi; what is new is the villagers' reluctant heroism and unwilling sacrifice.

Ah Cheng (b. 1949)

Ah Cheng is the pen-name of Zhong Acheng, the son of a well-known film critic, Zhong Dianfei. He was born and grew up in Beijing, where he attended one of the capital's best secondary schools, and for a time lived with his parents in the compound belonging to the Beijing Film Studio. During the Cultural Revolution, he was first sent to Inner Mongolia but managed to get transferred to the semi-tropics in the Xishuangbanna region of Yunnan in the far south-west. He returned to Beijing in 1979 and worked for the Chinese Book Import and Export Company before becoming an art editor at World Books. His first attempt at fiction was 'The King of Chess' in 1984, which set off a new interest in primitivism and sparked an 'Ah Cheng' fever that lasted for two years. Two more 'King' stories followed: 'The King of Trees' and 'The King of Children', both published in 1985. In the same year, Ah Cheng wrote a series of sketches entitled 'Romances of the Landscape' which describe the scenery and customs of border areas far from civilisation. During the mid-1980s he wrote film adaptations of works by other authors, such as Gu Hua's *A Small Town Called Hibiscus*. He migrated to the United States in 1986 where he still lives.

'The King of Chess' is based on the life of a group of educated youth in south-west China. The narrator at first feels superior to Wang Yisheng, who is from a poor family, but comes to respect his simplicity and talent. Wang Yisheng has two obsessions: chess and food. The group eke out their meagre grain rations with mice, snakes and wild herbs, cooking and sharing their food in friendship, laughter and good fun. While eating takes care of physical existence, chess provides the spiritual dimension which makes Wang Yisheng stand out morally and intellectually. Wang Yisheng's mentor, an elderly garbage collector, teaches him the secrets of chess in language borrowed from Daoism. The climax comes when he participates in a chess championship. Wang Yisheng takes on nine finalists at the same time by playing all nine games at once; eight are defeated outright, and the mysterious ninth player is forced to come out of seclusion and beg for a draw.

He turns out to be an elderly man who addresses Wang Yisheng in classical Chinese. The description of the championship and its aftermath is one of the finest passages in contemporary literature.

The narrator of 'The King of Children' is an educated youth nicknamed Beanpole, who works on a state farm. When he is chosen to teach at a village school, his friends make a special meal to celebrate. Laidi, a plump working-class girl from Shanghai who is in charge of cooking, displays her fondness for singing and for the narrator. At the school, Beanpole finds that there are no textbooks and children know little besides political slogans. Beanpole then develops his own teaching methods, setting the children to write free compositions on subjects drawn from their daily life. One boy, Wang Fu, displays a ferocious appetite for learning and has a keen memory. In a bet with Beanpole, he wins a dictionary lent to him by Laidi and sets about learning new characters by copying the dictionary page by page. Beanpole's unorthodox teaching incurs the displeasure of the authorities and he is dismissed. As a parting gift, he makes a present of the dictionary to Wang Fu to encourage him to learn by his own efforts. The film version by Chen Kaige has a very different ending: in a repudiation of rote learning whether Confucian or Communist, Beanpole tells Wang Fu not to copy the dictionary. 'The King of Trees' combines Daoism with conservationist ethics, and shows a preference for village superstition over political dogmatism.

The most striking aspect of the King stories is Ah Cheng's use of language and narrative, which draw heavily on traditional story-telling. Closely related is the skilful introduction of ideas drawn from Confucianism, Daoism and Buddhism. His descriptions of life in the countryside are also remarkable, avoiding both the self-pity of 'scar literature' and the idealised images of orthodox and pastoral writers. Because of his debts to traditional Chinese culture, Ah Cheng is usually included among the 'root-seeking' writers but he avoids their excessive emphasis on violence and brutality, while his adeptness in using the past to explore the present won the admiration of both conservatives and reformist writers.

Shi Tiesheng (b. 1951)

Born in Beijing, Shi Tiesheng was sent to Guanjia village near

Yan'an as an educated youth in 1969, but he became seriously ill and had to be returned to Beijing in 1972. In 1973–81 he worked in a neighbourhood factory, but his illness had left him with a permanent disability and eventually Shi was forced to stop working. It was at this point that Shi Tiesheng turned to writing fiction. His first short story, 'The Law Professor and His Wife', was published in 1979, and his first major success was the award-winning 'My Faraway Qingpingwan' in 1983; 'Granny's Star' also won a national prize for short stories in 1984. At a time when most writers of his generation were still depicting life in remote villages as barbaric, Shi Tiesheng's pastoral nostalgia struck an idyllic note (found also in fiction by Ah Cheng and Kong Jiesheng at this time) that was attractive to both the authorities and young readers disillusioned with their return to urban life.

Told in the first person, 'My Faraway Qingpingwan' looks back at the narrator's time in northern Shaanxi as an educated youth. His duty is to tend the water buffalo under the guidance of Bai, a kind old man who likes to sing the local folksongs. At the end of the story the narrator is in hospital in Beijing, paralysed from the waist down. Although he has no intention of leaving the capital, he recalls with affection the simple and natural world he left behind, its harsh beauty and the strengths and kindness of its impoverished inhabitants. Two lines from the story ('It was a scene that made me forget the times I lived in and reflect in silence on mankind's long and remote history. It seemed to me that this was exactly how we had walked through the centuries') and the verses sung by Bai inspired scenes in Chen Kaige's 1984 film *The Yellow Earth*.

Shi Tiesheng relates the life of an old woman with the same kind of nostalgia in 'Granny's Star'. This apparently autobiographical memoir of the author's grandmother overturns the political orthodoxy of the previous thirty years. Granny had been married into the Shi family, the wealthiest in the entire county, when she was only seventeen. Although she was treated like a servant, she was denounced by the local authorities as belonging to a landlord family and denied her civic rights. Her happiest time was in the early 1960s, when the landlord label was taken off her and she was allowed to clean the streets. During the Cultural Revolution, deprived again of the right to work, she took to sweeping the streets before dawn so that nobody would see her.

The narrator recalls Granny's belief that when someone dies on earth, a star is added to the heavens so that night travellers will have light to guide them. Shi Tiesheng shows former landlords and present-day neighbourhood committee busybodies as warm-hearted and gracious, qualities rarely depicted in the 1980s.

Shi Tiesheng's main contribution to contemporary fiction is his description of the disabled. Whereas other writers of the 1980s used the disabled either as symbols of China's degeneration or the shortcomings of individuals, Shi Tiesheng's disabled characters show compassion for others and steadfastly pursue meaning in life. 'A Winter's Evening' is about a disabled couple's support for each other as they hesitantly attempt to adopt a child, and 'Our Corner' depicts the unlikely but warm relationship of a group of young men in a sheltered workshop and a lively young woman who is temporarily assigned to help them. For all his lyricism, Shi Tiesheng is still acutely aware of frustration and injustice. The story 'Fate', for instance, describes in detail the bitterness of an ambitious young man whose spine is damaged in an accident. 'Original Sin', on the other hand, shows an almost mystical faith in the consolations of spiritual values.

Shi's most complex story on this theme is 'Strings of Life', which tells of two blind men, a wandering musician and his apprentice. Many years earlier, the old man was told by his own master that when he has worn out a thousand banjo strings, he can tear open the banjo's casing and find inside a prescription for medicine that will help him regain his sight. The story begins a few days before the old man breaks his thousandth string. His apprentice has other concerns, for he has fallen in love with a young woman in the village where they are playing. When the string finally breaks, the old man takes out the paper and asks people to read what is written on it. They all tell him it is blank. Shattered, his despair knows no bounds, until he suddenly realises the meaning of his master's act: not expecting him to live so long or play so energetically, he meant only to encourage him to put his heart into his playing. The old man returns to seek his apprentice but finds him lying in the snow, waiting to die: the young woman he had been courting had that day married. In his turn, the old man seals the blank paper in the young man's banjo case, telling him that he can only open it after he has worn out one thousand two hundred strings. Filmed by Chen Kaige under the title *Life on a String* with substantial additions and references to the June Fourth massacre, it proved a critical and box-office failure.

Kong Jiesheng (b. 1952)

Born in Guangzhou, Kong Jiesheng spent two years in a nearby village as an educated youth from the age of sixteen, and the next four years on a state farm in Hainan Island; returning to Guangzhou in 1974, he worked in a factory. His early fiction is based on his experiences of these years. 'A Destined Marriage' and 'Because of Her' won national prizes in 1978 and 1979 respectively; 'Across the River', also published in 1979, was more controversial. All three follow the current fashion for love stories, especially on hitherto taboo subjects. 'A Destined Marriage', for example, is about the romance between a factory worker and a returned Overseas Chinese. The status of Overseas Chinese and their relatives in China was still a very sensitive issue in the coastal areas of Guangdong: in Cultural Revolution fiction they were invariably objects of suspicion, and their appearance as desirable marriage partners in fiction was controversial. 'Across the River' even more daringly raised the spectre of incest as a result of the break-up and scattering of families during the 1960s and 1970s. A young man and a young woman, both educated youth from the city, are sent to Hainan; living on opposite sides of a river, they become friends and eventually lovers. A chance remark convinces them that they are brother and sister, but the revelation turns out to be false.

The novellas *The South Bank* (1982) and *Primeval Forest* (1984) are less sensational but still pioneering in dealing with contemporary social problems. *The South Bank* is one of the first stories to describe the dilemma faced by young people returning to the cities after the end of the Cultural Revolution: while they consider themselves fortunate to have returned, many cannot forget the companionship and excitement of their village days. The narrator works in a noodle shop in Guangzhou, run by a group of friends who knew each other in Hainan. His stories about his experiences in Hainan win the love of his old teacher's daughter, but he is in love with a young woman from a background similar to his own, whose first boyfriend died while working in a state forest.

Despite this unhappy omen, the two choose to leave the city and return to the state farm. Kong Jiesheng's nostalgia for Hainan dismayed some readers who found it too unrealistic.

As if to prove his knowledge of the potential cruelty of nature, Kong Jiesheng's *Primeval Forest* relates the disasters experienced by a team of five educated youth who are sent to investigate the possibility of growing rubber in a Hainan jungle. After losing their compass, they begin to fall ill, and by the end of the story four of them are dead. Under the strain, their relationships also become feverish, generating hate and love. The survivor vows to do her best to put an end to the authorities' unrealistic attempts to impose inappropriate agricultural policies for purely political and nationalist ends. This story of human impotence against the forces of nature is one of several mid-1980s works on conservationist themes, along with Ah Cheng's 'King of Trees' and Gao Xingjian's *The Wild Man*.

Kong Jiesheng went to the United States in the late 1980s. After the June Fourth massacre he started a new literary magazine with Chen Ruoxi and others for Chinese writers abroad but the venture was not a success, and Kong joined the editorial board of *Today* in 1990.

Han Shaogong (b. 1953)

Han Shaogong was born in Changsha, Hunan, and spent six years as an educated youth in the Hunan countryside. He began his career as a writer in 1974 while employed in a museum in a small town, and in 1978 entered Hunan Normal University to study Chinese. After graduation, he worked as an editor before becoming deputy chair of the Hunan Writers' Association in 1987. His short stories and novellas of 1978–85 followed the current fashion in criticising 'gang of four' policies, and two won national awards. 'Yuelan' (1979), about the disaster which befalls a conscientious peasant accused of wasting public grain because she lets her chickens feed in the paddy fields, is typical of his early, conventional work.

The first of his stories to show his predilection for writing about people with mental or physical handicaps is 'The Deaf-mute and His Suona' (1981). It relates the search of a profoundly deaf person for love. 'Pa Pa Pa' (1985) and 'Woman Woman Woman'

(1986) were even more fascinating and controversial to a readership which regarded the handicapped as weird and their sexual needs as abnormal. In 1985 he wrote an essay on seeking the roots of Chinese civilisation, after which he was regarded as a leader in the new 'root-seeking' school. By his own admission, Han Shaogong spent many years studying the pre-Confucian culture of the ancient state of Chu (roughly corresponding to present-day Hunan), seeking an alternative to mainstream Confucianism. (It is this aspect of his work which has particularly attracted the attention of Western critics.) His choice of bizarre subjects can be traced back to early Chinese short fiction, and critics also claim that he has been influenced by Latin American 'magic realism'. Whatever its source, Han Shaogong's version of primitivism is brutal and degenerate. Since 1988 he has been living in Hainan.

The setting of 'Pa Pa Pa' is a remote mountain village at an indeterminate time in the present, and the story traces the decline of a village through the life of Bing, a severely handicapped child whose only words are 'Papa' and 'x Mama' (presumably an obscenity). Bing is born retarded and he is disgusting to look at, with his dull eyes, huge head and slow movements. Bing's father disappeared before he was born; his mother is ugly and speaks with what the villagers consider to be an outlandish accent. Bing takes to calling all the men 'papa', and the villagers treat him as a figure of fun. When the local children torment him, Bing's mother curses them, but when she tries to comfort her son, the only words he can reply with is the vulgar expression 'x Mama'.

Bing's disability is a symbol of the village's economic troubles. Through years of misuse, the land has been drained of its nutrients, and by the time Bing appears, the people are close to starvation. Seeking the cause within their village, they decide to cut off Bing's head and present it as a sacrifice to the Rice God, but just as the cleaver is raised, there is a clap of thunder. The villagers believe that this is a sign that Bing should be spared and let him go. They next consult a sorcerer, who tells them that Cock's Head, the peak of Mount Cock, is pecking all the grain from their fields. The villagers decide to blow up Cock's Head, but the neighbouring village objects, fearing that it would bring bad luck. An all-out battle between the two villages ensues, with heavy losses on both sides. In one scene the body of a villager is boiled and Bing is forced to eat part of the lung. However, even cannibalism cannot help the village, and its members get thinner and thinner until eventually they capitulate. Poison is distributed to the old and weak, including Bing, while the young march off to another site to seek a new life. Miraculously, after all the villagers are gone and the people from the neighbouring village come to see what they can salvage, Bing is found to be still alive, calling 'Pa Pa Pa Pa Pa!'

'Woman Woman Woman' describes the life of an old woman, Aunt Yao, whose physical and mental faculties are in decline. At the beginning of the story she is reduced to ape-like grunts and follows instructions only when she is beaten. Later she crawls on all fours, impervious to hunger or cold, and in the end she comes to resemble a fish. In a reversal of evolution, Han Shaogong suggests that the human species can degenerate to a pre–primate state.

Jia Pingwa (b. 1953)

Jia Pingwa is one of the most influential members of the 'root-seeking' school, with a particular interest in sexual relationships. Born in Shaanxi, he studied Chinese literature at Northwest University and began writing fiction as an undergraduate. In 1975 he was assigned to work as an editor in the Shaanxi People's Publishing House, where he won several literary awards. He was transferred to the literary magazine *Chang'an* (Chang'an is the older name for Xi'an, Shaanxi's provincial capital) in 1980, and continued to write steadily throughout the decade. Short stories, novellas and novels such as 'Human Extremities', *Families of Jiwowa Village* (1984), *The Heavenly Hound* (1986) and *Shangzhou* (1987) established his reputation as a chronicler of the history and customs of Shangzhou, a rural district outside Xi'an. His novel *Turbulence* won the 1988 Pegasus Prize.

'Human Extremities' relates the story of two sworn brothers and the two women who come into their lives. The 'brothers' are poor peasants who rescue a young woman from the city during a flood. When one discovers that the other has raped her, he condemns the rapist, who then commits suicide in shame. The survivor falls into a deep depression and only regains his will to live when he rescues another woman, this time an abused peasant who is pregnant as a result of gang rape. They set up house together and he cares for both mother and child until she is taken back by her previous husband under whose cruelty she dies from maltreatment. Again despondent beyond words, the protagonist meets the first woman again. He an ignorant peasant and she a schoolteacher, they make an improbable but loving couple.

Families of Jiwowa Village describes the impact of the rural economic reforms of the late 1970s on the lives of two friends, Huihui and Hehe. Huihui is a conscientious worker who does not like taking risks. He and his wife Yanfeng are content to till the fields but regret having no children. Hehe is married to Mairong and has a child; he is ambitious and wants to raise silkworms. When Hehe's projects come to nought and the debt collectors are at their door, Hehe leaves home and goes to stay with his old friend. Huihui gets tired of bailing out Hehe as one reckless scheme after another fails, but Yanfeng has faith in his potential and thinks they should help him. This causes conflict between husband and wife, and Huihui and Yanfeng end up divorcing. Yanfeng and Hehe get married and have a child; Hehe's projects also come to fruition and earn vast amounts of money. As the story concludes, Huihui, who by this stage has married Mairong, has got steadily poorer and is forced to accept help from Hehe. The story's affirmation of Deng Xiaoping's policies of agricultural diversification and individual enterprise is underlined by Hehe's ability to get both women pregant. *Families of Jiwowa Village* is about economics and politics as much as wife-swapping but Jia Pingwa tells it without resorting to jargon or sermons, and it was made into an equally lively film.

The message that economic circumstances force changes in sexual relations is also found in *The Heavenly Hound*. The protagonist, Tiangou (Heavenly Hound), is apprenticed to a well-digger, who through an accident becomes paralysed from the waist down. Tiangou devotes his life to supporting his master's family, including his young wife and their son. When he is reduced to spending the money he had saved for buying a wife, his master and mistress devise a plan in which according to local custom, Tiangou is to become the second husband. Tiangou agrees but refrains from consummating the marriage. As the new ecomomic policies come into force, the family starts a business raising scorpions, an ingredient in traditional Chinese medicine, and the enterprise flourishes. The wife wants Tiangou to consummate their marriage, but he runs away. Only when Tiangou's master hangs himself to set them free does Tiangou sleep in his master's bed. Again, behaviour which might be seen as reprehensible is excused on the grounds of economic necessity or local custom.

Turbulence is about the experiences of Jingou, a demobilised soldier from a poor family, who on return to his home town becomes a successful boatman. Although he is in love with Han Xiaoshui, who also works on the river, he decides to go to the city and study to become a reporter. To do this, he has to agree to marry Yingying, niece of the village head. As a famous reporter, he recalls his background and resolves to expose corruption. After a series of melodramatic events, in which he divorces Yingying, he and a friend are gaoled, and Han Xiaoshui's husband is killed by a bear, the lovers are finally united. Compared with his earlier work, this novel suffers from an over-complicated plot and rather conventional moral framework.

Can Xue (b. 1953)

Can Xue, pen-name of Deng Xiaohua, is one of the leading writers of the 'nightmare' school, whose work features bizarre and meaningless events. Her early life in Changsha was marked by such nightmares, as her father, the editor of the *New Hunan News*, was labelled a Rightist in 1957, and she herself worked in a factory for ten years during the Cultural Revolution. Can Xue and her husband set up a tailor's shop in the early 1980s, and as the business flourished, she begin writing fiction. Among her most controversial works are the two novellas *Yellow Mud Street* (1983) and *Old Floating Cloud* (1986), both included in the collection *Dialogues in Paradise* (1988), along with eight short stories.

Can Xue's anti-realism makes considerable demands on readers: images of stagnation, decay and death fill her pages, the language is self-consciously crude, the plots lack coherence, the breakdown of self negates the very concept of character development, and even the narrator is likely to disappear from view. In *Yellow Mud Street*, the street is filled with piles of excrement and puddles of stinking black ooze. It seems to have an evil power: fruit begins to rot as soon as it is brought in, its inhabitants have boils and ulcers all over their bodies, a man's ear falls off for no reason, cats and dogs go crazy and bite people, and rats kill cats. People relate their nightmares to each other, even though it increases their own fears. The body of an old man who hangs himself cannot be found, but his voice can be heard at nights. A 'thing' called Wang Ziguang appears: nobody knows whether or not it is human. The residents become so corrupted that they are no longer distinguishable from the filth and waste which surround them.

Madness and loss of memory are also frequent tropes. *Old Floating Cloud* resembles Han Shaogong's 'Woman Woman Woman' in its depiction of the mental and physical disintegration of the protagonist but its background of nightmares and hallucinations gives it an additional dimension of philosophical delirium. As memory is lost or misunderstood and identity breaks down, the subject becomes a caged animal, forced to commune with a self that no longer holds any meaning.

Sometimes described as post-modernist, Can Xue's fiction is interpreted variously as a symbolic representation of China's nascent capitalism, a Freudian allegory of repressed sexuality, an exploration of female identity or a technical exercise in narrative fragmentation. Chinese critics are divided: Wang Meng, for instance, claims not to be able to read her stories to the end, and even early supporters such as Wang Xiaoming came to find her work unduly repetitive. Western critics are attracted by her distinctively individual voice, but her work lacks the parody usually associated with post-modernism.

Wang Anyi (b. 1954)

Like her mother, Ru Zhijuan, Wang Anyi began her literary career as an orthodox writer and became noted for defending the role of intellectuals in modern China. Born in Nanjing, Wang Anyi grew up in Shanghai and went to a village in Anhui as an educated youth in 1970. In 1972 she was admitted to the Xuzhou Art Workers' Troupe, where she began writing essays and short stories. Returning to Shanghai in 1978, she was appointed editor of the journal *Childhood Years*. The work which established her reputation as a writer is 'Rustling Rain' (1981), one of a series of stories about young women in search of love and happiness.

Wang Anyi's most famous work is a trilogy on love and extra-marital sex published in the mid-1980s: *Love on a Barren Mountain* (1986), *Love in a Small Town* (1986) and *Brocade Valley* (1987). Although not as radical as Can Xue, Wang Anyi introduces modernistic devices such as multiple narration and main characters without names, but her chief innovation is her preoccupation with female sexuality. The protagonist of *Love on a Barren Mountain* is a beautiful young woman who has learned to flirt from her mother and becomes a popular actress. She is courted by many young men but marries someone who pretends not to be attracted to her. They have a child and seem to be reasonably happy. Then her husband arranges for her to be transferred to the cultural bureau in the county town, where she meets and falls in love with a musician. The musician comes from a educated family and is married to a young woman with a similar background. They have two children and also appear to be happily married until he meets the heroine. Their affair soon becomes notorious. Her husband beats her, and his wife makes preparations to leave town. In desperation, the lovers climb up Barren Mountain, drink poison and die in each other's arms. The story is sympathetic to the man's repressed sexuality but gives most attention to the woman's romantic and impulsive behaviour.

In *Love in a Small Town*, a young woman discovers the meaning of love and responsibility through an affair with a man she has known since childhood. Both are members of a drama troupe, but growing up during the Cultural Revolution they receive little education and their bodies are distorted by the bad training they receive at that time. In order to continue as dancers, they have to be retrained, and every day they practice together, the sweat pouring from their tortured bodies. Eventually they discover the excitement of sexual attraction, but after each encounter they feel ashamed and guilty. When she becomes pregnant, she begins to find in her child the meaning of her existence. This is something he cannot share, and their relationship comes to an end.

The heroine of *Brocade Valley* is an editor in a publishing house whose marriage has lost much of its passion. At a writers' conference in the glamorous mountain resort of Lushan, she meets a famous novelist (a character based, it is said, on Zhang Xianliang) and finds herself intoxicated by feelings of passion which have not stirred in her for a long time. After she returns home to the same mundane surroundings, she waits for a letter from the writer.

Her frustration grows as she fails to hear from him, but finally she realises that she was not so much in love with him as with the 'she' that their unconsummated affair created. The most autobiographical of the three 'romances', the story shows little sense of feminism or sisterhood (the other women characters are either contemptible or sick), but is eloquent on the dreariness of the living conditions as well as emotional life of China's contemporary intellectuals.

Liu Heng (b. 1954)

Born in Beijing, Liu Heng came from an educated family and studied Russian at the school attached to the Foreign Languages Institute until the onset of the Cultural Revolution. He then obtained a posting to the navy, after which he was assigned to the Beijing Motor Factory. He began writing fiction in 1977 and became an editor for *Beijing Literature* in 1979. His output is considerable, but his fame dates from the publication of two novels in 1988.

Liu Heng specialises in exploring the psychological states of people whose lives are distorted by events beyond their control. His most famous work, *The Obsessed*, is a study of lust and violence within a small rural family in the 1940s. Yang Jinshan, an elderly widower without an heir after thirty years of marriage, buys the young and beautiful Wang Judou. Despite his repeated attempts to make her pregnant, however, Wang Judou remains barren, and the frustrated Yang Jinshan abuses her sadistically. His nephew, Yang Tianqing, orphaned and adopted by his uncle, is only four years younger than Wang Judou and feels great sympathy for her. Tianqing and Judou, who are at the peak of physical well-being, soon plunge into a passionate affair which they hide from the uncle, and when Judou gives birth to a son, Tianbai, Jinshan is overjoyed. After the old man falls down a cliff and becomes paralysed, Tianqing and Judou become more reckless and Jinshan realises what has been happening. He attempts to strangle Tianbai, but is caught by Tianqing and Judou, who then take turns in humiliating him. With Yang Jinshan paralysed, the lovers take elaborate precautions to prevent Judou from falling pregnant again, but painful methods prescribed by the village sorceress cause their passion to fade. When Tianbai grows older and discovers the relationship between his mother and his 'cousin', he is furious. Tianqing drowns himself in a water-vat in shame, and Judou gives birth to a weakling. The Chinese title indicates that this powerful tale of illicit love and incest can be read as a modern version of an ancient Chinese creation myth. Its sexual detail is unusually graphic, as in the image of Tianqing's penis dangling outside the vat. Zhang Yimou's film of the story became a huge international success under the title *Judou*.

Black Snow depicts petty crime in Beijing in the 1980s. The hero is Li Huiquan, a young man whose parents abandoned him and who was raised by foster parents who are both dead by the time the action begins. Li Huiquan is released from prison after three years for his involvement in a street fight. He is no more inclined to accept social norms than before, but an old prison guard has become a sort of mentor. With the help of a neighbour, he sets up a street stall to sell clothing, and at night frequents a karaoke bar where Zhao Yaqiu, a nineteen-year-old singer, is the main attraction. Li Huiquan becomes infatuated with her and acts as her 'bodyguard', although he later discovers that he is not the only one. In the same bar Li Huiquan meets Cui Yongli, a dealer in stolen goods and pornographic videos. He tries to recruit Li Huiquan as an accomplice but Li declines both this offer and sexual favours from one of Cui's women. Even when Zhao Yaqiu is revealed as another of Cui's girlfriends, Li cannot break free from her. Meanwhile he becomes aware that the gang loyalty which he had always upheld has been betrayed by one of his old companions, but when another gang member escapes from gaol seeking refuge at Li Huiquan's place, he cannot bring himself to betray the escapee. With his life collapsing around him, Li Huiquan wanders into a dark alley and is knifed to death by two young hooligans. Although both plot and characterisation suffer from inconsistency and ultimately fail to convince, *Black Snow* nevertheless compares favourably with Ke Yan's conventional and moralistic story of Beijing street crime, *The World Regained*, both of which were made into successful films.

The protagonist of the novella *Whirlpool*, which also appeared in 1988, is a successful intellectual with a good job at a Chinese medical research institute, an understanding wife and two lovely children, but the emptiness in his life and his hypocrisy are revealed through his affair with a colleague whose work he supervises. A modern-day version of 'Mr Hua Wei', the story is a nicely sustained satire although it lacks the humour of Zhang Tianyi's work. 'Unreliable Witness' is a remarkable tale on the theme of male impotence and imputations of homosexuality (matters of considerable anxiety in the 1980s) leading to suicide. As the first-person narrator tries to collect information on the suicide, he is faced repeatedly with the impossibility of understanding other people's lives. In the eyes of his contemporaries (the 'unreliable witnesses' who include the narrator), the protagonist's sexual problems seem overwhelming, ranging from a crush on an older woman to seduction by a young woman who has been jilted by her lover. His shameful secrets become the subject of intense gossip, and even his suicide is greeted with incomprehension and as much malice as sympathy. Liu Heng's revelations of obscure corners in contemporary life and insights into social attitudes give his work a universal appeal that goes beyond mere sociological reporting.

Liu Suola (b. 1955)

Born in Beijing, Liu Suola graduated from the Central Conservatory of Music in 1983. As a student she also began to write fiction, and has kept up her interests in both music and literature. Her 1985 novella *You Have No Other Choice* has been called the first example of Chinese post-modernism, and 'Blue Sky, Green Sea' and 'In Search of the King of Singers' were also influential. Liu Suola was based in London in the late 1980s and has travelled widely in the United States and Europe.

'You Have No Other Choice' profiles a group of music students, each with different personal histories and unfulfilled desires, but all feeling trapped in the academy with no choice but to pursue music as their career. Shi Bai mostly keeps to himself, heeding his professor's advice to cultivate his musical talent. Li Ming also keeps to himself, but out of hypochondria. Dai Qi, who wants to transfer from composing to the piano, quarrels with his girlfriend, Lili. These young people, full of self-doubt and rebelliousness, are presented as typical of the restless youth in a rapidly modernising society where all of the old values are under attack.

'Blue Sky, Green Sea' relates a day at a recording studio. Memories of her dead friend, Manzi, affect the first-person narrator so deeply that she becomes unable to sing. In contrast to the narrator, who longs for recognition, Manzi did not care for success or other worldly symbols but found joy in singing for its own sake. The conflict between art and fame is carried further in 'In Search of the King of Singers', in which the narrator's lover, a well-known composer, disappears in a primeval jungle while the narrator tries to make a success of her own career. Both stories consist chiefly of juxtaposed passages of interior monologue with few narrative links and almost no plot. Set in a glamorous and privileged milieu, Liu Suola's stories are frankly subjective and self-indulgent.

Mo Yan (b. 1956)

Mo Yan is the pen-name of Guan Moye, born in Gaomi, Shandong, and much of his fiction is based on the area around his hometown. Mo Yan joined the People's Liberation Army at the age of twenty, serving as political commissar and propaganda officer and at the same time beginning his literary career. A prolific writer, with several novels, dozens of novellas and many more short stories to his name, his best-known works date from 1985 and 1986.

The novella *Explosions* can be read as a critique of the current one-child policy, the cause of tremendous suffering in the Chinese countryside in the 1980s. The narrator forces his wife to terminate a second pregnancy. During her ordeal, he watches a group of people hunting a fox in the field outside the hospital, recalling folktales of foxes who make immortality pills. 'The Yellow-haired Baby' also juxtaposes traditional lore with current issues. Sun Tianqiu, a political commissar in the People's Liberation Army, spends his time in town ogling the statue of a naked fisherwoman through binoculars, while his neglected wife has an affair with a young albino peasant, Blondy. Blondy's attractiveness is heightened by his skills as a storyteller, entertaining Sun Tianqiu's mother and wife with tales of weird and fantastic happenings. The result of the affair is a yellow-haired baby. On discovering his wife in bed with Blondy when he returns to the village, Sun Tianqiu cold-bloodedly kills the baby by breaking its neck.

Mo Yan graduated from the People's Liberation Army Art Academy in 1986 and became a member of the Writers' Association; *Red Sorghum*, his most famous work, dates from that year. The history of a family in the 1930s, it is related in the first person some forty years later. The narrator is the grandson of Yu Zhan'ao, a sedan-chair bearer turned bandit. Hired to take Dai Fenglian to her husband's place on her wedding day, Yu kills a robber along the way and excites Dai's attention. Dai's husband is an older man rumoured to have leprosy, and on arriving at his home she refuses to let him touch her. On the third day, she goes back to visit her own parents as is customary. On the way, when she and her father pass through the sorghum fields, she is raped by Yu Zhan'ao. When she returns to her husband's home, she finds both her husband and her father-in-law murdered. Yu moves in to live with her, and their sorghum wine becomes famous throughout the area after he urinates in it during the fermentation process. Their son, Douguan, is born and grows into a brave boy. When the Japanese attack the village, Yu becomes a commander of the local militia. Both sides commit terrible atrocities, which are described in detail. For attempting to run away with the donkeys, for example, Uncle Arhat is skinned alive. Yu loses most of his men in a decisive battle when he is betrayed by another militia unit, and Dai is also shot dead. While the battle is won when the other militia arrives, bad blood is already sown among the Chinese fighters.

The novel is a mixture of many elements, with myths and legends intermingling with tales of grotesque cruelty. Its appeal to patriotism meshes neatly with currrent official policies, and its explicit descriptions also suits the current popular demand for sex and violence. Filmed by Zhang Yimou under the same title, it won several international awards and brought Mo Yan an international following.

Wang Shuo (b. 1958)

Born in Beijing, Wang Shuo joined the navy after he left school and was stationed at the seaside resort town of Qingdao, where he is reputed to have spent most of his time womanising and lazing about on the beach. His first story was published in *Liberation Army Literature and the Arts* in 1978. A series of odd jobs followed demobilisation, including a few years at the Beijing Pharmaceutical Company. From the mid-1980s, the royalties from his fiction, augmented by the film versions, gave him the means to pursue a hedonistic existence among like-minded friends. Wang Shuo's fiction is peopled by hooligans, idlers and rebellious youth: ir-reverent and cynical, they enjoy making fun of social norms. Among themselves, however, they foster a strong gang loyalty, and their frivolous attitudes expose the hypocrisy of the estab-lishment. The 1987 'The Rubber Man' and 'The Operators' per-haps best illustrate his predilection for irreverent farce.

The first-person narrator and protagonist of 'The Rubber Man' is an unemployed youth from the north who makes friends with a group of like-minded people in a southern city. His nickname, Rubber Man, indicates his chameleon nature and his complete lack of principle. The group live in high-class hotels and enjoy whatever life has to offer. Rubber Man sets up a deal with a Hong Kong businessman to buy and sell a batch of colour television sets, and when the businessman tries to con him, Rubber Man gives him a brutal beating. Pursued by a gang of thugs, he is arrested while making his escape. After his release, he finds that his friends have made a fortune dealing in cars, and one of them claims that she is in love with him. But the narrator feels alienated not just from society, but from his friends as well. Like a rubber man who can be bent to any shape, nothing is sacred to him, and nothing will bring him either happiness or pain.

Yu Guan, the protagonist of 'The Operators', is also a man without principles. The plot consists mainly of unconnected episodes where he and his friends Yang Zhong and Ma Qing sell their services as proxies to anyone willing to pay. Yang Zhong, for instance, meets a young woman on another man's behalf, while Ma Qing stands in for the husband of a quarrelsome wife. Wang Shuo's philosophy that there is nothing more to life than self-indulgence gained widespread popularity in the late 1980s, and his success encouraged other writers to take advantage of the new opportunities for commercial publication.

Su Tong (b. 1963)

Su Tong was born in Suzhou and studied Chinese literature at Beijing University. One of the most successful writers of the 1980s, his fiction tends to dwell on the more unpleasant aspects of the human condition. His most famous work is the novella *Wives and Concubines* (1987), set in a wealthy household in 1930s. Chen Zuoqian already has a wife and two concubines competing for his attention, but brings destruction on the household when he buys Lotus, a young student. Lotus tries to secure her position by bearing Chen a son but her inability to do so leaves her in disgrace. She learns that an earlier concubine has gone insane, and is forced to witness the murder of another concubine whose affair with a doctor is discovered. Lotus comes to realise that women are treated in the Chen household as mere toys, and herself goes insane by the end of the story. Zhang Yimou's Oscar-nominated film version *Raise the Red Lantern*, released in 1992, won him international fame.

Su Tong's taste for the weird and grotesque in Chinese culture is even more pronounced in the 1987 novella *Nineteen Thirty-four Escapes*. Like Mo Yan's *Red Sorghum*, it is the history of a family in the year 1934, told through the recollections of an adult who was a child at the time of the plot, and is filled with images of death and decay. *Nineteen Thirty-four Escapes*, however, is less an action story than a psychological study of degradation. The protagonist is the narrator's uncle, Chen Gouzai (Gouzai meaning 'puppy'). In 1934 Guozai is fifteen years old and collects dog droppings to raise money for a pair of rubber boots. The local landlord, Chen Wenzhi, who hoards young boys' semen in a white jade jar, gives him a pair of boots when Gouzai lets him masturbate him. Gouzai's father has moved into town where he lives with a young woman. Forced by poverty at home to seek him out, Gouzai spies on his father's lovemaking and is punished. Gouzai then dies as a result of accumulated mental and physical suffering. In 1934, also, plague swept through the narrator's village and corpses are left to rot in ditches, and the narrator describes his grandmother's intense pleasure as she throws the bodies of her five children into a pond and inhales the putrid smell of death. Critics have read stories such as this as symbolic of the decadence and moral bankruptcy of contemporary Chinese culture.

The most notable impact of the Cultural Revolution in fiction was the encouragement given to amateur authors and group authorship. Although most failed to survive the change of government after 1976, amateur writers from the early 1970s such Jiang Zilong, Feng Jicai, Shen Rong, Liu Xinwu and Gu Hua became professional writers in the late 1970s and 1980s. The non-traditional backgrounds of these writers and their experiences during the Cultural Revolution gave them a wide range of themes and characters to draw on. In this latter respect, they were similar to an older group of writers, the former Rightists from the 1950s who included most notably Wang Meng, Gao Xiaosheng and Zhang Xianliang. These two groups of writers were similar in their preoccupation with the past, and repudiating the attitudes displayed in their earlier work, they dominated the world of fiction in 1977–85. Most of these writers were conservative in their approach to writing, Wang Meng being one of the few to try out new techniques.

Despite their similarities, literary critics commonly distinguished between them on the basis of age, dividing them into two (occasionally three) 'generations' with a further generation of educated youth as their successors. Like the concept of the 'new era', this categorisation tended to blur the political differences between writers of the same 'generation': for instance, the radicalism of older writers such as Zhang Xianliang and the fundamental orthodoxy of young writers like Tie Ning (b. 1957).

Experimental fiction, which dates from the underground writers of the 1970s such as Zhao Zhenkai, flourished in the mid-1980s in the hands of writers like Ah Cheng and Can Xue, who grew up during the Cultural Revolution. Most of them spent their youth in the countryside and compensated for their lack of formal schooling by self-education (some were from culturally privileged backgrounds) and by what might be called first-hand anthropological investigation into remote corners of Chinese rural life or – what was even more foreign to previous Chinese fiction – gang life in China's cities.

Like their predecessors during the May Fourth period, writers in the 1980s were keen to reassess China's culture and traditions along with their fascination for Western ideas and ways of life. A new development was the gradual discovery on the mainland of post-1945 literary trends in Taiwan, including both modernists such as Chen Ruoxi (b. 1938) and Bai Xianyong (b. 1937) and 'native earth' writers such as Chen Yingzhen (b. 1937), Huang Chunming (b. 1939) and Wang Tuo (b. 1944).

Women writers became more active in the early 1980s than any other time in Chinese history. Writers from the 1950s and 1960s such as Ke Yan (b. 1929), Ru Zhijuan and Shen Rong reappeared with mildly unorthodox views, to be joined by new faces such as the more assertive Zhang Jie. At the same time, Zhang Kangkang (b. 1950), Zhang Xinxin (b. 1953), Can Xue, Wang Anyi and Liu Suola took advantage of the relaxation of controls in the mid- and late-1980s to challenge the limits of orthodoxy more defiantly. Women writers nevertheless still mostly came from a conventionally educated background, and even when the market economy of the late 1980s finally allowed reader preference for themes of sex and violence to surface, they tended to stick to experimental or conventional fiction, leaving male writers such as Wang Shuo and Jia Pingwa to dominate commercial publication.

In gender, social background, education and career expectations, the fiction writers of the 1960s, 1970s and 1980s were a more diverse group than perhaps ever before in the history of Chinese literature.

13

POETRY: THE CHALLENGE
OF MODERNITY

As the violence of the Cultural Revolution was brought under control in 1969, the gradual construction of a new culture became a top priority. Apart from isolated short stories and poems in the remaining newspapers, the new products were as yet hardly visible, but amateurs and professionals were organised and set to work. The third and final phase of the Cultural Revolution, from 1971 to 1976, was as remarkable as any in modern Chinese literary history. The hoped-for populist literature remained elusive, since the effective primary audience for it was still the cultural bureaucracy, but several tendencies emerged in poetry which were to influence the literary scene for the next two decades: a bogus folk revival, which nevertheless had the effect of encouraging a revived regionalism; the restoration to respectability of classical poetry; the final degradation of the official poets, now exposed as willing to lend their support to whatever regime was in power; the use of poetry as a vehicle for spontaneous political protest; and the development of poetry for personal expression. The first three trends took place on the official level; the last pair were part of a widespread and largely uncoordinated underground move-ment.

The main characteristic of the 1970s and 1980s (still ignored in orthodox Chinese accounts of the period) is the intensification of the gap between official and non-official writing that had its beginnings in the 1940s, 1950s and 1960s. A second major char-acteristic, marking it off from the previous period, is the wider range of audiences being addressed. The rate of illiteracy and semi-illiteracy had fallen dramatically from about 90 per cent at the beginning of the century to 38 per cent in 1964: the audience that could be addressed in print was much larger both in absolute numbers and as a proportion of the population. By the 1980s different kinds of audiences also came to be acknowledged, and the pretence of a single homogenised audience prevalent in the 1960s was maintained only at the highest ideological level. Writers still tended to come from families with a background of several generations of education, but access to publication was no longer their exclusive preserve. Certainly in the 1970s an extremely broad cross-section of the general public were being encouraged to regard writing poetry as a standard part of their adult daily life. Very little, of course, was regarded as worth distributing beyond the writer's own circle of friends and colleagues; and it could even be said that the widespread practice of poetry, associated with primitive rather than technologically advanced societies, was another manifestation of Mao's deep-seated nostalgia for China as a traditional peasant society.

A partial resumption of literary publications began in 1971 and became more pronounced in 1972 with the reappearance of provincial and city literary journals. To celebrate the Spring Festival, a small number of literary works were also reprinted or published for the first time. Among the poets with new or old work appearing in 1972 were He Jingzhi, Li Ying, and a worker poet, Li Xueao. Between 1972 and 1975, more than four hundred (mostly very slim) volumes of poetry were published. (A visitor to China in 1973 found fifty-seven literary titles on sale at bookshops throughout China, mostly collections of short stories or poems; none was by an author known before 1960.)

The revival of the old cultural magazines was organised during the summer of 1975: *Poetry* reappeared in January 1976, along with the revived *People's Literature*. The editorial board was not named, but Zang Kejia and Li Ying were among the contributors (Li Ji was named as editor in 1977, and may have taken on the position the previous year). Again, Mao contributed two poems, and his letter on poetry was quoted but with a new stress: this time, it was emphasised that although the main body of verse should be in the new (i.e. May Fourth or free-verse) style, old-style poetry could still be written, and poets were advised to create new poetry on the basis of the critical acceptance of classical and folk poetry – formerly sharply differentiated, these two were now clearly seen as complementary.

Other writers who appeared in the official press in the months before Mao's death in September 1976 were Zhu De (another old general who favoured classical verse), Zhao Puchu, Feng Zhi, Li Xueao and Feng Jingyuan (another worker poet). In the following year, the literary journals and columns also featured work by Zang Kejia, Li Ying, Zhao Puchu, Feng Zhi, Tian Jian, He Jingzhi, Guo Xiaochuan, Li Xueao, Feng Jingyuan and even Guo Moruo (it seems in an odd way fitting that Guo's last published poem should be in classical form). The immediate succession was smoothly achieved, and to the restored elites, it may have seemed that the old way of life before the Cultural Revolution could be revived without appreciable change. Others believed that the seeds of the Cultural Revolution were sown as far back as the 1940s and were determined to set the country in a new direction. Some of the most explicit articulations of the desire for fundamental change, making the passage from underground to non-official to above ground in a few short years, were in poetry.

The existence of a literary underground in modern China is a phenomenon of the 1970s and 1980s. In the first decades of the century, censorship by warlord and Nationalist governments was offset by the relative freedom of the foreign concessions and lack of an efficient bureaucracy. The May Fourth writers were mostly young men eager to establish themselves as professionals, and with a few exceptions (mainly during the war years), private circulation was neither necessary nor attractive. Books not approved by the authorities were circulated privately in the early 1950s but these were mainly older works, not products of the day. The 1980s revealed very little 'drawer' literature from earlier decades: although some undoubtedly existed, most was destroyed during the dangerous years of the early Cultural Revolution. The chief surviving examples were the classical verse of the old generals' and senior intellectuals' private poetry circles, which were only heterodox in choice of form.

The physical removal of the old cultural leadership and its replacement in the late 1960s by a band of extreme dogmatists had the effect of creating a vacuum in literature and the arts. At the same time, the dispersal of urban educated youth to the countryside and the general breakdown in social order allowed budding writers a kind of personal liberty, free from neigbourhood, school or Youth League supervision and control. Finally, the excesses which these potential recruits into the next generation of elites had either indulged in or witnessed brought about in some of them a deep revulsion against any form of support for the current leadership (including entry into the ranks of the official writers). Since political activity of any other kind was not only extremely dangerous but also implied a kind of radical anarchy which few Chinese have ever found attractive, the alternative for some of the restless young was to create their own literature and to circulate it among friends and friends of friends.

The first publication of underground writing was *Revelations That Move the Earth to Tears* (1974), an anthology of poetry and prose dating from 1970 to 1974 either smuggled out of China or written by refugee youth in Hong Kong. The editor, a former Red Guard, drew attention to the highly idealistic and personal nature of this writing, distinguishing it from the entertainment fiction then also in underground circulation on the mainland. Both classical and May Fourth styles are employed in poetry but not the jaunty folksong promoted by Cultural Revolution populists. Other Hong Kong publications carried underground poetry and fiction of similar kinds, plus information on its distribution within China. Private publication at first took the form of hand-copying; in the second half of the 1970s, mimeographed manuscripts of individual works or even journals were also circulated. The easiest kind of manuscript to circulate was poetry: poems could also be learned by heart and passed on orally. The writer and the audience converged.

Participation in underground publication implied at the very least a rebellious attitude on the part of the producers and their audiences, and although the writers generally avoided overt attacks on the system, the sense of rebelliousness is clear in their work. The Tiananmen protests of 1976, or the April Fifth Movement as it later became known with self-conscious reference to May Fourth, was the most spectacular demonstration of the political uses of poetry in modern Chinese history. Like the event itself, the poems written for the commemoration of Zhou Enlai on April Fifth seem to have been completely spontaneous. Several different collections of the poems circulated after the incident, including some poems which may have been added in the days immediately afterwards; none claimed to be wholly comprehensive. The best known, edited by 'Tong Huai Zhou' (Children Mourn Zhou), appeared in mimeographed form on the first anniversary of Zhou Enlai's death and was printed later the same month for limited circulation. An expanded and revised edition came out in May under the title *Revolutionary Poems from Tiananmen*, and in July a second volume appeared containing new material. Although not for sale, they quickly spread throughout China, and an official one-volume edition retitled *Revolutionary Poems* was finally released for the third anniversary of Zhou Enlai's death in 1979.

The Tiananmen poems have a single theme: opposition to the 1976 leadership after Zhou's death. It is difficult to establish the authenticity of all the included material or the representative nature of the collection as a whole: but taking it at least as an expression of 1978 sensibility, it is notable that the majority of the poems are in a classical or semi-classical style, and that they are arranged primarily by metrical type: a striking awareness of traditional formal values in the most highly charged political verse.

Underground publications increased in number and circulation during the excitements of the death of Mao and the arrest of the 'gang of four' in late 1976, the reinstatement of Deng Xiaoping in 1977 and the reversal of verdicts in late 1978 on the 1950s' Rightists and the April Fifth demonstrators. The democratic movement that surfaced on Democracy Wall in November 1978 traced its origins to the April Fifth demonstrations and exhibited a similar spontaneous expression of political concern in literary form. Beginning with posters, the movement soon turned to magazines which circulated openly but unofficially above ground. Most of the magazines included stories and poems along with articles on politics and society, and within a month literary magazines also made their appearance.

The materials in the unofficial magazines date back to the early 1970s. One of the earliest was 'The God of Fire Symphonic Poems', a series written between 1969 and 1972 by Huang Xiang (b.1941). The inflated imagery of divinities, fire, youth and the sea, the exaggerated and repetitive language, and the passionate yearning for emotional and intellectual liberation are dismayingly reminiscent of Guo Moruo's early poetry. Later examples use the same kinds of simplified classical forms as the Tiananmen poems. Given that nature of the unofficial publications and their contributors' links to former Party hierarchies, it is hardly surprising that these poems, unlike the examples published in Hong Kong from a less elevated social group, are unrelentingly public. They form an extension to the campaign poetry fostered by the Communist authorities since the outbreak of the War against Japan and intensified during the Cultural Revolution.

It was the literary journals on and around the Democracy Wall which confirmed the earlier impression that the underground literature of the 1970s was as much for the expression of personal emotion as for political protest. The most prominent was *Today*, published irregularly for nine issues between December 1978 and September 1980, and for a further three issues as 'study material' to the end of 1980. *Today* was built around the work of a poetry circle which had been formed in 1969 in the countryside around Beijing by former Red Guards from intellectual backgrounds. Mang Ke (pen-name of Jiang Shiwei; b. 1950) was its founder, and his co-editor of *Today*, Bei Dao, became its best-known member. Apart from work by the two editors, the first issue also featured a poem by Shu Ting and extracts from Huang Yongyu's 'Bestiary'; the second issue had Chen Maiping's first published story; and the third issue was prefaced by Ah Cheng's drawing of Zhou Enlai from 1976. Other members of the group were Jiang He (b.1949), Yan Li (b. 1954), Yang Lian, Duo Duo and Gu Cheng.

The avant-garde poetry of this group was characterised as 'obscure' (*menglong*, sometimes misleadingly translated as 'misty') by the hostile critic, Zhang Ming, in *Poetry* in 1980, but the term stuck, perhaps because after all it was not too derogatory: in its original sense the word evokes the half-light when the moon is obscured. 'Obscure poetry' became extremely influential in the 1980s, reaching an international audience never before granted to mainland writers in this century. Although direct political protest was voiced in their poems, the traditional themes of love, friendship, nature and history were uppermost. Their immediate inspiration was May Fourth modernism (including the Nine Leaves poets), which they read in volumes confiscated from public and private libraries, and the classical poetry which had become respectable again during the latter phases of the Cultural Revolution. Much later, these poets also became familiar with Western modernist poetry in translation, and during the 1980s all of them read widely in Western literature.

The unprecedented respite the avant-garde continued to enjoy from supervision from their elders, including literary critics, encouraged a tremendous upsurge in both official and non-official publications in 1978–80. The very possibility of publication itself inspired a new outburst of productivity and experimentation. In taking the step from underground to unofficial, the avant-garde poets simultaneously demanded that the authorities recognise their legitimacy and widened the audience on which their legitimacy was based. Their political activities in the period 1976–8 gave them a profound sense of their own moral worth in society, their ability to make correct judgements on the political process in their country, and their right or even their obligation to express their views on the society around them.

In addition to publishing, another important activity was the formation of poetry clubs or circles, sometimes consisting of only a few people, sometimes of several dozens in the bigger cities; poems were read and discussed at meetings, and open-air recitals were held in Beijing and elsewhere in the late 1970s. The semi-clandestine nature of these activities added greatly to the drama of the occasion, and poetry as a performance art was again invested with all the glamour of youthful rebellion.

After Deng Xiaoping closed down the Democracy Wall and the unofficial publications in March 1979, the *Today* poets, having established their credentials both for publication and for jobs in publishing, drifted into the fringes of the literary world. The official publications were themselves changing rapidly at this time, partly because of the recruitment of younger staff who themselves had been part of the underground or who sympathised with its aims; active in soliciting and selecting materials, from the periphery they inched in towards the centre. Family and social connections also protected younger poets and helped them find jobs in cultural organizations that gave them access to free stationery, the chance to meet influential cultural figures, and the leisure in which to write. Thirdly, there were many people in senior positions who, having also suffered from the excesses of Party policies, welcomed their critical and enquiring spirit: despite the gradual tightening in control between 1979 and 1983, there was still room for considerable discretion in patronage. In China, where social control is chiefly exercised through the workplace, assignment to jobs in literary or cultural organizations was one of the major ways in which the new poets were drawn into the literary world, influencing it and being influenced by it in turn.

After the initial enthusiasm for denouncing the 'gang of four', the official literary magazines gave prominence to writers who supported the Party's reformist aims of the late 1970s. Reformist poets included Ai Qing (b. 1910), newly rehabilitated in 1979 and at first eloquent on the subject of honesty and integrity; Huang Yongyu (b. 1924), a painter who found satirical verse an outlet for his indignation at the continuing conservatism of the restored authorities; Ye Wenfu (b. 1945), whose outraged exposure of military privilege in 'General, You Can't Do This' made him one of the most famous protesters of the period, and Luo Gengye (b. 1951), who expressed his frustration in the elaborately Whitmanesque 'Discontent'. With their experience as collaborators, witnesses and victims in the past decades, the reformist poets did not question Party control over culture, only rejecting excessive control or abuse of power. Believing that political stability was the basic need for post-Mao China and for themselves in the 1980s, they saw Deng's policies as the most promising force for reform within this framework. At the same time, encouraged by the demand for autonomy by the avant-garde, they sought the right to express their own opinions and perceptions in their professional activities, probing the limits of official control in their literary works.

The sudden attack on the literary world in the campaign against 'spiritual pollution' in 1983 had been heralded by warning signals that were taken seriously by the avant-garde, conscious that since 1979 they had been losing ground. 'Obscure poetry' was attacked in 1981 and 1982 by poets and critics including Ai Qing, Zang Kejia, Tian Jian and Li Ying; Yuan Kejia was one of the few who came out in support. To the reformists, however, worried about the possibility of a backlash, warnings from the top were as much comforting as threatening, especially when tempered with episodes such as the open-ended debate over modernism in 1981–2. The recruitment of writers into the Party also persuaded literary reformists that both elites still shared common goals.

In the autumn of 1983, however, when both the avant-garde and reformists came under attack from Party officials for spreading 'pollution', the reaction was swift. Ai Qing immediately sided with the establishment, joining in the denunciation of Bei Dao with the same kind of enthusiasm he had shown in denouncing Jiang Qing. The *Today* poets were one of the main targets of the campaign: their poetry was banned, their work privileges were withdrawn, some of their supporters in editorial or academic positions were demoted and some were suspended from duty.

After the recovery of 1984–5, the summer of 1986 represented a high point in literary experimentation and bureaucratic benevolence. The former underground poets had by now achieved respectability: their works were published, their material conditions greatly improved; they joined the professional associations and travelled abroad; they married, had children, and divorced. In their social activities they moved with a self-conscious weight, their original social and political engagement now augmented by the responsibility engendered by their domestic and foreign renown. Not surprisingly, this provoked accusations that they had become part of the establishment, but, strictly speaking, this was not true: the avant-garde did not in fact moderate their demands for autonomy and independence, and their poetry also moved on. Bei Dao discarded flowery language in a harsh world of mental hospitals and the decreptitude of old age, while Duo Duo dropped elaborate rhythms for blatantly disturbing imagery.

There were many new groups who complained about not getting published and who pressed their mimeographed, handbound publications into the hands of foreigners (without any apparent interference from police or other authorities) in all major cities throughout the country. The poetry circles of the 1970s had proliferated in the 1980s so that it was hardly possible to distinguish a common tendency except for the desire to outdo the *Today* poets as the avant-garde of the late 1980s. Above all, the new poets sought emancipation from the political engagement and moral seriousness of their predecessors, just as the latter had won emancipation from the political submissiveness and moral ambivalence of theirs.

Public attention was attracted to new trends in poetry by a 'Major Exhibition of Modernist Poems in China' in 1986. Styling them the 'third generation', one of their supporters, Cheng Weidong, published an article in *Wenhui Daily* in January 1987 called 'Goodbye, Shu Ting and Bei Dao'. In a telling comparison, Bei Dao's line, 'I want to go to the other side of the river' (a Buddhist nirvana? the West?), was matched by the assertion that for the 'third generation' there was no 'other side of the river'. The exhibition was sponsored by the *Shenzhen Youth Daily*, edited and supported by a group of former *Today* poets and critics from the north-east, including Xu Jingya (b. 1949), Cao Changqing (b. 1953) and Wang Xiaoni (b. 1955). One sub-group called themselves 'extremists'; another was the 'not-not' poets from Sichuan, who chose to escape from the high rhetoric and moral seriousness of 'obscure poetry' by adopting an attitude of amoral indifference expressed in an anti-heroic colloquial idiom about the vulgarity and trivia of everyday life, including dirt, vomit and excreta. Some 'third generation' poets condemned *Today*'s preoccupation with abstract and politicised concepts such as freedom and democracy, choosing instead to concern itself with the universe, lamenting humanity's alienation in existential anguish; the most articulate in this respect was a former student of philosophy at Sichuan University, Tang Yaping (b. 1964). Along with her fellow provincial, Zhai Yongming (b. 1952), Tang also demonstrates that sentimentality is no longer an automatic tag for poetry by women. The best-known of all was Hai Zi (b. 1964), whose suicide in March 1989 was regarded by his fellow poets as the ultimate expression of their shared nihilism.

November 1988 found the much-travelled *Today* poets back in Beijing to celebrate the tenth anniversary of the magazine's founding. Despite the immense changes in that decade, which saw rural incomes double, intellectuals saw their own status eroded by policies which favoured a combination of local entrepreneurship and central authoritarianism; in concentrating on rural economic reform, the Chinese rulers seemed deliberately to be ignoring demands for greater participation and influence in politics. When Fang Lizhi called for the release of Wei Jingsheng in January 1989, Bei Dao quickly followed up in February with a petition for his release signed in the course of one afternoon's rapid tour around Beijing by thirty-three members of the literary intelligentsia.

The student protest of the spring and its brutal suppression in the summer resembled in some ways the April Fifth demonstrations on a more massive scale. One difference was its lack of literary expression. A quotation from one of Bei Dao's poems was prominently displayed at the Square, and Chai Ling's statement of witness to the massacre also quoted from his poems; later, a pop song by Cui Jian became a kind of unofficial anthem. Great events do not necessarily call forth great literature, and literature about great events does not necessarily partake of greatness itself.

Several members of the *Today* group, including Bei Dao, were abroad again at the time of the massacre, and others joined them later that year and in 1990 (Mang Ke and Shu Ting were the only major *Today* poets to remain in China). Some of these poets were not so much exiles (they had not been expelled, and were welcome to return to stand trial) as expatriates. Many of them joined the pro-democracy organizations of Chinese abroad and contributed to their journals. To provide a forum for other exiled or expatriate writers and also for dissidents inside China, *Today* was re-established in Oslo early in 1990 under the editorship of Bei Dao and Chen Maiping; it moved to Stockholm with Chen Maiping in 1991. The new writing won sympathetic attention from Western readers, and poetry became at the end of the 1980s and beginning of the 1990s the main expression of China's dispossessed in the modern world.

Li Xueao (b. 1933) and Feng Jingyuan (b. 1941)

To appreciate the achievements of the Chinese poets of the last twenty years, it is helpful first to look at the kind of writing favoured by the official press at the beginning of this period. They are chosen for their typicality rather than for their merits, though both were singled out for particular praise at the time.

Li Xueao claims to have learned to read and write in a Children's Brigade of the Eighth Route Army in Hebei. At the age of fourteen he was taken on as a printer's apprentice in the Communist-controlled border region, followed the factory when it transferred to Beijing in 1949, and entered the Party the following year. He began writing in 1951, was appointed head of the factory's propaganda department in 1953, and in 1956 took part in a national young writers' workshop. While maintaining his status as a part-time writer, he produced several hundred poems over the next few years before being admitted to the Writers' Association in 1956. Appointment as a full-time writer in 1962 brought assignments to a commune, an army camp, the Vietnam front and a steel plant, celebrated in several volumes of poems published in the 1960s and 1970s. One of the most prolific writers of the Cultural Revolution, he was appointed to the editorial board of *Poetry* in 1975. He was still employed as a full-time writer in the early 1980s, but nothing is known of his present whereabouts.

Feng Jingyuan had the distinction of being the first poet to contribute an autobiographical sketch to the revived *Poetry* in 1976. Born in an industrial area north of Tianjin, he was first employed like his father in the local steelworks. He began writing poetry in the late 1950s, and by the time he joined the army around 1960, was ambitious enough to send them to the literary magazines for publication. Lack of success forced him to develop a more literary style, though he claims to have continued writing in simpler styles for his army comrades until demobilised in 1973. Recognition came with the Cultural Revolution, and a collection of his poems about steelworking was published in 1975. He continued to contribute to *Poetry* and *People's Literature* in 1976 and 1977, but has since disappeared from the literary scene.

Although both were much praised in the mid-1970s as proletarian poets of the new age, Li Xueao and Feng Jingyuan developed very different styles. Li employed a loose, colloquial line modelled on the folk ballads of north China, making use of traditional kinds of rhyme and metre; in the 1970s, he wrote mostly long narrative verse. Feng Jingyuan's poetry has a much denser texture, with elaborate verbal effects including repetition, parallelism and classical syntax, and an extensive, powerful vocabulary based on industrial technology. It is hard to say what the two poets made of their work: although it is obviously based on their own life experience, it remains impersonal, at the service of an orthodoxy dictated even if accepted. It is unlikely that it has anything but curiosity value now, and it probably never had a voluntary audience. The attempt to create worker poets in the 1950s, 1960s and 1970s was partly to break down the dominance of intellectuals in literary recruitment, production and distribution, but chiefly to consolidate factional political power through ideological controls.

Bei Dao (b. 1949)

By the time that the *Today* publications were closed down in 1980, Bei Dao was widely regarded by the cognoscenti as the leading non-official poet. Throughout the 1980s, he acted as a magnet for younger poets and readers, receiving immense quantities of mail, personal visits, and invitations to address student audiences. More than any other poet in this century except Mao Zedong himself, his work was learnt by heart and quoted by his contemporaries, and he came to stand as a symbol of a whole generation: the educated youth of the 1960s and 1970s who learnt through harsh experience to free themselves of the habits of orthodoxy that had bound their parents to state and Party policies. Mao Zedong had released them from formal schooling and encouraged them to rebel against authorities: they rebelled against his teachings.

Born in Beijing (Bei Dao is his pen-name, meaning 'north island'), Zhao Zhenkai had the best schooling that China could offer in the 1950s and early 1960s, and although his formal education ceased in 1966 in his first year at senior high school, he remains a typical intellectual in his habits and outlook (his description as a 'worker' on his first appearance in *Poetry* in 1979 is highly misleading). A Red Guard in the early days of the Cultural Revolution, instead of being sent to the countryside in 1969 he was assigned work in a construction company in the western suburbs of Beijing, as the eldest son and the main support of his family. He gained the privacy he needed for writing poetry in the photographic darkroom on site, and in 1972 he started also writing fiction.

Bei Dao's most famous poem is 'The Answer', written in response to the April Fifth demonstrations in which he was also a participant. The lines:

> I don't believe the sky is blue,
> I don't believe in the sound of thunder,
> I don't believe that dreams are false,
> I don't believe that death has no revenge

defy the absurd unreality of Party policies (including the tacked-on optimism of all literary works), the threats to those who refuse to submit, the denial of the individual's private world, and the brutality of the police state. The same defiance is expressed in 'Declaration':

> I will not kneel on the ground
> allowing the executioners to look tall
> the better to obstruct the wind of freedom

Before his name was ever mentioned openly in the press, Bei Dao became notorious for a 'poem' that was in fact only a stanza in the long poem, 'Notes from the City of the Sun'. The subtitle given to the verse was 'Living'; the verse itself consisted in Chinese of a single word: 'A net'. A creative misunderstanding read the line as a condemnation of the lack of freedom in Chinese life and the despair of those caught in its toils, while the authorities ridiculed the formal reductionism of such writing.

'Notes from the City of the Sun' consists of a series of very short stanzas, a set of reporter's notes on a visit to Utopia. The form was introduced by Mang Ke and was very popular among the underground poets. In Bei Dao's early work, it was used mostly for reflective poetry, but it is hard to draw a line between his public and his private world. The short poem 'Lost', for instance, reads like a search for the beloved, but as one critic pointed out, it can also be read as a quest whose object is enquiry itself. The word 'exploration' (the title of Wei Jingsheng's Democracy Wall journal) had become a slogan of the democratic movement.

Among Bei Dao's most popular works are his love poems, in which again he broke into forbidden ground, and poems celebrating friendship, like 'Head for Winter'. The latter was written for publication in *Today*, whose founding in late 1978 led Bei Dao to renewed productivity both in fiction and poetry. *Today* gained a national audience, and even the establishment started to take notice. 'The Answer' was reprinted from *Today* in *Poetry* in 1979, and in 1980 about a dozen of his poems were published in official magazines. He was also appointed to the first of his jobs in the official press.

As the reformist writers talked cheerfully of a new era in literature in the 1980s, Bei Dao noted the increasing pressures to conform in official policy and became more and more pessimistic. The attacks on him in the campaign against spiritual pollution targeted his nihilism, mostly quoting from his Cultural Revolution work, but his poems of the early 1980s were if anything darker in mood:

> *Freedom is nothing but the distance*
> *between the hunter and the hunted*

Nevertheless even Bei Dao was encouraged by the early end to the campaign and the promises of 1985 and 1986. He joined the Beijing Writers' Association, travelled abroad, published *Bei Dao's Collected Poems* in the official press, and took part in literary conferences. His sense of foreboding returned in 1987, and towards the end of 1988 he wrote the first version of a poem anticipating the violence of the coming year, 'The Bell'. In 'Requiem', however, written a few days after June Fourth, there is a note of hope: like other Chinese then abroad, he could only believe that the use of terror spelt the imminent end of the regime.

During the 1980s, Bei Dao's poems were translated into most European languages and Japanese, and he was frequently invited to poetry recitals and other literary gatherings throughout the world, where he has been regarded as a spokesman for his country. His editorship of the revived *Today* and his contributions to it have assured him a dominant position in contemporary Chinese literature, denied to him for so long in his homeland. His main collections in English translation are *The August Sleepwalker* (1988) and *Old Snow* (1991). After moving between Berlin, Oslo, Stockhom and Aarhus in the late 1980s and early 1990s, he took up residence in the United States. (*For Bei Dao's fiction, see section under Zhao Zhenkai in Chapter 12.*)

Shu Ting (b. 1952)

A poem by Shu Ting with the enigmatic title 'This Too Is All', published in *Poetry* in 1979, was used to attack Bei Dao in 1981 and 1982 by critics of 'obscure poetry'. Written in response to Bei Dao's 'All' (which had still not appeared in the official press), it seemed to offer a contemporary answer to Bei Dao's nihilism. Where Bei Dao wrote:

> All is fate
> All is cloud
> All is a beginning without end
> All is a search that dies at birth
> All joy lacks smiles
> All sorrow lacks tears
> All language is a repetition
> All contact a first encounter ...

Shu Ting replied:

> Not all trees
>
> are broken by the storm;

Not all seeds

> *are left rootless in the soil;*

Not all feelings

> *dry in the deserts of the heart;*

Not all dreams

> *let their wings be clipped;*

No, not all
is as you say....

Shu Ting's poem was also published in *Today*, and she was one of the first provincial writers to become identified with the group. But the gentler, more sentimental tone of her poetry made it from the beginning more acceptable both to the authorities and also to many younger readers who were baffled or alienated by Bei Dao's bitter irony. Her 1979 patriotic poem 'My Homeland, My Dear Homeland' won a national prize for poetry, and her love poetry also won her a devoted audience. Born in the former foreign concession of Gulangsu, a tiny island opposite Xiamen (formerly known in English as Amoy), Shu Ting (pen-name for Gong Peiyu) was brought up among books before being sent to the Fujian countryside during the Cultural Revolution. Later she worked in a light-bulb factory in Xiamen, where she wrote poetry under the wing of an older poet, Cai Qijiao (attacked in the 1950s as a Rightist). Her work was widely publicised in the debates on 'obscure poetry' in the early 1980s, and she was the first of the group to join the Writers' Association. During the mid-1980s she made several trips abroad, and distance from the capital undoubtedly helped her survive the upheavals of the 1980s.

Gu Cheng (1956–93)

In the debates on 'obscure poetry' in 1981 and 1982, where direct reference to Bei Dao by name was still forbidden, Gu Cheng featured as the most controversial of the new poets. The son of a high-ranking army poet, Gu Gong (b. 1927), Gu Cheng had enjoyed a sheltered life in Beijing but encountered a more brutal world with the onset of the Cultural Revolution, when his family was sent to the countryside. He returned to Beijing in 1974, where he was assigned work in a carpentry shop, and took part in the 1976 April Fifth Movement. Attracted to the Democracy Wall, he became a contributor to *Today* in early 1980. Like Shu Ting, who became a close friend and colleague, he made an easy transition to official publication. 'Farewell' (1981) is a typical example of his early verse:

> *Today*
> *you and I*
> *will step over the ancient threshhold*
> *don't wish me well*
> *don't say goodbye*
> *they're like a performance*
> *silence is best*
> *in reserve there's no deception*
> *leave thoughts of the past to the future*
> *like leaving dreams to the night*
> *tears to the sea*
> *wind to the sails on the night sea*

Gu Cheng was admitted to the Beijing branch of the Writers' Association in 1982 but came under attack the following year for lines like:

> *Grey the sky*
> *grey the road*
> *grey the tower*
> *grey the rain*
>
> *through deathly grey*
> *two children walk*
> *one bright red*
> *one light green*

('Impressions', 1980). The youngest of the original *Today* poets, he retained a note of innocence or naivety in his verse throughout the 1980s, lasping into a more eccentric idiom in the early 1990s. Gu Cheng's other characteristics include a vivid imagination and fondness for experimentation. The simple vocabulary and structure of his poems make them very suitable for recitals, at which he became an accomplished performer at home and abroad. Gu Cheng left China with his wife, Xie Ye, also a poet, in 1987. After a series of incidents in several countries involving domestic violence, he killed his wife and then committed suicide in New Zealand. His main collection in English translation is *Selected Poems* (1990).

Yang Lian (b. 1955)

As a poet, Yang Lian has always been preoccupied with Chinese history, searching through the past for China's former glory and a vision for the future. This tendency was fostered by an earlier *Today* poet, Jiang He, and Yang Lian's attraction to early Chinese mysticism is shared by Gu Cheng, but Yang Lian also shows a particular interest in the religions of China's ethnic minorities. His work contributed to the primitivist movement which swept through fiction, drama, film, painting and sculpture in the early 1980s. His own poetry is crammed with historical allusion and a grandiloquent vocabulary, and consists typically of long poems arranged in cycles to give form to his panoramic visions.

Yang Lian was born in Switzerland, where his parents worked at the Chinese Embassy, and grew up in Beijing. A contributor to *Today* since October 1979 (initially under the pen-name Fei Sha), he also became notorious as a literary 'hooligan', enjoying a flamboyant way of life under the protection of his parents' connections. At the same time he was also engaged in extensive study, widening the philosophical basis of his poetry. His celebration of the role of poet as shaman in the long poem 'Norlang' (1984) came under attack, and his work, previously praised as 'heroic', was described as 'unhealthy' in 1983. His reputation grew in the mid-1980s, attracting followers such as the Sichuan poet Ouyang Jianghe (b. 1955). Yang Lian's first visit to the West came in 1986, and he has lived abroad since 1988. His collections in English translation include *Masks and Crocodiles* (1990) and *The Dead in Exile* (1991).

Duo Duo (b. 1951)

Duo Duo's poetry was relatively late in achieving domestic and foreign recognition. Much of the early work is difficult to read (and more difficult to translate); some of it is bizarre; and some of it appears to confront the reader with unconcealed hostility. Its tensions reflect the author's own life, which has been marked with private tragedies. Born in Beijing, Li Shizheng (his real name) was an early member of Mang Ke's poetry circle but did not contribute to *Today* till 1980, under the pen-names Bai Ri and Bai Ye. He tried his hand at a number of occupations – opera singer, painter – before obtaining an editorial post on the newspaper *Agricultural Daily* in 1980. A steady stream of verse published in the official press brought invitations to read his poetry, and he developed a cool, offbeat style as an effective counter to the melodramatic style favoured at official readings. Invited to Britain in 1989, he managed to get on one of the last flights out of Beijing on the day after the massacre, and has lived abroad ever since. His main collection of poetry in English translation is *Looking Out from Death* (1989).

The literary revolution was a good time for poetry: it was the centre of attention in the new literary movement, and most of the celebrated writers and scholars of the twentieth century had a volume or two to their credit. In the 1950s and 1960s, one poet's work came to dominate, chiefly because of his political power but not without its own literary merit. It also achieved what might in 1921 or 1922 have seemed impossible: identification of the classical tradition as a central element in contemporary history. Again, but briefly, in 1976, in 1978–83 and in 1989, poetry was the medium that best voiced the crucial concerns of Chinese political and literary intellectuals, and it is no accident that China's main contender for the Nobel Prize in Literature since the mid-1980s has been a poet. As an everyday part of social life, however, poetry since the 1920s has increasingly given way to fiction and even (in the 1960s) to drama.

As we draw closer to our own time, it becomes harder to distinguish which of the trends, the works and the writers will survive their immediate present. Academic critics have their own criteria for appraising works, and what appeals to them does not necessarily find favour with readers – or vice versa. The interference of the Chinese authorities, who regard modern Chinese literature as their own property, also makes it difficult for outsiders to distinguish between what is central and what is marginal. The literature of dissent can be seen as more central than the official product, and yet the tiny percentage of its readership suggests that the peasantry, distant from the urban centres and still voiceless to them – may yet produce the new poetry for the next century. For the moment, the modernising, Westernising tendency, dating from the May Fourth Movement and most recently represented by 'obscure poery' and its successors, again seems irresistible; it would be foolish to assume that it will stay that way.

14

CONCLUSION

The young band of writers and reformers who set out early this century to create a new literature in China had several goals: it should be written in a new language, corresponding to standard (northern) spoken Chinese; it should disregard the former hierarchy of genres; it should reach a national audience; it should express the subjectivity of autonomous individuals; it should describe contemporary life and address contemporary social problems; and it should act as the moral conscience of a modern nation. Later in the century, writers set or accepted other goals: literature should serve the masses (at least those who were literate); it should serve political ends, supporting or opposing those in power; it should give vent to private obsessions or fantasies; it should perform the paradox of affirming nihilism; it should represent Chinese voices in the world. Less frequently acknowledged, literature was also created for the purpose of providing entertainment, titillation or aesthetic pleasure, and other uses, even less explicit: to further personal ambitions, whether academic or political, and to use as a weapon to destroy opponents. Perhaps none of these goals, strictly speaking, were entirely new, but literature in this century can nevertheless be credited with success in having created a distinctively new corpus of poetry, fiction and drama.

The achievements of twentieth-century Chinese literature are also related to its changing patterns of production, distribution and consumption. Attempts to control the passage of literary works between their authors and their readers reached their apogee in the 1960s but were almost immediately subverted and eventually abandoned. The extension of education from the 1910s on to reach all social levels and all parts of the country broadened the range of both authorship and readership, so that by the end of the 1980s neither was restricted to a tiny fraction of the population located mainly in the cities. Literary intellectuals at times viewed this process with alarm.

Chinese literature in this century (defining literature as artistic works in the form of written documents) has, like its predecessor, been dominated by writers with a university education or its equivalent. Many of the prominent writers had a family background over several generations among the former educated elite, the scholar-officials of imperial China. Except in brief periods, writers who lacked this background still acquired the education and occupations that fitted into the pattern established by the literary intellectuals.

One reason for this domination lies in the difficulty of mastering the compositional style of modern written Chinese. While by no means as complex as classical literary Chinese, it is still influenced by the nature of the Chinese script as an ideographic medium. Perceiving themselves as a privileged social group, intellectuals sought to protect the ranks of educators, writers, readers and literary publishers against political and commercial interests which threatened to displace them. Continually obliged to give way to the superior force of these interests, intellectuals nevertheless generally retained their exclusivist values.

In the context of China's internal and external weakness in the twentieth century, the scholar-official background of the writers led to an obsession with political and social reform in China, with particular attention to the role and status of intellectuals in a modernising society. The predominant tone is one of high moral concern: writing which is playful, humorous, imaginative, fanciful, or frankly fantastic can be found but is not common.

It is sometimes claimed that literature – especially poetry – has been marginalised in contemporary China. This is to define 'literature' by implicit reference to special interests rather than as a value-free term. Classical poetry was certainly at the core of classical literature in imperial China, but it was only ever practised and read by a tiny proportion of the population of the country; folk poetry was practised and heard by a larger number of people, including the educated elite, and can be called central to folk literature, although hardly (except perhaps in such special cases as courting poetry) to people's lives. In the same way, new poetry was at the core of the new literature, in the eyes of intellectuals as diverse as Hu Shi and Jiang Qing, as the voice of the new elites, and was just as thoroughly ignored by the majority of uneducated or poorly educated masses. As the numbers of educated people rose, giving rise to different strata within the elite, poetry became overshadowed by fiction as the preferred reading of the modern educated man and woman.

This remains broadly true throughout the whole of the twentieth century, with only very few isolated examples where poetry broke through the usual small circles of poetry readers to become a form of communication reaching several or even all strata of readers (for example, Mao Zedong's poetry during the Cultural Revolution, the Tiananmen poems of 1976, or Bei Dao's poems in 1978 and 1989). It makes more sense to talk of the marginalisation of the poet, seen as a paradigm of the marginalisation of humanistically educated men in the twentieth century. It is striking, however, how readily young poets attained high position throughout the twentieth century, frequently abandoning poetry once their professional status was assured. The Cultural Revolution was almost the only major challenge to privilege and power as a natural consequence of poetry-writing by educated men until the commercialism of the 1990s, but neither in the 1940s nor in the 1960s were villagers in the countryside the actual readers of 'mass literature': oral literature and other kinds of performing arts, joined eventually by feature films, still dominate cultural life in rural China.

Statements on readership, however, have to remain speculative since it is difficult to discuss twentieth-century Chinese readership other than conceptually or anecdotally, since statistically rigorous surveys of reader preferences are almost non-existent. Print-runs express the optimism of the literary groups that mainly sponsored publication of May Fourth literature in the 1920s, but how can we know reliably that Mao Dun was more (or less) widely read than Zhang Henshui (or read by whom)? Print-runs from the 1950s are even less informative about readers, although they tell a great deal about the pecking order within the Writers' Association. Were the poems by army or factory poets such as Li Ying or Feng Jingyuan read by their fellow soldiers or workers in the 1970s, and did those readers number more or fewer than the young men and women who scanned the literary magazines for new poems by Gu Cheng and Shu Ting a decade later? Who read Wang Anyi's stories of adultery among the literati: secondary school girls or middle-aged men, or both? In theatres, at least, the audience could stand up and be counted, and subtle distinctions of dress and deportment visually differentiated audiences for traditional local opera from those for spoken plays. In the decade from 1972 to 1982, however, theatres mainly subsisted on block bookings from organisations that rarely bothered to tell the ticket holders what was being performed.

The most attentive readers of twentieth-century literature have been the authors themselves and their fellow writers, who also form the cultural bureaucracy, either state or self-appointed, that chooses what is to be published and in what quantities. Literary critics and academics also play a major role as influential readers, but unlike their counterparts in Western countries, not only fame and power are at stake but even careers or lives if they make a wrong choice. Writers throughout this century have frequently pitched their work at these readers, whether consciously or not. A third influential group of readers have been secondary school and university students, along with recent graduates employed in educational or cultural organisations. It is partly their youth that has made them loyal readers: anecdotal evidence testifies to the lasting impact on young readers of what is now dismissed as hack work by state-subsidised orthodox writers of the 1950s like Du Pengcheng. To draw a comparison to Taiwan and Hong Kong fiction, which began to penetrate the mainland in the 1980s, the natural parallels to Qu Bo and Yang Mo are not Taiwan modernists like Bai Xianyong and Chen Ruoxi, but the Hong Kong and Taiwan popular writers like Jin Yong and Qiong Yao. There were brief episodes when distinctions between popular and serious literature seemed to be eclipsed – Ba Jin and Mao Zedong crossed boundaries, and in different ways so did Zhao Shuli and Shu Ting – but such cases are rare.

During the first and last periods into which this book is divided, we know relatively more about readers since what testimony there exists is less likely to suffer from positive or negative censorship. From accounts by writers of their own reactions as readers and of readers' direct responses to them as writers, it seems that large numbers of readers in the 1920s and 1930s, coming as they did from the same kind of background as the writers, shared their preoccupation with China and its intellectuals. To a large extent they also accepted without much conscious unease the assumptions that literature was fundamentally autobiographical (and that narrative expressed the author's own views), that it should be invested with emotions such as sincerity and express lofty moral ideas, that content and form were separate entities and that style was an affectation standing sometimes perversely between author and reader. Although the audience for the literature of this period may still have been small compared to the total population, or even compared to the literate population, it was nevertheless large and enthusiastic enough to sustain the writers' morale.

Like the writers in their role as readers, however, readers of this period also read for entertainment. Entertainment literature persisted throughout the century (although prohibited at times for political reasons) but was generally ignored by literary critics and scholars. While freely acknowledging the crossovers between folk, popular and classical literature in the past, Chinese critics and scholars were reluctant to pay attention to frankly commercial or entertainment literature of the present century, and were generally supported in this fastidiousness by political interests.

The audience for literature in the 1980s was different in many ways. It was larger, covered more varied social groups and was accessible to people with a wider range of educational levels. With some exceptions, there was little gender distinction among contemporary readers in their choice of literary reading. Younger readers still outnumbered the middle-aged and the elderly for contemporary literature, while older readers tended to prefer martial arts fiction or traditional novels and poetry.

Young readers still formed an enthusiastic audience: many readers were aspiring authors, writing to their favourite authors, asking for advice and help in publication. In the early 1980s, Bei Dao was deluged with manuscripts and Liu Xinwu even published a volume of letters from readers. In the mid-1980s, as writers mocked the establishment as much by their flamboyant behaviour as their literary work, writers like Liu Suola took the place of rock stars as popular celebrities.

Readers also modelled their behaviour and expectations on characters in fiction and drama, and took cues from poetry on identifying their moods and emotions. Although the 'model' functions of literature were now discredited in theory, Chinese youth still learnt what they should feel by reading poetry, how they should conduct themselves by watching drama, and how they should think by reading fiction. When they had the choice, they overwhelmingly preferred popular fiction, especially martial arts fiction and romances; other types of genre fiction, such as detective stories, thrillers and science fiction, had yet to reach the same mass readership. Up until recently, popular fiction came mainly from Hong Kong and Taiwan, but from the mid-1980s it was being produced inside China, often by authors previously considered literary. This is perhaps the most striking testimony to the changing relationship between writers and readers this century.

For the first half of the century, socially conscious writers wrote about people excluded by lack of education from their readership. The growth of literacy in the 1940s and 1950s made this phenomenon increasingly obsolete, and Chinese writers became aware that the people they were writing about were able now to read what was written about them. A story published in the early 1950s illustrates this twist in events. A young man writes to a well-known author through a newspaper column, asking for advice on how to be a writer, only to find out that she is none other than the beautiful bus-conductor who punches his ticket every morning (bus conductors and mail deliverers are the proletarian equivalent in the 1950s of the rickshaw-pullers of the 1920s and 1930s). This new situation presumably influenced the way in which the non-elites are portrayed, whether they are actual readers or merely the theoretical audience.

For their part, readers' expectations from the 1950s on may have been raised by Mao's emphasis in the Yan'an 'Talks' on the audience as the objective of literature and the arts. Young people educated on the 'Talks' during the Cultural Revolution saw it as natural that writers should respond to readers' requests, and in the 1980s, readers in their thousands also wrote to writers like Liu Binyan and Jiang Zilong urging them to raise specific topics or to describe certain types of characters. A new bond between readers and writers was being created.

For the first time in history, Chinese writers are also addressing non-Chinese readers. Especially since the open-door policy in 1978, the publication abroad (usually in translation) of Chinese works has been negotiated by private arrangements between the authors and Western translators, scholars and publishers. Official publishers such as the Foreign Languages Press took a few years longer to move from a producer-dominated list (chiefly determined

by the Writers' Association) to consumer-based selection, sometimes in direct agreement with foreign publishers. As a result,
some writers became notorious at home for writing with a speculative eye on the foreign market. All the stranger that even contemporary Chinese literature has not been very successful in attracting
Western readers.

Classical Chinese poetry and radical Chinese politics have
produced devoted followers this century; contemporary writers
from India, Japan and South America have overcome the barriers
of translations into English, French and German and of Western
xenophobia. The uncoordinated efforts of dozens of sinologists,
supported by the Foreign Languages Press since the 1950s, have
provided the material base for a foreign audience for modern
Chinese literature. But despite the crazes for things oriental – or
even specifically Chinese – that have taken place in Western
countries at various times this century, the only Chinese writer
whose works are well-known outside a small group of academics
and critics is Mao Zedong. Some of the reasons for this are trivial
and contingent; some are related to fundamental problems in the
literature itself.

To many Western readers (and to some Chinese readers as
well), modern Chinese writing suffers from its derivative Westernisation. Because of the time-lag common in cross-cultural contacts, by the time the Chinese products of Western influence
reached the West in the form of translations, they already seemed
dated. Introduced more or less simultaneously to nineteenth-century Western realism and romanticism leavened with relics of an
earlier age, Chinese writers throughout most of this century
wavered uncomfortably between the imitation of reality and the
imitation of an ideal. Most of the work described in these pages
falls outside the late-nineteenth- and twentieth-century movements
in Western literature and art (known collectively as modernism)
which have shaped Western tastes in our time.

Even when literary trends from both areas happened to correspond, however, Chinese works left no lasting impact on Western
readers. During the 1930s, for instance, Chinese writers became
confidently abreast of contemporary trends in Europe, Australia
and the United States. At that time, Western writing was going
through a strongly committed, realist, participatory, historically
minded phase, away from individual sensibility and towards col-

lective experience. Nevertheless, even the best writers of the time like Lu Xun and Wen Yiduo failed to gain a lasting audience. As the pendulum swung again back to modernism, the Chinese were cut off from Western contacts and only made contact again when modernism was itself giving way to post-modernism. During the 1970s, a form of cultural modernism took root and spread to such a degree that more conventional works were also affected by it; by the end of the 1980s, as contacts between China and the outside world developed at a breathtaking pace, there appeared its self-reflexive, self-conscious, post-modernist successor. Except through adaptation in film, this literature has yet to find a firm hold among foreign readers, but translations, poetry readings, and generous newspaper coverage of representative authors like Liu Suola and Zhang Xianliang have now taken their work beyond specialist audiences. Some may still regret that Chinese writers feel bound to adopt Western models at all; that they treat Western literature as a model to be copied rather than as a source of creative inspiration; that in many cases their works are so preoccupied with the problems of Chinese intellectuals that they lack relevance outside China; and finally, that even now some are so concerned with writing as a means for other purposes that they ignore its roles as entertainment and mythopeia.

The reaction of Western readers to Chinese literature is not simply a matter of concern to a few contemporary Chinese writers who hope to make a reputation abroad. The Chinese authorities tend to blame a lingering colonialist mentality for such things as the failure of the Swedish Academy to award a Nobel Prize to China, and to accuse Western transmitters of modern Chinese literature to select what shows China in a poor light. Chinese writers argue among themselves about the difference between internationalism (good) and cosmopolitanism (bad), patriotism (good) and nationalism (bad), tradition (good and bad) and modernity (bad and good). Audiences everywhere, in China and abroad, can take comfort in these debates, and in the flourishing literature to which they form a backdrop. Chinese readers themselves are now part of the modern world, and the literature they have supported with sometimes fretful devotion is also now part of world literature.

FURTHER READING

General: Anthologies and Critical Studies

Barlow, Tani E. (ed.), *Gender Politics in Modern China: Writing and Feminism* (Durham, NC: Duke University Press, 1993).

Benton, Gregor (ed.), *Wild Lilies, Poisonous Weeds: Dissident Voices from People's China* (London: Pluto Press, 1982).

China: The Revolution Is Dead, Long Live the Revolution, comp. and ed. by The 70s, with introduction by Kan San (Montreal: Black Rose Books, 1977).

Chow, Rey, *Women and Chinese Modernity: The Politics of Reading between West and East*, (Minneapolis: University of Minnesota Press, 1991).

Chung, Hilary (ed.), *In the Party Spirit: Socialist Realism and Literary Practice in the Soviet Union, East Germany and China* (Amsterdam: Rodopi, 1996).

Davis, A.R. *Search for Indentity: Modern Literature and the Creative Arts in Asia.* (Sydney: Angus and Robertson, 1974).

Denton, Kirk A. (ed.), *Modern Chinese Literary Thought: Writings on Literature, 1893–1945* (Stanford University Press, 1996).

Dillard, Annie, *Encounters with Chinese Writers* (Middletown, CT: Wesleyan University Press, 1984).

Duke, Michael S., *Blooming and Contending: Chinese Literature in the Post-Mao Era.* (Bloomington, IN: Indiana University Press, 1985).

——(ed.), *Modern Chinese Women Writers: Critical Appraisals* (Armonk, NY: M.E. Sharpe, 1989).

Eoyang, Eugene, *The Transparent Eye: Reflections on Translation, Chinese Literature, and Comparative Poetics* (Honolulu: University of Hawaii Press, 1992).

Fokkema, D.W., *Literary Doctrine in China and Soviet Influence, 1956–1960* (The Hague: Mouton, 1965).

Galik, Marian, *Milestones in Sino-Western Literary Confrontation (1898–1979)* (Wiesbaden: Harrassowitz, 1986).

—— (ed.), *Interliterary and Intraliterary Aspects of the May Fourth Movement 1919 in China* (Bratislava: Veda, 1990).

Goldblatt, Howard (ed.), *Chinese Literature for the 1980s: The Fourth Congress of Writers and Artists* (Armonk, NY: M.E. Sharpe, 1982).

—— (ed.), *Worlds Apart: Recent Chinese Writing and Its Audiences* (Armonk, NY: M.E. Sharpe, 1990).

Goldman, Merle, *Literary Dissent in Communist China* (Cambridge, MA: Harvard University Press, 1967).

—— (ed.), *Modern Chinese Literature in the May Fourth Era* (Cambridge, MA: Harvard University Press, 1977).

——, **Timothy Cheek and Carol Lee Hamrin** (eds), *China's Intellectuals and the State: In Search of a New Relationship* (Cambridge, MA: Harvard University Press, 1987).

Gunn, Edward M., *Unwelcome Muse: Chinese Literature in Shanghai and Peking, 1937–1945* (New York: Columbia University Press,1980).

Hamrin, Carol Lee, and Timothy Cheek (eds), *China's Establishment Intellectuals* (Armonk, NY: M.E. Sharpe, 1986).

Hegel, Robert E., and Richard C. Hessney (eds), *Expressions of Self in Chinese Literature* (New York: Columbia University Press, 1985).

Holm, David, *Art and Ideology in Revolutionary China* (Oxford: Clarendon, 1991).

Hsia, Tsi-An, *The Gate of Darkness: Studies on the Leftist Literary Movement in China* (Seattle, WA: University of Washington Press, 1968).

Hsu, Immanuel, *The Rise of Modern China* (Hong Kong: Oxford University Press, 1983).

Hsu Kai-yu (ed.), *Literature of the People's Republic of China* (Bloomington, IN: Indiana University Press, 1980).

Kao Hsin-sheng (ed.), *Nativism Overseas: Contemporary Chinese Women Writers* (New York: State University of New York Press, 1993).

Kingsbury, Diana B. (tr.), *I Wish I Were a Wolf: The New Voice in Chinese Women's Literature* (Beijing: New World Press, 1994).

Kinkley, Jeffrey C. (ed.), *After Mao: Chinese Literature and Society, 1978–1981* (Cambridge, MA: Harvard University Press, 1985).

Kubin, Wolfgang, and Rudolf Wagner (eds), *Essays in Modern Chinese Literature and Literary Criticism* (Bochum: Broekmeyer, 1982).

Larson, Wendy, *Literary Authority and the Modern Chinese Writer: Ambivalence and Autobiography* (Durham, NC: Duke University Press, 1991).

—— **and Anne Wedell-Wedellsborg** (eds), *Inside Out: Modernism and Postmodernism in Chinese Literary Culture* (Aarhus University Press, 1993).

Lau, Joseph S. M., and Howard Goldblatt (eds). *The Columbia Anthology of Modern Chinese Literature* (New York: Columbia University Press, 1995).

Lee, Gregory, *Troubadours, Trumpeters, Troubled Makers: Lyricism, Nationalism and Hybridity in China and its Others* (London: Hurst, 1996).

Lee, Leo Ou-fan, *The Romantic Generation of Modern Chinese Writers* (Cambridge, MA: Harvard University Press, 1973).

Leung Laifong, *Morning Sun: Interviews with Chinese Writers of the Lost Generation* (Armonk, NY: M.E. Sharpe, 1994).

Link, Perry (ed.), *Stubborn Weeds: Popular and Controversial Chinese Literature after the Cultural Revolution* (Bloomington, IN: Indiana University Press, 1983).

——, **Richard Madsen and Paul C. Pickowicz** (eds), *Unofficial China: Popular Culture and Thought in the People's Republic* (Boulder, CO: Westview Press, 1989).

Liu Kang and Xiaobing Tang (eds), *Politics, Ideology and Literary Discourse in Modern China: Theoretical Interventions and Cultural Critique* (Durham, NC: Duke University Press, 1993).

Lu Tonglin (ed.), *Gender and Sexuality in Twentieth-century Chinese Literature and Society* (Albany, NY: State University of New York Press, 1993).

Lynn, Richard John, *Guide to Chinese Poetry and Drama*, 2nd edn. (Boston, MA: G. K. Hall, 1984).

McDougall, Bonnie S., *The Introduction of Western Literary Theories into China, 1991–1925* (Tokyo: Centre for East Asian Cultural Studies, 1971).

——, *Mao Zedong's 'Talks at the Yan'an Conference on Literature and Art': A Translation of the 1943 Text with Commentary* (Ann Arbor, MI: University of Michigan Center for Chinese Studies, 1980).

——(ed.), *Popular Chinese Literature and Performing Arts in the People's Republic Of China* (Berkeley, CA: University of California Press, 1984).

MacFarquhar, Roderick, *The Hundred Flowers Campaign and the Chinese Intellectual* (New York: Praeger, 1960).

Malmquist, G. (ed.), *Modern Chinese Literature and its Social Context* (Stockholm: Nobel Symposium 32, 1977).

Martin, Helmut, and Jeffrey Kinkley (eds), *Modern Chinese Writers: Self-Portrayals* (Armonk, NY: M. E. Sharpe, 1992).

Moody, Peter R., *Opposition and Dissent in Contemporary China* (Stanford: Hoover Institution Press, 1977).

Nieh Hualing (ed. and co-tr.), *Literature of the Hundred Flowers*, 2 vols (New York: Columbia University Press, 1981).

Pollard, David E., *A Chinese Look at Literature: The Literary Values of Chou Tso-jen in Relation to the Tradition* (London: Hurst, 1973).

Prusek, Jaroslav (ed.), *Studies in Modern Chinese Literature* (Berlin: Akademie-Verlag, 1964).

Scott, A. C., *Literature and Arts in Twentieth-Century China* (London: Geo. Allen and Unwin, 1963).

Soong, Stephen C., and J. Minford (eds), *Trees on the Mountain: An Anthology of New Chinese Writing* (Hong Kong: Chinese University Press, 1984).

Spence, Jonathan, *The Gate of Heavenly Peace* (New York: Viking Press, 1981).

Tang Tao (ed.), *History of Modern Chinese Literature* (Beijing: Foreign Languages Press, 1993).

Wagner, Rudolph, *Inside a Service Trade: Studies in Contemporary Chinese Prose* (Cambridge, MA: Harvard University Council on East Asian Studies, 1992).

Wang, David Der-wei (ed.), *Running Wild: New Chinese Writers* (New York: Columbia University Press, 1994).

Wang, Mason Y.H. (ed.), *Perspectives in Contemporary Chinese Literature* (Michigan: Green River Press, 1983).

Whitfield, Susan (ed.), *After the Event: Human Rights and Their Future in China* (London: Wellsweep Press, 1993).

Widmer, Ellen, and David Der-wei Wang (eds), *From May Fourth to June Fourth* (Cambridge, MA: Harvard University Press, 1993).

Yang Li *et al.* (eds), *A Biographical Dictionary of Modern Chinese Writers* (Beijing: New World Press, 1994).

Poetry: Anthologies and Studies of Multiple Poets

Barnstone, Tony (ed.), *Out of the Howling Storm: The New Chinese Poetry* (Hanover, NH: University Press of New England, 1993).

Finkel, Donald (tr.), *A Splintered Mirror: Chinese Poetry from the Democracy Movement*, additional trans. Carolyn Kizer (San Francisco, CA: North Point Press, 1991).

Hockx, Michel, *A Snowy Morning: Eight Chinese Poets on the Road to Modernity* (Leiden: Research School CNWS, 1994).

Hsu Kai-yu (tr. & ed.), *Twentieth Century Chinese Poetry: An Anthology* (Ithaca, NY: Cornell University Press, 1970).

Ing, Nancy (tr. & ed.), *New Voices: Stories and Poems by Young Chinese Writers* (San Francisco, CA: Chinese Materials Center, 1980).

―――― (ed. & tr.), *Summer Glory: A Collection of Contemporary Chinese Poetry* (San Francisco, CA: Chinese Materials Center, 1982).

Lin, Julia C., *Modern Chinese Poetry: An Introduction* (Seattle, WA: University of Washington Press, 1972).

――――, *Essays on Contemporary Chinese Poetry* (Athens, OH: Ohio University Press, 1985).

――――, *Women of the Red Plain: An Anthology of Contemporary Women's Poetry* (London: Penguin, 1992).

Liu, James, *The Interlingual Critic: Interpreting Chinese Poetry* (Bloomington IN: Indiana University Press, 1982).

Lyrics from Shelters: Modern Chinese Poetry, 1930–1950 (New York: Garland, 1992).

Morin, Edward (ed.), *The Red Azalea: Chinese Poetry since the Cultural Revolution,* trans. Fang Dai, Dennis Ding and Edward Morin, with introduction by Leo Lee (Honolulu: University of Hawaii Press, 1990).

Sunflower Splendor: Three Thousand Years of Chinese Poetry (Bloomington, IN: Indiana University Press, 1990).

Tang Chao and Lee Robinson (ed. & tr.), *New Tide: Contemporary Chinese Poetry* (Toronto: Mangajin Books, 1992).

Woo, Catherine, *Crystal: Spectrums of Chinese Culture through Poetry* (New York: P. Lang, 1995).

Xiao Lan (ed. & tr.), *The Tiananmen Poems* (Beijing: Foreign Languages Press, 1979).

Yeh, Michelle, *Modern Chinese Poetry: Theory and Practice since 1917* (New Haven: Yale University Press, 1991).

—— (ed. & tr.), *Anthology of Modern Chinese Poetry* (New Haven, CT: Yale University Press, 1992).

Yu, Pauline, *The Reading of Imagery in the Chinese Poetic Tradition* (Princeton University Press, 1987).

Poetry: Collections and Studies of Individual Poets

Ai Qing, *Black Eel*, trans. Yang Xianyi and Robert C. Friend (Beijing: Chinese Literature, 1982).

Almberg, Shiu Pang, *The Poetry of Chen Jingrong: A Modern Chinese Woman Poet* (University of Stockholm, 1988).

Bei Dao, *The August Sleepwalker*, trans. Bonnie S. McDougall (London: Anvil Press, 1988).

——, *Old Snow: Poems*, trans. Bonnie S. McDougall and Chen Maiping (New York: New Directions Books, 1991).

——, *Forms of distance*, trans. David Hinton (New York: New Directions Books, 1994).

Duo Duo, *Looking Out from Death: From the Cultural Revolution to Tiananmen Square*, trans. by Gregory Lee and John Cayley (London: Bloomsbury, 1989).

——, *Statements: The New Chinese Poetry of Duo Duo*, trans. by Gregory Lee and John Cayley (London: Wellsweep Press, 1989).

Eoyang, Eugene (ed.), *Selected Poems of Ai Qing* (Bloomington, IN: Indiana University Press, 1982).

Gu Cheng (Ku Ch'eng), *Selected Poems*, ed. Sean Golden and Chu Chiyu (Hong Kong: Renditions Paperbacks, 1990).

Haft, Lloyd, *Pien Chih-lin: A Study in Modern Chinese Poetry* (Dordrecht: Foris Publications, 1983).

He Qifang (Ho Ch'i-fang), *Paths in Dreams: Selected Prose and Poetry of Ho Ch'i-fang*, trans. Bonnie S. McDougall (St Lucia: University of Queensland Press, 1976).

Hsu Kai-yu, *Wen I-to* (Boston: Twayne, 1980).

Kowallis, Jon, *The Lyrical Lu Xun: A Study of His Classical-style Verse* (Honolulu: University of Hawaii Press, 1995).

Lee, Gregory, *Dai Wangshu: The Life and Poetry of a Chinese Modernist* (Hong Kong: Chinese University Press, 1989).

McDougall, Bonnie S. (tr.), *Notes from the City of the Sun: Poems by Bei Dao* (Ithaca, NY: Cornell University East Asia Papers, 1983).

Mao Zedong (Mao Tse-tung), *The Poetry of Mao Tse-tung*, trans. Hua-ling, Nieh Engle and Paul Engle (London: Wildwood House, 1973).

Roy, David Tod, *Kuo Mo-jo: The Early Years* (Cambridge, MA: Harvard University Press, 1971).

'The 70s', *see China: The Revolution is Dead....*

Shu Ting, *Selected Poems: An Authorized Collection*, trans. Eva Hung *et al.* (Hong Kong: Research Centre for Transation, Chinese University of Hong Kong, 1994).

——, *Mist of My Heart: Selected Poems of Shu Ting*, trans. Gordon Osing (Beijing: Chinese Literature, 1995).

Wen Yiduo (Wen I-to), *Red Candle: Selected Poems*, trans. T.T. Sanders (London: Cape, 1972).

Yang Lian, *The Dead in Exile*, trans. Mabel Lee (Canberra: Tiananmen Publications, 1990).

——, *Masks and Crocodiles: A Contemporary Chinese Poet and His Poetry*, trans. Mabel Lee (Broadway, NSW: Wild Peony, 1990).

——, *Non-person Singular: Selected Poems of Yang Lian*, trans. Brian Holton (London: Wellsweep Press, 1994).

Fiction: Anthologies and Studies of Multiple Authors

Anderson, Marston, *The Limits of Realism: Chinese Fiction in the Revolutionary Period* (Berkeley, CA: University of California Press, 1990).

Barmé, Geremie, and Lee, Bennett (eds), *The Wounded: New Stories of the Cultural Revolution* (Hong Kong: Joint Publishing, 1979).

Berninghausen, John, and Ted Huters, *Revolutionary Literature in China: An Anthology* (Armonk, NY: M.E. Sharpe, 1977).

Chinese Stories from the Fifties (Beijing: Chinese Literature, 1984).

Contemporary Chinese Short Stories (Beijing, Chinese Literature, 1983).

Duke, Michael S. (ed.), *Contemporary Chinese Literature: An Anthology of Post-Mao Fiction and Poetry* (Armonk, NY: M.E. Sharpe, 1985).

——(ed.), *Worlds of Modern Chinese Fiction: Short Stories and Novellas from the People's Republic, Taiwan and Hong Kong* (Armonk, NY: M.E. Sharpe, 1991).

Galik, Marian, *Mao Tun and Modern Chinese Literary Criticism* (Wiesbaden: Franz Steiner, 1969).

Goldblatt, Howard (ed.), *Chairman Mao Would Not Be Amused: Fiction from Today's China* (New York: Grove, 1995).

Hanan, Patrick (ed.), *The Sea of Regret: Two Turn-of-the-Century Chinese Romantic Novels* (Honolulu: University of Hawaii Press, 1995).

Hsia, C. T., *A History of Modern Chinese Fiction, 1917–1957* (New Haven, CT: Yale University Press, 1961).

——— (ed.), *Twentieth Century Chinese Stories* (New York: Columbia University Press, 1971).

Hsia, Tsi-An, *Heroes and Hero-Worship in Chinese Communist Fiction* (Seattle, WA: University of Washington Press, 1968).

Huang, Joe C., *Heroes and Villains in Communist China: The Contemporary Novel as a Reflection of Life* (London: Hurst, 1973).

Huters, Theodore (ed.), *Reading the Modern Chinese Short Story* (Armonk, NY: M.E. Sharpe, 1990).

Jenner, W. J. F. (ed.), *Fragrant Weeds: Chinese Short Stories Once Labelled as Poisonous Weeds* (Hong Kong: Joint Publishing, 1983).

Lau, Joseph, C.T. Hsia and Leo Ou-fan Lee (eds), *Modern Chinese Stories and Novellas* (New York: Columbia University Press, 1981).

Lee Yee (ed.), *The New Realism: Writings From China after the Cultural Revolution* (New York: Hippocrene Books, 1983).

Link, Perry (ed.), *Mandarin Ducks and Butterflies: Popular Fiction in Early Twentieth-Century Chinese Cities* (Berkeley: University of California Press, 1981).

——— (ed.), *Roses and Thorns: The Second Blooming of the Hundred Flowers in Chinese Fiction* (Berkeley, CA: University of California Press, 1984).

Liu Nienling (trans.), *The Rose Coloured Dinner: New Works by Contemporary Chinese Women Writers* (Hong Kong: Joint Publishing, 1988).

Long Xu (ed.), *Recent Fiction from China, 1987–1988: Selected Stories and Novellas* (Lewiston: Mellen Press, 1991).

Louie, Kam, *Between Fact and Fiction: Essays on Post-Mao Chinese Literature and Society* (Broadway, NSW: Wild Peony, 1989).

——— **and Louise Edwards**, *Bibliography of English Translations and Critiques of Contemporary Chinese Fiction, 1945–1992* (Taipei: Center for Chinese Studies, 1993).

Lu Tonglin, *Misogyny, Cultural Nihilism and Oppositional Politics: Contemporary Chinese Experimental Fiction* (Stanford University Press, 1995).

Ng, Mau-sang, *The Russian Hero in Modern Chinese Fiction* (Hong Kong: Chinese University Press, 1988).

Nieh Hualing (ed. and co-trans.), *Literature of the Hundred Flowers; vol. II: Poetry and Fiction* (New York: Columbia University Press, 1981).

Registration and Other Stories (Beijing: Foreign Languages Press, 1954).

Roberts, R. A., and A. Knox (eds), *One Half of the Sky: Stories of Contemporary Women Writers of China* (London: Heinneman, 1987).

Seven Contemporary Chinese Women Writers (Beijing: Chinese Literature, 1982).

Siu, Helen F. (ed.), *Furrows – Peasants, Intellectuals, and the State: Stories and Histories from Modern China* (Stanford University Press, 1990).

—— **and Zelda Stern** (eds), *Mao's Harvest: Voices from China's New Generation* (New York: Oxford University Press, 1983).

Six Contemporary Chinese Women Writers (Beijing: Chinese Literature, 1995).

Stories from the Thirties, 2 vols (Beijing: Chinese Literature, 1982).

Tai, Jeanne (ed. and trans), *Spring Bamboo: A Collection of Contemporary Chinese Short Stories* (New York: Random House, 1989).

Wang, David Der-wei, *Fictional Realism in Twentieth-century China: Mao Dun, Lao She, Shen Congwen* (New York: Columbia University Press, 1992).

Yang, Winston L. Y., and Nathan K. Mao, *Stories of Contemporary China* (New York: Paragon Book Gallery, 1979.)

——(eds), *Modern Chinese Fiction: A Guide to its Study and Appreciation Essays and Bibliographies* (Boston, MA: G.K. Hall, 1981).

Ying Bian (ed.), *The Time Is Not Yet Ripe* (San Francisco, CA: China Books, 1991).

Yu Hua, *The Past and the Punishments*, trans. Andrew F. Jones (Honolulu, HA: University of Hawaii Press, 1996).

Zhao, Henry Y. H., *The Uneasy Narrator: Chinese Fiction from the Traditional to the Modern* (London: Oxford University Press, 1995).

—— (ed.), *The Lost Boat: Avant-garde Fiction from China* (London: Wellsweep, 1993).

—— **and John Cayley** (eds), *Under-sky Underground: Chinese Writing Today 1* (London: Wellsweep, 1994).

Zhu Hong (ed.), *The Chinese Western: Short Fiction from Today's China* (New York: Ballantine, 1988).

——(ed.), *The Serenity of Whiteness: Stories by and about Women in Contemporary China* (New York: Ballantine Books, 1991).

Fiction: Collections and Studies of Individual Authors

A Cheng (Ah Cheng), *Three Kings: Three Stories from Today's China*, trans. Bonnie S. McDougall (London: Collins Harvill, 1990).

Ai Wu, *Banana Vale* (Beijing: Chinese Literature Press, 1993).

Ba Jin, *Living Amongst Heroes* (Beijing: Foreign Languages Press, 1954).

——, *Cold Nights*, trans. Nathan Mao and Liu Ts'un-yan (Hong Kong: Chinese University, 1979).

——, *Autumn in Spring and Other Stories* (Beijing: Chinese Literature, 1981).

——, *The Family* (Beijing: Foreign Languages Press, 1958).

————, *Selected Works of Ba Jin*, 2 vols (Beijing: Foreign Languages Press, 1988).

Bai Hua, *The Remote Country of Women*, trans. Qingyun Wu and Thomas O. Beebee (Honolulu: University of Hawaii Press, 1994).

Børdahl, Vibeke, *Along the Broad Road of Realism: Qin Zhaoyang's World of Fiction* (London: Curzon Press, 1990).

Can Xue, *Dialogues in Paradise*, trans. Ronald R. Janssen and Jian Zhang (Evanston, IL: Northwestern University Press, 1989).

————, *Old Floating Cloud: Two Novellas*, trans. Ronald Janssen and Zhang Jian (Evanston, IL: Northwestern University Press, 1991).

Chang Jun-mei, *Ting Ling: Her Life and Her Work* (Taipei: Institute of International Relations, National Chengchi University, 1978).

Chi Li, *Apart from Love* (Beijing: Chinese Literature, 1994).

Deng Youmei, *Snuff-bottles and Other Stories*, trans. Gladys Yang (Beijing: Chinese Literature, 1986).

Ding Ling (Ting Ling), *The Sun Shines over the Sangkan River*, trans. Gladys Yang and Yang Xianyi (Beijing: Foreign Languages Press, 1954).

————, *Miss Sophie's Diary and Other Stories* (Beijing: Chinese Literature).

————, *I Myself Am a Woman*, ed. Tani E. Barlow (Boston, MA: Beacon Press, 1989).

Dolezalova, Anna, *Yu Ta-fu: Specific Traits of His Literary Creation* (Bratislava: Slovak Academy of Sciences/London: Hurst, 1971).

Duke, Michael S. (ed.), *Worlds of Modern Chinese Fiction: Short Stories and Novellas from the People's Republic, Taiwan and Hong Kong* (Armonk, NY: M.E. Sharpe, 1991).

Feng Jicai, *The Miraculous Pigtail* (Beijing: Chinese Literature, 1987).

————, *The Three-inch Golden Lotus*, trans. David Wakefield (Honolulu: University of Hawaii Press, 1994).

Feuerwerker, Yi-tsi Mei, *Ding Ling's Fiction: Ideology and Narrative in Modern Chinese Literature* (Cambridge, MA: Harvard University Press, 1982).

Gao Xiaosheng, *The Broken Betrothal* (Beijing: Chinese Literature, 1987).

Gu Hua, *A Small Town Called Hibiscus*, trans. Gladys Yang (Beijing: Chinese Literature, 1983).

————, *Pagoda Ridge and Other Stories* (Beijing: Chinese Literature, 1985).

Han Shaogong, *Homecoming? and Other Stories*, trans. Martha Cheung (Hong Kong: Renditions, 1992).

Jia Pingwa (Chia Ping-ao and Jia Ping'ao), *The Heavenly Hound* (Beijing: Chinese Literature, 1991).

————, *Turbulence*, trans. Howard Goldblatt (Baton Rouge, LA: Louisiana State University Press, 1991).

Jiang Zilong, *All the Colours of the Rainbow* (Beijing: Chinese Literature, 1983).

Kinkley, Jeffrey C., *The Odyssey of Shen Congwen* (Stanford University Press, 1987).

Lang, Olga, *Pa Chin and His Writings* (Cambridge, MA: Harvard University Press, 1967).

Lao She, *Cat Country: A Satirical Novel of China in the 1930s*, trans. William Lyell (Columbus, OH: Ohio State University Press, 1970).

——, *Beneath the Red Banner*, trans. Don J. Cohn (Beijing: Chinese Literature, 1982).

——, *Camel Xiangzi*, trans. Shi Xiaoqing (Beijing: Foreign Languages Press, 1981).

——, *Crescent Moon and Other Stories* (Beijing: Chinese Literature, 1985).

——, *The Two Mas*, trans. Kenny K. Huang and David Finkelstein (Hong Kong: Joint Publishing, 1984).

Lee, Leo Ou-fan, *Lu Xun and His Legacy* (Berkeley, CA: California University Press, 1985).

Li Boyuan, *Modern Times: A Brief History of Enlightenment*, trans. Douglas Lancashire (Hongkong: Chinese University of Hongkong, 1996).

Liu Binyan, *People or Monsters and Other Stories and Reportage from China after Mao*, ed. Perry Link (Bloomington, IN: Indiana University Press, 1983).

Liu E, *The Travels of Lao Can* (Beijing: Chinese Literature, 1983).

Liu Heng, *The Obsessed*, trans. David Kwan (Beijing: Chinese Literature, 1990), pp. 16–125.

——, *Black Snow*, trans. David Kwan (Beijing: Chinese Literature, 1991); Also trans. Howard Goldblatt (New York: Atlantic Monthly Press, 1993).

Liu Shaotang, *Catkin Willow Flats* (Beijing, Chinese Literature, 1984).

Liu Suola, *Blue Sky Green Sea and Other Stories*, trans. Martha Cheung (Hong Kong: Renditions, 1993).

——, *Chaos and All That*, trans. Richard King (Honolulu: University of Hawaii Press, 1994).

Liu Xinwu, *Black Walls and Other Stories,* ed. Don J. Cohn (Hong Kong: Renditions, 1990).

Lu Xun (Lu Hsun), *The Complete Stories of Lu Xun. Call to Arms, Wandering*, trans. Yang Hsien-yi and Gladys Yang (Bloomington, IN: Indiana University Press, 1981).

Mao Dun (Mao Tun), *Spring Silkworms and Other Stories*, trans. Sidney Shapiro (Beijing: Foreign Languages Press, 1956).

——, *Midnight*, trans. Hsu Meng-hsiung and A.C. Barnes (Beijing: Foreign Languages Press, 1957).

——, *The Vixen* (Beijing: Chinese Literature, 1987).

——, *Rainbow*, trans. Madeleine Zelin (Berkeley and Los Angeles, CA: University of California Press, 1992).

Mo Yan, *Explosions and Other Stories*, trans. Janice Wickeri (Hong Kong: Renditions, 1991).

Mo Yan, *Red Sorghum: A Novel of China*, trans. Howard Goldblatt (New York: Viking, 1993).

———, *Garlic Ballads*, trans. Howard Goldblatt (New York: Viking Penguin, 1996).

Ouyang Shan, *Uncle Kao*, trans. Kuo Mei-hua (Beijing: Foreign Languages Press, 1957).

———, 'Three-Family Lane', *Chinese Literature* 5 (May 1961), pp. 2–71; 6 (June 1961), pp. 3–68.

Qian Zhongshu, *Fortress Besieged* (Bloomington, IN: Indiana University Press, 1979).

Qu Bo (Ch'ü Po), *Tracks in the Snowy Forest*, trans. Sidney Shapiro (Beijing: Foreign Languages Press, 1965).

Ru Zhijuan, *Lilies and Other Stories* (Beijing: Chinese Literature, 1985).

Shen Congwen, *The Border Town and Other Stories* (Beijing: Chinese Literature, 1981).

Shen Rong, *At Middle Age* (Beijing: Chinese Literature, 1987).

Shi Tiesheng, *Strings of Life* (Beijing: Chinese Literature, 1991).

Shi Zhecun, *One Rainy Evening* (Beijing: Chinese Literature Press, 1994).

Su Manshu, *The Lone Swan*, trans. George Kin Leung (Shanghai: Commercial Press, 1924).

Su Tong, *Raise the Red Lantern: Three Novellas*, trans. Michael Duke (New York: William Morrow and Company, 1993).

Wang Anyi, *Lapse of Time* (San Francisco: China Books, 1988).

———, *Love in a Small Town*, trans. Eva Hung (Hong Kong: Renditions, 1988).

———, *Baotown*, trans. Martha Avery (New York: Viking, 1989).

———, *Love on a Barren Mountain*, trans. Eva Hung (Hong Kong: Renditions, 1991).

———, *Brocade Valley*, trans. Bonnie S. McDougall and Chen Maiping (New York: New Directions, 1992).

Wang Meng, *Butterfly and Other Stories* (Beijing: Chinese Literature, 1983).

———, *Bolshevik Salute: A Modernist Chinese Novel*, trans. Wendy Larson (Seattle, WA: University of Washington Press, 1989).

———, *Selected Works of Wang Meng; vol. 1: The Strain of Meeting* (Beijing: Foreign Languages Press, 1989).

———, *Selected Works of Wang Meng; vol. 2: Snowball* (Beijing: Foreign Languages Press, 1989).

Wang Shuo, *Playing for Thrills: A Mystery*, trans. Howard Goldblatt (New York: William Morrow, 1997).

Wang Zengqi, *Story after Supper* (Beijing: Chinese Literature, 1990).

Williams, Philip F., *Village Echoes: The Fiction of Wu Zuxiang* (Boulder, CO: Westview Press, 1993).

Xiao Hong, *The Field of Life and Death*, trans. Howard Goldblatt and Ellen Yeung; and *Tales of Hulan River*, trans. Howard Goldblatt (Bloomington: Indiana University Press, 1979).

————, *Selected Stories of Xiao Hong*, trans. Howard Goldblatt (Beijing: Chinese Literature, 1982).

Xiao Jun (T'ien Chün), *Village in August*, trans. Evan King (New York: Smith & Durrell, 1942).

Xiao Qian, *Chestnuts and Other Stories* (Beijing: Chinese Literature, 1984).

Yang Mo, *The Song of Youth* (Beijing: Foreign Languages Press, 1978).

Ye Shengtao, *The Schoolmaster Ni Huan-chi* (Beijing: Foreign Languages Press, 1958).

————, *How Mr Pan Weathered the Storm* (Beijing: Chinese Literature, 1987).

Yu Dafu, *Nights of Spring Fever and Other Stories* (Beijing: Chinese Literature, 1984).

Yuan Jing (Yuan Ching), *Daughters and Sons*, trans. Sidney Shapiro (Beijing: Foreign Languages Press, 1979).

Zhang Chengzhi, *The Black Steed* (Beijing: Chinese Literature, 1990).

Zhang Jie, *Love Must Not Be Forgotten* (San Francisco: China Books, 1986).

————, *Leaden Wings*, trans. Gladys Yang. (London: Virago, 1987); also trans. as *Heavy Wings* by Howard Goldblatt (New York: Grove Weidenfeld, 1989).

————, *As Long as Nothing Happens Nothing Will* (London: Virago, 1988).

Zhang Tianyi (Chang T'ien-yi), *Big Lin and Little Lin*, trans. Gladys Yang and Yang Hsien-yi (Beijing: Foreign Languages Press, 1958).

————, *Stories of Chinese Young Pioneers* (Beijing: Foreign Languages Press, 1962).

Zhang Xianliang, *Mimosa* (Beijing: Chinese Literature, 1985).

————, *Half of Man Is Woman*, trans. Martha Avery (London: Viking, 1987/and New York: W.W. Norton, 1988).

————, *Getting Used to Dying*, trans. Martha Avery (New York: Harper-Collins, 1991).

Zhao Shuli (Chao Shu-li), *Sanliwan Village*, trans. Gladys Yang (Beijing, Foreign Languages Press, 1957/1964).

————, *Rhymes of Li Yu-tsai and Other Stories*, trans. Sydney Shapiro (Beijing: Foreign Languages Press, 1954/1980).

Zhao Zhenkai (Bei Dao), *Waves*, ed. Bonnie S. McDougall (Hong Kong: Chinese University Press, 1985).

Zheng Wanlong, *Strange Tales from Strange Lands: Stories by Zheng Wanlong*, ed. Kam Louie (Ithaca: Cornell East Asia Series, 1993).

Zhou Erfu (Chou Er-fu), *Morning in Shanghai*, 2 vols, trans. A.C. Barnes (Beijing: Foreign Languages Press, 1962).

Zhou Libo (Chou Li-po), *The Hurricane*, trans. Meng-hsiung Hsu (Beijing: Foreign Languages Press, 1955).

———, *Great Changes in a Mountain Village: Volume 1*, trans. Derek Bryan (Beijing: Foreign Languages Press, 1961).

Drama: Anthologies and Studies of Multiple Playwrights

Chai, Ch'u, and Winberg Chai (eds), *A Treasury of Chinese Literature: A New Prose Anthology Including Fiction and Drama* (New York: Appleton-Century, 1965).

Eide, Elisabeth, *China's Ibsen: from Ibsen to Ibsenism* (London: Curzon Press, 1987).

Gu Zongyi (Ku Tsong-nee) (tr.), *Modern Chinese Plays* (Shanghai: Commercial Press, 1941).

Gunn, Edward M., (ed.), *Modern Chinese Drama: An Anthology* (Bloomington, IN: Indiana University Press, 1983).

Howard, Roger, *Contemporary Chinese Theatre* (London: Heinemann, 1978).

Lopez, Manuel D., *Chinese Drama: An Annotated Bibliography of Commentary, Criticism, and Plays in English Translation* (Metuchen, NJ: Scarecrow Press, 1991).

Mackerras, Colin, *The Chinese Theatre in Modern Times; From 1840 to the Present Day* (London: Thames and Hudson, 1975).

———, *The Performing Arts in Contemporary China* (London: Routledge & Kegan Paul, 1981).

———, *Chinese Theater: From its Origins to the Present Day* (Honolulu: University of Hawaii Press, 1983).

———, *Chinese Drama: A Historical Survey*, 1st edn. (Beijing: New World, 1990).

Mitchell, John D., *The Red Pear Garden: Three Dramas of Revolutionary China*, with an introduction by Richard E. Strassberg (Boston: David R. Godine, 1973).

Scott, A. C., *An Introduction to the Chinese Theater* (New York: Theater Arts Books, 1958).

———, *Actors Are Madmen: Notebook of a Theatregoer in China* (Madison: University of Wisconsin Press, 1982).

Snow, Lois Wheeler, *China on Stage: An American Actress in the People's Republic* (New York: Vintage Books, 1973).

Tung, Constantine, and Colin Mackerras (eds), *Drama in the People's Republic of China* (Albany, NY: State University of New York Press, 1987).

Wagner, Rudolf G., *The Contemporary Chinese Historical Drama: Four Studies* (Berkeley, CA: University of California Press, 1990).

Drama: Collections and Studies of Individual Playwrights

Cao Yu (Ts'ao Yu), *Peking Man*, trans. Leslie Nai-Kwai Lo (New York: Columbia University Press, 1986; based on 1954 edition).

———, *Thunderstorm*, trans. Wang Tso-liang and A. C. Barnes, preface by Cao Yu (Peking: Foreign Languages Press, 1958).

———, *Bright Skies*, trans. Chang Pei-chi (Beijing: Foreign Languages Press, 1960).

———, *The Wilderness*, trans. Christopher C. Rand and Joseph S. M. Lau (Hong Kong University Press, 1980).

Guo Moruo (Kuo Mo-jo), *Chu Yuan: A Play in Five Acts*, trans. Yang Hsien-yi and Gladys Yang (Beijing: Foreign Languages Press, 1953).

———, *Selected Works of Guo Moruo: Five Historical Plays*, trans. Bonnie S. McDougall *et al.* (Beijing: Foreign Languages Press, 1984).

Hu, John Y. H., *T'sao Yu* (New York: Twayne, 1972).

Lao She (Lao Sheh), *Dragon Beard Ditch: A Play in Three Acts* (Beijing: Foreign Languages Press, 1956).

Lau, Joseph S. M., *Ts'ao Yu: The Reluctant Disciple of Chekhov and O'Neill. A Study in Literary Influence* (Hong Kong University: Centre of Asian Studies, 1970).

Li Jianwu, *It's Only Spring and Thirteen Years: Two Early Plays by Li Jianwu*, trans. (with afterword and notes) Tony Hyder (London: Bamboo Publishing, 1989).

Tian Han (Tien Han), *Kuan Han-ching: A Play*, trans. Liao Hung-ying, preface by Tian Han (Beijing: Foreign Languages Press, 1961).

Xia Yan (Hsia Yen), *The Test: A Play in Five Acts* (Beijing: Foreign Languages Press, 1956).

Yao Xinnong (Hsin-nung; also known as **Yao Ke),** *The Malice of Empire*, trans. (intro. by) Jeremy Ingalls (Berkeley: University of California Press, 1970).

See also translations and critical studies in *Chinese Literature* (Beijing), Renditions (Hong Kong) and *Modern Chinese Literature* (Boulder, CO).

GLOSSARY OF TITLES AND AUTHORS

'About to Sail for Home' (*Dongshen guiguo de shihou*) 动身归国的时候

Acme (*Dingdian*) 顶点

'Across the River' (*Zai xiao he nabian*) 在小河那边

'Adventures of Little Swallow, The' (*Xiao yanzi wan li feixing ji*) 小燕子万里飞行集

'After Coming Home' (*Hui jia yihou*) 回家以后

'After Drinking' (*Jiu hou*) 酒后

'After Joining the Ranks' (*Ru wu hou*) 入武后

After-hours (*Fan yu ji*) 饭余集

Agricultural Daily (*Nongye ribao*) 农业日报

Ah Cheng 阿城

Ah, Humanity (*Ren a, ren*) 人啊, 人

'Ah Q spirit' (*A Q jingshen*) 阿Q精神

Ai Qing 艾青

Ai Wu 艾芜

'Alarm Bell, The' (*Luan zhong*) 乱钟

'All' (*Yiqie*) 一切

'All the Colours of the Rainbow' (*Chi cheng huang lü qing lan zi*) 赤橙黄绿青蓝紫

Analects, The (*Lunyu*) 论语

Annals of Sorrow, The (*Tong shi*) 痛史

Annals of the Theatre (*Xiju chunqiu*) 戏剧春秋

Annals of the Warring States (*Zhanguo ce*) 战国册

Announcement of Dawn (*Liming de tongzhi*) 黎明的通知

'Answer, The' (*Huida*) 回答

Anti-Japanese Drama Companies (*Kang Ri yanjuhui*) 抗日演剧会

Archaeology (*Kaogu*) 考古

Ardent Hearts (*Huore de xin*) 火热的心

Ark, The (*Fangzhou*) 方舟

463

Around the Time of Qingming (*Qingming qianhou*) 清明前后

'Artillery Commander's Son, The' (*Paobing siling de erzi*) 炮兵司令的
儿子

'Artist, The' (*Yishujia*) 艺术家

Arts Troupe (*Yishu jushe*) 艺术剧社

Ashes (*Jieyu hui*) 劫余灰

'At Middle Age' (*Ren dao zhongnian*) 人到中年

'At the Bridge Site' (*Zai qiaoliang de gongdi shang*) 在桥梁的工地上

'At the Paris Cinema' (*Bali daxituan*) 巴黎大戏团

'At the Precipice' (*Zai xuanya shang*) 在悬崖上

Autumn (*Qiu*) 秋

'Autumn' (*Qiu*) 秋

Autumn Harvest (*Qiu shou*) 秋收

'Autumn Moon, The' (*Qiu yue*) 秋月

Autumn Song (*Qiu sheng fu*) 秋声赋

'Awake, My Brother' (*Xinglai ba, didi*) 醒来吧，弟弟

Awakening (*Juewu*) 觉悟

Azalea Mountain (*Dujuanshan*) 杜鹃山

Ba Jin 巴金

Ballad of a Long Night (*Chang ye xing*) 长夜行

'Ballad of a Painter' (*Huazhe de xingyin*) 画者的行吟

Bamboo Ruler and Iron Hammer (*Zhuchi yu tiechui*) 竹尺与铁锤

Barriers (*Gemo*) 隔膜

'Battle of the Lowlands, The' (*Wadi shang de zhanyi*) 洼地上的战役

'Because of Her' (*Yinwei youle ta*) 因为有了她

'Before Dante's Tomb' (*Danding mu qian*) 但丁墓前

Before Dawn (*Qianxi*) 前夕

Before Dawn (*Weiming ji*) 未明集

Before I Die (*Si qian*) 死前

Before the Madonna (*Shengmu xiang qian*) 圣母像前

Begonia (*Qiuhaitang*) 秋海棠

'Behind the Screen' (*Pingfeng hou*) 屏风后

Bei Dao 北岛

Bei Dao's Collected Poems (*Bei Dao shi xuan*) 北岛诗选

'Beidaihe' (*Beidaihe*) 北戴河

Beijing Academy of Traditional Drama (*Beijing xiqu xueyuan*) 北京戏曲
学院

Beijing Arts Academy (*Beijing guoli yishu zhuanmen xuexiao*) 北京国
立艺术专门学校

Beijing Evening News (*Beijing wanbao*) 北京晚报

Beijing People's Art Theatre (*Beijing renmin yishu juyuan*) 北京人民艺术剧院

Beijing School of Traditional Drama (*Beijing xiqu xuexiao*) 北京戏曲学校

Beiping Love Songs (*Beiping qingge*) 北平情歌

'Bell, The' (*Zhongsheng*) 钟声

Beneath the Red Banner (*Zheng Hong Qi xia*) 正红旗下

'Besieged, The' (*Bei wei zhe*) 被围者

Best Chinese One-Act Plays of 1936 (*1936 nian Zhongguo zuijia dumuju*) 1936 年中国最佳独幕剧

'Bestiary' (*Dongwu pian*) 动物篇

Bian Zhilin 卞之琳

Big Circus, The (*Da maxituan*) 大马戏团

Big Dike River (*Dayan he*) 大堰河

'Big Dike River—My Wetnurse' (*Dayan he—wo de baomu*) 大堰河—我的保姆

Big Dipper (*Beidou*) 北斗

Big Land, The (*Da di*) 大地

'Big Sister Liu' (*Chuntao*) 春桃

Bing Xin 冰心

Bing Xin's Collected Poems (*Bingxin shiji*) 冰心诗集

'Biography of a Cart Driver, The' (*Ganche zhuan*) 赶车传

'Bird of Destiny' (*Mingming niao*) 命命鸟

'Bitter Crop' (*Kucai*) 苦菜

Bitter Struggle (*Ku dou*) 苦斗

Black Hands of Sin, The (*Zuie de heishou*) 罪恶的黑手

'Black Li and White Li' (*Hei Bai Li*) 黑白李

Black Slave's Cry to Heaven, The (*Hei nu yu tian lu*) 黑奴吁天录

Black Snow (*Hei de xue*) 黑的雪

'Black Steed' (*Hei junma*) 黑骏马

'Blood of the Yellow People' (*Huangren zhi xue*) 黄人之血

'Blue Sky, Green Sea' (*Lantian lühai*) 蓝天绿海

'Bolshevik Salute' (*Buli*) 布礼

Border Region Masses' Opera Troupe (*Bianqu minzhong jutuan*) 边区民众剧团

'Border Region Self-Defence Corps, The' (*Bianqu ziweijun*) 边区自卫军

Border Town (*Biancheng*) 边城

Boulder Bay (*Panshi wan*) 磐石湾

Boxers, The (*Yihequan*) 义和拳

Brand, The (Laoyin) 烙印

Breaking Out of the House of Ghosts (Dachu youling ta) 打出幽灵塔

Bridge, The (Qiao) 桥

Bright Flowers among the Willow Shades (Liu an hua ming) 柳暗花明

Bright Skies (Minglang de tian) 明朗的天

Bright Sunny Skies (Yanyang tian) 艳阳天

Brightness and Darkness (Guangming yu heian) 光明与黑暗

Brocade Valley (Jinxiugu zhi lian) 金绣谷之恋

'Broken Betrothal, The' *(Jieyue)* 解约

'Broken Hairpin, The' *(Sui zan ji)* 碎簪记

Bureaucracy Exposed, The (Guanchang xianxing ji) 官场现行集

Burning City, The (Huo shao de cheng) 火烧的城

Bus-stop, The (Che zhan) 车站

Butcher, The (Tuhu) 屠户

'Butterfly' *(Hudie)* 蝴蝶

'By an Unknown Roadside' *(Zai bu zhiming de dao pang)* 在不知名的道旁

'Cactus Flower' *(Tanhua)* 昙花

Call to Arms (Nahan) 呐喊

Camel Grass (Luotuo cao) 骆驼草

Camel Xiangzi (Luotuo Xiangzi) 骆驼祥子

Can Xue 残雪

Canary, The (Jinsique) 金丝雀

Cao Yu 曹禺

Carpenter's Shop, The (Mu chang) 木厂

'Carved Pipe, The' *(Diaohua yandou)* 雕花烟斗

Case of the Blood-stained Corpse, The (Xueshi an) 血尸案

Cat Country (Mao cheng ji) 猫城记

Catkin Willow Flats (Puliu renjia) 蒲柳人家

Central Academy of Drama (Zhongyang xiju xueyuan) 中央戏剧学院

Central China Post (Chu bao) 楚报

Central Daily (Zhongyang ribao) 中央日报

'Chairman of the Peasants' Association' *(Nongmin huizhang)* 农民会长

Changes in Li Village (Lijiazhuang de bianqian) 李家庄的变迁

Characters in Society (Jianghu xing) 江湖行

Chen Baichen 陈白尘

Chen Dabei 陈大悲

'Chen Huansheng's Adventure in Town' *(Chen Huansheng shang cheng)* 陈奂生上城

Chen Jingrong 陈敬容

Chen Mengjia 陈梦家
Chestnuts (Lizi) 栗子
'Child from the Forest, The' [also translated as 'Music of the Forest']
  (*Cong senlin li lai de haizi*) 从森林里来的孩子
Childhood Years (Ertong shidai) 儿童时代
Children (Xiaohai) 小孩
Children of the Rich (Caizhu de ernümen) 财主的儿女们
Children's Pagoda, The (Hair ta) 孩儿塔
China (Zhongguo) 中国
'China in October' (*Zhongguo de shiyue*) 中国的十月
China's New Poetry (Zhongguo xin shi) 中国新诗
Chinese National Federation of Writers and Artists (*Zhonghua quanguo
  wenxue yishujie lianhehui*) 中华全国文学艺术界联合会
Chinese National Federation of Anti-Japanese Writers and Artists (*Zhong-
  hua quanguo wenyijie kang di xiehui*) 中华全国文艺界抗敌协会
Chinese Shepherd Songs (Zhongguo mu ge) 中国牧歌
Chinese Village Tales (Zhongguo nongcun de gushi) 中国农村的故事
Chinese Youth Art Theatre (*Zhongguo qingnian yishu juyuan*) 中国青
  年艺术剧院
Chinese Youth News (Zhongguo qingnian bao) 中国青年报
Chongqing in Fog (Wu Chongqing) 雾重庆
Cicada (Tiaotang ji) 蜩螗集
'City in Spring' (*Chun cheng*) 春城
'civilised drama' (*wenming xi*) 文明戏
'Class Teacher' (*Ban zhuren*) 班主任
Clay Pot (Wa fu ji) 瓦釜集
'Clock' (*Zhong*) 钟
'Clouds' (*Yun*) 云
Clouds over Xishan (Xishan zhi yun) 西山之云
Coal Mines in May (Wuyue de kuangshan) 五月的矿山
Cold Nights (Han ye) 寒夜
College of Foreign Languages (*Tongwenguan*) 同文馆
'Come Here to Me' (*Dao wo zheli lai*) 到我这里来
'Coming Out of the Mountain' (*Chu shan*) 出山
Committee for Theatre Reform (*Xiju gaige weiyuanhui*) 戏剧改革委员
  会
Comrade, You've Taken the Wrong Path! (Tongzhi, ni zoucuole lu) 同
  志, 你走错了路
Confession (Kougong) 口供
Contemporaries (Tonglingren) 同龄人

Contemporary (Dangdai) 当代
Contemporary Review (Xiandai pinglun) 现代评论
Cosmos, The (Wan xiang) 万象
Country Above All, The (Guojia zhi shang) 国家至上
Country Girl (Cun gu) 村姑
Couples in Adversity (Huannan fuqi) 患难夫妻
Creation (Chuangzao) 创造
Creation Quarterly (Chuangzao jikan) 创造季刊
Creation Society (*Chuangzao she*) 创造社
Crescent Monthly (*Xinyue yuekan*) 新月月刊
'Crescent Moon, The' (*Yueyar*) 月牙儿
Crescent Press (*Xinyue shudian*) 新月书店
Crescent Society (*Xinyue she*) 新月社
Cricket, The (Qiu chong) 秋虫
'Crimson Silk, The' (*Jiang sha ji*) 绛纱记
Critical Review (Xueheng zazhi) 学横杂志
'critical realism' (*piping de xianshizhuyi*) 批评的现实主意
'criticise Lin Biao, criticise Confucius' (*pi Lin pi Kong*) 批林批孔
'Critique of the New Historical Play *Hai Rui Dismissed from Office*, A'
   (*Ping xinbian lishiju Hai Rui ba guan*) 评新编历史剧《海瑞罢官》
Crows and Sparrows (Wuya yu maque) 乌鸦与麻雀
Cry in the Wilderness, A (Kuangye de huhan) 旷野的呼喊
'Cuckoo, The' (*Bugu*) 布谷
Cultural Relics (Wenwu) 文物
Culture and Life Press (*Wenhua shenghuo chubanshe*) 文化生活出版
   社
'Curse, The' (*Duzhou*) 毒咒
Dai Wangshu 戴望舒
Dame aux camélias, La (Chahua nü) 茶花女
Dance (Wudao) 舞蹈
Dance Troupe of China (*Zhongguo wujutuan*) 中国舞剧团
Daughters and Sons (Xin ernü yingxiong zhuan) 新儿女英雄传
Dawn Daily, The (Liming bao) 黎明报
Dawn in the East (Dongfang yu xiao) 东方欲晓
'Day in the Life of the Head of the Electrical Equipment Bureau, A'
   (*Jidianjuzhang de yi tian*) 机电局长的一天
'Day of the Duststorm' (*Fengsha ri*) 风沙日
Dead Water (Sishui) 死水
'Deaf-mute and His Suona, The' (*Fengchui suona sheng*) 风吹唢呐声
'Dear Husband' (*Qin'ai de zhangfu*) 亲爱的丈夫

'Death of a Nazarene, The' (*Yi ge Nasaleren de si*) 一个拿撒勒人的死

'Death of a Star' (*Mingyou zhi si*) 明优之死

Death of Li Xiucheng (*Li Xiucheng zhi si*) 李秀成之死

'Death of Sister Wang, The' (*Wang Asao de si*) 王阿嫂的死

Decay (*Fushi*) 腐蚀

'Declaration' (*Xuangao*) 宣告

'Declaration by the Nationalist Literature Movement, A' (*Minzuzhuyi wenyi yundong xuanyan*) 民族主义文艺运动宣言

Defend the Marco Polo Bridge (*Baowei Lugouqiao*) 保卫芦沟桥

Deluge, The (*Hongshui*) 洪水

Deng Youmei 邓友梅

'Deserted Village, The' (*Huang cun*) 荒村

'Destined Marriage, A' (*Yinyuan*) 姻缘

Destruction (*Huimie*) 毁灭

Destruction (*Miewang*) 灭亡

'Devil's Road' (*Mo dao*) 魔道

Dialogues in Paradise (*Tiantang li de duihua*) 天堂里的对话

'Diary of a Madman' (*Kuangren riji*) 狂人日记

Ding Ling 丁玲

Ding Xilin 丁西林

Ding Yi 丁易

Dingding's Strange Journey (*Dingding de yici qiguai de lüxing*) 丁丁的一次奇怪的旅行

Discipline (*Duanlian*) 锻炼

'Discontent' (*Bu man*) 不满

'Disillusion' (*Huanmie*) 幻灭

Divorce (*Lihun*) 离婚

'Do Not Wash Away the Red' (*Xiu xi hong*) 休洗红

'Don't Pinch Me, Pain' (*Bie ning wo, teng*) 别拧我，疼

Dr Bethune (*Bai Qiuen daifu*) 白求恩大夫

Dragon Beard Ditch (*Longxugou*) 龙须沟

Drama [1921–22] (*Xiju*) 戏剧

Drama [1926] (*Jukan*) 剧刊

Drama News (*Xiju xinwen*) 戏剧新闻

Dream of the Red Chamber (*Honglou meng*) 红楼梦

'Dream of Three and a Half Days, A' (*San tian ban de meng*) 三天半的梦

'Dreams and Poetry' (*Meng yu shi*) 梦与诗

Driven to Join the Liangshan Rebels (*Bi shang Liangshan*) 逼上梁山

Drum Tower (*Zhonggu lou*) 钟鼓楼

'Drunk' (*Zuile*) 醉了
Duanmu Hongliang 端木蕻良
Duck Bill Fall (*Yazui lao*) 鸭嘴崂
Duo Duo 多多
Dust (*Chentu ji*) 尘土集
'Early Summer' (*Chu xia*) 初夏
East is Red, The (*Dongfang hong*) 东方红
'Echo in the Valley' (*Shengu huisheng*) 深谷回声
Eclipse (*Shi*) 蚀
'eight-legged essay' (*bagu wen*) 八股文
'Eighteen Hundred Piculs' (*Yiqian babai dan*) 一千八百担
Eighteen Springs (*Shiba chun*) 十八春
'Eighteen, The' (*Shiba ge*) 十八个
'Elegy of Yan Zhao' (*Yan Zhao beige*) 燕赵悲歌
'Embroidered Pillows' (*Xiu zhen*) 绣枕
Endangered City (*Weicheng ji*) 危城记
'enlightened drama' (*kaiming xi*) 开明戏
Enlightenment Dramatic Society (*Kaiming yanju hui*) 开明演剧会
'Entering the Ranks' (*Ruwu*) 入伍
Eternal Words (*Yong yan ji*) 永言集
'Eve of the Mid-Autumn Festival, The' (*Zhongqiu wan*) 中秋晚
'Evening Appointment' (*Wan hui*) 晚会
'Evening Chats at Yanshan' (*Yanshan ye hua*) 燕山夜话
'Evening Drizzle' (*Meiyu zhi xi*) 霉雨之夕
Evergreen (*Wan nian chun*) 万年春
Everlasting Youth (*Wannian qing*) 万年青
Experimental Drama Troupe (*Shiyan jutuan*) 实验剧团
Experiments (*Changshi ji*) 尝试集
Exploration Team, The (*Tansuo zhe*) 探索者
'Explosions' (*Baozha*) 爆炸
Families of Jiwowa Village (*Jiwowa de renjia*) 鸡窝洼的人家
'Family on the Other Side of the Mountain, The' (*Shan na mian renjia*)
　山那面人家
'Fan, The' (*Shan*) 扇
'Fan Hamlet' (*Fanjiapu*) 樊家铺
Fang Ji 方纪
Fang Jing 方敬
'Fangfang and Tom' (*Fangfang he Tangmu*) 芳芳和汤姆
'Farewell' (*Zeng bie*) 赠别
Fascist Bacillus, The (*Faxisi xijun*) 法西斯细菌

'Fate' (*Mingyun*) 命运
Fate (*Shengsi yuan*) 生死缘
Fate in Tears and Laughter (*Tixiao yinyuan*) 啼笑因缘
'Father and Son' (*Fu zi lia*) 父子俩
Feng Jicai 冯骥才
Feng Jingyuan 冯景元
Feng Naichao 冯乃超
Feng Xuefeng 冯雪峰
Feng Zhi 冯至
Feng Zhi's Selected Poems (*Feng Zhi shi wen xuanji*) 冯至诗文选集
Fengling Ferry (*Fengling du*) 风陵渡
Field of Life and Death, The (*Shengsi chang*) 生死场
Fifteen Strings of Cash (*Shiwu guan*) 十五贯
Fighter's News (*Bingtuan zhanshi bao*) 兵团战士报
Fighting on the Plains (*Pingyuan zuozhan*) 平原作战
Fine Art (*Meishu*) 美术
Fire (*Huozai*) 火灾
Fish Eyes (*Yu mu ji*) 鱼目集
Flag, The (*Qi*) 旗
'Flag, The' (*Qi*) 旗
'Flesh and Soul' (*Ling yu rou*) 灵与肉
'Flight' (*Chuben*) 出奔
Flood, The (*Shui*) 水
Flourishing the Whip (*Yang bian ji*) 扬鞭集
Flower City (*Huacheng*) 花成
Flower in an Ocean of Sin, A (*Niehai hua*) 孽海花
Flowerlike Sin (*Hua yiban de zuie*) 花一般的罪恶
Flowing Clouds (*Liu yun xiao shi*) 流云小诗
'Flyover, The' (*Liti jiaochaqiao*) 立体交叉桥
Fog (*Yanyun ji*) 烟云集
Fog in Chongqing (*Wu Chongqing*) 雾重庆
'Footprints in the Sand' (*Sha shang de jiaoyin*) 沙上的脚印
'For the Battlers' (*Gei zhandouzhe*) 给战斗者
'forbidden areas' (*jinqu*) 禁区
Foreign Graduate, The (*Yang zhuangyuan*) 洋状元
Fortress Besieged (*Weicheng*) 围城
Four Generations Under One Roof (*Sishi tong tang*) 四世同堂
Fragments (*Lingluan cao*) 零乱草
Fragrant Flowers on the Horizon (*Fangcao tianya*) 芳草天涯
'free people' (*ziyou ren*) 自由人

Friendship Daily (*Youhao bao*) 友好报

'From Guling to Tokyo' (*Cong Guling dao Dongjing*) 从牯岭到东京

'From Literary Revolution to Revolutionary Literature' (*Cong wenxue geming dao geming wenxue*) 从文学革命到革命文学

'Funerals' (*Song zang*) 送葬

Gall and the Sword, The (*Dan jian pian*) 胆剑篇

'Galloping Legs' (*Yinziche de minyun*) 印子车的命运

Gao Lan 高兰

Gao Lan's Verses for Declamation (*Gao Lan langsong shi*) 高兰朗诵诗

Gao Xiaosheng 高晓声

Gao Xingjian 高行健

Garden of the Future (*Jianglai de huayuan*) 将来的花园

'General, You Can't Do This' (*Jiangjun, bu neng zheyang zuo*) 将军, 不能这样做

Getting Used to Dying (*Xiguan siwang*) 习惯死亡

Ghostland Diary (*Guitu riji*) 鬼土日记

Ghostly Love (*Guilian*) 鬼恋

'Goats' (*Yang*) 羊

'God of Fire Symphonic Poems, The' (*Huoshen jiaoxiang shi*) 火神交响诗

'God's Dream' (*Shangdi de meng*) 上帝的梦

Goddesses, The (*Nüshen*) 女神

Gods, Spirits and Men (*Shen, gui, ren*) 神·鬼·人

'Going to Heaven's Bridge' (*Shang Tianqiao qu*) 上天桥去

Gold Rush (*Taojin ji*) 淘金记

'Golden Cangue, The' (*Jinsuo ji*) 金锁记

Golden Road, The (*Jinguang dadao*) 金光大道

'Good Son, The' (*Hao erzi*) 好儿子

'Goodbye, Shu Ting and Bei Dao' (*Biele, Shu Ting Bei Dao*) 别了, 舒婷北岛

'Granny's Star' (*Nainai de xingxing*) 奶奶的星星

Grass, The (*Caor*) 草儿

Gravitation (*Yinli*) 引力

Great Changes in a Mountain Village (*Shanxiang jubian*) 山乡巨变

'Great Exhibition of Poems by Modernist Groups in China' (*Zhongguo xiandaizhuyi shiqun da zhan*) 中国现代主意诗群大展

Great Stage of the Twentieth Century, The (*Ershi shiji da wutai*) 二十世纪大舞台

'Greatest Event in Life, The' (*Zhongshen dashi*) 终身大事

Green Branches (*Qingzhi lüye*) 青枝绿叶

Gu Cheng 顾城

Gu Hua 古华

Guangdong Institute for Theatre Studies (*Guangdong xiju yanjiusuo*) 广东戏剧研究所

Guangdong Literature (*Guangdong wenxue*) 广东文学

'Guanguan's Tonic' (*Guanguan de bupin*) 官官的补品

Guangzhou Literature (*Guangzhou wenxue*) 广州文学

Guo Moruo 郭沫若

Guo Moruo's Selected Works (*Guo Moruo xuanji*) 郭沫若选集

Guo Xiaochuan 郭小川

Hai Rui Dismissed from Office (*Hai Rui ba guan*) 海瑞罢官

'Half a Cartload of Straw Short' (*Cha ban che maijie*) 差半车麦秸

Half a Life (*Bansheng yuan*) 半生缘

Half a Man Is Woman (*Nanren de yiban shi nüren*) 男人的一半是女人

Han Garden, The (*Han yuan ji*) 汉园集

Han Shaogong 韩少功

Hang Yuehe 杭约赫

Hao Ran 浩然

Happiness (*Xingfu*) 幸福

'Has Civilisation Shaken Out the Candlelight?' (*Wenming yaojinle zhuguang?*) 文明摇尽了烛光

Hatred (*Zenghen*) 憎恨

He Jingzhi 贺敬之

He Qifang 何其芳

'Head for Winter' (*Zou xiang dongtian*) 走向冬天

'Heartbeats' (*Xintiao*) 心跳

Heaven and Earth (*Tiandi*) 天地

Heaven and May (*Tiantang yu wuyue*) 天堂与五月

Heavenly Hound (*Tiangou*) 天狗

Hebei Daily (*Hebei ribao*) 河北日报

Hebei Youth (*Hebei qingnian bao*) 河北轻年报

Heibei Literature and Art (*Hebei wenyi*) 河北文艺

Herdsman's Story, The (*Muma ren*) 牧马人

'Heroes and Little Troublemakers' (*Zhong yingxiong he xiao daodan*) 众英雄和小捣蛋

Hesitation (*Panghuang*) 彷徨

Hidden Grass (*Qian cao*) 浅草

'Homecoming Stranger, The' (*Guilai de moshengren*) 归来的陌生人

Hong Shen 洪深

Hope (*Xiwang*) 希望

Hot Blood (*Re xue*) 热血
How to Get Promoted (*Sheng guan tu*) 升官图
Hu Shi 胡适
Huang Baiwei 黄白薇
'Human Extremities' (*Ren ji*) 人极
'Humble Sacrifice, A' (*Bodian*) 薄奠
Hurricane, The (*Baofeng zhouyu*) 暴风骤雨
'I Came Out of a Café' (*Wo cong Cafe zhong chulai*) 我从Cafe中出来
'I Curse that Smile of Yours' (*Wo zuzhou ni name yi xiao*) 我诅咒你那么一笑
'I've Returned to my Country' (*Wo guilai le, wo de guguo*) 我归来了，我底故国
If I Were Real (*Jiaru wo shi zhende*) 假如我是真的
Illustrated Fiction (*Xiuxiang xiaoshuo*) 绣像小说
'Immortals' Cave, The' (*Wei Li Jin tongzhi ti suo she Lushan Xianrendong zhao*) 为李进同志题所摄庐山仙人洞照
Impartial, L' (*Da gong bao*) 大公报
'Impressions' (*Ganjue*) 感觉
'Improve Yourself Through Training' (*Duanlian duanlian*) 锻炼锻炼
In a Land of Silence (*Yu wusheng chu*) 于无声处
In Iron Chains (*Zai tielian zhong*) 在铁链中
In Praise of the Setting Sun (*Luori song*) 落日颂
'In Qixiangju Teahouse' (*Zai Qixiangju chaguan li*) 在其香居茶馆里
In Search of Love (*Qiu ai*) 求爱
'In Search of the King of Singers' (*Xunzhao gewang*) 寻找歌王
'In the Ruins' (*Zai feixu shang*) 在废墟上
'Inside News' (*Ben bao neibu xiaoxi*) 本报内部消息
'Inspiration' (*Linggan*) 灵感
'Intersection' (*Jiaochadian*) 交叉点
It's Only Spring (*Zhe buguo shi chuntian*) 这不过是春天
Jia Pingwa 贾平凹
'Jiang Boy, The' (*Xiao Jiang*) 小蒋
Jiang Guangci 蒋光慈
Jiang Zilong 蒋子龙
Jin Yi 靳以
'jottings' (*biji*) 笔记
Journeying Clouds (*Xing yun ji*) 行云集
July Society (*Qiyue she*) 七月社
Juvenescence (*Qingchun*) 青春
Kang Baiqing 康白情

Ke Lan 柯蓝

Ke Zhongpin 柯仲平

'King of Chess, The' (*Qi wang*) 棋王

'King of Children, The' (*Haizi wang*) 孩子王

'King of Trees, The' (*Shu wang*) 树王

'Kite Streamers' (*Fengzheng piaodai*) 风筝飘带

Kong Jiesheng 孔捷生

Kong Jue 孔厥

Korchin Banner Steppe, The (*Keerqin qi caoyuan*) 科尔沁旗草原

kunqu 昆曲

Lakeside (*Hu pan*) 湖畔

'Lakeside Tragedy, A' (*Hu shang de beiju*) 湖上的悲剧

Lament for China, A (*Ai Zhongguo*) 哀中国

'Lament for Sun Yatsen' (*Ku Sun Zhongshan*) 哭孙中山

Land (*Diban*) 地板

'Land of Wonder and Mystery, A' (*Zhe shi yi pian shenqi de tudi*) 这是
一片神奇的土地

Lanzhi and Zhongqing (*Lanzhi yu Zhongqing*) 兰芝与仲卿

Lao She 老舍

'Laundry Song' (*Xi yi ge*) 洗衣歌

'Law Professor and His Wife, The' (*Faxue jiaoshou ji qi furen*) 法学教
授及其妇人

Lawsuit Brought by Liu Qiaor, The (*Liu Qiaor gao zhuang*) 刘巧儿告状

Leaden Wings (*Chenzhong de chibang*) 沉重的翅膀

Leaf, A (*Yi ye*) 一叶

League of Left-Wing Dramatists (*Zuoyi xijujia lianmeng*) 左翼戏剧家联
盟

League of Left-wing Writers (*Zuoyi zuojia lianmeng*) 左翼作家联盟

Leave it to Me (*Bao de xing*) 包得行

Leaves of Three Autumns (*Sanqiu cao*) 三秋草

Letters to Young Readers (*Ji xiao duzhe*) 寄小读者

Li Boyuan 李伯元

Li Guangtian 李广田

Li Ji 李季

Li Jianwu 李健吾

Li Jinfa 李金发

'Li Shunda Builds a House' (*Li Shunda zao wu*) 李顺大造屋

Li Xueao 李雪鳌

Li Ying 李瑛

Liang Xiaosheng 梁晓声

Liang Yuanda (*Liang Yuanda*) 梁元达
Liberation Army Daily (*Jiefangjun bao*) 解放军报
Liberation Army Literature and the Arts (*Jiefangjun wenyi*) 解放军文艺
'Life' (*Shenghuo*) 生活
Life Gone Through (*Xingguo zhi shengming*) 行过之生明
Life in The Capital (*Chunming waishi*) 春明外史
'Life of Light, A' (*Guangming de yi sheng*) 光明的一生
Life of Wu Xun, The (*Wu Xun zhuan*) 武训传
Life on a String (*Bian chang bian zou*) 边唱边走
Life on Reed Lake (*Weitang jishi*) 苇塘纪事
'Life, A' (*Yi sheng*) 一生
Light of the Setting Sun (*Luo ri guang*) 落日光
Light Rain (*Wei yu*) 微雨
'Lilies' (*Baihe hua*) 白合花
'Lin Family Shop, The' (*Linjia puzi*) 林家铺子
Ling Shuhua 凌叔华
Lingering Fog (*Canwu*) 残雾
Literary Gazette (*Wenyi bao*) 文艺报
Literary Renaissance (*Wenyi fuxing*) 文艺复兴
Literary Review (*Wenxue pinglun*) 文学评论
Literary Works (*Zuopin*) 作品
literary language (*wen yan*) 文言
Literature Miscellany (*Wenxue congkan*) 文学丛刊
Literature Quarterly (*Wenxue jikan*) 文学季刊
Literature Ten-daily (*Wenxue xunkan*) 文学旬刊
'Little Bean' (*Xiao Dour*) 小豆儿
'Little Bell' (*Xiao lingr*) 小铃儿
Little Brothers (*Xiao ger lia*) 小哥儿俩
Liu Binyan 刘宾雁
Liu Dabai 刘大白
Liu E 刘鹗
Liu Fu 刘复
Liu Heng 刘恒
Liu Shaotang 刘绍棠
Liu Suola 刘索拉
Liu Xinwu 刘心武
'Log Cabin Overgrown with Creepers, The' (*Paman qingteng de muwu*)
  爬满青藤的木屋
Lone Swan, The (*Duanhong lingyan ji*) 断鸿零雁记
Lonely Country, The (*Jimo de guo*) 寂寞的国

Long Live the Chinese People (*Minzu wan sui*) 民族万岁
Long Live Youth (*Qingchun wan sui*) 青春万岁
Long River, The (*Changhe*) 长河
Looking West to Chang'an (*Xi wang Chang'an*) 西往长安
'Lost' (*Mitu*) 迷途
'Loushan Pass' (*Loushanguan*) 娄山关
Love in a Small Town (*Xiao cheng zhi lian*) 小城之恋
Love in Redland (*Chidi zhi lian*) 赤地之恋
'Love Must Not Be Forgotten' (*Ai, shi bu neng wangji de*) 爱, 是不能忘记的
'Love of Sons and Daughters, The' (*Ernü qing*) 儿女情
Love on a Barren Mountain (*Huangshan zhi lian*) 荒山之恋
'Love Story of a Young Monk, The' (*Shoujie*) 受戒
'Love's Inspiration' (*Ai de linggan*) 爱的灵感
Lu Ling 路翎
Lu Xun 鲁迅
Lucky (*Fugui*) 福贵
'Lucky One, The' (*You fuqi de ren*) 有福气的人
'Lute Music on a Cold Dawn' (*Hanxiao de qinge*) 寒晓的琴歌
Lute, The (*Pipa ji*) 琵琶记
Ma Bole (*Ma Bole*) 马伯乐
Magic Cube, The (*Mofang*) 魔方
'Magpies Perch on Branches' (*Xique dengzhi*) 喜鹊登枝
Malice of Empire, The (*Qing gong yuan*) 清宫怨
'Man Who Ate Stones, The' (*Chi shitou de ren*) 吃石头的人
Man with Movable Parts, The (*Huodong bianrenxing*) 活动变人形
'Manager Qiao Assumes Office' (*Qiao changzhang shangren ji*) 乔厂长上任记
Mao Dun 茅盾
Mao Zedong 毛泽东
'March 18' (*Sanyue shiba*) 三月十八
Marching Forward in the Fields (*Zai tianye shang, qianjin*) 在田野上, 前进
Marco Polo Bridge (*Lugouqiao*) 芦沟桥
'Marriage of Young Blacky, The' (*Xiao Erhei jiehun*) 小二黑结婚
Mass Literature and the Arts (*Dazhong wenyi*) 大众文艺
Masses Magazine Company (*Qunzhong zazhi gongsi*) 群众杂志公司
Masses' Opera Troupe (*Minzhong jutuan*) 民众剧团
Mayor Chen Yi (*Chen Yi shizhang*) 陈毅市长
'Melody' (*Xuanlü*) 旋律

Men and Women in Troubled Times (*Luanshi nannü*) 乱世男女
Men, Beasts and Ghosts (*Ren shou gui*) 人·兽·鬼
Mental Illness (*Xinbing*) 心病
'Merchant's Wife, The' (*Shangren fu*) 商人妇
Metamorphosis (*Tuibian*) 蜕变
Midnight (*Ziye*) 子夜
Mimosa (*Lühuashu*) 绿花树
'Miracle' (*Qiji*) 奇迹
'Miraculous Pigtail, The' (*Shenbian*) 神鞭
'Miserable People' (*Shouku ren*) 受苦人
'Miss Sophie's Diary' (*Shafei nüshi de riji*) 莎菲女士的日记
'Miss Winter' (*Dongr guniang*) 冬儿姑娘
Miss Youlan (*Youlan nüshi*) 幽兰女士
Mission, The (*Shiming*) 使命
Mo Yan 莫言
'model revolutionary theatrical works' (*yangbanxi*) 样板戏
'Modern Age in a Small Cabin, The' (*Xiaocang zhong de xiandai*) 小舱中的现代
Modern Press (*Xiandai shuju*) 现代书局
modern revolutionary dance-drama (*geming xiandai wuju*) 革命现代舞剧
modern revolutionary Peking opera (*geming xiandai jingju*) 革命现代京剧
Modern Tales of Chivalrous Heroes (*Jindai xiayi yingxiong zhuan*) 近代侠义英雄传
Modern Times (*Xiandai*) 现代
Modern Times: A Brief History of Enlightenment (*Wenming xiao shi*) 文明小史
Modern Writing Series (*Xiandai chuangzuo congkan*) 现代创作丛刊
Monthly Fiction (*Yueyue xiaoshuo*) 月月小说
Moon Breaks Out from Behind the Clouds, The (*Chongchu yunwei de yueliang*) 冲出云围的月亮
'Moon on the Manuscript' (*Gaozhi shang de yueliang*) 槁纸上的月亮
'Moonlight Sonata, The' (*Yueguang qu*) 月光曲
Morning in Shanghai (*Shanghai de zaochen*) 上海的早晨
Morning Post (*Chenbao*) 晨报
Morning Post Supplement (*Chenbao fukan*) 晨报副刊
Moruo's Complete Works (*Moruo wenji*) 沫若文集
'Most Precious, The' (*Zui baogui de*) 最宝贵的
Mother (*Muqin*) 母亲

Mount Miaofeng (Miaofeng shan) 妙峰山
Mountain Rain (Shan yu) 山雨
'Moving South' *(Nan qian)* 南迁
'Mr Hua Wei' *(Hua Wei xiansheng)* 华威先生
'Mr Pan in Difficulty' *(Pan xiansheng zai nan zhong)* 潘先生在难中
Mu Dan 穆旦
Mu Dan's Collected Poems (Mu Dan shiji) 穆旦诗集
Mu Mutian 穆木天
Mulan Joins the Army (Mulan cong jun) 木兰从军
'My Education' *(Wo de jiaoyu)* 我的教育
'My Faraway Qingpingwan' *(Wo de yaoyuan de Qingpingwan)* 我的遥
    远的清平湾
'My Homeland, My Dear Homeland' *(Zuguo a, wo qin'ai de zuguo)* 祖国
    啊, 我亲爱的祖国
My Memories (Wo de jiyi) 我的记忆
'Nameless People' *(Meiyou mingzi de ren)* 没有名字的人
Nannan and Uncle Whiskers (Nannan he huzi bobo) 南南和胡子伯伯
Nation Above All, The (Guojia zhi shang) 国家至上
National Academy of Drama *(Guoli xiju zhuanke xuexiao)* 国立戏剧专
    科学校
National Dance Academy *(Quanguo tiaowu xueyuan)* 全国跳舞学院
National Dance School *(Quanguo tiaowu xuexiao)* 全国跳舞学校
'national defence literature' *(guofang wenxue)* 国防文学
Nationalist Daily (Minguo ribao) 民国日报
'nationalist literature' *(minzuzhuyi wenxue)* 民族主义文学
'nationalist revolutionary literature' *(minzu geming wenxue)* 民族革命
    文学
'New Daughter-in-Law, The' *(Xin xifu)* 新媳妇
New Drama Fellowship *(Xinju tongzhi hui)* 新剧同志会
New Dream, A (Xin meng) 新梦
New Fiction (Xin xiaoshuo) 新小说
New Peach Blossom Fan, The (Xin taohua shan) 新桃花扇
New People's Miscellany (Xinmin congbao) 新民丛报
New Poems and Songs (Xin shige) 新诗歌
'New Poetry' *(Xin shi)* 新诗
New Poetry Monthly (Xin shi yuekan) 新诗月刊
New Tide (Xin chao) 新潮
'New Year's Sacrifice' *(Zhufu)* 祝福
New Youth (Xin qingnian) 新青年
'new drama' *(xin ju)* 新剧

'new opera' (*xin xi*) 新戏

Nie Ying 聂嫈

Night (*Ye*) 夜

'Night at Xiang River, A' (*Xiangjiang yi ye*) 湘江一夜

Night in Florence, A (Feilengcui de yi ye) 翡冷翠的一夜

Night in the South, A (Nanguo zhi ye) 南国之夜

Night Inn, The (Ye dian) 夜店

'Night Songs' *(Ye ge)* 夜歌

Night Songs (*Ye ge*) 夜歌

Night Songs and Songs of Day (*Ye ge he baitian de ge*) 夜歌和白天的歌

'Night the Tiger Was Caught, The' (*Huo hu zhi ye*) 获虎之夜

'Night Xujia Village Roared, The' (*Paoxiao de Xujiatun*) 咆哮的许家屯

'Nights of Spring Fever' (*Chunfeng chenzui de wanshang*) 春风沉醉的晚上

Nine Leaves group (*Jiu ye pai*) 九叶派

'Nineteen Thirty-four Escapes' (*Yijiusansi nian de taowang*) 一九三四年的逃亡

'No. 13 Happiness Street' (*Xingfu dajie shisan hao*) 幸福大街十三号

'Norlang' (*Nuorilang*) 诺日朗

North, The (Beifang) 北方

North-west Battleground Service Corps (*Xibei zhandi fuwutuan*) 西北战地服务团

Northern Journey and Other Poems, The (Bei you ji qita) 北游及其他

'Not-not' (*Feifei*) 非非

'Notes from the City of the Sun' (*Taiyang cheng zhaji*) 太阳城札记

'obscure poetry' (*menglong shi*) 朦胧诗

Obsessed, The (Fuxi Fuxi) 伏羲伏羲

October (Shiyue) 十月

Ode to Yimeng (*Yimeng song*) 沂蒙颂

Old Dreams (Jiu meng) 旧梦

'Old Floating Cloud' (*Canglao de fuyun*) 苍老的浮云

'Old Stick's Wineshop' (*Lao Bangzi jiuguan*) 老棒子酒馆

Old Tales Retold (*Gushi xinbian*) 故事新编

'On 'Love' and 'Patience' Among Comrades' (*Lun tongzhi zhi 'ai' yu 'nai'*) 论同志之 "爱" 与 "耐"

'On Proletarian Literature' (*Lun wuchanjieji wenyi*) 论无产阶级文艺

On the Docks (Haigang) 海港

On the Plains (*Pingyuan shang*) 平原上

'On The Relationship Between Fiction and Ruling the Masses' (*Lun xiaoshuo yu qunzhi zhi guanxi*) 论小说与群制之关系

'On the Hunger Line' (*Ji'e xian shang*) 饥饿线上

'On the Oxcart' (*Niuche shang*) 牛车上

'On the Subjectivity of Literature' (*Lun wenxue de zhutixing*) 论文学的主题性

'On the Yalu River' (*Yalujiang shang*) 鸭绿江上

One Man's Troubles (*Yi ge ren de fannao*) 一个人的烦恼

'One Night in a Café' (*Kafeidian zhi yi ye*) 咖啡店之一夜

One-eyed Tiger (*Danyan hu*) 单眼虎

'Open Your Eyes' (*Zhengda ni de yanjing*) 睁大你的眼睛

'Operators, The' (*Wanzhu*) 玩主

'Oppression' (*Yapo*) 压迫

Orchid Wind (*Hui de feng*) 蕙的风

'Our Army Commander' (*Women de junzhang*) 我们的军长

'Our Corner' (*Women de jiaoluo*) 我们的角落

Outside the Window (*Chuang wai*) 窗外

Ouyang Shan 欧阳山

Ouyang Yuqian 欧阳予倩

'Pa Pa Pa' (*Ba ba ba*) 爸爸爸

'Pages from a Factory Secretary's Diary' (*Yi ge gongchang mishu de riji*) 一个工厂秘书的日记

Painstaking Work (*Keyi ji*) 刻意集

Pale Chimes (*Cangbai de zhongsheng*) 苍白的钟声

Palm, The (*Shouzhang ji*) 手掌集

'Palm, The' (*Shouzhang*) 手掌

Pan Mohua 潘漠华

'Passer-by, The' (*Guo ke*) 过客

Past Life (*Guoqu de shengming*) 过去的生命

'Path Through the Grassland, The' (*Caoyuan shang de xiao lu*) 草原上的小路

Patriotic Heart, A (*Yi pian aiguo xin*) 一片爱国心

Peach Blossom Fan (*Taohua shan*) 桃花扇

Peaches and Plums in the Spring (*Tao li chun feng*) 桃李春风

'Peacock Flies South-east, The' (*Kongque dongnan fei*) 孔雀东南飞

Peacock Gall (*Kongque dan*) 孔雀胆

Pearls (*Zhubei ji*) 珠贝集

Peking Man (*Beijing ren*) 北京人

Peking Opera Troupe of Beijing (*Beijing jingjutuan*) 北京京剧团

Peking Opera Troupe of China (*Zhongguo jingjutuan*) 中国京剧团

Peking Opera Troupe of Shandong (*Shandong sheng jingjutuan*) 山东省京剧团

Peking Opera Troupe of Shanghai (*Shanghai jingjutuan*) 上海京剧团

'People or Monsters?' (*Ren yao zhi jian*) 人妖之间

People's Cinema (*Renmin diangying*) 人民电影

People's Dramatic Society (*Minzhong xiju she*) 民众戏剧社

People's Literature (*Renmin wenxue*) 人民文学

People's Music (*Renmin yinyue*) 人民音乐

People's Theatre (*Renmin xiju*) 人民戏剧

Performance Arts (*Quyi*) 曲艺

'Personal Grief' (*Siren du qiaocui*) 斯人独憔悴

'Philatelist, The' (*Youpiao*) 邮票

Philosophy of Lao Zhang, The (*Lao Zhang zhexue*) 老张哲学

Picking Star Grass (*Xie xing cao*) 撷星草

'Piece of Broken Ship, A' (*Yi kuai po chuan pian*) 一块破船片

pingju 评剧

Pioneers (*Tuohuangzhe*) 拓荒者

'Pipa Tune in an Alley at Midnight' (*Yeban shen xiang pipa*) 夜半深巷琵琶

'Place of Love, The' (*Aiqing de weizhi*) 爱情的位置

Playscripts (*Juben*) 剧本

Pleasure Garden (*Qiyuan*) 憩园

Plum Blossom Party (*Meihua dang*) 梅花党

Poems of a Decade [Bian Zhilin] (*Shinian shi cao*) 十年诗草

Poems of a Decade [Zang Kejia] (*Shinian shi xuan*) 十年诗选

Poems of Grace (*Yingying ji*) 盈盈集

Poems Without Titles (*Wu ti cao*) 无题草

Poetry Creation (*Shi chuangzao*) 诗创造

Poetry [1926] (*Shi juan*) 诗卷

Poetry [1957–1964, 1976–] (*Shikan*) 诗刊

Poetry [Jan 1922–May 1923] (*Shi*) 诗

Popular Arts Drama School (*Renyi xiju zhuanmen xuexiao*) 人益戏剧专门学校

Popular Drama Society (*Minzhong xiju she*) 民众戏剧社

'Postprandial' (*Yan ba*) 宴罢

Pot of Gold (*Jin tanzi*) 金坛子

'Precious Horse, The' (*Bao ma*) 宝马

'Primeval Forest' (*Da linmang*) 大林莽

Princess Wencheng (*Wencheng gongzhu*) 文成公主

'Process' (*Guocheng*) 过程

Progress Troupe (*Jinhua tuan*) 进化团
Prophecy, The (*Yuyan*) 预言
Pu Feng 葡风
Public Opinion (*Qingyi bao*) 清议报
'Put Down Your Whip' (*Fangxia ni de bianzi*) 放下你的鞭子
Qian Zhongshu 钱钟书
Qin Shouou 秦瘦鸥
Qin Zhaoyang 秦兆阳
Qu Bo 曲波
Quiet Maternity Hospital, The (*Jingjing de chanyuan*) 静静的产院
'Quiet Night' (*Jingye*) 静夜
Raid on the White Tiger Regiment (*Qixi Baihutuan*) 奇袭白虎团
Rainbow, The (*Hong*) 虹
Rainscapes (*Yujing*) 雨景
'Rainy Alley, The' (*Yu xiang*) 雨巷
'Rainy Evening, A' (*Yuxi*) 雨夕
'Rainy Season, The' (*Mei yu*) 梅雨
'Random Notes from the Three Family Village' (*Sanjiacun zhaji*) 三家村
    札记
Rao Mengkan 饶孟侃
Real Man, The (*Lu nanzi*) 鲁男子
'Realism—The Broad Road' (*Xianshizhuyi—guangkuo de daolu*) 现实
    主意一广阔的大路
Records of a Nightmare (*Emeng lu*) 噩梦录
'records of the strange' (*zhiguai*) 志怪
Recovery (*Huifu*) 恢复
Red and Black (*Hong yu hei*) 红与黑
Red Black (*Hong hei*) 红黑
Red Candle (*Hong zhu*) 红烛
Red Communications Route (*Hongse jiaotong xian*) 红色交通线
Red Detachment of Women, The (*Hongse niangzi jun*) 红色娘子军
Red Flag (*Hong qi*) 红旗
Red Gauze Lantern, The (*Hongsha deng*) 红纱灯
Red Guards (*hong weibing*) 红卫兵
Red Lantern, The (*Hong deng ji*) 红灯记
Red Leaves over the Mountains (*Hongye, zai shan nabian*) 红叶, 在山
    那边
Red Nose, The (*Hong bizi*) 红鼻子
Red Sorghum (*Hong gaoliang*) 红高粱
Reducing Rent (*Jian zu*) 减租

'Reed Pipe' (*Lu di*) 芦笛

'Registration' (*Dengji*) 登记

Reminiscences (*Suixiang lu*) 随想录

Reminiscences (*Yi*) 忆

'Remorse' (*Shangshi*) 伤逝

Renaissance (*Xinchao*) 新潮

'Reply to Li Shuyi' (*Da Li Shuyi*) 答李淑一

'Requiem' (*Wange*) 挽歌

Resistance Literature and the Arts (*Kangzhan wenyi*) 抗战文艺

Retainer and Hard Times (*Shike yu xiongnian*) 食客与凶年

Return on a Snowy Night (*Fengxue ye guiren*) 风雪夜归人

'Return to the South' (*Nan gui*) 南归

'Return to Yan'an' (*Hui Yan'an*) 回延安

Returning from the West (*Xi huan*) 西还

Revelations That Move the Earth to Tears (*Gan you geyin dong di ai*)
    敢有歌吟动地哀

Revived Earth, The (*Fuhuo de tudi*) 复活的土地

'Revolution and Literature' (*Geming yu wenxue*) 革命与文学

'revolution in fiction' (*xiaoshuojie geming*) 小说界革命

'revolution in literature' (*wenjie geming*) 文界革命

'revolution in poetry' (*shijie geming*) 诗界革命

Revolutionary Army, The (*Geming jun*) 革命军

Revolutionary Poems from Tiananmen (*Tiananmen geming shi chao*)
    天安门革命诗抄

'revolutionary war literature' (*geming zhanzheng de wenxue*) 革命战争
    的文学

'Rhymes of Li Youcai' (*Li Youcai banhua*) 李有才板话

Rice-sprout Song, The (*Yangge*) 秧歌

'right the wrongs' (*pingfan*) 平反

'Rising poets: on the modernist tendencies in Chinese poetry' (*Jueqide
    shiqun—ping woguo shige de xiandai qingxiang*) 崛起的诗群一评
    我国诗歌的现代倾向

River Crossing (*Guodu*) 过渡

River of Iron, The (*Tieshui benliu*) 铁水奔流

'Rivers of the North' (*Beifang de he*) 北方的河

Riverside (*He bian*) 河边

Rocks and Reeds (*Panshi yu puwei*) 磐石与蒲苇

Romance of a Generation (*Yi dai fengliu*) 一代风流

'Romances of the Landscape' (*Biandi fengliu*) 遍地风流

'root-seekers' (*xungen*) 寻根

Ru Zhijuan 茹志鹃
'Rubber Man, The' (*Xiangpi ren*) 橡皮人
'ruins fiction' (*feixu xiaoshuo*) 废墟小说
'Rustling Rain' (*Yu, shashasha*) 雨, 沙沙沙
Rustling Wind, The (*Feng xiaoxiao*) 风萧萧
Sacred Land, The (*Sheng di*) 圣地
'Sacrifice to the Kitchen God' (*Ji zao*) 祭灶
Sanliwan (*Sanliwan*) 三里湾
'scar literature' (*shanghen wenxue*) 伤痕文学
'Scar, The' (*Shanghen*) 伤痕
Scarecrow, The (*Daocaoren*) 稻草人
Scenery Here, The (*Zhebian fengjing*) 这便风景
Scenes from Northern Shaanxi (*Shaanbei fengguang*) 陕北风光
Sea of Earth, The (*Dadi de hai*) 大地的海
Sea of Regret (*Henhai*) 恨海
'Search, The' (*Zhuiqiu*) 追求
'Second Farewell to Cambridge, A' (*Zai bie Kangqiao*) 再别康乔
Second Handshake, The (*Di-er ge woshou*) 第二个握手
'Second Kind of Loyalty, The' (*Di-er zhong zhongcheng*) 第二种忠诚
Secret History of the Qing Palace, The (*Qing gong mi shi*) 清宫秘史
Secret Life of Marx, The (*Makesi mishi*) 马克思秘史
'Secret Love' (*Siqing*) 私情
Secret to Becoming Rich, The (*Facai mijue*) 发财秘诀
'Self' (*Ziji*) 自己
'Send-off, The' (*Song che*) 送车
'Severed Finger, A' (*Duan zhi*) 断指
Sha Ting 沙汀
Sha Yexin 沙叶新
Shajiabang (*Shajiabang*) 沙家浜
Shanghai at Night (*Ye Shanghai*) 夜上海
Shanghai Dance School (*Shanghai shi wudao xuexiao*) 上海市舞蹈学校
Shanghai Dramatic Association (*Shanghai xiju xieshe*) 上海戏剧协社
Shanghai Literary Gazette (*Zilin Hubao*) 字林沪报
Shanghai Literature (*Shanghai wenxue*) 上海文学
Shanghai opera (*huju*) 沪剧
Shanghai Pacific News (*Taipingyang bao*) 太平洋报
Shanghai People's Art Theatre (*Shanghai renmin yishu juyuan*) 上海人民艺术剧院
Shanghai Theatre Arts Association (*Shanghai juyi she*) 上海剧艺社

Shao Xunmei 邵洵美
She Is a Weak Woman (*Ta shi yi ge ruo nüzi*) 她是一个弱女子
'She Too Will Kill' (*Ta ye yao sha ren*) 她也要杀人
Shen Congwen 沈从文
Shen Rong 谌容
Shenzhen Youth Daily (*Shenzhen qingnian bao*) 深圳青年报
Shi Dakai's Road to Ruin (*Shi Dakai de molu*) 石达开的末路
Shi Tiesheng 史铁生
Shi Tuo 师陀
Shi Zhecun 施蛰存
Short Story Monthly (*Xiaoshuo yuebao*) 小说月报
'Shrew, The' (*Pofu*) 泼妇
Shu Ting 舒婷
'Silver-Grey Death' (*Yinhuise de si*) 银灰色的死
'Singer, The' (*Gezhe*) 歌者
Singing for Joy (*Wei xingfu er ge*) 为幸福而歌
'Sinking' (*Chenlun*) 沉沦
'Sister Apricot' (*Xingmei*) 杏妹
Six Chapters from a Cadre School (*Ganxiao liu ji*) 干校六记
Sketches Gathered at My Native Place (*Limen shiji*) 里门拾记
Sketches of Hulan River (*Hulanhe zhuan*) 呼兰河传
Small Town Called Hibiscus, A (*Furongzhen*) 芙蓉镇
'Smuggling' (*Zousi*) 走私
'Snow' (*Xue*) 雪
Snow City (*Xuecheng*) 雪城
Snowstorm in the Faraway Sky (*Yuantian de bingxue*) 远天的冰雪
Snowy Morning, A (*Xue zhao*) 雪朝
Snuff-bottles (*Yanhu*) 烟壶
'socialist realism' (*shehuizhuyi xianshizhuyi*) 社会主义现实主义
Society of Harmonious Fists (*Yi he tuan*) 义和团
'Some Tentative Suggestions for the Reform of Chinese Literature'
    (*Wenxue gailiang chuyi*) 文学改良刍议
'Son of the Earth' (*Di zhi zi*) 地之子
'Song of August 1' (*Ba-yi zhi ge*) 八一之歌
'Song of Lei Feng' (*Lei Feng zhi ge*) 雷锋之歌
Song of Reality (*Zhenshi zhi ge*) 真实之歌
Song of Returning Spring, The (*Hui chun zhi qu*) 回春之曲
Song of the Dragon River (*Longjiang song*) 龙江颂
Song of the Great Wind (*Da feng ge*) 大风歌
'Song of the Great Wind' (*Da feng ge*) 大风歌

Song of Youth, The (Qingchun zhi ge) 青春之歌
Song to the Spirit of Honour (Zheng qi ge) 正气歌
Song Zhidi 宋之的
Songs of a Stroller (Xingyin de ge) 行吟的歌
Songs of the Red Flag (Hongqi geyao) 红旗歌谣
Songs of Yesterday (Zuori zhi ge) 昨日之歌
Sonnets (Shisihang ji) 十四行集
Sons and Daughters of Xisha (Xisha ernü) 西沙儿女
Sorrow for the Fall of the Ming (Mingmo yihen) 明末遗恨
Sorrows of Lisa, The (Lisha de aiyuan) 丽莎的哀怨
Sound of War, The (Zhan sheng ji) 战声集
Sounds (Shengyin) 声音
'South Bank, The' *(Nanfang de an)* 南方的岸
Southern Arts Academy *(Nanguo yishu xueyuan)* 南国艺术学院
'Southern Night, A' *(Nanfang zhi ye)* 南方之夜
Southern Society *(Nanguo she)* 南国社
'Souvenir' *(Jinian)* 纪念
Sparks amid the Reeds (Ludang huozhong) 芦荡火种
Spiritual Fire (Ling yan) 灵焰
'spiritual pollution' *(jingshen wuran)* 精神污染
'spoken plays' *(huaju)* 话剧
Spring (Chun) 春
Spring Fields and the Window (Chun ye yu chuang) 春野于窗
'Spring Forever' *(Yongyuan shi chuntian)* 永远是春天
Spring in Edo (Jianghu zhi chun) 江户之春
'Spring Silkworms' *(Chuncan)* 春蚕
Spring Songs (Chun de geji) 春的歌集
Spring Sun Society *(Chunyang she)* 春阳社
Spring Waters (Chun shui) 春水
Spring Willow Society *(Chunliu she)* 春柳社
Spring Willow Theatre *(Chunliu juchang)* 春柳剧场
Sprouts Monthly (Mengya yuekan) 萌芽月刊
Starry Sky, The (Xingkong) 星空
Stars (Fanxing) 繁星
Starving Guo Su'e, The (Ji'e de Guo Sue) 饥饿的郭素娥
Stone Gate, The (Shimen ji) 石门集
Story of Earthworm and Bee, A (Qiuyin he mifeng de gushi) 蚯蚓和蜜
蜂的故事
Story of Little Black Horse, The (Xiao Heima de gushi) 小黑马的故事
'Story of Luo Wenying, The' *(Luo Wenying de gushi)* 罗文应的故事

'Story Out of Sequence, A' (*Jianji cuole de gushi*) 剪辑错了的故事
Story-telling (*Shuoshuo changchang*) 说说唱唱
Strange Case of Ninefold Murder, The (*Jiuming qiyuan*) 九命奇冤
'Strange Encounter' (*Qiyu*) 奇遇
Strange Events Witnessed During the Last Twenty Years (*Ershi nian mudu zhi guai xianzhuang*) 二十年目睹之怪现状
Strange Knight-errant of the Shanghai Concessions, The (*Yangjingbang qixia*) 洋泾浜奇侠
'Strange Tales from Strange Lands' (*Yixiang yiwen*) 异乡异闻
Street theatre (*Jietou yanju*) 街头演剧
'Strings of Life' (*Ming ruo qinxian*) 命若琴弦
Study Lamp (*Xue deng*) 学灯
Studying in Japan (*Liu Dong waishi*) 留东外史
Su Jinsan 苏金伞
Su Manshu 苏曼殊
Su Tong 苏童
'Suicide' (*Zisha*) 自杀
'Summary of the Meeting on People's Liberation Army Work in Literature and the Arts Held by Jiang Qing with the Endorsement of Lin Biao' (*Lin Biao weituo Jiang Qing zhaokai de budui wenyi gongzuo zuotanhui jiyao*) 林彪委托江青召开的部队文艺工作座谈会纪要
Summer (*Xiatian*) 夏天
'Summer Vacation' (*Shujia zhong*) 暑假中
Sun Dayu 孙大雨
Sun Shines over the Sanggan River, The (*Taiyang zhao zai Sangganhe shang*) 太阳照在桑干河上
Sun Society (*Taiyang she*) 太阳社
Sun Yutang 孙毓棠
Sunken Bell, The (*Chen zhong*) 沉钟
'Sunless Morning, A' (*Meiyou taiyang de zaochen*) 没有太阳的早晨
Sunrise (*Richu*) 日出
'Superman' (*Chaoren*) 超人
'Suzhou Night's Tale, A' (*Suzhou yehua*) 苏州夜话
Swallow's Nest, The (*Yan ni ji*) 燕泥集
'Swimming' (*Youyong*) 游泳
Symphony, A (*Jiaoxiang ji*) 交响集
Taking Tiger Mountain by Strategy (*Zhiqu Weihushan*) 智取威虎山
'Tale of Big Nur' (*Danao jishi*) 大淖记事
'Tale Which is Not a Dream, The' (*Fei meng ji*) 非梦记

Tales Under the Old Mulberry Tree (*Lao sangshu xia de gushi*) 老桑树下的故事

'tales of the wondrous' (*chuanqi*) 传奇

Tall Aspens (*Gaogao de baiyang shu*) 高高的白杨树

'Tang Xiaoxi in Next Time Port' (*Tang Xiaoxi zai Xia Ci Kaichuangang*) 唐小西在下次开船港

Tao Jun 陶骏

Teahouse (*Chaguan*) 茶馆

Temple of Flowers, The (*Hua zhi si*) 花之寺

'Ten Years Deducted' (*Jianqu shi sui*) 减去十岁

Test, The (*Kao yan*) 考验

'That Night' (*Na yi ye*) 那一夜

'There Is a Snowstorm Tonight' (*Jinye you baofengyu*) 今夜有暴风雨

'There Is a Youth' (*You yi ge qingnian*) 有一个青年

'Third Kind of People, The' (*di-san zhong ren*) 第三种人

'This Is a Coward's World' (*Zhe shi yi ge qienuo de shijie*) 这是一个怯懦的世界

'This Too Is All' (*Zhe ye shi yiqie*) 这也是一切

'Thoughts on March Eighth' (*San-ba jie you gan*) 三八节有感

Thread of Talk (*Yu si*) 语丝

Thread of Talk Society (*Yusi she*) 语丝社

'Three Dollars, National Currency' (*San kuai qian guobi*) 三块钱国币

Three Family Lane (*San jia xiang*) 三家巷

Three-inch Golden Lotus (*San cun jin lian*) 三寸金莲

Three Rebellious Women (*San ge panni de nüxing*) 三个叛逆的女性

'three prominences' (*san tuchu*) 三突出

Thrice Ascending Peach Peak (*San shang Taofeng*) 三上桃峰

Thunderstorm (*Leiyu*) 雷雨

Tian Han 田汉

Tian Jian 田间

Tianjin Daily News (*Tianjin riri xinwen*) 天津日日新闻

Tiger Tally, The (*Hufu*) 虎符

Tiger Weekly, The (*Jiayin zhoukan*) 甲寅周刊

Tiger, The (*Menghu ji*) 猛虎集

'Tips' (*Xiao zhang*) 小帐

To Set an Example (*Yi shen zuo ze*) 以身作则

To the Muse (*Ji shihun*) 寄诗魂

Today (*Jintian*) 今天

'Tong Huai Zhou' (*Tong Huai Zhou*) 童怀周

Torrent (*Jiliu*) 激流

Torrents (*Benliu*) 奔流
Totems of Life, The (*Shengming de tuteng*) 生命的图腾
Towards the Sun (*Xiang taiyang*) 向太阳
Traces (*Zongji*) 踪迹
Track, The (*Guidao*) 轨道
Tracks in the Snowy Forest (*Linhai xueyuan*) 林海雪原
'Traitor's Offspring, The' (*Hanjian de zisun*) 汉奸的子孙
Traveller's Heart, The (*Lü xin*) 旅心
Travelling Dramatic Troupe of China (*Zhongguo lüxing jutuan*) 中国旅
　行剧团
Travels in the South (*Nanxing ji*) 南行记
Travels of Lao Can (*Lao Can youji*) 老残游记
Trendsetter, The (*Cai feng bao*) 采风报
Trilogy of Contemporary Youth (*Dangdai qingnian san bu qu*) 当代青年
　三部曲
Trilogy of Love (*Aiqing de san bu qu*) 爱情的三部曲
'True Story of Ah Q' (*A Q zheng zhuan*) 阿Q正传
Turbulence (*Fuzao*) 浮躁
'Turk, The' (*Tuerqi*) 土耳其
Twenty-eight Black Letters (*Hei zi ershiba*) 黑字二十八
Twin Blossoms (*Tangdi zhi hua*) 棠棣之花
'Two Families' (*Liang ge jiating*) 两个家庭
Two Mas, The (*Er Ma*) 二马
Ugly Duckling (*Chou xiaoya*) 丑小鸭
Uncle Gao (*Gao ganda*) 高干大
Under Shanghai Eaves (*Shanghai wuyan xia*) 上海屋檐下
Under the Fence (*Li xia ji*) 篱下集
'Underdog, The' (*Renxiaren*) 人下人
'Unfired Bullet, The' (*Yi ke wei chu tang de qiangdan*) 一颗未出膛的枪
　弹
'Unforgettable 1976, The' (*Nanwang de yijiuqiliu*) 难忘的一九七六
Unnamed Society (*Weiming she*) 未名社
'Unrequited Love' (*Kulian*) 苦恋
'Vacillation' (*Dongyao*) 动摇
'Vain Labours of a Spider, The' (*Zhui wang laozhu*) 缀网劳蛛
Valley, The (*Gu*) 谷
Valley of Dreams (*Meng zhi gu*) 梦之谷
Vanguard Monthly, The (*Qianfeng yuebao*) 前锋月报
Vanguard Weekly, The (*Qianfeng zhoubao*) 前锋周报
Vanguard, The (*Qianmao*) 前茅

Vase, The (*Ping*) 瓶
Venice (*Weinishi*) 威尼市
'Verdant Bamboo Hermitage, The' (*Luzhu shanfang*) 菉竹山房
Victims' Verses (*Shounanzhe de duanqu*) 受难者的短曲
'Victorious in Death' (*Shengli de si*) 胜利的死
Village in August (*Bayue de xiangcun*) 八月的乡村
Village Sketches (*Nongcun sanji*) 农村散记
Village Trilogy, A (*Nongcun san bu qu*) 农村三部曲
'Visitor, The' (*Lai fang zhe*) 来访者
'Voices of Spring' (*Chun zhi sheng*) 春之声
W.E. (*W.M. women*) W·M (我们)
Wandering in the Clouds (*Yun you*) 云游
Wang Anyi 王安忆
Wang Duqing 王独清
Wang Gui and Li Xiangxiang (*Wang Gui he Li Xiangxiang*) 王贵和李香香
Wang Jingzhi 汪静之
Wang Meng 王蒙
Wang Peigong 王培公
Wang Shuo 王朔
Wang Tongzhao 王统照
Wang Xindi 王辛笛
Wang Yaping 王亚平
Wang Zengqi 汪曾祺
Wang Zhaojun 王昭君
Wang Zhongxian 汪仲贤
Wangshu's Drafts (*Wangshu cao*) 望舒草
War Drums (*Zhangu*) 战鼓
Ward Four (*Di-si bingshi*) 第四病室
Warning Signal (*Juedui xinhao*) 绝对信号
'Wasp, A' (*Yi zhi mafeng*) 一只马蜂
'Water Buffalo' (*Niu*) 牛
Weeds (*Ye cao*) 野草
Wen Yiduo 闻一多
Wenhui Daily (*Wenhui bao*) 文汇报
West Willow Village (*Xiliu ji*) 西柳集
Western-style opera (*geju*) 歌剧
'What's Wrong with Him?' (*Ta you shenme bing?*) 他有什么病
'When I Was in Xia Village' (*Wo zai Xiacun de shihou*) 我在霞村的时候

'When Your Eaves Are Low' (*Aiyan*) 矮檐
Whirlpool (*Baiwo*) 白涡
White Snake, The (*Bai she zhuan*) 白蛇传
White-haired Girl, The (*Bai mao nü*) 白毛女
'Why Herdsmen Sing About Mother' (*Qishou wei shenme gechang mu-qin*) 骑手为什么歌唱母亲
'Why This Kind of Criticism?' (*Wei shenme hui you zheyang de piping?*) 为什么会这样的批评
'Wild Lilies' (*Ye baihe hua*) 野白合花
Wild Man, The (*Ye ren*) 野人
Wilderness, The (*Caomang ji*) 草莽集
Wilderness, The (*Yuanye*) 原野
'Will, The' (*Yizhu*) 遗嘱
Wind and Fire Mountains (*Feng huo shan*) 风火山
Wind and Sand Literary Society (*Feng sha wenyi she*) 风沙文艺社
Windswept Blossoms (*Feng xu*) 风絮
Winter in the City (*Dushi de dong*) 都市的冬
Winter Night (*Dong ye*) 冬夜
'Winter Rain' (*Dong yu*) 冬雨
'Winter's Evening, A' (*Zai yi ge dongtian de wanshang*) 在一个冬天的晚上
Wintertide (*Suihan tu*) 岁寒图
'With My Injured Hand' (*Wo yong cansun de shouzhang*) 我用残损的手掌
'Wives and Concubines' (*Qiqi qieqie*) 妻妻妾妾
'Woman Woman Woman' (*Nü nü nü*) 女女女
'Woman, A' (*Yi ge nüxing*) 一个女性
Women (*Nüren*) 女人
Women, Women (*Nüren nüren*) 女人女人
'World at Peace, The' (*Tianxia taiping*) 天下太平
'Written on a Prison Wall' (*Yu zhong ti bi*) 狱中题壁
Wu Han 吴晗
Wu Woyao 吴沃尧
Wu Zuguang 吴祖光
Wu Zuxiang 吴祖湘
Xia Yan 夏衍
Xiang Kairan 向恺然
Xiao Hong 萧红
Xiao Jun 萧军
Xiao Po's Birthday (*Xiao Po de shengri*) 小坡的生日

Xiao Qian 萧乾
Xinjiang Literature and Art (Xinjiang wenyi) 新疆文艺
Xiong Foxi 熊佛西
Xu Dishan 许地山
Xu Xu 徐圩
Xu Yunuo 徐玉诺
Xu Zhimo 徐志摩
Yama Zhao (Zhao Yanwang) 赵阎王
Yan Wenjing 严文井
Yang Jiang 杨绛
Yang Lian 杨炼
Yang Mo 杨沫
yangge 秧歌
Yangtze Literary Compendium (Changjiang wenxue congkan) 长江文
　　学丛刊
Yao Ke 姚克
Yao Xueyin 姚雪垠
Yao Zhongming 姚仲明
Ye Shengtao 叶圣陶
'Year of Spoken Drama, The' (*huaju nian*) 话剧年
Years of Disaster (Zainan de suiyue) 灾难的岁月
Yellow Earth, The (Huang tudi) 黄土地
'Yellow Mud Street' (*Huang ni jie*) 黄泥街
'Yellow Smoke' (*Huang yan*) 黄烟
'Yellow-haired Baby, The' (*Jinfa ying'er*) 金发婴儿
Yin Fu 殷夫
Ying Xiuren 应修人
'You Have No Other Choice' (*Ni bie wu xuanze*) 你别无选择
Young China (Shaonian Zhongguo) 少年中国
Young Man with a Hoe, The (Chutou jian'er) 锄头健儿
'Young Newcomer in the Organisation Department, The' (*Zuzhibu xinlai
　　de nianqing ren*) 组织部新来的年轻人
Young Wanderer, The (Shaonian piaobozhe) 少年飘泊者
Yu Dafu 郁达夫
Yu Ling 于伶
Yu Pingbo 俞平伯
Yuan Changying 袁昌英
Yuan Jing 袁静
Zang Kejia 臧克家
Zeng Pu 曾朴

Zero Degree of Life, The (*Shengming de lingdu*) 生命的零度
Zhang Ailing 张爱玲
Zhang Chengzhi 张承志
Zhang Henshui 张恨水
Zhang Jie 张洁
Zhang Tianyi 张天翼
Zhang Xianliang 张贤亮
Zhao Shuli 赵树理
Zhao Zhenkai 赵振开
Zhao Ziyue (*Zhao Ziyue*) 赵子曰
Zheng Min 郑敏
Zheng Min's Poems (*Zheng Min shi ji*) 郑敏诗集
Zheng Wanlong 郑万隆
Zhimo's Poems (*Zhimo de shi*) 志摩的诗
Zhou Erfu 周而复
Zhou Libo 周立波
Zhou Zuoren 周作人
Zhu Xiang 朱湘
Zhu Ziqing 朱自清
Zhuo Wenjun (*Zhuo Wenjun*) 卓文君
Zong Baihua 宗白华
Zong Fuxian 宗复先
Zou Difan 邹荻帆

INDEX

Ah Cheng (Zhong Acheng), 212, 370, 397, 400-1, 402, 405, 419, 426
Ai Qing, 69, 72-4, 193, 196, 203, 264, 270, 271, 273, 283, 332, 337, 428
Ai Wu, 134-6, 208, 218
Ajia, 355
April Fifth Movement (1976), 331, 333, 342, 362, 424-5, 430, 433, 437
Anti-Rightist campaign, *see under* campaigns
Aying (Qian Xingcun), 172, 287, 315
Azalea Mountain, 346, 361-2

Ba Jin: 28, 70, 75, 128-30, 134, 152, 184, 185, 199, 215-17, 231, 239, 243, 286, 332, 343, 351, 444; *The Family*, 129-30, 185, 216, 288, 306
Ba Ren, 202
Bai Fengxi, 351
Bai Hua, 336
Bai Juyi, 39
Bai Xianyong, 419, 444
Bei Dao (Zhao Zhenkai), 214, 247, 333, 337, 369, 397-8, 419, 426, 428-31, 432-5, 436, 442, 445
Beijing Academy School of Traditional Drama, 292
Beijing Film Studio, 398, 400
Beijing People's Art Theatre, 169, 292, 302, 303, 306, 310, 317, 353, 364
Bian Zhilin, 28, 74-6, 77-8, 202, 218, 219, 263, 264, 271, 273-4
Bing Xin, 48-9, 74, 119-21
Book of Songs, The, 32, 38, 42-43, 264, 299
bourgeois liberalisation, *see under* campaigns
Boxer Rebellion (1900): 13-14, 85, 89,
99, 115, 181, 211, 295, 313, 327, 390; Boxer Indemnity, 24
Boulder Bay, 346
Buddhism, 70, 75, 85, 91, 100-1, 136, 401, 429

Cai Qijiao, 436
Cai Wenji, 301
Cai Yuanpei, 93
campaigns: 200, 206-7, 239-40, 257, 260, 336, 338; Rectification (1942), 193-4, 200, 222, 290; Rectification (1957), 224; Hundred Flowers (1957-8), 202-3, 213, 246, 254-7, 292, 294, 303, 319; Great Leap Forward (1958), 204-5, 257, 264, 274, 294, 296, 306, 320, 353, 355, 358, 360, 373; poetry-writing (1958), 264, 274-5; Anti-Rightist (1957-8), 148, 203, 207, 219, 232, 246-7, 248, 254-7, 271, 273, 278, 312, 332, 374, 375, 380, 383, 394, 409, 419, 425, 436; against spiritual pollution (1983-4), 213-14, 311, 337, 342, 351, 365, 428, 434; against bourgeois liberalisation (1981-7), 254, 336-7, 339-40, 342, 391
Can Xue, 370, 409-10, 411, 419, 420
Cao Baohua, 70, 271
Cao Changqing, 430
Cao Cao, 301
Cao Yu: 28, 157-8, 167, 177-81, 182, 210, 285-6, 290, 292, 293, 305-7, 311, 351; *Thunderstorm*, 160, 164, 173, 177-80, 185, 305, 306, 362
Capital Theatre, 292, 301, 306, 309, 352, 364, 365
Carlton Theatre, 160, 313

495